W9-CRN-092

TAKING SIDES

Clashing Views on Controversial

Issues in Anthropology

SECOND EDITION

TAKING SIDES

Clashing Views on Controversial

Issues in Anthropology

SECOND EDITION

Selected, Edited, and with Introductions by

Kirk M. Endicott
Dartmouth College

and

Robert L. Welsch
Dartmouth College

McGraw-Hill/Dushkin
A Division of The McGraw-Hill Companies

For Karen and Sarah

Photo Acknowledgment
Cover image: © 2003 by PhotoDisc, Inc.

Cover Art Acknowledgment
Charles Vitelli

Manufactured in the United States of America

Second Edition

123456789BAHBAH6543

Library of Congress Cataloging-in-Publication Data
Main entry under title:
Taking sides: clashing views on controversial issues in anthropology/selected, edited, and with
introductions by Kirk M. Endicott and Robert L. Welsch.—2nd ed.
Includes bibliographical references and index.
1. Anthropology. I. Endicott, Kirk M., *comp.* II. Welsch, Robert L., *comp.*
306
0-07-282276-7
ISSN: 1530-0757

Printed on Recycled Paper

Preface

Many courses and textbooks present anthropology as a discipline that largely consists of well-established facts. In *Taking Sides: Clashing Views on Controversial Issues in Anthropology* we present the discipline in quite a different light. Here we focus on active controversies that remain unresolved. These issues represent the kind of arguments and debates that have characterized anthropology for more than a century. They show the varied ways that anthropologists approach the subject of their research and the kinds of anthropological evidence needed to bolster an academic argument.

Generally, we have chosen selections that express strongly worded positions on two sides of an issue. For most issues, several other reasonable positions are also possible, and we have suggested some of these in our introductions and postscripts that accompany each issue.

Taking Sides: Clashing Views on Controversial Issues in Anthropology is a tool to encourage and develop critical thinking about anthropological research questions, methods, and evidence. We have selected a range of readings and issues to illustrate the kinds of topics that anthropologists study. Another goal of this volume is to provide opportunities for students to explore how anthropologists frame and defend their interpretations of anthropological evidence. We have also chosen issues that raise questions about research methods and the quality or reliability of different kinds of data. All of these complex matters go into shaping the positions that anthropologists debate and defend in their writings. We hope that in discussing these issues students will find opportunities to explore how anthropologists think about the pressing theoretical issues of the day.

Plan of the book This book is made up of 18 issues that deal with topics that have provoked starkly different positions by different anthropologists. We have divided the volume into five Parts reflecting the discipline's four main subfields (Biological Anthropology, Archaeology, Linguistic Anthropology, and Cultural Anthropology) as well as another Part dealing with Ethics in Anthropology. Each issue begins with an *introduction,* which sets the stage for the debate as argued in the YES and NO selections. Following these two selections is a *postscript* that makes some final observations and points the way to other questions related to the issue. In reading an issue and forming your own opinions, you should remember that there are often alternative perspectives that are not represented in either the YES or NO selections. Most issues have reasonable positions that might appear to be intermediate between the two more extreme viewpoints represented here in the readings. There are also reasonable positions that lie totally outside the scope of the debate presented in these selections, and students should consider all of these possible positions. Each postscript also contains *suggestions for further reading* that will help you find further resources to continue your study of any topic. Students researching any of these issues or related ones for a research paper will find these further readings (as well as their bibliographies) a useful place to begin a more intensive analysis. At the end of the book we have also included a list of all the *contributors to this volume,* which will give you information on the anthropologists and other commentators whose views are debated here. An *On the Internet* page accompanies each part opener. This page gives you Internet site addresses (URLs) that are relevant to the issues discussed in that part of the book. Many of these sites contain links to related sites and bibliographies for further study.

Changes to this edition   This edition has been updated to reflect the latest controversies. There are six completely new issues: *Did Neandertals Interbreed With Modern Humans?* (Issue 2); *Does Language Determine How We Think?* (Issue 8); *Is It Natural for Adopted Children to Want to Find Out About Their Birth Parents?* (Issue 12); *Has the Islamic Revolution in Iran Subjugated Women?* (Issue 13); *Is Ethnic Conflict Inevitable?* (Issue 14); and *Did Napoleon Chagnon and Other Researchers Harm the Yanomami Indians of Venezuela?* (Issue 17). In addition, the NO selection in Issue 10 (*Are San Hunter-Gatherers Basically Pastoralists Who Have Lost Their Herds?*) has been replaced to bring the debate up-to-date. In all, there are 13 new selections. A new part has been added, Linguistic Anthropology, to reflect that subfield. Part introductions, issue introductions, postscripts, and *On the Internet* pages have been revised as necessary.

A word to the instructor   An *Instructor's Manual With Test Questions* (multiple-choice and essay) is available through the publisher for the instructor using *Taking Sides* in the classroom. A general guidebook, called *Using Taking Sides in the Classroom,* which discusses methods and techniques for integrating the pro-con approach into any classroom setting, is also available. An online version of *Using Taking Sides in the Classroom* and a correspondence service for Taking Sides adopters can be found at http://www.dushkin.com/usingts/.

Taking Sides: Clashing Views on Controversial Issues in Anthropology is only one of many titles in the Taking Sides series. If you are interested in seeing the table of contents for any of the other titles, please visit the Taking Sides Web site at http://www.dushkin.com/takingsides/.

Acknowledgments   We received many helpful comments and suggestions from many friends and colleagues, including Hoyt Alverson, Colin Calloway, Dale Eickelman, Samuel B. Fee, Jana Fortier, Alison Galloway, Ridie Ghezzi, Rosemary Gianno, Paul Goldstein, Alberto Gomez, Robert Gordon, Allen Hockley, Judy Hunt, Sergei Kan, Steve Kangas, Kenneth Korey, Christine Kray, Marilyn Lord, Deborah Nichols, Lynn Rainville, Jeanne Shea, Robert Tonkinson, John Watanabe, Adrienne Zihlman, Elizabeth Carpenter, Brian Didier, Katherine Keith, Laura Litton, Lynn MacGillivray, Kevin Reinhart, John Terrell, Robin Torrence, Lindsay Whaley, and J. Peter White. We also want to thank John Cocklin, Lucinda Hall, Francis X. Oscadal, Cindy Shirkey, Reinhart Sonnenberg and Amy Witzel, members of the Baker Library Reference Department, all of whom have helped track down many of the sources we have used. We also want to thank our student research assistants Whitney Wilking and Rachel Yemeni and our President Scholars/student research assistants Tate LeFevre and Lauren Weldon. We also want to thank Ted Knight and Juliana Gribbins at McGraw-Hill/Dushkin for their constant assistance, suggestions, patience, and good humor. We also wish to thank our wives, Karen L. Endicott and Sarah L. Welsch, for their support and encouragement during the preparation of this volume.

Kirk M. Endicott
Dartmouth College
Robert L. Welsch
Dartmouth College

Contents In Brief

PART 1   Biological Anthropology   1

Issue 1.   Did *Homo Sapiens* Originate Only in Africa?   2
Issue 2.   Did Neandertals Interbreed With Modern Humans?   24
Issue 3.   Are Humans Inherently Violent?   42

PART 2   Archaeology   65

Issue 4.   Did People First Arrive in the New World After the Last Ice
              Age?   66
Issue 5.   Was There a Goddess Cult in Prehistoric Europe?   86
Issue 6.   Were Environmental Factors Responsible for the Mayan
              Collapse?   108

PART 3   Linguistic Anthropology   127

Issue 7.   Can Apes Learn Language?   128
Issue 8.   Does Language Determine How We Think?   144

PART 4   Cultural Anthropology   169

Issue 9.   Should Cultural Anthropology Model Itself on the Natural
              Sciences?   170
Issue 10.   Are San Hunter-Gatherers Basically Pastoralists Who Have
              Lost Their Herds?   194
Issue 11.   Do Sexually Egalitarian Societies Exist?   216
Issue 12.   Is It Natural for Adopted Children to Want to Find Out About
              Their Birth Parents?   234
Issue 13.   Has the Islamic Revolution in Iran Subjugated Women?   254
Issue 14.   Is Ethnic Conflict Inevitable?   278

PART 5   Ethics in Anthropology   301

Issue 15.   Should the Remains of Prehistoric Native Americans Be
              Reburied Rather Than Studied?   302
Issue 16.   Should Anthropologists Work to Eliminate the Practice of
              Female Circumcision?   324
Issue 17.   Did Napoleon Chagnon and Other Researchers Harm the
              Yanomami Indians of Venezuela?   344
Issue 18.   Do Museums Misrepresent Ethnic Communities Around the
              World?   370

Contents

Preface   i

Introduction: xiii

PART 1   BIOLOGICAL ANTHROPOLOGY   1

Issue 1.   Did *Homo Sapiens* Originate Only in Africa?   2

YES: **Christopher Stringer and Robin McKie,** from *African Exodus: The Origins of Modern Humanity* (Henry Holt & Company, 1996)   *4*

NO: **Alan G. Thorne and Milford H. Wolpoff,** from "The Multiregional Evolution of Humans," *Scientific American* (April 1992)   *12*

Paleoanthropologist Christopher Stringer and science writer Robin McKie argue that recent analysis of mitochondrial DNA evidence dates the evolution of anatomically modern humans to about 200,000 years ago. They assert that *Homo sapiens* originated from a single African population, which then spread over the rest of that continent and ultimately dispersed to all parts of the Old World, replacing all earlier hominid populations. Paleoanthropologists Alan G. Thorne and Milford H. Wolpoff counter that models derived from mitochondrial DNA evidence do not agree with the fossil and archaeological evidence. They maintain that *Homo erectus* populations had dispersed to all parts of the Old World by one million years ago. As the populations dispersed, they maintained contact and interbred enough so that the populations gradually evolved throughout the Old World to become anatomically modern humans.

Issue 2.   Did Neandertals Interbreed With Modern Humans?   24

YES: **João Zilhão,** from "Fate of the Neandertals," *Archaeology* (July/August 2000)   *26*

NO: **Jean-Jacques Hublin,** from "Brothers or Cousins?" *Archaeology* (September/October 2000)   *34*

Archaeologist João Zilhão discusses the recently found remains of a young child who was buried in a rock shelter in Portugal about 25,000 years ago. He concludes that the Lagar Velho child was a hybrid with mixed Neandertal and early modern human ancestry. Biological anthropologist Jean-Jacques Hublin maintains that the Lagar Velho child was merely one variant within the diverse early modern human population. He argues that there was some cultural influence from early modern humans to Neandertals but little or no interbreeding between them.

Issue 3.   Are Humans Inherently Violent?   42

YES: **Richard Wrangham and Dale Peterson,** from *Demonic Males: Apes and the Origins of Human Violence* (Houghton Mifflin Company, 1996)   *44*

NO: **Robert W. Sussman,** from "Exploring Our Basic Human Nature," *Anthro Notes* (Fall 1997) *52*

Biological anthropologist Richard Wrangham and science writer Dale Peterson maintain that sexual selection, a type of natural selection, has fostered an instinct for male aggression because males who are good fighters mate more frequently and sire more offspring than weaker and less aggressive ones. Biological anthropologist Robert W. Sussman regards the notion that human males are inherently violent as a Western cultural tradition, not a scientifically demonstrated fact.

PART 2 ARCHAEOLOGY   65

Issue 4.   Did People First Arrive in the New World After the Last Ice Age? 66

YES: **Stuart J. Fiedel,** from *Prehistory of the Americas,* 2d ed. (Cambridge University Press, 1992) *68*

NO: **Thomas D. Dillehay,** from "The Battle of Monte Verde," *The Sciences* (January/February 1997) *77*

Archaeologist Stuart J. Fiedel supports the traditional view that humans first reached the Americas from Siberia at the end of the last Ice Age. He argues that there are currently no convincing sites dated before that time and is skeptical of statements by other archaeologists who date human occupation of sites significantly earlier. Archaeologist Thomas D. Dillehay asserts that the site he has excavated at Monte Verde proved that humans reached the New World well before the end of the last Ice Age, possibly as early as 30,000 years ago.

Issue 5.   Was There a Goddess Cult in Prehistoric Europe?   86

YES: **Marija Gimbutas,** from "Old Europe in the Fifth Millennium B.C.: The European Situation on the Arrival of Indo-Europeans," in Edgar C. Polomé, ed., *The Indo-Europeans in the Fourth and Third Millennia* (Karoma Publishers, 1982) *88*

NO: **Lynn Meskell,** from "Goddesses, Gimbutas, and 'New Age' Archaeology," *Antiquity* (March 1995) *96*

Archaeologist Marija Gimbutas argues that the civilization of pre–Bronze Age "Old Europe" was matriarchal—ruled by women—and that the religion centered on the worship of a single great Goddess. Archaeologist Lynn Meskell considers the belief in a supreme Goddess and a matriarchal society in prehistoric Europe to be an unwarranted projection of some women's utopian longings onto the past.

Issue 6.   Were Environmental Factors Responsible for the Mayan Collapse?   108

YES: **Richard E. W. Adams,** from *Prehistoric Mesoamerica,* rev. ed. (University of Oklahoma Press, 1991) *110*

NO: **George L. Cowgill,** from "Teotihuacan, Internal Militaristic Competition, and the Fall of the Classic Maya," in Norman Hammond and Gordon R. Willey, eds., *Maya Archaeology and Ethnohistory* (University of Texas Press, 1979)   *117*

Archaeologist Richard E. W. Adams argues that while military factors must have played some role in the collapse of the Classic Maya states, a combination of internal factors combined with environmental pressures were more significant. Archaeologist George L. Cowgill agrees that no single factor was responsible for the demise of the Classic Maya civilization, but he contends that military expansion was far more significant than scholars had previously thought.

PART 3   LINGUISTIC ANTHROPOLOGY   127

Issue 7.   Can Apes Learn Language?   128

YES: **E. S. Savage-Rumbaugh**, from "Language Training of Apes," in Steve Jones, Robert Martin, and David Pilbeam, eds., *The Cambridge Encyclopedia of Human Evolution* (Cambridge University Press, 1999)   *130*

NO: **Joel Wallman**, from *Aping Language* (Cambridge University Press, 1992)   *136*

Psychologist and primate specialist E. S. Savage-Rumbaugh argues that, since the 1960s, attempts to teach chimpanzees and other apes symbol systems similar to human language have resulted in the demonstration of a genuine ability to create new symbolic patterns. Linguist Joel Wallman counters that attempts to teach chimps and other apes sign language or other symbolic systems have demonstrated that apes are very intelligent animals, but up to now these attempts have not shown that apes have any innate capacity for language.

Issue 8.   Does Language Determine How We Think?   144

YES: **John J. Gumperz and Stephen C. Levinson**, from "Introduction: Linguistic Relativity Re-examined" and "Introduction to Part 1," in John J. Gumperz and Stephen C. Levinson, eds., *Rethinking Linguistic Relativity* (Cambridge University Press, 1996)   *146*

NO: **Steven Pinker**, from *The Language Instinct: How the Mind Creates Language* (Perennial Classics, 2000)   *157*

Sociolinguists John J. Gumperz and Stephen C. Levinson contend that recent studies of language and culture suggest that language structures human thought in a variety of ways that most linguists and anthropologists had not believed possible. Cognitive neuropsychologist Steven Pinker draws on recent studies in cognitive science and neuropsychology to support the notion that previous studies have examined language but have said little, if anything, about thought.

PART 4   CULTURAL ANTHROPOLOGY   169

Issue 9.   Should Cultural Anthropology Model Itself on the Natural Sciences?   170

YES: **Marvin Harris,** from "Cultural Materialism Is Alive and Well and Won't Go Away Until Something Better Comes Along," in Robert Borofsky, ed., *Assessing Cultural Anthropology* (McGraw-Hill, 1994) *172*

NO: **Clifford Geertz,** from *The Interpretation of Cultures: Selected Essays by Clifford Geertz* (Basic Books, 1973) *182*

Cultural anthropologist Marvin Harris argues that anthropology has always been a science and should continue to be scientific. He contends that anthropology's goal should be to discover general, verifiable laws as in the other natural sciences. Cultural anthropologist Clifford Geertz views anthropology as a science of interpretation. He believes that anthropology's goal should be to generate deeper interpretations of diverse cultural phenomena, using what he calls "thick description," rather than attempting to prove or disprove scientific laws.

Issue 10.   Are San Hunter-Gatherers Basically Pastoralists Who Have Lost Their Herds?   194

YES: **James R. Denbow and Edwin N. Wilmsen,** from "Advent and Course of Pastoralism in the Kalahari," *Science* (December 19, 1986) *196*

NO: **Richard B. Lee,** from *The Dobe Ju/'hoansi,* 3rd ed. (Wadsworth Thomson Learning, 2003) *206*

Archaeologists James R. Denbow and Edwin N. Wilmsen argue that the San of the Kalahari Desert in southern Africa have been involved in pastoralism, agriculture, and regional trade networks since at least A.D. 800. They imply that the San, who were hunting and gathering in the twentieth century, were descendants of pastoralists who lost their herds due to subjugation by outsiders, drought, and livestock disease. Cultural anthropologist Richard B. Lee counters that evidence from oral history, archaeology, and ethnohistory shows that the Ju/'hoansi group of San living in the isolated Nyae Nyae-Dobe area of the Kalahari Desert were autonomous hunter-gatherers until the twentieth century. Although they carried on some trade with outsiders before then, it had minimal impact on their culture.

Issue 11.   Do Sexually Egalitarian Societies Exist?   216

YES: **Maria Lepowsky,** from *Fruit of the Motherland: Gender in an Egalitarian Society* (Columbia University Press, 1993) *218*

NO: **Steven Goldberg,** from "Is Patriarchy Inevitable?" *National Review* (November 11, 1996) *227*

Cultural anthropologist Maria Lepowsky argues that among the Vanatinai people of Papua New Guinea, the sexes are basically equal, although minor areas of male advantage exist. Sociologist Steven Goldberg contends that in all societies men occupy most high positions in hierarchical organizations and most high-status roles, and they dominate women in interpersonal relations. He states that this is because men's hormones cause them to compete more strongly than women for high status and dominance.

Issue 12.   Is It Natural for Adopted Children to Want to Find Out About Their Birth Parents?   234

YES: **Betty Jean Lifton,** from *Journey of the Adopted Self: A Quest for Wholeness* (Basic Books, 1994)   *236*

NO: **John Terrell and Judith Modell,** from "Anthropology and Adoption," *American Anthropologist* (March 1994)   *242*

Adoptee and adoption rights advocate Betty Jean Lifton argues that there is a natural need for human beings to know where they came from. Adoption is not a natural human state, she asserts, and it is surrounded by a secrecy that leads to severe social and psychological consequences for adoptees, adoptive parents, and birth parents. Anthropologists John Terrell and Judith Modell, who are each the parent of an adopted child, contend that the "need" to know one's birth parents is an American (or Western European) cultural construct. They conclude that in other parts of the world, where there is less emphasis placed on biology, adoptees have none of the problems said to be associated with being adopted in America.

Issue 13.   Has the Islamic Revolution in Iran Subjugated Women?   254

YES: **Parvin Paidar,** from "Feminism and Islam in Iran," in Deniz Kandiyoti, ed., *Gendering the Middle East: Emerging Perspectives* (Syracuse University Press, 1996)   *256*

NO: **Erika Friedl,** from "Sources of Female Power in Iran," in Mahnaz Afkhami and Erika Friedl, eds., *In the Eye of the Storm: Women in Post-Revolutionary Iran* (Syracuse University Press, 1994)   *266*

Iranian historian Parvin Paidar considers how the position of women suffered following the 1979 Iranian Revolution because of the imposition of Islamic law (shari'a), as interpreted by conservative male clerics. She contends that the Islamic Revolution marked a setback in the progressive modernist movements, which had improved women's rights during the secular regime of the Shah; new rights and opportunities have emerged since 1979 only in opposition to conservative interpretations of Islamic law. American anthropologist Erika Friedl asserts that men in Iran have consistently tried to suppress women's rights since the 1979 Iranian Revolution. Despite these efforts to repress them, women in all levels of society have access to many sources of power. In fact, argues Friedl, women have considerably more power available to them than either Western or Iranian stereotypes might suggest, even though they must work within Islamic law to obtain this power.

Issue 14.   Is Ethnic Conflict Inevitable?   278

YES: **Sudhir Kakar,** from "Some Unconscious Aspects of Ethnic Violence in India," in Veena Das, ed., *Mirrors of Violence: Communities, Riots and Survivors in South Asia* (Oxford University Press, 1990)   *280*

NO: **Anthony Oberschall,** from "The Manipulation of Ethnicity: From Ethnic Cooperation to Violence and War in Yugoslavia," *Ethnic and Racial Studies* (November 2000)   *288*

Indian social researcher Sudhir Kakar analyzes the origins of ethnic conflict from a psychological perspective to argue that ethnic differences are deeply held distinctions that from time to time will inevitably erupt as ethnic conflicts. He maintains that anxiety arises from preconscious fears about cultural differences. In his view, no amount of education or politically correct behavior will eradicate these fears and anxieties about people of differing ethnic backgrounds. American sociologist Anthony Oberschall considers the ethnic conflicts that have recently emerged in Bosnia and contends that primordial ethnic attachments are insufficient to explain the sudden emergence of violence among Bosnian ethnic groups. He adopts a complex explanation for this violence, identifying circumstances in which fears and anxieties were manipulated by politicians for self-serving ends. It was only in the context of these manipulations that ethnic violence could have erupted, concludes Oberschall.

PART 5   ETHICS IN ANTHROPOLOGY   301

Issue 15.   Should the Remains of Prehistoric Native Americans Be Reburied Rather Than Studied?   302

YES: **James Riding In**, from "Repatriation: A Pawnee's Perspective," *American Indian Quarterly* (Spring 1996)   *304*

NO: **Clement W. Meighan**, from "Some Scholars' Views on Reburial," *American Antiquity* (October 1992)   *313*

Assistant professor of justice studies and member of the Pawnee tribe James Riding In argues that holding Native American skeletons in museums and other repositories represents a sacrilege against Native American dead and, thus, all Indian remains should be reburied. Professor of anthropology and archaeologist Clement W. Meighan believes that archaeologists have a moral and professional obligation to the archaeological data with which they work. Such data is held in the public good and must be protected from destruction, he concludes.

Issue 16.   Should Anthropologists Work to Eliminate the Practice of Female Circumcision?   324

YES: **Merrilee H. Salmon**, from "Ethical Considerations in Anthropology and Archaeology, or Relativism and Justice for All," *Journal of Anthropological Research* (Spring 1997)   *326*

NO: **Elliott P. Skinner**, from "Female Circumcision in Africa: The Dialectics of Equality," in Richard R. Randolph, David M. Schneider, and May N. Diaz, eds., *Dialectics and Gender: Anthropological Approaches* (Westview Press, 1988)   *335*

Professor of the history and philosophy of science Merrilee H. Salmon argues that clitoridectomy (female genital mutilation) violates the rights of the women on whom it is performed. Professor of anthropology Elliott P. Skinner accuses feminists who want to abolish clitoridectomy of being ethnocentric. He argues that African women themselves want to participate in the practice, which functions like male initiation, transforming girls into adult women.

Issue 17.   Did Napoleon Chagnon and Other Researchers Harm the Yanomami Indians of Venezuela?   344

YES: Patrick Tierney, from "The Fierce Anthropologist," *The New Yorker* (October 9, 2000)   *346*

NO: John Tooby, from "Jungle Fever," *Slate,* http://slate.msn.com/?id=91946 (October 25, 2000)   *362*

Investigative journalist Patrick Tierney contends that geneticist James Neel caused a measles epidemic among the Yanomami Indians of Venezuela by inoculating them with a virulent measles vaccine. He also states that Neel's collaborator, anthropologist Napoleon Chagnon, exaggerated Yanomami aggressiveness and actually caused violence by indiscriminately giving machetes to tribesmen who helped him, sometimes even inducing them to break their own taboos. Anthropologist John Tooby counters that medical experts agree that it is impossible to produce communicable measles with the vaccine that Neel used. He also argues that Tierney systematically distorts Chagnon's views on Yanomami violence and exaggerates the amount of disruption caused by Chagnon's activities compared to that of such others as missionaries and gold miners.

Issue 18. Do Museums Misrepresent Ethnic Communities Around the World?   370

YES: James Clifford, from *The Predicament of Culture: Twentieth-Century Ethnography, Literature, and Art* (Harvard University Press, 1988)   *372*

NO: Denis Dutton, from "Mythologies of Tribal Art," *African Arts* (Summer 1995)   *381*

Postmodernist anthropologist James Clifford argues that the very act of removing objects from their ethnographic contexts distorts the meaning of objects held in museums. Exhibitions misrepresent ethnic communities by omitting important aspects of contemporary life, especially involvement with the colonial or Western world. Anthropologist Denis Dutton asserts that no exhibition can provide a complete context for ethnographic objects, but that does not mean that museum exhibitions are fundamentally flawed.

Contributors   392
Index   397

Introduction

Kirk M. Endicott

Robert L. Welsch

Anthropology is the study of humanity in all its biological, social, cultural, and linguistic diversity. Some of the founders of American anthropology, like Franz Boas, made important contributions to the understanding of human biology, culture, and language. But few such Renaissance men and women can be found today. To master the concepts, methods, and literatures involved in studying the different aspects of human variation, anthropologists have had to specialize. At times it may seem that no two anthropologists actually study the same things, yet they all are working toward a greater understanding of the commonalties and differences that define the human species.

Today, anthropology encompasses four major subdisciplines—biological anthropology, prehistoric archaeology, linguistic anthropology, and cultural anthropology—and several smaller subdisciplines. Controversial issues in each of these subfields are included in the first four parts of this volume.

Biological anthropology, also called *physical anthropology,* concerns the anatomy, physiology, mental capabilities, and genetics of humans and our nearest relatives, the primates. Traditionally, biological anthropologists, like other biologists, have understood human variation in evolutionary terms. Increasingly, as geneticists have introduced new ways of analyzing genetic data encoded in our DNA, biological anthropologists have described and explained human biological variation at the molecular level.

Fundamental questions for biological anthropologists include: How did our species evolve from early non-human primates? When did our species take on attributes that are associated with anatomically modern humans? Where did our species arise? What were the evolutionary forces that contributed to our anatomical and behavioral evolution? How and why did the hominids develop the capacity for culture—socially learned and transmitted patterns of behavior, thought, and feeling?

Paleoanthropologists (students of humankind's ancient ancestors) search for and excavate fossil bone fragments of long-dead primates, reconstruct their skeletons, and make inferences about their behavior patterns from bones, teeth, and other clues. They also use sophisticated dating techniques, computer models, and studies of living primates, both in the laboratory and in their natural environments, to create plausible models of human evolution and the relationships among the different branches of the primate order.

Archaeology, which is also referred to as *prehistory,* involves documenting, understanding, and explaining the history of human communities and civilizations that existed before written records. Unlike most historians who can turn to documents and papers to detail the life and times of their subjects, archaeologists must usually find evidence for their reconstructions of the past through excavations of sites where people formerly lived or worked.

One issue at the heart of most archaeological controversies is how we can or should interpret these varied kinds of data to reconstruct the ways of life of earlier times. Recurrent questions include: What is the use and meaning of an artifact? To what extent can we use current lifeways of tribal or foraging groups as analogies for how prehistoric communities lived?

A set of questions that archeologists continue to ask is when, why, and how people first settled different parts of the world. They also ask why innovations like agriculture developed at particular times and in particular places. Why did some societies develop into complex civilizations, while others remained village-based societies, free of centralized political authority?

A frequent point of debate among archaeologists concerns the dating of archaeological deposits. Accurate dating, even if only relative to other artifacts in a site, is clearly essential for accurate interpretations, although dating alone does not reveal the processes that led to particular changes in the archaeological record. Stratification—the principle that the lower layers of a deposit are older than the upper layers—is still the most reliable basis for relative dating within a site. Now archaeologists also draw on a wide battery of high-tech absolute dating methods—including carbon 14, potassium-argon, and thermoluminescence dating—which have varying degrees of accuracy for different time spans. Dating always requires interpretation because, for example, carbon samples may be contaminated by more recent organic material like tree roots, and scholars do not always agree on the correct interpretation.

Linguistic anthropology includes the study of language and languages, especially non-Western and unwritten languages, as well as the relationship between language and other aspects of culture. Language provides the categories within which culture is expressed. Some anthropologists regard linguistic anthropology as a subdivision of cultural anthropology because language is a part of culture and is the medium by which much of culture is transmitted from one generation to the next. A classic question for linguistic anthropologists has been: Do the categories of a language shape how humans perceive and understand the world? This question was first proposed by linguistic anthropologists Edward Sapir and Benjamin Whorf early in the twentieth century but continues to be one of the central questions of interest to linguistic anthropologists. Issue 8, "Does Language Determine How We Think?" addresses this question. Another question that linguistic anthropologists have debated for several decades concerns whether chimpanzees and other apes have the innate ability to use symbols in ways that resemble human language. This question is asked in Issue 7, "Can Apes Learn Language?" and is important because if apes are capable of complex symbolic activity, then language and culture are probably not the exclusive capabilities of humans but have their origins in our primate past.

Cultural anthropology, which is also called *social anthropology* in Great Britain or sometimes *sociocultural anthropology* in the United States, is concerned with the cultures and societies of living communities. Cultural anthropologists have proposed many different definitions of *culture.* Most emphasize that cultural behavior, thought, and feeling are socially created and learned, rather than generated by biologically transmitted instincts. Anthropologists differ considerably on the relative weight they assign to culture and instincts in explaining human behavior, as some of the issues in this volume show. Because cultures are human creations, they differ from one society to another.

Data for most cultural anthropologists come from observations, informal conversations, and interviews made while living within a study community. The hallmark of cultural anthropology is *fieldwork,* in which the anthropologist lives with another cultural group, learns their language, their customs, and their patterns of interaction. Anthropological fieldwork involves *participant observation*—observing while participating in the life of the community.

As in the other subfields of anthropology, cultural data must be interpreted. Interpretation begins with the creation of the research questions themselves. This reflects what investigators consider as being important to discover and directs their observations and questions in the field. At each step of data collection and analysis, the investigators' theories and interests shape their understanding of other cultures.

Much explanation in cultural anthropology is based on the comparison of cultural features in different societies. Some anthropologists explicitly make cross-cultural comparisons, using statistics to measure the significance of apparent correlations between such things as childrearing practices and adult personalities. Even anthropologists who concentrate on explaining or interpreting features of particular cultures use their knowledge of similar or different features in other societies as a basis for insights.

Like other anthropologists, cultural anthropologists look for uniformities in human behavior as well as variations. Understanding what patterns of human behavior are possible has been at the center of many controversies in cultural anthropology. Questions touched on in this book include: Is gender equality possible? Is violence inevitable? Can small-scale hunting and gathering societies live in contact with more powerful food-producing societies without being dominated by them?

Recently, cultural anthropologists have begun asking questions about possible biases in the ways anthropologists depict and represent other cultures through writing, films, and other media. This movement has been called *post-modern anthropology* or *critical anthropology.* Post-modernists ask, among other things: Do our theories and methods of representation inadvertently portray the people we study as exotic "Others," in exaggerated contrast with Western peoples? This is the question that lies behind Issue 18, "Do Museums Misrepresent Ethnic Communities Around the World?"

Ethics in anthropology Concerns about the ethics of research have become increasingly important in contemporary anthropology. The American Anthropological Association has developed a Code of Ethics covering both research and teaching (see the American Anthropological Association Web site at http://www.aaanet.org). It recognizes that researchers sometimes have conflicting obligations to the people and animals studied, host countries, the profession, and the public. One basic principle is that researchers should do nothing that could harm or distress the people or animals they study. Cultural anthropologists must be aware of the possibility of harming the living people with whom they work, but similar considerations also affect archaeologists and biological anthropologists because the artifacts of past communities often represent the ancestors of living communities. Here the interests of anthropologists and native peoples may diverge. For example, in Issue 15 we ask, "Should the Remains of Prehistoric Native Americans Be Reburied Rather Than Studied?" Similarly, we may ask what the ethical responsibilities of Western anthropologists should be when they find certain cultural practices of other peoples abhorrent or unjust. For example, Issue 16 asks, "Should Anthropologists Work to Eliminate the Practice of Female Circumcision?"

Some Basic Questions

On the surface, the issues presented in this book are very diverse. Anthropologists from different subfields tend to focus on their own specialized problems and to work with different kinds of evidence. Most of the controversial issues we have chosen for this volume can be read as very narrow, focused debates within a subfield. But many of the issues that confront anthropologists in one subfield arise in other subfields as well. What has attracted us to the issues presented here is that each raises much broader questions that affect the entire discipline. In this section we briefly describe some of the basic questions lying behind specific issues.

Is Anthropology a Science or a Humanity?

Science is a set of ideas and methods intended to describe and explain phenomena in a naturalistic way, seeing individual things and events as the outcome of discoverable causes and as conforming to general laws. Anthropologists taking a scientific approach are concerned with developing broad theories about the processes that lead to observed patterns of variation in human biology, language, and culture. The humanities, on the other hand, are concerned with understanding people's cultural creations in terms of their meanings to their creators and the motivations behind their creation.

Biological anthropology seeks the reasons for human evolution and biological diversity largely in the processes of the natural world, and it uses the methods of the physical sciences for investigating those phenomena. Archaeology, too, uses natural science concepts and methods of investigation, but it also draws on understandings of human behavior that take account of culturally-influenced motivations, values, and meanings. Cultural anthropologists are divided over whether cultural anthropology should model itself on the natural sciences or on the humanities. Some cultural anthropologists try to discover the causes of particular cultural forms occurring at specific places and times, while others try to interpret the meanings (to the people themselves) of cultural forms in other societies in ways that are intelligible to Western readers. Issue 9, "Should Cultural Anthropology Model Itself on the Natural Sciences?" directly addresses the question of whether anthropology is part of the sciences or humanities.

Is Biology or Culture More Important in Shaping Human Behavior?

Most anthropologists accept that both genetically transmitted behavioral tendencies (instincts) and cultural ideas and norms influence human behavior, thought, and emotion. However, anthropologists diverge widely over the amount of weight that they assign to these two influences. *Biological determinists* believe that all human behavior is ultimately determined by the genes, and that culture merely lends distinctive coloration to our genetically driven behaviors. At the other extreme, *cultural determinists* believe that any instincts humans may have are so weak and malleable that cultural learning easily overcomes them. The conflict between supporters of the two extreme views, called the *nature-nurture debate,* has been going on for many years and shows no sign of being resolved soon.

Several of the issues in this volume deal directly with the nature-nuture question, including Issue 3, "Are Humans Inherently Violent?"; Issue 7, "Can Apes Learn Language?"; Issue 11, "Do Sexually Egalitarian Societies Exist?"; and Issue 12, "Is It Natural for Adopted Children to Want to Find Out About Their Birth Parents?"

Is the Local Development of Culture or Outside Influence More Important in Shaping Cultures?

In trying to explain the form a particular culture takes, different anthropologists place different amounts of emphasis on the local development of culture and on outside influence. Those who favor local development emphasize unique innovations and adaptations to the natural environment, while those favoring outside influences emphasize the borrowing of ideas from neighbors (*diffusion*) and changes forced upon a people by more powerful groups (*acculturation*). Most anthropologists recognize some influence from both sources, but some attribute overriding importance to one or the other.

The debate between proponents of local development of culture and proponents of outside influence plays a major role in two of the issues in this volume: Issue 6, "Were Environmental Factors Responsible for the Mayan Collapse?" and Issue 10, "Are San Hunter-Gatherers Basically Pastoralists Who Have Lost Their Herds?"

Is a Feminist Perspective Needed in Anthropology?

Although female anthropologists—like Margaret Mead and Ruth Benedict—have been very influential in the development of anthropology, there was a bias in early anthropological studies toward emphasizing the social and political lives of men. Over the past 30 years feminist anthropologists have argued that these male-biased accounts have overlooked much of what goes on in traditional societies because male anthropologists have been preoccupied with men's activities and the male point of view.

Issue 5, "Was There a Goddess Cult in Prehistoric Europe?" considers one possible male bias in interpreting prehistoric religions. Issue 11, "Do Sexually Egalitarian Societies Exist?" considers whether or not a feminist perspective is needed to recognize sexual equality. Feminist anthropologists have also asserted that male bias has affected the choice of research topics and methodologies. In recent years, female anthropologists have investigated gender roles in different societies. Issue 13, "Has the Islamic Revolution in Iran Subjugated Women?" considers how religion and politics have influenced the role of women in contemporary Iran.

Some Theoretical Approaches

Anthropologists draw on many theories of widely varying scope and type. We present brief summaries of a number of theoretical approaches used by authors in this book so that you will recognize and understand them when you see them. We have arranged these theories in a rough continuum from most scientific in approach to most humanistic.

Biological evolution   Biological anthropology is based predominantly on the modem theory of biological evolution. This builds upon the ideas that Charles Darwin developed in the mid-nineteenth century. Darwin combined the idea of evolution—the development of species by means of incremental changes in previous species—with the concept of natural selection. Natural selection means that in a variable population those individuals best adapted to the environment are most likely to survive and reproduce, thus passing on their favorable characteristics (called *survival of the fittest*). The modem theory of biological evolution adds an understanding of genetics, including the concepts of *genetic drift* (random variation in gene frequencies) and *gene flow* (transmission of genes between populations). Most biological anthropologists today also subscribe to the notion of *punctuated equilibrium,* which states that evolutionary change takes place in fits and starts, rather than at an even pace.

Virtually all biological anthropologists use the modem theory of evolution, so their disagreements arise not over which theory to use, but over interpretations of evidence and questions of how the theory applies to specific cases.

Sociobiology   Sociobiology is a theory that attempts to use evolutionary principles to explain all behavior of animals, including humans. The best-known practitioner is biologist E. O. Wilson, whose book *Sociobiology: The New Synthesis* (Harvard University Press, 1975) sets out the basic concepts. Sociobiologists believe that human behavior is determined by inherited behavioral tendencies. The genes promoting behaviors that lead to survival and successful reproduction are favored by natural selection and thus tend to become more common in a population over the generations. For sociobiologists such behaviors as selfishness, altruism to close kin, violence, and certain patterns of marriage are evolutionarily and biologically determined. They see individual and cultural ideas as mere rationalizations of innate patterns of behavior. In their view, no culture will persist that goes against the "wisdom of the genes."

Cultural evolution Drawing on an analogy with biological evolution, nineteenth-century cultural anthropologists developed the idea that complex societies evolve out of simpler ones. The unilineal schemes of such cultural evolutionists as Lewis Henry Morgan, E. B. Tylor, and James G. Fraser postulated that all societies pass through a fixed series of stages, from savagery to civilization. They regarded contemporary simple societies, like the tribal peoples of the Amazon, as "survivals" from earlier stages of cultural evolution.

Unilineal schemes of cultural evolution have now been discredited because they were speculative, ignored differences in patterns of culture change in different places, and were blatantly ethnocentric, regarding all non-Western cultures as inferior to those of Europe. But some archaeologists and cultural anthropologists still espouse more sophisticated versions of cultural evolution regarding at least some aspects of culture change.

Cultural ecology The theory of cultural ecology was developed by cultural anthropologist Julian Steward in the 1930s as a corrective to the overly simple schemes of cultural evolution. Emphasizing the process of adaptation to the physical environment, he postulated that societies in different environments would develop different practices, though the general trend was toward higher levels of complexity, a process he called *multilinear evolution*. His idea of adaptation, like natural selection, explained why some societies and practices succeeded and were perpetuated, while other less well-adapted ones died out.

Many archaeologists and cultural anthropologists use versions of cultural ecology to explain why certain practices exist in certain environments. Marvin Harris's widely-used theory of *cultural materialism* is a further development of cultural ecology. The basic idea behind all versions of cultural ecology is that societies must fulfill their material needs if they are to survive. Therefore those institutions involved with making a living must be well adapted to the environment, while others, like religions, are less constrained by the environment.

Culture history One of the founders of American cultural anthropology, Franz Boas, rejected the cultural evolution schemes of the nineteenth century, with their fixed stages of cultural development. He pointed out that all societies had unique histories, depending on local innovations and diffusion of ideas from neighboring societies. Also, change is not always toward greater complexity; civilizations crumble as well as rise. Boas advocated recording the particular events and influences that contributed to the makeup of each culture.

World system theory   The world system theory, which has gained great prominence in the social sciences in recent years, asserts that all societies, large and small, are—and long have been—integrated in a single worldwide political-economic system. This approach emphasizes the connections among societies, especially the influence of politically powerful societies over weak ones, as in colonialism, rather than local development of culture.

Cultural interpretation   Humanist anthropologists emphasize their role as interpreters, not explainers, of culture. They focus on the task of describing other cultures in ways that are intelligible to Western readers, making sense of customs that at first glance seem incomprehensible. The most prominent practitioner of cultural interpretation is Clifford Geertz, who coined the term *thick description* for this process. This approach is used especially for dealing with aspects of culture that are products of human imagination, like art and mythology, but even the institutions involved in physical survival, like families and economic processes, have dimensions of meaning that warrant interpretation.

Feminist anthropology   Feminist anthropology began in the 1970s as an approach meant to correct the lack of coverage of women and women's views in earlier anthropology. It has now developed into a thoroughgoing alternative approach to the study of culture and society. Its basic idea is that gender is a cultural construction affecting the roles and meanings of the sexes in particular societies. The aim of feminist anthropology is both to explain the position of women and to convey the meanings surrounding gender. Feminist anthropologists emphasize that all social relations have a gender dimension.

How Anthropologists Reach Conclusions

None of the issues considered in this volume have been resolved, and several are still the subject of heated, and at times, acrimonious debate. The most heated controversies typically arise from the most extreme points of view. When reading these selections students should bear in mind that only two positions are presented formally, although in the introductions and postscripts we raise questions that should guide you to consider other positions as well. We encourage you to question all of the positions offered before coming to any conclusions of your own. Remember, for more than a century anthropology has prided itself on revealing how our own views of the world are culturally biased. Try to be aware of how your own background, upbringing, ethnicity, religion, likes, and dislikes affect your assessments of the arguments presented here.

In our own teaching we have often used controversial issues as a way to help students understand how anthropologists think about research questions. We have found that five questions often help students focus on the most important points in these selections:

1. Who is the author?
2. What are the author's assumptions?
3. What methods and data does an author use?
4. What are the author's conclusions?
5. How does the author reach his or her conclusions from the data?

For each issue we suggest that you consider what school of thought, what sort of training, and what sort of research experience each author has. We often find it useful to ask why this particular author finds the topic worth writing about. Does one or the other author seem to have any sort of bias? What assumptions does each author hold? Do both authors hold the same assumptions?

For any anthropological debate, we also find it useful to ask what methods or analytical strategies each author has used to reach the conclusions he or she presents. For some of the issues presented in this book, authors share many of the same assumptions and are generally working with the same evidence, but disagree as to how this evidence should be analyzed. Some authors disagree most profoundly on what kinds of data are most suitable for answering a particular research question. Some even disagree about what kinds of questions anthropologists should be asking.

Finally, we suggest that you consider how the author has come to his or her conclusions from the available data. Would different data make any difference? Would a different kind of evidence be more appropriate? Would different data likely lead to different conclusions? Would different ways of analyzing the data suggest other conclusions?

If you can answer most of these questions about any pair of selections, you will be thinking about these problems anthropologically and will understand how anthropologists approach controversial research questions. After weighing the various possible positions on an issue you will be able to form sound opinions of your own.

On the Internet . . .

Human Origins and Evolution in Africa

Jeanne Sept, an anthropology professor at Indiana University who has done
fieldwork on the question of human origins in Africa, created this Web site,
which is entitled Human Origins and Evolution in Africa. The site contains much
information and provides links to related Web sites.

> http://www.indiana.edu/~origins/

Fossil Evidence for Human Evolution in China

The Fossil Evidence for Human Evolution in China Web site was created by
the Center for the Study of Chinese Prehistory. This site includes a catalog of
Chinese human fossil remains; provides links to other sites dealing with paleontology, human evolution, and Chinese prehistory; and includes other resources
that may be useful for gaining a better understanding of China's role in the
emergence of humankind.

> http://www.chineseprehistory.org

Neanderthals

This site provides information on the differences between Neanderthals (also
spelled *Neandertals*) and modern humans and on the emergence of modern humans. It also includes links to other sites offering further information
on Neanderthals.

> http://www.neanderthal.de/e_thal/fs_1.htm

Fossil Hominids: The Evidence for Human Evolution

Created by Jim Foley, this site is entitled Fossil Hominids: The Evidence for Human Evolution, and it provides links to recent articles about human evolution
and the question of whether or not Neandertals and early modern humans interbred. A discussion of creationism and the Biblical interpretation of the origins
of life is also presented.

> http://www.talkorigins.org/faqs/homs/

PART 1

Biological Anthropology

*B*iological anthropologists, also called physical anthropologists, study the bodies, bones, and genetics of humans and of our nearest relatives, the other primates. Their basic goals are to understand human evolution scientifically and to explain contemporary human diversity. Fundamental questions include: How did our species evolve from early nonhuman primates? When did our species take on attributes that are associated with anatomically modern humans? Where did our species develop as a species, and what were the evolutionary forces that contributed to our anatomical evolution? These questions have traditionally required detailed comparisons of bones from living species and fossilized bones from extinct species. However, increasingly anthropologists asking these kinds of questions are developing new models about evolution from observing and studying living primates either in the laboratory or in their natural environment.

- Did *Homo Sapiens* Originate Only in Africa?

- Did Neandertals Interbreed With Modern Humans?

- Are Humans Inherently Violent?

ISSUE 1

Did *Homo Sapiens* Originate Only in Africa?

YES: Christopher Stringer and Robin McKie, from *African Exodus: The Origins of Modern Humanity* (Henry Holt & Company, 1996)

NO: Alan G. Thorne and Milford H. Wolpoff, from "The Multiregional Evolution of Humans," *Scientific American* (April 1992)

ISSUE SUMMARY

YES: Paleoanthropologist Christopher Stringer and science writer Robin McKie argue that recent analysis of mitochondrial DNA evidence dates the evolution of anatomically modern humans to about 200,000 years ago. They assert that *Homo sapiens* originated from a single African population, which then spread over the rest of that continent and ultimately dispersed to all parts of the Old World, replacing all earlier hominid populations.

NO: Paleoanthropologists Alan G. Thorne and Milford H. Wolpoff counter that models derived from mitochondrial DNA evidence do not agree with the fossil and archaeological evidence. They maintain that *Homo erectus* populations had dispersed to all parts of the Old World by one million years ago. As the populations dispersed, they maintained contact and interbred enough so that the populations gradually evolved throughout the Old World to become anatomically modern humans.

Few debates in biological anthropology have been as heated as the debate concerning when and where anatomically modern humans evolved. At the heart of the debate are two distinct sets of biological data.

The first data set consists of the fossil record of early hominids and associated archaeological evidence of stone tools. Models of human evolution have remained fairly stable in spite of the fact that in recent years the number of fossilized hominid skeletons available to paleoanthropologists for study has increased substantially.

The second data set consists of mitochondrial DNA—genetic material that has only recently been deciphered by molecular biologists. Nuclear DNA from each parent combines at conception so that a child shares half of his or her DNA with each parent. This fact also means that half of the child's DNA differs from that of each parent. In this way nuclear, or recombinant, DNA continues to recombine with each generation so that after five generations, a child shares only a very small part of his or her DNA with each of its 32 great-great-great grandparents. But mitochondrial DNA is different; it comes exclusively from the mother and does not recombine with the father's DNA at all. It is passed on intact from mothers to daughters forming female lineages called matrilines. Mitochondrial DNA changes only through mutation.

In the 1950s early fossil skeletons were discovered along the Rift Valley in Africa by Louis and Mary Leakey. Since then paleoanthropologists have found many *Australopithecus* remains, thus proving that Africa is where our human lineage split off from that of the great apes. This gave rise to Robert Ardrey's book *African Genesis* (Atheneum, 1961), which stated that our first bipedal ancestors originated in Africa. Scholars today accept that *Homo erectus* spread out from Africa to settle in most of the Old World by at least one million years ago. These conclusions about *Homo erectus* have been confirmed by new fossil evidence both within Africa and elsewhere, and no paleoanthropologists or geneticists challenge this theory.

But where and how *Homo erectus* evolved to become *Homo sapiens* has been a fiercely contested matter. Two theories have been put forward: (1) the "out-of-Africa" theory and (2) the "multiregional" theory.

The "out-of-Africa" theory was first proposed in 1987 by a group of geneticists and molecular anthropologists in Berkeley, California. They interpreted their analysis of human mitochondrial DNA as indicating that all humans living today are members of the same mitochondrial DNA matrilineage that originated roughly 200,000 years ago.

In their selection, Christopher Stringer and Robin McKie discuss what is known as the "African Eve." They argue that by calibrating the rate of mutations in mitochondrial DNA, they can date the founding mother of all living human beings.

In the second selection, Alan G. Thorne and Milford H. Wolpoff support the "multiregional" theory. According to this theory, after *Homo erectus* spread across the Old World, the species continued to evolve as a single species to become *Homo sapiens*. The shift from *Homo erectus* to *Homo sapiens* was gradual and at no time were *Homo erectus* and *Homo sapiens* competing for the same resources or ecological niches.

These selections raise a number of questions for anthropologists: How reliable is DNA evidence? What assumptions are built into these DNA models? How can the rates of genetic mutation be calibrated? Does mitochondrial DNA mutate at the same rate as nuclear DNA? How complete is the fossil record? Do paleoanthropologists also have assumptions about how fossils change that might be incorrect? What evidence in the fossil or archaeological record should be found if *Homo sapiens* replaced *Homo erectus*? Can anthropologists find some middle ground between these two models that will account for all of the current data?

Christopher Stringer
and Robin McKie

 **YES**

The Mother of All Humans?

$\mathbf{I}$t is not the gorilla, nor the chimpanzee, nor the orangutan, that is unusual. . . .
Each enjoys a normal spectrum of biological variability. It is the human race
that is odd. We display remarkable geographical diversity, and yet astonishing genetic unity. This dichotomy is perhaps one of the greatest ironies of
our evolution. Our nearest primate relations may be much more differentiated with regard to their genes but today are consigned to living in a band of
land across Central Africa, and to the islands of Borneo and Sumatra. We, who
are stunningly similar, have conquered the world.

This revelation has provided the unraveling of our African origins with
one of its most controversial chapters. And it is not hard to see why. The realization that humans are biologically highly homogeneous has one straightforward
implication: that mankind has only recently evolved from one tight little group
of ancestors. We simply have not had time to evolve significantly different patterns of genes. Human beings may look dissimilar, but beneath the separate
hues of our skins, our various types of hair, and our disparate physiques, our
basic biological constitutions are fairly unvarying. We are all members of a
very young species, and our genes betray this secret.

It is not this relative genetic conformity per se that has caused the fuss
but the results of subsequent calculations which have shown that the common
ancestor who gave rise to our tight mitochondrial DNA lineage must have lived
about 200,000 years ago. This date, of course, perfectly accords with the idea of
a separate recent evolution of *Homo sapiens* shortly before it began its African
exodus about 100,000 years ago. In other words, one small group of *Homo sapiens* living 200 millennia ago must have been the source of all our present, only
slightly mutated mitochondrial DNA samples—and must therefore be the fount
of all humanity. Equally, the studies refute the notion that modern humans
have spent the last one million years quietly evolving in different parts of the
globe until reaching their present status. Our DNA is too uniform for that to be
a realistic concept. . . .

Not surprisingly, such intercessions into the hardened world of the fossil hunter, by scientists trained in the "delicate" arts of molecular biology and
genetic manipulation, have not gone down well in certain paleontological circles. The old order has reacted with considerable anger to the interference of

these "scientific interlopers." The idea that the living can teach us anything about the past is a reversal of their cherished view that we can best learn about ourselves from studying our prehistory. Many had spent years using fossils to establish their interpretations of human origins, and took an intense dislike to being "elbowed aside by newcomers armed with blood samples and computers," as *The Times* (London) put it. "The fossil record is the real evidence for human evolution," announced Alan Thorne and Milford Wolpoff in one riposte (in *Scientific American*) to the use of mitochondrial DNA to study our origins. "Unlike the genetic data, fossils can be matched to the predictions of theories about the past without relying on a long list of assumptions." Such a clash of forces has, predictably, generated a good many sensational headlines, and triggered some of the most misleading statements that have ever been made about our origins. Scientists have denied that these genetic analyses reveal the fledgling status of the human race. Others have even rejected the possibility of ever re-creating our past by studying our present in this way. Both views are incorrect, as we shall see. Even worse, the multiregionalists have attempted to distort the public's understanding of the Out of Africa theory by deliberately confusing its propositions with the most extreme and controversial of the geneticists' arguments. By tarnishing the latter they hope to diminish the former. This [selection] will counter such propaganda and highlight the wide-ranging support for our African Exodus provided, not just by the molecular biologists, but by others, including those who study the words we speak and who can detect signs of our recent African ancestry there. We shall show not only that the majority of leading evolutionists and biologists believe in such an idea but that their views raise such serious questions about the multiregional hypothesis that its future viability must now be very much in doubt.

Unraveling the history of human migration from our current genetic condition is not an easy business, of course. It is a bit like trying to compile a family tree with only an untitled photograph album to help you. "Our genetic portrait of humankind is necessarily based on recent samplings, [and] it is unavoidably static," says Christopher Wills of the University of San Diego. "Historical records of human migrations cover only a tiny fraction of the history of our species, and we know surprisingly little about how long most aboriginal people have occupied their present homes. We are pretty close to the position of a viewer who tries to infer the entire plot of *Queen Christina* from the final few frames showing Garbo's rapt face."

It is an intriguing image. Nevertheless, biologists are beginning to make a telling impact in unraveling this biological plot and in understanding *Homo sapiens'* African exodus. And they have done this thanks to the development of some extraordinarily powerful techniques for splitting up genes, which are made of stands of DNA (deoxyribonucleic acid) and which control the process of biological inheritance....

[T]his is exactly what Allan Wilson, Rebecca Cann, and Mark Stoneking, working at the University of California, Berkeley, did in 1987. They took specimens from placentas of 147 women from various ethnic groups and analyzed each's mitochondrial DNA. By comparing these in order of affinity, they assembled a giant tree, a vast family network, a sort of chronological chart for mankind, which linked up all the various samples, and therefore the world's races, in a grand, global genealogy.

The study produced three conclusions. First, it revealed that very few mutational differences exist between the mitochondrial DNA of human beings, be they Vietnamese, New Guineans, Scandinavians, or Tongans. Second, when the researchers put their data in a computer and asked it to produce the most likely set of linkages between the different people, graded according to the similarity of their mitochondrial DNA, it created a tree with two main branches. One consisted solely of Africans. The other contained the remaining people of African origin, and everyone else in the world. The limb that connected these two main branches must therefore have been rooted in Africa, the researchers concluded. Lastly, the study showed that African people had slightly more mitochondrial DNA mutations compared to non-Africans, implying their roots are a little older. In total, these results seemed to provide overwhelming support for the idea that mankind arose in Africa, and, according to the researchers' data, very recently. Their arithmetic placed the common ancestor as living between 142,500 and 285,000 years ago, probably about 200,000 years ago. These figures show that the appearance of "modern forms of *Homo sapiens* occurred first in Africa" around this time and "that all present day humans are descendants of that African population," stated Wilson and his team.

The Berkeley paper outlining these findings was published in the journal *Nature* in January 1987, and made headlines round the world, which is not surprising given that Wilson pushed the study's implications right to the limit. He argued that his mitochondrial tree could be traced back, not just to a small group of *Homo sapiens,* but to one woman, a single mother who gave birth to the entire human race. The notion of an alluring fertile female strolling across the grasslands of Africa nourishing our forebears was too much for newspapers and television. She was dubbed "African Eve"—though this one was found, not in scripture, but in DNA. (The honor of so naming this genetic mother figure is generally accorded to Charles Petit, the distinguished science writer of the *San Francisco Chronicle.* Wilson claimed he disliked the title, preferring instead, "Mother of us all" or "One lucky mother.")

The image of this mitochondrial matriarch may seem eccentric but it at least raises the question of how small a number of *Homo sapiens* might have existed 200,000 years ago. In fact, there must have been thousands of women alive at that time. The planet's six billion inhabitants today are descendants of many of these individuals (and their male partners), not just one single super-mother. As we have said, we humans get our main physical and mental characteristics from our nuclear genes, which are a mosaic of contributions from myriad ancestors. We appear to get our mitochondrial genes from only one woman, but that does not mean she is the only mother of all humans.

"Think of it as the female equivalent of passing on family surnames," states Sir Walter Bodmer, the British geneticist. "When women marry they usually lose their surname, and assume their husband's. Now if a man has two children, there is a 25 percent chance both will be daughters. When they marry, they too will change their name, and his surname will disappear. After twenty generations, 90 percent of surnames will vanish this way, and within 10,000 generations—which would take us from the time of 'African Eve' to the present day—there would only be one left." An observer might assume that this vast, single-named clan bore a disproportionately high level of its originator's genes. In fact, it would contain a fairly complete blend of all human genes. And the same effect is true for mitochondrial DNA (except of course it is the man who is "cut out"). The people of the world therefore seem to have basically only one mitochondrial "name." Nevertheless, they carry a mix of all the human genes that must have emanated from that original founding group of *Homo sapiens.* It is a point that Wilson tried, belatedly, to make himself. "She wasn't the literal mother of us all, just the female from whom all our mitochondrial DNA derives." . . .

And there we have it. The blood that courses through our veins, the genes that lie within our cells, the DNA strands that nestle inside our mitochondrial organelles, even the words we speak—all bear testimony to the fact that 100,000 years ago a portion of our species emerged from its African homeland and began its trek to world dominion. (The other part, which stayed behind, was equally successful in diversifying across the huge African continent, of course.) It may seem an exotic, possibly unsettling, tale. Yet there is nothing strange about it. This process of rapid radiation is how species spread. The real difference is just how far we took this process—to the ends of the earth. A species normally evolves in a local ecology that, in some cases, provides a fortuitously fertile ground for honing a capacity for survival. Armed with these newly acquired anatomies, or behavior patterns, it can then take over the niches of other creatures. This is the normal course of evolution. What is abnormal is the supposed evolution of mankind as described by the multiregionalists. They place their faith in a vast global genetic link-up and compare our evolution to individuals paddling in separate corners of a pool. . . . According to this scheme, each person maintains their individuality over time. Nevertheless, they influence one another with the spreading ripples they raise—which are the equivalent of genes flowing between populations.

Let us recall the words of Alan Thorne and Milford Wolpoff. . . .
They state that:

> The dramatic genetic similarities across the entire human race do not reflect a recent common ancestry for all living people. They show the consequences of linkages between people that extend to when our ancestors first populated the Old World, more than a million years ago. They are the results of an ancient history of population connections and mate exchanges that has characterised the human race since its inception. Human evolution happened everywhere because every area was always part of the whole.

Gene flow is therefore crucial to the idea that modern humans evolved separately, for lengthy periods, in different corners of the earth, converging somehow into a now highly homogeneous form. Indeed, the theory cannot survive without this concept—for a simple reason. Evolution is random in action and that means that similar environmental pressures—be they associated with climate change, or disease, or other factors—often generate different genetic responses in separate regions. Consider malaria, a relatively new disease that spread as human populations became more and more dense after the birth of agriculture. Our bodies have generated a profusion of genetic ripostes for protection in the form of a multitude of partially effective inherited blood conditions. And each is unique to the locale in which it arose. In other words, separate areas produced separate DNA reactions. There has been no global human response to malaria.

Nevertheless, multiregionalism maintains that gene flow produces just such a global response. Given enough time gene exchange from neighboring peoples will make an impact, its proponents insist. This phenomenon, they say, has ensured that the world's population has headed towards the same general evolutionary goal, *Homo sapiens;* though it is also claimed that local selective pressure would have produced some distinctive regional physical differences (such as the European's big nose). And if the new dating of early *Homo erectus* in Java is to be believed (as many scientists are prepared to), then we must accept that this web of ancient lineages has been interacting—like some ancient, creaking international telephone exchange—for almost two million years.

Now this is an interesting notion which makes several other key assumptions: that there were enough humans alive at any time in the Old World over that period to sustain interbreeding and to maintain the give and take of genes; that there were no consistent geographical barriers to this mating urge; that the different human groups or even species that existed then would have wished to have shared their genes with one another; and that this rosy vision of different hominids evolving globally towards the same happy goal has some biological precedent.

So let us examine each supposition briefly, starting with the critical question of population density. According to the multiregionalists, genes had to be passed back and forward between the loins of ancient hominids, from South Africa to Indonesia. And this was done, not by rapacious, visiting males spreading their genotype deep into the heart of other species or peoples (a sort of backdoor man school of evolution), but by local interchange. In neighboring groups, most people would have stayed where they were, while some individuals moved back and forward, or on to the next group as they intermarried. In other words, populations essentially sat still while genes passed through them. But this exchange requires sufficient numbers of neighboring men and women to be breeding in the first place. By any standard, hominids—until very recent times—were very thin on the ground. One calculation by Alan Rogers, a geneticist at the University of Utah, in Salt Lake City, and colleagues uses mitochondrial DNA mutations to assess how many females the species possessed as it evolved. The results he produced are striking. "The multiregional model implies that modern humans evolved in a population that spanned several continents, yet the present results imply that this population contained fewer than 7,000 females," he states in *Current Anthropology.* It is therefore implausible, he adds, that a species so thinly spread could have spanned three continents and still have been connected by gene flow.

Then there is the question of geography. To connect humanity throughout the Old World, genes would have had to flow ("fly" might be a better word) back and forth up the entire African continent, across Arabia, over India, and down through Malaysia; contact would therefore have had to have been made through areas of low population density such as mountains and deserts, coupled with some of the worst climatic disruptions recorded in our planet's recent geological past. Over the past 500,000 years, the world was gripped by frequent Ice Ages: giant glaciers would have straddled the Himalayas, Alps, Caucasus Mountains; meltwater would have poured off these ice caps in torrents, swelling inland lakes and seas (such as the Caspian) far beyond their present sizes; while deserts, battered by dust storms, would have spread over larger and larger areas. Vast regions would have been virtually blocked to the passage of humans. At times our planet was extremely inhospitable while these straggling hordes of humans were supposed to be keeping up the very busy business of cozy genetic interaction. "Even under ecologically identical conditions, which is rarely the case in nature, geographically isolated populations will diverge away from each other and eventually become reproductively isolated. . . . It is highly improbable that evolution would take identical paths in this multi-dimensional landscape," writes the Iranian researcher Shahin Rouhani.

[Luca] Cavalli-Sforza agrees: "What is very difficult to conceive is a parallel evolution over such a vast expanse of land, with the limited genetic exchange that there could have been in earlier times." He acknowledges that it is theoretically possible that the genes of west European humans would have been compatible with those of east Asia despite their ancient separation. Barriers to fertility are usually slow to develop: perhaps a million years or more in mammals. However, he adds, "barriers to fertility of a cultural and social nature may be more important than biological ones." Two very different looking sets of people may have been able to interbreed physically but would have considered such action as breaking a gross taboo.

In other words, we are expected to believe that a wafer-thin population of hominids, trudging across continents gripped by Ice Ages, were supposed to be ready to mate with people they would have found extraordinarily odd-looking and who behaved in peculiar ways. Cavalli-Sforza, for one, does not buy this. "Proponents of the multiregional model simply do not understand population genetics," he states. "They use a model that requires continuous exchange of genes, but it requires enormous amounts of time to reach equilibrium. There has been insufficient time in human history to reach that equilibrium." The spread of modern humans over a large fraction of the earth's surface is more in tune with a specific expansion from a nuclear area of origin, he adds.

Now this last point is an important one, for it is frequently presented in the popular press that the Out of Africa theory represents a divergence from the natural flow of biological affairs, that its protagonists are somehow on the fringes of orthodoxy, proposing strange and radical notions. The reverse is true —the large number of scientists quoted [here] indicates the wide intellectual support now accorded the theory. It is a very new idea, admittedly. It is only a little more than a decade since it was first proposed, on the basis of fossils, by scientists like [Gunter] Bräuer and [Chris] Stringer. Yet its precepts now affect many areas of science, and its implications are accepted by their most distinguished practitioners. We are witnessing a rare moment in science, the replacement of a redundant orthodoxy by a formerly heretical vision. Hence the words of Yoel Rak as he staggered from a multiregionalists' symposium in 1991. "I feel like I have just had to sit through a meeting of the Flat Earth Society," he moaned.

Of course, Rak became an African Exodus proselytizer many years ago. A more damning convert, if you are multiregionalist, is that of *Science,* a journal noted for its dispassion and conservatism. "The theory that all modern humans originated in Africa is looking more and more convincing," it announced in March 1995, "and the date of the first human exodus keeps creeping closer to the present... the evidence coming out of our genes seems to be sweeping the field."

In fact, the idea that the opposition—the multiregionalists—represent the norm in biological thinking is to present the story of human origins "ass backwards," as Stephen Jay Gould succinctly puts it.

> Multi-regionalism... is awfully hard to fathom. Why should populations throughout the world, presumably living in different environments under varying regimes of natural selection, all be moving on the same evolutionary pathway? Besides, most large, successful, and widespread species are stable for most of their history, and do not change in any substantial directional sense at all. For non-human species, we never interpret global distribution as entailing preference for a multiregional view of origins. We have no multiregional theory for the origin of rats or pigeons, two species that match our success and geographical spread. No one envisions proto-rats on all continents evolving together toward improved ratitude. Rather we assume that *Rattus rattus* and *Columbia livia* initially arose in a single place, as an entity or isolated population, and then spread out, eventually to cover the globe. Why uniquely for humans, do we develop a multiregional theory and then even declare it orthodox, in opposition to all standard views about how evolution occurs?

The answer to that critical question has much to do with an outlook that has pervaded and bedeviled science throughout history. We have, at various times, been forced to abandon species-centric scientific notions that we live at the center of the cosmos, and that we were specially created by a supreme being. A last vestige of this urge to self-importance can be seen in multiregionalism, which holds that our brain development is an event of all-consuming global consequence towards which humanity strived in unison for nearly two million years. It argues that *Homo sapiens'* emergence was dictated by a worldwide tendency to evolve large braincases, and share genes and "progress." Humanity is the product of a predictable proclivity for smartness, in other words, so we cannot possibly be the outcome of some local biological struggle. Surely that would demean us. To believe that humanity could be the product of a small, rapidly evolving African population who struck it lucky in the evolution stakes is therefore viewed as being worse than apostasy by these people. Unfortunately for them, there is little proof to support their specialist, global promotion of mankind—as we have seen. Once again we must adopt the simplest scientific explanation (i.e., the one for which the facts best fit) as the superior one. As this [selection] has made clear, there is no good genetic evidence to sustain an argument that places humanity on a plinth of global superiority. To do so is to indulge in mysticism. *Homo sapiens* is not the child of an entire planet, but a creature, like any other, that has its roots in one place and period—in this case with a small group of Africans for whom "time and chance" has only just arrived. Nor is our species diminished in any way by such interpretations. Indeed, we are enriched through explanations that demonstrate our humble origins, for they place us in an appropriate context that, for the first time, permits proper self-evaluation and provides an understanding of the gulf we are crossing from a clever ape to a hominid that can shape a planet to its requirements—if only it could work out what these are.

Alan G. Thorne and
Milford H. Wolpoff

 **NO**

The Multiregional Evolution of Humans

Two decades ago paleoanthropologists were locked in a debate about the origin of the earliest humans. The disagreement centered on whether the fossil *Ramapithecus* was an early human ancestor or ancestral to both human and ape lineages. Molecular biologists entered that discussion and supported the minority position held by one of us (Wolpoff) and his students that *Ramapithecus* was not a fossil human, as was then commonly believed. Their evidence, however, depended on a date for the chimpanzee-human divergence that was based on a flawed "molecular clock." We therefore had to reject their support.

Today the paleoanthropological community is again engaged in a debate, this time about how, when and where modern humans originated. On one side stand some researchers, such as ourselves, who maintain there is no single home for modern humanity—humans originated in Africa and then slowly developed their modern forms in every area of the Old World. On the other side are workers who claim that Africa alone gave birth to modern humans within the past 200,000 years. Once again the molecular geneticists have entered the fray, attempting to resolve it in favor of the African hypothesis with a molecular clock. Once again their help must be rejected because their reasoning is flawed.

Genetic research has undeniably provided one of the great insights of 20th-century biology: that all living people are extremely closely related. Our DNA similarities are far greater than the disparate anatomic variations of humanity might suggest. Studies of the DNA carried by the cell organelles called mitochondria, which are inherited exclusively from one's mother and are markers for maternal lineages, now play a role in the development of theories about the origin of modern human races.

Nevertheless, mitochondrial DNA is not the only source of information we have on the subject. Fossil remains and artifacts also represent a monumental body of evidence—and, we maintain, a much more reliable one. The singular importance of the mitochondrial DNA studies is that they show one of the origin theories discussed by paleontologists must be incorrect.

With Wu Xinzhi of the Institute of Vertebrate Paleontology and Paleoanthropology in Beijing, we developed an explanation for the pattern of human evolution that we described as multiregional evolution. We learned that some of the features that distinguish major human groups, such as Asians, Australian

Aborigines and Europeans, evolved over a long period, roughly where these peoples are found today.

Multiregional evolution traces all modern populations back to when humans first left Africa at least a million years ago, through an interconnected web of ancient lineages in which the genetic contributions to all living peoples varied regionally and temporally. Today distinctive populations maintain their physical differences despite interbreeding and population movements; this situation has existed ever since humans first colonized Europe and Asia. Modern humanity originated within these widespread populations, and the modernization of our ancestors was an ongoing process.

An alternative theory, developed by the paleontologist William W. Howells of Harvard University as the "Noah's ark" model, posited that modern people arose recently in a single place and that they subsequently spread around the world, replacing other human groups. That replacement, recent proponents of the theory believe, must have been complete. From their genetic analyses, the late Allan C. Wilson and his colleagues at the University of California at Berkeley concluded that the evolutionary record of mitochondrial DNA could be traced back to a single female, dubbed "Eve" in one of his first publications on the issue, who lived in Africa approximately 200,000 years ago. Only mitochondrial DNA that can be traced to Eve, these theorists claim, is found among living people.

⋅◈⋅

How could this be? If Eve's descendants mixed with other peoples as their population expanded, we would expect to find other mitochondrial DNA lines present today, especially outside Africa, where Eve's descendants were invaders. The most credible explanation for the current absence of other mitochondrial DNA lineages is that none of the local women mixed with the invading modern men from Africa—which means that Eve founded a new species. Wilson's reconstruction of the past demands that over a period of no more than 150,000 years there was a complete replacement of all the preexisting hunter-gatherers in Africa and the rest of the then inhabited world; later, the original African features of the invading human species presumably gave way to the modern racial features we see in other regions.

An analogy can highlight the difference between our multiregional evolution theory and Wilson's Eve theory. According to multiregional evolution, the pattern of modern human origins is like several individuals paddling in separate corners of a pool; although they maintain their individuality over time, they influence one another with the spreading ripples they raise (which are the equivalent of genes flowing between populations). In contrast, the total replacement requirement of the Eve theory dictates that a new swimmer must jump into the pool with such a splash that it drowns all the other swimmers. One of these two views of our origin must be incorrect.

Mitochondrial DNA is useful for guiding the development of theories, but only fossils provide the basis for refuting one idea or the other. At best, the genetic information explains how modern humans might have originated if the assumptions used in interpreting the genes are correct, but one theory cannot be used to test another. The fossil record is the real evidence for human evolution, and it is rich in both human remains and archaeological sites stretching back for a million years. Unlike the genetic data, fossils can be matched to the predictions of theories about the past without relying on a long list of assumptions.

The power of a theory is measured by how much it can explain; the scientific method requires that we try to incorporate all sources of data in an explanatory theory. Our goal is to describe a theory that synthesizes everything known about modern human fossils, archaeology and genes. The Eve theory cannot do so.

The Eve theory makes five predictions that the fossil evidence should corroborate. The first and major premise is that modern humans from Africa must have completely replaced all other human groups. Second, implicit within this idea is that the earliest modern humans appeared in Africa. Third, it also follows that the earliest modern humans in other areas should have African features. Fourth, modern humans and the people they replaced should never have mixed or interbred. Fifth, an anatomic discontinuity should be evident between the human fossils before and after the replacement.

⌒⊙⌒

We are troubled by the allegations that beginning about 200,000 years ago one group of hunter-gatherers totally replaced all others worldwide. Although it is not uncommon for one animal species to replace another locally in a fairly short time, the claim that a replacement could occur rapidly in every climate and environment is unprecedented.

We would expect native populations to have an adaptive and demographic advantage over newcomers. Yet according to the Eve theory, it was the newcomers who had the upper hand. How much of an advantage is necessary for replacement can be measured by the survival of many hunter-gatherer groups in Australia and the Americas; they have persisted despite invasions by Europeans, who during the past 500 years arrived in large numbers with vastly more complex and destructive technologies.

If a worldwide invasion and complete replacement of all native peoples by Eve's descendants actually took place, we would expect to find at least some archaeological traces of the behaviors that made them successful. Yet examining the archaeology of Asia, we can find none. For instance, whereas the hand ax was a very common artifact in Africa, the technologies of eastern Asia did not include that tool either before or after the Eve period. There is no evidence for the introduction of a novel technology.

Geoffrey G. Pope of the University of Illinois has pointed out that six decades of research on the Asian Paleolithic record have failed to unearth any indication of intrusive cultures or technologies. Types of artifacts found in the earliest Asian Paleolithic assemblages continue to appear into the very late Pleistocene. If invading Africans replaced the local Asian populations, they must have adopted the cultures and technologies of the people they replaced and allowed their own to vanish without a trace.

Archaeological evidence for an invasion is also lacking in western Asia, where Christopher B. Stringer of the Natural History Museum in London and a few other researchers believe the earliest modern humans outside of Africa can be found at the Skhūl and Qafzeh sites in Israel. The superb record at Qafzeh shows, however, that these "modern" people had a culture identical to that of their local Neanderthal contemporaries: they made the same types of stone tools with the same technologies and at the same frequencies; they had the same stylized burial customs, hunted the same game and even used the same butchering procedures. Moreover, no evidence from the time when Eve's descendants are supposed to have left Africa suggests that any new African technology emerged or spread to other continents. All in all, as we understand them, the Asian data refute the archaeological predictions implied by the Eve theory.

Perhaps that refutation explains why Wilson turned to a different advantage, asserting that the invasion was successful because Eve's descendants carried a mitochondrial gene that conferred language ability. This proposal is yet to be widely accepted. Not only does it conflict with paleoneurology about the language abilities of archaic humans, but if it were true, it would violate the assumption of Wilson's clock that mitochondrial mutations are neutral.

The remaining predictions of the Eve theory relate to abrupt anatomic changes and whether the earliest recognizably modern humans resembled earlier regional populations or Africans. With the fossil evidence known at this time, these questions can be unambiguously resolved in at least two and possibly three regions of the world. The most convincing data are from southern and northern Asia.

The hominid fossils from Australasia (Indonesia, New Guinea and Australia) show a continuous anatomic sequence during the Pleistocene that is uninterrupted by African migrants at any time. The distinguishing features of the earliest of these Javan remains, dated to about one million years ago, show they had developed when the region was first inhabited.

Compared with human fossils from other areas, the Javan people have thick skull bones, with strong continuous browridges forming an almost straight bar of bone across their eye sockets and a second well-developed shelf of bone at the back of the skull for the neck muscles. Above and behind the brows, the forehead is flat and retreating. These early Indonesians also have large projecting faces with massive rounded cheekbones. Their teeth are the largest known in archaic humans from that time.

A series of small but important features can be found on the most complete face and on other facial fragments that are preserved. These include such things as a rolled ridge on the lower edge of the eye sockets, a distinctive ridge on the cheekbone and a nasal floor that blends smoothly into the face.

This unique morphology was stable for at least 700,000 years while other modern characteristics continued to evolve in the Javan people. For example, the large fossil series from Ngandong, which recent evidence suggests may be about 100,000 years old, offers striking proof that the Javans of that time had brain sizes in the modern range but were otherwise remarkably similar to much earlier individuals the region.

⋅⋗⊙⋖⋅

The first inhabitants of Australia arrived more than 60,000 years ago, and their behavior and anatomy were clearly those of modern human beings. Their skeletons show the Javan complex of features, along with further braincase expansions and other modernizations. Several dozen well-preserved fossils from the late Pleistocene and early Holocene demonstrate that the same combination of features that distinguished those Indonesian people from their contemporaries distinguishes modern Australian Aborigines from other living peoples.

If the earliest Australians were descendants of Africans, as the Eve theory required, the continuity of fossil features would have to be no more than apparent. All the features of the early Javans would need to have evolved a second time in the population of invaders. The repeated evolution of an individual feature would be conceivable but rare; the duplication of an entire set of unrelated features would be unprecedentedly improbable.

Northern Asia also harbors evidence linking its modern and ancient inhabitants. Moreover, because the similarities involve features different from those significant in Australasia, they compound the improbability of the Eve theory by requiring that a second complete set of features was duplicated in a different population.

The very earliest Chinese fossils, about one million years old, differ from their Javan counterparts in many ways that parallel the differences between north Asians and Australians today. Our research with Wu Xinzhi and independent research by Pope demonstrated that the Chinese fossils are less robust, have smaller and more delicately built flat faces, smaller teeth and rounder foreheads separated from their arched browridges. Their noses are less prominent and more flattened at the top. Perhaps the most telling indication of morphological continuity concerns a peculiarity of tooth shapes. Prominently "shoveled" maxillary incisors, which curl inward along their internal edges, are found with unusually high frequency in living east Asians and in all the earlier human remains from that area. Studies by Tracey L. Crummett of the University of Michigan show that the form of prehistoric and living Asian incisors is unique.

This combination of traits is also exhibited at the Zhoukoudian cave area in northern China, where fully a third of all known human remains from the Middle Pleistocene have been found. As Wu Rukang of the Chinese Academy of Sciences has pointed out, even within the 150,000 or more years spanned by the Zhoukoudian individuals, evolutionary changes in the modern direction, including increases in brain size, can be seen. Our examinations of the Chinese specimens found no anatomic evidence that typically African features ever replaced those of the ancient Chinese in these regions. Instead there is a smooth transformation of the ancient populations into the living peoples of east Asia.

Paleontologists have long thought Europe would be the best source of evidence for the replacement of one group, Neanderthals, by more modern humans. Even there, however, the fossil record shows that any influx of new people was neither complete nor without mixture. In fact, the most recent known Neanderthal, from Saint-Césaire in France, apparently had the behavioral characteristics of the people who succeeded the Neanderthals in Europe. The earliest post-Neanderthal Europeans did not have a pattern of either modern or archaic African features. Clearly, the European Neanderthals were not completely replaced by Africans or by people from any other region.

Instead the evidence suggests that Neanderthals either evolved into later humans or interbred with them, or both. David W. Frayer of the University of Kansas and Fred H. Smith of Northern lllinois University have discovered that many allegedly unique Neanderthal features are found in the Europeans who followed the Neanderthals—the Upper Paleolithic, Mesolithic and later peoples. In fact, only a few Neanderthal features completely disappear from the later European skeletal record.

Figure 1

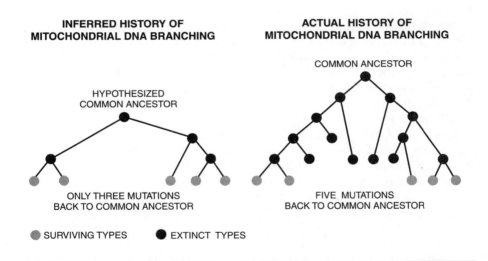

INFERRED HISTORY OF MITOCHONDRIAL DNA BRANCHING

ACTUAL HISTORY OF MITOCHONDRIAL DNA BRANCHING

COMMON ANCESTOR

HYPOTHESIZED COMMON ANCESTOR

ONLY THREE MUTATIONS BACK TO COMMON ANCESTOR

FIVE MUTATIONS BACK TO COMMON ANCESTOR

SURVIVING TYPES   EXTINCT TYPES

Maternal lineage reconstructions based solely on the mitochondrial DNA types found today are inherently flawed. A hypothetical tree inferred from only five surviving types (*left*) leaves out the branches and mutational histories of extinct lines (*right*). Consequently, it sets the date for a common ancestor much too recently by presenting evidence of too few mutations.

Features that persist range from highly visible structures, such as the prominent shape and size of the nose of Neanderthals and later Europeans, to much more minute traits, such as the form of the back of the skull and the details of its surface. A good example is the shape of the opening in the mandibular nerve canal, a spot on the inside of the lower jaw where dentists often give a pain-blocking injection. The upper part of the opening is covered by a broad bony bridge in many Neanderthals, but in others the bridge is absent. In European fossils, 53 percent of the known Neanderthals have the bridged form; 44 percent of their earliest Upper Paleolithic successors do, too, but in later Upper Paleolithic, Mesolithic and recent groups, the incidence drops to less than 6 percent.

In contrast, the bridged form is seen only rarely in fossil or modern people from Asia and Australia. In Africa the few jaws that date from the suggested Eve period do not have it. This mandibular trait and a number of others like it on the skull and the rest of the skeleton must have evolved twice in Europe for the Eve theory to be correct.

In sum, the evolutionary patterns of three different regions—Australasia, China and Europe—show that their earliest modern inhabitants do not have the complex of features that characterize Africans. There is no evidence that Africans completely replaced local groups. Contrary to the Eve theory predictions, the evidence points indisputably toward the continuity of various skeletal features between the earliest human populations and living peoples in different regions.

⋖◈⋗

If Africa really were the "Garden of Eden" from which all living people emerged, one would expect to find evidence for the transition from archaic to modern forms there—and only there. Following the lead of the German worker Reiner Protsch of Goethe University in Frankfurt, some paleontologists did argue that modern *Homo sapiens* originated in Africa because they believed the earliest modern-looking humans were found there and that modern African racial features can be seen in these fossils. But the African evidence is sparse, fragmentary and for the most part poorly dated; it includes materials that do not seem to fit the Eve theory.

Early human remains from Africa, such as the Kabwe skull from Zambia, are extremely rare and are presumed to be at least 150,000 years old. Later transitional fossils from Morocco, Ethiopia, Kenya and South Africa confirm the expectation that local modernization occurred in Africa, as it did everywhere else. No pattern in the fossils, however, indicates the previous emergence of skeletal features that uniquely characterize modern humans generally or even modern Africans in particular.

The evidence for a great antiquity of modern-looking people is based primarily on the interpretation of bones from three sites: the Omo site in Ethiopia and the Klasies River and Border Cave sites in South Africa. Some of the Omo and Border Cave individuals resemble modern humans, but all the remains are fragmentary. Most of the Omo remains were found on the surface, not in datable strata. The estimate of their age, which is based on inappropriate dating techniques, is widely considered to be unreliable. Some of the Border Cave bones, including the most complete cranium, were dug out by local workmen looking for fertilizer and are of unknown antiquity. Other human bones found at a 90,000-year-old level are chemically different from animal bones found there. They may actually be more recent burials dug into the cave.

The best excavated remains are from the Klasies River Mouth Cave and are securely dated to between 80,000 and 100,000 years ago. Some of the skull fragments are small and delicate and are said to "prove" that modern humans were present. Yet a comparative analysis of the entire sample by Rachel Caspari of Albion College showed that others are not modern-looking at all. Two of the four lower jaws do not have chins, so thorough proof of a modern jaw is lacking. The single cheekbone from the site is not only larger than those of living Africans but also larger and more robust than those of both the earlier transitional humans and the archaic humans found in Africa. The claim that this sample contains modern Africans is highly dubious and does not justify the proposal that the earliest modern humans arose in Africa.

❦

With the disproof of the unique African ancestry theory for the living people of most areas and the lack of evidence showing that modern people first appeared in Africa, we conclude that the predictions of the Eve theory cannot be substantiated. We must wonder why the analysis of mitochondrial DNA suggested a theory so contrary to the facts. Perhaps the mitochondrial DNA has been misinterpreted.

The basic difficulty with using mitochondrial DNA to interpret recent evolutionary history stems from the very source of its other advantages: in reproduction, the mitochondrial DNA clones itself instead of recombining. Because mitochondrial DNA is transmitted only through the maternal line, the potential for genetic drift—the accidental loss of lines—is great: some mitochondrial DNA disappears every time a generation fails to have daughters.

The problem is analogous to the way in which family surnames are lost whenever there is a generation without sons. Imagine an immigrant neighborhood in a large city where all the families share a surname. An observer might assume that all these families were descended from a single successful immigrant family that completely replaced its neighbors (just as Eve's descendants are supposed to have replaced all other humans). An alternative explanation is that many families immigrated to the neighborhood and intermarried; over time, all the surnames but one were randomly eliminated through the occasional appearance of families that had no sons to carry on their names. The surviving family name would have come from a single immigrant, but all the immigrants would have contributed to the genes of the modern population. In the same way, generations without daughters could have extinguished some lines of mitochondrial DNA from Eve's descendants and her contemporaries.

Any interpretation of the surviving mitochondrial DNA mutations in populations consequently depends on a knowledge of how the size of the populations has changed over time and how many maternal lines may have vanished. Random losses from genetic drift alter a reconstruction of the tree of human mitochondrial DNA branching by pruning off signs of past divergences. Each uncounted branch is a mutation never taken into account when determining how long ago Eve lived.

Changes in population sizes have been dramatic. In parts of the Northern Hemisphere, some human populations shrank because of climate fluctuations during the Ice Ages. Archaeological evidence from both Africa and Australia suggests that similar population reductions may have taken place there as well. These reductions could have exacerbated genetic drift and the loss of mitochondrial DNA types.

At the end of the Ice Ages, along with the first domestication of animals and plants, some populations expanded explosively throughout a wide band of territory from the Mediterranean to the Pacific coast of Asia. Although the number of people expanded, the number of surviving mitochondrial DNA lines could not—those lost were gone forever.

Human populations with dissimilar demographic histories can therefore be expected to preserve different numbers of mutations since their last common mitochondrial DNA ancestor. They cannot be used together in a model that assumes the lengths of mitochondrial lineages reflect the age of their divergence. One cannot assume, as Wilson does, that all the variation in a population's mitochondrial DNA stems solely from mutations: the history of the population is also important.

◆

A major problem with the Eve theory, therefore, is that it depends on an accurate molecular clock. Its accuracy must be based on mutation rates at many different loci, or gene positions. Yet genes in the mitochondrial DNA cannot recombine as genes in the nucleus do. All the mitochondrial DNA genes are the equivalent of a single locus. The molecular clock based on mitochondrial DNA is consequently unreliable.

Mitochondrial DNA may not be neutral enough to serve as the basis for a molecular clock, because some data suggest that it plays a role in several diseases. Because of random loss and natural selection some vertebrate groups—cichlid fish in Lake Victoria in Africa, American eels, hardhead catfish and redwing blackbirds, for example—have rates of mitochondrial DNA evolution that are dramatically slower than Wilson and his colleagues have claimed for humans. A number of molecular geneticists disagree with Wilson's interpretation of the mitochondrial genetic data.

The molecular clock of Wilson and his colleagues has, we believe, major problems: its rate of ticking has probably been overestimated in some cases and underestimated in others. Rebecca L. Cann of the University of Hawaii at Manoa and Mark Stoneking of Pennsylvania State University, two of Wilson's students, admitted recently that their clock was able to date Eve only to between 50,000 and 500,000 years ago. Because of the uncertainty, we believe that for the past half a million years or more of human evolution, for all intents and purposes, there is no molecular clock.

Putting aside the idea of a clock, one can interpret the genetic data in a much more reasonable way: Eve, the ultimate mitochondrial ancestor of all living humans, lived before the first human migrations from Africa at least one million years ago. The spread of mitochondria would then mark the migration of some early human ancestors into Eurasia when it contained no other hominids. Such an interpretation can fully reconcile the fossil record with the genetic data. We propose that future research might more productively focus on attempts to disprove this hypothesis than on attempts to recalibrate a clock that clearly does not work.

The dramatic genetic similarities across the entire human race do not reflect a recent common ancestry for all living people. They show the consequences of linkages between people that extend to when our ancestors first populated the Old World, more than a million years ago. They are the results of an ancient history of population connections and mate exchanges that has characterized the human race since its inception. Human evolution happened everywhere because every area was always part of the whole.

Neither anatomic nor genetic analyses provide a basis for the Eve theory. Instead the fossil record and the interpretation of mitochondrial DNA variation can be synthesized to form a view of human origins that does fit all the currently known data. This synthetic view combines the best sources of evidence about human evolution by making sense of the archaeological and fossil record and the information locked up in the genetic variation of living people all over the world. The richness of human diversity, which contrasts with the closeness of human genetic relationships, is a direct consequence of evolution. We are literally most alike where it matters, under the skin.

POSTSCRIPT

Did *Homo Sapiens* Originate Only in Africa?

The debate between the "multiregional" and the "out-of-Africa" theorists has not been resolved since these selections were first published. Nor have tensions between proponents of these two positions diminished. This acrimony has been intensified by the fact that some commentators have seen the "multiregional" theory as merely a racist attempt to deny Africa its status as the place of origin for all humankind. It should be noted, however, that the multiregionalists continue to see African origins for *Homo erectus* and earlier hominids, but have argued that *Homo sapiens* evolved more-or-less simultaneously in Africa, Asia, Europe, and Australia. For a discussion of these issues see Milford H. Wolpoff and Rachel Caspari's *Race and Human Evolution: A Fatal Attraction* (Simon & Schuster, 1996).

Another issue separating these two groups of scientists concerns the data used for determining whether anatomically modern humans evolved uniquely in one place or simultaneously in all inhabited places. Either the mitochondrial evidence is poorly interpreted or the analysis of fossils is flawed, since both theories cannot be correct. Currently, our knowledge of mitochondrial DNA evolution is still imperfect, and the use of mitochondrial DNA as a clock for dating the emergence of *Homo sapiens* carries with it some uncertainty. There is now consensus that mitochondrial DNA and nuclear DNA mutate at different rates, but it is still uncertain as to how fast mitochondrial DNA mutates. The debate between the "multiregionalists" and the "out-of-Africa" theorists parallels a similar divide between paleontologists who support a gradualist model and paleontologists who support a punctuated equilibrium model. For a discussion of the paleontological issues, see Stephen Jay Gould's *Dinosaur in a Haystack: Reflections in Natural History* (Harmony Books, 1995), pp. 101–107, in which he supports the African origins model of this debate for much the same reasons that he supports a punctuated equilibrium model concerning other species.

For one of the earliest statements framing the "out-of-Africa" theory, see Rebecca L. Cann, Mark Stoneking, and A. C. Wilson's "Mitochondrial DNA and Human Evolution," *Nature* (1987). Also see Allan C. Wilson and Rebecca L. Cann's statement, "The Recent African Genesis of Humans," *Scientific American* (1992). Michael H. Brown's *The Search for Eve* (Harper & Row, 1990) offers a popular account of the early research, while Stringer and McKie's *African Exodus: The Origins of Modern Humanity* (Henry Holt & Company, 1996), from which the Yes-side selection was excerpted, provides a more extended discussion. For background on mitochondrial DNA research, see J. N. Spuhler's paper

"Evolution of Mitochondrial DNA in Monkeys, Apes and Humans," *American Journal of Physical Anthropology Yearbook* (1988).

For an early assessment of the "out-of-Africa" theory and the "multiregional" theory, see Wolpoff and Thorne's article entitled, "The Case Against Eve," *New Scientist* (June 22, 1991); Alan R. Templeton's "The 'Eve' Hypotheses: A Genetic Critique and Reanalysis," *American Anthropologist* (1993); and Leslie C. Aiello's "The Fossil Evidence for Modern Human Origins in Africa: A Revised View," *American Anthropologist* (1993). For background on the "multiregional" theory and the fossil record see Fred H. Smith and Frank Spencer's edited volume, *The Origins of Modern Humans: A World Survey of the Fossil Evidence* (Alan R. Liss, 1984).

Several years after Cann, Stoneking, and Wilson released their findings on mitochondrial DNA, M. F. Hammer reported identifying a single male lineage of Y chromosomes. See his "A Recent Common Ancestry for Human Y Chromosomes," *Nature* (1995) and another paper by M. F. Hammer et al., "The Geographic Distribution of Human Y Chromosome Variation," *Genetics* (1997). Hammer and his colleagues contend that the "African Adam" from whom we all descend lived about 200,000 years ago. Not surprisingly, multiregionalists have raised many of the same issues here as they have with "Eve," arguing that Hammer and his colleagues have incorrect assumptions and weak calibration of the rate at which the Y chromosome mutates. For a recent review of both mitochondrial DNA and Y chromosome research, see Joanna L. Mountain's "Molecular Evolution and Modern Human Origins," *Evolutionary Anthropology* (1998).

ISSUE 2

Did Neandertals Interbreed With Modern Humans?

YES: João Zilhão, from "Fate of the Neandertals," *Archaeology* (July/August 2000)

NO: Jean-Jacques Hublin, from "Brothers or Cousins?" *Archaeology* (September/October 2000)

ISSUE SUMMARY

YES: Archaeologist João Zilhão discusses the recently found remains of a young child who was buried in a rock shelter in Portugal about 25,000 years ago. He concludes that the Lagar Velho child was a hybrid with mixed Neandertal and early modern human ancestry.

NO: Biological anthropologist Jean-Jacques Hublin maintains that the Lagar Velho child was merely one variant within the diverse early modern human population. He argues that there was some cultural influence from early modern humans to Neandertals but little or no interbreeding between them.

The image of Neandertals (also spelled *Neanderthals*) has fluctuated widely since the mid-nineteenth century, when scholars first recognized that the fossil bones being unearthed in Europe were those of early humans and not just deformed individuals. The scientists who reconstructed the Neandertal skeletons were influenced by the theory of evolution introduced by Charles Darwin in his books *Origin of Species* (John Murray, 1859) and *Descent of Man* (John Murray, 1871). Some scientists pictured Neandertals as the "missing link" between humans and the apes. This view was exemplified by French scientist Marcellin Boule's 1909 analysis of a skeleton from Chapelle-aux-Saints, popularly known as the "Old Man." Classifying Neandertals as a separate species from humans, Boule illustrated the Chapelle-aux-Saints man in a slouching, bent-kneed posture, which he contrasted with the upright carriage of an Australian Aborigine, then thought to be the most primitive form of modern humans. Other scholars considered Neandertals the ancestors of Europeans or even of all humanity, positing a "Neandertal stage" of human evolution. For example, the eminent anatomist Sir Arthur Keith analyzed the same Chapelle-aux-Saints remains and concluded that the Old Man was a full member of the human family. These sharply contrasting images express the enigmatic nature of Neandertals: they were both like us and not like us.

Evidence accumulated over the last 100 years has partially resolved the question of the status of the Neandertals. The notions of both a missing link and a global Neandertal stage of human evolution have been discarded. Today the predominant theories of recent human evolution are the "out of Africa" theory and the "multiregional evolution" theory. According to proponents of the out of Africa theory, Neandertals were a dead-end branch of humanity, which evolved out of *Homo erectus* in Europe and met its demise when modern humans arrived from Africa and outcompeted or killed the Neandertals off. Multiregionalists contend that Neandertals were descendants of part of the widespread *Homo erectus* population that evolved as a whole into modern humans. In their view Neandertals were local variants of the early human species who probably interbred with the incoming variants from Africa and whose genes were eventually mixed into the gene pool of modern Europe. Scientists are now seeking direct evidence of interbreeding in the bones, genes, stone tools, and behavior patterns of Neandertals and early modern humans in Europe.

João Zilhão discusses the recent find in Portugal of a fossil skeleton of a child, which appears to combine Neandertal features (e.g., short, thick limb bones) and modern human features (e.g., modern teeth and chin). He considers this child to be direct evidence that Neandertals interbred with the early modern humans who entered Europe after about 36,500 years ago. He argues that Neandertals created the sophisticated Châtelperronian stone tool industry before the arrival of modern humans, thus showing their intellectual similarity to the newcomers. Zilhão maintains that the Neandertals disappeared by being absorbed into the larger early modern human population.

Jean-Jacques Hublin, on the other hand, doubts that the Lagar Velho child resulted from interbreeding between Neandertals and early modern humans, implying that it could have been just one variant of a diverse early modern population. He maintains that Neandertals borrowed ideas and exchanged products with early modern humans to a limited extent—thus accounting for the sophisticated Châtelperronian tool kit of the Neandertals—but that they remained biologically separate. He believes that Neandertals eventually died out because early modern humans outcompeted them for scarce resources during the last glacial period.

This dispute shows how scientists can draw opposing conclusions from the same evidence. How convincing do you find the writers' interpretations? Do you think it is likely that Neandertals borrowed tool-making techniques from early modern humans but did not interbreed with them? What kinds of evidence do you think scholars need to decisively answer the question of whether Neandertals and modern humans interbred? Are there other possible explanations for the disappearance of Neandertals that these authors do not consider? Does this question have any wider significance?

João Zilhão

Fate of the Neandertals

T he bones of a four-year-old child, buried for millennia in the rear of a rock-shelter in the Lapedo Valley 85 miles north of Lisbon, Portugal, comprised the first complete Palaeolithic skeleton ever dug in Iberia. Our November 28, 1998, find made national news, but an even greater surprise was in store when my colleague, Washington University anthropologist Erik Trinkaus, who measured the bones weeks after the discovery, reported that the child's anatomy could only have resulted from a mixed Neandertal-early modern human ancestry. Here, finally, was proof that Neandertals did not simply disappear from Europe 28,000 years ago. Instead, they interbred with modern humans and became part of our family.

The discovery was made by João Maurício and Pedro Souto, archaeology field assistants and members of a local archaeology group, who visited the valley at my request to check on reports that a student from a nearby village had found some prehistoric paintings. The reports turned out to be genuine. The student showed them a few small, red anthropomorphic figures in a style characteristic of the Copper Age (fourth and third millennia B.C.) painted on the back wall of a shallow rock-shelter on the north side of the valley.

While they were there, João and Pedro decided to inspect a larger shelter they saw on the opposite side of the valley. When they got there, the first thing they noticed was that archaeological deposits in the shelter had recently been destroyed; we later learned that in 1992 the landowner had bulldozed the upper six to nine feet of the shelter's fill to widen a rural trail used to reach property located farther up the valley. All that was left was a foot-and-a-half remnant of the original deposit in a fissure running along most of the length of the shelter's back wall. This remnant corresponds to a section of the original stratigraphic sequence lying between two and three feet below the former ground surface.

The remnant was extremely rich in charcoal, stone tools, and animal remains, including fossilized horse teeth, all suggesting an Upper Palaeolithic age (between 30,000 and 10,000 years ago) for the site. While collecting surface material that had fallen from the remnant, João and Pedro inspected a recess in the back wall. In the loose sediments they recovered several small bones stained with red ochre they thought could be human. Recognizing the potential significance of the discovery, they stopped investigating and reported their finds to me.

The following weekend, on December 6, I went to the site with my colleagues Cristina Araújo, a fellow archaeologist, and Cidália Duarte, a bioarchaeologist specializing in burial taphonomy (how bodies are buried and preserved). João and Pedro presented their finds and two things almost immediately became clear. First, the bones they thought could be human were indeed the left forearm and hand bones of a young child. Second, stone tools found in the fissure dated the deposit to the Middle Solutrean and the Proto-Solutrean, that is, the period between 20,000 and 22,000 years ago. Since the juvenile human bones that lay some nine feet below this remnant belonged to a single individual and were very well preserved, the implication was obvious: a child had been buried at the site either in late Middle Palaeolithic or in early Upper Palaeolithic times, between 40,000 and 25,000 years ago. The ochre staining of the bones (a feature of all burials from the Gravettian period between 25,000 and 27,000 years ago) and rough estimates of the rate of sedimentation at the site led us to believe that a date closer to 25,000 years ago was more likely.

❧

This conclusion prompted me to start a salvage excavation of the site, which we called the Lagar Velho rock-shelter after the ruin of an ancient olive-oil press at its entrance. The excavation began on December 12, 1998, continuing without interruption through Christmas and the New Year until January 7, 1999. Subsequently, in July and August, deep testing of the preserved deposits under the burial and in the central part of the shelter further documented the site's stratigraphy. The surface of the site was also excavated and extensively screened, enabling the recovery of many of the child's missing teeth and skull fragments. We realized the bulldozer had come within an inch or two of the skeleton, leaving it miraculously intact except for the skull, which had been crushed into more than 100 pieces. The presence of ancient fractures in the cranial fragments suggests that natural processes had collapsed it inward not long after burial, but fresh breaks show that further fragmentation occurred when the site was bulldozed, scattering skull fragments east of the burial.

The broken left side of the child's lower jaw, including the chin region, had been recovered at the outset in a very thin layer of disturbed deposits overlying the burial. The chin featured the characteristic "snow-plow" shape found in Cro-Magnon people, the first anatomically modern humans, whose appearance on the European continent coincides with the disappearance of Neandertals. The day after that lower jaw was recovered, discovery of a pierced marine shell of the species *Littorina obtusata,* the most common ornament in the Upper Palaeolithic of Portugal, reinforced the hypothesis that this was an early Upper Palaeolithic burial. The shell was found near the neck vertebrae, suggesting that the dead child was wearing it as a pendant when he was buried. As the excavation continued, we were able to uncover a nearly complete, *in situ* skeleton (minus an intact skull), and establish that the body had been laid on its back, left side parallel to the cliff base, head to the east, feet crossed. Four red deer (*Cervus elaphus*) canines pierced through the root were found with the cranial remains. They suggest that the child was buried with some kind of decorated head wear. Pierced red deer canines have also been found on the skulls of Gravettian period people buried in Italy and Moravia.

The skeleton, especially the skull pieces, were heavily stained with red ochre as was the sediment in which the bones lay. This, and the fact that both the upper and the lower surfaces of the bones were stained, indicates that the body must have been wrapped in a shroud of ochre-painted skin, whose subsequent decay caused the transfer of the mineral pigment to the skeleton and sediment. The presence of a semi-rigid durable wrap around the body would also have provided the space for the post-mortem collapse of the child's ankle ligaments, evident in the position of the feet. At the base of the pit, immediately below and in contact with the child's legs, there was a thin black lens of charcoal, which belonged to a single branch of Scots pine. This suggests that a ritual fire was lit before the deposition of the body; the adjacent deposits contained no traces of charcoal.

Red deer bones found in association with the burial pit are distinct from those found in the surrounding and immediately underlying sediments. The latter present eroded surfaces, have a shine suggesting they were chewed and digested by carnivores, often display actual teeth punctures, and are associated with coprolites. In contrast, the deer bones found by the head and feet of the child's skeleton are well preserved, show no evidence of being mauled by carnivores, were in direct contact with the body, and provided a C14 date showing contemporaneity with the burial. Furthermore, no artifacts or other evidence of habitation were recovered at this level in this part of the shelter. The simplest explanation is that these bones belonged to parts of deer carcasses deposited in the grave as food offerings. The same may be true of the rabbit bones that overlay the child's right leg (three vertebrae, four ribs, and one sacrum fragment). They were also stained red, and two of the ribs were complete, suggesting that they were originally joined to the vertebrae.

Throughout the 1998–1999 salvage work we were able to count on the invaluable advice of Erik Trinkaus, to whom I e-mailed digital pictures of the excavation daily. Realizing the potential significance of the burial, Cidália Duarte and I invited him to the site to study the skeleton. An authority on Neandertals and early modern humans, Erik was already involved in analyzing Palaeolithic human material from Portugal.

While Cidália and I completed the fieldwork, Erik began to clean and reassemble the skeleton and work toward a preliminary anatomical description. After returning to the United States, he was able to compare the bones with his extensive data base on Neandertals and early modern humans. On January 25, I got a message from him which began with the ominous words: "The end of last week I made some quick comparisons of the Lagar Velho [child's] leg bone proportions with some data that I have, and it comes out looking like a Neandertal!" Other resemblances with Neandertals followed, but throughout this initial stage Cidália and I kept in mind Erik's cautionary remark in that first message: "unless I have made some silly mistake."

We decided to check and double check all the measurements ourselves, and eventually concluded that Erik had made no mistake—the child did present a mosaic of Neandertal and modern human features. Most prominent among the former, the arctic body proportions (with short limbs, especially the lower parts of the arms and legs), the robusticity of the limb bones and the angle at which the jaw bones meet at the chin; among the latter, the characteristic "snow-plow" chin and the size of the dentition. Body proportions are particularly important in this regard because the study of present-day populations has proved that they are genetically inherited and that the basic patterns of body shape are already established in the fetal stage of development. This makes it possible to compare the bones of the Lagar Velho child not only with those of other children but also with available adult skeletons from the same time period. Among the two possible ancestral populations of the group to which this child belonged, it is well-established that all Neandertals had arctic body proportions. On the contrary, all European early modern humans had tropical body proportions (long limbs), betraying their recent (in evolutionary time) African origin, in spite of the fact that they had been living for many millennia in the very cold steppe-tundra environments then present throughout the unglaciated parts of the continent located north of the Pyrenees.

In the following months, after discussing our suspicions with human palaeontologists and primate biologists who study natural hybrids, we grew increasingly convinced: the child possessed an anatomy that could only be explained as the result of a mixed Neandertal-early modern human ancestry. Then, in early April, the first radiocarbon results started to arrive. Obtained from samples from the charcoal lens under the child's legs and from the animal bones associated with the grave, they confirmed our earlier estimates that the age of the burial was ca. 25,000 years old, some 3,000 years after Neandertals presumably disappeared from western Iberia. This made it clear that the mosaic of anatomical features in the Lagar Velho child could not have been the result of a rare, chance encounter producing a hybrid descendant from a Neandertal mother and a modern human father (or vice versa). On the contrary, it had to represent a mixture of populations. Put another way, Neandertals had not simply disappeared without descendants, they had been absorbed, through extensive interbreeding, into the modern human groups that had started to take over Iberia ca. 30,000 years ago. They had contributed to the gene pool of subsequent early Upper Palaeolithic populations of the peninsula and, therefore, had to be counted among our ancestors: they were family.

This conclusion contrasts with the prevailing view of the Neandertals as an evolutionary dead end, a side branch of the human tree, that has become so popular in the wake of the Eve hypothesis based on mitochondrial DNA (mtDNA). First proposed in 1987, this hypothesis states that Europeans descended entirely from anatomically modern human populations that gradually evolved in Africa from an ancestral *Homo erectus* stock after 250,000 years ago. Having begun to spread from there to the rest of the world some 50,000 years ago, these anatomically modern groups eventually replaced, without admixture, all indigenous anatomically archaic human forms of Eurasia. Thus, Neandertals became extinct with no descendants.

This view received strong support from the publication, in 1997, by Svante Päabo of the University of Munich and his colleagues, of a comparison between mtDNA extracted from the original Feldhofer Cave Neandertal type specimen found in 1856 and that of present-day human populations. It inferred that the difference was so significant as to put Neandertals outside the range of modern humanity, suggesting that they had belonged to an altogether different biological species and that interbreeding, although conceivable, could not have been significant. Possible support for this view comes from the mtDNA analysis of the rib of a 29,000-year-old fetal or neo-natal skeleton from Mezmaiskaya Cave, in the northern Caucasus, recently published in the journal *Nature*. The significance of the latter, however, remains to be seen. It is reported as a Neandertal infant, but its classification is in fact uncertain.

Analysis of the Lagar Velho child's mtDNA would certainly help to test our interpretation. Unfortunately, this is likely to be impossible, due to the chemical weathering undergone by the child's fragile bones. However, as we prepared the preliminary publication of the burial and of our interpretation of the child's anatomy, the journal to which we had submitted it (*Proceedings of the National Academy of Sciences USA*) published a major paper on the variability of the DNA of African apes, our closest living relatives. This work showed that contemporary interbreeding populations of chimpanzees are genetically more diverse than modern humans and our Late Pleistocene fossil ancestors, including the one Neandertal specimen Päabo analyzed. By primate standards, therefore, the results obtained by Päabo's team indicated that present-day humans ought to be considered abnormally homogeneous. This low DNA variability is consistent with a single recent origin for modern humans (the Out-of-African model), but does not imply that Neandertals were a different species. It simply confirms, from genetic data, what palaeontologists have established for about a century on the basis of fossil bones: that Neandertals, as a separate, well-defined geographic variant of humanity that became differentiated during the Middle Pleistocene, are now extinct. That does not mean that they did not contribute to the gene pool of subsequent populations. The Lagar Velho child's anatomical mosaic suggests that they did, even if such a contribution eventually became so diluted as to become unrecognizable today.

Recent developments in the archaeology of the last Neandertals and the earliest modern humans in Europe point to a similar conclusion. Ever since the original Neander Valley fossil was discovered, most researchers have doubted that the Neandertals were capable of using symbols or manufacturing complex bone and ivory objects. While modern humans are thought to have created cave art and delicate carvings and to have engaged in specialized hunting, Neandertals have been viewed as scavengers or opportunistic hunters. When cultural remains found in late Neandertal sites suggested otherwise, the evidence was dismissed.

The earliest modern humans in Europe are associated with characteristic stone and bone tool-kits, called Aurignacian, whose first appearance in the archaeological record has been assumed for the last decade to date to ca. 40,000 years ago. In France and northern Spain, local Neandertals were thought to have copied some of the stone and bone tools of their new neighbors, the Aurignacian moderns, as well as their personal ornaments, giving rise to a new Neandertal cultural entity, the Châtelperronian. It was argued, however, that such an imitation would have been carried out with no real understanding of the underlying symbolic meaning of the objects.

Other kinds of explanations postulated post-depositional disturbance of sites to deny Neandertals any role in the manufacture of those items. Scholars such as Yvette Taborin of the University of Paris I and Randall White of New York University, for instance, suggested that the presence of personal ornaments and bone tools at the key site of Grotte du Renne, in Burgundy, France, would have been the result of a mixing of archaeological strata. Others, such as Jean-Jacques Hublin of Paris' Musée de l'Homme and Paul Mellars of Cambridge University suggested as an alternative explanation that such a presence might be due to Neandertals having collected or traded for objects manufactured by neighboring moderns.

The reassessment of the evidence from Grotte du Renne by Francesco d'Errico of the University of Bordeaux I, myself, and other colleagues showed that Châtelperronian Neandertals were indeed the makers of the personal ornaments and bone tools found there. Moreover, the grooved or perforated teeth of fox, wolf, bear, hyena, red deer, horse, marmot, bear, and reindeer recovered at the Grotte du Renne and other sites (such as Quinçay, in the Charente, France) were made with techniques different from those used by Aurignacian modern humans. The same is true of the different knapping techniques and tool types that appear among late Neandertals in various regions of Europe. These innovations everywhere fail to show any influence from the Aurignacian, while maintaining affinities with preceding Neandertal traditions.

D'Errico and I have also closely examined the archaeological record to verify whether the arrival of early modern humans in western Europe did indeed predate these Neandertal innovations, as had to be the case if the emergence of the innovations had been triggered by contact with the newcomers. We found, however, that wherever archaeological layers of both cultures are represented at the same sites, the Châtelperronian always underlies the Aurignacian. Similarly, research on hundreds of radiometric datings available for this period in Europe and the Near East shows that, wherever the context of the dated samples is well established, the first Aurignacian ones date to no earlier than ca. 36,500 years ago. The same radiometric data, however, indicate that, by then, Neandertals had already accomplished their own transition to behavioral modernity. In others words, there is no doubt that the Châtelperronian and other late Neandertal cultures emerged in Europe well before any modern humans established themselves in neighboring areas.

This autonomous development included the manufacture and use of symbolic objects created for visual display on the body that reflected, as often observed in present-day traditional societies, different social roles. It is also at about 40,000 years ago that the earliest evidence for personal ornaments appears in the anatomically modern human populations of eastern and southern Africa. Thus, "modern" behavior seems to have appeared independently in different regions and among different groups of humans, much as would happen later in history with the invention of agriculture, writing, and social organization. On the strength of available data, our hypothesis that late Neandertal groups invented their own tools and ornaments is firmly supported. The notion that we were the only human type capable of developing a symbolic culture has collapsed.

If the two groups did not represent biologically different species and had attained a similar level of cultural achievement, why then did modern humans prevail? Why was it that the immigrants absorbed the locals and not the other way around? These are the really interesting questions for archaeologists and geneticists to ask. Biogeographic and demographic explanations may provide the answers. In the Pleistocene period, under climatic conditions much colder than today's, most of Eurasia was uninhabitable. The northernmost areas were covered by ice sheets and barren tundras, and population densities in the settled areas must have been much lower than in Africa. Erik Trinkaus' palaeodemographic analysis of Neandertal remains reveals those populations were highly unstable. Therefore, it is quite likely that between 100,000 and 40,000 years ago a large majority of all the planet's human beings lived in Africa, where the modern morphological form evolved.

If these African groups also had a higher fertility, as is commonly the case with warm climate populations of the same species when compared with those from colder climates, we can plausibly explain what happened. Africans started to disperse into the neighboring regions, a process that must have been hastened by a warming period between ca. 50,000 and ca. 30,000 years ago, during which the savannas of eastern Africa, and their faunas, spread into the Middle East. Given enough time, even a very small difference in fertility would put the much smaller and more scattered populations of Neandertals at a demographic disadvantage, especially if interbreeding were common.

Once modern humans became established throughout most of the European continent, their absorption of remnant Neandertal populations was just a matter of time. Radiometric data suggest that isolated Neandertal communities existed until quite late, not only in Iberia, where the evidence is the strongest, but also in Croatia and Crimea. In the case of southwestern Europe, the Ebro River in northern Spain seems to have represented some sort of biocultural "frontier" separating Aurignacian modern humans established north of the Cantabrian-Pyrenean mountains since ca. 36,500 years ago from Neandertals surviving south of them until ca. 28,000 years ago. That Neandertals held on for so long shows just how well-adapted they must have been. No wonder that, when modern humans started to cross that "frontier," they saw them as fellow human beings and interbred, as demonstrated by the Lagar Velho child.

If, for our anatomically modern ancestors, Neandertals were just people—perhaps a little funny-looking, but people nonetheless—why should we believe otherwise and persist, against all available biological and cultural evidence, in trying to put them in an entirely different category?

 **NO**

Brothers or Cousins?

Meeting a male Neandertal face to face would be an unforgettable experience. He would have the bodily proportions of an Eskimo, with a long trunk and incredibly powerful shoulders and arms. He would weigh a muscular 200 pounds, and have a huge head with a long face, a big projecting nose, no chin, receding cheeks, and big eye sockets surmounted by a continuous browridge. Neandertal facial characteristics are so distinct that even primary school children can distinguish a Neandertal skull from a modern one.

Discovered more than a century-and-a-half ago, Neandertals are the most studied group of fossil hominids. The debate over the causes of their extinction and their relation to modern humans is one of the most passionate in the field of palaeoanthropology. Indeed, the Neandertals are not a remote species of extinct primates, but rather our closest neighbors in the hominid family tree. Discussing their biology and behavior means talking about our own. Interestingly, scholars and the public have viewed Neandertals differently over the years. While in the past Neandertals were often (but not always) imagined as ape-like hairy brutes, there is now a tendency to depict them as pacific, crafty hunter-gatherers just a shade stockier than modern humans but otherwise much like us. That Neandertals and early modern humans coexisted in Europe for 10,000 years and shared culture and technology while representing different species or sub-species of hominids is for some an uncomfortable fact. The present need among some researchers to integrate the Neandertals' behavior and biology with that of modern humans is a misguided response.

Debated Biology

Most palaeoanthropologists think Neandertals belong to a group clearly separate from modern humans. For more than 400,000 years in Europe, they adapted to their cool-to-cold climate, far from the majority of hominids living in tropical areas. Their physical uniqueness also resulted from geographical and genetic isolation. However, for more than a century some palaeoanthropologists argued that Neandertals were the ancestors of modern Europeans. When fully modern humans contemporary or even older than European Neandertals were discovered in the Near East and Africa, this hypothesis was abandoned.

Today it is widely accepted that the sudden emergence in Europe of ancient modern humans, called Cro-Magnons, between 40,000 and 35,000 years ago resulted instead from their migration from warmer geographical areas. Most of the debate on the Neandertals now focuses on their exact biological relationship to us and on the possibility of genetic and behavioral exchange between them and the modern invaders.

The Neandertals' genetic signature has been revealed in DNA studies on individuals from the Feldhofer site in Germany, where Neandertals were first identified in the mid-nineteenth century, and from Mezmaskaya cave in the Caucasus, where a newborn Neandertal was found associated with Middle Palaeolithic artifacts. Genetic analysis of fossil hominids, however, is still in its infancy and very many questions remain. Only tiny samples of mitochondrial DNA can be analyzed, but the results from Feldhofer and Mezmaskaya are very similar even though the two individuals lived far apart. On average the Neandertal specimens differ more from those of modern humans around the world than they do from each other. This reinforces the view that the Neandertals have no close connection with modern European populations. At the moment it is very frustrating not to be able to compare Neandertal DNA with that of Cro-Magnons; Palaeolithic human DNA remains very difficult to find, and so far genetic evidence still does not provide us with a firm standard to decide whether Neandertals represented a distinct sub-species of *Homo sapiens,* or a very close sister species, *Homo neanderthalensis.*

Closer Encounters

Changes in stone-artifact production accompanied the replacement of Neandertals by modern invaders some 40,000 years ago. Mousterian tool kits produced by Neandertals were supplanted by new assemblages, but the most spectacular changes did not take place in stone technology. After millennia of very slow development, there was a burst of innovation: composite weapons made of bone, wood, and flint appeared; social organization evolved; and the structure of dwellings improved. Trade developed, as did the clear expression of symbolic thought revealed by arts and ornaments, and there was likely some sort of linguistic advancement. Recent studies of the Middle Stone Age (100,000 years B.P.) in south and central Africa suggest that some of these changes may in fact have begun a long time ago outside of Europe. The image we have of a disruptive "cultural revolution" in Europe may have resulted from an invasion by tropical hunter-gatherers who brought new techniques and behaviors with them.

While Neandertals and hominids display clear biological differences, the European archaeological record yields several "transitional" Neandertal assemblages between the Middle and Upper Palaeolithic. In the late 1970s, it was widely believed that European Neandertals had created only Mousterian (Middle Palaeolithic) artifacts predating 40,000 B.P. Later, Upper Palaeolithic assemblages, including the transitional ones, were all assigned to "Cro-Magnons," i.e., anatomically modern humans. Transitional tool kits such as the Châtelperronian in France and northern Spain, the Uluzzian in Italy, and the Szeletian in Central Europe, were considered early Upper Palaeolithic assemblages. French and Spanish Châtelperronian assemblages are composed of truly Mousterian artifacts together with elongated blades for making knives and spearpoints. Their most indisputable "Upper Palaeolithic" feature is the rare but clear occurrence of decorated bone objects and body ornaments. Arcy-sur-Cure, 60 miles southeast of Paris, yielded a rather complete series of these artifacts on a floor stained with pigments where distinct huts had been located. In all respects this stratum contrasts dramatically with the amorphous underlying Mousterian floor.

For decades it was difficult to reconcile the almost total replacement of population in Europe 35,000 years ago with some kind of in situ cultural evolution. In the spring of 1979, the discovery of a new Neandertal specimen resolved the dilemma and completely changed our view of the last Neandertals. I still vividly remember those exciting weeks. My Ph.D. at the Science University Pierre and Marie Curie in Paris was just finished and a new and very unusual Neandertal skeleton was being examined on a large table in palaeoanthropologist Bernard Vandermeersch's office. In the following months Saint-Césaire, the cave site not far from the Cognac vineyards north of Bordeaux where the remains were discovered, would become world famous among palaeoanthropologists.

The Saint-Césaire Neandertal burial belonged to Châtelperronian strata and was well separated from the underlying Mousterian. Neandertals were thus the makers of the so-called transitional assemblages. The end of the Neandertals, we learned, did not coincide with the beginning of Upper Palaeolithic but was to be found within this transitional period. In the years following the Saint-Césaire discovery, several scholars, including myself, proposed a new explanation for these transitional industries. In our view, they resulted from interaction of the last Neandertals with the first modern Europeans over a significant period of time. While in some places Neandertals stayed away from the modern invaders and pursued their traditional way of life, they adopted new behaviors in areas of closer contact.

The first tool industry securely assigned to modern humans in Europe is the Aurignacian. One of its most remarkable features is the development of bone artifacts and especially standardized spearheads. The flint bladelets Cro-Magnon hunters produced were also likely part of bone and wood projectiles. The Aurignacians were the first European population to produce figurative art, and they did it in the most spectacular way, from stunning statues like the ivory figurines from Vogelherd, Germany, to the recently discovered painted images of animals at the Chauvet Cave in south-central France. The Chauvet Cave demonstrates that more than 31,000 years ago these groups had already mastered all rock-art techniques. Aurignacian assemblages are identified in eastern Europe before 40,000 B.P. and are also present in the West soon after.

Châtelperronian sites are centered in southwestern France and northern Spain. In some caves, at the periphery of this area, archaeologists have observed interstratifications between Châtelperronian and Aurignacian tools, suggesting that Neandertals and modern humans occupied the area at different times. Throughout the Palaeolithic, southwestern France was a favorable place to live, and when the first modern humans arrived, it was probably the European area most densely peopled by Neandertals. The last Châtelperronian assemblages are located in Quinçay in west-central France and at Arcy-sur-Cure. Palaeoanthropologists have even observed a longer persistence of Neandertals at the site of Zafarraya in Andalucia (Spain), where I excavated in the early 1990s. There, we dated Mousterian layers after 30,000 B.P., and several other sites have produced dates indicating that the southern Iberian peninsula was a refuge where late Neandertals survived apart from any Cro-Magnon cultural influence. Neandertals post-dating 30,000 B.P. have also been documented in the Balkans and Caucasus.

For some 10,000 years, Neandertals and modern humans shared a mosaic of territories in Europe though they didn't actually live in the same areas at the same time. The Palaeolithic world was an empty one and a Neandertal probably had little chance to meet the "aliens" within his or her lifetime. Very likely Neandertals and modern humans did not exploit their environment in the same way, encouraging the segregation of their territories. Researchers will have to write a different history for the disappearance of the Neandertals for each region of Europe. In some cases Neandertals were isolated from modern groups for thousands of years and were not influenced by them. In others, Neandertals adopted some innovations, maybe trading some objects. But on the whole these influences were rather limited and are mainly demonstrated by the Neandertals' use of bone objects and ornaments.

The exact age of the earliest Aurignacian sites, interpretation of sites where Châtelperronian and Aurignacian layers have been found, and the biological characteristics of the first Aurignacian modern humans have been the subject of all sorts of discussions. Although criticized, the "acculturation model," in which transitional industries result from the interaction between local Neandertals and modern invaders, is still the most widely accepted explanation for the cultural evolution of the last Neandertals. So far, only modern humans have been found associated with Aurignacian assemblages in Europe, and only Neandertals associated with Mousterian and Châtelperronian. The important points are that there is clearly a chronological overlap between the two groups of hominids, and after at least 400,000 years of separate evolution the Neandertals developed the use of decorated bone objects and body ornaments only at this time.

Recently Francesco D'Errico of the University of Bordeaux I and João Zilhão of the Instituto Português de Arqueologia have argued that the handful of pierced teeth and beads collected at some Châtelperronian sites could have been invented "independently" by Neandertals, just before the arrival of Aurignacians carrying thousands of virtually identical objects. This view seems to result from a strange political correctness toward our extinct cousins. They compare the Neandertals' supposed invention of these objects with the independent invention of agriculture in the Old World and Mesoamerica. This comparison is difficult to comprehend. If there were any indication that a Near Eastern group had sailed to the Americas in the Early Neolithic, long before farming appeared in the New World, nobody would dare claim Precolumbian agriculture was invented "independently." More likely the meeting of modern humans and Neandertals in Europe spurred production of body ornaments, objects, and behavior related to individual and group identification.

Hybridization and Extinction

Were Neandertals a distinct sub-species of *Homo sapiens* or a very close but separate species? In either case, it is possible, even expected, that some inter-breeding occurred between the two groups. In nature, close species such as coyotes and wolves interbreed when their ranges overlap. Among Neandertals and modern humans, there is little if any evidence of such a phenomenon. This is not surprising considering the rarity of specimens studied from the range of time when the two groups coexisted in Europe. In 1995, Fred Spoor of University College, London, Marc Braun of the University of Nancy, and I described morphological differences between the inner ear of Neandertals, modern humans, and fossil and extant hominoids such as gorillas and chimpanzees. The form of this organ in the skull base is set after six months of embryological development, and our findings suggested strong genetic differences between the groups. The inner ear of a baby from Arcy-sur-Cure's Châtelperronian layers was fully Neandertal with no hybrid characteristics. Some Aurignacian modern human remains display a high degree of robusticity, but no demonstrably Neandertal characteristics. If some genes were exchanged, they are not more visible in ancient modern human populations than a drop of milk in a cup of coffee.

The 25,000 year-old Lagar Velho child in Portugal, studied by Erik Trinkaus of Washington University in St. Louis, is said to show Neandertal features after the extinction of the group and thus is supposed to indicate earlier interbreeding (see ARCHAEOLOGY, July/August 2000, pp. 24–31). The issue is hotly debated and considering the anatomical variation in early modern humans and Neandertals, evaluating whether or not some physical character-istics are hybridized is a difficult task. In the case of the four-year-old Lagar Velho child, its youth makes this type of interpretation even more difficult. Between 40,000 and 30,000 years ago, there is not one well preserved speci-men, Neandertal or Cro-Magnon, of the same age known in Europe that would allow us to evaluate how for example the body proportions of the Lagar Velho child compare with the variation of Upper Palaeolithic modern children. The comparisons that have been made have been restricted to some Neander-tal specimens and to later or living modern humans. If the southern Iberian peninsula represented a long-lasting area of hybridization between Neandertals and modern humans, further discoveries will prove it. For now, across Europe, Neandertals and modern humans reveal themselves as two groups interacting in a limited way, exchanging even fewer genes than bone-carving techniques.

The Lagar Velho controversy presents another problem: the exact time and process of extinction of the last Neandertals. The long coexistence of Ne-andertals and modern humans in Europe demonstrates that modern humans were not overwhelmingly superior. Indeed, Neandertals prospered in Europe for hundreds of millennia and initially were probably better adapted to local conditions than their warm-weather challengers. In fact, it took a long time for modern humans to adapt biologically to their new environment; it was only toward the end of the Upper Palaeolithic that their body proportions lost all the features (such as long limbs) reminiscent of their tropical origin. Their technical skills, however, were much better than those of the Neandertals. For the first time, humans were able to sustain themselves in periglacial environments at very high latitudes. The spectacular site of Sungir north of Moscow, dating to more than 22,000 years ago, is at a latitude where continuous Middle Palaeolithic settlements did not occur. Modern humans' technical innovations, such as the eyed needle, allowed them to make complex clothing that probably played a major role in this success, as did their establishment of social networks and new strategies for the appropriation and storage of food.

Several scenarios have been proposed to explain Neandertal extinction. Scholars have considered epidemic diseases resulting from contact with modern invaders, but nothing occurred like the decimation of Native Americans by viruses imported from Europe. Some kind of genocide has also been imagined. Although violence is difficult to demonstrate in the archaeological record, the interactions between the two groups may not always have been friendly. The extinction of the Neandertals was most likely a slow process that took some 10,000 years. Differences in mortality and fecundity rates between populations of small sizes also can lead to the replacement of one by the other. It is very possible there were several simultaneous causes.

I emphasize the role of climatic changes in the demise of the Neandertals. In the past 450,000 years, Europe periodically witnessed glacial episodes. Neandertals and their ancestors adapted biologically to the cool-to-cold environment but, because of their limited technical skills, mainly responded to these climatic changes by scaling back their geographic domain. At the peak of the last glacial era, some 20,000 to 18,000 years ago, even modern humans with their needles, sophisticated housing, and new social organization had to yield large portions of the territory they had settled in Europe, surviving in southern refuges. Previous glacial periods must have placed a greater strain on Neandertals, who suffered dramatic reductions of their territories and population, but always re-colonized the lost lands during milder periods.

Between 40,000 and 35,000 years ago, modern humans had invaded some parts of Europe during a long and unstable interglacial stage and co-existed with the Neandertals in a fragile environmental equilibrium. But in the freeze that accompanied the beginning of the last glacial age, habitable Europe shrunk again and competition for land increased between the groups. The equilibrium was subverted. Refuges where Neandertals survived during previous glacial crises were partly occupied by challengers who proved themselves better at responding to environmental change. In the more favorable refuges, Neandertals must have felt heavy pressure from their modern neighbors. Competition for natural resources, violent interactions, and differences in the ability to respond to the new environmental challenge all likely led to the extinction of the Neandertals. The age of the very last pockets of Neandertals recently documented at Zafarraya (Spain), possibly Vindjia (Croatia), and Mezmaskaya (Caucasus) matches the beginning of falling temperatures in western Europe, between 28,000 and 24,000 years ago. The places the Neandertals last gathered are significantly located in remote and mountainous areas that are natural refuges in southern Europe. It is in these places that the Neandertals' 400,000-year history came to an end.

POSTSCRIPT

Did Neandertals Interbreed
With Modern Humans?

The debate rages on between those, like Zilhão, who believe that Neandertals interbred with early modern humans in Europe and those, like Hublin, who believe that Neandertals were a separate species or subspecies that became extinct. Resolving whether or not Neandertals and early modern humans interbred will probably require more direct evidence of how the two groups arose from *Homo erectus*—whether or not they formed separate species—and how they interacted when they met in Europe. Fortunately, new fossil and archaeological evidence is coming in fast. The discovery of the possibly mixed Lagar Velho child in Portugal in 1998 is just one especially dramatic example. A mitochondrial DNA test of Neandertal bones from central Europe proved similar to earlier results from the Neander Valley specimen, indicating that the earlier results were reliable and that Neandertals formed a closely related population. But resolving whether or not they were a separate species depends on obtaining mitochondrial DNA profiles of early modern humans from the same period for comparison.

There is a huge and rapidly growing literature on Neandertals. Because new evidence is coming in so fast, students should try to get the most recent possible sources. The Web site of the Neanderthal Museum in Germany, at http://www.neanderthal.de, is especially useful in this respect. It provides general information, the latest scholarly reports, and links to related sites. Because of the enormous public interest in Neandertals, most popular science magazines—including *Natural History, Archaeology,* and *Scientific American*—feature regular updates on the Neandertal controversy. An excellent recent overview of the controversy is Kate Wong's article "Who Were the Neanderthals?" *Scientific American* (April 2000). Recent books arguing against interbreeding theories include Christopher Stringer and Clive Gamble's *In Search of the Neanderthals* (Thames & Hudson, 1993), Ian Tattersall's *The Last Neanderthal* (Westview Press, 1999), and Ian Tattersall and Jeffrey H. Schwartz's *Extinct Humans* (Westview Press, 2000). Scholarly journals periodically devote parts of issues to the debate over the Neandertals. Recent examples include the *Current Anthropology* special supplement, "The Neanderthal Problem and the Evolution of Human Behavior" (vol. 39, 1998) and the *Current Anthropology* Forum on Theory in Anthropology, "The Neanderthal Problem Continued" (vol. 40, no. 3, 1999), in which anthropologists Paul Mellars, Marcel Otte, Laurence Straus, João Zilhão, and Francesco D'Errico present conflicting views of recent Neandertal evidence.

ISSUE 3

Are Humans Inherently Violent?

YES: Richard Wrangham and Dale Peterson, from *Demonic Males: Apes and the Origins of Human Violence* (Houghton Mifflin Company, 1996)

NO: Robert W. Sussman, from "Exploring Our Basic Human Nature," *Anthro Notes* (Fall 1997)

ISSUE SUMMARY

YES: Biological anthropologist Richard Wrangham and science writer Dale Peterson maintain that male humans and chimpanzees, our closest nonhuman relatives, have an innate tendency to be aggressive and to defend their territory by violence. They state that sexual selection, a type of natural selection, has fostered an instinct for male aggression because males who are good fighters mate more frequently and sire more offspring than weaker and less aggressive ones.

NO: Biological anthropologist Robert W. Sussman rejects the theory that human aggression is an inherited propensity, arguing instead that violence is a product of culture and upbringing. He also rejects the contention that male chimpanzees routinely commit violent acts against other male chimps. Sussman regards the notion that human males are inherently violent as a Western cultural tradition, not a scientifically demonstrated fact.

Human history is rife with wars between groups of all types, from clans to nation-states, and interpersonal violence is common enough that all societies attempt to control it. But is violence a part of human nature, or is violence merely one of many human capabilities that may be either encouraged or discouraged by cultures?

The question of whether or not humans have an instinct for aggression has been around since the formative years of anthropology, and it is still being debated today. Some nineteenth-century scholars interpreted Darwin's concepts of "natural selection" and "survival of the fittest" to mean that the strong would kill off the weak. The strongest and most aggressive individuals, therefore, would have the most offspring, and their strength and instinct for aggression would gradually come to predominate in the population.

Most cultural anthropologists from the 1950s onward rejected the explanation of human aggression in terms of instincts, emphasizing instead the social and cultural causes of violence. They pointed out that the amount of aggression tolerated varies widely from one society to another and that individuals can become aggressive or peaceful depending on how they are raised. They held up such groups as the Semai of Malaysia (see Robert K. Dentan, *The Semai: A Nonviolent People of Malaya* [Holt, Rinehart & Winston, 1968]) as proof that culture could create a people who abhorred all forms of aggression and coercion. Whatever instinct for aggression humans might have, they argued, must be very weak indeed.

The question behind this issue concerns the nature of human nature. Have we a set of innate behavioral predispositions that, when set off by certain stimuli, are very likely to be expressed? Or, are any such predispositions at best weak tendencies that can be shaped or even negated by cultural conditioning? Many apparently innate behaviors in humans turn out to be highly variable in their strength and form. While the sucking instinct of babies operates predictably in all newborns, a hypothesized "mothering instinct" seems quite diverse in expression and variable in strength from one woman to another. The question, then, is whether the hypothesized aggression instinct is a powerful drive that all human males must express in one way or another or a weak and pliable tendency that some males may never act upon.

Richard Wrangham and Dale Peterson argue that human wars and interpersonal violence are driven by inherited behavioral tendencies that have evolved under pressure of sexual selection—natural selection of traits that enhance the reproductive success of one sex. Among both humans and chimpanzees, males who are aggressive use their fighting ability to dominate other males and to prevent them from mating with the available females. Therefore the genes causing aggression are passed on to succeeding generations in greater numbers than the genes causing nonaggressive behavior.

Robert W. Sussman rejects Wrangham and Peterson's assertion that natural selection favors aggressive human males and that aggressiveness is an inherited tendency rather than a result of environment and upbringing. He contends that human hunter-gatherers and most apes are remarkably nonaggressive, as were our earliest human ancestors, the australopithecines. He sees the evidence that chimpanzee males routinely attack other males as weak, and he questions the relevance of chimpanzee behavior for humans.

These selections raise a number of questions with regard to the nature and causes of human aggression. How can we determine whether a person's aggressive act is due to instinct, upbringing, or both? If male aggression in humans is based on instinct, how can scholars explain variations in the amount and type of aggression found in different individuals and cultures? If male aggression is not based on instinct, why is violence between men so widespread? What role did women have in the evolution of an instinct for male violence? To what extent can studies of animal behavior be applied to humans?

**Richard Wrangham
and Dale Peterson**

Demonic Males: Apes and the Origins of Human Violence

Paradise Lost

The killer ape has long been part of our popular culture: Tarzan had to escape from the bad apes, and King Kong was a murderous gorilla-like monster. But before the Kahama observations [in which males of one chimpanzee group killed the males of a neighboring group], few biologists took the idea seriously. The reason was simple. There was so little evidence of animals killing members of their own species that biologists used to think animals killed each other only when something went wrong—an accident, perhaps, or unnatural crowding in zoos. The idea fit with the theories of animal behavior then preeminent, theories that saw animal behavior as designed by evolution for mutual good. Darwinian natural selection was a filter supposed to eliminate murderous violence. Killer apes, like killers in any animal species, were merely a novelist's fantasy to most scientists before the 1970s.

And so the behavior of people seemed very, very different from that of other animals. Killing, of course, is a typical result of human war, so one had to presume that humans somehow broke the rules of nature. Still, war must have come from somewhere. It could have come, for example, from the evolution of brains that happened to be smart enough to think of using tools as weapons, as Konrad Lorenz argued in his famous book, *On Aggression,* published in 1963.

However it may have originated, more generally war was seen as one of the defining marks of humanity: To fight wars meant to be human and apart from nature. This larger presumption was true even of nonscientific theories, such as the biblical concept of an original sin taking humans out of Eden, or the notion that warfare was an idea implanted by aliens, as Arthur C. Clarke imagined in *2001: A Space Odyssey.* In science, in religion, in fiction, violence and humanity were twinned.

The Kahama killings were therefore both a shock and a stimulus to thought. They undermined the explanations for extreme violence in terms of uniquely human attributes, such as culture, brainpower, or the punishment of an angry god. They made credible the idea that our warring tendencies go back into our prehuman past. They made us a little less special.

And yet science has still not grappled closely with the ultimate questions raised by the Kahama killings: Where does human violence come from, and why? Of course, there have been great advances in the way we think about these things. Most importantly, in the 1970s, the same decade as the Kahama killings, a new evolutionary theory emerged, the selfish-gene theory of natural selection, variously called inclusive fitness theory, sociobiology, or more broadly, behavioral ecology. Sweeping through the halls of academe, it revolutionized Darwinian thinking by its insistence that the ultimate explanation of any individual's behavior considers only how the behavior tends to maximize genetic success: to pass that individual's genes into subsequent generations. The new theory, elegantly popularized in Richard Dawkins's *The Selfish Gene,* is now the conventional wisdom in biological science because it explains animal behavior so well. It accounts easily for selfishness, even killing. And it has come to be applied with increasing confidence to human behavior, though the debate is still hot and unsettled. In any case, the general principle that behavior evolves to serve selfish ends has been widely accepted, and the idea that humans might have been favored by natural selection to hate and to kill their enemies has become entirely, if tragically, reasonable.

Those are the general principles, and yet the specifics are lacking. Most animals are nowhere near as violent as humans, so why did such intensely violent behavior evolve particularly in the human line? Why kill the enemy, rather than simply drive him away? Why rape? Why torture and mutilate? Why do we see these patterns both in ourselves and chimpanzees? Those sorts of questions have barely been asked, much less addressed.

Because chimpanzees and humans are each other's closest relatives, such questions carry extraordinary implications, the more so because the study of early human ancestry, unfolding in a fervor as we approach the century's end, is bringing chimpanzees and humans even closer than we ever imagined. Three dramatic recent discoveries speak to the relationship between chimpanzees and humans, and all three point in the same direction: to a past, around 5 million years ago, when chimpanzee ancestors and human ancestors were indistinguishable.

First, fossils recently dug up in Ethiopia indicate that over 4.5 million years ago there walked across African lands a bipedal ancestor of humans with a head strikingly like a chimpanzee's.

Second, laboratories around the world have over the last decade demonstrated chimpanzees to be genetically closer to us than they are even to gorillas, despite the close physical resemblance between chimpanzees and gorillas.

And third, both in the field and in the laboratory, studies of chimpanzee behavior are producing numerous, increasingly clear parallels with human behavior. It's not just that these apes pat each other on the hand to show affection, or kiss each other, or embrace. Not just that they have menopause, develop lifelong friendships, and grieve for their dead babies by carrying them for days or weeks. Nor is it their ability to do sums like 5 plus 4, or to communicate with hand signs. Nor their tool use, or collaboration, or bartering for sexual favors.

Nor even that they hold long-term grudges, deliberately hide their feelings, or bring rivals together to force them to make peace.

No, for us the single most gripping set of facts about chimpanzee behavior is what we have already touched on: the nature of their society. The social world of chimpanzees is a set of individuals who share a communal range; males live forever in the groups where they are born, while females move to neighboring groups at adolescence; and the range is defended, and sometimes extended with aggressive and potentially lethal violence, by groups of males related in a genetically patrilineal kin group.

What makes this social world so extraordinary is comparison. Very few animals live in patrilineal, male-bonded communities wherein females routinely reduce the risks of inbreeding by moving to neighboring groups to mate. And only two animal species are known to do so with a system of intense, male-initiated territorial aggression, including lethal raiding into neighboring communities in search of vulnerable enemies to attack and kill. Out of four thousand mammals and ten million or more other animal species, this suite of behaviors is known only among chimpanzees and humans.

Humans with male-bonded, patrilineal kin groups? Absolutely. *Male bonded* refers to males forming aggressive coalitions with each other in mutual support against others—Hatfields versus McCoys, Montagues versus Capulets, Palestinians versus Israelis, Americans versus Vietcong, Tutsis versus Hutus. Around the world, from the Balkans to the Yanomamö of Venezuela, from Pygmies of Central Africa to the T'ang Dynasty of China, from Australian aborigines to Hawaiian kingdoms, related men routinely fight in defense of their group. This is true even of the villages labeled by anthropologists as "matrilineal" and "matrilocal," where inheritance (from male to male) is figured out according to the mother's line, and where women stay in their natal villages to have children—such villages operate socially as subunits of a larger patrilineal whole. In short, the system of communities defended by related men is a human universal that crosses space and time, so established a pattern that even writers of science fiction rarely think to challenge it.

When it comes to social relationships involving females, chimpanzees and humans are very different. That's unsurprising. Discoveries in animal behavior since the 1960s strongly suggest that animal societies are adapted to their environments in exquisitely detailed ways, and obviously the environments of chimpanzees and humans are a study in contrast. But this just emphasizes our puzzle. Why should male chimpanzees and humans show such similar patterns?

Is it chance? Maybe our human ancestors lived in societies utterly unlike those of chimpanzees. Peaceful matriarchies, for example, somewhat like some of our distant monkey relatives. And then, by a remarkable quirk of evolutionary coincidence, at some time in prehistory human and chimpanzee social behaviors converged on their similar systems for different, unrelated reasons.

Or do they both depend on some other characteristic, like intelligence? Once brains reach a certain level of sophistication, is there some mysterious logic pushing a species toward male coalitionary violence? Perhaps, for instance, only chimpanzees and humans have enough brainpower to realize the advantages of removing the opposition.

Or is there a long-term evolutionary inertia? Perhaps humans have re-tained an old chimpanzee pattern which, though it was once adaptive, has now acquired a stability and life of its own, resistant even to new environments where other forms of society would be better.

Or are the similarities there, as we believe, because in spite of first ap-pearances, similar evolutionary forces continue to be at work in chimpanzee and human lineages, maintaining and refining a system of intergroup hostility and personal violence that has existed since even before the ancestors of chim-panzees and humans mated for the last time in a drying forest of eastern Africa around 5 million years ago? If so, one must ask, what forces are they? What bred male bonding and lethal raiding in our forebears and keeps it now in chimpanzees and humans? What marks have those ancient evolutionary forces forged onto our twentieth-century psyches? And what do they say about our hopes and fears for the future? . . .

Sexual selection, the evolutionary process that produces sex differences, has a lot to answer for. Without it, males wouldn't possess dangerous bod-ily weapons and a mindset that sanctions violence. But males who are better fighters can stop other males from mating, and they mate more successfully themselves. Better fighters tend to have more babies. That's the simple, stupid, selfish logic of sexual selection. So, what about us? Is sexual selection ulti-mately the reason why men brawl in barrooms, form urban gangs, plot guerrilla attacks, and go to war? Has it indeed designed men to be especially aggressive?

Until we have carefully examined the evidence, our answer should be: not necessarily. Because the social, environmental, genetic, and historical cir-cumstances for any single species are so extremely complex, we can't assume a priori that sexual selection has acted in any particular way for any single species. Among the 10 million or more animal species on earth, you can find interest-ing exceptions to almost every rule. On the one hand, you can find species like spotted hyenas, where such extraordinary ferocity has evolved among females that it outshines even the stark sexual aggression shown by males. And on the other, you will discover the pacifists. . . .

So there is no particular reason to think that human aggression is all cultural, or that our ancestors were as pacific as muriquis [nonaggressive mon-keys of South America]. The only way to find out whether sexual selection has shaped human males for aggression is to leave the theory and go back to the ev-idence. There are two places to look for an answer. We can look at our bodies, and we can think about our minds. The easier part is our bodies.

A biologist from Mars looking at a preserved human male laid out on a slab might find it hard to imagine our species as dangerous. Lined up next to male specimens from the other apes, or from virtually any other mammal species, human males don't look as if they are designed to fight at all. They are rather slender, their bones are light, and they appear to have no bodily weapons.

People don't think of humans in the same way that they think of dangerous animals. That first impression is misleading, however. Humans are indeed designed to fight, although in a different way from most of the other primates.

Here's one clue. Men are a little larger and more heavily muscled than women. For other primate species, larger male size links strongly to male aggression. But with humans, that apparent evidence seems to conflict with the absence of fighting canine teeth. Could it be that humans break the general rule linking larger males to an evolved design for aggression?

Consider our teeth. The upper canines of most primates are longer and sharper than any other tooth. These long teeth are obvious weapons, bright daggers ground to a razor-sharp edge against a special honing surface on a pre-molar tooth in the lower jaw. Baboons, for example, have canines five to six centimeters long. Male baboons trying to impress each other grind their canines noisily, occasionally showing off their teeth in huge, gaping yawns. When male baboons make those display yawns, they are acting like cowboys twirling their revolvers.

By comparison, human canines seem tiny. They barely extend beyond the other teeth, and in males they are no longer than in females. Those canines may help us bite an apple, we love to imagine them elongated for the Halloween scare, and we unconsciously display them when we sneer, but our canines virtually never help us fight. In fact, the fossil record indicates that ever since the transition from rainforest ape to woodland ape, our ancestors' canines have been markedly smaller than they are in chimpanzees. In the woodlands, those teeth quickly became muriqui-like in appearance—one reason why some people wonder if woodland apes were as pacific as modern muriquis are.

But we should not allow ourselves to become misled by the evidence of canine teeth. The importance of a species' canines depends entirely on how it fights....

Apes can fight with their fists because they have adapted to hanging from their arms, which means that their arms can swing all around their shoulders, the shoulder joint being a flexible multidirectional joint. So chimpanzees and gorillas often hit with their fists when they fight, and they can keep most canine-flashing opponents at bay because their arms are long. If chimpanzees and gorillas find punching effective, then surely the woodland apes, who were standing up high on hind legs, would have fought even better with their arms.

Fists can also grasp invented weapons. Chimpanzees today are close to using hand-held weapons. Throughout the continent, wild chimpanzees will tear off and throw great branches when they are angry or threatened, or they will pick up and throw rocks. Humphrey, when he was the alpha male at Gombe, almost killed me once by sending a melon-size rock whistling less than half a meter from my head. They also hit with big sticks. A celebrated film taken in Guinea shows wild chimpanzees pounding meter-long clubs down on the back of a leopard. (Scientists were able to get that film because the leopard was a stuffed one, placed there by a curious researcher. The chimpanzees were lucky to find a leopard so slow to fight back.) Chimpanzees in West Africa already have a primitive stone tool technology, and there could well be a community of chimpanzees today, waiting to be discovered, who are already using heavy sticks as clubs against each other. Certainly we can reasonably imagine that the woodland apes did some of these things.

... The shoulders of boys and girls are equally broad until adolescence; but at puberty, shoulder cartilage cells respond to testosterone, the male sex hormone newly produced by the testes, by growing. (In an equivalent way, pubertal girls get wider hips when their hip cartilage cells respond to estrogen, the female sex hormone.) The result is a sudden acceleration of shoulder width for boys around the age of fourteen, associated with relative enlargement of the upper arm muscles. In other words, the shoulders and arms of male humans—like the neck muscles of a red deer, the clasping hands of a xenopus frog, or the canine teeth of many other primates—look like the result of sexual selection for fighting. All these examples of male weaponry respond to testosterone by growing. They are specialized features that enlarge for the specific purpose of promoting fighting ability in competition against other males. Small wonder, then, that men show off to each other before fights by hunching their shoulders, expanding their muscles, and otherwise displaying their upper-body strength. . . .

If the bipedal woodland apes fought with fists and sometimes with weapons, those species should have had especially broad shoulders and well-muscled arms, like modern men. We haven't enough fossils yet to know if that's true. Indeed, it is not yet absolutely certain that male woodland apes were larger than females, though most of the current fossil evidence suggests so. If they were, we can confidently imagine that the males were designed for aggression. Perhaps the early development of club-style weapons might also explain why the skulls of our ancestors became strikingly thicker, particularly with *Homo erectus* at 1.6 to 1.8 million years ago. That's a guess, but it's clear in any case that our present bodies carry the same legacy of sexual selection as other mammals whose males fight with their upper bodies. The broad shoulders and powerful, arching torso we so admire in Michelangelo's *David* are the human equivalent of antlers. The mark of Cain appears in our shoulders and arms, not in our teeth.

◦◦◦

What about our minds? Has sexual selection shaped our psyches also, in order to make us better fighters? Can sexual selection explain why men are so quick to bristle at insults, and, under the right circumstances, will readily kill? Can our evolutionary past account for modern war?

Inquiry about mental processes is difficult enough when we deal just with humans. Comparison with other species is harder still. The supposed problem is that animals fight with their hearts, so people say, whereas humans fight with their minds. Animal aggression is supposed to happen by instinct, or by emotion, and without reason. Wave a red rag in a bull's face and the bull charges thoughtlessly—that's the model. Human wars, on the other hand, seem to emerge, so Karl von Clausewitz declared, as "the continuation of policy with the admixture of other means." According to historian Michael Howard,

human wars "begin with conscious and reasoned decisions based on the calculation, made by both parties, that they can achieve more by going to war than
by remaining at peace." The principle seems as true for the measured deliber-
ations on the top floor of the Pentagon as for the whispered councils among
the Yanomamö, and it suggests a wholly different set of psychological processes
from the supposedly rigid, instinctual, emotional drives of animals. The fact
that we possess consciousness and reasoning ability, this theory says, takes us
across a chasm into a new world, where the old instincts are no longer important. If there is no connection between these two systems, the rules for each
cannot be the same. In other words, aggression based on "conscious and reasoned decisions" can no longer be explained in terms of such evolutionary
forces as sexual selection.

The argument sounds fair enough, but it depends on oversimplified thinking, a false distinction between animals acting by emotion (or instinct) and
humans acting by reason. Animal behavior is not purely emotional. Nor is human decision-making purely rational. In both cases, the event is a mixture.
And new evidence suggests that even though we humans reason much more
(analyze past and present context, consider a potential future, and so on) than
nonhuman animals, our essential process for making a decision still relies on
emotion....

People have always accepted that animals act from emotions; humans...
can never act without them. Suddenly the apparent chasm between the mental processes of chimpanzees and our species is reduced to a comprehensible
difference. Humans can reason better, but reason and emotion are linked in
parallel ways for both chimpanzees and humans. For both species, emotion sits
in the driver's seat, and reason (or calculation) paves the road.

We are now ready to ask what causes aggression. If emotion is the ultimate arbiter of action for both species, then what kinds of emotions underlie
violence for both? Clearly there are many. But one stands out. From the raids
of chimpanzees at Gombe to wars among human nations, the same emotion
looks extraordinarily important, one that we take for granted and describe most
simply but that nonetheless takes us deeply back to our animal origins: pride.

Male chimpanzees compete much more aggressively for dominance than
females do. If a lower-ranking male refuses to acknowledge his superior with
one of the appropriate conventions, such as a soft grunt, the superior will
become predictably angry. But females can let such insults pass. Females are certainly capable of being aggressive to each other, and they can be as politically
adept as males in using coalitions to achieve a goal. But female chimpanzees
act as if they just don't care about their status as much as males do.

By contrast, we exaggerate only barely in saying that a male chimpanzee
in his prime organizes his whole life around issues of rank. His attempts to
achieve and then maintain alpha status are cunning, persistent, energetic, and
time-consuming. They affect whom he travels with, whom he grooms, where
he glances, how often he scratches, where he goes, and what time he gets up in
the morning....

Eighteenth-century Englishmen used less dramatic tactics than wild chimpanzees, but that acute observer Samuel Johnson thought rank concerns were

as pervasive: "No two people can be half an hour together, but one shall acquire an evident superiority over the other." Pride obviously serves as a stimulus for much interpersonal aggression in humans, and we can hypothesize confidently that this emotion evolved during countless generations in which males who achieved high status were able to turn their social success into extra reproduction. Male pride, the source of many a conflict, is reasonably seen as a mental equivalent of broad shoulders. Pride is another legacy of sexual selection....

Our ape ancestors have passed to us a legacy, defined by the power of natural selection and written in the molecular chemistry of DNA. For the most part it is a wonderful inheritance, but one small edge contains destructive elements; and now that we have the weapons of mass destruction, that edge promotes the potential of our own demise. People have long known such things intuitively and so have built civilizations with laws and justice, diplomacy and mediation, ideally keeping always a step ahead of the old demonic principles. And we might hope that men will eventually realize that violence doesn't pay.

The problem is that males are demonic at unconscious and irrational levels. The motivation of a male chimpanzee who challenges another's rank is not that he foresees more matings or better food or a longer life. Those rewards explain why sexual selection has favored the desire for power, but the immediate reason he vies for status is simpler, deeper, and less subject to the vagaries of context. It is simply to dominate his peers. Unconscious of the evolutionary rationale that placed this prideful goal in his temperament, he devises strategies to achieve it that can be complex, original, and maybe conscious. In the same way, the motivation of male chimpanzees on a border patrol is not to gain land or win females. The temperamental goal is to intimidate the opposition, to beat them to a pulp, to erode their ability to challenge. Winning has become an end in itself.

It looks the same with men.

Robert W. Sussman

 **NO**

Exploring Our Basic Human Nature

Are human beings forever doomed to be violent? Is aggression fixed within our genetic code, an inborn action pattern that threatens to destroy us? Or, as asked by Richard Wrangham and Dale Peterson in their recent book, *Demonic Males: Apes and the Origins of Human Violence,* can we get beyond our genes, beyond our essential "human nature"?

Wrangham and Peterson's belief in the importance of violence in the evolution and nature of humans is based on new primate research that they assert demonstrates the continuity of aggression from our great ape ancestors. The authors argue that 20–25 years ago most scholars believed human aggression was unique. Research at that time had shown great apes to be basically non-aggressive gentle creatures. Furthermore, the separation of humans from our ape ancestors was thought to have occurred 15–20 million years ago (Mya). Although Raymond Dart, Sherwood Washburn, Robert Ardrey, E.O. Wilson and others had argued through much of the 20th century that hunting, killing, and extreme aggressive behaviors were biological traits inherited from our earliest hominid hunting ancestors, many anthropologists still believed that patterns of aggression were environmentally determined and culturally learned behaviors, not inherited characteristics.

Demonic Males discusses new evidence that killer instincts are not unique to humans, but rather shared with our nearest relative, the common chimpanzee. The authors argue that it is this inherited propensity for killing that allows hominids and chimps to be such good hunters.

According to Wrangham and Peterson, the split between humans and the common chimpanzee was only 6–8 Mya. Furthermore, humans may have split from the chimpanzee-bonobo line after gorillas, with bonobos *(pygmy chimps)* separating from chimps only 2.5 Mya. Because chimpanzees may be the modern ancestor of all these forms, and because the earliest australopithecines were quite chimpanzee-like, Wrangham speculates (in a separate article) that "chimpanzees are a conservative species and an amazingly good model for the ancestor of hominids" (1995, reprinted in Sussman 1997:106). If modern chimpanzees and modern humans share certain behavioral traits, these traits have "long evolutionary roots" and are likely to be fixed, biologically inherited parts of our basic human nature and not culturally determined.

Wrangham argues that chimpanzees are almost on the brink of human-ness:

> Nut-smashing, root-eating, savannah-using chimpanzees, resembling our ancestors, and capable by the way of extensive bipedalism. Using ant-wands, and sandals, and bowls, meat-sharing, hunting cooperatively. Strange para-dox . . . a species trembling on the verge of hominization, but so conservative that it has stayed on that edge. . . . (1997:107).

Wrangham and Peterson (1996:24) claim that only two animal species, chimpanzees and humans, live in patrilineal, male-bonded communities "with intense, male initiated territorial aggression, including lethal raiding into neigh-boring communities in search of vulnerable enemies to attack and kill." Wrang-ham asks:

> Does this mean chimpanzees are naturally violent? Ten years ago it wasn't clear. . . . In this cultural species, it may turn out that one of the least variable of all chimpanzee behaviors is the intense competition between males, the violent aggression they use against strangers, and their willingness to maim and kill those that frustrate their goals. . . . As the picture of chimpanzee soci-ety settles into focus, it now includes infanticide, rape and regular battering of females by males (1997:108).

Since humans and chimpanzees share these violent urges, the implication is that human violence has long evolutionary roots. "We are apes of nature, cursed over six million years or more with a rare inheritance, a Dostoyevskyan demon . . . The coincidence of demonic aggression in ourselves and our closest kin bespeaks its antiquity" (1997: 108–109).

Intellectual Antecedents

From the beginning of Western thought, the theme of human depravity runs deep, related to the idea of humankind's fall from grace and the emergence of original sin. This view continues to pervade modern "scientific" interpretations of the evolution of human behavior. Recognition of the close evolutionary rela-tionship between humans and apes, from the time of Darwin's *Descent of Man* (1874) on, has encouraged theories that look to modern apes for evidence of parallel behaviors reflecting this relationship.

By the early 1950s, large numbers of australopithecine fossils and the dis-covery that the large-brained "fossil" ancestor from Piltdown, in England, was a fraud, led to the realization that our earliest ancestors were more like apes than like modern humans. Accordingly, our earliest ancestors must have behaved much like other non-human primates. This, in turn, led to a great interest in using primate behavior to understand human evolution and the evolutionary basis of human nature. The subdiscipline of primatology was born.

Raymond Dart, discoverer of the first australopithecine fossil some thirty years earlier, was also developing a different view of our earliest ancestors. At first Dart believed that australopithecines were scavengers barely eking out an existence in the harsh savanna environment. But from the fragmented and dam-aged bones found with the australopithecines, together with dents and holes in these early hominid skulls, Dart eventually concluded that this species had used bone, tooth and antler tools to kill, butcher and eat their prey, as well as to kill one another. This hunting hypothesis (Cartmill 1997:511) "was linked from the beginning with a bleak, pessimistic view of human beings and their ancestors as instinctively bloodthirsty and savage." To Dart, the australopithecines were:

> confirmed killers: carnivorous creatures that seized living quarries by vio-
> lence, battered them to death, tore apart their broken bodies, dismembered
> them limb from limb, slaking their ravenous thirst with the hot blood of
> victims and greedily devouring livid writhing flesh (1953:209).

Cartmill, in a recent book (1993), shows that this interpretation of early human morality is reminiscent of earlier Greek and Christian views. Dart's (1953) own treatise begins with a 17th century quote from the Calvinist R. Baxter: "of all the beasts, the man-beast is the worst/ to others and himself the cruellest foe."

Between 1961–1976, Dart's view was picked up and extensively popularized by the playwright Robert Ardrey (*The Territorial Imperative, African Genesis*). Ardrey believed it was the human competitive and killer instinct, acted out in warfare, that made humans what they are today. "It is war and the instinct for territory that has led to the great accomplishments of Western Man. Dreams may have inspired our love of freedom, but only war and weapons have made it ours" (1961: 324).

Man the Hunter

In the 1968 volume *Man the Hunter*, Sherwood Washburn and Chet Lancaster presented a theory of "The evolution of hunting," emphasizing that it is this behavior that shaped human nature and separated early humans from their primate relatives.

> To assert the biological unity of mankind is to affirm the importance of
> the hunting way of life.... However much conditions and customs may
> have varied locally, the main selection pressures that forged the species were
> the same. The biology, psychology and customs that separate us from the
> apes... we owe to the hunters of time past... for those who would under-
> stand the origins and nature of human behavior there is no choice but to
> try to understand "Man the Hunter" (1968:303).

Rather than amassing evidence from modern hunters and gatherers to prove their theory, Washburn and Lancaster (1968:299) use the 19th-century concept of cultural "survivals": behaviors that persist as evidence of an earlier time but are no longer useful in society.

> Men enjoy hunting and killing, and these activities are continued in sports
> even when they are no longer economically necessary. If a behavior is im-
> portant to the survival of a species... then it must be both easily learned
> and pleasurable (Washburn & Lancaster, p. 299).

Man the Dancer

Using a similar logic for the survival of ancient "learned and pleasurable" behaviors, perhaps it could easily have been our propensity for dancing rather than our desire to hunt that can explain much of human behavior. After all, men and women love to dance; it is a behavior found in all cultures but has even less obvious function today than hunting. Our love of movement and dance might explain, for example, our propensity for face-to-face sex, and even the evolution of bipedalism and the movement of humans out of trees and onto the ground.

Could the first tool have been a stick to beat a dance drum, and the ancient Laetoli footprints evidence of two individuals going out to dance the "Afarensis shuffle"? Although it takes only two to tango, a variety of social interactions and systems might have been encouraged by the complex social dances known in human societies around the globe.

Sociobiology and E.O. Wilson

In the mid-1970s, E.O. Wilson and others described a number of traits as genetically based and therefore human universals, including territoriality, male–female bonds, male dominance over females, and extended maternal care leading to matrilineality. Wilson argued that the genetic basis of these traits was indicated by their relative constancy among our primate relatives and by their persistence throughout human evolution and in human societies. Elsewhere, I have shown that these characteristics are neither general primate traits nor human universals (Sussman 1995). Wilson, however, argued that these were a product of our evolutionary hunting past.

For at least a million years—probably more—Man engaged in a hunting way of life, giving up the practice a mere 10,000 years ago. . . . Our innate social responses have been fashioned through this life style. With caution, we can compare the most widespread hunter-gatherer qualities with similar behavior displayed by some of the non-human primates that are closely related to Man. Where the same pattern of traits occurs in . . . most or all of those primates— we can conclude that it has been subject to little evolution. (Wilson 1976, in Sussman 1997: 65–66).

Wilson's theory of sociobiology, the evolution of social behavior, argued that:

1. the goal of living organisms is to pass on one's genes at the expense of all others;
2. an organism should only cooperate with others if:

    (a) they carry some of his/her own genes (kin selection) or
    (b) if at some later date the others might aid you (reciprocal altruism).

To sociobiologists, evolutionary morality is based on an unconscious need to multiply our own genes, to build group cohesion in order to win wars. We should not look down on our warlike, cruel nature but rather understand its success when coupled with "making nice" with *some* other individuals or groups. The genetically driven "making nice" is the basis of human ethics and morality.

> Throughout recorded history the conduct of war has been common... some of the noblest traits of mankind, including team play, altruism, patriotism, bravery... and so forth are the genetic product of warfare (Wilson 1975:572–3).

The evidence for any of these universals or for the tenets of sociobiology is as weak as was the evidence for Dart's, Ardrey's and Washburn and Lancaster's theories of innate aggression. Not only are modern gatherer-hunters and most apes remarkably non-aggressive, but in the 1970s and 1980s studies of fossil bones and artifacts have shown that early humans were not hunters, and that weapons were a later addition to the human repertoire. In fact, C.K. Brain (1981) showed that the holes and dents in Dart's australopithecine skulls matched perfectly with fangs of leopards or with impressions of rocks pressing against the buried fossils. Australopithecines apparently were the hunted, not the hunters (Cartmill, 1993, 1997).

Beyond Our Genes

Wrangham and Peterson's book goes beyond the assertion of human inborn aggression and propensity towards violence. The authors ask the critical question: Are we doomed to be violent forever because this pattern is fixed within our genetic code or can we go beyond our past?—get out of our genes, so to speak.

The authors believe that we can look to the bonobo or pygmy chimpanzee as one potential savior, metaphorically speaking.

Bonobos, although even more closely related to the common chimpanzee than humans, have become a peace-loving, love-making alternative to chimpanzee-human violence. How did this happen? In chimpanzees and humans, females of the species select partners that are violent... "while men have evolved to be demonic males, it seems likely that women have evolved to prefer demonic males... as long as demonic males are the most successful reproducers, any female who mates with them is provided with sons who themselves will likely be good reproducers" (Wrangham and Peterson 1996:239). However, among pygmy chimpanzees females form alliances and have chosen to mate with less aggressive males. So, after all, it is not violent males that have caused humans and chimpanzees to be their inborn, immoral, dehumanized selves, it is rather, poor choices by human and chimpanzee females.

Like Dart, Washburn, and Wilson before them, Wrangham and Peterson believe that killing and violence is inherited from our ancient relatives of the past. However, unlike these earlier theorists, Wrangham and Peterson argue this is not a trait unique to hominids, nor is it a by-product of hunting. In fact, it is just this violent nature and a natural "blood lust" that makes both humans and chimpanzees such good hunters. It is the bonobos that help the authors come to this conclusion. Because bonobos have lost the desire to kill, they also have lost the desire to hunt.

> ... do bonobos tell us that the suppression of personal violence carried with it the suppression of predatory aggression? The strongest hypothesis at the moment is that bonobos came from a chimpanzee-like ancestor that hunted monkeys and hunted one another. As they evolved into bonobos, males lost their demonism, becoming less aggressive to each other. In so doing they lost their lust for hunting monkeys, too... Murder and hunting may be more closely tied together than we are used to thinking (Wrangham and Peterson 1996:219).

The Selfish Gene Theory

Like Ardrey, Wrangham and Peterson believe that blood lust ties killing and hunting tightly together but it is the killing that drives hunting in the latter's argument. This lust to kill is based upon the sociobiological tenet of the selfish gene. "The general principle that behavior evolves to serve selfish ends has been widely accepted; and the idea that humans might have been favored by natural selection to hate and to kill their enemies has become entirely, if tragically, reasonable" (Wrangham and Peterson 1996:23).

As with many of the new sociobiological or evolutionary anthropology theories, I find problems with both the theory itself and with the evidence used to support it. Two arguments that humans and chimpanzees share bio-logically fixed behaviors are: (1) they are more closely related to each other than chimpanzees are to gorillas; (2) chimpanzees are a good model for our earliest ancestor and retain conservative traits that should be shared by both.

The first of these statements is still hotly debated and, using various ge-netic evidence, the chimp-gorilla-human triage is so close that it is difficult to tell exact divergence time or pattern among the three. The second statement is just not true. Chimpanzees have been evolving for as long as humans and gorillas, and there is no reason to believe ancestral chimps were similar to present-day chimps. The fossil evidence for the last 5–8 million years is ex-tremely sparse, and it is likely that many forms of apes have become extinct just as have many hominids.

Furthermore, even if the chimpanzee were a good model for the ancestral hominid, and was a conservative representative of this phylogenetic group, this would not mean that humans would necessarily share specific behavioral traits. As even Wrangham and Peterson emphasize, chimps, gorillas, and bonobos all behave very differently from one another in their social behavior and in their willingness to kill conspecifics.

Evidence Against "Demonic Males"

The proof of the "Demonic Male" theory does not rest on any theoretical grounds but must rest solely on the evidence that violence and killing in chim-panzees and in humans are behaviors that are similar in pattern; have ancient, shared evolutionary roots; and are inherited. Besides killing of conspecifics,

Wrangham "includes infanticide, rape, and regular battering of females by males" as a part of this inherited legacy of violent behaviors shared by humans and chimpanzees (1997:108).

Wrangham and Peterson state: "That chimpanzees and humans kill members of neighboring groups of their own species is... a startling exception to the normal rule for animals" (1996:63). "Fighting adults of almost all species normally stop at winning: They don't go on to kill" (1996:155). However, as Wrangham points out there are exceptions, such as lions, wolves, spotted hyenas, and I would add a number of other predators. In fact, most species do not have the weapons to kill one another as adults.

Just how common is conspecific killing in chimpanzees? This is where the real controversy may lie. Jane Goodall described the chimpanzee as a peaceful, non-aggressive species during the first 24 years of study at Gombe (1950–1974). During one year of concentrated study, Goodall observed 284 agonistic encounters: of these 66% were due to competition for introduced bananas, and only 34% "could be regarded as attacks occurring in 'normal' aggressive contexts" (1968:278). Only 10 percent of the 284 attacks were classified as 'violent', and "even attacks that appeared punishing to me often resulted in no discernable injury.... Other attacks consisted merely of brief pounding, hitting or rolling of the individual, after which the aggressor often touched or embraced the other immediately (1968:277).

Chimpanzee aggression before 1974 was considered no different from patterns of aggression seen in many other primate species. In fact, Goodall explains in her 1986 monograph, *The Chimpanzees of Gombe,* that she uses data mainly from after 1975 because the earlier years present a "very different picture of the Gombe chimpanzees" as being "far more peaceable than humans" (1986:3). Other early naturalists' descriptions of chimpanzee behavior were consistent with those of Goodall and confirmed her observations. Even different communities were observed to come together with peaceful, ritualized displays of greeting (Reynolds and Reynolds 1965; Suguyama 1972; Goodall 1968).

Then, between 1974 and 1977, five adult males from one subgroup were attacked and disappeared from the area, presumably dead. Why after 24 years did the patterns of aggression change? Was it because the stronger group saw the weakness of the other and decided to improve their genetic fitness? But surely there were stronger and weaker animals and subgroups before this time. Perhaps we can look to Goodall's own perturbations for an answer. In 1965, Goodall began to provide "restrictive human-controlled feeding." A few years later she realized that

> the constant feeding was having a marked effect on the behavior of the chimps. They were beginning to move about in large groups more often than they had ever done in the old days. Worst of all, the adult males were becoming increasingly aggressive. When we first offered the chimps bananas the males seldom fought over their food;.... now... there was a great deal more fighting than ever before.... (Goodall 1971:143).

The possibility that human interference was a main cause of the unusual behavior of the Gombe chimps was the subject of an excellent, but generally ig-

nored book by Margaret Power (1991). Wrangham and Peterson (1996:19) foot-
note this book, but as with many other controversies, they essentially ignore
its findings, stating that yes, chimpanzee violence might have been unnatural
behavior if it weren't for the evidence of similar behavior occurring since 1977
and "elsewhere in Africa" (1996:19).

Further Evidence

What is this evidence from elsewhere in Africa? Wrangham and Peterson provide only four brief examples, none of which is very convincing:

(1) Between 1979–1982, the Gombe group extended its range to the south
and conflict with a southern group, Kalande, was suspected. In 1982, a "raiding" party of males reached Goodall's camp. The authors state: "Some of these
raids may have been lethal" (1996:19). However, Goodall describes this "raid"
as follows: One female "was chased by a Kalande male and mildly attacked. . . .
Her four-year-old son . . . encountered a second male—but was only sniffed"
(1986:516). Although Wrangham and Peterson imply that these encounters were
similar to those between 1974–77, no violence was actually witnessed. The authors also refer to the discovery of the dead body of Humphrey; what they do
not mention is Humphrey's age of 35 and that wild chimps rarely live past 33
years!

(2) From 1970 to 1982, six adult males from one community in the
Japanese study site of Mahale disappeared, one by one over this 12 year period. None of the animals were observed being attacked or killed, and one was
sighted later roaming as a solitary male (Nishida et al., 1985:287–289).

(3) In another site in West Africa, Wrangham and Peterson report that
Boesch and Boesch believe "that violent aggression among the chimpanzees is
as important as it is in Gombe" (1986:20). However, in the paper referred to,
the Boesches simply state that encounters by neighboring chimpanzee communities are more common in their site than in Gombe (one per month vs. 1 every
4 months). There is no mention of violence during these encounters.

(4) At a site that Wrangham began studying in 1984, an adult male was
found dead in 1991. Wrangham states: "In the second week of August, Ruizoni
was killed. No human saw the big fight" (Wrangham & Peterson 1996:20).
Wrangham gives us no indication of what has occurred at this site over the
last 6 years.

In fact, this is the total amount of evidence of warfare and male-male
killing among chimpanzees after 37 years of research!! The data for infanticide
and rape among chimpanzees is even less impressive. In fact, data are so sparse
for these behaviors among chimps that Wrangham and Peterson are forced to
use examples from the other great apes, gorillas and orangutans. However, just
as for killing among chimpanzees, both the evidence and the interpretations
are suspect and controversial.

Can We Escape Our Genes?

What if Wrangham and Peterson are correct and we and our chimp cousins are inherently sinners? Are we doomed to be violent forever because this pattern is fixed within our genetic code?

After 5 million years of human evolution and 120,000 or so years of *Homo sapiens* existence, is there a way to rid ourselves of our inborn evils?

> What does it do for us, then, to know the behavior of our closest relatives? Chimpanzees and bonobos are an extraordinary pair. One, I suggest shows us some of the worst aspects of our past and our present; the other shows an escape from it.... Denial of our demons won't make them go away. But even if we're driven to accepting the evidence of a grisly past, we're not forced into thinking it condemns us to an unchanged future (Wrangham 1997:110).

In other words, we can learn how to behave by watching bonobos. But, if we can change our inherited behavior so simply, why haven't we been able to do this before *Demonic Males* enlightened us? Surely, there are variations in the amounts of violence in different human cultures and individuals. If we have the capacity and plasticity to change by learning from example, then our behavior is determined by socialization practices and by our cultural histories and not by our nature! This is true whether the examples come from benevolent bonobos or conscientious objectors.

Conclusion

The theory presented by Wrangham and Peterson, although it also includes chimpanzees as our murdering cousins, is very similar to "man the hunter" theories proposed in the past. It also does not differ greatly from early European and Christian beliefs about human ethics and morality. We are forced to ask:

Are these theories generated by good scientific fact, or are they just "good to think" because they reflect, reinforce, and reiterate our traditional cultural beliefs, our morality and our ethics? Is the theory generated by the data, or are the data manipulated to fit preconceived notions of human morality and ethics?

Since the data in support of these theories have been weak, and yet the stories created have been extremely similar, I am forced to believe that "Man the Hunter" is a myth, that humans are not necessarily prone to violence and aggression, but that this belief will continue to reappear in future writings on human nature. Meanwhile, primatologists must continue their field research, marshaling the actual evidence needed to answer many of the questions raised in Wrangham and Peterson's volume.

References

Ardrey, Robert. 1961. *African Genesis: A Personal Investigation into Animal Origins and Nature of Man.* Atheneum.
_____. *The Territorial Imperative.* Atheneum, 1966.

Brain, C.K. 1981. *The Hunted or the Hunter? An Introduction to African Cave Taphonomy.* Univ. of Chicago.

Dart, Raymond. 1953. "The Predatory Transition from Ape to Man." *International Anthropological and Linguistic Review* 1:201–217.

Darwin, Charles. 1874. *The Descent of Man and Selection in Relation to Sex.* 2nd ed. The Henneberry Co.

Cartmill, Matt 1997. "Hunting Hypothesis of Human Origins." In *History of Physical Anthropology: An Encyclopedia,* ed. F. Spencer, pp. 508–512. Garland.

_____. 1993. *A View to a Death in the Morning: Hunting and Nature Through History.* Harvard Univ.

Goodall, Jane. 1986. *The Chimpanzees of Gombe: Patterns of Behavior.* Belknap.

_____. 1971. *In the Shadow of Man.* Houghton Mifflin.

Goodall, Jane. 1968. "The Behavior of Free-Living Chimpanzees in the Gombe Stream Reserve." *Animal Behavior Monographs* 1:165–311.

Nishida, T., Hiraiwa-Hasegawa, M., and Takahtat, Y. "Group Extinction and Female Transfer in Wild Chimpanzees in the Mahali Nation Park, Tanzania." *Zeitschrift für Tierpsychologie* 67:281–301.

Power, Margaret. 1991. *The Egalitarian Human and Chimpanzee: An Anthropological View of Social Organization.* Cambridge University.

Reynolds, V. and Reynolds, F. 1965. "Chimpanzees of Budongo Forest." In *Primate Behavior: Field Studies of Monkeys and Apes,* ed. I. DeVore, pp. 368–424. Holt, Rinehart, and Winston.

Suguyama, Y. 1972. "Social Characteristics and Socialization of Wild Chimpanzees." In *Primate Socialization,* ed. F.E. Poirier, pp. 145–163. Random House.

Sussman, R.W., ed. 1997. *The Biological Basis of Human Behavior.* Simon and Schuster.

Sussman, R.W. 1995. "The Nature of Human Universals." *Reviews in Anthropology* 24:1–11.

Washburn, S.L. and Lancaster, C. K. 1968. "The Evolution of Hunting." In *Man the Hunter,* eds. R. B. Lee and I. DeVore, pp. 293–303. Aldine.

Wilson, E. O. 1997. "Sociobiology: A New Approach to Understanding the Basis of Human Nature." *New Scientist* 70(1976):342–345. (Reprinted in R.W. Sussman, 1997.)

_____. 1975. Sociobiology: *The New Synthesis.* Cambridge: Harvard University.

Wrangham, R.W. 1995. "Ape, Culture, and Missing Links." *Symbols* (Spring):2–9, 20. (Reprinted in R. W. Sussman, 1997.)

Wrangham, Richard and Peterson, Dale. 1996. *Demonic Males: Apes and the Origins of Human Violence.* Houghton Mifflin.

POSTSCRIPT

Are Humans Inherently Violent?

W rangham and Peterson's argument that human males have an innate tendency toward aggressive behavior is a classic sociobiological explanation. Sociobiological explanations consist of two basic assertions: (1) that all human behavior is ultimately driven by instincts, and (2) that those instincts result from natural selection favoring the behaviors they cause. Sociobiology, which has become very popular in recent years, began in biology and ethology (the study of animal behavior) and spread to the social sciences, including psychology, where it is called "evolutionary psychology." Its popularity is probably due to its attempt to explain many confusing variations in behavior by using a few simple, scientific principles. Any human social behavior—from selfishness to altruism—can be explained by sociobiology. It's all in the genes. Why are human males aggressive? Sociobiology would say it is because natural selection favored our more aggressive ancestors, allowing them to have more children than less aggressive individuals, thus ensuring that the tendency for male aggression increased in our species.

To learn more about sociobiology in general, the best starting point is probably E. O. Wilson's seminal book *Sociobiology: The New Synthesis* (Harvard University Press, 1975). Works explaining the human propensity for violence in terms of instincts include—besides Wrangham and Peterson's book *Demonic Males* (Houghton Mifflin, 1996)—Konrad Lorenz's classic book *On Aggression* (Harcourt, Brace & World, 1967), Martin Daly and Margo Wilson's book *Homicide* (A de Gruyter, 1988), and Michael Ghiglieri's book *The Dark Side of Man: Tracing the Origins of Male Violence* (Perseus Books, 1999). Carrying sociobiological reasoning a step further, Randy Thornhill and Craig T. Palmer argue in their book *A Natural History of Rape: Biological Bases of Sexual Coercion* (MIT Press, 2000) that human males have an instinct for rape because in the evolution of hominids rape was an effective way for males to pass on their genes.

Sussman's argument that human violence is basically a product of social and cultural conditions comes from the tradition of cultural anthropology. He challenges Wrangham and Peterson's assumptions that human behaviors are driven by instincts. Sussman says that the behaviors that Wrangham and Peterson, following E. O. Wilson, attribute to instinct, such as territoriality and male dominance over females, are not in fact universal among humans and lower primates. He also rejects Wrangham and Peterson's contention that an instinct exists if a behavior is universal to the human species, is easy to learn, and is pleasurable to perform. By these criteria, Sussman says, dancing must also be caused by an instinct to dance. Presumably a long list of similar activities, such as playing games and telling jokes, must also have their governing instincts. Sussman also rejects Wrangham and Peterson's contention that aggressive males would have been favored by natural (sexual) selection during hominid evolution. If this were so, he implies, why aren't all males equally aggressive today? How could the genes for nonaggressive behavior have survived countless generations of selection against them? Further, Sussman ridicules the notion that female hominids (or chimpanzees) would deliberately select aggressive males to father their offspring.

Important works challenging the sociobiological explanation of human violence include Ashley Montagu's book *The Nature of Human Aggression* (Oxford University Press, 1976), Richard Lewontin, Leon Kamin, and Stephen Rose's book *Not in Our Genes: Biology, Ideology, and Human Nature* (Pantheon Books, 1984), Kenneth Bock's book *Human Nature and History: A Response to Sociobiology* (Columbia University Press, 1980), and Matt Cartmill's book *A View to a Death in the Morning: Hunting and Nature Through History* (Harvard University Press, 1993). For descriptions and analyses of societies in which aggression is minimized, see Leslie E. Sponsel and Thomas A. Gregor's edited volume *The Anthropology of Peace and Nonviolence* (L. Rienner, 1994) and Signe Howell and Roy Willis's volume *Societies at Peace: Anthropological Perspectives* (Routledge, 1989).

On the Internet . . .

Archaeology Magazine

This is the Web site of *Archaeology* magazine. This site has a searchable database with links to various articles about recent issues in archaeology, including a number of articles on the goddess cult in Europe.

http://www.archaeology.org

Center for the Study of the First Americans

The Center for the Study of the First Americans works to promote interdisciplinary scholarly dialogue and to stimulate public interest concerning the colonization of the Americas. This Web site provides articles that describe several theories on how the Americas were first colonized.

http://www.centerfirstamericans.com/cat.html?c=4

The Maya of Guatemala

The Maya of Guatemala Web site provides general information on the Maya using the latest techniques in digital photography. This site contains links to information on Maya archaeology and on museums that focus on Maya culture. Explore the media links to view both high-quality photographs and QuickTime movies.

http://maya-archaeology.org

PART 2

Archaeology

*A*rchaeologists are prehistorians concerned with questions about the unrecorded history of human communities and civilizations. Like other historians, archaeologists seek evidence about how people lived, what they subsisted on, and the kinds of social institutions they established. But, unlike most historians who can turn to documents and papers to detail the life and times of their subjects, archaeologists must find evidence in excavations. Over the past century, archaeologists have developed specialized methods for excavating and analyzing artifacts, stone tools, animal bones, shells, pollen, and carbon from old fires to determine a great deal about the environment, vegetation, subsistence patterns, living arrangements, and also when sites were occupied. At issue is how these varied kinds of data from ancient sources can be interpreted to reconstruct the lifeways of earlier times. A traditional set of questions that archeologists ask is when, why, and how did people first settle different parts of the world, such as the Americas. They also ask questions about the meaning and significance of certain kinds of artifacts, such as the goddess figures of ancient Europe and the Middle East. Archaeologists also ask questions about why complex civilizations rose and fell.

- Did People First Arrive in the New World After the Last Ice Age?

- Was There a Goddess Cult in Prehistoric Europe?

- Were Environmental Factors Responsible for the Mayan Collapse?

ISSUE 4

Did People First Arrive in the New World After the Last Ice Age?

YES: Stuart J. Fiedel, from *Prehistory of the Americas,* 2d ed. (Cambridge University Press, 1992)

NO: Thomas D. Dillehay, from "The Battle of Monte Verde," *The Sciences* (January/February 1997)

ISSUE SUMMARY

YES: Archaeologist Stuart J. Fiedel supports the traditional view that humans first reached the Americas from Siberia at the end of the last Ice Age (perhaps 14,000 years ago). He argues that there are currently no convincing sites dated before that time and is skeptical of statements by other archaeologists who date human occupation of sites such as Meadowcroft in Pennsylvania and Monte Verde in Chile significantly earlier.

NO: Archaeologist Thomas D. Dillehay asserts that the site he has excavated at Monte Verde, a complex site in Chile, proves that humans reached the New World well before the end of the last Ice Age, possibly as early as 30,000 years ago. He contends that those archaeologists who are skeptical about his carbon-14 dates and other findings are so entrenched in traditional thinking that they refuse to accept the solid evidence that Monte Verde provides.

For more than a century archaeologists have asked, When and how did human beings first arrive in the Americas? The conventional view is that humans arrived from Asia via an ancient land bridge across the Bering Strait, which connected Siberia and Alaska during the last Ice Age. This traditional view has several components that Stuart J. Fiedel analyzes in his selection. First, the land bridge existed because ocean water was trapped in glacial ice. But this same glacial ice would also have presented an impenetrable barrier to human passage until glacial ice began to recede at the very end of the Ice Age. A narrow corridor between two separate ice sheets appears to have opened up about 14,500 years ago. Second, once human populations had passed through this ice corridor, they found large populations of woolly mammoth, saber-toothed tiger, and other megafauna, and these species became extinct soon after the ice pack retreated. Third, the archaeological association of certain kinds of stone projectile points (called Clovis points) with the bones of several of these extinct species has suggested that humans hunted them for food. Some archaeologists have argued that excessive human hunting caused their extinction (the overkill hypothesis).

Convincing radiocarbon dating of many sites on both continents suggests that if humankind first arrived in the Americas at the end of the Ice Age, they had spread throughout both continents within a thousand years or so. For many years, archaeologists have disputed whether or not this was enough time for this sort of human dispersal across many different ecological zones.

In his selection, Fiedel surveys the history of the search for the earliest Americans and focuses on two of the most promising candidates for acceptance as pre-Clovis sites: the Meadowcroft shelter in Pennsylvania and an upland coastal site in south-central Chile called Monte Verde. Fiedel is skeptical that either will prove unambiguously to be pre-Clovis, but he recognizes that, unlike most other sites thought to be early, neither of these can be firmly dismissed as postglacial, although for different reasons. His skepticism emerges from several angles simultaneously, and considers the question: If humans had settled the New World significantly before the last Ice Age, why have archaeologists not identified dozens of pre-Clovis sites before now?

Thomas D. Dillehay is probably best known for his archaeological excavations at Monte Verde, a site he has worked on for more than 20 years. He contends that this site is complex. One part fits what one might expect a genuine pre-Clovis site to look like: It was occupied for a relatively short time by a hunting-and-gathering group, and the tool kit is significantly simpler than that of most Clovis sites. But simple or not, this assemblage has now been dated to significantly earlier than the date that the corridor through the northern glacial ice pack appeared, which means that human settlement of the Americas must have occurred before the last glacial maximum.

Dillehay suggests that skeptics of the quality of his carbon-14 dates are largely reacting defensively to his findings because the findings would force archaeologists to abandon models about the early settlement of the Northern Hemisphere that they have held for many years. What one can see in these two selections is a clash of paradigms.

Fiedel and Dillehay raise a number of questions of general interest to archaeologists. Are the authors defending different theoretical models of New World settlement, or are the "facts of the case" genuinely problematic? Are early carbon-14 dates sufficient to establish the Monte Verde site as genuinely pre-Clovis, or do Dillehay and his colleagues need to work out the artifact sequences before we can accept their findings? As with other controversies in archaeology, the arguments here seem to be about the facts of Monte Verde, but are these archaeologists actually arguing about their own models? Would it be appropriate for a nonpartisan team of archaeologists to visit Monte Verde and assess Dillehay's findings either to demonstrate problems in the data or to establish the site as an early one once and for all?

Stuart J. Fiedel

 **YES**

The Paleo-Indians

Archaeological Evidence of the First Americans

In the latter part of the nineteenth century, American scholars and amateurs, inspired by Darwin's theories and the Stone Age discoveries made in Europe, sought evidence of early man in the New World. Sure enough, they turned up a great many stone tools. The crudeness of some of these suggested that they were very ancient, belonging either to the Pleistocene or even to some earlier epoch. In addition, human remains were found, and for these, too, great antiquity was claimed. However, the eminent Czech-born physical anthropologist, Aleš Hrdlička, ruthlessly demolished these claims, demonstrating that all the American skeletal finds represented humans of modern type. On the basis of this conclusion, Hrdlička asserted that Ice Age man had not lived in the Americas; he set the initial entry at about 3000 B.C. No one seems to have pointed out at the time that humans of modern type had lived during late glacial times in Europe, where their remains had been found at Cro-Magnon and elsewhere; so the absence of pre-*sapiens* fossils in the Americas did not preclude a Pleistocene occupation. Hrdlička's conservative view prevailed in scholarly circles until an astonishing discovery in 1927 rendered it untenable.

George McJunkin, a black cowhand, had noticed some bones protruding from the side of a gulley near Folsom, New Mexico. This find was brought to the attention of J. D. Figgins of the Denver Museum of Natural History, who excavated the site. The bones turned out to belong to a large, long-horned species of bison (*Bison antiquus*), which became extinct at the end of the Pleistocene. In 1926, Figgins found a stone spearpoint embedded in clay near the bones. This point was initially dismissed by other archaeologists as intrusive. But in 1927, Figgins came upon another point, this time lying between two bison ribs. He left the point in place, and invited several prestigious archaeologists to examine the new find. They agreed that the Folsom site presented an indisputable association of man-made artifacts with the remains of extinct Pleistocene animals. Initially, archaeologists could only guess the age of the Folsom remains; but, since 1950, a series of C14 dates for sites where stone points of the same type have been excavated place the Folsom culture at about 9000 to 8000 B.C.

Many more Folsom sites have been discovered since 1927. At a few of them, artifacts were recovered from geological strata lying *below* those that yielded Folsom points. The distinctive artifact type of these earlier assemblages is the Clovis point. Clovis points were first excavated at the Blackwater Draw site near Clovis, New Mexico; here, and at several other sites, they were found in association with the remains of mammoths. The Clovis or "Llano" culture of the western United States has been dated to about 9500 to 9000 B.C. Clovis-like fluted points have a very wide geographic distribution, having been found throughout the United States and in Canada and Central America. The striking similarity of these points, found over such a vast area, has led many archaeologists to conclude that the points were made and used by closely related hunting bands.

We can envision one or several ancestral bands entering the northern Plains through the ice-free corridor, thus stumbling upon a hunter's paradise, teeming with game that had never experienced the terrible cunning and tenacity of the human predator. In such a favorable situation, the original human population would have grown rapidly: where growth is not constrained by food or space limitations, population can double or even triple in each successive generation. We can estimate, using some speculative yet reasonable calculations, the minimum length of time necessary for the Americas to have been filled to capacity with hunting bands. We start with figures derived from ethnographic studies of extant hunting and gathering groups. These studies indicate that, irrespective of environmental differences, the typical hunting band consists of 25 to 50 people. These studies also reveal a range of population densities, from 0.4 to 9.6 persons per 100 square km (1 to 25 persons per 100 square miles). Pleistocene densities may have exceeded the upper end of this range; we can use a figure of 0.4 persons per square km (one person per square mile). North and South America, south of the glacial margins at 10,000 B.C., contained roughly 26 million square km (10 million square miles). Ignoring for the moment environmental differences that made areas more or less suitable for human habitation, and applying the 0.4 per square km (one per square mile) density figure, we get 10,000,000 as the potential hunting population of the Americas. If we assume that a band of 25 people passed through the corridor into North America, and that this population doubled in each successive generation (every 30 years or so), we reach the 10,000,000 figure in about 500 years. In reality, judging from the scarcity of their typical artifacts, Paleo-Indian populations probably did not reach even one-tenth of this level. In any case, assuming an exponential growth rate, the difference is insignificant; the 1 million level could have been attained in about 350 years.

... It has sometimes been assumed that thousands of years must have elapsed between the initial entry of humans into North America and their arrival at Fell's Cave [in Patagonia]; however, our calculations have shown how rapidly population expansion could have occurred. The distance from the base of the corridor to Tierra del Fuego is about 13,000 km (8,000 miles). If the expansion of human population to the limits of the continents took as little as 500 years, we would have to assume that the rate of migration was about 26 km (16 miles) a year, or 780 km (480 miles) per generation. Such movement is quite feasible, particularly in light of evidence that Paleo-Indians sometimes made tools of flint that they had carried from sources located several hundred kilometers away (as, for example, at the Shoop site in Pennsylvania and the Wapanucket site in Massachusetts). The southward movement was probably wavelike, constantly widening on its southern front. The impact of this human wave on the herd animals of the Americas may well have contributed to their extinction. . . .

So, we see that the presence of man at "the end of the road," Tierra del Fuego, by about 9000 B.C., is consistent with an initial entry through the ice-free corridor as late as 9500 B.C. However, the widespread and easily recognized Clovis culture was not necessarily the earliest in the Americas. The archaeological record offers tantalizing hints of earlier occupation.

Over the years, thousands of crude stone tools have been found in North America. These closely resemble the chopper-chopping tools of East Asia; as you may recall, the latter were produced from hundreds of thousands of years ago until quite recently. Some archaeologists have suggested that the American choppers must be older than the Clovis points, that they in fact represent a "pre-projectile point horizon." The absence of points in the supposedly pre-Clovis industries has been interpreted as evidence of a subsistence pattern involving less specialized hunting of large mammals and greater reliance on small game and plant foods.

However, claims for a preprojectile horizon must be regarded with skepticism. Most of the crude choppers have been surface finds, whose age cannot be determined. Others have been found in datable geological contexts, but they are so formless that they are almost certainly not artifacts at all. Still other choppers are definitely man-made, but are associated with relatively late, more delicate artifacts. Such choppers were probably used for tasks that did not require more finely made tools. Some crudely retouched bifaces found in North America superficially resemble the Acheulian handaxes of Europe and Africa; but the American pieces have been shown to be "blanks," stones retouched into rough form at a quarry site with a view toward later, finer modification into a desired tool. . . .

The most convincing evidence of pre-Clovis occupation in North America, south of the Pleistocene ice margins, comes from the Meadowcroft rockshelter in western Pennsylvania. Here, stone tools and waste flakes from the earliest culture-bearing layer (Stratum IIa) have been dated, by eight radiocarbon determinations, between 17,000 and 11,000 B.C. C14 dates for the overlying strata form a consistent sequence, and are appropriate for the Archaic and Woodland period cultural material with which they are associated. However, the geologist C. Vance Haynes has suggested that the early dates from the lowest level might be the result of contamination by old carbon from coal deposits in the vicinity of the site. This attempt to explain away the early dates has been vigorously disputed by the excavator of Meadowcroft, James Adovasio, and his colleagues. But there is other evidence that casts doubt on the dates for Stratum IIa. Flotation of soil samples from this layer yielded abundant remains of plants—pits, nutshells, and carbonized fragments. These remains clearly indicate that the prevailing environment at the time of the Stratum IIa occupation was the same as that which existed during later periods—a deciduous forest including oak, walnut, and hickory trees. But at the time indicated by the C14 dates for Stratum IIa, the front of the Laurentide ice sheet was only 83 km (50 miles) to the north of the rockshelter. It is almost certain that Meadowcroft lay within a band of tundra, bordered by forests of spruce and pine, at about 15,000 B.C. It was not until about 8500 B.C. that the tundra and boreal forest were replaced by deciduous forest, spreading up from the south. An earlier presence of deciduous forest around Meadowcroft at the height of the Wisconsin glaciation would be very surprising. The few animal bones from Stratum IIa do not resolve the apparent contradiction between the radio-carbon dates and the paleo-botanical evidence. Among the highly fragmented bones was a piece of antler that could be confidently assigned to the white-tailed deer. Other identified specimens represent passenger pigeon and southern flying squirrel. All three species usually inhabited temperate deciduous forests. No remains of extinct Pleistocene mammals such as horse, mastodon, or mammoth, nor remains of tundra-dwelling caribou, have been found at Meadowcroft.

The stone tools from the lowest levels of Meadowcroft rockshelter do not appear to be typical of eastern Paleo-Indian assemblages, but neither do they represent a preprojectile horizon. Small blades are common. Also found were a bifacially retouched flake knife (called "Mungai" by Adovasio) and a projectile point. This point is lanceolate in shape like a Clovis point, but it is neither fluted like Clovis points nor as finely retouched as they usually are. Haynes, who questions the pre-Clovis dating of this material, suggests that the point is basically similar to unfluted, post-Clovis Plano points. Adovasio, on the other hand, sees similarities to points from a few western sites, such as Fort Rock Cave, which may be earlier than 10,000 B.C. He suggests that the Meadowcroft point might represent the prototype from which Clovis and Plano points were derived.

The Upper Paleolithic character of the Meadowcroft lithic assemblage is obvious. This is not the first discovery of blades in an early context in North America; well-made blades were reported in 1963 from the Clovis site of Blackwater Draw in New Mexico. These had been detached from a cone-shaped core by striking a bone or antler punch, resting on the core's basal rim, with a stone hammer. The small blades from Meadowcroft were made in the same way. In the Old World, this technique probably developed out of Middle Paleolithic Levallois flaking from prepared cores; but blades, retouched into numerous tool types, first became dominant in Upper Paleolithic assemblages. But, as we have seen, some archaeologists have argued that the first Americans were exclusively users of crude chopper-chopping tools and broken bones; according to this view, they made neither bifacially flaked points nor blades. The development from these simple Lower Paleolithic tools to the elegantly made Clovis point would have been an indigenous process, unrelated to cultural developments in Eurasia. This seems to me a very unlikely course of events. Even if Clovis points were an American innovation—and to date, nothing like them has turned up in Asia—they were products of an Upper Paleolithic technological tradition, incorporating methods of blade production and retouching, which were developed in Eurasia. . . .

Two caves in the western United States may have been occupied before 10,000 B.C. In a deep level of a stratified sequence in Wilson Butte Cave, in southern Idaho, a bifacially worked, bipointed point and a blade have been C14 dated, using samples of associated bones, at about 12,500 B.C. It is conceivable that the dated bone was contaminated by older carbon in the surrounding soil, or that it was brought in from earlier deposits by rodents. At Fort Rock Cave in south-central Oregon, a charcoal concentration lying on Pleistocene lake gravels has been C14 dated at 11,200 B.C. Nearby were two projectile points, several scrapers and gravers, and some flakes, as well as a milling stone and a hand-stone fragment. These ground stone artifacts are suggestive of the processing of collected seeds, a subsistence activity that is well attested in the Desert Archaic culture of this region after about 8000 B.C. However, grinding stones do not occur at Paleo-Indian sites that are earlier than 8000 B.C. Therefore, some doubt exists as to the association of the dated charcoal and the lithic finds. But since an overlying level was C14 dated at 8200 B.C., it seems indisputable that the artifacts are at least that old.

Clovis

... The Clovis culture ... appears distinctive in several important respects from known Siberian Paleolithic cultures. Cultural change and innovation must have occurred during the migration of the ancestral Paleo-Indians across Beringia and through the corridor. It seems, on present evidence, that the fluted point was invented in North America.

If we accept the evidence from Valsequillo, Meadowcroft, and the few other sites that indicate that man was present in the Americas as early as 20,000 B.C., the rapid spread of Clovis-style lithic industries around 9500–9000 B.C. becomes more difficult to explain. We must choose among several plausible models for Clovis expansion:

1. Pre-Clovis occupation was ultimately unsuccessful; earlier inhabitants vanished or were restricted to a few isolated areas before the Clovis point-makers arrived.
2. Pre-Clovis occupation was widespread and successful. Somewhere in North America, fluted points began to be made. Then, (a) this new technology spread quickly as it was adopted by local hunting groups, who found it useful in hunting big game, or (b) the fluted point gave its inventors such an adaptive advantage that they rapidly expanded, encroaching upon and replacing the original inhabitants of other areas.

Model 2(a) seems the least likely explanation. There are no significant regional distinctions among Clovis tool kits, such as would indicate the addition of point-making to ongoing local flint-working traditions. The known distribution of Clovis points causes problems for model 2(b). It seems unlikely that fluted points would have been decisively advantageous in all of the diverse environments—tundra, grassland, boreal and deciduous forests—that Paleo-Indians occupied at the end of the Pleistocene. Model 1 poses an obvious problem: Why should hunters equipped with a sophisticated Upper Paleolithic technology, including effective stone projectile points (found at most of the convincing pre-Clovis sites), and resourceful enough to have endured a trek through Beringia and the glacial corridor, have been any less successful than the Clovis hunters? The paleontologist Paul S. Martin has wryly suggested an answer to this problem: "Given the biology of the species, I can envision only one circumstance under which an ephemeral discovery of America might have occurred. It is that, sometime before 12,000 years ago, the earliest early man came over the Bering Strait without early woman."

Martin has proposed an elegant model of Paleo-Indian migration. His theory would account at once for the rapidity of occupation of North and South America, the uniformity of Clovis tool kits, and the extinction of many species of large mammals at the end of the Pleistocene. Discounting claims of earlier sites, Martin assumes that the makers of Clovis points were the first humans to pass through the ice-free corridor into North America. Here they encountered herds of animals that had no experience of human predation, and so had developed neither defensive nor reproductive strategies to deal with this new threat. Taking advantage of the seemingly limitless supply of game, the Clovis hunters multiplied rapidly, their numbers doubling with each generation. As their numbers grew, the hunters also pushed southward, their movement taking the form of a great wave of advance, with the greatest density of population at its front. After a brief bottleneck in Central America, the same sort of expansion occurred in South America. Martin calculates that the descendants of an original band of 100 people who emerged from the ice-free corridor could have finished off the large Pleistocene mammals in North America. He estimates that the maximum total animal biomass for unglaciated North America at the end of the Pleistocene was some 230 million metric tons. Human population in North America could have reached a maximum of 600,000, at a density of 0.4 per square km (one per square mile), in about 250 years. If, at the front of the wave of advance, one person did all of the hunting for himself and three others (as might the adult male in a small nuclear family), and if this hunter killed only one animal weighing 450 kilograms (or 992 pounds—about the weight of a young modern bison) per week, the animals at the front would have been wiped out in less than ten years. At this rate, all of the large mammals in the Americas could have been slaughtered in about 500 to 1,000 years—as long as it took for the Paleo-Indians to reach Tierra del Fuego.

Numerous objections have been raised against Martin's "overkill" hypothesis. However, scientists agree that there is a basic fact that requires explanation: at the end of the Pleistocene, some 32 genera of American mammals became extinct. These included the mammoth, the mastodon, the giant sloth, the armadillolike glyptodon, the camel, the horse, the saber-toothed "tiger" and the dire wolf. Clearly, these extinctions must be connected in some way with the major environmental and climatic changes that were caused by the retreat of the Wisconsin ice sheets. However, the ice sheets had retreated before, in previous interglacial episodes, but these events had not resulted in the extinction of so many species. As Martin points out, the unique factor present during the last glacial retreat was human hunting. . . .

Paleontologists have proposed several alternative explanations for the late Pleistocene extinctions. Most have seen climate change as the primary cause. Dramatic shifts in temperature and rainfall patterns led to contraction of the habitats of at least some Pleistocene mammals. Over-specialized animals could not adjust to the new environments, and large animals, with their greater food and space requirements, could not compete with smaller species for which readaptation was easier. But this theory does not account for the extinction of those mammals whose habitats changed very little as the ice sheets retreated. . . .

It has also been suggested that the late Pleistocene opening of the glacial corridor permitted not only human hunters but also an assortment of new parasites and disease organisms to invade North America. But epidemics did not cause widespread extinction during previous interglacials. Generally, after initial high fatality rates, populations became resistant, and more stable disease-host relationships set in before extinction of the host. So diseases are unlikely to have been the critical factor in the Pleistocene extinctions.

The problem of Pleistocene extinctions is a challenging one, and none of the suggested solutions is entirely satisfactory. Many scientists would probably grant that Paleo-Indian hunters might have delivered the *coup de grâce* to several species, but would also emphasize that these and other mammals were already seriously weakened by climatic and environmental stress. . . .

Paleo-Indians in South America

Carbon dates from Fell's Cave in Patagonia indicate that man had reached the southernmost tip of South America by about 9000 or 8700 B.C. As we have seen, these dates are not inconsistent with an initial entry into South America only a few hundred years earlier. However, there have been claims that a few sites demonstrate occupation of the continent before 10,000 B.C. Clearly, if it can be proven that any South American sites are really that old, claims of pre-Clovis habitation of North American will gain credibility. . . .

An extraordinarily well-preserved and apparently very early site has been excavated at Monte Verde, in south central Chile. Twelve wooden structures, abundant plant remains, and bones of butchered mastodon and guanaco, all buried under a layer of peat, have been C14 dated to between 13,650 ± 250 and 11,790 ± 200 B.P. (ca. 11,700 to 9800 B.C.). A lower layer of the site yielded broken stones and charcoal that possibly represent remains of human activity more than 30,000 years ago. The long hiatus between this dubious occupation and the late Pleistocene reuse of the vicinity has not been convincingly explained. The houses, made of planks and small tree trunks, are thought to have been covered with hides. Clay-lined hearths had been excavated outside the houses. Wooden mortars and grinding stones were used to process plant food. Actual plant remains include wild potatoes, medicinal plants, and salt-rich plants that must have been brought from the coast, 30 km distant from the site. The stone tool kit is reported to be a very simple one, consisting mostly of split pebble choppers and flakes. Some roughened stones may have been tied together with leather thongs and used as bolas. Hunting devices of this sort would have been a necessity if stone spearpoints were unknown to this culture. In fact, however, two well-made, thin lanceolate spearpoints, chipped from basalt, have been found at Monte Verde. They bear some resemblance to the El Jobo points of Venezuela, which are associated with comparably early, but controversial, radiocarbon dates. At present, too little is known about the Monte Verde culture to compare it with any others. Apart from the mastodon remains, the lifeway represented seems more Archaic than Paleo-Indian. The 2,000-year range of the radiocarbon dates is surprisingly wide for a site that is thought to have been created during a single brief occupation. Acceptance of the most recent dates would take the site into the period of Clovis immigration. However, the predominantly simple stone tool kit attested at Monte Verde is not very similar to typical Clovis assemblages. Nevertheless, if the early C14 dates are verified by further research, Monte Verde will have provided irrefutable evidence of a human presence in the Americas about 1,000 years before the Clovis migration (or diffusion). If Monte Verde and other South American sites really do predate 10,000 B.C., archaeologists will have to explain the puzzling absence of proven sites of comparable antiquity in North America.

South America was occupied around 9000 B.C. by Paleo-Indians who made fluted points, stylistically distinctive from, yet obviously related to, the Clovis points of North America. In the 1930s, Junius Bird found "fishtail" points, many of them fluted, at Fell's Cave. Similar points have been discovered at El Inga, in the highlands of Ecuador. Unlike North American fluted points, these broad-bodied points taper to markedly thinner stems, which take up more than a third of the points' length. However, some Clovis-like points from the south-eastern United States have very similar fishtail-shaped bases, and are constricted just above the base so that they almost appear to have stems. A link between these northern and southern points is provided by several surface finds from Central America. Short, broad fishtail points of the type found at Fell's Cave, are known from Panama (Madden Lake) and Costa Rica (Turrialba). Somewhat thinner fishtail points, more similar to the Clovis-like points of eastern North America, have been found at the same sites, and also in western Costa Rica, Guatemala, and Durango, Mexico. Recently, a Clovis point like those found in the southwestern United States was collected from a site in the Quiche Basin, in the highlands of Guatemala; similar points are reported from recently excavated sites in Belize. Lacking firm chronological controls, we cannot be sure that the more slender of the Central American points represent a transitional phase in the stylistic evolution of fishtail points from North American Clovis prototypes; but this seems to be the best explanation of the existing evidence. The close resemblance of fishtail points from sites in Costa Rica and Patagonia, separated by more than 6,400 km (4,000 miles), implies a very rapid migration of Paleo-Indians along the mountainous spine of western South America. As in North America, such a rapid migration seems to imply that there was no previous human occupation of the region; alternatively, if the pre-10,000 B.C. dates are valid, the earlier population must have been so small and scattered that they could be easily replaced or absorbed by the makers of fluted points.

It should be noted that there have been finds in South America of leaf-shaped and lanceolate points that seem to be as old as the fishtail points. Some archaeologists argue that such points, of which the best known examples are the El Jobo points from Venezuela, may in fact be older than the fishtail type; however, this argument rests primarily on a few dubious radiocarbon dates. The closest North American parallels to the leaf-shaped points are the Lerma points of Texas and Mexico, and the San Dieguito points of California and the Great Basin; these types are dated to between 9000 and 6000 B.C.

Apart from fluted points, other items in the tool kit of the South American Paleo-Indians—scrapers, gravers, and knives—suggest a derivation from North American forms. The probable use of these tools in the processing of meat and hides further implies a continuation of the ancestral North American Paleo-Indians' pursuit of big game.

The South American Paleo-Indians' big game-hunting orientation is confirmed by associations of artifacts with remains of extinct Pleistocene mammals at several sites. There is evidence of the hunting of horse, mastodon, and giant ground sloth. The Paleo-Indians also hunted animals of modern species—deer and guanaco, various rodents, rabbits, and birds, particularly the ground-dwelling tinamou. The Paleo-Indians probably turned increasingly to such small game as the Pleistocene megafauna disappeared. Bones found at Los Toldos, Argentina, and Tagua Tagua in Chile hint at the early domestication of the dog, which would have been helpful in hunting the tinamou. In addition to small animals, plants became more important as a food source after 9000 B.C. There is evidence at Guitarrero Cave that beans and peppers were cultivated, and various tubers and fruits were collected, perhaps as early as 8500 B.C. and certainly before 7000 B.C. This dietary diversification in the Andean highlands is comparable to the broad spectrum adaptations that developed after the extinction of the Pleistocene megafauna in North America and Mesoamerica.

NO

Thomas D. Dillehay

The Battle of Monte Verde

In archeology the simplest questions are often the hardest to answer. Two such questions—who were the first Americans and when did they reach the New World?—have tormented investigators for more than a century. Archaeologists have long believed that Asian immigrants, crossing the Bering land bridge in pursuit of big game, pioneered the New World about 11,000 years ago. Known as the Clovis people, after the site in New Mexico where their elaborate, fluted projectile points were first discovered, the immigrants gradually worked their way south. They were skilled hunters, and when their travels brought them to places teeming with an astonishing variety of prey, the result was a human population explosion. In a matter of centuries Clovis hunters moved throughout the Americas, helping to wipe out bison, woolly mammoths, camelids and other species in the so-called Pleistocene die-off.

Or perhaps not. In recent years a wave of discoveries outside North America has brought nearly every aspect of the migration theory under intense scrutiny. Fresh insights on the peopling of China, Japan and Siberia are redrawing the debate about the first Americans on a much broader canvas, framed by the entire Pacific Rim. And in South America a rash of controversial early dates has suggested that the Americas were settled even earlier than 11,000 years ago. Several sites in Tierra del Fuego, for instance, have been convincingly shown to be about 11,000 years old.

How could people have arrived in North America and at the southern tip of South America at approximately the same time? Did they journey through Alaska before the Clovis hunters, or did they sail across the seas to reach South America just as Clovis hunters were crossing the Bering land bridge? Faced with such questions, New World archaeologists have divided into Clovis and pre-Clovis camps. The dispute between the two has become so emotionally charged that one archaeologist has likened it to the debate between creationists and evolutionists.

Twenty years ago I was drawn into the fray when I began excavating Monte Verde, a site near the town of Puerto Montt, in south-central Chile. Monte Verde had been discovered accidentally in 1976 by some local lumbermen clearing paths for their ox carts. They had been cutting back the banks of a small creek in a marshy area when they literally stumbled on some large bones and

From Thomas D. Dillehay, "The Battle of Monte Verde," The Sciences, vol. 37, no. 1 (January/February 1997). Copyright © 1997 by The New York Academy of Sciences. Reprinted by permission of The Sciences.

buried wood. The bones were later determined to be the remains of mastodons. In 1977, when the find was brought to my attention, I was head of the anthropology department at the Southern University of Chile in Valdivia. That year I formed an international interdisciplinary team, which eventually grew to eighty members, and we began to excavate the site.

Early on, we knew that Monte Verde was an exceptional site. But we also knew that our finds would provoke a barrage of skepticism, not least because of their age. According to firm radiocarbon dates, the most impressive remains date from 1,500 years before Clovis hunters are said to have discovered North America. The possible remains of human habitation in Monte Verde's deepest levels are nearly 20,000 years older than that.

⚜

Archaeologists are, by necessity, masters of inference. From the meanest, most innocuous of things—discarded oyster shells, broken pots, the subtle bands of color and texture in an excavation wall—we try to re-create an entire world and its inhabitants. To the uninitiated, the process may seem as occult as counting the angels on the head of a pin. How does this standing stone signify religion? Why is that "chopper" not just a rock? How can so much be made of so little?

Thanks to some happy accidents of nature, the remains at Monte Verde are of a far more evocative kind. Some 12,500 years ago the site was an open-air settlement on the banks of what is now Chinchihuapi Creek. All around were sandy knolls, small bogs and a cool, damp forest. As the bogs spread into the adjacent creek bed, they buried the abandoned settlement under a layer of fibrous peat, preserving it like an exotic specimen pickled in formaldehyde. The water protected the remains from the wear and tear of changing humidity. It also prevented oxygen from reaching the remains, thereby keeping bacteria from digesting them.

Once it was carefully drained and stripped of its layers of protective peat, the site revealed much more than the usual cache of bones and stone tools. From wood structures to medicinal plants to hunks of meat, it held a wealth of organic debris that normally disappears from the archaeological record. More than any other early site in the Americas, Monte Verde would enable us to reconstruct life in the Ice Age.

⚜

At the beginning of the project, we put together a team that included geologists, botanists, forestry scientists and zoologists to study the fauna and flora preserved at the site. Our digging uncovered the remains of a sixty-foot-long tentlike structure sturdy enough to house twenty or thirty people, some of them year-round. The frame was made of logs and planks anchored by stakes, and the walls consisted of poles covered with hides (from mastodons and paleo-llamas, judging by the bones we excavated). The entire structure was bound together with cordage and string made of junco reed. Inside the tent, planks and poles apparently set off individual living spaces, each of which had a brazier pit lined with clay. Hundreds of microscopic flecks of hide, embedded in the dirt, suggest that the floor was probably covered with skins.

Outside the tent we found two large communal hearths, a supply of firewood, and wooden mortars with their grinding stones. Near the hearths, we uncovered two brown, sopping hunks of meat next to some mastodon bones. The most dramatic remains, however, are of a more delicate variety. About 12,000 years ago one of the Monte Verdeans walked across some soft, wet clay brought to the site for refurbishing the hearths. As the clay hardened, it preserved three footprints for posterity. In one print the toes, heel and arch of a foot were clearly visible. On the basis of the print's size and shape, specialists from our team of forensic anthropologists think it was made by a small adult or a large adolescent.

West of the main building, we found a wishbone-shaped structure made of wooden uprights set into a foundation of sand and gravel hardened with animal fat. Mastodon carcasses were butchered inside the structure, hides were prepared and tools were manufactured. Because the medicinal parts of certain plants were found next to those remains, we think the Monte Verdeans may have also gone there to practice healing.

In southern Chile today the Mapuche people use medicinal plants to treat rheumatism, stomach aches, dysentery, infected cuts and pulmonary problems, among other ailments, as well as to induce abortions. The twenty-three kinds of medicinal plants found at Monte Verde are all still used to treat various problems. Boldo leaf (*Peumus boldus*), for instance, is used for intestinal ailments and hallucinations, natre leaf (*Solanum crispum*) reduces fever, and *Lycopodium* (a kind of club moss) gives a natural talcum powder that soothes skin infections. Some of the plants are native to the area, but about half come from the coast, and one is found only in arid regions to the north.

To modern sensibilities, the most intriguing plants preserved at the site are the ones that now seem most commonplace: potatoes. Many explorers and scientists, Charles Darwin among them, have noted the wide variety and abundance of wild potatoes in southern Chile. On the basis of studies done on wild potatoes in the region, Soviet botanists in the 1930s speculated that potatoes originally came from that area and from Peru. The presence of the tuber at Monte Verde, in the cracks and pits of wooden mortars and in food storage pits in the corners of shelters, confirms the Soviet hypothesis and underlines the importance of southern Chile in the evolution of the potato.

The smorgasbord of food scraps the Monte Verdeans left behind suggests that the bulk of their diet was made up of meat from mastodons, paleo-llamas, small animals and freshwater mollusks, together with aquatic plants from freshwater marshes and other areas. Most of those foods are found in ecological zones thirty-five miles from Monte Verde, along the Pacific shoreline and in the Andean mountains. Three varieties of seaweed—a rare occurrence on the southern coast—were probably scavenged some fifty miles to the west or received in trade. Salt, pebbles worn flat and round by ocean waves (ideal for polishing animal hides or grinding food), and bitumen used to attach stone tools to wooden hafts were also found at the site, demonstrating that the Monte Verdeans brought back more than food from the coast.

To make use of so many resources from so many ecological zones, the Monte Verdeans devised a sophisticated division of labor. Residential areas are separate from non-residential areas at the site, and certain areas are associated with specific tools and food remains. In one living space, for instance, quartz artifacts for cutting and scraping were found with the remains of fruits and tubers that grow only in brackish estuaries, which suggests that the occupants specialized in collecting resources from the coast. In another area of the tent, stone scrapers and pieces of skin indicate that people worked animal hides there.

⋘⊙⋙

Our excavations at Monte Verde have revealed a much more complex social and economic organization than archeologists have come to expect of early New World cultures. The excavations also call into question the commonly accepted idea that all Ice Age bands were nomadic. Our evidence shows that some of the people at the site's younger settlement remained there year-round, living off a wide variety of plants and animals. Although few sites contemporaneous with Monte Verde have been found so far, we think the Monte Verdeans probably belonged to a scattered group of colonizers accustomed to temperate wetlands and forests. The fact that they used many river resources suggest that they came from the Maullín River basin, seven miles to the north, into which Chinchihuapi Creek discharges.

For all their surprising sophistication, the Monte Verdeans had fairly crude tools. True, our excavations uncovered some artifacts made of wood, such as digging sticks, as well as some bone artifacts, such as a baton for striking flakes off stones and gouges made of mastodon tusks. But many of the tools we found were simply pebbles from the creek bed or distant ocean beaches. Their damaged edges, coated with residues from food plants, identify them as tools that were picked up, used and then discarded. Other stones were simply split or struck to remove a few flakes. Only a few stone specimens, such as bifacially flaked projectile points and chopping tools, grooved sling stones and grinding stones, would be universally accepted as human tools even if they had been discovered in a different setting with no corroborating evidence.

Our findings should serve as a cautionary tale for archaeologists seeking indisputable artifacts in ancient sites. If, as it sometimes seems, we deceive ourselves by thinking that rocks are tools, we may just as often mistake tools for rocks. The oldest, deepest levels at Monte Verde are a case in point. Four feet below the latest settlement, in another area of the site, we found twenty-four fractured pebbles and three shallow depressions, lined with clay, containing burned wood and seeds. Seven of the pebbles were probably flaked by people; four of the twenty-four pebbles show polish or striations on their sharp edges from the cutting and scraping of meat, hides and plants. Charcoal from two of the depressions has been radiocarbon-dated to about 33,000 years ago.

Were the charcoal and the pebbles around it made by people? The evidence is inconclusive. But if the answer is yes, the faint traces the early Monte

Verdeans left behind suggest that they were probably transient explorers. The paleo-ecological evidence indicates that 33,000 years ago the region was going through an interglacial period. As the climate warmed up and moors and beech forests began to appear, southern Chile would have grown increasingly hospitable to colonists.

***

[In] January [1997] a multidisciplinary research team will be at the University of Kentucky for two days to inspect the Monte Verde artifacts and to discuss the site in greater detail. The team will then travel to Chile for a three-day visit to examine the site setting and the stratigraphy. I have mixed feelings about the visit. Although we have been calling for a site visit since 1979, no one has accepted our offer. Given that the military government of General Augusto Pinochet was in power throughout the 1970s and 1980s, some archaeologists were understandably reluctant to visit us. Even more of them, however, were put off by the late Junius B. Bird of the American Museum of Natural History.

Dean of paleo-Indian research in South America, Bird was sent to inspect the site in 1979, when the National Geographic Society was funding our excavations. He arrived at the site early, when we were still establishing our base camp and grid system. Bird stayed for just two days, during which time we screened dirt only from the site's sterile upper layers. He later told colleagues in the United States and Chile that he did not see any cultural materials at Monte Verde and that the site was still of questionable value.

As far as artifacts were concerned, Bird spoke the truth. If he had stayed just two more weeks at the site, however, he would have seen us uncover the dramatic 12,500-year-old remains. As a result of that visit, unfortunately, the archaeological community—particularly Thomas F. Lynch of Cornell University in Ithaca, New York, and other strong advocates of the Clovis paradigm—joined Bird in dismissing the site.

***

Much of the debate about the existence of pre-Clovis peoples in the Americas hinges on standards of archaeological evidence. Clovis advocates maintain, with some justification, that most pre-Clovis sites are nothing more than jumbled deposits of old soil and much younger artifacts and plant remains. Pre-Clovis advocates counter that their opponents are isolationists and chauvinists, that they too often reject sites without proper evidence of disproof. If the same standards were applied to Clovis sites, they go on to say, many of those sites would not be accepted either.

In the years since Bird's visit, Clovis proponents, led by Lynch, have criticized Monte Verde on nearly every count. The site's 12,500-year-old layers, they say, must be contaminated by younger artifacts that worked their way down with burrowing animals, tree roots or through cracks in the ground. The material that was radiocarbon-dated must be contaminated by petroleum. The wood and bone artifacts must have been picked up from another site and washed into Monte Verde by floods.

None of those claims have been backed up by any geological or archaeological evidence. In the fifteen years that our team worked at the site, we did not find a single artifact above the 12,500-year-old level. There is one Archaic site, between 8,000 and 5,000 years old, about a third of a mile upstream from Monte Verde. But those deposits are buried several hundred yards inland, in an intact stratum not subject to erosion or flooding. The artifacts from that site, in any case, are made of raw materials entirely different from those at Monte Verde. Moreover, there is no geological, archaeological or other evidence to indicate that the younger Monte Verde remains were ever disturbed. The footprints, house floors, tied and knotted strings and other materials we found—all of them intact—verify the site's high archaeological integrity.

In recent years, as we have published more data on the site, much of the criticism of it has subsided. Even Lynch, to his credit, has conceded that the younger level of the site is valid, though he and others reserve final judgement until all the archaeological data is published. I can only hope that my second volume of findings from Monte Verde, due to be published by Smithsonian Institution Press [in] February [1997], will put their remaining doubts to rest.

⋘⊙⋙

Support for pre-Clovis colonization of the Americas is starting to come from other disciplines as well, though each new theory brings its own guesses, loose ends and inconsistencies. The linguist Richard A. Rogers of the University of Kansas in Lawrence thinks native North American languages are too various to have evolved only in the past 11,000 years. Given the rate at which languages diversify, he suggests that people were living in southern parts of the continent substantially more than 18,000 years ago, when the Pleistocene ice sheets had reached their greatest extent.

The bioanthropologist Christy G. Turner II of Arizona State University in Tempe has proposed an alternate scenario. On the basis of a comparison of teeth from 9,000 skeletons discovered in Eurasia and in America, he has proposed that the first immigrants entered Alaska from northern China more than 12,000 years ago. Their descendants then rapidly colonized the Americas, all the way to Tierra del Fuego. Other biological evidence, such as the high incidence of shovel-shaped incisors, the absence of blood group B and the rarity of group A, shows that all Native Americans except the recently arrived Eskimos and Aleuts are closely related to one another and clearly distinct from their Asiatic ancestors.

Some biological anthropologists suggest that Native Americans are genetically similar because the first colonizers were few in number—perhaps only a single band of hunters and foragers. But the diverse lineages indicated by the genetic data also suggests that people arrived in the Americas more than 11,000 years ago, and that more genetic variability exists among members of the Native American population than anyone had previously estimated. It may be that instead of a massive migration of big-game hunters at the end of the Ice Age, between 12,000 and 11,000 years ago, several small bands walked from Siberia to Alaska much earlier. To avoid the massive ice sheets that mantled Alaska until about 13,000 years ago, they may have skirted the Pacific coast on foot or by boat.

The migration to the Americas represents the last step in a worldwide human dispersion. Recent findings of fossil skeletons and genetic data indicate that people physically identical to ourselves lived in Africa and the Near East at least 90,000 years ago. From there they spread out across the face of Europe and Asia in slowly advancing waves, reaching China, Japan and Australia about 30,000 years ago. Many archaeologists believe that only fully modern humans had the skills and tools necessary to adapt successfully to the harsh, arid grasslands of Siberia and, later, to push into the coldest reaches of North America.

The big picture of modern human origins has become clearer, but the debate about allegedly pre-Clovis peoples remains as contentious as it was when the first Ice Age sites were discovered more than fifty years ago. Monte Verde demonstrates conclusively that people were living in the Americas more than 12,000 years ago. But archaeologists still have little solid evidence to suggest that people made it to the New World before 15,000 years ago.

ॐ

Although I was braced for some criticism when we first began excavating Monte Verde, I was taken aback by how quickly our work was cast into the middle of the pre-Clovis controversy. Every few months, it seems, a new instant analysis of Monte Verde and other pre-Clovis sites appeared, all without a site visit or a review of all the evidence. Given that many good archaeologists, including the late Ruth Simpson and Louis S. B. Leakey, have lost some of their standing as "objective" scientists by championing failed pre-Clovis sites, the skepticism is understandable. And to be honest, I have been guilty of some instant analysis of my own—for example, when questioning finds at the Pedra Furada site in Brazil, which are said to be between 15,000 and 45,000 years old. Instant-opinion-hurling has become something of a sport in the study of the first Americans—a sport that reveals our arbitrary understanding of little-known sites and of the peopling of the Americas.

Much of the bickering, I believe, has served only to trivialize the processes of scientific proof, criticism and debate. In the case of many early sites, it has distracted archaeologists from the cultural value of their findings and from the interdisciplinary research methods they have employed. More important, it has led to a neglect of questions such as, Why did people migrate to the New World in the first place? And how did they adapt so quickly to environments ranging from the frozen wastes of Alaska to the equatorial rain forests of South America? In archaeology, it sometimes seems, a single priority—the omnipotent radiocarbon date—still overshadows any other information about a site.

Admittedly, the date that people first arrived in the New World is a key to how they managed to do so. Depending on when they arrived, the first Americans might have had to navigate an ocean or traverse glaciers, build snow shelters against the cold or thatched huts against the tropical rains. Yet the dating game has little importance if one cannot assign wider cultural and historical meaning to an archaeological site.

Archaeologists will probably never find the remains of the very first Americans. Even if they do, they may not recognize those remains for what they are. Like the Mapuche's ancestors, those of us who study them are bound to go down many long paths that lead nowhere, and sometimes to turn on one another in frustration. But if we give as much attention to the pattern and process of human dispersion as we do to its timing, perhaps we can get better at choosing the good paths—and at making the journey a joyful one.

POSTSCRIPT

Did People First Arrive in the New World After the Last Ice Age?

Even if one accepts Monte Verde as a genuine pre-Clovis site, how widespread across the hemisphere were such pre-Clovis settlements? Were the Monte Verde settlers with their simple technologies in use 14,000 years ago ancestors of peoples living in the region who had a more sophisticated Clovis technology? Do Monte Verde and Clovis sites represent two distinct migrations into the New World or the rapid cultural evolution of a single people? Moreover, dating Monte Verde to 14,000 years ago does not explain where the Monte Verde people came from, how long they had been in the Americas, or how they got there.

The debate over Monte Verde raises many questions that will continue to challenge archaeologists for many years to come. It will continue to raise issues about the limits of carbon-14 dating and more generally about the standards of archaeological evidence. But it also raises questions about archaeological models. Why have early sites been so difficult to locate? Are archaeologists looking for the right kinds of artifacts? Do we have reasonable models of human settlement patterns that would allow us to find occupation sites used by people 30,000 years ago?

Those interested in the early debate about Monte Verde and the question of whether any preglacial sites exist in the New World should consult Dillehay's first report, "Early Rainforest Archaeology in Southwestern South America: Research Context, Design, and Data at Monte Verde," in B. A. Purdy, ed., *Wet Site Archaeology* (Telford Press, 1988), together with Thomas Lynch's assessment, "Glacial-Age Man in South America? A Critical Review," *American Antiquity* (vol. 55, 1990); Dillehay and Michael B. Collins's "Monte Verde, Chile: A Comment on Lynch," *American Antiquity* (vol. 56, 1991); Ruth Gruhn and Alan L. Bryan's "A Review of Lynch's Descriptions of South American Pleistocene Sites," *American Antiquity* (vol. 56, 1991); and Lynch's "Lack of Evidence for Glacial-Age Settlement of South America: Reply to Dillehay and Collins and to Gruhn and Bryan," *American Antiquity* (vol. 56, 1991).

Students may also find two recent popular articles about the first Americans of interest: *Archaeology* (November/December 1999) published a book review essay by Mark Rose, which outlines the current debate, and *Scientific American's Discovering Archaeology* (February 2000) devoted a special section to "The Puzzle of the First Americans," dealing with a variety of current research problems and theoretical concerns.

ISSUE 5

Was There a Goddess Cult in Prehistoric Europe?

YES: Marija Gimbutas, from "Old Europe in the Fifth Millennium B.C.: The European Situation on the Arrival of Indo-Europeans," in Edgar C. Polomé, ed., *The Indo-Europeans in the Fourth and Third Millennia* (Karoma Publishers, 1982)

NO: Lynn Meskell, from "Goddesses, Gimbutas, and 'New Age' Archaeology," *Antiquity* (March 1995)

ISSUE SUMMARY

YES: Archaeologist Marija Gimbutas argues that the civilization of pre–Bronze Age "Old Europe" was matriarchal—ruled by women —and that the religion centered on the worship of a single great Goddess. Furthermore, this civilization was destroyed by patriarchal Kurgan pastoralists (the Indo-Europeans), who migrated into southeastern Europe from the Eurasian steppes in the fifth to third millennia B.C.

NO: Archaeologist Lynn Meskell considers the belief in a supreme Goddess and a matriarchal society in prehistoric Europe to be an unwarranted projection of some women's utopian longings onto the past. She regards Gimbutas's interpretation of the archaeological evidence as biased and speculative.

T he idea that prehistoric societies were matriarchal and worshiped a supreme Goddess has deep roots in European thought. The Greeks, like the Babylonians, regarded the earth as feminine and associated it with goddesses, a notion preserved in our expressions "Mother Earth" and "Mother Nature." In the nineteenth century some cultural evolutionists, like J. J. Bachofen (*Das Mutterrecht*, Benno Schwabe, 1861) and John Ferguson MacLellan (*Primitive Marriage: An Inquiry Into the Origin of the Form of Capture in Marriage Ceremonies*, 1865), postulated that the earliest human societies were woman-centered, but they became patriarchal ("male-governed") before the beginning of written records. Coincidentally some classicists began to see a single great Goddess lying behind the goddesses of classical Greece, and they linked this Goddess to the female figurines ("Venus figures") being turned up in archaeological sites in the Balkans and southeastern Europe. In 1903 the prominent classicist Jane Ellen Harrison drew the threads together, postulating that in prehistoric southeastern Europe there existed a peaceful, woman-centered civilization where people lived in harmony with nature and worshiped a single female deity. This civilization was later destroyed by patriarchal invaders from the north, who brought war and male deities. By the 1950s most archaeologists specializing in Europe accepted the view that a Goddess religion and matriarchal social system had spread throughout Europe before being replaced by the male-centered societies of the Bronze Age. But in the 1960s a young archaeologist, Peter Ucko, challenged this view on the basis of extensive analyses of figurines from throughout eastern Europe and the eastern Mediterranean. He saw that there was great variation among figurines in time and space, and far from all were female. This led the archaeological establishment to retreat to a more agnostic view, once again reserving judgment over the nature of the earliest European religions.

One archaeologist who retained and even elaborated on the theory of the ancient matriarchal society and the Goddess, however, was the late Marija Gimbutas. In the following selection, Gimbutas presents her version of the theory and some of the evidence for it. She bases her interpretation on a large body of archaeological materials, especially the remains of buildings, clay models of buildings, and figurines. She contends that this matrifocal ("woman-focused") culture was destroyed by the invasions of patriarchal, nomadic pastoralists from the steppes of southern Russia, but traces of the earlier culture linger among the non–Indo-European peoples of Europe, like the Basques, and were mixed into the later patriarchal culture.

Lynn Meskell, however, criticizes Gimbutas and her followers for adopting a highly speculative gynocentric ("female-centered") interpretation of the evidence, one that she believes consistently ignores contrary evidence and other possible interpretations. Meskell argues that Gimbutas has allowed her desire to affirm the existence of an ancient feminist utopia to color and distort her interpretation of the archaeological record, leading her, for example, to overlook the large numbers of figurines that are male or ambiguous in gender. She suggests that the current popularity of Gimbutas's view is due to "New Age" feminists hoping to ground their utopian visions in a past that they see as having been unfairly destroyed by men.

These selections raise a number of questions that are important not only for our understanding of the prehistory of Europe, but for archaeological interpretation in general. Are any other interpretations of this evidence possible? If so, how can we choose among the different possible readings? Can archaeologists insulate themselves from social and political currents of their day and provide "objective" interpretations of their findings? What is the proper role of imagination in creating a comprehensive picture of a vanished way of life from the small set of clues that have survived the vicissitudes of time?

Old Europe in the Fifth Millennium B.C.

With the growing realization of the necessity to distinguish the Neolithic and Copper Age pre-Indo-European civilization from the "Indo-Europeanized" Europe of the Bronze Age, I coined, ten years ago, the new term "Old Europe." This term covers, in a broad sense, all Europe west of the Pontic Steppe before the series of incursions of the steppe (or "Kurgan") pastoralists in the second half of the fifth, of the fourth, and the beginning of the third millennium B.C., for in my view Europe is not the homeland of the Indo-European speakers. In a narrower sense, the term Old Europe applies to Europe's first civilization, i.e., the highest Neolithic and Copper Age culture focused in the southeast and the Danubian basin, gradually destroyed by repeated Kurgan infiltrations....

The two cultural systems are very different: the first is sedentary, matrifocal, peaceful, art-loving, earth- and sea-bound; the second is patrifocal, mobile, warlike, ideologically sky-oriented, and indifferent to art. The two systems can best be understood if studied before the period of their clash and mélange, i.e., before ca. 4500–4000 B.C....

Social Organization

Theocratic monarchies? Old European societies were unstratified: there were no contrasting classes of rulers and laborers, but there was a rich middle class which rose as a consequence of metallurgy and expansion of trade. Neither royal tombs, distinct in burial rites from those of the rest of the population, nor royal quarters, distinguished by extravagance, have been discovered. I see no evidence of the existence of a patriarchal chieftain system with pronounced ranking of the Indo-European type. Instead, there are in Old Europe a multitude of temples with accumulations of wealth—gold, copper, marble, shells, and exquisite ceramics. The goods of highest quality, produced by the best craftsmen, belonged not to the chief, as is customary in chiefdoms, but to the Goddess and to her representative, the queen-priestess. The social organization represented by the rise of temples was a primary centrifugal social force.

The question of government organization is as yet difficult to answer. Central areas and secondary provinces can be observed in each culture group. Some of the foci were clearly more influential than others, but whether centralized government existed we do not know. I favor the theory of small theocratic king-doms or city-states, analogous to Etruscan *lucomonies* and Minoan palaces, with a queen-priestess as ruler, and her brother or husband as supervisor of agricul-ture and trade. The basis of such a structure was more social and religious in character than civil, political, or military.

The matrilinear society.   There is absolutely no indication that Old European society was patrilinear or patriarchal. Evidence from the cemeteries does not indicate a subordinate position of women. There was no ranking along a patri-archal masculine-feminine value scale as there was in Europe after the infiltra-tion of steppe pastoralists who introduced the patriarchal and the patrilinear systems. The study of grave equipment in each culture group suggests an egal-itarian society. A division of labor between the sexes is demonstrated by grave goods, but not a superiority of either. The richest graves belong to both men and women. Age was a determining factor; children had the lowest number of objects.

A strong support for the existence of matrilinearity in Old Europe is the historic continuity of matrilinear succession in the non-Indo-European soci-eties of Europe and Asia Minor, such as the Etruscan, Pelasgian, Lydian, Carian, and Basque. Even in Rome during the monarchy, royal office passed regularly through the female line—clearly a non-Indo-European tradition most probably inherited from Old Europe, Polybius, in the second century B.C., speaking of the Greek colony, Lokroi, on the toe of Italy, says, "all their ancestral honors are traced through women." Furthermore, we hear from Greek historians that the Etruscans and prehistoric Athenians had "wives in common" and "their chil-dren did not know their own fathers." The woman in such a system is free to marry the man of her choice, and as many as she pleases (there is no ques-tion of adultery—that was a male invention), and she retains control of her children with regard to their paternity. This evidence led George Thomson to the assumption that group marriage was combined with common ownership in prehistoric Aegean societies. Matrilinear succession on some Aegean islands (e.g., Lesbos, Skyros) is reported by written records in the eighteenth century and continues in partial form to this very day. Matrilinear succession to real property and prenuptial promiscuity were practiced in isolated mountainous regions of southwestern Yugoslavia up to the twentieth century. Such customs are certainly unthinkable in present patriarchal society; only a very deeply rooted tradition could have survived for millennia the counter-influence of the patrilinearity of surrounding tribes.

A matrifocal society is reflected by the types of Old European goddesses and their worship. It is obvious that goddesses, not gods, dominated the Old European pantheon. Goddesses ruled absolutely over human, animal, and plant life. Goddesses, not male gods, spontaneously generated the life-force and cre-ated the universe. As demonstrated by the thousands of figurines and temples from the Neolithic through the Copper Ages, the male god was an adjunct of the female goddess, as consort or son. In the models of house-shrines and temples, and in actual temple remains, females are shown as supervising the preparation and performance of rituals dedicated to the various aspects and functions of the

Goddess. Enormous energy was expended in the production of cult equipment and votive gifts. Some temple models show the grinding of grain and the baking of sacred bread. The routine acts of daily existence were religious rituals by virtue of replicating the sacred models. In the temple workshops, which usually constitute half the building or occupy the floor below the temple proper, females made and decorated quantities of the various pots appropriate to different rites. Next to the altar of the temple stood a vertical loom on which were probably woven the sacred garments and temple appurtenances. The most sophisticated creations of Old Europe—the most exquisite vases, sculptures, etc., now extant—were women's work (the equipment for decoration of vases so far is known only from female graves). Since the requirements of the temple were of primary importance, production for the temple must have doubled or tripled the general level of productivity, both stimulating and maintaining the level of feminine craftsmanship.

Religion

Temples.   The tradition of temple buildings begins in the seventh millennium B.C. A remarkable series of temple models and actual rectangular temples from the sixth and fifth millennia B.C. bear witness to a great architectural tradition.

At present about 50 models from various culture groups and phases are known. They are more informative than the actual temple remains, since they present details of architecture, decoration, and furnishings otherwise unavailable to prehistoric archaeology. Actual remains of sanctuaries suggest that miniature models in clay were replicas of the real temples. They almost always were found at the altars, probably as gifts to the goddess.

The seventh and sixth millennia temple models seemed to have conceived of the temple as literally the body or the house of the deity. Shrine models from Porodin near Bitola in Macedonia, for instance, have a cylindrical "chimney" in the middle of the roof upon which is modeled the masked features of a large-eyed Bird Goddess, a necklace encircling her neck ("chimney"). Other models have round openings fit for the goddess to enter in the shape of a bird or are made in the form of a bird's nest....

The figurines portrayed (in clay models) and found in actual shrines are shown to perform various cult activities—ritual grinding, baking of sacred bread, attending sacrifices—or are seated on the altar, apparently used for the reenactment of a particular religious ceremony. In the mid-fifth millennium Cucuteni (Early Tripolye) shrine at Sabatinivka in the valley of Southern Bug in the Ukraine, 16 figurines were sitting on chairs on the altar, all with snake-shaped heads and massive thighs. One held a baby snake. The other group of 15 were in action—baking, grinding, or standing at the dish containing remains of a bull sacrifice. In the corner next to the altar stood a life-size clay throne with horned back support, perhaps for a priestess to supervise the ceremony. At Ovčarovo near Trgovište, northeastern Bulgaria, 26 miniature cult objects were found within the remains of a burned shrine. They included four figurines with upraised arms, three altar screens (or temple facades) decorated with symbols, nine chairs, three tables, three lidded vessels, three drums, and several dishes larger than figurines. Such objects vividly suggest ceremonies with music and dances, lustrations, and offerings.

The production of an enormous variety of cult paraphernalia—exquisite anthropomorphic, zoomorphic, and ornithomorphic vases, sacrificial containers, lamps, ladles, etc.—is one of the very characteristic features of this culture and may be viewed as a response to the demands of a theocentric culture where most production centered around the temple. The consideration of these creations is unfortunately beyond the scope of this article. Regarding the technological and aesthetic skills, nothing similar was created in the millennia that followed the demise of Old Europe.

Ceremonial costume and mask.   A wealth of costume details is preserved on the clay figurines. Deep incisions encrusted with white paste or red ochre affirm the presence of hip-belts, fringe, aprons, narrow skirts, blouses, stoles, a variety of hair styles, and the use of caps, necklaces, bracelets, and medallions. Whether these fashions were commonly worn, or were traditional garb for priestesses or other participants in ritual celebrations, can only be conjectured. The latter was probably the case; most of the figurines seem to have been characters in tableaux of ritual. But, ritual or not, the costumes reflect stylistic conventions of dress and taste characteristic of the period.

In the female costume several dress combinations recur persistently: partly dressed figures wear only a hip-belt, or a hip-belt from which hangs an apron or panels of an entire skirt of fringe, resembling a hula skirt; others wear a tight skirt with shoulder straps or a blouse.

A number of figurines show incised or painted stoles over the shoulders and in front and back. The skirt, which generally begins below the waist and hugs the hips, has a decorative texture of white encrusted incisions, showing net-pattern, zigzags, checkerboard, or dots. The skirt narrows below the knees, and on some figurines wrappings around the legs are indicated. It may be that the skirt was slit in front below the knees and fastened between the legs with woven bands. This type of skirt gives the impression of constraining movement and quite likely had a ritualistic purpose.

The figurines tell little about male attire; males are usually portrayed nude, except for a large V-shaped collar and a belt. In the last phase of the Cucuteni culture male figures wear a hip-belt and a strap passing diagonally across the chest and back over one of the shoulders. . . .

Special attention to coiffure and headgear is evidenced. The Bird and Snake Goddess in particular, or devotees associated with their images, had beautiful coiffures, a crown, or decorative headbands. Vinča and Butmir figurines have hair neatly combed and divided symmetrically in the center, the two panels perhaps separated by a central ribbon. Late Cucutenian figurines, primarily nude, but some wearing hip-belt and necklace, have a long, thick coil of hair hanging down the back and ending in a large, circular bun or with an attached disc, reminiscent of the style favored by Egyptian ritual dancers of the third millennium B.C. A typical item of dress is a conical cap on which radial or horizontal parallel incisions perhaps represent its construction of narrow ribbon-like bands.

Figurines were portrayed wearing masks representing certain goddesses, gods, or their sacred animals, or else they were simply shown as bird-headed (with beaked faces on a cylindrical neck), snake-headed (with a long mouth, round eyes, and no nose), or ram- or other animal-headed. Frequently-occurring perforations of the mask were obviously intended to carry some sort of organic attachment. Plumes, flowers, fruits, and other materials could have been employed in this way. . . .

Deities worshipped.   In the literature on prehistoric religion the female figures of clay, bone, and stone are usually considered to be the "Mother Goddess." Is she indeed nothing more than an image of motherhood? The term is not entirely a misnomer if we understand her as a creatress or as a cosmogenic woman. It must be emphasized that from the Upper Paleolithic onward the persona of the Goddess splintered the response to the developing economy, and the images of deities portray not only the single maternal metaphor of the deity. Study of the several stereotypical shapes and postures of the figurines and of the associated symbolism of the signs incised upon them clearly shows that the figurines intend to project a multiplicity of divine aspects and a variety of divine functions.

There are, in my opinion, two primary aspects of the Goddess (not necessarily two Goddesses) presented by the effigies. The first is, "She who is the Giver of All"—Giver of Life, Giver of Moisture, of Food, of Happiness; she is also "Taker of All," i.e., Death. The second aspect of the Goddess is connected with the periodic awakening of nature: she is springtime, the new moon, rebirth, regeneration, and metamorphosis. Both go back to the Upper Paleolithic. The significance of each aspect is visually supported on the figurines by appropriate symbols and signs. The first aspect of the Goddess as Giver and Taker of All, that is, as both beginning and end of life, is accompanied by aquatic symbols —water birds, snakes, fish, frogs, all animals associated with water—and representations of water itself in the form of zigzag bands, groups of parallel lines, meanders, nets, checkerboards, and running spirals. The second aspect of the Goddess as Rebirth, Renewal, and Transcendance is accompanied by the symbols of "becoming": eggs, uteri, phalluses, whirls, crescents, and horns which resemble cornucopias. The Goddess often appears in the form of a bee, a butterfly, or a caterpillar. This second group involves male animals such as bulls and dogs.

The Giver of All, the Fish, Water Bird, and Snake Goddess

Hybrids of the human female with bird or snake dominated mythical imagery throughout the Upper Paleolithic, Neolithic, Chalcolithic, and Copper Ages from ca. 26,000 to the end of Old Europe at ca. 3000 B.C., but lingered in the Aegean and Mediterranean regions through the Bronze Age and later—at least 40 percent of the total number of figurines belong to this type. The Fish, Bird, and Snake Goddesses were interrelated in meaning and function. Each is

Creatress and Giver. They are, therefore, inseparable from cosmogonic and cosmogenic myths such as water birds carrying cosmic eggs. She as the Mother or *Source* is the giver of rain, water, milk, and meat (sheep, their skin and wool). Her portrayals usually show exaggerated breasts marked with parallel lines, or a wide-open beak or round hole for a mouth. Her large eyes are a magical source, and are surrounded by aquatic symbolism (usually groups of parallel lines). Beginning in the Neolithic, the ram (the earliest domesticated animal, a vital source of food and clothing) became her sacred animal. The symbols of this goddess on spindle whorls and loom weights suggest that she was the originator or guardian of the crafts of spinning and weaving. Metaphorically, as "the spinner and weaver of human life," she became the Goddess of Fate.

Along with the life-giving aspect of the Goddess, her life-taking or death-giving aspect must have developed in preagricultural times. The images of vultures and owls are known from the Upper Paleolithic and from the earliest Neolithic (in the frescoes of Çatal Hüyük, in central Anatolia, vultures appear above headless human beings). The figurine type of the nude goddess with large pubic triangle, folded arms, and face of an owl, well known from Old European graves, may be representative of the Goddess in the aspect of night and death.

In early agricultural times, the Giver of All developed another function, a function vital to tillers of the soil—namely, that of "Giver of Bread." Her images were deposited in grain silos or in egg-shaped vases, where they were indispensable insurance for the resurgence of plant life. She also appears as a pregnant woman, her ripe body a metaphor of the fertile field. She was worshipped with her sacred animal, the pig. The fattening of the pig encouraged the growth and ripening of crops or fertility in general.

Richly represented throughout the Neolithic, Chalcolithic, and Copper Ages, still another aspect of the Goddess is, by natural association, that of "Birth-giving Goddess." She is portrayed with outstretched legs and upraised arms in a naturalistic birth-giving posture. This stereotypic image appears in relief on large vases and on temple walls; carved in black and green stone or alabaster, it was worn as an amulet.

The "Periodic Regeneration" aspect of the Goddess may be as ancient as the Giver of All aspect, since symbols of "becoming" are present in the Upper Paleolithic: crescents and horns appear in association with Paleolithic nudes. To regenerate the life-force was her main function; therefore, the Goddess was flanked by male animals noted for physical strength—bulls, he-goats, dogs. In her incarnation as a crescent, caterpillar, bee, or butterfly, she was a symbol of new life; she emerged from the body or horns of the bull as a bee or butterfly.

The female principle was conceived as creative and eternal, the male as spontaneous and ephemeral. The male principle was represented symbolically by male animals and by phalluses and ithyphallic animal-masked men—goat-men or bull-men. They appear as adjuncts of the Goddess. The figurines of ecstatic dancers, goat- or bull-masked, may represent worshippers of the Goddess in rituals enacting the dance of life. . . .

Conclusion: The Kurgan Penetration

Old Europe was rapidly developing into an urban culture, but its growth was interrupted and eventually stopped by destructive forces from the east—the steadily increasing infiltration of the semi-nomadic, horse-riding pastoralists from the Pontic steppes. Periodic waves of infiltration into civilized Europe effected the disintegration of the first European civilization. Only on the islands, like Crete, Thera, and Malta, did the traditions of Old Europe survive for almost two millennia. The Bronze Age culture that followed north of the Aegean was an amalgam of the substrate and totally different elements of an eastern culture.

Thanks to a growing number of radiocarbon dates, archaeologists can ascertain the periods of Kurgan penetration into Europe. There was no single massive invasion, but a series of repeated incursions concentrated into three major thrusts:

- Wave No. 1, ca. 4400–4200 B.C.
- Wave No. 2, ca. 3400–3200 B.C.
- Wave No. 3, ca. 3000–2800 B.C.

The steppe (or "Kurgan") people were, above all, pastoralists. As such, their social system was composed of small patrilinear units that were socially stratified according to the strategic services performed by its male members. The grazing of large herds over vast expanses of land necessitated a living pattern of seasonal settlements or small villages affording sufficient pasturage for animals. The chief tasks of a pastoral economy were executed by men, not by women as was characteristic of the indigenous agricultural system.

It was inevitable that an economy based on farming and another which relied on stock breeding would produce unrelated ideologies. The upheaval of the Old European civilization is registered in the abrupt cessation of painted pottery and figurines, the disappearance of shrines, the termination of symbols and signs.

Old European ceramics are readily identified with the rich symbolic signs and decorative motifs that reflect an ideology concerned with cosmogony, generation, birth, and regeneration. Symbols were compartmentalized or interwoven in a myriad combination—meanders and spirals, chevrons and zigzags, circles, eggs, horns, etc. There were a multitude of pictorial and sculptural representations of goddesses and gods, of worshippers, and sacred animals. Kurgan pottery is devoid of symbolic language and of aesthetic treatment in general because it obviously did not serve the same ceremonial purposes as that of Old Europe. The stabbing and impressing technique is quite primitive and seems to focus on only one symbol, the sun. Occasionally, a schematized fir tree occurs which may symbolize a "tree-of-life."

Mythical images that were in existence on the Eurasiatic steppe dispersed now over a large part of Europe, and continued to the beginning of Christianity and beyond. The new ideology was an apotheosis of the horseman and warrior. The principal gods carry weapons and ride horses or chariots; they are figures of inexhaustible energy, physical power, and fecundity. In contrast to the pre-Indo-European cultures whose myths centered around the moon, water, and the female, the religion of pastoral, semi-sedentary Indo-European peoples was oriented toward the rotating sky, the sun, stars, planets, and other sky phenomena such as thunder and lightning. Their sky and sun gods were shining, "bright as the sky"; they wore starry cloaks adorned with glittering gold, copper, or amber pendants, torques, chest plates, belts. They carried shining daggers, swords, and shields. The Indo-Europeans glorified the magical swiftness of arrow and javelin and the sharpness of the blade. Throughout the millennia, the Indo-Europeans exulted in the making of weapons, not pottery or sculpture. The touch of the ax blade awakened the powers of nature and transmitted the fecundity of the Thunder God; by the touch of his spear tip, the god of war and the underworld marked the hero for glorious death.

Goddesses, Gimbutas, and 'New Age' Archaeology

For a century a notion of a prehistoric Mother Goddess has infused some perceptions of ancient Europe, whatever the realities of developing archaeological knowledge. With the reverent respect now being given to Marija Gimbutas, and her special vision of a perfect matriarchy in Old Europe, a daughter-goddess is now being made, bearer of a holy spirit in our own time to be set alongside the wise mother of old.

Introduction

The field of archaeology, like many others, is prone to fads and fictions within the academic community and general public alike. A recurrent interest since the 19th century has been the notion of an omnipotent Mother Goddess, whose worship symbolizes a cultural continuity from the Palaeolithic era to modern times. The principle advocate for this theory over the past two decades, Marija Gimbutas, is seen to offer archaeological validity to these claims as a result of her recognized academic standing and long history of fieldwork in southeast European sites. From the material particulars of archaeology in her earlier work she moved toward an ideal vision of prehistory (compare Gimbutas 1965; 1970; 1971a; 1973 with interpretations in 1974; 1981; Gimbutas et al. 1989; 1989a; 1989b; 1991; 1992). Her widely published theories appeal to those committed to ecofeminism and the 'New Age' range of esoteric concerns, which include ancient religion and mythology. Whilst this vision of the past appears to embrace aspects of cognitive, gender and even feminist archaeologies, the interpretations it presents are simply hopeful and idealistic creations reflecting the contemporary search for a social utopia.

The concept of The Goddess is entangled within a larger, more complex, political phenomenon that involves regional and nationalist struggles (Chapman 1994; Anthony in press), linguistic aetiology (Renfrew 1987; Mallory 1989: 81), contemporary gender struggles and the feminist cause (Hallett 1993; Passman 1993). However, the revisionist histories on offer (Eisler 1987; Gimbutas 1974; 1989a; 1989b; 1991; 1992; Orenstein 1990; Spretnak 1992; etc.) do not aim for a more complete understanding of ancient societies *in toto*. Rather, they provide altogether alternative historical projections of what certain groups see as desirable. Re-writing the past from an engendered perspective is certainly long overdue, yet re-weaving a fictional past with claims of scientific proofs (e.g. Gimbutas 1992) is simply irresponsible. Such 'new and improved' histories are more telling of contemporary socio-sexual concerns rather than their ancient antecedents.

Why the Goddess and Why Now?

Why has there been a proliferation of studies devoted to the concept of a Mother Goddess in recent years? Why has this appeal been so persistent, particularly to the general public? Whereas the academic study of figurines is usually integrated within regional culture studies, the notion of the Goddess has assumed larger proportions to the wider community. As a result, the literature of the Goddess lies at the interface where academic scholarship meets New Age gynocentric, mythologized interpretations of the past (Eisler 1987; Gimbutas 1974; 1989a; 1992; Spretnak 1992). This is a radically burgeoning field in women's studies and New Age literature, and its books must far outsell their scholarly counterparts. Since achieving icon status, The Goddess has been linked with movements and disciplines as diverse as christianity, feminism and ecofeminism, environmentalism, witchcraft and archaeology. In each of these the Goddess phenomenon is taken as a given rather than one speculative interpretation to be considered with alternative hypotheses. The past is being used in the present as an historical authority for contemporary efforts to secure gender equality (or superiority?) in spiritual and social domains.

... The current interest in the Goddess is not purely academic, but stems from a desire to remedy the results of millennia of misogyny and marginalization (Frymer-Kensky 1992: vii) in both religious and secular spheres. My contention is that the connection has materialized in response to female disempowerment in our own recent history, particularly within religious power bases. The Goddess serves as a vehicle for women's groups and activists to reinforce legitimization of their position by means of an ancient antecedent. Contrary to the bloodied, materialist history and overt androcentrism of the Church, she is earth-centered, offering refuge and a counterbalance to the remote, punitive male god of western religions (Frymer-Kensky 1992; Spretnak 1992).

... Many of these initial gynocentric theories of prehistory share a fundamental commonality to prior androcentric premises since they both employ 'sexist' paradigms in re-constru(ct)ing the past. Thus they do not promote credibility: rather they damage and delimit the positive attributes of gender-based research, due to their poor scholarship, ahistorical interpretations, fictional elements and reverse sexism. I see no detriment to current quests if we acknowledge that inequality was operative in the past, as it was in the historic cultures of the Near East and Mediterranean.

The Figurines as Archaeological Data

Figurines collectively termed Mother Goddesses or Venuses emanate from various regions and span an immense time-depth from the Palaeolithic to the Bronze Age and into historical periods, with considerable variability in form, style, decoration and context. This class of artefact—if that is an appropriate term—appears throughout much of Europe and southwest Asia, primarily southeast Europe and the Mediterranean islands from the Cyclades to Crete, Malta and Majorca (Ehrenberg 1989: 65; Malone *et al.* 1992: 76). The figures are generally accorded the status of 'art', although ethnographic evidence suggests that they do not form a distinct category. In a further tendency to project 20th-century biases of what constitutes 'good art', it has been suggested that carefully made sculptures were produced for important occasions by priestesses or mother figures (Gimbutas *et al.* 1989: 220). Conversely, the simple, schematic examples could have been made by any member of the community (male?). Figurines have been objectified, taken as devoid of spatial and cultural specificity; yet objects do not have inherent meaning divorced from their historically specific context of production and use (Hodder 1991; Dobres 1992a; 1992b).

For many figurines, provenience and context are lost due to poor excavation or non-archaeological recovery (for Cycladic figures see Gill & Chippindale 1993). Runnels (1990) and McPherron (1991) have noted the limits of excavation and recording by Gimbutas for her own site at Achilleion (Gimbutas *et al.* 1989), on which much of the larger picture is reliant. Dating, methodology, testing, typological and statistical analyses have all come under fire, not to mention artistic licence and over-interpretation. Weaknesses in scholarship have prevented Gimbutas' attempts, and the question of gender studies, to be taken seriously in archaeological circles (Tringham 1991: 97; 1993).

As part of a gynocentric agenda, female figurines have been considered largely to the exclusion of male and sexless examples (Gimbutas 1971b; 1974; 1986; 1989a; 1989b; 1992; Gimbutas *et al.* 1989), this selection shaping the vision of a single, omnipresent female deity. Her position is clear: male divinities were not prominent before the Indo-European invasion (see van Leuven 1993: 84). Many are undeniably female. Many are also male, androgynous, zoomorphic or indeterminate (see Marinescu-Bîlcu 1981; Hodder 1990; Milojkovic 1990; Pavlovic 1990; Talalay 1993); these are dismissed.

To her credit, Gimbutas assembled a large corpus of southeast European figurines in English publications, with copious photographs and illustrations. She aimed to investigate figurine attributes such as raw materials, production and form to some degree. However, studies of production have been undertaken more systematically by other scholars (Murray 1970), coupled with analyses of decorative motifs and positioning (Ucko 1968; Marinescu Bîlcu 1981; Pogozheva 1983) and patterns of breakage. It is unfortunate that Gimbutas did not incorporate findings from these studies into her later publications.

Mediterranean Matriculture
and the Indo-European Debate

One key debate in 19th-century anthropology, currently experiencing a revival, hinges on the traditional matriarchal view of cultural evolution. Eminent scholars such as Morgan, Engels and Bachofen led the early debate, influenced by their own socio-intellectual biases, though failing to make the distinction between matriarchy, matrilinearity and matrilocality. Bachofen's evolutionist interpretations, long since discredited within academia, have now resurfaced in the Goddess literature. . . .

It has become popular in the past decade to view Neolithic cultures as matriarchal or matrifocal (Hayden 1986: 17), and to depict them as peaceful, harmonious and artistic in contrast to the more aggressive, destructive patriarchal societies that followed (Chapman 1991; Tringham 1991; Conkey & Tringham in press): the overthrowing of matriarchy by patriarchial society was the real Fall which has beleaguered Europe ever since. Childe raised a powerful analogue, arguing that using female figurines to substantiate matriarchal or matrilineal society was as accurate an indicator as the image of the Virgin Mary in the modern patriarchy (Childe 1951: 65). We should not ignore the possibility of matriarchy; rather we are not clear what form such evidence would take.

This line of reasoning ties directly into the polemic debate surrounding Indo-European archaeology and linguistics, in which Gimbutas was a major player (see Renfrew 1987: xiii; Mallory 1989: 182). Briefly, her view of Old Europe in the Neolithic period was characterized by its unfortified settlements (*contra* Marinescu Bîlcu 1981; Anthony in press) where a peaceful existence prevailed without threat of violence or fear of death itself. Within the matriarchy there were no husbands, yet men fulfilled important roles in construction, crafts and trade. Women's lives were liberal, socially and sexually, and inextricably bound to the rich religious system which ensured their prominence (Gimbutas 1992). Old Europe is portrayed as culturally homogeneous (*contra* Pavlovic 1988: 33; Mallory 1989: 22), socially egalitarian (*contra* Tringham 1990: 605; Anthony in press), devoid of human or animal sacrifice (*contra* Marinescu Bîlcu 1981; Anthony in press). Accordingly, this utopian existence was abruptly destroyed by Indo-European invasions: more specifically by the equocentric Kurgan culture from the Russian steppe. . . .

There is a striking congruence between Gimbutas' own life and her perception of Old Europe. Born in Lithuania, she witnessed two foreign occupations by 'barbarian invaders'; however, those from the East stayed. This prompted her immigration to the United States during which time the Soviet occupation of the Baltic states continued almost up until her death in 1994. In her own words, 'history is showing us between eight and ten million women had to die for her [the Goddess] . . . the wise people of the time . . . so it reminds me of the same [*sic*] what happened in Stalin's Europe when the cream of the society had to be removed and only fools were left to live. What happened in the twentieth century is the greatest shame of human history' (Gimbutas

1992). This strongly mirrors her view of Old Europe, a creative, matriarchal and *good* society which was invaded by men with weapons from the East.

Other writers (see Eisler 1987; Passman 1993) have run with Gimbutas' theories by stressing the superiority of assumed matristic cultures in Old Europe, Anatolia, Egypt and Minoan Crete on the basis of their peaceful, egalitarian, non-fortified communities and even their predisposition to vegetarianism (?) (Passman 1993: 187). Such a scenario is not borne out archaeologically. Walls and ditches at Nea Nikomedia, Dimini and Sesklo may have defensive functions. Both Neolithic and Chalcolithic sites like Tîrpesti, Ovcharovo, Polyanitsa and Tripolye clearly demonstrate fortification (Marinescu-Bîlcu 1981; Anthony in press: 20). Sites such as Dimini and Agia Sophia (Demoule & Perlès 1993) suggests status differentiation within communities, as does Selevac (Tringham & Krstic 1990: 206), with more evidence of social hierarchy from the cemeteries at Varna, Durankulak and other East Balkan sites (Anthony in press: 20). In addition, there is evidence of human sacrifice at Traian-Dealui, Fîntînilor (Marinescu-Bîlcu 1981: 135) and later from Knossos (Wall *et al.* 1986); animal sacrifices are attested at Poiana în Pisc and Anza. Artefactual evidence from Egypt indicates that weapons, in addition to items displaying battle scenes, were amongst the most common in the predynastic repertoire (see Davis 1992).

Even without the overwhelming archaeological data, historical evidence from Greece (Humphreys 1983; Hallett 1993), Egypt (Robins 1993) and Mesopotamia (Frymer-Kensky 1992) plus numerous ethnographic accounts suggest that cultures with strong female deities—if indeed they are deities—may still regard women in the profane world as a low-status group. The romanticized view of antiquity many feminists and pseudo-feminists present has more to do with creating an idealized past to contrast with our own secular, impersonal and industrialized present than with archaeological facts (Hays 1993: 84). Their visionary work links notions of 'ancient' and 'future', so enabling a richly figured heritage, once lived and lost, to be experienced again (Passman 1993: 182). This political reconstruction of a matristic past furnishes the seed for a return to Edenic conditions, ecological balance, healing the planet and matriculture itself, in opposition to the forecasts of Armageddon and the second coming (Starhawk 1982; Orenstein 1990; Passman 1993).

Cultic Figurines From a Sexist Perspective

Although proponents of post-processualism (e.g. Hodder 1987; 1990; 1991; Shanks & Tilley 1987) aim to understand symbolic systems, they still regard the archaeological record as a polysemous text that can be read (Hays 1993). Some have taken their position as reader to the extreme. Herein lies Gimbutas' attraction for a New Age audience, since she adopts the role of translator (channeller?) for a symbolic language stretching back millennia into the Neolithic mindset. In answer to Onians' claim that figurines represent ancient erotica, Gimbutas argues that 'love-making is clearly far from the thoughts of the ancient artist' (1981: 32). Knowing 'our European prehistoric forefathers were more philosophical than we seem to think' (1981: 39), she understands how they would be stunned to hear these new hypotheses. She further claims that the Achilleion figurines 'represent deities and their sacred animals, witness to continuous ritual performances in temples and at ovens in courtyards' (Gimbutas *et al.* 1989: 335). Her typological analysis was narrowed to fit these criteria, without mention of other functional interpretations. Similarly, she dismissed alternative explanations of Cycladic figures from mortuary contexts in favour of the Great Goddess (or stiff White Goddess) from a deeply rooted European tradition (1974: 158; 1992).

From the 1970s onwards Gimbutas presented arguments, with increasing fervour, to challenge a balanced and complementary view of the sexes in sacred and profane spheres (Hayden 1986; Chapman 1991). Her publications, including site reports (where one expects some attempt to discuss the data without a charged interpretation), were devoted to the Goddess and her manifestations; the gods are overlooked. At Anza 'only one [figurine] can possibly be male' (1976: 200), at Sitagroi 'only 1% can be considered as possibly portraying men' (1986: 226), at Achilleion the divine creatrix does not require male fecundity since 'her divine bisexuality stresses her absolute power' (Gimbutas *et al.* 1989: 196). In these reports every figure that is not phallic—and some that clearly are—are taken as symbols of the Goddess. This includes parallel lines, lozenges, zigzags, spirals, double axes, butterflies, pigs and pillars. Why this miscellany are self-evidently emblems of a female , much less a deity, is never explained. And indeed even the *male* may be symbolically *female:* 'although the male element is attached, these figurines remain essentially female' (1989a: 232). Gimbutas denied that phallicism was symbolic of procreation since Neolithic peoples did not understand the nature of biological conception (1974: 237).

Gimbutas was emphatic that Neolithic mythology was not polarized into male and female, due to the supremacy of the Mother. From this assumption she extrapolated, concomitantly, the role of women was not subordinate to men (Gimbutas 1974: 237; see Chapman 1991; Tringham 1991). Yet male, sexless and zoomorphic figures do exist, which makes the notion of an omnipotent Mother Goddess difficult to support. Ucko's examination of the later Knossos figurines demonstrated that androgynous examples were equal in number to the identifiable female statuettes (1968: 316; see Conkey & Tringham in press). Ucko (1968: 417) further concluded that most scholars treat male figures as exceptions, dismiss the sexless examples and regard female figurines as a singular deity without convincing explanation for their obvious variation.

The Goddess Contextualized

In addressing the archaeological context of finds at Anza, Sitagroi and Achilleion, Gimbutas interpreted partially excavated dwellings as 'house-shrines' and 'cult-places', and benches as 'altars' (1981; 1986; Gimbutas *et al.* 1989). She concluded human activities like grinding grain, baking bread, weaving and spinning were inseparable from divine participation (Gimbutas *et al.* 1989: 213–15). To Gimbutas it was 'obvious that the Goddess ruled over human, animal and plant life' (Gimbutas *et al.* 1989: 220). Perhaps these areas represented dwellings or workshops in view of associated finds like spindle whorls, a needle, awl and pottery discs? Indeed, few artefacts and features from these sites are assigned a mundane status (1981: 198–200; Gimbutas *et al.* 1989: 36–46, 213–15).

... Evidence from Anza, Selevac, Tîrpesti and Achilleion (see Gimbutas 1981; Gimbutas *et al.* 1989; Marinescu-Bîlcu 1981; Hodder 1990; Tringham 1990) indicates that figurines are found in every kind of context—refuse pits included. This would signify, as Gimbutas prefers, that the sacred is everywhere. Conversely, it could demonstrate that these figures are not sacred at all; or they may have multiple meanings which change as a figure is made, used and discarded.

Alternative Hypotheses

Recent work in Kephala (northern Greece) uncovered figurines near graves, which would indicate a possible function as territorial markers to reinforce ancestral ties in the Neolithic period (Talalay 1991: 49). Ethnographic reports from Africa over the past 200 years also suggest this kind of placement may be associated to ancestor cults. Further functions proposed include dolls, toys, tokens of identification, primitive contracts, communication or as part of birthing rituals (Talalay 1993: 40–43). Other plausible interpretations include teaching devices, tools of sorcery, magic, healing or initiation (Ehrenberg 1989: 75). Talalay proposes that clay legs from the northern Peloponnese served to symbolize social and economic bonds among communities like those of marriage contracts or identification of trading partners (1987: 161–2). These alternatives, as opposed to a universal deity, may explain the practice of discard. To assume *a priori* that there is a Goddess behind every figurine is tantamount to interpreting plastic figures of Virgin Mary and of 'Barbie' as having identical ideological significance....

Conclusion: The Goddess, Pseudo-Feminism and Future Research

Whilst the concept of gender as a structuring principle is relatively new to archaeology, many progressive and scholarly studies have emerged in the last few years (e.g. Gero & Conkey 1991; Wylie 1991; Dobres 1992a; 1992b; Bacus *et al.* 1993; Brown 1993; Conkey & Tringham in press). However, many feminists feel that the establishment of an originary myth of the basis of scientific historical reality will facilitate the restoration of women's power. It then follows that the patriarchy will be dismantled and the lost pre-patriarchal culture can be regained (Passman 1993: 187). Matriculture is seen to give feminism the legitimacy the system demands.

Contrary to this position I argue, as feminist and archaeologist, that the approaches of Gimbutas and her advocates contrast markedly to many feminists (Brown 1993: 254), especially those involved in archaeological discourse. This is not to say that Gimbutas claimed to do feminist archaeology; rather that she has been adopted as an icon within the movement, more ardently outside archaeological circles. However, some feminists do not accept her methodology, since she was so steeped within the 'establishment' epistemological framework of polar opposites, rigid gender roles, barbarian invaders and cultural stages (Fagan 1992; Brown 1993) which are now regarded as outmoded. It is unfortunate that many archaeologists interested in gender are drawn to historical fiction and emotional narratives, which either replace or accompany serious archaeological dialogues. At this juncture sound feminist scholarship needs to be divorced from methodological shortcomings, reverse sexism, conflated data and pure fantasy, since this will only impede the feminist cause and draw attention away from the positive contribution offered by gender and feminist archaeologies. Gero & Conkey (1991: 5) assert that we are now in a position to draw from and contribute to emergent theoretical developments within archaeology, particularly post-processual directions that see social and symbolic theories as central. Gender, however, cannot be separated from other archaeological considerations and become the type of speciality area Gimbutas created.

In future studies we should not expect to delineate a rigid and unitary code which holds for all contexts (Hodder 1987), but rather to identify the dimensions of meaning pertaining to particular societies and to comprehend their social locus. It may prove more informative to ask 'how did the social production of this object contribute to its meanings and uses?', 'how did these meaningful objects enhance people's understanding of their lives?' and 'what other associated activities were operative that can inform us about social context?' (Dobres 1992a: 17–18). Naturally the multiplicity of manifestations relative to their archaeological contexts must be considered, coupled with the socioeconomic concerns of their manufacturers.

To conclude, academic and popular audiences alike need to review critically the evidence for a solitary universal Mother Goddess, along with other plausible interpretations. Although the post-processualists have stressed notions of pluralism, most now advocate that not *all* pasts are equal. The gynocentric narratives discussed above reveal more about our relationship(s) with the past and certain contemporary ideologies (Conkey 1992) than how these figurines were deployed in antiquity.

The Mother Goddess metanarrative presents a possible challenge to feminist archaeologies in that solidarity can often prevent us from contesting theories presented by women which seem to espouse pro-female notions: even if the evidence would suggest otherwise. Loyalty to a misrepresented picture of the past and our human heritage by dismissing or misconstruing the archaeological record cannot be supported under the guise of any political standpoint. Needless to say, many men feel that they are not in a position to engage in these issues and that only other women can do so. This exclusivity is not conducive to scholarly development; neither is failing to counter claims of a gendered superiority supported by 'scientific' archaeology that ultimately has filtered into mainstream society. An engendered re-balancing of the scales is long overdue and critically important to the trajectory of the discipline. However, emphasis on one sex to the exclusion of the other is not only detrimental to serious gender/feminist studies, but threatens the interpretative integrity of archaeology.

References

ANTHONY, D. W. In press. Nazi and ecofeminist prehistories: ideology and empiricism in Indo-European archaeology, in P. Kohl & C. Fawcett (ed.), *Nationalism, politics and the practice of archaeology*: 1–32. Cambridge: Cambridge University Press.

BACUS, E.A. *et al.* 1993. *A gendered past: a critical review of gender in archaeology.* Ann Arbor (MI): University of Michigan Press.

BROWN, S. 1993. Feminist research in archaeology. What does it mean? Why is it taking so long?, in Rabinowitz & Richlin (ed.): 238–71.

CHAPMAN, J. 1991. The creation of social arenas in the Neolithic and copper age of SE Europe: the case of Varna, in P. Garwood *et al* (ed.). *Sacred and profane*: 152–71. Oxford: Oxford University Committee for Archaeology, Monograph 32.

— 1994. Destruction of a common heritage: the archaeology of war in Croatia. Bosnia and Hercegovina, *Antiquity* 68: 120–26.

CHILDE, V. G. 1951. *Social evolution.* London: Watts.

CONKEY, M. W. 1992. Mobilising ideologies: the archaeologics of Paleolithic 'art'. Paper delivered to the American Anthropological Association, San Francisco.

CONKEY, M. W. & R. E. TRINGHAM. In press. Archaeology and the Goddess: exploring the contours of feminist archaeology, in A. Stewart & D. Stanton (ed.), *Feminism in the academy: rethinking the disciplines.* Ann Arbor (MI): University of Michigan Press.

DAVIS, W. 1992. *Masking the blow: the scene of representation in late prehistoric Egyptian art.* Berkeley (CA): University of California Press.

DEMOULE, J.-P. & C. PERLES. 1993. The Greek Neolithic: a new review, *Journal of World Prehistory* 7(4): 355–416.

DOBRES, M.-A. 1992a. Re-presentations of Palaeolithic visual imagery: simulacra and their alternatives, *Kroeber Anthroplogical Society Papers* 73–4: 1–25.

EHRENBERG, M. 1989. *Women in prehistory.* London: British Museum Publications.

EISLER, R. 1987. *The chalice and the blade: our history, our future.* San Francisco (CA): Harper Row.

FAGAN, B. M. 1992. A sexist view of prehistory, *Archaeology* 45(2): 14–16, 18, 66.

FRYMER-KENSKY, T. 1992. *In the wake of the goddess: women, culture and the biblical transformation of pagan myth.* New York (NY): Ballantine.

GERO, J. M. & M. W. CONKEY. 1991. Tensions, pluralities and engendering archaeology: an introduction to women and prehistory, in Gero & Conkey (ed.): 2–29.

GERO, J. M. & M. W. CONKEY (ed.). 1991. *Engendering archaeology: women and prehistory.* Oxford: Basil Blackwell.

GILL, D. W. J. & C. CHIPPINDALE. 1993. Material and intellectual consequences of esteem for Cycladic figures, *American Journal of Archaeology* 97: 601–59.

GIMBUTAS, M. 1965. *The Bronze Age cultures in central and eastern Europe.* The Hague: Mouton.

— 1970. Proto-Indo-European culture: the Kurgan culture during the 5th, 4th and 3rd millennium BC in G. Cardona *et al.* (ed.), *Indo-European and Indo-Europeans*: 155–97. Philadelphia (PA): University of Pennsylvania Press.

— 1971a. *The Slavs.* London: Thames & Hudson.

— 1971b (ed). *Neolithic Macedonia: as reflected by excavations at Anza, southeast Yugoslavia.* Los Angeles (CA): UCLA Institute of Archaeology. Monumenta Archaeologica 1.

— 1973. The beginning of the Bronze Age in Europe and the Indo-Europeans— 3500–2500 BC, *Journal of Indo-European Studies* 1(2): 163–214.

— 1974. *Gods and goddesses of old Europe.* London: Thames & Hudson.

— 1981. Vulvas, breasts and buttocks of the Goddess Creatress: commentary on the origins of art, in G. Buccellati & C. Speroni (ed.), *The shape of the past. Studies in honour of Franklin D. Murphy:* 19–40. Los Angeles (CA): UCLA Institute of Archaeology.

— 1986. Mythical imagery of Sitagroi society, in Renfrew *et al.* (ed.): 225–301.

—— 1989a. *The language of the Goddess: unearthing hidden symbols of western civilisation*. London: Thames and Hudson.

—— 1989b. Women and culture in Goddess-oriented Old Europe, in J. Plaskow & C. C. Christ (ed.), *Weaving the visions*: 63–71. San Francisco (CA): Harpers.

—— 1991. *The civilization of the Goddess: the world of Old Europe*. San Francisco (CA): Harpers.

—— 1992. *The age of the Goddess: ancient roots of the emerging feminine consciousness*. Boulder (CO): Sounds True Recordings. Audio tape #A192.

GIMBUTAS, M., S. WINN & D. SHIMABUKU. 1989. *Achilleion: a Neolithic settlement in Thessaly, Greece 6400–5600 BC*. Los Angeles (CA): UCLA Institute of Archaeology.

HALLETT, J. P. 1993. Feminist theory, historical periods, literary canons, and the study of Greco-Roman antiquity, in Rabinowitz & Richlin (ed.): 44–72.

HAYDEN, B. 1986. Old Europe: sacred matriarchy or complimentary opposition in A. Bonanno (ed.), *Archaeology and fertility cult in the Mediterranean*: 17–41. Amsterdam: B. R. Grunner.

HAYS, K. A. 1993. When is a symbol archaeologically meaningful?: meaning, function and prehistoric visual arts, in N. Yoffee and S. Sherratt (ed.), *Archaeological theory: who sets the agenda?*: 81–92. Cambridge: Cambridge University Press.

HODDER, I. R. 1987. Contextual archaeology: an interpretation of Çatal Hüyük and a discussion of the origins of agriculture. *University of London Institute of Archaeology Bulletin* 24: 43–56.

—— 1990. *The domestication of Europe: structure and contingency in Neolithic societies*. Oxford: Basil Blackwell.

HUMPHREYS, S. C. 1983. *The family, women and death: comparative studies*. London: Routledge & Kegan Paul.

MCPHERRON, A. 1991. Review of Gimbutas *et al.* (1989), *American Antiquity* 56(3): 567–8.

MALLORY, J. P. 1989. *In search of the Indo-Europeans*. London: Thames & Hudson.

MALONE, C., A. BONANNO, T. GOULDER, S. STODDART & D. TRUMP. 1993. The death cults of prehistoric Malta. *Scientific American* (December): 76–83.

MARINESCU-BILCU. 1981. *Tirpesti: from prehistory to history in eastern Romania*. Oxford: British Archaeological Reports. International series 107.

MILOJKOVIC, J. 1990. The anthropomorphic and zoomorphic figurines, in Tringham & Krstic (ed.): 397–436.

MURRAY, J. 1970. *The first European agriculture, a study of the osteological and botanical evidence until 2000 BC*. Edinburgh: Edinburgh University Press.

ORENSTEIN, G. F. 1990. *The reflowering of the Goddess*. New York (NY): Pergamon Press.

PAVLOVIC, M. 1990. The aesthetics of Neolithic figurines, in *Vinca and its world: international symposium. The Danubian region from 6000 to 3000 BC. Belgrade, Smederevska Palanka, October 1988*: 33–4. Belgrade: Academy of Arts and Sciences.

PASSMAN, T. 1993. Out of the closet and into the field: matriculture, lesbian perspective and feminist classics, in Rabinowitz & Richlin (ed.): 181–208.

POGOZHEVA, A. P. 1983. *Antropomorfnaya plastika Tripol'ya*. Novosibirsk: Akademiia Nauk, Sibirskoe Otdelenie.

RENFREW, C. 1987. *Archaeology and language: the puzzle of Indo-European origins*. London: Jonathan Cape.

ROBINS, G. 1993. *Women in ancient Egypt*. London: British Museum Press.

RUNNELS, C. 1990. Review of Gimbutas *et al.* (1989), *Journal of Field Archaeology* 17: 341–5.

SHANKS, M. & C. Tilley. 1987. *Re-constructing archaeology: theory and practice*. Cambridge: Cambridge University Press.

SPRETNAK, C. 1992. *Lost goddesses of early Greece*. Boston (MA): Beacon Press.

STARHAWK. 1982. *Dreaming the dark: magic, sex and politics*. Boston (MA): Beacon Press.

TALALAY, L. E. 1991. Body imagery of the ancient Aegean. *Archaeology* 44(4): 46–9.

—— 1993. *Dolls, deities and devices. Neolithic figurines from Franthchi cave, Greece.* Bloomington (IN): Indiana University Press. Excavations at Franchthi Cave, Greece 9.

TRINGHAM, R. E. 1991. Households with faces: the challenge of gender in prehistoric architectural remains, in Gero & Conkey (ed.): 93–131.

—— 1993. Review of Gimbutas (1991). *American Anthropologist* 95: 196–7.

TRINGHAM, R. E. & D. KRSTIC (ed.). 1990. *Selevac: a Neolithic village in Yugoslavia.* Los Angeles (CA): UCLA Institute of Archaeology Monumenta Archaeologica 15.

UCKO, P. J. 1968. *Anthropomorphic figures of predynastic Egypt and Neolithic Crete with comparative material from the prehistoric Near East and Mainland Greece.* London: Andrew Szmidla.

VAN LEUVEN, J. 1993. Review of Gimbutas (1991). *Journal of Prehistoric Religion 7*: 83–4.

WALL, S. M., J. H. MUSGRAVE & P. M. WARREN. 1986. Human bones from a late Minoan 1b house at Knossos. *Annual of the British School at Athens* 81: 333–88.

WYLIE, M. A. 1991. Gender theory and the archaeological record: why is there no archaeology of gender?, in Gero & Conkey (ed.): 31–47.

POSTSCRIPT

Was There a Goddess Cult in Prehistoric Europe?

O ver the past 20 years a popular women's movement, the "Goddess Move-ment," has grown up, especially in the United States, around the idea that the earliest organized religion was based on worship of a supreme Goddess. This is largely a reaction against the perceived androcentrism and antifemale bias of Christianity, Judaism, Islam, and other world religions and of the civilizations they underpin. Proponents believe that by reviving this religion, they can undo the cultural and psychological harm inflicted on women (and men) by our long history of patriarchal religions and cultures.

Many feminist archaeologists are ambivalent toward the Goddess Move-ment and Gimbutas's contribution to it. They believe, on the one hand, that Gimbutas's work helps to correct the imbalance in conventional presentations of human prehistory, in which women are usually portrayed as minor bit play-ers. But they are concerned about the quality of her methodology and theories. Feminist archaeologists also worry that Gimbutas's "old-fashioned" ideas, such as the notion of universal stages of cultural evolution and her static view of gender relations, do not contribute to an archaeology in which feminist views are an integral part.

For background on the Goddess Movement's roots in European thought, see Ronald Hutton's "The Neolithic Great Goddess: A Study in Modern Tradi-tion," *Antiquity* (vol. 71, 1997). Also see Jane Ellen Harrison's *Prolegomena to the Study of Greek Religion* (Cambridge University Press, 1903).

For elaboration of Gimbutas's views, see her books *The Language of the Goddess* (Harper & Row, 1989), *The Civilization of the Goddess* (Harper & Row, 1991), and *The Living Goddesses* (University of California Press, 1999).

For critiques of the Goddess theory see Peter Ucko's works: his article "The Interpretation of Prehistoric Anthropomorphic Figurines," *Journal of the Royal Anthropological Institute* (vol. 92, 1962) and his monograph *Anthropomor-phic Figurines of Predynastic Egypt and Neolithic Crete With Comparative Material From the Prehistoric Near East and Mainland Greece* (Royal Anthropological Insti-tute, 1968). Also see Anne Baring and Jules Cashford's *The Myth of the Goddess* (Viking Press, 1991) and Margaret Conkey and Ruth Tringham's "Archaeology and the Goddess: Exploring the Contours of Feminist Archaeology," in D. C. Stanton and A. J. Stewart, eds., *Feminisms in the Academy* (University of Michi-gan Press, 1995). Conkey and Tringham's article also gives an excellent overview of the controversy and discussion of its significance for feminist archaeology.

ISSUE 6

Were Environmental Factors Responsible for the Mayan Collapse?

YES: Richard E. W. Adams, from *Prehistoric Mesoamerica*, rev. ed. (University of Oklahoma Press, 1991)

NO: George L. Cowgill, from "Teotihuacan, Internal Militaristic Competition, and the Fall of the Classic Maya," in Norman Hammond and Gordon R. Willey, eds., *Maya Archaeology and Ethnohistory* (University of Texas Press, 1979)

ISSUE SUMMARY

YES: Archaeologist Richard E. W. Adams argues that while military factors must have played some role in the collapse of the Classic Maya states, a combination of internal factors combined with environmental pressures were more significant.

NO: Archaeologist George L. Cowgill agrees that no single factor was responsible for the demise of the Classic Maya civilization, but he contends that military expansion was far more significant than scholars had previously thought.

The discovery of vast ancient ruins in the tropical rainforests of lowland southern Mexico and northern Central America in the nineteenth century posed a major question for archaeologists and historians. Spanish explorers discovered major cities and ceremonial centers complete with pyramids that were reminiscent of complexes in ancient Egypt. The explorers realized that these cities were ancestral to the Maya societies they encountered. What caused the disappearance of this pre-Hispanic civilization that had a complex system of hieroglyphic writing, an accurate calendar, elaborate sculpture, and major ceremonial complexes?

Over the past century, archaeologists, linguists, and a variety of other researchers have worked with national and regional governments in Mexico, Guatemala, Belize, and Honduras to excavate and interpret these early sites. Using radiocarbon and other dating methods, researchers have established certain facts: (1) beginning around the fourth century, the preclassic Maya began to form a series of small states, each centered around regional centers; (2) by about 650 C.E. these states began to flourish, with the Maya building enormous architectural complexes and erecting stone monuments to their elites; and (3) soon after 900 C.E. all of the centers in the southern lowlands seem to have been abandoned although cities in the northern lowlands flourished for several more centuries.

Although it is now clear to most researchers that the Maya collapse represents a complex combination of factors, two major theories have emerged. Richard E. W. Adams argues that the Maya collapse could only have occurred because of a complex interplay of internal factors, culminating in an ecological collapse on a regional scale. He sees the seventh- and eighth-century architectural developments as evidence of the flourishing of Classic Maya civilization. But he argues that this development went too far too fast to sustain the large populations that the grand building programs of the elite required. He contends that crop failures, epidemics, and other environmental factors led to a decline in population from 12 million to fewer than 2 million. Once individual states stopped using their ceremonial centers, a thick, thorny secondary growth jungle covered the sites, making them much more difficult to cultivate. As a result, the Maya abandoned these sites for land that was much easier to cultivate.

While George L. Cowgill accepts that environmental factors played a role in the decline and ultimate collapse of the Classic Maya states, he argues that these factors would probably not have had such a profound impact had the various polities not been so heavily engaged in military activity. He contends that the eighth-century Maya "florescence" was not a time of Maya prosperity, but instead a period of impending crisis. To understand conditions in the Maya lowlands, Cowgill compares the prehistoric pattern found in the central Mexican highland site of Teotihuacan, which had a strong central authority for many centuries, with the Classic Maya sites. The Maya had many competing local elites. His view is that smaller polities were fundamentally unstable over the long term. He argues that the Maya political development during the preclassic period could survive with many regional elites and no centralized authority. However, once these small city-states grew in population and developed elaborate ritual centers, local leaders sought to become a central authority by defeating their smaller neighbors. Military conflict during the Classic Maya period turned out to be an unsuccessful attempt to meld a single centralized state from many competing centers. As local populations were drawn into local wars, it was only a matter of time before poor crop yields, epidemics, or other regional environmental problems brought an end to these Maya centers.

The following selections suggest a number of questions for consideration. Is there evidence that the Classic Maya were warlike and participated in conflicts with neighboring Maya groups? Was the local elite so preoccupied with exotic, high-status goods that they were willing to compete with neighbors to get these objects? Did Classic Maya religion encourage local elites to ignore the impending crises that ultimately befell them? Would environmental degradation accompanied by short-term environmental changes have been sufficient to bring about the nearly complete collapse of this civilization?

Richard E. W. Adams  **YES**

Transformations

The Classic Maya Collapse

According to what we now know, Maya civilization began to reach a series of
regional peaks about A.D. 650. By A.D. 830, there is evidence of disintegration
of the old patterns, and by A.D. 900, all of the southern lowland centers had
collapsed. An understanding of the Maya apocalypse must be based in large part
on an understanding of the nature of Maya civilization. During the Terminal
Classic period, A.D. 750 to 900, cultural patterns of the lowlands can be briefly
characterized as follows. Demographically, a high peak had been reached at
least as early as A.D. 600 and perhaps earlier. This population density and size in
turn led to intensive forms of agriculture and the establishment of permanent
farmsteads in the countryside. Hills were terraced, swamps were drained and
modified, water impoundments were made by the hundreds, and land became
so scarce that walls of rock were built both as boundaries and simply as the
results of field clearance. These masses of people were also highly organized
for political purposes into region-state units, which fluctuated in size. These
states were more than simple aggregations of cities and were characterized by
hierarchical and other complex relationships among them.

Society was organized on an increasingly aristocratic principle by A.D.
650. Dynasties and royal lineages were at the top of the various Maya states and
commanded most of the resources of Maya economic life. Most of the large
architecture of the cities was for their use. Groups of craft specialists and civil
servants supported the elite, with the mass of the population engaged in either
part-time or full-time farming. Trade was well organized among and within the
states. Military competition was present but was controlled by the fact that it
had become mainly an elite-class and prestige activity which did not greatly
disturb the economic basis of life. Thus, Maya culture at the ninth century
A.D. seems to have been well-ordered, adjusted, and definitely a success. Yet a
devastating catastrophe brought it down.

Characteristics of the Collapse

It sometimes seems that the accumulation of weighty theoretical formulations
purporting to explain the collapse of Maya civilization will eventually, instead,

cause the collapse of Maya archaeology. A refreshingly skeptical and clear-sighted book by John Lowe reviews the major theories and tests them as well. We will not be as thorough in the following section but, it is to be hoped, just as convincing. A brief characterization of the collapse includes the following features:

1. It occurred over a relatively short period of time: 75 to 150 years.
2. During it the elite-class culture failed, as reflected in the abandonment of palaces and temples and the cessation of manufacture of luxury goods and erection of stelae.
3. Also during the period there was a rapid and nearly complete depopulation of the countryside and the urban centers.
4. The geographical focus of the first collapse was in the oldest and most developed zones, the southern lowlands and the intermediate area. The northern plains and Puuc areas survived for a while longer.

In other words, the Maya collapse was a demographic, cultural, and social catastrophe in which elite and commoner went down together. Drawing on all available information about the ancient Maya and comparable situations, the 1970 Santa Fe Conference developed a comprehensive explanation of the collapse. This explanation depends on the relatively new picture of the Maya summarized above. That is, we must discard any notion of the Maya as the "noble savage" living in harmony with nature. Certainly, the Maya lived more in tune with nature than do modern industrial peoples, but probably not much more so than did our nineteenth-century pioneer ancestors. As we shall see, some dissonance with nature was at least partly responsible for its failure. More than this, however, data have been further developed since the conference which strengthen some assumptions and weaken others. Therefore, the explanation which follows is a modified version of that which appears in the report of the Santa Fe Conference.

Stresses

Maya society had a number of built-in stresses, many of which had to do with high populations in the central and southern areas. Turner's and other studies indicate that from about A.D. 600 to 900 there were about 168 people per square kilometer (435 per square mile) in the Río Bec zone. The intensive agricultural constructions associated with this population density are also found farther south, within 30 kilometers (19 miles) of Tikal. They are also to be found to the east in the Belize Valley, and there are indications elsewhere to the south that high populations were present. According to Saul's studies of Maya bones from the period, the population carried a heavy load of endemic disease, including malaria, yellow fever, syphilis, and Chagas's disease, the latter a chronic infection which leads to cardiac insufficiency in young adulthood. Chronic malnutrition is also indicated by Saul's and Steele's studies. Taken altogether, these factors indicate the precarious status of health even for the elite. Average lifespan in the southern lowlands was about thirty-nine years. Infant mortality was high; perhaps as many as 78 percent of Maya children never reached the age of twenty. Endemic disease can go epidemic with just a rise in malnutrition. In other words, the Maya populace carried within itself a biological time bomb which needed only a triggering event such as a crop failure to go off.

With population pressing the limits of subsistence, management of land and other resources was a problem, and one which would have fallen mainly on the elite. If food were to be imported, or if marginal lands were to be brought into cultivation, by extensive drainage projects, for example, then the elite had to arrange for it to be done. There were certain disadvantages to this arrangement. Aristocratic or inherited leadership of any kind is a poor means to approach matters that require rational decisions. One need only consider the disastrous manner in which seventeenth-century European armies were mishandled by officers whose major qualifications were their lineages. There is a kind of built-in variation of the Peter Principle in such leadership: one is born to his level of incompetence. Maya aristocracy apparently was no better equipped to handle the complex problems of increasing populations than were European aristocrats. There were no doubt capable and brilliant nobles, but there was apparently no way in which talent could quickly be taken to the top of society from its lower ranks. Lowe's model of the collapse of Maya civilization emphasizes the management-administrative aspects of the problem and essentially considers the collapse as an administrative breakdown.

There are also signs in the Terminal Classic period of a widening social gulf between elite and commoners. At the same time, problems were increasing in frequency and severity. The elite class increased in size and made greater demands on the rest of Maya society for its support. This created further tensions. Intensive agriculture led to greater crop yields, but also put Maya food production increasingly at hostage to the vagaries of weather, crop disease, insects, birds, and other hazards. Marginal and complex cultivation systems require large investments of time and labor and necessitate that things go right more often than not. A run of bad weather or a long-term shift in climate might trigger a food crisis. Recent work on tree rings and weather history from other sources indicates that a Mesoamerica-wide drought may have begun about A.D. 850. In addition, there are periodic outbreaks of locusts in the Maya Lowlands.

These stresses were pan–Maya and occurred to a greater or lesser degree in every region. No matter whether one opts for the city-state or the regional state model, competition over scarce resources among the political units of the Maya resulted from these stressful situations. The large southern center of Seibal was apparently taken by a northern Maya elite group about A.D. 830. Evidence is now in hand of military intrusions from north to south at Rio Azul, at the Belize sites of Nohmul, Colha, and Barton Ramie, and at Quirigua in the Motagua Valley. At least at Rio Azul and Colha a period of trade preceded the raids, presaging the later Aztec *pochteca* pattern. The patterns and nature of the intrusions indicate that the raids were probably from the Puuc zone and that a part of the motivation, as suggested by Cowgill, was to capture populations. Warfare increased markedly along the Usumacinta River during the ninth century A.D., according to hieroglyphic texts and carved pictures from that area.

There are also hints that the nature of Maya warfare may have changed during this last period. A lintel from Piedras Negras appears to show numerous soldiers in standard uniforms kneeling in ranks before an officer. In other words, organized violence may have come to involve many more people and much more effort and therefore may have become much more disruptive. Certainly competition over scarce resources would have led to an increasingly unstable situation. Further, the resultant disorganization would have led to vulnerability to outside military intervention, and that seems to have been the case as well.

There were also external pressures on the Maya. Some were intangible and in the form of new ideas about the nature of human society as well as new ideologies from the Gulf Coast and Central Mexico. The northern Maya elites seem to have absorbed a number of these new ideas. For example, they included the depiction of Mexican Gulf Coast deities on their stelae as well as some Mexican-style hieroglyphs. Altar de Sacrificios was invaded by still another foreign group from the Gulf Coast about A.D. 910. These people may have been either a truly Mexican Gulf Coast group or Chontal Maya, who were non-Classic in their culture.

A progressive pattern of abandonment and disaster in the western lowlands is suggestive. Palenque, on the southwestern edges of the lowlands, was one of the first major centers to go under; it was abandoned about A.D. 810. The major Usumacinta cities of Piedras Negras and Yaxchilan (Bird-Jaguar's City) were the next to go. They put up their last monuments about A.D. 825. Finally, it was Altar de Sacrificios's turn about A.D. 910. Clearly, there was a progressive disintegration from west to east, and it seems likely that it was caused by pressures from militaristic non–Maya groups. These peoples, in turn, were probably being jostled in the competitive situation set up after the fall of Teotihuacan and may have been pushed ahead of peoples such as the Toltecs and their allies. Perhaps the Epi-Classic states discussed above were involved, as well as some mercenary groups. In any case, it appears certain that these groups were opportunists. They came into an area already disorganized and disturbed and were not the triggering mechanism for the catastrophe but part of the following process.

At any one Maya city or in any one region, the "mix" of circumstances was probably unique. At Piedras Negras there is evidence that the elite may have been violently overthrown from within. Faces of rulers on that site's stelae are smashed, and there are other signs of violence. Invasion finished off Altar de Sacrificios. Rio Azul was overrun by Maya groups from the north, perhaps including Toltec allies, as were a number of Maya centers along the Belize coast and down to Quirigua. At other centers, such as the regional capital of Tikal, the elite were apparently abandoned to their fate. Without the supporting populations, remnants of the Maya upper classes lingered on after the catastrophe. At Colha and Seibal, northern Maya acting as new elites attempted to continue the southern economic and political systems, but they abandoned these attempts after a relatively short time. The general demographic catastrophe and disruption of the agricultural systems were apparently too great to cope with.

In short, ecological abuse, disease, mismanagement, overpopulation, militarism, famines, epidemics, and bad weather overtook the Maya in various combinations. But several questions remain. What led to the high levels of populations which were the basis of much of the disaster?

The Maya were much more loosely organized politically during the Late Formative than during the Classic period. The episodes of interstate competition and of Teotihuacan's intervention seem to have led them to try new, more centralized political arrangements. These seem to have worked well for a time, in the case of the Early Classic expansion of Tikal. After the suggested civil wars of the sixth century there seems to have been a renewed and still stronger development of centralized states, which were probably monarchical.

Using general historical and anthropological experience, Demitri Shimkin observed that village-level societies approach population control very differently than do state-level societies. Relatively independent villages are oriented plainly and simply toward survival. There are many traditional ways of population control, female infanticide being a favorite practiced widely even in eighteenth-century England. Use of herbal abortion, late marriage, ritual ascetisicism, and other means keep population within bounds for a village. A state-level society, on the other hand, is likely to encourage population growth for the benefit of the directing elite. The more manpower to manipulate, the better. In the case of the Maya, we have noted a certain megalomania in their huge Late Classic buildings. Unfinished large construction projects at Tikal and Uaxactun were overtaken by the collapse. Such efforts required immense manpower reserves and a simultaneous disregard for the welfare of that workforce. The Maya appear to have shifted gears into a more sophisticated and ultimately maladaptive state organization.

Another question to be considered is, Why did the Maya not adjust to cope with the crises? The answer may lie in the nature of religiously sanctioned aristocracies. Given a crop failure, a Maya leadership group might have attempted to propitiate the ancestors and gods with more ritual and more monuments. This response would have exacerbated the crisis by taking manpower out of food production. Inappropriate responses of this sort could easily have been made, given the ideology and worldview that the Maya seem to have held. On the other hand, if the crisis were a long-term drought, with populations dangerously high and predatory warfare disrupting matters even more, perhaps any response would have been ineffectual.

The rapid biological destruction of the Maya is an important aspect of the collapse. From a guessed-at high of 12 million, the population was reduced within 150 years to an estimated remnant of about 1.8 million. The disease load and the stress of malnutritional factors indicate that a steady diminishment of Maya population probably started by A.D. 830 and rapidly reached a point of no recovery. An average increase of 10 to 15 percent in the annual mortality rate will statistically reduce 12 million to 1.8 million in 75 years. Obviously there was not anything like a steady decline, but the smoothed-out average over the period had to have been something of that order, or perhaps the decline began earlier, at A.D. 750, when Maya civilization reached its peak.

The disruptive nature of population declines can be easily understood if one considers the usual effects of epidemics. In such catastrophic outbreaks of disease, those first and most fatally affected are the young and the old. Even if the main working population survives relatively untouched, the social loss is only postponed. The old take with them much of the accumulated experience and knowledge needed to meet future crises. The young will not be there to mature and replace the adult working population, and a severe manpower shortage will result within fifteen to twenty years. Needless to say, much more work on population estimates and studies of the bones and the general health environment of the ancient Maya needs to be done to produce a really convincing statement on this aspect of the collapse.

A last, although not by any means final, question concerns the failure to recover. This feature may involve climatic factors. If shifts of rainfall belts were responsible for triggering the collapse, then the answer might be the persistence of drought conditions until there were too few people left to sustain the Classic cultural systems. As now seems probable, the Maya were confronted with the situation of having overcultivated their soils and having lost too much surface water. Temporary abandonment of fields would have led to their being rapidly overrun by thick, thorny, second-growth jungle, which is harder to clear than primary forest. Thus, a diminished population may have been faced with the problem of clearing heavily overgrown, worn-out soils, of which vast amounts were needed to sustain even small populations. Second-growth forest springs up overnight and is even today a major problem in maintaining archaeological sites for tourists.

Another possible answer to the question of recovery is that the Maya may have been loathe to attempt the sort of brilliant effort that had ultimately broken them. Just as they preferred to revert to swidden agriculture rather than maintain intensive techniques, they probably found it a relief to live on a village level instead of in their former splendid but stressful state of existence.

The above is an integrated model of the Maya collapse. It explains all the features of the collapse and all the data now in hand, but it is not proved by any means, and in some respects is more of a guide to future research than a firm explanation. If the model is more or less correct, however, it should be largely confirmed within the next ten years of research. Indeed, this process of confirmation has already begun. The 1970 conference which developed the model could explain certain features of the archaeological record only by assuming much higher levels of ancient population than were otherwise plausible at the time. The 1973 Rio Bec work of Turner and Eaton turned up a vast amount of data which indicate that higher levels of ancient populations indeed had been present. Recent work at Colha and Rio Azul has indicated the importance of militarism in the process. All of these findings lend credibility to the model.

Delayed Collapse in the North

The vast and very densely distributed centers of the Puuc area survived for a time. These Puuc cities, possibly a regional state with a capital at Uxmal, appear to have turned into predators on the southern cities. As noted before, part of the motivation may have been for the capture and enslavement of southern populations. Even so, it seems that large centers such as Uxmal, Kabah, Sayil, and Labna lasted only a century longer than the southern cities. Northern Maya chronology is much more disputed than that in the south, but it now seems likely that outsiders, including Toltec, were in Yucatan by A.D. 900 and perhaps earlier, and there are clear indications that Uxmal was absorbing Mexican ideas much earlier. Certain motifs, such as eagles or vultures, appear on Puuc building facades late in the Classic period.

We are now faced with at least three possible explanations of the Puuc collapse: they may have succumbed to the same combination of factors that brought down the southern Maya centers; the Toltec may have conquered them; or a combination of these factors may have been at work. At this time, it appears that the northern florescence was partly at the expense of the southern area.... [E]vidence for Toltec conquest now appears even stronger, and this is presently the favored explanation for the Puuc collapse.

Chichen Itza, in north central Yucatan, is a center which was culturally allied with the Puuc cities in architecture and probably politically as well. Puuc centers have been found even in the far northeast of the peninsula. At Chichen Itza, Puuc architecture is overlaid and succeeded by Toltec architecture. Un-mapped defensive walls surround both Chichen and Uxmal. The data available now make it likely that the Toltec and other groups may have appeared in Yucatan by A.D. 800 and thereafter, perhaps brought in as mercenaries, as so often happened later in Maya history. In whatever capacity they arrived, they appear to have established themselves at Chichen Itza by A.D. 950 as the controlling power. As has happened in history elsewhere, the mercenaries became the controlling forces. Toltec raids, battles, and sieges, combined with the internal weaknesses of Classic Maya culture and perhaps with changing environmental factors, brought about a swift collapse in the Puuc.

The aftermath of the collapse was also devastating. Most of the southern Maya Lowlands have not been repopulated until the last fifty years. Eleven hundred years of abandonment have rejuvenated the soils, the forests, and their resources, but modern man is now making inroads on them. Kekchi Maya Indians have been migrating into the lowlands from the northern Guatemalan highlands as pioneer farmers for the past century, and the Mexican government has colonized the Yucatan, Campeche, and Quintana Roo area with dissatisfied agriculturists from overpopulated highland areas. The forests are being logged and cut down. Agricultural colonies have failed in both Guatemala and Mexico, and some zones are already abandoned. In other areas, the inhabitants have turned to marijuana cultivation. Vast areas have been reduced to low scrub jungle, and large amounts of land are now being converted to intensive agriculture. One looks at the modern scene and wonders. Fortunately, in 1988 a movement began to set aside the remnants of the once immense monsoon forests, and it may be that a series of protected zones in the form of contiguous national parks will soon be in existence in Guatamala, Mexico, and Belize.

NO

George L. Cowgill

Teotihuacan, Internal Militaristic Competition, and the Fall of the Classic Maya

In very broad terms, the Teotihuacan civilization, centered in the Mexican Highlands, and the Classic civilization of the Southern Maya Lowlands exhibit a similar developmental trajectory. That is, both enjoyed a period of development, flourished for a time, and then collapsed. But as soon as one looks beyond these gross generalities, the evidence from each region shows striking differences in the pace and timing of events. These differences are of interest in their own right, and one of my objectives is to call attention to them. In addition, however, they help to direct our attention to some of the distinctive features of the Maya trajectory which are relevant for understanding the functioning of Late Classic Maya society and for explaining its collapse. My main concern is to point out difficulties in some recently proposed explanations . . . and to suggest that escalating internal warfare may have been more a cause than a consequence of serious trouble for the Maya. I do not suggest warfare as a mono-causal explanation for the Maya collapse, but I do think it may have been an important contributing factor, and old evidence should be re-examined and new evidence sought with this possibility in mind.

Emphasis on Maya warfare is part of a widespread recognition that the Maya were not the gentle pacifists that some archaeologists would have them be. But there is a difference between sporadic raiding, with occasional enslavement or sacrifice or captives, and what David Webster calls *militarism*: institutionalized warfare intended for territorial aggrandizement and acquisition of other capital resources, with military decisions part of the conscious political policy of small elite, semiprofessional warriors, and lethal combat on a large scale. Webster and I both argue that the Late Classic Maya may have become militaristic in this sense, but we differ about the probable dynamics and consequences of Maya militarism.

Although it is clear that there were important contacts between the Highlands and the Southern Maya Lowlands, I should stress that I am *not* arguing that either Teotihuacan intervention or the withdrawal of Teotihuacan contacts played a decisive role in the Maya collapse. Direct or indirect contacts with

From George L. Cowgill, "Teotihuacan, Internal Militaristic Competition, and the Fall of the Classic Maya," in Norman Hammond and Gordon R. Willey, eds., *Maya Archaeology and Ethnohistory* (University of Texas Press, 1979). Copyright © 1979 by University of Texas Press. Reprinted by permission. References omitted.

Teotihuacan are important and extremely interesting, but I doubt if they explain much about either the rise or the fall of the Lowland Maya. In any case, my use of the Teotihuacan data here is purely as a contrastive example.

It is often assumed that Teotihuacan developed rather steadily up to a distinct peak somewhere around A.D. 500 to 600, after which it soon began a fairly rapid decline.... [L]argely through the data obtained by the comprehensive surface survey and limited test excavations completed by the Teotihuacan Mapping Project, under the direction of René Millon, evidence for a very different pattern has emerged....

Briefly, it appears that the city of Teotihuacan enjoyed an early surge of extremely rapid growth, followed by a four-to-five-century "plateau" during which growth was very much slower or may even have ceased altogether. Then, probably not before the eighth century A.D., the city collapsed, apparently rather rapidly. This pattern is most clearly suggested by the dates of major monumental construction in the city, but it is also suggested by the demographic implications of quantities and areal spreads of ceramics of various periods, both in the city itself and in all parts of the Basin of Mexico which have been systematically surveyed. Further support comes from data on Teotihuacan obsidian industry.

In contrast, the Maya site of Tikal was settled at least as early as Teotihuacan but developed more irregularly to a modest Late Preclassic climax, followed apparently by something of a pause. There seems to have been a second peak in Early Classic times, and then a distinct recession for a century or so. Then there was a relatively brief burst of glory in the seventh and eighth centuries, immediately followed by rapid decline and very drastic population loss. Tikal population may have been relatively stable from about A.D. 550 until after A.D. 800, or it may have shot up rapidly during the 600's to a short-lived maximum in the 700's. In either case, however, it seems clear that the Late Classic population of Tikal was larger than that at any previous time. Other major sites in the Southern Maya Lowlands had rather different trajectories, but they also generally peaked during the Late Classic and collapsed during the ninth or tenth centuries.

There are also striking contrasts in spatial patterns. The early growth of Teotihuacan is concomitant with rapid and marked decline in the number and size of other settlements in the Basin of Mexico. Teotihuacan quickly achieved, and for several centuries maintained, a size probably twenty or more times larger than any other known Basin of Mexico settlement. Even Cholula, in the Valley of Puebla some ninety kilometers away, does not seem to have covered more than a sixth of the area of Teotihuacan, and other settlements in the Tlaxcala–Northern Puebla area were much smaller. In the Southern Maya Lowlands there were other major centers comparable in size to Tikal, and below these there was a hierarchy of other sites ranging from fairly large secondary centers to small hamlets and individual households. (In contrast to Marcus, Hammond argues that present evidence is insufficient for assigning specific sites to specific hierarchical levels, although hierarchies probably existed. The very fact of the controversy points up the contrast with Teotihuacan, where there is no dispute at all about its primacy in the settlement hierarchy.) There is no suggestion that Tikal or other major centers ever drew people away from other sites or monopolized power to anywhere near the extent that Teotihuacan did in central Mexico. . . .

Implications of the Teotihuacan Evidence

Several implications of the Teotihuacan pattern suggest themselves. The long duration of Teotihuacan seems unreasonable unless economic and political power were quite strong and quite effectively centralized in the city, and much other evidence also suggest this. In contrast, both the more or less concomitant development of many Lowland Maya centers and the dynastic evidence so far gleaned from inscriptions indicate that no single Southern Lowland Maya center ever gained long-term firm political or economic control of any very large region, although there is plenty of evidence for brief domination of one center by another, and of political alliances often bolstered by dynastic marriages.

The obvious next step is to suggest that Teotihuacan was long-lived and highly centralized because it was a "hydraulic" state, based on intensive irrigation agriculture in a semiarid environment, while the Southern Maya Lowlands was politically less centralized and enjoyed a much briefer climax because of critical deficiencies in its tropical forest environment. I do not think that environmental considerations are unimportant, but I do feel that there are extremely serious difficulties with these explanations.

Discussions of Teotihuacan irrigation usually do not deal adequately with its *scale*. Evidence for pre-Toltec irrigation in the Teotihuacan Valley remains circumstantial rather than direct, but it seems quite likely that canal irrigation there does date back to Patlachique or Cuanalan times. But the maximum area available for permanent canal irrigation is less than four thousand hectares. This is not a very large area, nor does it call for large or complex canals, dikes, or flood-control facilities. Assuming a peak population of 125,000, there would have been about one irrigated hectare for 30 people. It is clear that the city grew well beyond any population limits set by irrigation agriculture, and a substantial fraction of its subsistence must have come from other sources, including riskier and much less productive alternative forms of agriculture, and collecting and hunting wild plants and animals. Faunal analyses and paleoethnobotanical studies provide evidence that Teotihuacanos ate a wide variety of wild as well as domesticated plants and wild animals.

It seems unlikely that there were any environmental or purely technical factors which would have made it impossible for the Teotihuacanos to have practiced intensive chinampa agriculture in the southern part of the Basin of Mexico. Chinampas were an important subsistence source for the Aztec population, which was much larger than the Teotihuacan population. Yet there is no evidence for extensive use of chinampas in Teotihuacan times. It is tempting to speculate that technical difficulties in assembling food for more people in one place may be at least part of the reason that Teotihuacan grew so little after Tzacualli times (a point also made by J. R. Parsons). If indeed there were environmental reasons, such as a change in lake levels, which prevented extensive chinampa exploitation in Teotihuacan times, then Teotihuacan is an instance of a population which expanded until it approached a perceived subsistence limit and then stabilized, rather than disastrously exceed that limit. If, as seems more likely, there was no environmental reason why the Teotihuacanos could not have fed more people by simply moving part of the population down to the chinampa area and investing in chinampa developments, their apparent failure to do so must have been for social or political reasons. If so, Teotihuacan population growth in the Basin of Mexico halted at a level well below the number of people it would have been technically possible to feed.

Teotihuacan's behavior has particular significance for the Maya because Culbert suggests that the Maya collapsed because they were unable to control runaway expansion which caused them to "overshoot" disastrously the productive limits of their environment.

Whether or not I am right in suspecting that Teotihuacan population growth leveled off before environmental limits were approached, it is logically inescapable that it was biologically possible for Teotihuacan population to have continued to expand until it "overshot" all technically feasible subsistence possibilities. If it were simply the case that rapid development tends to acquire a sort of momentum which carries it beyond environmental limits and into disaster before it can be stopped, then the ability of the Teotihuacanos to slow down and stop short of disaster would be puzzling.

An extended discussion of Teotihuacan's eventual collapse is not possible here, but I should add that I do not know of any convincing evidence that even the end of Teotihuacan was primarily due to climatic deterioration or other environmentally generated subsistence difficulties. Growing competition from other Highland centers was probably important, and I suspect that Teotihuacan may have collapsed for political, economic, and military reasons, rather than purely ecological reasons.

Proponents of either "population pressure" or "hydraulic" explanations for early states may perhaps argue that Teotihuacan "plateaued" instead of overshooting because the power of the state was very much stronger and more centralized than in the Maya cities, so that when the disastrous consequences of further expansion of the city became evident, the state had the power to intervene effectively and halt further population growth. Possibly this may be part of the explanation, but I do not think this explanation is required. The main reason may have been that there was simply no advantage in further expansion that would have offset attendant inconveniences. There is much evidence that population growth rates are very responsive to shifts in other variables. Assuming the Southern Lowland Maya did indeed "overshoot" their environment, even in the face of growing subsistence difficulties, it is the Maya behavior which is puzzling—far more puzzling than Culbert assumes—and it is the Maya "overshoot" rather than the Teotihuacan "plateau" which is most in need of explanation.

Culbert's "overshoot" explanation of the Maya collapse is one of the least unsatisfactory suggestions made so far. Culbert himself cogently disposes of most previous explanations. And archaeological evidence for the Southern Maya Lowlands in the eighth century does suggest a population so large that, in spite of evidence for terraces, ridged fields, and tree and root crops in addition to swidden, a subsistence crisis seems a real possibility. Nevertheless, there are serious problems with Culbert's explanation. He speaks of many causal factors, but inspection shows that excessive population growth plays a central role in his model. And, in his 1974 book, he offers no particular explanation for the population growth itself. More recently he has attributed population growth to economic development. But the question remains: what would have driven the Maya to expand population and/or environmental exploitation to the point where a subsistence crisis was produced? And if, instead, there was little population growth after about A.D. 550, as Haviland (1970 and personal communication) argues, then the postponement of collapse for some 250 years seems even more puzzling.

A different explanation for the Maya collapse suggests that the eighth-century Maya "florescence" was not, in fact, a time of Maya prosperity at all, but instead an attempt to cope with already serious troubles. This theory, if I understand it correctly, suggests that ability to obtain foreign goods by trade was critical for elite Maya prestige, for the power that derived from that prestige, and as a means of providing incentives for local production. Exclusion of central Peten elites from developing Mesoamerican trade networks supposedly precipitated a crisis for these elites, in which they attempted to offset their sagging prestige by even more ambitious monumental construction projects. But clearly nothing indispensable for subsistence was lacking, and prestige games can be played with whatever one defines as status markers, as Sanders points out. Goods need not be obtained by long-distance trade in order to be scarce and valuable. Furthermore my guess is that the decline of Teotihuacan, if anything, expanded the possibilities for profitable trade by Southern Lowland Maya elites. Webb's postulated development of new Mesoamerican trading networks following the decline of Teotihuacan seems, in very broad outline, a reasonable possibility. But I am much less persuaded than either Webb or Rathje that, at least at first, the Southern Lowland Maya were unable to participate in these new developments. The scale and substance of Late Classic Maya material civilization argues that they *were* able to profit from the situation, at least for a time. To be sure, there is some evidence for poor nutritional status for some Lowland Maya, but the same was probably true for much of the English and Western European population at the height of rapid economic growth in the early decades of the Industrial Revolution. It may well be that Late Classic Maya wealth was very unevenly distributed, and it also may be that the Late Classic Maya of the Southern Lowlands were increasingly "living off ecological capital," but this does not mean that the elites were already badly off, or were doing what they did in order to cope with resource pressures or an unfavorable balance of trade. The argument that the Late Classic Maya were already in serious trouble in the seventh or eighth centuries is unconvincing. Exclusion from trade networks does seem a good explanation for nonrecovery after the collapse, but not for the collapse itself....

It seems likely that in Late Classic times there was general economic development in a number of regional centers in the Southern Maya Lowlands, perhaps at least in part because of the weakening of Highland states such as Teotihuacan and Monte Alban. More speculatively, the elites of the individual centers may have increasingly seen it as both feasible and desirable to extend strong control over a relatively large surrounding area—a control based more on conquest and annexation than on political alliance and elite intermarriage. Population growth may well have been a concomitant of this economic and political development. My argument here and previously is not that population growth rarely occurs, nor that population growth does not have important reciprocal effects on other variables. My objections, instead, are to the idea that population can be counted on to increase for no reason except human procreative proclivities, and to the idea that competition and militaristic warfare would intensify mainly as a response to subsistence shortages. Instead, I suggest that if population was increasing, it was because it was useful either to elites, to peasant households, or to both. And I suggest that intensified militaristic competition is a normal extension of intensified economic competition.

Mayanists are accustomed to assuming that the political institutions of the Classic Maya Lowlands were marginally statelike. I suggest that we should seriously consider the possibility that by the seventh and eighth centuries the combination of economic development, population growth, and social changes was leading to the emergence of more highly developed and more centralized governmental structures—the kinds of structures which would make the incorporation of many small states into a single reasonably stable empire seem a realistic possibility. I would not venture to make further conjectures about the specific forms of these new political and economic developments. However, archaeological and epigraphical evidence promises not only to test the general proposition, but also to shed a great deal of further light on the precise forms of Maya political and economic organization.

What I suggest, then, is that eventually the major Maya centers may have begun to compete for effective political mastery of the whole Southern Lowlands. This postulated "heating up" of military conflict, for which there is some support in Late Classic art and inscriptions, may have played a major role in the Maya collapse. If, indeed, population growth and/or utilization of the environment expanded beyond prudent limits, the spur may have been provided by militaristic competition. And even if population and production did not expand beyond feasible steady-state values (under peaceful conditions), intensified warfare may have precipitated disaster through destruction of crops and agricultural facilities and through disruption of agricultural labor cycles. Clearly, internal warfare is not "the" single cause of the Maya collapse, but I believe it deserves renewed consideration as a contributing factor.

Webster also places new stress on the role of warfare in Maya history, but our views and emphases differ in several important ways. First, he is mainly concerned with Preclassic and Early Classic warfare as one of the causes of the *rise* of Maya civilization. This is a topic I have not discussed here. My feeling is that Webster makes some good points—there is certainly clear evidence for some Maya warfare quite early—but he probably overestimates the explanatory importance of early warfare. Second, Webster tends to see warfare largely as a response to shortages in land or other subsistence resources. I believe that this underestimates other incentives for warfare, especially for large-scale militaristic warfare. Third, Webster places much less stress than I do on Late Classic economic development, and he differs sharply on the matter of political integration. He feels that even the largest autonomous political units were never more than forty to sixty thousand people and that incorporation of further large increments of population, especially at considerable distances, proved unworkable. Presumably, although Webster does not explicitly discuss the matter, he would assume that serious attempts to incorporate many more people and more land and other resources within single states did not play a significant role in Maya history. He does feel that warfare may have contributed to the Maya collapse, but he explains intensified warfare mainly as a consequence of the manipulation of militarism by the Maya elite for bolstering their control of their own subject populations, rather than for any extensive conquests of other states. He says that conflicts may also have intensified over strategic resources, especially capital improvements for intensified agriculture, in the intermediate zones between major centers, but he does not suggest that there may have been major attempts to expand beyond the intermediate zones to gain control of the other centers as well. He does not suggest, as I do, that an important contributory element in the Maya collapse may have been a struggle—violent, protracted, and unsuccessful—to bring into being something like the kind of polity Teotihuacan had succeeded in creating several centuries earlier.

POSTSCRIPT

Were Environmental Factors Responsible for the Mayan Collapse?

Recent archaeological research on the Maya tends to focus on the complex interplay of many variables rather than emphasizing the prominent role of any single causal factor in the collapse of Classic lowland Maya civilizations. In these selections, Adams and Cowgill draw on several factors and differ primarily in the way they interweave these forces into an overall model. At one level, both models are incomplete because they draw on the experiences of different Maya centers. Moreover, as we learn about more Maya sites, archaeologists have begun to recognize regional variations within the Maya lowlands. The decline of some centers may actually be the result of specific local factors. The Maya collapse increasingly appears far more complex than most early scholars who sought single-factor explanations had suggested.

There is fairly strong evidence that military conquest by neighboring states brought down some centers. Human occupation appears to end abruptly and the memorial stone stelae are defaced, suggesting a hostile takeover by enemies. It is also clear that environmental changes such as heavy soil erosion in some areas were the result of human activities. While there is no question that the Maya population experienced a major decline from 800 C.E. up to the time of the Spanish conquest, it is not clear whether this decline was a sudden response to epidemics or a more gradual reduction that resulted from the combined effects of poorer nutrition, slightly lower fertility rates, and an increase in mortality rates over an extended period. As suggested earlier, each of these factors may have had different local expressions and may have affected different centers in diverse ways. What this means is that there may be no single answer to the question: What caused the Maya collapse?

There are many books and articles about the Maya and their demise. *The Classic Maya Collapse,* edited by T. Patrick Culbert (University of New Mexico Press, 1983) offers a collection of readings by scholars, each dealing with a different aspect. Charles Gallenkamp's *Maya: The Riddle and Rediscovery of a Lost Civilization* (Penguin Books, 1987), Robert J. Sharer's *The Ancient Maya,* 5th ed. (Stanford University Press, 1994), and John Henderson's *The World of the Ancient Maya,* 2d ed. (Cornell University Press, 1997), offer up-to-date accounts of what we now know about Maya civilization.

Two recent collaborative studies by teams of researchers show how complex the issue of the Maya collapse continues to be for archaeologists. The first is by a group of scholars working out of Vanderbilt University who have excavated at Petexbatun, a peripheral center in southwestern Peten (Guatemala). In a special section of the journal *Ancient Mesoamerica* (vol. 8, no. 2, Fall 1997), Arthur

Demarest and his colleagues and students report on their excavations at Petex-batun from 1989 to 1995. They argue that interest in the Maya and the Maya collapse has overemphasized the dynastic histories of the literate Maya elites and has largely ignored the regional impact of Maya civilization on the environment, demography, and subsistence patterns. A similar collaborative project, based at Pennsylvania State University and headed by David Webster, excavated at the major center Copan in Honduras from 1980 to 1984. A very useful survey of their findings is *Copan: The Rise and Fall of an Ancient Maya Kingdom* (Harcourt Brace, 2000). While this study considers the role of environmental factors, it emphasizes the interplay of political and military factors.

A number of videos about the Maya can be found. *Out of the Past,* directed by David Webster et al. (Annenberg CPB Project, 1993) and *Central America: The Burden of Time,* from Michael Wood's Legacy series (Ambrose Video Publishing, Inc., 1991) offer thoughtful analysis about the Maya and the archaeological issues that researchers still face.

The Chimpanzee and Human Communication Institute Home Page

The Chimpanzee and Human Communication Institute provides information on this site about current research on teaching American Sign Language to chimpanzees. The site includes information about experiments with chimps as well as links to other sites dealing with the question of whether apes can learn a language.

http://www.cwu.edu/~cwuchci/

Language in Apes

This Web site contains an essay entitled, "Language in Apes: How Much Do They Know and How Much Should We Teach Them?" This essay explores the ethical issues that are involved when teaching apes to learn language. Also included is a summary of various language experiments on apes and the theories concerning the results of these experiments.

http://www.math.uwaterloo.ca/~dmswitze/apelang.html

UsingEnglish.com

UsingEnglish.com contains a page that has information on the Sapir-Wharf hypothesis. Also on this page is a link to a discussion on this topic. Numerous links to sites on the subject from various sides can also be found on this page.

http://www.usingenglish.com/speaking-out/linguistic-whorfare.html

The Language of Thought Hypothesis

The Language of Thought Hypothesis site provides a description of the hypothesis, which proposes that thought and thinking take place in a mental language. This site also contains a summary of arguments that support and refute this hypothesis.

http://www.seop.leeds.ac.uk/entries/language-thought/

PART 3

Linguistic Anthropology

*L*inguistic anthropologists study languages, particularly non-Western and unwritten languages. They also investigate the complex relationship between language and other aspects of culture. Language provides the categories within which culture is expressed and is the medium by which much of culture is transmitted from one generation to the next. Here we consider two classic questions that have confronted linguistic anthropologists for several decades. The first concerns whether chimpanzees and other apes have the innate ability to use symbols in ways that resemble human language. This question is important because if apes are capable of complex symbolic activity, then language and culture are probably not the exclusive capabilities of humans but have their origins in our primate past. The second question concerns whether categories of a language shape how humans perceive and understand the world. Although first proposed early in the twentieth century, this issue continues to be one of the central questions in linguistic anthropology.

- Can Apes Learn Language?

- Does Language Determine How We Think?

ISSUE 7

Can Apes Learn Language?

YES: E. S. Savage-Rumbaugh, from "Language Training of Apes," in Steve Jones, Robert Martin, and David Pilbeam, eds., *The Cambridge Encyclopedia of Human Evolution* (Cambridge University Press, 1999)

NO: Joel Wallman, from *Aping Language* (Cambridge University Press, 1992)

ISSUE SUMMARY

YES: Psychologist and primate specialist E. S. Savage-Rumbaugh argues that, since the 1960s, attempts to teach chimpanzees and other apes symbol systems similar to human language have resulted in the demonstration of a genuine ability to create new symbolic patterns.

NO: Linguist Joel Wallman counters that attempts to teach chimps and other apes sign language or other symbolic systems have demonstrated that apes are very intelligent animals, but up to now these attempts have not shown that apes have any innate capacity for language.

For more than a century anthropologists have generally assumed that humankind's ability to make tools and use language are two characteristics that distinguish humans from other animals. In the 1960s and 1970s Jane Goodall and other primatologists convincingly demonstrated that chimpanzees, our nearest biological relatives, made simple tools, thus narrowing the gap between apes and humans. Beginning in the 1940s a series of other scientists have worked with gorillas, chimps, and most recently the bonobo (or pygmy chimp), attempting to teach these apes simple forms of human-like language.

In the 1950s psychologist B. F. Skinner argued that human children learn natural language through conditioning, such that positive responses to utterances from proud parents and other adults essentially train children to recognize both grammatical patterns and vocabulary. But in the 1960s linguist Noam Chomsky disproved Skinner's theory, showing that human language is so highly complex that it must require some innate biological capability, which he called a "language acquisition device." In several respects, all of the ape-language experiments since then have sought to understand when this biological capacity for language learning evolved in primates.

The early years of the ape-language projects encountered one major difficulty. Try as they might, trainers could not get apes to vocalize human words reliably. This difficulty was a consequence of the fact that a chimp's vocal apparatus simply does not allow the possibility of human utterances.

Since Chomsky's studies of human language, linguists have generally accepted that the manipulation of symbols in systematic grammatical ways, rather than the ability to make utterances, is the most important and complex aspect of human language. Thus, if apes could manipulate symbols in linguistic ways, researchers hoped they could demonstrate that the ability to acquire language is a biological trait shared by at least certain species of the apes and humans.

If true, the ability to learn and use language, the last barrier that separates human beings from our nonhuman primate relatives, has fallen away. This view has its supporters and detractors, many of whom—largely on political or religious grounds—would either like to see humans as just another of the great apes or would prefer to view human beings as unique in the animal kingdom. But at issue is whether or not the long series of ape-language projects has demonstrated that apes can learn to manipulate signs and symbols.

E. S. Savage-Rumbaugh and her husband Duane Rumbaugh have been among the most innovative researchers in their field at the intersection of anthropology, linguistics, and cognitive psychology. They argue that of all the great apes a certain species of pygmy chimps, the bonobo, is biologically closest to *Homo sapiens*. Their recent work with a bonobo named Kanzi has been among the most successful of these ape-language projects. After tracing the history of these projects, Savage-Rumbaugh concludes that Kanzi's ability to use symbols closely resembles similar abilities observed among young human children.

Joel Wallman interprets the evidence very differently from Savage-Rumbaugh. He acknowledges that the various gorillas, chimps, and bonobos are clever animals, which have learned to respond to their trainers. But he argues that these animals have not learned anything resembling human language. However, chimps and bonobos are clever animals, and while they do not have full linguistic abilities, their abilities to use mental abstractions suggest that at least modest versions of these mental processes arose before our branch of the hominoid lineage split off from the lineage of the great apes.

These selections raise a number of questions about the similarities and differences between apes and humans. What kind of linguistic ability do these ape learners exhibit? Do their symbolic strings genuinely parallel early childhood language acquisition? Most importantly, do these ape-language studies show that apes and human beings genuinely share a common ability for language? What are the minimal features that make up any natural language?

Language Training of Apes

Can apes learn to communicate with human beings? Scientists have been attempting to answer this question since the late 1960s when it was first reported that a young chimpanzee named Washoe in Reno, Nevada had been taught to produce hand signs similar to those used by deaf humans.

Washoe was reared much like a human child. People made signs to her throughout the day and she was given freedom to move about the caravan where she lived. She could even go outdoors to play. She was taught how to make different signs by teachers who moved her hands through the motions of each sign while showing her the object she was learning to 'name'. If she began to make a portion of the hand movement on her own she was quickly rewarded, either with food or with something appropriate to the sign. For example, if she was being taught the sign for 'tickle' her reward was a tickling game.

This training method was termed 'moulding' because it involved the physical placement of Washoe's hands. Little by little, Washoe became able to produce more and more signs on her own. As she grew older, she occasionally even learned to make new signs without moulding. Once Washoe had learned several signs she quickly began to link them together to produce strings of signs such as 'you me out'. Such sequences appeared to her teachers to be simple sentences.

Many biologists were sceptical of the claims made for Washoe. While they agreed that Washoe was able to produce different gestures, they doubted that such signs really served as names. Perhaps, to Washoe, the gestures were just tricks to be used to get the experimenter to give her things she wanted; even though Washoe knew how and when to make signs, she really did not know what words meant in the sense that people do.

The disagreement was more than a scholarly debate among scientists. Decades of previous work had demonstrated that many animals could learn to do complex things to obtain food, without understanding what they were doing. For example, pigeons had been taught to bat a ball back and forth in what looked like a game of ping pong. They were also taught to peck keys with such words as 'Please', 'Thank you', 'Red' and 'Green' printed on them. They did this in a way that made it appear that they were communicating, but they

From E. S. Savage-Rumbaugh, "Language Training of Apes," in Steve Jones, Robert Martin, and David Pilbeam, eds., *The Cambridge Encyclopedia of Human Evolution* (Cambridge University Press, 1999). Copyright © 1999 by Cambridge University Press. Reprinted by permission.

were not; they had simply learned to peck each key when a special signal was given.

This type of learning is called *conditioned discrimination* learning, a term that simply means that an animal can learn to make one set of responses in one group of circumstances and another in different circumstances. Although some aspects of human language can be explained in this way, such as 'Hello', 'Goodbye', 'Please' and 'Thank you', most cannot. Human beings learn more than what to say when: they learn what words stand for.

If Washoe had simply signed 'drink' when someone held up a bottle of soda, there would be little reason to conclude that she was doing anything different from other animals. If, however, Washoe used the sign 'drink' to represent any liquid beverage, then she was doing something very different—something that everyone had previously thought only humans could do.

It was difficult to determine which of these possibilities charcterised her behaviour, as the question of how to distinguish between the 'conditioned response' and a 'word' had not arisen. Before Washoe, the only organisms that used words were human beings, and to determine if a person knew what a word stood for was easy: one simply asked. This was impossible with Washoe, because her use of symbols was not advanced enough to allow her to comprehend complex questions. One- and two-year-old children are also unable to answer questions such as these. However, because children are able to answer such questions later on, the issue of determining how and when a child knows that words have meanings had not until then been seen as critical.

Teaching Syntax

Several scientists attempted to solve this problem by focusing on sentences instead of words. Linguists argue that the essence of human language lies not in learning to use individual words, but rather in an ability to form a large number of word combinations that follow the same set of specific rules. These rules are seen as a genetic endowment unique to humans. If it could be shown that apes learn syntactical rules, then it must be true that they were using symbols to represent things, not just perform tricks.

Three psychologists in the 1970s each used a different method in an attempt to teach apes syntax. One group followed the method used with Washoe and began teaching another chimpanzee, Nim, sign language. Another opted for the use of plastic symbols with the chimpanzee Sarah. Still another used geometric symbols, linked to a computer keyboard, with a chimpanzee named Lana. Both Lana and Sarah were taught a simple syntax, which required them to fill in one blank at a time in a string of words. The number of blanks was slowly increased until the chimpanzee was forming a complete 'sentence'. Nim was asked to produce syntactically correct strings by making signs along with his teacher.

Without help from his teachers, Nim was unable to form sentences that displayed the kind of syntactical rules used by humans. Nim's sign usage could best be interpreted as a series of 'conditioned discriminations' similar to, albeit more complex than, behaviours seen in many less-intelligent animals. This work suggested that Nim, like circus animals but unlike human children, was using words only to obtain rewards.

However, the other attempts to teach sentences to apes arrived at a different conclusion, perhaps because a different training method was used. Both Sarah and Lana learned to fill in the blanks in sentences in ways that suggested they had learned the rules that govern simple sentence construction. Moreover, 6 per cent of Lana's sentences were 'novel' in that they differed from the ones that she had been taught. Many of these sentences, such as 'Please you move coke in cup into room', followed syntactical rules and were appropriate and meaningful communications. Other sentences followed the syntactical rules that Lana had learned, but did not make sense; for example, 'Question you give beancake shut-open'. Thus, apes appeared to be able to learn rules for sentence construction, but they did not generalise these rules in a way that suggested full comprehension of the words.

By 1980, Washoe had matured and given birth. At this time there was great interest in whether or not she would teach her offspring to sign. Unfortunately, her infant died. However, another infant was obtained and given to Washoe. This infant, Loulis, began to imitate many of the hand gestures that Washoe used, though the imitations were often quite imprecise. Washoe made few explicit attempts to mould Loulis's hands. Although Loulis began to make signs, it was not easy to determine why he was making them or what, if anything, he meant. Loulis has not yet received any tests like those that were given to Washoe to determine if he can make the correct sign when shown an object. It is clear that he learned to imitate Washoe, but it is not clear that he learned what the signs meant.

The question of whether or not apes understand words caused many developmental psychologists to study earlier and earlier aspects of language acquisition in children. Their work gave, for the first time, a detailed insight into how children use words during the 'one-word' stage of language learning and showed that children usually learn to understand words before they begin to use them. At the same time, there was a new approach to the investigation of ape language. Instead of teaching names by pairing an object with its sign or symbol and rewarding correct responses, there was a new emphasis on the communicative aspect of symbols. For example, to teach a symbol such as 'key', a desirable item was locked in a box that was given to the chimpanzee. When the chimpanzee failed to open it, he was shown how to ask for and how to use a key. On other occasions, the chimpanzee was asked to retrieve a key for the teacher, so that she might open the box.

This new approach was first used with two chimpanzees named Sherman and Austin. It resulted in a clearer symbolic use of words than that found in animals trained by other methods. In addition, because these chimpanzees were taught comprehension skills, they were able to communicate with one another and not just with the experimenters. Sherman and Austin could use their symbols to tell each other things that could not be conveyed by simple glances or by pointing. For example, they could describe foods they had seen in another room, or the types of tools they needed to solve a problem. Although other apes had been reported to sign in each other's presence, there was no evidence that they were intentionally signing to each other or that they responded to each other's signs.

Most important, Sherman and Austin began to show an aspect of symbol usage that they had not been taught; they used symbols to say what they were going to do *before* they did it. Symbol use by other apes had not included descriptions of intended actions; rather, communications had been begun by a teacher, or limited to simple requests.

Sherman and Austin also began to use symbols to share information about objects that were not present and they passed a particularly demanding test, which required them to look at symbols and answer questions that could be answered only if they knew what each symbol represented. For example, they could look at printed lexigram symbol such as 'key', 'lever', 'stick', 'wrench', 'apple', 'banana', 'pineapple' and 'juice', and state whether each lexigram belonged to the class of 'food' words or 'tool' words. They could do this without ever being told whether these lexigram symbols should be classified as foods or tools. These findings were important, because they revealed that by using symbols an ape can describe what it is about to do.

How Similar Is Ape Language to Human Language?

Even though it was generally agreed that apes could do something far more complex than most other animals, there still remained much disagreement as to whether ape's symbols were identical to human symbols. This uncertainty arose for two reasons: apes did not acquire words in the same manner as children —that is, by observing others use them; and apes did not appear to use true syntactical rules to construct multiple-word utterances.

The first of these differences between ape and child has recently been challenged by a young pygmy chimpanzee or bonobo named Kanzi. Most previous studies had focused on common chimpanzees because pygmy chimpanzees are very rare (they are in great danger of having their habitat destroyed in the coming decade and have no protected parks).

In contrast to other apes, Kanzi learned symbols simply by observing human beings point to them while speaking to him. He did not need to have his arms placed in position, or to be rewarded for using a correct symbol. More important, he did not need to be taught to comprehend symbols or taught that symbols could be used for absent objects as well as those present. Kanzi spontaneously used symbols to announce his actions or intentions and, if his meaning was ambiguous, he often invented gestures to clarify it, as young children do.

Kanzi learned words by listening to speech. He first comprehended certain spoken words, then learned to read the lexigram symbols. This was possible because his caretakers pointed to these symbols as they spoke. For example, Kanzi learned 'strawberries' as he heard people mention the word when they ran across wild strawberries growing in the woods. He soon became able to lead people to strawberries whenever they asked him to do so. He similarly learned the spoken names of many other foods that grew outdoors, such as wild grapes, honeysuckle, privet berries, blackberries and mushrooms, and could take people to any of these foods upon spoken request.

Unlike previous apes reared as human children, Kanzi was reared in a semi-natural woodland. Although he could not produce speech, he understood much of what was said to him. He could appropriately carry out novel spoken requests such as 'Will you take some hamburger to Austin?', 'Can you show your new toy to Kelly?' and 'Would you give Panzee some of your melon?'. There appeared to be no limit to the number of sentences that Kanzi could understand as long as the words in the sentences were in his vocabulary.

During the first 3 or 4 years of his life, Kanzi's comprehension of spoken sentences was limited to things that he heard often. However, when he was 5 years old, he began to respond to novel sentences upon first hearing them. For example, the first time he heard someone talk about throwing a ball in the river, he suddenly turned and threw his ball right in the water, even though he had never done this before. Similarly, when someone suggested, for fun, that he might then try to throw a potato at a turtle that was nearby, he found a potato and tossed it at the turtle. To be certain that Kanzi was not being somehow 'cued' inadvertently by people, he was tested with headphones. In this test he had to listen to a word and point to a picture of the word that he heard. Kanzi did this easily, the first time he took the test.

About this time, Kanzi also began to combine symbols. Unlike other apes, he did not combine symbols ungrammatically to get the experimenter to give something that was purposefully being held back. Kanzi's combinations had a primitive English word order and conveyed novel information. For example, he formed utterances such as 'Ball go group room' to say that he wanted to play with a specific ball—the one he had seen in the group room on the previous day. Because the experimenter was not attempting to get Kanzi to say this, and was indeed far from the group room, such a sentence conveyed something that only Kanzi—not the experimenter—knew before Kanzi spoke.

Thus Kanzi's combinations differed from those of other apes in that they often referred to things or events that were absent and were known only to Kanzi, they contained a primitive grammar and were not imitations of the experimenter. Nor did the experimenter ask rhetorical questions such as 'What is this?' to elicit them, Kanzi's combinations include sentences such as 'Tickle bite', 'Keep-way balloon' and 'Coke chase'. As almost nothing is yet known of how pygmy chimpanzees communicate, they could use a form of simple language in the wild. Kanzi understands spoken English words, so the ability that is reflected in language comprehension is probably an older evolutionary adaptation than is the ability to talk.

Studying ape language presents a serious challenge to the long-held view that only humans can talk and think. Certainly, there is now no doubt that apes communicate in much more complex and abstract ways than dogs, cats and other familiar animals. Similarly, apes that have learned some language skills are also able to do some remarkable non-linguistic tasks. For example, they can recognise themselves on television and even determine whether an image is taped or live. They can also play video games, using a joystick to catch and trap a video villain.

Scientists have only just begun to discover ways of tapping the hidden talents for language and communication of our closest relatives. Sharing 98 per cent of their DNA with human beings, it has long been wondered why African apes seem so much like us at a biological level, but so different when it comes to behaviour. Ape-language studies continue to reveal that apes are more like us than we ever imagined.

Joel Wallman

Aping Language

Experiments carried out over the past two decades . . . attempted to impart a language, either natural or invented, to an ape. The debate engendered by these projects has been of interest—consuming for some, passing for others—to all of those whose concerns include the enduring questions of human nature, among them anthropologists, psychologists, linguists, biologists, and philosophers.

An adequate treatment of the linguistic capabilities of apes entails consideration of a number of related issues, each of which is an interesting problem in its own right. Continuities in primate mentality, the relationship between language and thought in the individual and in the species, and the origin of language . . . are themes that . . . recur throughout this [debate].

. . . [N]one of the ape-language projects succeeded, despite employing years of tutelage far more intense than that experienced by most children, in implanting in an ape a capacity for language equal to that of a young child, let alone an adult. . . .

Why the Ape-Language Controversy Is a Controversy

All scientific arguments have in common at least these elements: (1) a minimum of two positions regarding the subject in dispute, positions generally held to be irreconcilable, and (2) an intensification of the normal emotional investment of the scientist in his or her position, due in some measure to the contending itself but perhaps also related to the ideological significance of the subject within the larger society. If, in addition, the argument includes suggestions of fraudulent or quasi-fraudulent procedures, the disagreement becomes a controversy. To the extent that this is an accurate characterization of scientific controversies, the ape-language debate is an exemplary one.

The radical opposition of opinion about the achievement of the various ape-language projects is well conveyed by the following quotations:

> [Washoe] learned a natural human language and her early utterances were highly similar to, perhaps indistinguishable from the early utterances of human children. (Gardner and Gardner 1978, p. 73)

The evidence we have makes it clear that even the brightest ape can acquire not even so much as the weak grammatical system exhibited by very young children. (Premack and Premack 1983, p. 115)

On measures of sign performance (form), sign order (structure), semantic relations (meaning), sign acts (function) and sign acquisition (development), apes appear to be very similar to 2 to 3 year old human children learning sign . . . Apes also appear to be very similar to 2 to 3 year old human children learning to speak. (Miles 1978, p. 114)

[The experimental chimpanzees] show, after years of training and exposure to signing, not the slightest trace of homological development parallel to that of human children. (Leiber 1984, p. 84)

After years of gentle teaching Koko has learned to use American Sign Language—the very same sign language used by the deaf. With her new-found vocabulary, Koko is now providing us with an astounding wealth of knowledge about the way animals view the world. (Patterson 1985a, p. 1) . . .

There are several sources of the stridency of the debate.
. . . [L]anguage, at least in the European intellectual tradition, is the quintessential human attribute, at once evidence and source of most that is transcendent in us, distinguishing ours from the merely mechanical nature of the beast. Language is regarded as the *sine qua non* of culture, and its presence in our species is the most salient behavioral difference between us and the other hominoids—with the relinquishing of tool use and, more recently, tool making (Goodall 1971; Beck 1980) as uniquely human capabilities, the significance of language as a separator has grown. And resistance to losing our quintessential attributes is, arguably, itself one of those uniquely human traits. Hence, some ape partisans (Linden 1974; Gysens-Gosselin 1979) have argued, the prevalent reluctance to accord the talking apes their due. An occasional variant of this interpretation is the accusation that those who refuse to recognize ape language are insufficiently committed to the Darwinian perspective or, worse, are anti-Darwinian. Thus Linden (1987) depicts those who question the likelihood of ape–human linguistic continuities as latter-day Wilberforces, averse to investigating "creatures who threaten to paralyze us by shedding light on the true nature and origins of our abilities" (p. 8).
    A countervailing vector of our ideology, perhaps peculiar to our culture but possibly pancultural, consists of careless anthropomorphic projection and an irrepressively attractive vision of communication between our own and other species. In fact, it seems correct to observe that, at least until recently in the debate and probably up to the present, the majority opinion, both lay and scientific, regarding the linguistic capabilities of the apes has been positive. People seem not only accepting but positively desirous of the possibility of ape language.
    Even if language did not have the sacrosanct status it does in our conception of human nature, the question of its presence in other species would

still promote argument, for we are lacking any universally accepted, unassailable diagnostic criteria for language. There is no shortage of candidates for the indispensable attribute of language. For Katz (1976) and Limber (1977), the projective capability is crucial, the provision of language for the articulation of any conceivable new proposition through a novel combination of words. Savage-Rumbaugh (1981) holds the referential nature of individual symbols to be the essence of language, while Premack (1984) and Marshall (1971) see the capacity for representation of real-world situations to be paramount, and so on. The property most commonly invoked as definitive of language is its predication on a system of abstract rules for the production and interpretation of utterances—in other words, grammar. Hockett's (1959, 1960, 1963; Hockett and Altmann 1968) famous list of so-called design features of language—including rapid fading, duality of patterning, and displacement—has provided a useful orientation for those trying to capture the differences between human and nonhuman natural systems of communication. What is wanting, nonetheless, is consensus on what the necessary and sufficient, as distinguished from inessential, property or properties of language are and hence on how we might unequivocally identify language in another species.

This problem of defining features is more severe where the language of the young child is concerned, and it is the child's language that is taken by most parties to the debate to be the proper material for comparison with the apes. If the young child is not, in fact, capable of linguistically encoding anything she can think of, if her production and understanding of utterances do not suggest abstract grammatical constituents and processes, then can it be said that the child has language? Limber (1977) and Lightfoot (1982), at least, would say no.

This is a defensible position, its major problem found in the fact that the young child's language, which may not yet be language, will eventually become language. How is this discontinuity in development to be bridged? The difficulty is not the existence of a discontinuity per se—there are a number of others in human development. The physiological transition from prepubescence to pubescence, for example, poses a similar problem—the two developmental phases are identifiably distinct, yet there are no two adjacent points in time about which it could be said that the child was prepubescent in the first but pubescent in the second.

What makes the transition from "nonlanguage" (... early language) to language more problematic is that, unlike the case of puberty, in which the first phase is defined largely by the absence of characteristics of the later one, early language has its own, very salient features. Moreover, there are some striking functional and possibly structural similarities between these features and those of adult language.... And, contrary to those who would deny language to the young child, there is extensive evidence for grammatical structure in the earliest word combinations (Bloom 1970; Brown 1973), and, some have suggested (De Laguna 1927; McNeill 1970), in single-word utterances as well. (The proper characterization of this structure, however, is the subject of ongoing debate in developmental psycholinguistics—in fact, this may be the dominant concern of the field. ...

Language, in summary, is central to our self-definition as a species, even though we have yet to derive an adequate definition of language itself, one that includes the essential but excludes the merely contingent.

Behaviorist Roots of the Ape-Language Experiments

There is an additional source of the contention surrounding the ape-language question. The issues in the debate tend to resonate along the longstanding cleavage within the behavioral sciences between those who advocate study of cognition and/or innately determined behavior, on the one hand, and those, on the other, who are behaviorist in method and theory.

Behaviorism, or stimulus–response psychology, came into being in the early decades of this century as an avowed antidote to the introspectionist trend in turn-of-the-century psychological investigation. Knowledge, thought, intention, affect, and all other unobservable mental phenomena were banished in favor of overt behavior as the only proper subject of a scientific psychology. To explain the behavior of animals, behaviorism, like the eighteenth-century empiricism from which it descends, posits a bare minimum of cognitive apparatus: (1) perception, (2) a capacity to represent in durable format the results of perception, and (3) the ability to form associations among those representations. In the behaviorist paradigm, the acquisition and strengthening of such associations constitute learning.

An association may be formed between a perceptual stimulus and an inborn response if that stimulus consistently accompanies another one that is innately connected to the response, as in the celebrated conjunction of the ticking of a metronome, food, and salivation in Pavlov's dogs. Or an animal may form an association between one of its own actions and a subsequent stimulus, as when a pigeon comes reliably to peck a button because its activation results in the dispensing of food. In this process, an association is created between an action and a following stimulus that "reinforces" that action. To qualify as a reinforcing stimulus, a consequence need not be one that we would regard a priori as satisfying or pleasant—in fact, any stimulus that increases the probability of the organism emitting the behavior that preceded it is, by definition, reinforcing.

In the behaviorist conception, all behavior is determined either by current stimuli or by past consequences. Language is verbal behavior; words function both as responses to stimuli and as stimuli themselves, eliciting further responses. Thus a sentence can be interpreted as a chain of stimulus–response events, each word a response to the preceding one and also a stimulus evoking the next, with the first word elicited by an environmental stimulus or an internal one, a "private event." Or, in some formulations, the entire sentence is regarded as one complex response to a stimulus.

The orthodox behaviorist account of learning has little use for traditional distinctions among types of behavior. Nor are species differences in behavioral mechanisms acknowledged. Although sometimes touted as such, the latter attitude is not an appreciation of evolutionary continuity, with the selectively and historically wrought similarities and divergences in behavior that such a theoretical affirmation entails. Rather, it reflects a commitment to cross-species *homogeneity,* a rejection of the notion that there are important differences across species in the processes that underlie the development and causation of behavior. . . .

Like other contemporary adherents of behaviorism, the ape-language experimenters embraced the various concessions to reality that the most primitive versions of behaviorism were forced to make over the years. The Gardners, for example, acknowledge that some parts of the innate behavioral repertoire of a species are more plastic and hence more readily conditioned than others, and also that species differ in their intrinsic propensities for various behaviors. Thus the chimpanzee's inborn motivation to communicate obviates conditioning as laborious as another behavior might require. That language acquisition in the chimpanzee and in the child are similarly dependent on extensive molding, shaping, and imitation, however, is an assumption that is fundamental to their research, and fundamentally erroneous. Indeed, their suggestion that the linguistic performance of the preschool child requires "intensive training" (1971, p. 188) is the *opposite* of one of the few claims to which virtually all language-acquisition researchers would assent. . . .

Lastly, it may be worth observing that the potential personal rewards of the ape projects have been substantial and emotional commitment commensurately high—the first person or team to give language to another species would certainly attain scientific immortality.

⋅⟨⊙⟩⋅

. . . In describing their aspirations for Washoe, the first of the modern ape-language pupils, the Gardners expressed pessimism about a direct assault on the question "Can an ape talk?" and . . . adopted instead an unabashedly behavioristic goal: "We wanted to develop behavior that could be called conversation" (1969, p. 665). And critics . . . have maintained that Washoe and her peers, though they may have simulated conversation, acquired neither a human language nor something crucially like one, but rather a system of habits that are crude facsimiles of the features of language.

Refuting the claim that apes have the ability to learn a language logically entails proving that they do *not* have it. This [selection] has not succeeded in doing something that cannot be achieved: proving that something does not exist. The relevant refutable claim, rather, is that one or more of the animals featured in these pages learned a language. Refuting this unequivocally, however, presupposes a set of definitive criteria for language and a demonstration that at least one of them was not met by each of the animals in question. . . . [S]uch criteria do not yet exist, either for adult forms or for children's forms of language. So it is not possible in principle to show that no ape *could* learn a language, and it is not possible in practice to show that none *has* learned a language. . . .

The ape-language experiments confirmed what students dating back at least as far as the gestalt psychologist Wolfgang Kohler have repeatedly demonstrated, which is that apes are highly intelligent creatures, probably second only to us, on measures of human intelligence. We may wonder how the evolutionary process engendered such a powerful mentality in the midst of the African rain forests, asking, like Humphrey (1976), of what use "conditional oddity discrimination" is to an ape in the jungle. But the cognitive prowess of the apes is a fact regardless of our inability to account for it.

That the apes, too, are reflexive and capable of impressively abstract mentation suggests that at least modest versions of these faculties arose before the ancestral hominoid lineage diversified into the African apes on the one hand and us on the other. Consider a modest assertion: a capacity for culture requires at least ape-level powers of abstraction. And a case could be made for self-awareness, too, as prerequisite to culture. To the extent that Freud's understanding of humanity's cultural creations as "immortality projects" is sound, an ego is presupposed. If the capacity for language, too, had arisen prior to that last hominoid divergence, then linguistics might have been a branch of comparative psychology, the ape-language experiments would never have been conceived, and this [selection] would have been about something else, say patterns of interspecies marriage. But, for that matter, had language arisen prior to the split that produced them and us—had we all spoken the same language—there might not have been a them and an us.

POSTSCRIPT

Can Apes Learn Language?

The two sides on the issue of ape-language ability remain widely separated. At the heart of the issue are several questions about (1) the biological nature of human beings and their nearest primate relatives; (2) the character of language and cognition, particularly among children who are just beginning to acquire language; and (3) the best and most unbiased methods for investigating ape-language abilities.

One of the strongest critics of the ape-language experiments is the cognitive psychologist Steven Pinker, who outlines his arguments in his book *The Language Instinct* (HarperCollins, 1994). Pinker argues that ape trainers have inadvertently used very subtle conditioning to train their primates. The sequences of symbols produced by even the most talented of the apes are far simpler than normal children's linguistic abilities. His view is that Savage-Rumbaugh and other trainers have overinterpreted the primate symbolic sequences and ignored numerous random "utterances." Chimps and bonobos may be clever animals, he concedes, but their cleverness is conditioned along the lines that Skinner had proposed; it is not linguistic behavior as understood by Chomsky and most linguists. If true, Pinker's criticism suggests that all of the ape-language projects have been failures, and at best trainers have tricked themselves into believing that apes can use symbols in linguistic ways.

Do the ape-language experiments introduce bias by interpreting symbolic strings too broadly and ambiguously? Are detractors of these experiments themselves biased, refusing to believe that apes are capable of any human-like linguistic or cognitive processes? And even if these experiments do not demonstrate an ability to use symbols in ways that precisely parallel child language use, can they not tell us a great deal about general patterns of cognition relevant to both humans and primates?

If Pinker is correct that humans use a different part of the brain for language than do apes when making natural vocalizations, then the efforts to demonstrate language ability in even the brightest of the great apes may ultimately be unsuccessful. Nevertheless, as Wallman and Savage-Rumbaugh suggest, however primitive apes' use of symbols may be, researchers may still learn a great deal about certain kinds of cognitive processes. If research does convincingly show that apes have some kind of language capability, there is still much to be learned about ape cognition in several of the areas that Savage-Rumbaugh has suggested.

Such advances are possible only if ape-language researchers can develop research methods that are completely free from bias and inadvertent human conditioning of their ape subjects. While Savage-Rumbaugh and the other researchers have tried to minimize the possibility of conditioning on their subject animals, as Pinker suggests, the context of the training makes it difficult to exclude the possibility of conditioning.

Up to now none of the ape-language projects have been able to tell us much, if anything, about ape communication in natural settings because all of the projects were conducted in laboratory settings. Even though no language-like communication has been identified among wild chimps or bonobos, there is still much to be learned about how these species communicate. Such studies, particularly if they can be linked to the ape-language experiments, may have a great deal to offer about primate cognition, and they may ultimately offer insights about the process of language acquisition in human children.

For a discussion of Washoe and other early ape-language projects, see R. Allen Gardner and Beatrice T. Gardner's essay "Communication With a Young Chimpanzee: Washoe's Vocabulary," in Rémy Chauvin, ed., *Modèles Animaux du Comportement Humain* (Centre National de la Recherche Scientifique), Herbert S. Terrace's *Nim* (Knopf, 1979), and David Premack and Ann Premack's *The Mind of an Ape* (W. W. Norton, 1983). On Kanzi, see Savage-Rumbaugh and Roger Lewin's *Kanzi: The Ape at the Brink of the Human Mind* (Wiley, 1994). On child language acquisition, see Pinker's *Language Learnability and Language Development* (Harvard University Press, 1984). For Skinner's original behavorist model of language learning, see his *Verbal Behavior* (Appleton-Century-Crofts, 1957) and Chomsky's critique *Syntactic Structures* (Mouton, 1957). Students may also enjoy Pinker's most recent analysis of what defines language in *Words and Rules: The Ingredients of Language* (Basic Books, 1999). For recent views about the state of ape-language experiments, see Savage-Rumbaugh, Stuart G. Shaker, and Talbot J. Taylor's *Apes, Language, and the Human Mind* (Oxford University Press, 1998), Barbara J. King, ed., *The Origins of Language: What Nonhuman Primates Can Tell Us* (SAR Press, 1999), and Barbara J. King's *The Information Continuum: Evolution of Social Information Transfer in Monkeys, Apes, and Hominids* (SAR Press, 1994).

ISSUE 8

Does Language Determine How We Think?

YES: John J. Gumperz and Stephen C. Levinson, from "Introduction: Linguistic Relativity Re-examined" and "Introduction to Part 1," in John J. Gumperz and Stephen C. Levinson, eds., *Rethinking Linguistic Relativity* (Cambridge University Press, 1996)

NO: Steven Pinker, from *The Language Instinct: How the Mind Creates Language* (Perennial Classics, 2000)

ISSUE SUMMARY

YES: Sociolinguists John J. Gumperz and Stephen C. Levinson contend that recent studies of language and culture suggest that language structures human thought in a variety of ways that most linguists and anthropologists had not believed possible.

NO: Cognitive neuropsychologist Steven Pinker draws on recent studies in cognitive science and neuropsychology to support the notion that previous studies have examined language but have said little, if anything, about thought.

For more than a century, anthropologists and linguists have observed that the world's languages differ in a number of significant ways. While some languages, such as French or Spanish, require speakers to mark the gender of most nouns, English does not. Some languages in Africa, New Guinea, and Latin America have only two, three, or four basic color terms, while English has eleven. Some languages are rich in cover terms such as tree, bird, or animal, while others have many terms for the different species but may lack any single term that would include all kinds of trees, birds, or animals. Do such differences among the world's languages have any effect on how different people think about the world in which they live?

The idea that human thought changes with different languages has come to be known as the question of linguistic relativity. It is most widely associated with the linguistic anthropologist Edward Sapir and his sometime student Benjamin Lee Whorf. Early in the twentieth century Sapir had drawn on his studies of Native American languages to suggest that different lexical (vocabulary) items and different grammatical features did lead various Indian groups to view the world differently from white English-speaking Americans. By the 1950s the idea that the language people spoke shaped the way they were inclined to think about the world had become known as the Sapir-Whorf hypothesis.

Although the Sapir-Whorf hypothesis had been generally accepted by most American anthropologists, few accepted the hypothesis in its strongest and most deterministic form. Derived from Whorf's writings, the strong version implied that humans were prisoners of their native language and could only think in terms of that language's grammatical and lexical categories. Since most anthropologists learned these exotic languages and with training were themselves able to understand both the words and the exotic worldviews, most anthropologists recognized that language could not be so deterministic. On the other hand, most anthropologists recognized that their informants approached the world quite differently from themselves.

The first formal test of linguistic relativity came in 1969 when cognitive anthropologist Brent Berlin and Paul Kay published *Basic Color Terms* (Berkeley, University of California Press). Examining the color terminologies of more than 100 languages from around the world, they concluded that the number of key or basic color terms a language might have is highly variable, from as few as two to as many as twelve. But the particular hues that would be coded was highly predictable and not at all random. Berlin and Kay suggested that all people perceive colors the same, but how they assign particular color chips to different color terms is anything but arbitrary.

In the 1970s these and other studies of how different people classified their natural, biological, and social worlds suggested to most anthropologists that language's role in culture was primarily limited to prescribing how people classified the world they inhabited rather than on people's thought processes. Thus, for about two decades the Sapir-Whorf hypothesis was relegated to the dustbin of bad anthropological theories. But in the 1990s a growing number of linguists and linguistic anthropologists began to reevaluate the hypothesis, and a growing number has come to see the relationship between language and thought in a variety of new ways.

The first selection, by John J. Gumperz and Stephen C. Levinson, examines some new studies, suggesting that new findings on the issue of linguistic relativity are emerging from many quarters in linguistics and anthropology. Accepting a nondeterministic reading of Sapir and Whorf, they explore some of the directions this new research is taking.

As anthropologists and linguists began to reexamine Sapir-Whorf, new criticisms have arisen from the new field of cognitive neuroscience. Here, Steven Pinker evaluates the linguistic relativity question, drawing on recent studies by cognitive neuroscience. He tends to view the relativity problem in more determinist terms than do Gumperz and Levinson, as well as most of the anthropologists who are currently working on this problem.

John J. Gumperz and
Stephen C. Levinson

 YES

Rethinking Linguistic Relativity

Introduction: Linguistic Relativity Re-Examined

Language, Thinking, and Reality

Every student of language or society should be familiar with the essential idea of linguistic relativity, the idea that culture, *through* language, affects the way we think, especially perhaps our classification of the experienced world. Much of our experience seems to support some such idea, for example the phenomenology of struggling with a second language, where we find that the summit of competence is forever over the next horizon, the obvious absence of definitive or even accurate translation (let alone the ludicrous failure of phrasebooks), even the wreck of diplomatic efforts on linguistic and rhetorical rocks.

On the other hand, there is a strand of robust common sense that insists that a stone is a stone whatever you call it, that the world is a recalcitrant reality that imposes its structure on our thinking and our speaking and that the veil of linguistic difference can be ripped aside with relative ease. Plenty of subjective experiences and objective facts can be marshalled to support this view: the delight of foreign friendships, our ability to "read" the military or economic strategies of alien rivals, the very existence of comparative sciences of language, psychology, and society.

These two opposing strands of "common sense" have surfaced in academic controversies and intellectual positions over many centuries of Western thought. If St. Augustine (354–430) took the view that language is a mere nomenclature for antecedently existing concepts, Roger Bacon (1220–92) insisted, despite strong views on the universal basis of grammar, that the mismatch between semantic fields in different languages made accurate translation impossible. The Port Royal grammarians of the seventeenth century found universal logic thinly disguised behind linguistic difference, while the German romantics in a tradition leading through to Humboldt in the nineteenth century found a unique *Weltanschauung*, "world view," in each language. The first half of our own century was characterized by the presumption of radical linguistic and cultural difference reflecting profound cognitive differences, a presumption to be found in anthropology, linguistics and behaviourist psychologies, not to mention philosophical emphasis on meaning as use. The second half of the century has been dominated by the rise of the cognitive sciences, with their treatment of mind as inbuilt capacities for information processing, and their associated universalist and rationalist presuppositions. St. Augustine would probably recognize the faint echoes of his views in much modern theorizing about how children acquire language through prior knowledge of the structure of the world.

There is surely some spiral ascent in the swing of this pendulum. Nevertheless it is important to appreciate how little real scientific progress there has been in the study of lexical or morphosyntactic meaning—most progress in linguistics has been in the study of syntax and sound systems, together with rather general ideas about how the meaning of phrases might be composed out of the meaning of their constituents. Thus there is still much more opinion (often ill-informed) than solid fact in modern attitudes to "linguistic relativity."

There are three terms in the relation: language, thought, and culture. Each of these are global cover terms, not notions of any precision. When one tries to make anything definite out of the idea of linguistic relativity, one inevitably has to focus on particular aspects of each of these terms in the relation. This [selection] will show how each can be differently construed and, as a consequence, the relation reconsidered. In addition the connecting links can be variously conceived. Thus by the end of the [selection] the reader will find that the aspects of language and thinking that are focused on are selective, but also that the very relation between culture and community has become complex. Readers will find the original idea of linguistic relativity still live, but functioning in a way that differs from how it was originally conceived.

Linguistic Relativity Re-Examined

The original idea, variously attributable to [Wilhelm von] Humboldt, [Franz] Boas, [Edward] Sapir, [and Benjamin Lee] Whorf, was that the semantic structures of different languages might be fundamentally incommensurable, with consequences for the way in which speakers of specific languages might think and act. On this view, language, thought, and culture are deeply interlocked, so that each language might be claimed to have associated with it a distinctive worldview.

These ideas captured the imagination of a generation of anthropologists, psychologists, and linguists, as well as members of the general public. They had deep implications for the way anthropologists should conduct their business, suggesting that translational difficulties might lie at the heart of their discipline. However, the ideas seemed entirely and abruptly discredited by the rise of the cognitive sciences in the 1960s, which favoured a strong emphasis on the commonality of human cognition and its basis in human genetic endowment. This emphasis was strengthened by developments within linguistic anthropology, with the discovery of significant semantic universals in color terms, the structure of ethnobotanical nomenclature, and (arguably) kinship terms.

However, there has been a recent change of intellectual climate in psychology, linguistics, and other disciplines surrounding anthropology, as well as within linguistic anthropology, towards an intermediate position, in which more attention is paid to linguistic and cultural difference, such diversity being viewed within the context of what we have learned about universals (features shared by all languages and cultures). New work in developmental psychology, while acknowledging underlying universal bases, emphasizes the importance of the socio-cultural context of human development. Within sociolinguistics and linguistic anthropology there has also been increasing attention to meaning and discourse, and concomitantly a growing appreciation of how interpretive differences can be rooted as much in the systematic uses of language as in its structure.

. . .[T]he ideas we associate today so especially with Whorf and Sapir have a long and distinguished lineage on the one hand, while perhaps being no more than one of two opposing perennial strands of thought, universalism vs. relativism, on the other. Nevertheless, they crystallized in a particular fashion in American intellectual life of the 1940s. The idea of a close link between linguistic and conceptual categories took on a new meaning in the context of three further background assumptions characteristic of the first half of the century. One was the presumption of a (sometimes tempered) empiricist epistemology, that is, the view that all knowledge is acquired primarily through experience. The other was the structuralist assumption that language forms a system of oppositions, such that formal distinctions directly reflect meaning distinctions. The third was the idea of an unconscious mental life, and thus the possibility of linguistic effects beyond conscious awareness. It was the conjunction of these background ideas together with the specific formulation of the "linguistic relativity" hypothesis that gave the hypothesis its particular character in the history of ideas.

Sapir may have originated the phrase, but the *locus classicus* (though by no means the most careful statement) of the concept of linguistic relativity is the popular articles by Whorf, where the following oft-quoted passages may be found which illustrate all the central themes.

Epistemology

We dissect nature along lines laid down by our native languages. The categories and types that we isolate from the world of phenomena we do not find there because they stare every observer in the face; on the contrary, the world is presented in a kaleidoscopic flux of impressions which has to be organized by our minds—and this means largely by the linguistic systems of our minds.

— (1956:213) . . .

Unconscious Thought

[T]he phenomena of language are to its own speakers largely of a background character and so are outside the critical consciousness and control of the speaker.

— (1956:211)

Linguistic Relativity

> The phenomena of language are background phenomena, of which the talkers are unaware or, at most, dimly aware... These automatic, involuntary patterns of language are not the same for all men but are specific for each language and constitute the formalized side of the language, or its "grammar"...
>
> From this fact proceeds what I have called the "linguistic relativity principle," which means, in informal terms, that users of markedly different grammars are pointed by their grammars toward different types of observations and different evaluations of externally similar acts of observation, and hence are not equivalent as observers, but must arrive at somewhat different views of the world.

> — (1956:221)...

The boldness of Whorf's formulation prompted a succession of empirical studies in America in the 1950s and early 1960s aimed at elucidating and testing what now became known as the Sapir–Whorf hypothesis. Anthropological and linguistic studies by Trager, Hoijer, Lee, Casagrande, and others have been well reviewed elsewhere. These studies hardly touched on cognition, but in the same period a few psychologists (notably Lenneberg, Brown, Stefflre) did try to investigate the relation between lexical coding and memory, especially in the domain of color, and found some significant correlations. This line of work culminated, however, in the celebrated demonstration by Berlin & Kay of the language-independent saliency of "basic colors," which was taken as a decisive anti-relativist finding, and effectively terminated this tradition of investigations into the Sapir-Whorf hypothesis. There followed a period in which Whorf's own views in particular became the butt of extensive criticism.

It is clear from this background that the "Sapir-Whorf" hypothesis in its classical form arose from deep historical roots but in a particular intellectual climate. Even though (it has been closely argued by Lucy the original hypothesis has never been thoroughly tested, the intellectual milieu had by the 1960s entirely changed. Instead of empiricism, we now have rationalistic assumptions. Instead of the basic tenets of structuralism, in which each linguistic or social system must be understood first in internal terms before comparison is possible, modern comparative work (especially in linguistics) tends to presume that one can isolate particular aspects or traits of a system (e.g. aspect or subjecthood) for comparison. The justification, such as it is, is that we now have the outlines of a universal structure for language and perhaps cognition, which provides the terms for comparison. It is true that the assumption of unconscious processes continues, but now the emphasis is on the unconscious nature of nearly all systematic information processing, so that the distinctive character of Whorf's habitual thought has been submerged.

In this changed intellectual climate, and in the light of the much greater knowledge that we now have about both language and mental processing, it would be pointless to attempt to revive ideas about linguistic relativity in their original form. Nevertheless, there have been a whole range of recent intellectual shifts that make the ground more fertile for some of the original seeds to grow into new saplings. It is the purpose of this [selection] to explore the implications of some of these shifts in a number of different disciplines for our overall view of the relations between language, thinking, and society.

The Idea Behind the Present [Selection]

This [selection] explores one chain of reasoning that is prompted by these recent changes in ideas. The line of argument runs in the following way.

Linguistic relativity is a theory primarily about the nature of meaning, the classic view focusing on the lexical and grammatical coding of language-specific distinctions. In this theory, two languages may "code" the same state of affairs utilizing semantic concepts or distinctions peculiar to each language; as a result the two linguistic descriptions reflect different construals of the same bit of reality. These semantic distinctions are held to reflect cultural distinctions and at the same time to influence cognitive categorizations, an issue re-examined... below.

Assuming that there is such a link between linguistic structure and conceptual categories, the possibility of conceptual relativity would seem at first sight to depend on whether linguistic codings are significantly different across languages. Very little, however, is actually known about substantive semantic or conceptual universals. It is true that there are demonstrations of universal semantic principles in a few domains like color terminology, ethnobiological taxonomies, perhaps also in systems of kinship terminology. However, these demonstrations carry no necessary general implications, and the same holds for studies of grammatical meaning....

Yet, on further reflection, distinctive linguistic (grammatical or lexical) codings are not the only ways in which "meanings" or interpretations can vary systematically across cultures. This is brought out by recent developments in the theory of meaning. These developments show that "meaning" is not fully encapsulated in lexicon and grammar, which provide only schematic constraints on what the speaker will be taken to have meant in a particular utterance....

A large part of the burden of interpretation is thus shifted from theories of context-free lexical and grammatical meaning to theories of use in context. Some important principles of the use of language may plausibly be argued to be universal.... Yet others seem much more clearly culture-specific. For example, the ethnography of speaking has shown how diverse can be the principles governing the production and interpretation of utterances in specific speech events—court proceedings, formal greetings, religious rituals, councils, and the like....

This [selection] therefore spans a large terrain, from the classic Whorfian issues of the relation of grammar to thought on the one hand to consideration of language use in sociolinguistic perspective on the other. One key idea that supports this span is the notion of indexicality, conceived not just in terms of the contextual dependence of deictic items, but also in the broader Peircean sense, as a broad relationship between interpreters, signals, and the context of interpretation. Indexicality necessarily anchors meaning and interpretation to the context of language use and thus to wider social organization. Issues of linguistic relativity are in this way directly related to the variable cultural structuring of contexts. . . .

Introduction to Part I . . .

The Very Idea: Causal Links Between Language and Thinking

Might the language we speak affect the way we think? Generations of thinkers have been intrigued by this idea. Aarsleff summarized Humboldt's influential views thus: "Humboldt's entire view of the nature of language is founded on the conviction that thinking and speaking, thought and language form so close a union that we must think of them as being identical, in spite of the fact that we can separate them artificially. Owing to this identity, access to one of the two will open nearly equal access to the other."

Whorf, as we saw [earlier], brought to the idea a new and heady mix of an empiricist epistemology, an insistence on the underlying systematicity of language as a structured semantical system, and an emphasis on the unconscious influence of language on habitual thought. . . .

The phrase "linguistic determinism" has come to stand for these views that there is a causal influence from linguistic patterning to cognition. Despite phrases like "linguistic conditioning," "linguistic legislation," "inexorable control," etc., Whorf's own considered position seems to have been that language influences unconscious habitual thought, rather than limiting thought potential. Thus the phrase "linguistic determinism" should be understood to imply that there is *at least some* causal influence from language categories to nonverbal cognition; it was not intended to denote an exclusive causal vector in one direction—probably no proponent has held the view that what cannot be said cannot be thought.

The idea that language could determine (however weakly) the nature of our thinking nowadays carries more than a faint whiff of anachronism; rather it seems to belong to an altogether different age, prior to the serious study of mind as an information processing device. That device, in the predominant metaphor of our time, is instantiated in "wetware," whose properties are in turn dictated by the genetic code of the species. Although those properties are only dimly understood, still it is generally presumed, as Fodor has influentially put it, that the mind is "modular," composed of subsystems specialized to the automatic unconscious processing of particular kinds of information, visual, auditory, haptic, and so on. Since we can, for example, talk about what we see, the output of these specialized systems must, it seems, be available to some central information processing system, where "thinking," in the sense of ratiocination and deliberation, occurs. This picture (a close analogy of course to the computers of the day) of a single generalized central processor with specialized input/output devices is beginning to give way to a more complex version: each specialized input/output device is itself a system of modules, while "central processes" may themselves be differentiated into different "languages of thought" (propositional, imagistic, and so on). . . . Nevertheless the essentials of the Fodorean view are very generally held.

Thus, on this widespread view, we can expect thinking in all essentials to have universal properties, to be couched in an inner language structurally the same for all members of the species, and to be quite unrelated to the facts of linguistic diversity. The tenor of the anti-Whorfian assumptions can be gauged from the following quotations: "For the vocabulary of the language, in and of its self, to be a moulder of thought, lexical dissections and categorizations of nature would have to be almost accidentally formed, rather as though some Johnny Appleseed had scattered named categories capriciously over the earth"; "Whorf's hypothesis [of linguistic determinism] has engendered much confusion, and many circular arguments. Its converse often seems more plausible" and "there is no evidence for the strong version of the hypothesis—that language imposes upon its speakers a particular way of thinking about the world"; "The discussions that assume that language determines thought carry on only by a collective suspension of disbelief."

In short, many authors find the thesis of linguistic determinism wildly adventurous or even ridiculous. On the other hand, others have recently claimed to find it sober and plausible. It is therefore useful to attempt to clarify the issues by dissecting the relativity hypothesis into its component parts, and in particular by isolating the "determinism" hypothesis from other linked ideas. Clearly, the hypothesis of linguistic relativity relies on the presumption of linguistic difference. Thus the discovery of universals may have a bearing on that hypothesis. But the hypothesis that linguistic categories might determine aspects of non-linguistic thinking is quite independent of facts about linguistic difference. Let us therefore spell out the nexus of interlinked hypotheses (where the numbers *[1]* and *[2]* refer to the premises and the number *[3]* to an implied conclusion).

[1] Linguistic Difference

Languages differ substantially in their semantic structure: both the intensions (the senses) and extensions (the denotations) of lexical and morpho-syntactic categories may differ across languages (and may do so independently).

[2] Linguistic Determinism

Linguistic categorizations, implicit or explicit, may determine or codetermine or influence aspects of non-linguistic categorization, memory, perception or thinking in general.

This is often said to have a "strong" and a "weak" form: under the strong claim, linguistically uncoded concepts would be unattainable; under the weak form, concepts which happen to be linguistically coded would be facilitated or favored (e.g. would be more accessible, easier to remember, or the default coding for non-linguistic cognition).

❧

The mechanisms whereby semantic distinctions may have an influence on cognition can be left open; a prior task is to show that there is indeed some correlation. Whorf himself of course held the view that the unconscious "compulsive patterning" of grammatical oppositions would play a special role in habitual unreflective patterns of thought.

Linguistic Relativity
Given that:

(1) differences exist in linguistic categories across languages;
(2) linguistic categories determine aspects of individuals' thinking;
     then:
(3) aspects of individuals' thinking differ across linguistic communities according to the language they speak.

Note that the conclusion here will hold even under the weakest versions of (1) and (2). Thus if there is *at least some* aspect of semantic structure that is not universal, *and at least some* cognitive effect of such distinctive semantic properties, then there must be *at least some* systematic cognitive variation in line with linguistic difference. That would seem ... to be as trivially true as the strongest version of linguistic relativity (that one's semantic inventory of concepts provides one's total vocabulary of thoughts) is trivially false. Thus the central problem is to illuminate the degrees of language difference, and the ways in which semantics and cognitive categories and processes interact.

Now notice that modern views complicate this picture by apparently subscribing to various aspects of these propositions while robustly denying the conclusion in the syllogism above. For example, a common modern stance is:

(1') languages differ in semantic structure, but only at a molecular level—at an atomic level, the conceptual "atoms" (e.g. "male," "adult," etc.) are identical, and are merely assembled into some culture-specific notion like "uncle";
(2') "determinism" between semantic categories and conceptual categories is in a sense trivially complete, since they are one and the same—the meanings of words are expressed in a "language" that is identical to the "language of thought." ...

Thus although the identity of linguistic and conceptual categories in (2') alone might be thought to entail linguistic relativity, it is in fact usually associated with some claim (often implicit) like that in (1'), allowing subscribers to presume that the "language of thought" (alias: system of semantic representations) is universal. Then the conclusion in (3) no longer follows. In schematic form we may now oppose the two views thus:

The Whorfian Syllogism
(1) Different languages utilize different semantic representation systems which are informationally non-equivalent (at least in the sense that they employ different lexical concepts);

(2) semantic representations determine aspects of conceptual representations;
>   *therefore*

(3) users of different languages utilize different conceptual representations.

The Anti-Whorfian Syllogism

(1′) Different languages utilize the same semantic representation system (if not at the molecular then at least at the atomic level of semantic primes);

(2′) universal conceptual representations determine semantic systems, indeed THE semantic representation system just is identical to THE propositional conceptual system (the innate "language of thought");
>   *therefore*

(3′) users of different languages utilize the identical conceptual representation system.

Despite the fact that the doctrines appear diametrically opposed, they are nevertheless, on suitable interpretations, *entirely compatible*, as long as one subscribes to the distinction between atomic and molecular levels of semantic representation. Then, on an atomic level, semantic representations, and their corresponding conceptual representations, are drawn from a universal language of thought, while on the molecular level there are language-specific combinations of universal atomic primitives, which make up lexical meanings (and meanings associated with morpho-syntactic distinctions) and which may have specific conceptual effects.

Most semantic analysts in practice work with an assumption of such "semantic decomposition" of linguistic expressions. But it is worth pointing out that there are in fact fundamental problems with that assumption which have long been recognized, and some of those who subscribe enthusiastically to (2′) might lose some of their enthusiasm if they realized that without (1′), (2′) implies the strongest version of linguistic relativity.

Let us take stock. Proposition (1) is evidently true, in the sense that languages clearly employ distinct lexical meanings. (1′) may or may not be tenable, but is in fact compatible with (1). Likewise (2) and (2′) are compatible if we make a distinction between atomic and molecular concepts: the inventory of concepts in the language of thought could determine the range of possible lexical concepts, but such lexical concepts once selected could in turn determine the concepts we employ when solving non-linguistic problems. (3) would be the conclusion from (1) and (2). All thus hinges on (2). Is it even remotely plausible?

Although the thesis of linguistic determinism seems at first sight to have an anachronistic flavor, it can easily be brought to bear on modern theorizing in a way that makes it look anything but silly. First, note that there is considerable psychological evidence that our working memory is restricted to about half a dozen chunks of information, but is indifferent to the underlying complexity of those chunks. Thus mental operations are facilitated by grouping elementary concepts into larger chunks. And this is just what lexical items do for us. Thus there is every reason to think that such chunks might play an important role in our thinking. . . .

Within such a framework, it is quite easy to show that in certain respects and for certain phenomena linguistic determinism *beyond* thinking-for-speaking is not only plausible, but must be correct. The reasoning can be exemplified as follows. Consider a language that has no words for 'in front,' 'behind,' 'left,' 'right,' and so on, preferring instead to designate all such relations, however microscopic in scale, in terms of notions like 'North,' 'South,' 'East,' 'West,' etc. Now a speaker of such a language cannot remember arrays of objects in the same way as you or I, in terms of their relative location from a particular viewing angle. If I think of the visual array currently in front of me, I think of it as, say, "boy in front of tree, dog to left of tree." Later I can so describe it. But that will not do for the speaker of the language with 'North'/'South'/'East'/'West' notions: remembering the array in terms of notions like 'front' and 'left' will not allow him to reconstruct the cardinal directions. So if he remembers it that way, he will not be able to describe it later; while if he remembers the array in a way congruent with the linguistic coding (in terms of 'North' and 'East', etc.), then he will be able to code it linguistically. So it seems *prima facie* quite clear that the speaker of such a language and I simply MUST code our experiences differently for memory in order to speak our different languages. In short, thinking in a special way for speaking will not be enough: we must mentally encode experiences in such a way that we can describe them later, in the terms required by our language.

There are in fact just such languages that require the use of cardinal directions. Furthermore, this *prima facie* argument about the cognitive consequences of speaking such different languages can be backed up by empirical investigation: it turns out that in non-linguistic tasks speakers of languages that use 'North'/'South'/'East'/'West' systems instead of 'front'/'back'/'left'/'right' systems do indeed remember spatial arrays differently, in ways that can be demonstrated experimentally and observationally.

Is this a peculiar case? One needs to think afresh to assess the possibilities. From the perspective of speech production, there are three different kinds of ways in which a particular language might determine how we think. First, the grammatical or lexical categories may force a specific way of thinking at the time of speaking (the "regimentation" of thoughts described above). Second, such thinking-for-speaking may itself require the coding of situations in specific forms at the time that they are experienced. This is clearly so in the North/South/East/West case above. It is also clearly so in many other cases: for example, obligatory coding of number in languages with plural marking will require noticing for all possible referents whether or not they are singletons—some languages without plural marking will let one say in effect "I saw bird on the lawn," but in English I must say either a *bird* or *birds* and must therefore have remembered how many relevant birds there were; or in systems of honorifics based on relative age, I must have ascertained before speaking whether the referent is senior or junior to me; or in systems of aspect requiring distinctions between perfective and imperfective, I must attend to the exact nature of event-overlap. These are language-specific distinctions that seem to require noticing special properties of the world so that one is ready to encode them linguistically should the need arise. Such examples suggest that those theorists who reluctantly subscribe to a relativity in thinking-for-speaking, will have also to subscribe to a consequent relativity in thinking at the time at which events are experienced. Thirdly, one may also go on to consider the consequences, or after-effects, of thinking-for-speaking in a particular way. There may for example be memory effects: it may be easier to remember aspects of events that have been coded for speaking during prior verbalization (hence we may indulge in speaking-for-thinking). Since some languages will enforce particular codings (e.g. in systems of aspect, honorifics, number-marking, etc.), they may ensure that their speakers recall certain features of situations better than others.

NO

Steven Pinker

Mentalese

Is thought dependent on words? Do people literally think in English, Chero-kee, [or] Kivunjo...? Or are our thoughts couched in some silent medium of the brain—a language of thought, or "mentalese"—and merely clothed in words whenever we need to communicate them to a listener? No question could be more central to understanding the language instinct.

In much of our social and political discourse, people simply assume that words determine thoughts. Inspired by [George] Orwell's essay "Politics and the English Language," pundits accuse governments of manipulating our minds with euphemisms like *pacification* (bombing), *revenue enhancement* (taxes), and *nonretention* (firing). Philosophers argue that since animals lack language, they must also lack consciousness—[Ludwig] Wittgenstein wrote, "A dog could not have the thought 'perhaps it will rain tomorrow' "—and therefore they do not possess the rights of conscious beings. Some feminists blame sexist thinking on sexist language, like the use of *he* to refer to a generic person. Inevitably, reform movements have sprung up. Many replacements for *he* have been suggested over the years, including *E, hesh, po, tey, co, jhe, ve, xe, he'er, thon,* and *na*. The most extreme of these movements is General Semantics, begun in 1933 by the engineer Count Alfred Korzybski and popularized in long-time best-sellers by his disciples Stuart Chase and S. I. Hayakawa. (This is the same Hayakawa who later achieved notoriety as the protest-defying college president and snoozing U.S. senator.) General Semantics lays the blame for human folly on insidious "semantic damage" to thought perpetrated by the structure of language. Keep-ing a forty-year-old in prison for a theft he committed as a teenager assumes that the forty-year-old John and the eighteen-year-old John are "the same per-son," a cruel logical error that would be avoided if we referred to them not as *John* but as *John$_{1972}$* and *John$_{1994}$*, respectively. The verb *to be* is a particu-lar source of illogic, because it identifies individuals with abstractions, as in *Mary is a woman*, and licenses evasions of responsibility, like Ronald Reagan's famous nonconfession *Mistakes were made*. One faction seeks to eradicate the verb altogether.

And supposedly there is a scientific basis for these assumptions: the fa-mous Sapir-Whorf hypothesis of linguistic determinism, stating that people's thoughts are determined by the categories made available by their language, and its weaker version, linguistic relativity, stating that differences among languages cause differences in the thoughts of their speakers. People who remember little else from their college education can rattle off the factoids: the languages that carve the spectrum into color words at different places, the fundamentally different Hopi concept of time, the dozens of Eskimo words for snow. The implication is heavy: the foundational categories of reality are not "in" the world but are imposed by one's culture (and hence can be challenged, perhaps accounting for the perennial appeal of the hypothesis to undergraduate sensibilities).

But it is wrong, all wrong. The idea that thought is the same thing as language is an example of what can be called a conventional absurdity: a statement that goes against all common sense but that everyone believes because they dimly recall having heard it somewhere and because it is so pregnant with implications. (The "fact" that we use only five percent of our brains, that lemmings commit mass suicide, that the *Boy Scout Manual* annually outsells all other books, and that we can be coerced into buying by subliminal messages are other examples.) Think about it. We have all had the experience of uttering or writing a sentence, then stopping and realizing that it wasn't exactly what we meant to say. To have that feeling, there has to be a "what we meant to say" that is different from what we said. Sometimes it is not easy to find *any* words that properly convey a thought. When we hear or read, we usually remember the gist, not the exact words, so there has to be such a thing as a gist that is not the same as a bunch of words. And if thoughts depended on words, how could a new word ever be coined? How could a child learn a word to begin with? How could translation from one language to another be possible?

The discussions that assume that language determines thought carry on only by a collective suspension of disbelief....

As we shall see in this [selection], there is no scientific evidence that languages dramatically shape their speakers' ways of thinking. But I want to do more than review the unintentionally comical history of attempts to prove that they do. The idea that language shapes thinking seemed plausible when scientists were in the dark about how thinking works or even how to study it. Now that cognitive scientists know how to think about thinking, there is less of a temptation to equate it with language just because words are more palpable than thoughts. By understanding *why* linguistic determinism is wrong, we will be in a better position to understand how language itself works....

◦⟨◉⟩◦

The linguistic determinism hypothesis is closely linked to the names Edward Sapir and Benjamin Lee Whorf. Sapir, a brilliant linguist, was a student of the anthropologist Franz Boas. Boas and his students (who also include Ruth Benedict and Margaret Mead) were important intellectual figures in this century, because they argued that nonindustrial peoples were not primitive savages but had systems of language, knowledge, and culture as complex and valid in their world view as our own. In his study of Native American languages Sapir noted that speakers of different languages have to pay attention to different aspects of reality simply to put words together into grammatical sentences. For example, when English speakers decide whether or not to put -*ed* onto the end of a verb, they must pay attention to tense, the relative time of occurrence of the event they are referring to and the moment of speaking. Wintu speakers need not bother with tense, but when they decide which suffix to put on their verbs, they must pay attention to whether the knowledge they are conveying was learned through direct observation or by hearsay.

Sapir's interesting observation was soon taken much farther. Whorf was an inspector for the Hartford Fire Insurance Company and an amateur scholar of Native American languages, which led him to take courses from Sapir at Yale. In a much-quoted passage, he wrote:

> We dissect nature along lines laid down by our native languages. The categories and types that we isolate from the world of phenomena we do not find there because they stare every observer in the face; on the contrary, the world is presented in a kaleidoscopic flux of impressions which has to be organized by our minds—and this means largely by the linguistic systems in our minds. We cut nature up, organize it into concepts, and ascribe significances as we do, largely because we are parties to an agreement to organize it in this way—an agreement that holds throughout our speech community and is codified in the patterns of our language. The agreement is, of course, an implicit and unstated one, *but its terms are absolutely obligatory*; we cannot talk at all except by subscribing to the organization and classification of data which the agreement decrees.

What led Whorf to this radical position? He wrote that the idea first occurred to him in his work as a fire prevention engineer when he was struck by how language led workers to misconstrue dangerous situations. For example, one worker caused a serious explosion by tossing a cigarette into an "empty" drum that in fact was full of gasoline vapor. Another lit a blowtorch near a "pool of water" that was really a basin of decomposing tannery waste, which, far from being "watery," was releasing inflammable gases. Whorf's studies of American languages strengthened his conviction. For example, in Apache, *It is a dripping spring* must be expressed "As water, or springs, whiteness moves downward." "How utterly unlike our way of thinking!" he wrote.

But the more you examine Whorf's arguments, the less sense they make. Take the story about the worker and the "empty" drum. The seeds of disaster supposedly lay in the semantics of *empty*, which, Whorf claimed, means both "without its usual contents" and "null and void, empty, inert." The hapless worker, his conception of reality molded by his linguistic categories, did not distinguish between the "drained" and "inert" senses, hence, flick... boom! But wait. Gasoline vapor is invisible. A drum with nothing but vapor in it looks just like a drum with nothing in it at all. Surely this walking catastrophe was fooled by his eyes, not by the English language.

The example of whiteness moving downward is supposed to show that the Apache mind does not cut up events into distinct objects and actions. Whorf presented many such examples from Native American languages. The Apache equivalent of *The boat is grounded on the beach* is "It is on the beach pointwise as an event of canoe motion." *He invites people to a feast* becomes "He, or somebody, goes for eaters of cooked food." *He cleans a gun with a ramrod* is translated as "He directs a hollow moving dry spot by movement of tool." All this, to be sure, is utterly unlike our way of talking. But do we know that it is utterly unlike our way of thinking?

As soon as Whorf's articles appeared, the psycholinguists Eric Lenneberg and Roger Brown pointed out two non sequiturs in his argument. First, Whorf did not actually study any Apaches; it is not clear that he ever met one. His assertions about Apache psychology are based entirely on Apache grammar—making his argument circular. Apaches speak differently, so they must think differently. How do we know that they think differently? Just listen to the way they speak.

Second, Whorf rendered the sentences as clumsy, word-for-word translations, designed to make the literal meanings seem as odd as possible. But looking at the actual glosses that Whorf provided, I could, with equal grammatical justification, render the first sentence as the mundane "Clear stuff—water—is falling." Turning the tables, I could take the English sentence "He walks" and render it "As solitary masculinity, leggedness proceeds." Brown illustrates how strange the German mind must be, according to Whorf's logic, by reproducing Mark Twain's own translation of a speech he delivered in flawless German to the Vienna Press Club:

> I am indeed the truest friend of the German language—and not only now, but from long since—yes, before twenty years already.... I would only some changes effect. I would only the language method—the luxurious, elaborate construction compress, the eternal parenthesis suppress, do away with, annihilate; the introduction of more than thirteen subjects in one sentence forbid; the verb so far to the front pull that one it without a telescope discover can. With one word, my gentlemen, I would your beloved language simplify so that, my gentlemen, when you her for prayer need, One her yonder-up understands.
>
> ... I might gladly the separable verb also a little bit reform. I might none do let what Schiller did: he has the whole history of the Thirty Years' War between the two members of a separate verb inpushed. That has even Germany itself aroused, and one has Schiller the permission refused the History of the Hundred Years' War to compose—God be it thanked! After all these reforms established be will, will the German language the noblest and the prettiest on the world be.

Among Whorf's "kaleidoscopic flux of impressions," color is surely the most eye-catching. He noted that we see objects in different hues, depending on the wavelengths of the light they reflect, but that physicists tell us that wavelength is a continuous dimension with nothing delineating red, yellow, green, blue, and so on. Languages differ in their inventory of color words: Latin lacks generic "gray" and "brown"; Navajo collapses blue and green into one word; Russian has distinct words for dark blue and sky blue; Shona speakers use one word for the yellower greens and the greener yellows, and a different one for the bluer greens and the nonpurplish blues. You can fill in the rest of the argument. It is language that puts the frets in the spectrum; Julius Caesar would not know shale from Shinola.

But although physicists see no basis for color boundaries, physiologists do. Eyes do not register wavelength the way a thermometer registers temperature. They contain three kinds of cones, each with a different pigment, and the cones are wired to neurons in a way that makes the neurons respond best to red patches against a green background or vice versa, blue against yellow, black against white. No matter how influential language might be, it would seem preposterous to a physiologist that it could reach down into the retina and rewire the ganglion cells.

Indeed, humans the world over (and babies and monkeys, for that matter) color their perceptual worlds using the same palette, and this constrains the vocabularies they develop. Although languages may disagree about the wrappers in the sixty-four crayon box—the burnt umbers, the turquoises, the fuchsias— they agree much more on the wrappers in the eight-crayon box—the fire-engine reds, grass greens, lemon yellows. Speakers of different languages unanimously pick these shades as the best examples of their color words, as long as the language has a color word in that general part of the spectrum. And where languages do differ in their color words, they differ predictably, not according to the idiosyncratic taste of some word-coiner. Languages are organized a bit like the Crayola product line, the fancier ones adding colors to the more basic ones. If a language has only two color words, they are for black and white (usually encompassing dark and light, respectively). If it has three, they are for black, white, and red; if four, black, white, red, and either yellow or green. Five adds in both yellow and green; six, blue; seven, brown; more than seven, purple, pink, orange, or gray. But the clinching experiment was carried out in the New Guinea highlands with the Grand Valley Dani, a people speaking one of the black-and-white languages. The psychologist Eleanor Rosch found that the Dani were quicker at learning a new color category that was based on fire-engine red than a category based on an off-red. The way we see colors determines how we learn words for them, not vice versa.

The fundamentally different Hopi concept of time is one of the more startling claims about how minds can vary. Whorf wrote that the Hopi language contains "no words, grammatical forms, constructions, or expressions that refer directly to what we call 'time,' or to past, or future, or to enduring or lasting." He suggested, too, that the Hopi had "no general notion or intuition of TIME as a smooth flowing continuum in which everything in the universe proceeds at an equal rate, out of a future, through a present, into a past." According to Whorf, they did not conceptualize events as being like points, or lengths of time like days as countable things. Rather, they seemed to focus on change and process itself, and on psychological distinctions between presently known, mythical, and conjecturally distant. The Hopi also had little interest in "exact sequences, dating, calendars, chronology."

What, then, are we to make of the following sentence translated from Hopi?

Then indeed, the following day, quite early in the morning at the hour when people pray to the sun, around that time then he woke up the girl again.

Perhaps the Hopi are not as oblivious to time as Whorf made them out to be. In his extensive study of the Hopi, the anthropologist Ekkehart Malotki, who reported this sentence, also showed that Hopi speech contains tense, metaphors for time, units of time (including days, numbers of days, parts of the day, yesterday and tomorrow, days of the week, weeks, months, lunar phases, seasons, and the year), ways to quantify units of time, and words like "ancient," "quick," "long time," and "finished." Their culture keeps records with sophisticated methods of dating, including a horizon-based sun calendar, exact ceremonial day sequences, knotted calendar strings, notched calendar sticks, and several devices for timekeeping using the principle of the sundial. No one is really sure how Whorf came up with his outlandish claims, but his limited, badly analyzed sample of Hopi speech and his long-time leanings toward mysticism must have contributed.

Speaking of anthropological canards, no discussion of language and thought would be complete without the Great Eskimo Vocabulary Hoax. Contrary to popular belief, the Eskimos do not have more words for snow than do speakers of English. They do not have four hundred words for snow, as it has been claimed in print, or two hundred, or one hundred, or forty-eight, or even nine. One dictionary puts the figure at two. Counting generously, experts can come up with about a dozen, but by such standards English would not be far behind, with *snow, sleet, slush, blizzard, avalanche, hail, hardpack, powder, flurry, dusting,* and a coinage of Boston's WBZ-TV meteorologist Bruce Schwoegler, *snizzling.*

Where did the myth come from? Not from anyone who has actually studied the Yupik and Inuit-Inupiaq families of polysynthetic languages spoken from Siberia to Greenland. The anthropologist Laura Martin has documented how the story grew like an urban legend, exaggerated with each retelling. In 1911 Boas casually mentioned that Eskimos used four unrelated word roots for snow. Whorf embellished the count to seven and implied that there were more. His article was widely reprinted, then cited in textbooks and popular books on language, which led to successively inflated estimates in other textbooks, articles, and newspaper columns of Amazing Facts.

The linguist Geoffrey Pullum, who popularized Martin's article in his essay "The Great Eskimo Vocabulary Hoax," speculates about why the story got so out of control: "The alleged lexical extravagance of the Eskimos comports so well with the many other facets of their polysynthetic perversity: rubbing noses; lending their wives to strangers; eating raw seal blubber; throwing Grandma out to be eaten by polar bears." It is an ironic twist. Linguistic relativity came out of the Boas school, as part of a campaign to show that nonliterate cultures were as complex and sophisticated as European ones. But the supposedly mind-broadening anecdotes owe their appeal to a patronizing willingness to treat other cultures' psychologies as weird and exotic compared to our own. As Pullum notes,

> Among the many depressing things about this credulous transmission and elaboration of a false claim is that even if there *were* a large number of roots for different snow types in some Arctic language, this would *not*, objectively, be intellectually interesting; it would be a most mundane and

unremarkable fact. Horsebreeders have various names for breeds, sizes, and ages of horses; botanists have names for leaf shapes; interior decorators have names for shades of mauve; printers have many different names for fonts (Carlson, Garamond, Helvetica, Times Roman, and so on), naturally enough.... Would anyone think of writing about printers the same kind of slop we find written about Eskimos in bad linguistics textbooks? Take [the following] random textbook..., with its earnest assertion "It is quite obvious that in the culture of the Eskimos... snow is of great enough importance to split up the conceptual sphere that corresponds to one word and one thought in English into several distinct classes..." Imagine reading: "It is quite obvious that in the culture of printers... fonts are of great enough importance to split up the conceptual sphere that corresponds to one word and one thought among non-printers into several distinct classes..." Utterly boring, even if true. Only the link to those legendary, promiscuous, blubber-gnawing hunters of the ice-packs could permit something this trite to be presented to us for contemplation.

If the anthropological anecdotes are bunk, what about controlled studies? The thirty-five years of research from the psychology laboratory is distinguished by how little it has shown. Most of the experiments have tested banal "weak" versions of the Whorfian hypothesis, namely that words can have some effect on memory or categorization. Some of these experiments have actually worked, but that is hardly surprising. In a typical experiment, subjects have to commit paint chips to memory and are tested with a multiple-choice procedure. In some of these studies, the subjects show slightly better memory for colors that have readily available names in their language. But even colors without names are remembered fairly well, so the experiment does not show that the colors are remembered by verbal labels alone. All it shows is that subjects remembered the chips in two forms, a nonverbal visual image and a verbal label, presumably because two kinds of memory, each one fallible, are better than one. In another type of experiment subjects have to say which two out of three color chips go together; they often put the ones together that have the same name in their language. Again, no surprise. I can imagine the subjects thinking to themselves, "Now how on earth does this guy expect me to pick two chips to put together? He didn't give me any hints, and they're all pretty similar. Well, I'd probably call those two 'green' and that one 'blue,' and that seems as good a reason to put them together as any." In these experiments, language is, technically speaking, influencing a form of thought in some way, but so what? It is hardly an example of incommensurable world views, or of concepts that are nameless and therefore unimaginable, or of dissecting nature along lines laid down by our native languages according to terms that are absolutely obligatory...

◦◦◦◦◦

People can be forgiven for overrating language. Words make noise, or sit on a page, for all to hear and see. Thoughts are trapped inside the head of the thinker. To know what someone else is thinking, or to talk to each other about the nature of thinking, we have to use—what else, words! It is no wonder that many commentators have trouble even conceiving of thought without words—or is it that they just don't have the language to talk about it?

As a cognitive scientist I can afford to be smug about common sense being true (thought is different from language) and linguistic determinism being a conventional absurdity. For two sets of tools now make it easier to think clearly about the whole problem. One is a body of experimental studies that break the word barrier and assess many kinds of nonverbal thought. The other is a theory of how thinking might work that formulates the questions in a satisfyingly precise way....

⤞◈⤝

Now we are in a position to pose the Whorfian question in a precise way. Remember that a representation does not have to look like English or any other language; it just has to use symbols to represent concepts, and arrangements of symbols to represent the logical relations among them, according to some consistent scheme. But though internal representations in an English speaker's mind don't *have* to look like English, they *could*, in principle, look like English—or like whatever language the person happens to speak. So here is the question: Do they in fact? For example, if we know that Socrates is a man, is it because we have neural patterns that correspond one-to-one to the English words *Socrates, is, a,* and *man,* and groups of neurons in the brain that correspond to the subject of an English sentence, the verb, and the object, laid out in that order? Or do we use some other code for representing concepts and their relations in our heads, a language of thought or mentalese that is not the same as any of the world's languages? We can answer this question by seeing whether English sentences embody the information that a processor would need to perform valid sequences of reasoning—without requiring any fully intelligent homunculus inside doing the "understanding."

The answer is a clear no. English (or any other language people speak) is hopelessly unsuited to serve as our internal medium of computation. Consider some of the problems.

The first is ambiguity. These headlines actually appeared in newspapers:

- Child's Stool Great for Use in Garden
- Stud Tires Out
- Stiff Opposition Expected to Casketless Funeral Plan
- Drunk Gets Nine Months in Violin Case
- Iraqi Head Seeks Arms...

Each headline contains a word that is ambiguous. But surely the thought underlying the word is *not* ambiguous; the writers of the headlines surely knew which of the two senses of the words *stool, stud,* and *stiff* they themselves had in mind. And if there can be two thoughts corresponding to one word, thoughts can't be words.

The second problem with English is its lack of logical explicitness. Consider the following example, devised by the computer scientist Drew McDermott:

> Ralph is an elephant.
> Elephants live in Africa.
> Elephants have tusks.

Our inference-making device, with some minor modifications to handle the English grammar of the sentences, would deduce "Ralph lives in Africa" and "Ralph has tusks." This sounds fine but isn't. Intelligent you, the reader, knows that the Africa that Ralph lives in is the same Africa that all the other elephants live in, but that Ralph's tusks are his own. . . .

A third problem is called "co-reference." Say you start talking about an individual by referring to him as *the tall blond man with one black shoe*. The second time you refer to him in the conversation you are likely to call him *the man*; the third time, just *him*. But the three expressions do not refer to three people or even to three ways of thinking about a single person; the second and third are just ways of saving breath. Something in the brain must treat them as the same thing, English isn't doing it.

A fourth, related problem comes from those aspects of language that can only be interpreted in the context of a conversation or text—what linguists call "deixis." Consider articles like *a* and *the*. What is the difference between *killed a policeman* and *killed the policeman*? Only that in the second sentence, it is assumed that some specific policeman was mentioned earlier or is salient in the context. Thus in isolation the two phrases are synonymous, but in the following contexts (the first from an actual newspaper article) their meanings are completely different:

- A policeman's 14-year-old son, apparently enraged after being disciplined for a bad grade, opened fire from his house, *killing a policeman* and wounding three people before he was shot dead.
- A policeman's 14-year-old son, apparently enraged after being disciplined for a bad grade, opened fire from his house, *killing the policeman* and wounding three people before he was shot dead.

Outside of a particular conversation or text, then, the words *a* and *the* are quite meaningless. They have no place in one's permanent mental database. Other conversation-specific words like *here, there, this, that, now, then, I, me, my, here, we,* and *you* pose the same problems, as the following old joke illustrates:

First guy: I didn't sleep with my wife before we were married, did you?

Second guy: I don't know. What was her maiden name? . . .

These examples (and there are many more) illustrate a single important point. The representations underlying thinking, on the one hand, and the sentences in a language, on the other, are in many ways at cross-purposes. Any particular thought in our head embraces a vast amount of information. But when it comes to communicating a thought to someone else, attention spans are short and mouths are slow. To get information into a listener's head in a reasonable amount of time, a speaker can encode only a fraction of the message into words and must count on the listener to fill in the rest. But *inside a single head*, the demands are different. Air time is not a limited resource: different parts of the brain are connected to one another directly with thick cables that can transfer huge amounts of information quickly. Nothing can be left to the imagination, though, because the internal representations *are* the imagination.

We end up with the following picture. People do not think in English or Chinese or Apache; they think in a language of thought. This language of thought probably looks a bit like all these languages; presumably it has symbols for concepts, and arrangements of symbols that correspond to who did what to whom. . . . But compared with any given language, mentalese must be richer in some ways and simpler in others. It must be richer, for example, in that several concept symbols must correspond to a given English word like *stool* or *stud*. There must be extra paraphernalia that differentiate logically distinct kinds of concepts, like Ralph's tusks versus tusks in general, and that link different symbols that refer to the same thing, like *the tall blond man with one black shoe* and *the man*. On the other hand, mentalese must be simpler than spoken languages; conversation-specific words and constructions (like *a* and *the*) are absent, and information about pronouncing words, or even ordering them, is unnecessary. Now, it could be that English speakers think in some kind of simplified and annotated quasi-English, with the design I have just described, and that Apache speakers think in a simplified and annotated quasi-Apache. But to get these languages of thought to subserve reasoning properly, they would have to look much more like each other than either one does to its spoken counterpart, and it is likely that they are the same: a universal mentalese.

Knowing a language, then, is knowing how to translate mentalese into strings of words and vice versa. People without a language would still have mentalese, and babies and many nonhuman animals presumably have simpler dialects. Indeed, if babies did not have a mentalese to translate to and from English, it is not clear how learning English could take place, or even what learning English would mean.

POSTSCRIPT

Does Language Determine How We Think?

In many respects the two positions on linguistic relativity differ largely on whether they accept the "strong" version of Sapir-Whorf or the more widely held "weaker" version in which language provides people with the concepts with which they can view the world. It is not clear that anyone, including Whorf, ever accepted the most deterministic position that has often been attributed to him. Sapir's writings on the subject are ambiguous but have generally been interpreted as a weaker formulation. Pinker and other critics from neuropsychology typically frame the question in its strongest and most deterministic reading. See Paul Kay and Willett Kempton's 1984 article "What Is the Sapir-Whorf Hypothesis?" *American Anthropologist* (vol. 86) for a similar view by anthropologists. Cognitive psychologist Jerry A. Fodor takes a similar point of view in *The Language of Thought* (Harvard University Press, 1975). Such differences in approach raise the question of whether or not these two groups of scholars are actually talking past one another. Since the strong version of the hypothesis is rarely accepted, would it not be more productive to explore the limits of the weaker version?

In mainstream anthropology the relativity question has often been framed in terms of language's effect on a people's worldview, which is another version of the weak hypothesis. See, for example, Jane Hill and Bruce Mannheim's "Language and World View," *Reviews in Anthropology* (vol. 21, 1992). Two books by linguists suggest ways in which the weak version of linguistic relativity can help us understand the relationship between language and culture even in our own language: George Lakoff's *Women, Fire and Dangerous Things* (University of Chicago Press, 1987) and George Lakoff and Mark Johnson's *The Metaphors We Live By* (University of Chicago Press, 1980).

The most important early statements by Whorf are to be found in a volume of his papers from the 1930s, collected in 1956 by John B. Carroll in *Language, Thought, and Reality: Selected Writings* (Technology Press). For a more recent and detailed survey of anthropological approaches to the Sapir-Whorf hypothesis, see John A. Lucy's review article, "Linguistic Relativity," *Reviews in Anthropology* (vol. 26, 1997).

On the Internet . . .

Cultural Materialism

The Cultural Materialism Web site, created by Dr. M. D. Murphy of the University of Alabama, features an explanation of cultural materialism, a summary of the history of cultural materialism, and a list of pertinent scholars. This site also gives links to other relevant Web sites.

http://www.as.ua.edu/ant/Faculty/murphy/cultmat.htm

The !Kung of the Kalahari Desert

The !Kung of the Kalahari Desert Web site contains general information about this group of people who are now called the Ju/'hoansi by most scholars.

http://www.ucc.uconn.edu/~epsadm03/Kung.html

Islam for Today

Islam for Today is a Web site that provides basic information about Islam for non-Muslims. Explore the links to basic Islamic beliefs, Muslim history and civilizations, and articles on Islam.

http://www.islamfortoday.com

Collisions of Religions and Violence: Redux

Collisions of Religions and Violence: Redux is a Web site that contains a special issue of the journal *Cross Currents* and deals specifically with the question of whether or not conflict and violence emerge from immutable religious and ethnic differences.

http://www.crosscurrents.org/violencespecial.htm

PART 4

Cultural Anthropology

*C*ultural anthropologists study the culture and society of living communities. Like other anthropologists, cultural anthropologists are concerned with developing and testing models about the human condition and the range of human possibilities, such as whether gender inequality or violence are inevitable in human societies. Some anthropologists have asked whether the lives of small hunting-gathering bands resemble the lifeways of early human groups with similar technologies. Other anthropologists have asked about the strength of other people's religious beliefs. But at the heart of anthropological debate today is whether anthropology should model itself on the natural sciences or whether anthropologists should see their role more as interpreters of human cultures.

- Should Cultural Anthropology Model Itself on the Natural Sciences?

- Are San Hunter-Gatherers Basically Pastoralists Who Have Lost Their Herds?

- Do Sexually Egalitarian Societies Exist?

- Is It Natural for Adopted Children to Want to Find Out About Their Birth Parents?

- Has the Islamic Revolution in Iran Subjugated Women?

- Is Ethnic Conflict Inevitable?

ISSUE 9

Should Cultural Anthropology Model Itself on the Natural Sciences?

YES: Marvin Harris, from "Cultural Materialism Is Alive and Well and Won't Go Away Until Something Better Comes Along," in Robert Borofsky, ed., *Assessing Cultural Anthropology* (McGraw-Hill, 1994)

NO: Clifford Geertz, from *The Interpretation of Cultures: Selected Essays by Clifford Geertz* (Basic Books, 1973)

ISSUE SUMMARY

YES: Cultural anthropologist Marvin Harris argues that anthropology has always been a science and should continue to be scientific. He contends that the most scientific approach to culture is cultural materialism, which he has developed specifically to be a "science of culture." Anthropology's goal should be to discover general, verifiable laws as in the other natural sciences, concludes Harris.

NO: Cultural anthropologist Clifford Geertz views anthropology as a science of interpretation, and as such he argues that anthropology should never model itself on the natural sciences. He believes that anthropology's goal should be to generate deeper interpretations of diverse cultural phenomena, using what he calls "thick description," rather than attempting to prove or disprove scientific laws.

For more than a century, anthropologists have viewed their discipline as a science of humankind or as a science of culture. But not all anthropologists agree about what being a science should mean. At issue has been the question: Just what kind of science is anthropology?

Nineteenth- and early-twentieth-century anthropologists generally viewed anthropology as one of the natural sciences, and most early theorists, such as Edward Tylor, James Fraser, and Lewis Henry Morgan, saw anthropology as an extension of biology. Like biology, anthropology is a comparative discipline, and ethnographic descriptions of particular societies resemble the systematic descriptions that biologists provide about different species. Most early anthropologists were also attracted to the theories of the naturalist Charles Darwin, whose theory of natural selection attempted to explain how natural species evolved. For anthropologists evolution meant explaining how one social form evolved into another, how one kind of society developed into another.

With the rise of functionalism in the 1920s, evolutionary models became much less important as sociocultural anthropologists made detailed studies of individual societies, conducting ethnographic fieldwork lasting a year or two. Research became a total immersion into the culture, and anthropologists were expected to learn the local language, conduct participant observation, and try to understand the indigenous culture from the "native's point of view."

Although many anthropologists abandoned evolutionary questions in the 1920s, several new kinds of evolutionary models emerged after the Second World War. Leslie White proposed a unilineal model, arguing that cultural evolution could be explained in terms of how much energy a people could capture with their technology. Julian Steward proposed a rather different multilinear model to explain how societies in widely scattered parts of the world respond similarly to environmental and ecological constraints.

Building on these kinds of evolutionary models, Marvin Harris developed an approach he has called "cultural materialism." For Harris cultural materialism makes anthropology a science that parallels the evolutionary and biological sciences. But whereas biologists try to explain the physical evolution of species through natural selection, Harris argues that anthropologists should explain cultural evolution by understanding "cultural selection." Some cultural practices, whether actual behaviors or ideas, directly influence the community's successful adaptation to its material environment. Harris contends that anthropology's research agenda should be to establish regular, predictable, and verifiable laws just as scientists in other scientific fields do.

In his selection, Clifford Geertz argues that anthropologists should not attempt any kind of positivist science at all and that it is futile to seek scientific laws to explain human behavior. He contends that such laws would be either so general as to be meaningless, so obvious as to be trivial, or so specific to particular cultural settings as to have no relevance to other communities. The interpretation of cultures requires "thick description," in which the anthropologist is sensitive to cultural meanings and can provide a nuanced understanding of what he or she has observed, heard, and experienced in the field. Thus, for Geertz, anthropology should develop as a science of interpretation, and by definition such a science of interpretation cannot consist of verifiable laws; instead, it depends on the personal interpretive abilities of each individual anthropologist.

These selections pose several questions that lie at the heart of all sociocultural anthropology. Should anthropologists focus their attention on developing evolutionary theories, such as the kinds of cultural materialist explanations Harris seeks? Or, should anthropology primarily seek a more modest role in the multicultural world of today, attempting to translate and make sense of other people's cultural practices? And finally, is anthropology big enough to hold both of these perspectives and others as well?

Marvin Harris

 **YES**

Cultural Materialism Is Alive and Well and Won't Go Away Until Something Better Comes Along

Cultural materialism is a paradigm whose principles are relevant to the conduct of research and the development of theory in virtually all of the fields and subfields of anthropology. Indeed, it has been guesstimated (Thomas 1989:115) that half of the archaeologists in the United States consider themselves to be cultural materialist to some degree. For cultural materialists, whether they be cultural anthropologists, archaeologists, biological anthropologists, or linguists, the central intellectual experience of anthropology is not enthnography but the exchange of data and theories among different fields and subfields concerned with the global, comparative, diachronic, and synchronic study of humankind: the origin of the hominids, the emergence of language and culture, the evolution of cultural differences and similarities, and the ways in which biocultural, mental, behavioral, demographic, environmental and other nomothetic processes have shaped and continue to shape the human world.

Culture

... The culture in cultural materialism refers to the socially conditioned repertories of activities and thoughts that are associated with particular social groups or populations. This definition of culture stands opposed to the fixed, "essentialist" notions that inspire those who define culture as a realm of pure and uniform ideas hovering over the hub-bub of the daily life of specific individuals. For cultural materialists, culture elements are constructed (more specifically, abstracted) from the bedrock of the immensely variable thoughts and behavior of specific individuals (Harris 1964a).... [C]ultural materialists have long argued that culture is at bottom an unfolding material process (*viz.* the concept of "behavior stream") rather than an emanation of a platonic archetype.... Yet, it would be completely self-defeating to limit the definition of culture and the scope of the social sciences ... to the bedrock of individual thought and activity. Although we cannot see or touch entities such as a mode of production or a transnational corporation or a sociocultural system, to the extent that these are logical and empirical abstractions built up out of the observation of individual-level events, they possess a reality that is not inferior to any other reality. Indeed, it is imperative for human survival and well-being that we learn to rise above individual thoughts and actions to the level at which we can begin to examine the aggregate effects of social life and the behavior of such higher-order entities as institutions and whole sociocultural systems. Political economies are as real as the individuals who fall under their sway, and a lot more powerful.

Paradigms

Paradigms stipulate the principles which govern the conduct of research. Principles fall into two classes: rules for acquiring, testing, and validating knowledge (i.e., epistemological principles) and rules for generating and evaluating theories (i.e., theoretical principles). A widely misunderstood aspect of scientific paradigms is that neither the epistemological or theoretical principles nor the paradigm as a whole has the status of a scientific theory. Principles such as creationism, natural selection, or the priority of infrastructure are not falsifiable. This does not mean however that paradigms are "ships that pass in the night." Paradigms can be compared with each other and evaluated from two standpoints: (1) their logical structure and internal coherence and (2) their respective abilities to produce scientific theories in conformity with the criteria discussed below. From this vantage point, the alternatives to cultural materialism presented in this [selection] offer slight hope of safe passage. I see a lot of sunken ships in the muddy waters of post-postmodernism—ships built out of flawed accounts of the history of anthropological theory, parochial agendas, inchoate conceptions of the nature of human society and human cultures, and a lack of well-formed epistemological and theoretical principles or useful substantive achievements that might justify a future—any future—for anthropology.

Epistemological Principles: Science

Cultural materialism is based on certain epistemological principles which are held in common by all disciplines which claim to have scientific knowledge. Scientific knowledge is obtained by public, replicable operations (observations and logical transformations). The aim of scientific research is to formulate explanatory theories which are (1) predictive (or retrodictive), (2) testable (or falsifiable), (3) parsimonious, (4) of broad scope, and (5) integratable or cumulative within a coherent and expanding corpus of theories.

The same criteria distinguish scientific theories which are more acceptable from those which are less acceptable. Scientific theories find acceptance in accordance with their relative powers of predictability, testability, parsimony, scope, and integratability as compared with rival theories about the same phenomena. Since one can only approach, but never completely reach, perfection in this regard, scientific theories are held as tentative approximations, never as "facts."

This view of science derives from the logical positivist and empiricist philosophical traditions.... Note that it makes no claim to being "value free." Rather it proposes to overcome the inevitable biases of all forms of knowledge by methodological rules that insist upon opening to public scrutiny the operations by which particular facts and theories come to be constructed. The oft-repeated charge by postmodernist science-bashers that there is no community of observers who can or do scrutinize anthropological, especially ethnographic operations... is belied by the intense criticisms to which crucial facts and theories are regularly subjected in the pages of anthropology's principal journals. Challenges by other observers to the ethnographic accuracy of the work of Boas, Mead, Benedict, Redfield, Evans-Pritchard, Malinowski, Lee, Vayda, and Chagnon just for starters, whether based on fresh fieldwork or written sources, clearly do fulfill the scientific model for independent testing by other observers.... It may take awhile, but ethnographers working in the same region if not the same village do help to keep each other in touch with basic ethnographic facts. However, I certainly agree... that the future of ethnography lies in greatly expanding the use of field teams and the number of restudies rather than, as Marcus proposes... increasing the number of experimental, personalistic, and idiosyncratic field studies carried out by untrained would-be novelists and ego-tripping narcissists afflicted with congenital logo-diarrhea.

... The reason that cultural materialists favor knowledge produced in conformity with the epistemological principles of science is not because science guarantees absolute truth free of subjective bias, error, untruths, lies, and frauds. It is because science is the best system yet devised for reducing subjective bias, error, untruths, lies, and frauds....

Following the lead of Clifford Geertz and under the direct influence of postmodern philosophers and literary critics such as Paul De Man, Jacques Derrida, and Michel Foucault, interpretationist anthropologists have adopted an increasingly arrogant and intolerant rhetoric aimed at ridding anthropology of all vestiges of scientific "totalizing" paradigms. According to Stephen Tyler, for example, sociocultural anthropologists should abandon

> the inappropriate mode of scientific rhetoric that entails "objects," "facts," "descriptions," "inductions," "generalizations," "verification," "experiment," "truth," and like concepts that, except as empty invocations, have no parallels either in the experience of ethnographic fieldwork or in the writing of ethnographies. The urge to conform to the canons of scientific rhetoric has made the easy realism of natural history the dominant mode of ethnographic prose, but it has been an illusory realism, promoting, on the one hand, the absurdity of "describing" nonentities such as "culture" or "society" as if they were fully observable, though somewhat ungainly, bugs, and, on the other, the equally ridiculous behaviorist pretense of "describing" repetitive patterns in isolation from the discourse that actors use in constituting and situating their action, and all in simpleminded surety that the observers' grounding discourse is itself an objective form sufficient to the task of describing acts. (1986:130)

Tyler's totalizing renunciation of the search for objects, facts, descriptions, inductions, generalizations, verification, experiment, truth, and "like concepts"(!) in human affairs mocks itself so effectively that any attempt at rebuttal would be anticlimactic. I do think it may be useful, however, to point out that the "simpleminded surety" with which positivists and behaviorists are alleged to view human social life flagrantly distorts the entire history of science in general, during which all sureties, simpleminded or not, have been subject to relentless skepticism, and the history of logical positivism in particular, during which the struggle to create objective data languages has constituted the central focus of a vast and continuing philosophical effort.

Anthropology's dedicated science-bashers are not mollified by the assurance that cultural materialists seek probabilities rather than certainties, generalizations rather than laws....

Questions and Answers

The fallacies that embolden these queries are so transparent that one must wonder if the interlocutors really intend to be taken seriously....

Question: Just how often does something have to recur in order for it to serve as the basis for a generalization?

Answer: The more times the better.

Question: If generalizations cannot be expected to be applicable to any specific case, what good are they?

Answer: The better the generalization, the more *probable* its applicability to the particular case, the more useful it is. (It is definitely useful to know that a particular person who smokes four packs of cigarettes a day is ten times more likely to get lung cancer than one who doesn't smoke, even though not all heavy smokers get lung cancer.)

Question: Why must science be equated with generalizing?

Answer: Because science is by definition a generalizing form of knowledge.

Question: Is the mandate to generalize nothing but a "procedural rule"?

Answer: Of course. And anyone is free to ignore the rule but to do so is to cease doing science. (It is also likely to get you killed the next time you step off the curb against the light, or the next time you strike a match to look inside your gas tank.)

Last question: Instead of generalizing, why not consider "all the particularity of the individual case"?

Answer: Because there are no limits to particularity. Any project that proposes to deliver *all* the particularities of any macrophysical event, human or not human, therefore makes a preposterous claim on our time and resources. For this reason, in science endless particularity is the exact equivalent of endless ignorance.

Epistemological Principles: Emics and Etics

In addition to the general epistemological principles shared with other scientific disciplines, cultural materialism is also based on epistemological principles which are specific to the study of human sociocultural systems. These involve: (1) the separation of mental events (thoughts) from behavior (actions of body parts and their environmental effects) and (2) the separation of emic from etic views of thoughts and behavior... The reason for the epistemological distinction between mental and behavioral events is that the operations (observational procedures) used to obtain knowledge of mental events are categorically distinct from those needed to obtain knowledge of behavioral events. In the former, observers depend directly or indirectly on participants to communicate what is going on inside their heads; in the latter observers are not dependent on actors to identify the actor's body motions and the environmental effects of those motions. The reason for the further distinction between emic and etic events is that the separation of mental from behavioral events does not exhaustively specify the epistemological status of the categories (data language) employed in the identification of mental or behavioral events. Observers have the option of describing both kinds of events in terms of categories that are defined, identified, and validated by the community of participants (emics) or by the community of observers (etics). Four types of knowledge stem from these distinctions: (1) emics of thought; (2) emics of behavior; (3) etics of behavior; (4) etics of thought.

To illustrate, consider the practice of indirect infanticide in northeast Brazil: (1) A sample of economically and socially deprived mothers condemns and abhors infanticide. (2) These mothers insist that their own behavior has been devoted to sustaining the life of their infants. (3) Observers note, however, that some of these mothers actually withhold food and drink from certain infants, especially from infants that are first and last born. (4) On the basis of the observed occurrence of maternal neglect and high infant mortality, it can be inferred that these disadvantaged women have thoughts that are contrary to or that modify their elicited emics of thought and behavior.... Emic and etic versions of social life are often but not necessarily contradictory.... But failure to distinguish between emic and etic and between mental and behavior data renders much of the sociocultural literature of cultural anthropology useless by literally preventing researchers from understanding the referential significance of their descriptive discourse (Harris 1968; Marano 1982; Headland, Pike, and Harris 1990).

Despite a persistent barrage of uninformed or malicious assertions to the contrary, cultural materialists insist that the proper study of humankind is both emics and etics and both thought and behavior....

While no cultural materialist has ever advocated making the subject matter of cultural anthropology exclusively etic or behavioral, the postmodernists and their idealist predecessors have relentlessly advocated essentialist exclusions with regard to what cultural anthropologists ought to study....

Theoretical Principles

These rest on the assumption that certain categories of behavioral and mental responses are more directly important to the survival and well-being of human individuals than others and that it is possible to measure the efficiency with which such responses contribute to the achievement of an individual's survival and well-being. This assumption lies at the basis of the "costing" of alternative patterns of behavior which in turn is essential for identifying optimizing behavior and thought ... and the development of materialist theories of the causes of sociocultural differences and similarities.

The categories of responses whose costs and benefits underwrite cultural selection and cultural evolution are empirically derived from the biological and psychological sciences that deal with the genetically given needs, drives, aversions, and behavioral tendencies of *Homo sapiens*: sex, hunger, thirst, sleep, language acquisition, need for affective nurturance, nutritional and metabolic processes, vulnerability to mental and physical disease and to stress by darkness, cold, heat, altitude, moisture, lack of air, and other environmental hazards. This list is obviously not intended to encapsulate the whole of human nature. It remains open-ended and responsive to new discoveries about the human biogram and population-specific genetic differences ....

Infrastructure, Structure, and Superstructure

The components of social life which most directly mediate and facilitate the satisfaction of biogram needs, drives, aversions, and behavioral tendencies constitute the causal center of sociocultural systems. The burden of this mediation is borne by the conjunction of demographic, technological, economic, and ecological processes—the modes of production and reproduction—found in every socio-cultural system. More precisely, it is the etic behavioral aspect of the demo-techno-econo-environmental conjunction that is salient.... Infrastructure constitutes the interface between nature in the form of unalterable physical, chemical, biological, and psychological constraints on the one hand, and culture which is *Homo sapiens*'s primary means of optimizing health and well-being, on the other.... Cultural optimizations and adaptations must in the first and last instance conform to the restraints and opportunities of the environment and of human nature.

In addition to infrastructure, every human sociocultural system consists of two other major subsystems: structure and superstructure, each with its mental/behavioral and emic/etic aspects. Structure denotes the domestic and political subsystems, while superstructure denotes the realm of values, aesthetics, rules, beliefs, symbols, rituals, religions, philosophies, and other forms of knowledge including science itself.

The basic theoretical principles of cultural materialism can now be stated: (1) optimizations of the cost/benefits of satisfying biogram needs probabilistically (i.e. with more than chance significance) determine (or select for) changes in the etic behavioral infrastructure; (2) changes in the etic behavioral infrastructure probabilistically select for changes in the rest of the sociocultural system. The combination of 1 and 2 is the principle of the primacy of infrastructure.

As a guide to theory-making, the primacy of infrastructure enjoins anthropological researchers concerned with the explanation of sociocultural differences and similarities to concentrate on and to give priority to the formulation of hypotheses and theories in which components of the etic behavioral infrastructure are treated as independent variables while components of structure and superstructure are treated as dependent variables. The practical consequence of such a commitment of research effort is that the search for causal infrastructural variables will be conducted with decisively greater persistence and in greater detail than is likely under the auspices of alternative paradigms. The history of anthropological theory demonstrates that those who lack a paradigmatic commitment inevitably "quit early" when confronted with difficult, puzzling phenomena....

Another aspect of the principle of the primacy of infrastructure that is surrounded by misinformation is the feedback between infrastructure and structure or superstructure. It would be convenient for materialist-bashers if the principle of the primacy of infrastructure meant that cultural materialists regard the mental, emic, and symbolic-ideational aspects of sociocultural systems as mere mechanical reflexes or epiphenomena of infrastructure. ("Harris thinks ideas, symbols, values, art, and religion are unimportant aspects of human life. Ugh!") Again I quote from Murphy's paper: "As for the materialists, they fail to recognize that cultural forms have lives of their own and are not mere epiphenomena of underlying 'infrastructures'" (page 57). The attempt by Murphy and others to portray cultural materialism as a paradigm in which "the ideas by which men [sic] live have no importance for their action" (Bloch 1985b:134) is totally at variance with the prominence of the phrase "sociocultural system" in the specification of cultural materialist principles. Why does one bother to talk about the systemic role of structure and superstructure if infrastructure alone has importance for action? Do cultural materialists propose that people go about producing and reproducing at random and without an idea in their heads? Could sociocultural life as we know it exist if there was nothing but infrastructure? Certainly not. No more than one can imagine people living without an infrastructure, i.e., living on ideas alone.... The issue is not whether thought is important for action, but whether thoughts and actions are equally important in the explanation of the evolution of sociocultural systems. Cultural materialism—indeed any genuinely materialist paradigm in the social sciences—says no. The system is asymmetrical. Infrastructural variables are more determinative of the evolution of the system. But this does not mean that the infrastructure can do without its superstructure....

To illustrate, consider the changes in U.S. family life since World War II with reference to the disappearance of the male breadwinner role, the demise of the multiparous stay-at-home housewife, and the rise of feminist ideologies emphasizing the value of sexual, economic, and intellectual independence for women. As I have proposed elsewhere (Harris 1981a), these structural and superstructural transformations are the determined outcome of a shift from goods-producing industrialism to service-and-information-producing industrialism, mediated by the call-up of a reserve army of housewives into low-paying service-and-information nonunion jobs. The infrastructural transformations themselves were related to the use of electronic technologies and to declining productivity in the unionized smokestack industries which had created and sustained the male-breadwinner-stay-at-home-housewife families. The rise of a feminist ideology which glamorized the wage labor market and the intellectual, sexual, and emotional independence of women was the determined outcome of the same infrastructural force. However, it is clear that both the structural and superstructural changes have exerted and continue to exert an amplifying, positive-feedback effect on the infrastructural transformations. As the consequences of the call-up of the female labor force manifest themselves in higher divorce rates, lower first marriage rates, and historically low fertility rates, service-and-information industrialism is in turn amplified into an ever-more dominant mode of production and reproduction. Similarly, as feminist ideologies continue to raise consciousness against the vestiges of male breadwinner sexism, men and women find themselves locked into the labor force as competitors, wages for both are driven down, unions are driven out, and the profitability of the service-and-information industries rises, encouraging more diversion of capital from goods-producing enterprises into service-and-information production. . . .

Power and Cultural Materialist Theories

For proposing that changes in sociocultural systems are selected for in conformity with optimizing principles, cultural materialism has been caricatured as a form of functionalism in which all is for the best in the best of all possible worlds (Diener, Nonini, and Robkin 1978). This accusation cannot be reconciled with cultural materialism's long-standing focus on problems of class, caste, racial, and sexual inequality and exploitation. . . .

The fact that modes of production and reproduction are selected for in conformity with optimizing principles does not mean that every member of a society benefits equally from this selection process. Where marked differences of power have evolved as between sexes and stratified groups, the benefits may be distributed in a completely lopsided and exploitative fashion. Under such circumstances, the costs and benefits must be reckoned not only with respect to individuals in their infrastructural context but with respect to the political-economic decisions of power holders. This does not mean that all changes which benefit ruling-class interests necessarily have adverse effects on everyone else, as Marxists have wanted us to believe. For example, as indicated above, the rise of the service and information sectors in hyperindustrial mixed economies reflects the higher rates of profit to be obtained from unorganized labor. Thus, an increasing portion of the industrial labor force consists of women who have to some extent risen above their previous condition as unpaid housewife-mothers dominated by blue-collar male chauvinist husbands. There is no contradiction involved in holding that the greater advantages accruing to U.S. capitalist interests are facilitated by a lesser but still favorable balance of benefits over costs accruing to women. The behavior of both strata exhibits the predicted optimizations even though one might hold that the gain for most women, especially for minority women, is slight by comparison.

Cultural materialism is thus no less emphatic about the importance of political-economic inequality as a modifier of optimization process than are various Marxist theoreticians who claim to have a monopoly on the defense of the oppressed (Harris 1991).... One can never escape the question of benefits for whom or of costs for whom. Far from neglecting or "covering up" the effects of political factors on optimizations, cultural materialists recognize regular systemic feedbacks from the structural to the infrastructural level which give rise to political economy, political demography, political technology, and political ecology. One cannot for example explain the adoption and spread of technological devices such as shotguns, of new varieties of wheat and rice, tractors, or solar cell generators apart from the interests of trading companies, agribusiness, and petrochemical transnational corporations, local landowners, banks, etc....

Where Is Cultural Anthropology Going?

A popular myth among interpretationist science-bashers is that positive anthropology deservedly collapsed because of its failure to produce a coherent body of scientific theories about society and culture. Marcus and Fischer for example assert that there is a crisis in anthropology and related fields because of the "disarray" in the "attempt to build general and comprehensive theories that would subsume all piecemeal research" (1986:118). This implies that the postmodernists have made a systematic study of the positivist corpus of theories that deal with the parallel and convergent evolution of sociocultural systems. But they have not done this. It was only after World War II that nonbiological, positivist cultural and archaeological paradigms gained acceptance among anthropologists. In the ensuing years unprecedented strides have been made in solving the puzzles of sociocultural evolution through a genuinely cumulative and broadening corpus of sophisticated and powerful theories based on vastly improved and expanded research methods. The cumulative expansion of knowledge has been especially marked within archaeology and at the interface between archaeology and cultural anthropology (see e.g. Johnson and Earle 1987). It is ironic, then, that at the very moment when anthropology is achieving its greatest scientific successes, anthropologists who have never tested the positivist theoretical corpus which they condemn hail the death of positivist anthropology and the birth of a "new" humanistic paradigm. Only those who know little about the history of anthropological theories could hail such a paradigm as "new," much less as "a refiguration of social thought" (Darnell 1984:271).

This raises the question of why antipositivistic humanism has become so attractive to a new generation of anthropologists (and other practitioners of social "science"). One reason may be that the generation of students reared during the 1960s and early 1970s believes that positivist social science is responsible for such twentieth-century scourges as fascism, Stalinism, U.S. imperialism, corpocracies, and the educational-industrial-military complex. No doubt hyperindustrialism, high tech, and the "technological fix" lead to feelings of dehumanization and alienation. But the association between all of this and positivist social science is spurious. The problem is not that we have had too much of positivist social science but that we have had too little (Harris 1974:264ff). The atrocities of the twentieth century have been carried out precisely by people who were ignorant of or vehemently opposed to positivist social science (e.g., Lenin, Stalin, Hitler, Mussolini). Too many anthropologists seem to have forgotten that there is a flip side to relativism, phenomenology, and antipositivism—the side on which relativists who denounce reason and scientific knowledge construct the world in their own image.

 **NO**

Thick Description: Toward an Interpretive Theory of Culture

I

[Here I argue] for a narrowed, specialized, and, so I imagine, theoretically more powerful concept of culture to replace E. B. Tylor's famous "most complex whole," which, its originative power not denied, seems to me to have reached the point where it obscures a good deal more than it reveals.

The conceptual morass into which the Tylorean kind of *pot-au-feu* theorizing about culture can lead, is evident in what is still one of the better general introductions to anthropology, Clyde Kluckhohn's *Mirror for Man.* In some twenty-seven pages of his chapter on the concept, Kluckhohn managed to define culture in turn as: (1) "the total way of life of a people"; (2) "the social legacy the individual acquires from his group"; (3) "a way of thinking, feeling, and believing"; (4) "an abstraction from behavior"; (5) a theory on the part of the anthropologist about the way in which a group of people in fact behave; (6) a "storehouse of pooled learning"; (7) "a set of standardized orientations to recurrent problems"; (8) "learned behavior"; (9) a mechanism for the normative regulation of behavior; (10) "a set of techniques for adjusting both to the external environment and to other men"; (11) "a precipitate of history"; and turning, perhaps in desperation, to similes, as a map, as a sieve, and as a matrix. In the face of this sort of theoretical diffusion, even a somewhat constricted and not entirely standard concept of culture, which is at least internally coherent and, more important, which has a definable argument to make is (as, to be fair, Kluckhohn himself keenly realized) an improvement. Eclecticism is self-defeating not because there is only one direction in which it is useful to move, but because there are so many: it is necessary to choose.

The concept of culture I espouse . . . is essentially a semiotic one. Believing, with [German sociologist and political economist] Max Weber, that man is an animal suspended in webs of significance he himself has spun, I take culture to be those webs, and the analysis of it to be therefore not an experimental science in search of law but an interpretive one in search of meaning. It is explication I am after, construing social expressions on their surface enigmatical. But this pronouncement, a doctrine in a clause, demands itself some explication.

II

... [I]f you want to understand what a science is, you should look in the first instance not at its theories or its findings, and certainly not at what its apologists say about it; you should look at what the practitioners of it do.

In anthropology, or anyway social anthropology, what the practitioners do is ethnography [the study of human cultures]. And it is in understanding what ethnography is, or more exactly *what doing ethnography is,* that a start can be made toward grasping what anthropological analysis amounts to as a form of knowledge. This, it must immediately be said, is not a matter of methods. From one point of view, that of the textbook, doing ethnography is establishing rapport, selecting informants, transcribing texts, taking genealogies, mapping fields, keeping a diary, and so on. But it is not these things, techniques and received procedures, that define the enterprise. What defines it is the kind of intellectual effort it is: an elaborate venture in, to borrow a notion from [British philosopher] Gilbert Ryle, "thick description."

Ryle's discussion of "thick description" appears in two recent essays of his (now reprinted in the second volume of his *Collected Papers*) addressed to the general question of what, as he puts it, *"Le Penseur"* is doing: "Thinking and Reflecting" and "The Thinking of Thoughts." Consider, he says, two boys rapidly contracting the eyelids of their right eyes. In one, this is an involuntary twitch; in the other, a conspiratorial signal to a friend. The two movements are, as movements, identical; from an I-am-a-camera, "phenomentalistic" observation of them alone, one could not tell which was twitch and which was wink, or indeed whether both or either was twitch or wink. Yet the difference, however unphotographable, between a twitch or wink is vast; as anyone unfortunate enough to have had the first taken for the second knows. The winker is communicating, and indeed communicating in a quite precise and special way: (1) deliberately, (2) to someone in particular, (3) to impart a particular message, (4) according to a socially established code, and (5) without cognizance of the rest of the company. As Ryle points out, the winker has now done two things, contracted his eyelids and winked, while the twitcher has done only one, contracted his eyelids. Contracting your eyelids on purpose when there exists a public code in which so doing counts as a conspiratorial signal *is* winking. That's all there is to it: a speck of behavior, a fleck of culture, and—*voilà!*—a gesture.

That, however, is just the beginning. Suppose, he continues, there is a third boy, who, "to give malicious amusement to his cronies," parodies the first boy's wink, as amateurish, clumsy, obvious, and so on. He, of course, does this in the same way the second boy winked and the first twitched: by contracting his right eyelids. Only this boy is neither winking nor twitching, he is parodying someone else's, as he takes it, laughable, attempt at winking. Here, too, a socially established code exists (he will "wink" laboriously, overobviously, perhaps adding a grimace—the usual artifices of the clown); and so also does a message. Only now it is not conspiracy but ridicule that is in the air. If the others think he is actually winking, his whole project misfires as completely, though with somewhat different results, as if they think he is twitching. One can go further: uncertain of his mimicking abilities, the would-be satirist may practice at home before the mirror, in which case he is not twitching, winking, or parodying, but rehearsing; though so far as what a camera, a radical behaviorist, or a believer in protocol sentences would record he is just rapidly contracting his right eyelids like all the others. Complexities are possible, if not practically without end, at least logically so. The original winker might, for example, actually have been fake-winking, say, to mislead outsiders into imagining there was a conspiracy afoot when there in fact was not, in which case our descriptions of what the parodist is parodying and the rehearser rehearsing of course shift accordingly. But the point is that between what Ryle calls the "thin description" of what the rehearser (parodist, winker, twitcher . . .) is doing ("rapidly contracting his right eyelids") and the "thick description" of what he is doing ("practicing a burlesque of a friend faking a wink to deceive an innocent into thinking a conspiracy is in motion") lies the object of ethnography: a stratified hierarchy of meaningful structures in terms of which twitches, winks, fake-winks, parodies, rehearsals of parodies are produced, perceived, and interpreted, and without which they would not (not even the zero-form twitches, which, *as a cultural category,* are as much nonwinks as winks are nontwitches) in fact exist, no matter what anyone did or didn't do with his eyelids.

Like so many of the little stories Oxford philosophers like to make up for themselves, all this winking, fake-winking, burlesque-fake-winking, rehearsed-burlesque-fake-winking, may seem a bit artificial.

. . . In finished anthropological writings, . . . this fact—that what we call our data are really our own constructions of other people's constructions of what they and their compatriots are up to—is obscured because most of what we need to comprehend a particular event, ritual, custom, idea, or whatever is insinuated as background information before the thing itself is directly examined. . . . There is nothing particularly wrong with this, and it is in any case inevitable. But it does lead to a view of anthropological research as rather more of an observational and rather less of an interpretive activity than it really is. Right down at the factual base, the hard rock, insofar as there is any, of the whole enterprise, we are already explicating: and worse, explicating explications. Winks upon winks upon winks.

. . . The point for now is only that ethnography is thick description. What the ethnographer is in fact faced with—except when (as, of course, he must do) he is pursuing the more automatized routines of data collection—is a multiplicity of complex conceptual structures, many of them superimposed upon or knotted into one another, which are at once strange, irregular, and inexplicit, and which he must contrive somehow first to grasp and then to render. And this is true at the most down-to-earth, jungle field work levels of his activity: interviewing informants, observing rituals, eliciting kin terms, tracing property lines, censusing households . . . writing his journal. Doing ethnography is like trying to read (in the sense of "construct a reading of") a manuscript—

foreign, faded, full of ellipses, incoherencies, suspicious emendations, and tendentious commentaries, but written not in conventionalized graphs of sound but in transient examples of shaped behavior.

III

Culture, this acted document, thus is public, like a burlesqued wink or a mock sheep raid. Though ideational, it does not exist in someone's head; though unphysical, it is not an occult entity. The interminable, because unterminable, debate within anthropology as to whether culture is "subjective" or "objective," together with the mutual exchange of intellectual insults ("idealist!" —"materialist!"; "mentalist!"—"behaviorist!"; "impressionist!"—"positivist!") which accompanies it, is wholly misconceived. Once human behavior is seen as (most of the time; there *are* true twitches) symbolic action—action which, like phonation in speech, pigment in painting, line in writing, or sonance in music, signifies—the question as to whether culture is patterned conduct or a frame of mind, or even the two somehow mixed together, loses sense. The thing to ask about a burlesqued wink or a mock sheep raid is not what their ontological status is. It is the same as that of rocks on the one hand and dreams on the other—they are things of this world. The thing to ask is what their import is: what it is, ridicule or challenge, irony or anger, snobbery or pride, that, in their occurrence and through their agency, is getting said.

This may seem like an obvious truth, but there are a number of ways to obscure it. One is to imagine that culture is a self-contained "super-organic" reality with forces and purposes of its own; that is, to reify it. Another is to claim that it consists in the brute pattern of behavioral events we observe in fact to occur in some identifiable community or other; that is, to reduce it. But though both these confusions still exist, and doubtless will be always with us, the main source of theoretical muddlement in contemporary anthropology is a view which developed in reaction to them and is right now very widely held— namely, that, to quote [anthropologist] Ward Goodenough, perhaps its leading proponent, "culture [is located] in the minds and hearts of men."

Variously called ethnoscience, componential analysis, or cognitive anthropology (a terminological wavering which reflects a deeper uncertainty), this school of thought holds that culture is composed of psychological structures by means of which individuals or groups of individuals guide their behavior. "A society's culture," to quote Goodenough again, this time in a passage which has become the *locus classicus* of the whole movement, "consists of whatever it is one has to know or believe in order to operate in a manner acceptable to its members." And from this view of what culture is follows a view, equally assured, of what describing it is—the writing out of systematic rules, an ethnographic algorithm, which, if followed, would make it possible so to operate, to pass (physical appearance aside) for a native. In such a way, extreme subjectivism is married to extreme formalism, with the expected result: an explosion of debate as to whether particular analyses (which come in the form of taxonomies, paradigms, tables, trees, and other ingenuities) reflect what the natives "really" think or are merely clever simulations, logically equivalent but substantively different, of what they think.

As, on first glance, this approach may look close enough to the one being developed here to be mistaken for it, it is useful to be explicit as to what divides them. If, leaving our winks and sheep behind for the moment, we take, say, a Beethoven quartet as an, admittedly rather special but, for these purposes, nicely illustrative, sample of culture, no one would, I think, identify it with its score, with the skills and knowledge needed to play it, with the understanding of it possessed by its performers or auditors, nor, to take care, *en passant,* of the reductionists and reifiers, with a particular performance of it or with some mysterious entity transcending material existence. The "no one" is perhaps too strong here, for there are always incorrigibles. But that a Beethoven quartet is a temporarily developed tonal structure, a coherent sequence of modeled sound—in a word, music—and not anybody's knowledge of or belief about anything, including how to play it, is a proposition to which most people are, upon reflection, likely to assent.

To play the violin it is necessary to possess certain habits, skills, knowledge, and talents, to be in the mood to play, and (as the old joke goes) to have a violin. But violin playing is neither the habits, skills, knowledge, and so on, nor the mood, nor (the notion believers in "material culture" apparently embrace) the violin. To make a trade pact in Morocco, you have to do certain things in certain ways (among others, cut, while chanting Quranic Arabic, the throat of a lamb before the assembled, undeformed, adult male members of your tribe) and to be possessed of certain psychological characteristics (among others, a desire for distant things). But a trade pact is neither the throat cutting nor the desire. . . .

Culture is public because meaning is. You can't wink (or burlesque one) without knowing what counts as winking or how, physically, to contract your eyelids, and you can't conduct a sheep raid (or mimic one) without knowing what it is to steal a sheep and how practically to go about it. But to draw from such truths the conclusion that knowing how to wink is winking and knowing how to steal a sheep is sheep raiding is to betray as deep a confusion as, taking thin descriptions for thick, to identify winking with eyelid contractions or sheep raiding with chasing woolly animals out of pastures. The cognitivist fallacy—that culture consists (to quote another spokesman for the movement, [anthropologist] Stephen Tyler) of "mental phenomena which can [he means "should"]—be analyzed by formal methods similar to those of mathematics and logic"—is as destructive of an effective use of the concept as are the behaviorist and idealist fallacies to which it is a misdrawn correction. Perhaps, as its errors are more sophisticated and its distortions subtler, it is even more so.

The generalized attack on privacy theories of meaning is, since early [Edmund] Husserl and late [Ludwig] Wittgenstein, so much a part of modern thought that it need not be developed once more here. What is necessary is to see to it that the news of it reaches anthropology; and in particular that it is made clear that to say that culture consists of socially established structures of meaning in terms of which people do such things as signal conspiracies and join them or perceive insults and answer them, is no more to say that it is a psychological phenomenon, a characteristic of someone's mind, personality, cognitive structure, or whatever, than to say that Tantrism, genetics, the progressive form of the verb, the classification of wines, the Common Law, or the notion of "a conditional curse" ... is. What, in a place like Morocco, most prevents those of us who grew up winking other winks or attending other sheep from grasping what people are up to is not ignorance as to how cognition works ... as a lack of familiarity with the imaginative universe within which their acts are signs....

IV

... [T]he aim of anthropology is the enlargement of the universe of human discourse. That is not, of course, its only aim—instruction, amusement, practical counsel, moral advance, and the discovery of natural order in human behavior are others; nor is anthropology the only discipline which pursues it. But it is an aim to which a semiotic concept of culture is peculiarly well adapted. As interworked systems of construable signs (what, ignoring provincial usages, I would call symbols), culture is not a power, something to which social events, behaviors, institutions, or processes can be causally attributed; it is a context, something within which they can be intelligibly—that is, thickly—described....

In short, anthropological writings are themselves interpretations, and second and third order ones to boot. (By definition, only a "native" makes first order ones: it's *his* culture.) They are, thus, fictions; fictions, in the sense that they are "something made," "something fashioned"—the original meaning of *fictiō* —not that they are false, unfactual, or merely "as if" thought experiments....

V

Now, this proposition, that it is not in our interest to bleach human behavior of the very properties that interest us before we begin to examine it, has sometimes been escalated into a larger claim: namely, that as it is only those properties that interest us, we need not attend, save cursorily, to behavior at all. Culture is most effectively treated, the argument goes, purely as a symbolic system (the catch phrase is, "in its own terms"), by isolating its elements, specifying the internal relationships among those elements, and then characterizing the whole system in some general way—according to the core symbols around which it is organized, the underlying structures of which it is a surface expression, or the ideological principles upon which it is based. Though a distinct improvement over "learned behavior" and "mental phenomena" notions of what culture is, and the source of some of the most powerful theoretical ideas in contemporary anthropology, this hermetical approach to things seems to me to run the danger (and increasingly to have been overtaken by it) of locking cultural analysis away from its proper object, the informed logic of actual life. There is little profit in extricating a concept from the defects of psychologism only to plunge it immediately into those of schematicism.

Behavior must be attended to, and with some exactness, because it is through the flow of behavior—or, more precisely, social action—that cultural forms find articulation. They find it as well, of course, in various sorts of arti-facts, and various states of consciousness; but these draw their meaning from the role they play (Wittgenstein would say their "use") in an ongoing pattern of life, not from any intrinsic relationships they bear to one another....

A further implication of this is that coherence cannot be the major test of validity for a cultural description. Cultural systems must have a minimal de-gree of coherence, else we would not call them systems; and, by observation, they normally have a great deal more. But there is nothing so coherent as a paranoid's delusion or a swindler's story. The force of our interpretations can-not rest, as they are now so often made to do, on the tightness with which they hold together, or the assurance with which they are argued. Nothing has done more, I think, to discredit cultural analysis than the construction of impeccable depictions of formal order in whose actual existence nobody can quite believe.

If anthropological interpretation is constructing a reading of what hap-pens, then to divorce it from what happens—from what, in this time or that place, specific people say, what they do, what is done to them, from the whole vast business of the world—is to divorce it from its applications and render it vacant. A good interpretation of anything—a poem, a person, a history, a ritual, an institution, a society—takes us into the heart of that of which it is the inter-pretation. When it does not do that, but leads us instead somewhere else—into an admiration of its own elegance, of its author's cleverness, or of the beau-ties of Euclidean order—it may have its intrinsic charms; but it is something else than what the task at hand—figuring out what all that rigamarole with the sheep is about—calls for....

The ethnographer "inscribes" social discourse; *he writes it down*. In so do-ing, he turns it from a passing event, which exists only in its own moment of occurrence, into an account, which exists in its inscriptions and can be reconsulted....

The situation is even more delicate, because, as already noted, what we inscribe (or try to) is not raw social discourse, to which, because, save very marginally or very specially, we are not actors, we do not have direct access, but only that small part of it which our informants can lead us into under-standing....

VI

So, there are three characteristics of ethnographic description: it is interpretive; what it is interpretive of is the flow of social discourse; and the interpreting involved consists in trying to rescue the "said" of such discourse from its per-ishing occasions and fix it in perusable terms. The *kula* is gone or altered; but, for better or worse, *The Argonauts of the Western Pacific* remains. But there is, in addition, a fourth characteristic of such description, at least as I practice it: it is microscopic.

This is not to say that there are no large-scale anthropological interpre-tations of whole societies, civilizations, world events, and so on. Indeed, it is such extension of our analyses to wider contexts that, along with their theoretical implications, recommends them to general attention and justifies our constructing them. . . .

It is merely to say that the anthropologist characteristically approaches such broader interpretations and more abstract analyses from the direction of exceedingly extended acquaintances with extremely small matters. He confronts the same grand realities that others—historians, economists, political scientists, sociologists—confront in more fateful settings: Power, Change, Faith, Oppression, Work, Passion, Authority, Beauty, Violence, Love, Prestige; but he confronts them in contexts obscure enough . . . to take the capital letters off them. These all-too-human constancies, "those big words that make us all afraid," take a homely form in such homely contexts. But that is exactly the advantage. There are enough profundities in the world already.

Yet, the problem of how to get from a collection of ethnographic miniatures—. . . an assortment of remarks and anecdotes—to wall-sized culturescapes of the nation, the epoch, the continent, or the civilization is not so easily passed over with vague allusions to the virtues of concreteness and the down-to-earth mind. For a science born in Indian tribes, Pacific islands, and African lineages and subsequently seized with grander ambitions, this has come to be a major methodological problem, and for the most part a badly handled one. The models that anthropologists have themselves worked out to justify their moving from local truths to general visions have been, in fact, as responsible for undermining the effort as anything their critics—sociologists obsessed with sample sizes, psychologists with measures, or economists with aggregates—have been able to devise against them.

Of these, the two main ones have been: the Jonesville-is-the-USA "microcosmic" model; and the Easter-Island-is-a-testing-case "natural experiment" model. Either heaven in a grain of sand, or the farther shores of possibility.

The Jonesville-is-America writ small (or America-is-Jonesville writ large) fallacy is so obviously one that the only thing that needs explanation is how people have managed to believe it and expected others to believe it. The notion that one can find the essence of national societies, civilizations, great religions, or whatever summed up and simplified in so-called "typical" small towns and villages is palpable nonsense. What one finds in small towns and villages is (alas) small-town or village life. If localized, microscopic studies were really dependent for their greater relevance upon such a premise—that they captured the great world in the little—they wouldn't have any relevance.

But, of course, they are not. The locus of study is not the object of study. Anthropologists don't study villages (tribes, towns, neighborhoods . . .); they study *in* villages. You can study different things in different places, and some things—for example, what colonial domination does to established frames of moral expectation—you can best study in confined localities. But that doesn't make the place what it is you are studying. . . .

The "natural laboratory" notion has been equally pernicious, not only because the analogy is false—what kind of a laboratory is it where *none* of the parameters are manipulable?—but because it leads to a notion that the data derived from ethnographic studies are purer, or more fundamental, or more solid, or less conditioned (the most favored word is "elementary") than those derived from other sorts of social inquiry. The great natural variation of cultural forms is, of course, not only anthropology's great (and wasting) resource, but the ground of its deepest theoretical dilemma: how is such variation to be squared with the biological unity of the human species? But it is not, even metaphorically, experimental variation, because the context in which it occurs varies along with it, and it is not possible (though there are those who try) to isolate the y's from x's to write a proper function....

The methodological problem which the microscopic nature of ethnography presents is both real and critical. But it is not to be resolved by regarding a remote locality as the world in a teacup or as the sociological equivalent of a cloud chamber. It is to be resolved—or, anyway, decently kept at bay—by realizing that social actions are comments on more than themselves; that where an interpretation comes from does not determine where it can be impelled to go. Small facts speak to large issues, winks to epistemology, or sheep raids to revolution, because they are made to.

VII

There is an Indian story—at least I heard it as an Indian story—about an Englishman who, having been told that the world rested on a platform which rested on the back of an elephant which rested in turn on the back of a turtle, asked (perhaps he was an ethnographer; it is the way they behave), what did the turtle rest on? Another turtle. And that turtle? "Ah, Sahib, after that it is turtles all the way down."

... Cultural analysis is intrinsically incomplete. And, worse than that, the more deeply it goes the less complete it is. It is a strange science whose most telling assertions are its most tremulously based, in which to get somewhere with the matter at hand is to intensify the suspicion, both your own and that of others, that you are not quite getting it right. But that, along with plaguing subtle people with obtuse questions, is what being an ethnographer is like.

There are a number of ways to escape this—turning culture into folklore and collecting it, turning it into traits and counting it, turning it into institutions and classifying it, turning it into structures and toying with it. But they *are* escapes. The fact is that to commit oneself to a semiotic concept of culture and an interpretive approach to the study of it is to commit oneself to a view of ethnographic assertion as, to borrow W. B. Gallie's by now famous phrase, "essentially contestable." Anthropology, or at least interpretive anthropology, is a science whose progress is marked less by a perfection of consensus than by a refinement of debate. What gets better is the precision with which we vex each other....

My own position in the midst of all this has been to try to resist subjectivism on the one hand and cabbalism on the other, to try to keep the analysis of symbolic forms as closely tied as I could to concrete social events and occasions, the public world of common life, and to organize it in such a way that the connections between theoretical formulations and descriptive interpretations were unobscured by appeals to dark sciences. I have never been impressed by the argument that, as complete objectivity is impossible in these matters (as, of course, it is), one might as well let one's sentiments run loose. As [economist] Robert Solow has remarked, that is like saying that as a perfectly aseptic environment is impossible, one might as well conduct surgery in a sewer. Nor, on the other hand, have I been impressed with claims that structural linguistics, computer engineering, or some other advanced form of thought is going to enable us to understand men without knowing them. Nothing will discredit a semiotic approach to culture more quickly than allowing it to drift into a combination of intuitionism and alchemy, no matter how elegantly the intuitions are expressed or how modern the alchemy is made to look.

The danger that cultural analysis, in search of all-too-deep-lying turtles, will lose touch with the hard surfaces of life—with the political, economic, stratificatory realities within which men are everywhere contained—and with the biological and physical necessities on which those surfaces rest, is an ever-present one. The only defense against it, and against, thus, turning cultural analysis into a kind of sociological aestheticism, is to train such analysis on such realities and such necessities in the first place. It is thus that I have written about nationalism, about violence, about identity, about human nature, about legitimacy, about revolution, about ethnicity, about urbanization, about status, about death, about time, and most of all about particular attempts by particular peoples to place these things in some sort of comprehensible, meaningful frame.

To look at the symbolic dimensions of social action—art, religion, ideology, science, law, morality, common sense—is not to turn away from the existential dilemmas of life for some empyrean realm of de-emotionalized forms; it is to plunge into the midst of them. The essential vocation of interpretive anthropology is not to answer our deepest questions, but to make available to us answers that others... have given, and thus to include them in the consultable record of what man has said.

POSTSCRIPT

Should Cultural Anthropology Model Itself on the Natural Sciences?

Cultural anthropology is often viewed as a big tent capable of embracing many diverse points of view, as the selections by Harris and Geertz suggest. One can see a number of parallels between anthropology and biology in this respect as well. Biology has always included those who provide systematic descriptions of natural species as well as theoretical biologists who develop and test evolutionary models. Some view anthropology in a similar way, arguing that Geertz's interpretive anthropology is merely the descriptive side of anthropology, while Harris's cultural materialism together with other evolutionary and ecological approaches provide the theoretical grounding. As Harris notes, most biological anthropologists and archaeologists either explicitly or implicitly draw on some form of cultural materialist theory, and it is this shared evolutionary theory that unifies the three main subfields of anthropology.

Geertz strongly disagrees with this view of anthropology, arguing that any positivist, nomothetic anthropology misses the nuance and subtlety that makes human cultures worth studying in the first place. But while Geertz is the most prominent champion of this viewpoint, he is not the harshest critic of efforts to turn anthropology into a law-based science. A number of younger scholars, such as James Clifford, George Marcus, and Stephen Tylor, have been much more vocal in their attacks on positivism in anthropology. Many of their arguments have origins in the interpretive approach developed by Geertz in the 1960s, but they have urged anthropology to become a self-reflective social science, which is often referred to as "critical theory." For these scholars, anthropologists should illuminate the implicit, underlying assumptions that have motivated anthropologists. Sometimes called "postmodernism," this perspective encourages anthropologists to deconstruct the assumptions of Western cultures. Some have suggested that critical theorists are more concerned with studying the culture of anthropology than with understanding anthropology's traditional subjects. In this sense, positivism in anthropology has become one of their most visible targets.

Cultural materialism is one direction for an evolutionary science of culture to develop, but it is not the only kind of "scientific" anthropology that has been proposed. Another evolutionary anthropology is "sociobiology," which takes a somewhat different approach from Harris. Sociobiologists argue that humans, like all animals, are genetically programmed to respond in certain ways, and cultural practices are just an external manifestation of inner biological drives. For example, sociobiologists argue that, like other species, humans are internally driven to pass on their genes to the next generation. Thus, they expect individuals to be altruistic toward their offspring as well as others who are closely related to them and therefore share some of the same genetic material. Increasingly, sociobiologists have developed theories that they maintain are both testable and verifiable.

Must all anthropologists have the same perspective, or is the discipline strengthened by having diverse theoretical points of view? Is there some middle ground between cultural materialism and an interpretive (or even a critical) anthropology?

For an extended treatment of Harris's views, see his *Cultural Materialism: The Struggle for a Science of Culture* (Random House, 1979). Two of Harris's other books put his theories into practice: *Cows, Pigs, Wars, and Witches* (Random House, 1974) and *Cannibals and Kings: The Origins of Cultures* (Random House, 1977).

Geertz's *The Interpretation of Cultures* (Basic Books, 1973), for which his selection was written, is the most coherent statement outlining the breadth and scope of an interpretive anthropology. It contains what is probably his best-known interpretive essay, "Deep Play: Notes on the Balinese Cockfight." Students should also consult his *Local Knowledge: Further Essays in Interpretive Anthropology* (Basic Books, 1983) and *Works and Lives: The Anthropologist as Author* (Stanford University Press, 1988). Michael Fisher's review essay "Interpretive Anthropology," *Reviews in Anthropology* (vol. 4, no. 4, 1977) offers a useful overview.

For background on sociobiology, see Edmund O. Wilson's *Sociobiology: The New Synthesis* (Belknap Press, 1975), Daniel G. Freedman's *Human Sociobiology: a Holistic Approach* (Free Press, 1979), and Georg Breuer's *Sociobiology and the Human Dimension* (Cambridge University Press, 1992). For an alternative view, see Marshall Sahlins's critique *The Use and Abuse of Biology: An Anthropological Critique of Sociobiology* (University of Michigan Press, 1976).

Important essays from a critical perspective are contained in two edited volumes: George E. Marcus and Michael M. J. Fisher's *Anthropology as Cultural Critique: An Experimental Moment in the Human Sciences* (University of Chicago Press, 1986) and James Clifford and George E. Marcus's *Writing Culture: The Poetics and the Politics of Anthropology* (University of California Press, 1986).

ISSUE 10

Are San Hunter-Gatherers Basically Pastoralists Who Have Lost Their Herds?

YES: James R. Denbow and Edwin N. Wilmsen, from "Advent and Course of Pastoralism in the Kalahari," *Science* (December 19, 1986)

NO: Richard B. Lee, from *The Dobe Ju/'hoansi*, 3rd ed. (Wadsworth Thomson Learning, 2003)

ISSUE SUMMARY

YES: Archaeologists James R. Denbow and Edwin N. Wilmsen argue that the San of the Kalahari Desert in southern Africa have been involved in pastoralism, agriculture, and regional trade networks since at least A.D. 800. They imply that the San, who were hunting and gathering in the twentieth century, were descendants of pastoralists who lost their herds due to subjugation by outsiders, drought, and livestock disease.

NO: Cultural anthropologist Richard B. Lee counters that evidence from oral history, archaeology, and ethnohistory shows that the Ju/'hoansi group of San living in the isolated Nyae Nyae-Dobe area of the Kalahari Desert were autonomous hunter-gatherers until the twentieth century. Although they carried on some trade with outsiders before then, it had minimal impact on their culture.

Can hunter-gatherers (also called "foragers") be economically self-sufficient and politically autonomous even when in contact with more powerful food-producing peoples? This is the basic question behind the "Great Kalahari Debate," which is illustrated by the following selections.

Even in the late nineteenth century, hunting-and-gathering peoples living outside the disruptive influence of complex societies and colonialism were scarce. By then most Native American hunter-gatherers were on reservations or incorporated into the fur trade, and others, like the Veddas of Sri Lanka, had been absorbed and transformed by the dominant societies that surrounded them. The most striking exception was the Australian Aborigines, who were still nomadic hunter-gatherers using stone tools at the time of European contact.

Aborigines became the model of the earliest stage of cultural evolution as discussed by Emile Durkheim in *The Elementary Forms of the Religious Life* (George Allen and Unwin Ltd., 1915) and Sigmund Freud in *Totem and Taboo* (Moffat, Yard, 1918). By the 1950s, however, most Aborigines, too, had been settled on ranches, missions, or government settlements, and their cultures had been radically disrupted. Anthropologists' waning hopes of studying other "pristine" foragers were suddenly raised when an American family, the Marshalls, found and studied a group of Ju/'hoansi (!Kung) San living by independent foraging in the Kalahari Desert of Southwest Africa (now Namibia). Lorna Marshall's scholarly articles (later collected in her book *The !Kung of Nyae Nyae* [Harvard University Press, 1976]), her daughter Elizabeth Marshall Thomas's popular book *The Harmless People* (Knopf, 1959) and her son John's films (e.g., *The Hunters*) attracted great attention to the San.

In 1963 then-graduate student Richard B. Lee went to northwestern Bechuanaland (now Botswana) in search of an independent foraging San group. He found such a group in the Ju/'hoansi at Dobe waterhole. Although he recognized that they interacted with Bantu-speaking herding people in the region, his research focused on their adaptation to the natural environment. His findings led to a radically new image of the San and, eventually, of foragers in general. Once thought to live in a precarious struggle for survival, he found that the Ju/'hoansi actually needed to work less than 22 hours a week to get an adequate amount of food. The key to their success was their dependence on plant foods, mostly gathered by women, rather than meat, and the emphasis placed on food sharing.

By the early 1970s, however, some anthropologists had begun to question the popular image of San as isolated people with a continuous history of independent foraging since preagricultural times. In their selection, James R. Denbow and Edwin N. Wilmsen make the case that the Kalahari San have long participated in the regional economy and political system. They argue that the Ju/'hoansi and other inhabitants of the Kalahari Desert were agropastoralists (farmer-herders) and commodity traders until the late nineteenth century, when dominating outsiders, drying climate, and livestock diseases caused some of them to lose their herds and revert (temporarily) to full-time foraging.

Richard B. Lee responds that some San groups—such as the Ju/'hoansi of the Nyae Nyae-Dobe area—were quite isolated from outsiders until the late nineteenth century, when Europeans and Bantu-speaking Africans began to make occasional journeys into their homeland. Thus, his research suggests that foraging societies can live in contact with food-producers without being economically or politically subjugated by them.

This debate raises a number of important questions. Can small-scale, politically weak societies have economic and political ties with powerful outsiders without being dominated and fundamentally changed? Can one generalize from one case like the Dobe Ju/'hoansi to other foraging peoples? If foragers were herders or farmers in the past, can they still tell us something about the hunting-and-gathering way of life before the advent of agriculture?

James R. Denbow and
Edwin N. Wilmsen

Advent and Course of Pastoralism in the Kalahari

It has long been thought that farming and herding were compara-
tively recent introductions into the Kalahari and that it has been a
preserve of foraging "Bushmen" for thousands of years. Agropastoral
Bantu-speakers were thought to have entered this region only within
the last two centuries. However, fully developed pastoralism and metallurgy are now shown to have been established in the Kalahari from
A.D. 500, with extensive grain agriculture and intracontinental trade
added by A.D. 800. Archeological, linguistic, and historical evidence
delineates the continuation of mixed economies in the region into the
present. Consequences of this revised view for anthropological theory
and for policy planning concerning contemporary Kalahari peoples
are indicated.

When the principal ethnographic studies of southern African peoples,
then called "Bushmen" (1), were undertaken in the 1950's and 1960's, very little
was known of their prehistory or of the history of their association with herding and farming peoples; a similar lack of historic depth characterized earlier
southern Bantu studies (2). At the time, it was universally assumed that Bantu-
speaking farming-herding peoples had intruded into the Kalahari no more than
two or three centuries ago. The region was presumed to have been peopled previously only by San-speaking foragers who had, until then, remained isolated
from external influences.

Before the mid-1970's, only two systematic archeological investigations
had been carried out in Botswana, an area approximately the size of Texas
(575,000 square kilometers); only one attempt had been made to integrate the
history of relations among hunting and herding Kalahari peoples. In addition, the climatic history of the Kalahari and its potential influence on local
economies was entirely unknown. Likewise, linguistic studies, with their implications for revealing the history of social interaction and diversification in
the region, were in their infancy. The assumption that pastoralism and social
heterogeneity in the Kalahari were very recently introduced appeared to be
correct.

Current work in archeology, geology, linguistics, and anthropology renders that assumption untenable. Since 1975, excavations have been carried out at 34 archeological sites in Botswana as well as at other sites in Zimbabwe and Namibia. Seventy-nine radiocarbon dates now delineate the chronology of domesticated food production in Botswana during the past 2000 years. These investigations indicate that cattle (*Bos taurus*) and ovicaprids were introduced along with ceramics into the northern Kalahari in the final centuries B.C. and first centuries A.D. Slightly later, grain cultivation and metallurgy were part of the economic repertoire of Early Iron Age (EIA) pastoralists in the region. By the ninth century, these peoples were engaged in trade networks that brought exotic goods such as glass beads and marine shells from the Indian Ocean into the Kalahari.

Geologic evidence suggests that significantly higher rainfall may have created an environment that encouraged the initial establishment of pastoral economies in the region. Linguistic evidence points to the diversification of Khoisan and southern Bantu languages coincident with this agropastoral expansion. Archival sources from the 18th and 19th centuries as well as oral histories document varying conjunctions of pastoralism and foraging in the economies of both Khoisan and Bantu-speakers that existed in precolonial time and characterize the region to this day. These sources also confirm the continued involvement of these peoples in ancient intracontinental trade networks that were not dominated by European colonial merchants until the second half of the 19th century. As a result of these studies, relations among hunters and herders in the Kalahari are shown to be both of longer duration and more integrated than has been thought.

The Context of Initial Pastoralism

Excavations of Late Stone Age (LSA) sites in the Kalahari reveal forager subsistence patterns differing from those recorded ethnographically among San in the region. Brooks and Helgren report that, in at least some LSA sites in the Makgadikgadi Pans area, fish and other aquatic resources complemented land animals in the subsistence of foragers between 4000 and 2000 years ago. At Lotshitshi, on the southeastern edge of the Okavango Delta, a LSA stratum dating within this period was found to contain fish, bullfrogs, and turtles along with large land mammals. Reconnaissance in the Makgadikgadi complex located over 50 additional LSA sites; two of these include small quantities of Bambata ceramics in their assemblages; eight others contain somewhat later EIA Gokomere or Kumadzulo pottery types. At Bambata Cave, in Zimbabwe, ceramics with remains of domesticated sheep are dated tentatively as early as the second century B.C. Maunatlala, in eastern Botswana, has ceramics and pole-and-clay hut remains at the end of the fourth century A.D.

The middle LSA level of Lotshitshi dates in the third century A.D. Faunal remains from this component indicate a broadly based economy including cattle (*B. taurus*) along with zebra, wildebeest, duiker, warthog, smaller game, and fish. Ceramics from this site are too fragmented for accurate identification, but their thin, charcoal-tempered fabric and finely incised decoration are compatible with Bambata types. Farther westward, in Namibia, ceramics (not Bambata ware) were present before A.D. 400 at Mirabib (with domestic sheep) and Falls Rock. Of the sites mentioned thus far, only Maunatlala has yielded evidence of metal use.

Radiocarbon dates placing sheep, and possibly cattle, but not metal, as far south as the Cape of Good Hope in the first century A.D. have been available for some years, consequently, a gap in data existed between these very early pastoralist manifestations in the far south and older centers north of the Okavango and Zambezi Rivers. The early pastoralist sites in the Kalahari and its margins begin to fill that gap. Consistent association of ceramics and domestic animals with LSA assemblages and their early dates indicate that pastoralist elements were introduced from the north into indigenous foraging economies here before the currently documented beginning of the Iron Age in southern Africa.

Recently acquired geomorphological evidence for fluctuating climates in the region has implications for these changes in LSA economies. At the Cwihaba caverns in western Ngamiland, periodically more humid climatic conditions are indicated by episodes of rapid sinter formation. In order to account for these episodes, Cooke suggests that rainfall in western Ngamiland reached 300 percent of the present annual mean between 2500 and 2000 years ago and again around 750 years ago. In general, these dates parallel those obtained for the sequence of beach levels found around the Makgadikgadi, Ngami, and Mababe basins where a number of higher lake levels with intervening regressions are indicated between 3000 and 1500 years ago.

Although it cannot be assumed that these high lake levels were caused solely by increased rainfall, Shaw argues for generally wetter conditions over the delta at dates congruent with those of Cwihaba. He estimates that rainfall over the Okavango increased between 160 and 225 percent. Under such a regime, many currently ephemeral pans and springs would also have contained more constant supplies of available water. Brain and Brain found evidence, in the form of microfaunal proportions, for episodes of climatic amelioration between about 4000 and 500 years ago at Mirabib in Namibia. Thus, several independent studies indicate higher rainfall during the millennium embracing the initial spread of agropastoral economies through the region 2500 to 1500 years ago.

In recent years, studies of Khoe (Central Khoisan) languages have proliferated in the Kalahari; all lead to an estimate that Khoe diversification in this region began about 2000 years ago. Vossen finds words for cattle and milking with apparent Proto-Khoe roots in the Khoe languages of north central Botswana. Köhler finds such words, along with a Khoe crop vocabulary, among the Kxoe (Khoe-speakers of northern Namibia). Both conclude that pastoralism must have been familiar to these peoples for a long time.

Ehret also argues that the basic separation of Khoi and Central Khoisan languages took place in the Botswana-Angola border region shortly after 500 B.C. He proposed further, from lexical evidence, that the basic pastoralist vocabulary of southern Bantu is derived through a Khoisan intermediary in this area, implying that these Bantu-speakers, but not others farther north, acquired cattle and sheep from Khoisan-speaking peoples. Pfouts suggests diversification of the Bantu languages of Namibia and southern Angola beginning about 1500 to 2000 years ago, whereas Ehret and Kinsman specifically place diversification of Proto-southeast Bantu in the EIA of this time frame. These authors suggest that economic factors contributed to this process of linguistic differentiation; their conclusions are compatible with the archeological evidence regarding initiation of pastoralism and socioeconomic heterogeneity in southern Africa. Elphick reconstructs historical data to reach a similar conclusion.

The Early Iron Age

The western sandveld.   The presence of Iron Age agropastoral communities in the Kalahari by the middle of the first millennium is now attested for Ngamiland as well as for eastern Botswana. At Tsodilo Hills, in the sandveld, 70 kilometers west of the Okavango, extensive excavations have uncovered settlements that span the period from the 6th to the 11th centuries A.D. Ceramics from the earliest (A.D. 550–730) of these sites, Divuyu, indicate that it belongs to an EIA variant, the distribution of which appears to extend northward into Angola. There are no close parallels in known EIA assemblages to the south, either in Zimbabwe or South Africa. Common decoration motifs consist of multiple parallel bands of combstamping separated by spaces that are either blank or filled-in with incised motifs. Divuyu ceramics are charcoal tempered but have substantial inclusions of calcrete.

A wide variety of iron and copper implements and ornaments were recovered from Divuyu but only a single stone tool. The presence of slag and bloomery waste indicates that metal working took place on the site. An amorphous scatter of friable burned clay fragments with stick impressions marks the probable location of a pole-and-clay hut. Fragments of perforated ceramic strainers indicate that salt was extracted from local sources. Unidentified marine shells provide firm evidence for coastal links, possibly through Angolan sites. Local trade with peoples of the Okavango system is indicated by the presence of fish bones and river mollusk shells (*Unio* sp. or *Aspartharin* sp.). Domesticated ovicaprids made up a large portion of the diet at Divuyu; domesticated *Bos* was rare. Large quantities of carbonized mongongo nut shells (*Ricinodendron rautanenii*) attest to the importance of foraging in the economy.

In the second Iron Age site at Tsodilo, Nqoma, a lower stratum contains Divuyu ceramics contemporary with the final dates at Divuyu itself. The major components at Nqoma stratigraphically overlie this material and are dated in the ninth and tenth centuries. Ceramics from these later components are uniformly charcoal tempered with few inclusions of other materials; decoration is most often applied as bands of interlocking triangles or in pendent triangles filled with hatching, combstamping, or linear punctuating. False-relief chevron designs occur frequently. Only a few dated sites are presently available for comparison. We see affinities with Sioma, in southwestern Zambia, and Dundo, in northeastern Angola, dated to the sixth through eighth centuries in the range of Divuyu and the beginning of Nqoma occupations at Tsodilo, but systematic ceramic comparisons of these sites have yet to be undertaken. Nqoma ceramics are similar to those from the ninth century site at Kapako on the Okavango River in Namibia; charcoal-tempered ceramics have been dated to the same period far out in the sandveld at NxaiNxai and are found in adjacent parts of Botswana and Namibia.

Evidence for metal working is attested at Nqoma by the presence of tuyeres as well as slag and bloom. Iron and copper ornaments are common and include finely made chains and necklaces with alternating links of copper and iron as well as bracelets with designs sometimes preserved by rust and oxidation. Moderate numbers of stone tools of LSA types are present. Dense areas of burned clay with pole and stick impressions mark the locations of substantial house structures.

Cattle (*Bos taurus*) were paramount in the pastoral economy of Nqoma; preliminary analysis suggests they outnumber ovicaprids by a factor of 2. Bifid thoracic vertebrae indicate that at least some of these cattle were of a hump-backed variety. Carbonized seeds of sorghum (*Sorghum bicolor* caffra), pearl millet (*Pennisetum americannum* thyphoides), and perhaps melons (*Cucurbita* sp.) provide direct evidence for cultivation. Remains of wild game along with carbonized mongongo nuts and *Grewia* seeds indicate that foraging continued to form an important part of the diet of this Iron Age population. Fish bones and river mollusk shells document continuing trade connections with the Okavango to the north and east.

Many glass beads and marine shells, primarily cowrie, along with worked ivory, one piece in the shape of a conus shell, provide evidence that Nqoma was an important local center in an intracontinental trade network extending to the Indian Ocean in the ninth century.

The river systems.   Although the origins of the EIA communities at Tsodilo point consistently northward to Angola, contemporary agropastoralist sites on the eastern margins of the Okavango Delta as well as on the Chobe River belong firmly within the Kumadzulo-Dambwa complex documented by Vogel for the Victoria Falls area. This complex forms a regional facies of the widespread Gokomere tradition of western Zimbabwe and northeastern Botswana. Kumadzulo-Dambwa complex ceramics and small clay figurines of hump-backed cattle were found at the eighth century site of Serondela, on the Chobe River, and cattle bones along with LSA lithics and similar ceramics were recovered at Hippo Tooth on the Botletle River dating to the early ninth century. At the island site of Qugana, in the eastern delta, the same ceramic complex with burned, reed-impressed clay hut remains dates to the eighth century; as yet, no domestic fauna have been recovered from this site.

Matlhapaneng, on the southeastern Okavango, is an extensive site dated between the late seventh and tenth centuries, contemporary with the Nqoma sequence at Tsodilo. Ceramics are charcoal tempered with Kumadzulo-Dambwa decoration motifs. Pole-and-clay structures, iron, copper, and ivory ornaments, slag, and bloomery waste mark this as a fully formed EIA community. LSA stone tools are also present. Although this site is not as rich as Nqoma, long-distance trade connections are attested by the presence of cowrie shells and glass beads. Carbonized remains of sorghum (*S. bicolor caffra*), millet (*P. americanum typhoides*), and cow peas (*Vigna unguiculata*) provide evidence for agriculture; cattle and ovicaprids dominate faunal remains. Foraging was important here as it was at Tsodilo; carbonized marula (*Sclerocarya caffra*) and *Grewin* seeds are present and wild animal remains are common.

The eastern hardveld.   Similar developments took place simultaneously in the eastern hardveld where thick kraal dung deposits vitrified by burning have been found at more than 200 sites, indicating that large herds were kept in the region. The same EIA suite of materials already described is present, although ceramics are of Gokomere-Zhizo types with affinities eastward to Zimbabwe and northern Transvaal. East coast trade, documented by glass beads and marine shells, is dated in the late first millennium at a number of these sites as well as at contemporary sites in Zimbabwe and the Transvaal.

Major chiefdoms developed along this eastern margin of the Kalahari at the end of the first millennium, marking a transition to later centralized state development. A tripartite hierarchy of settlement size and complexity is discernible at this time. Large towns of approximately 100,000 square meters, Toutswe, K2, and Mapungubwe, dominated extensive hinterlands containing smaller villages and many small hamlets. Rulers of these chiefdoms succeeded in controlling the Indian Ocean trade into the Kalahari; it is possible that a system supplying valued goods in tribute to these chiefdoms from the western sandveld was instituted at this time, displacing previous exchange relations in which foreign imports as well as local exports had circulated widely.

Supporting evidence for changes in social relations of economic production is found in a comparison of age distributions of cattle and ovicaprid remains at the middle-order sites, Nqoma, Matlhapaneng and Taukome, with those at the capital towns, Mapungubwe and K2. At the first set of sites, a bimodal culling pattern is found similar to that of present-day cattle posts in Botswana, where slaughter is highest in nonreproductive age classes. Such a strategy conserves breeding stock and emphasizes rates of herd growth rather than meat production. Producers and consumers of herd products at these sites probably belonged to the same local social units.

In contrast, at Mapungubwe and K2, both primary centers, the majority of cattle slaughtered were in prime age classes; offtake appears not to have followed the conservative strategy found at the secondary sites. In other studies, this form of distribution has been associated with differential social stratification among occupants of a site. This appears to be the most plausible explanation for the contrasting culling patterns observed in our study. Elites at primary centers appear to have been selective consumers of prime rather than very old animals, many of which would have been produced elsewhere.

The Kalahari in the Second Millennium

These eastern Kalahari chiefdoms collapsed around the beginning of the 13th century. Great Zimbabwe emerged at this time, supplanting the political role played earlier at Toutswe, K2, and Mapungubwe. The extent of this new hegemony is indicated by stone-walled Zimbabwe-Khami outposts found far out in the Kalahari on the margins of the Makgadikgadi Pans. Control of trade became the prerogative of this kingdom. The final component at Toutswe (A.D. 1500) is devoid of exotic goods and no long-distance trade items have been recovered from two rock shelters, Qomqoisi and Depression, excavated at Tsodilo and dated to the 16th and 17th centuries, nor in an upper stratum at Lotshitshi, which, though undated, probably falls in this period.

Glass beads reappear at Xaro in Ngamiland at the beginning of the 17th century. These and cowrie shells are abundant at the 18th century site, Kgwebe, as well as in a probably contemporary (though not yet dated) upper stratum at Nqoma. Portuguese, through their Atlantic trade into the Kongo and Angola, were the probable source of these beads, which reached the interior along trade routes that had functioned since the Early Iron Age. Many of the first Europeans to enter the region from the Cape record that this trade in Portuguese goods was active south of the Orange River and to the east at least as far as the Zambezi by the 18th century. Native peoples including San-speakers, not Portuguese themselves, are specified in these records as the interior agents of this trade.

Archival records as well as oral histories testify to the importance of pastoralism throughout the Kalahari long before Europeans arrived. Every European who first observed the region from the 18th century on reports the presence of peoples of different languages, appearance, and group designation —Bantu and Khoissan—everywhere they went. Virtually every one of these Europeans remarks on the importance of pastoralism in all parts of the region and on the involvement of San-speakers in herding; several specifically mention San owners of livestock. Indeed, the herds of subsequently subjugated peoples were one inducement for Tswana expansion into Ngamiland in 1795. So rich in cattle was the northwestern Kalahari that 12,000 head were exported annually from it alone to the Cape during the 1860's through the 1880's, while unknown but apparently large numbers of interior cattle had been supplied to the Atlantic trade since the late 18th century.

In addition to cattle, 100,000 pounds of ivory along with many bales of ostrich feathers and hides are recorded to have been exported annually from the region as a whole during those decades in exchange for guns, tobacco, sugar, coffee, tea, cloth, beads, and other European goods. These were newly developed markets, but the trade networks they followed were continuations of Iron Age systems. Both Khoisan- and Bantu-speakers are reliably recorded by many observers to have been thoroughly involved in production for precolonial regional exchange networks. When first seen by Europeans in the 19th century, the copper mines and salt pans of northern Namibia were exclusively under San control; 50 to 60 tons of ore were estimated to be taken annually from those mines and traded to Bantu smiths. Trade routes were linked to wider subcontinental networks. Salt, manufactured into loaves, was traded far into the interior and is reported to have been at least as important an exchange commodity as copper.

In extension of this economic activity, San are credited with producing the bulk of ivory and ostrich feathers exported through Bantu and Nama middlemen during the 19th century. Relations of production and exchange were thus not strictly bounded by ethnic or linguistic divisions but cut across them. More than anything else, it is this negotiable lattice of relations among peoples and production that characterizes the last two millennia in the Kalahari.

Discussion

We have summarized a large body of data pertaining to prehistoric and historic economies of Kalahari peoples, and those surrounding them, which has been accumulated by a number of investigators.... We have concentrated on the early introduction and subsequent local transformations of agropastoralism in the region because these have been the least known aspects of those economies. Pastoralism has been treated in the ethnographies cited at the beginning of this article as if its history in and adjacent to the Kalahari has been recent and separate from that of indigenous foraging. A guiding assumption of these anthropological studies was that 20th-century foraging there is a way of life that has remained unchanged for millennia. Practitioners of these segregated economies have been rather strictly supposed to have had distinct ethnic and racial origins, in contact only for the last two centuries or less. This position can no longer be supported.

Many problems remain to be investigated. Much of the central Kalahari is unexplored archeologically, and the extent to which Iron Age pastoralism penetrated this area is unknown. A hiatus exists in our knowledge of the entire region between the 12th and 16th centuries. While large centralized states with many satellite communities flourished in the east, few if any sites are presently known for this period in the entire western half of southern Africa, with some possible exceptions at the Cape. Drier conditions may have led to shifts in settlement size and location, making detection of sites in the Kalahari difficult under present conditions. A reasonable hypothesis posits a concentration of population along the river systems and permanent springs leaving less densely peopled the drier hinterland, where foraging may have waxed and waned in accordance with changing environmental and regional economic conditions, particularly after European influence penetrated the region. It is unlikely that herders withdrew entirely from the sandveld; more likely, they at least continued to exploit seasonal surface water and grazing. At present, there is no evidence either to support or refute these propositions.

All of the peoples of the Kalahari during the past two millennia have been linked by extensive social and economic networks; thus, during this period of time, the Kalahari was never the isolated refuge of foragers it has been thought to be. It was the vastly intensified extraction of commoditized animal products in the colonial period, abetted by a drying climatic trend and stock diseases, especially rinderpest, which killed 75 percent of all cattle and antelope in southern Africa at the end of the 19th century, that combined to pauperzie the region. These forces became factors leading to increased labor migration

to the newly opened South African mines. In the process, the dues and privileges of earlier native states became increasingly translated into private family
fortunes of a colonially favored aristocracy, while previously flexible relations
among Khoisan and Bantu-speakers were transformed into ethnic categories defined by criteria of race, language, and economic class. The resultant divisions
gave, to anthropological observers in the 20th century, the false impression of
a Kalahari eternally empty, its peoples long segregated and isolated from each
other.

An unresolved problem concerns the presence of Bantu-speakers in the
western half of the subcontinent, a presence that now appears to have been
more pervasive and much earlier than previously assumed. There is no doubt
that the introduction of EIA economies from central Africa brought with it
a complex interdigitation of people south of the Zambezi-Okavango-Cunene
Rivers. In the eastern half of the subcontinent, it is well established that Iron
Age Bantu agropastoralists gained a dominant position over indigenous foragers and pastoralists, ultimately subjugating, absorbing, or eliminating them.
This did not happen in the west where, in fact, Khoi-speaking (Nama) herders
dominated a large part of the area when first encountered by Europeans. It has
been thought that a major reason for this difference lay in the short history of
association of these peoples in the west. The perceived isolating severity of the
Kalahari environment has been seen as a primary factor protecting San foragers
from Bantu pastoralist domination. Neither supposition finds support in the
research reported here.

This research has profound implications for understanding relations
among contemporary southern African peoples. In particular, those relegated
to the ethnographic categories "Bushman" and "hunter-gatherers" are seen to
have a history radically different from that hitherto assumed. It is clear that,
rather than being static, uniform relics of an ancient way of life, San societies and cultures have undergone transformations in the past 2000 years that
have varied in place and time in association with local economic and political
alterations involving a variety of peoples.

Two important consequences flow from this new understanding. The first
forces reevaluation of models of social evolution based on assumptions brought
to the anthropological study of these peoples. At the very least, ethnographic
analogies formulated on modern San "foragers" and applied to studies of evolving social forms must be modified to take into account the millennia-long
association of these peoples with both pastoralism and Bantu-speakers. Following on this, and more immediately important, is the need to bring the results of
this research into the arena of policy planning. In this arena, San are routinely
dismissed as rootless "nomads," without legitimate claim to full participation
in modern national politics because they are conceived to be unprepared by
history to cope with complex decisions involving economic and political alternatives. That this is no more true of them than of any other peoples should be
clear in even this brief account of their recent past.

Notes

1. Etymologies of the terms "Bushmen" and "San" are debated; a long-standing derogatory connotation is acknowledged for the first of these, but San, as also "Bantu," has acquired segregating racial and ethnic overtones. To avoid such implications, we use Khoisan and Bantu as adjectives to designate speakers of two different language families, retaining San only where necessary to specify peoples so labeled in ethnographies. We use Setswana spelling, in which c and x represent the front clicks and q the back clicks of Khoisan words.

2. L. Marshall, *The !Kung of NyaeNyae* (Harvard Univ. Press, Cambridge, MA, 1976); R. Lee, *The !Kung San* (Harvard Univ. Press, Cambridge, MA, 1979); J. Tanaka, *The San* (Univ of Tokyo Press, Tokyo, 1980); G. Silberbauer, *Hunter and Habitat in the Central Kalahari Desert* (Cambridge Univ. Press, Cambridge, 1981); I. Schapera, *The Bantu-Speaking Tribes of Southern Africa* (Routledge, London, 1937); W. Hammond-Tooke, Ed., *The Bantu-Speaking Peoples of Southern Africa* (Routledge, London, 1974).

Richard B. Lee

The Kalahari Debate: Ju/'hoan Images of the Colonial Encounter

The Kalahari Debate, also known as Kalahari revisionism, sprung up in the late 1980s and early 1990s, and has been a topic of discussion among anthropologists ever since. What is at stake in the Kalahari Debate is the question of who the San peoples are historically—autonomous foragers or dependent serfs. The position taken [here] is that the Ju/'hoansi of the Dobe area, despite recent changes, show an unbroken history as independent hunters and gatherers that can be traced back far into the past. The "revisionists" argue that the Nyae Nyae and Dobe area Ju/'hoansi have been bound into regional trade networks and dominated by distant power holders for centuries. In this view they were not even hunters in the past but cattle-keepers, or servants of cattle people, raising the possibility that the Ju/'hoansi's unique cultural features of sharing and egalitarianism come not from their hunting and gathering traditions, but rather from being outcasts, at the bottom of a social hierarchy.

Curiously, until recently, neither the revisionists or their opponents had bothered to systematically ask the Ju people themselves for their views of their own history. How do the Ju/'hoansi interpret their past and how does that picture square with the evidence from archaeology and history? . . .

Beginning in 1986–1987 when the revisionist debate began to heat up, I started to ask Botswana Ju elders focused questions about the time they refer to as *n//a k'aishe* or "first time." The goal was to elicit collective memories of their pre-colonial past, a time we could date historically to the pre-1870s. Subsequently I returned for two more periods of interviewing, in 1995 and 1997, with informants from the Nyae Nyae and Cho/ana areas of Namibia. Now there are five major areas of Ju settlement represented in the oral history accounts. In this discussion, I will draw on three bodies of evidence on the Nyae Nyae-Dobe area Ju/'hoansi: their own oral histories, archaeology, and ethnohistory. . . .

Oral Histories

During my fieldwork in the Dobe area starting in the 1960s, the Ju/'hoansi were acutely aware that they were living under the gaze and control of the Tawana chiefdom and, beyond it, the British colonial authority. However in speaking of the area's past, Ju/'hoansi informants spoke of their own autonomy in the nineteenth century as a given: they were foragers who lived entirely on their own without agriculture or domesticated animals.

The existence of many Later Stone Age archeological sites in the Dobe area with thousands of stone artifacts and debris supports this view. But left unexplained is the presence on these same sites of small quantities of pottery and iron, indicating Iron Age presence or contact with Iron Age cultures. The Ju/'hoansi themselves explain the presence of these goods in terms of their long-standing trade relations with riverine peoples. On the other hand, Kalahari revisionists have argued that these archeological traces are proof positive of domination of the Dobe area by Iron Age peoples and the incorporation of the Ju/'hoansi into a regional polity. Wilmsen has further argued that people labeled Bushmen had raised cattle in centuries past:

> [I]n this century... an overwhelming majority of peoples so labeled have pursued a substantially pastoral way of life in symbiosis with, employed by, or enserfed to Bantu-speaking cattle owners... this is equally true of earlier centuries.

Remarkably, in all the voluminous writings on the Kalahari Debate..., neither side had systematically investigated how the Ju/'hoansi themselves articulate their own history.

An Interview With Kumsa N ≠whin

Kumsa n≠whin, a 70-year-old Dobe man, was a former tribal policeman and famous healer I interviewed in 1987. I began by asking him if long ago his ancestors had lived with cattle.

"No," he replied. "My father's father saw them for the first time. My father's father's father did not know them. The first non-San to come to the region were Europeans, not Blacks. We worked for them, got money and obtained our first cattle from the Tswana with that money. The Whites first came to !Kubi [south of Dobe], killed elephants and pulled their teeth [i.e., ivory]. In the old days the Ju/'hoansi also killed elephants with spears for the meat. At least 15 men were required for a hunt. They dumped the tusks [they didn't have a use for them].

"The Whites came by ≠dwa-/twe [lit. "giraffe-horse" [i.e., camels]. The Whites had no cattle, they had horses and camels. 'Janny' came from the south. Another one made a well at Qangwa [also called Lewisfontein]. My father said 'Oh, can water come out of there?' They used metal tools but not engines. This well is not used today. They spoke Burusi [Afrikaans]."

I asked, "Before the Whites came did you know 'Ju sa jo' [Black people] here?" His response was unequivocal: "No. We only knew ourselves. Ju/'hoansi exclusively."

"But when the Blacks did come, who was first?"

"The first Black was Mutibele, a Tswana, and his older brother, Mokgomphata. They came from the east following the paths made by the Whites going in the opposite direction. They were shown the waterholes by Ju/'hoansi including my father/Twi. They were shown the killing sites of the elephants, where the bones lay, the sites where Whites killed. And they said 'Oh, the Whites have already got the n!ore [territory] from us.' Then [Mutibele's] father claimed the land and all the Ju/'hoansi on it, but he deceived us."

"How did he deceive you? When the Tswana claims he is master of you all, do you agree?"

"If he was the master, he didn't give us anything, neither clothes nor pots, or even one calf. The Europeans had given the Ju/'hoansi guns. When the Tswana saw this they decided to give guns to other Ju/'hoansi, so that they could hunt eland and giraffe."

Later in the conversation I explored the nature of San-Black interactions in the precolonial period. What had they received from the Blacks?

"When I was young," Kumsa replied, "we had no iron pots. We used the clay pots of the Goba. We couldn't make them ourselves."

"Then how do you account for the fact that there are many potsherds on old Ju/'hoansi sites around here?"

"Our fathers' fathers and their fathers' fathers got them from the Gobas. They would trade for them with skins. The Gobas didn't come up here. They stayed where they were [on the rivers] and we went to them. This went on for a very long time [so that is why there are so many potsherds]."

"We [always] got two things from them: iron and pots. If you go to Danega today you will find the right earth. But the Gobas didn't come here. We always went to them."

⋘◉⋙

Kumsa's statements are congruent with a model of autonomy. Others had also made the point that a long-standing trade existed with riverine peoples *in which the Ju did the travelling*. It would be hard to argue that the Blacks could dominate the Dobe area without any physical presence, but I suppose it is not impossible. The trading trips made by the Ju to the east and elsewhere would certainly account for the presence of Iron Age materials on the Dobe area sites. In fact Polly Wiessner has argued that the levels of iron and pottery found on Dobe area Later Stone Age (LSA) sites can be accounted for by *hxaro* trade, a traditional form of delayed exchange still practiced by the Ju/'hoansi that historically has been a vehicle for long-distance trade.

One suggestive point was Kumsa's intriguing statement that the precolonial Ju hunted elephant but discarded the tusks; remarkable because it indicates that the Dobe Ju/'hoansi were hunting elephant for subsistence and were not part of a mercantile *or* a tributary network, since in either case elephant ivory would have been a prime valuable item.

Also interesting is Kumsa's rather dismissive view of the Tswana as overlords. For Kumsa the criterion for being a chief [lit. in San, "wealth-person"] is giving away in this context, not exercising power *per se*. The Europeans were chiefs because they gave guns, the Tswana were "deceivers" because in Kumsa's terms they claimed chiefly status but gave nothing.

A !Goshe Commentary on the Early Days of Contact

/Ti!kai-n!a, aged 80 at the time of the interview (1987), and /Ti!kai-tsau ("tooth") age 63, were two of the leading men of !Goshe, 16 kilometers east of Qangwa, and the easternmost and most economically "progressive" of the Dobe area villages. !Goshe is the jumping-off point for travel to the east, and the village has kept Tswana cattle since the 1910s. With their strong ties to the east where most Blacks reside, !Goshe people, by reason of history and geography, are the most attuned to links to "Iron Age" peoples.

"Certain Europeans in Gaborone," I began, "argue that long ago you Ju/ 'hoansi, [that is] your fathers' fathers' fathers' fathers had cattle. Do you agree?"

"No! Not a bit!" was the younger /Ti!kai's emphatic answer. "Long ago our fathers' fathers' fathers' fathers, the only meat *they* had was what they could shoot with arrows. We only got cows from the Tswana."

I persisted. "But when you dig holes deep down beneath where you live, you find pieces of pottery. Where did they come from?"

"Oh those pots were our own work!" replied the elder /Ti!kai. "Our ancestors made them. They would put them on the fire and cook with them. But since we got iron pots from you Europeans we lost the knowledge of pottery making."

Shifting the topic, I asked, "What about iron?"

"We got that from the Mbukushu," said /Ti!kai. "But we learned how to work it ourselves.... You stick it in the fire, heat it up, and hammer it.... We did it ourselves. We saw how the Gobas did it and we learned from them."

"Where did you get the iron itself from?"

Their answer surprised me. "The Europeans," said /Ti!kai. "The Tswana and Gobas didn't have it. They also got it from the Europeans."

I had to disagree. "But," I said, "in the oldest abandoned villages of the Gobas, iron is there. Long before the Europeans came."

At this point the older /Ti!kai intervened. "Yes! /Tontah is right. Long ago the Mbukushu had the pieces of iron that they worked."

The younger /Ti!kai turned to the older and asked, incredulously, "Well, where did they get the iron from?"

Matter-of-factly, the older man replied, "From the earth."

Much discussion followed on this point. The younger man was unconvinced that the Gobas had iron before the Europeans, but old /Ti!kai stuck to his story.

Shifting topic again, I asked, "Long long ago, did your fathers' fathers' fathers' fathers practice //hara [farming]?"

There was no disagreement on this point. "No, we didn't. We just ate the food that we collected from the bush."

The older /Ti!kai added, "When I was a boy we had learned about //hara from the Tswanas. They showed us how [to do it]."

The !Goshe interviews corroborate the account of Kumsa on the absence of cattle and agriculture before the twentieth-century arrival of the Tswana. They add detail on Ju/'hoan understandings of the history of pottery and iron use. In the first case they spoke of Ju manufacture of pottery, whereas other informants spoke of it as only imported. In the second case there was an intriguing difference of opinion. There was agreement that iron was imported from the Gobas but only in the recent past, but some believed that iron was so recent that the Gobas only obtained iron *after* the arrival of the Europeans, a view that we were to encounter elsewhere.

N!ae and /Kunta at Cho/ana

Another round of oral history interviews took place in 1995 at Cho/ana, a former Ju/'hoan waterhole, 65 kilometers northwest of Dobe, now located in Namibia's Kaudom Game Reserve. The informants were N!ae and her husband /Kunta (/Tontah) one of my namesakes. Cho/ana has long been known to historians as a meeting point for Ju/'hoansi from several regions. It was a convenient water hole for Ju/'hoan parties engaged in *hxaro* trade to meet.

In tracing the earliest history of the place, /Kunta saw the original owners as Ju/'hoansi, not Blacks or any other ethnic group. In the beginning, asserted /Kunta, only Ju/'hoansi lived here; there were no Gobas. Ju people would come from Nyae Nyae and from the north, to do *hxaro* here. It was a waterhole that always held water. People from the South (Nyae Nyae) would bring /*do* (ostrich eggshell beads). People from the North brought /*an* (glass beads). In /Kunta's words, "*Hxaro* brought them together."

A point of emphasis in our interviews was the question of whether the Gobas made trips to the interior to trade or to make their presence felt. /Kunta was emphatic: "No, [they didn't come to us] we went to them. We saw pots on their fires and wanted them, so they gave us some."

"And what did you give them in return?"

"We gave Gobas /*do* in exchange for pots."

The interior Ju/'hoansis' proximity to Iron Age peoples on their periphery and the use of iron as a marker of Iron Age overlordship has been a particular point of emphasis for the revisionists. I was anxious to hear /Kunta and N!ae's views of the pre-colonial use of iron and its source.

"Did your ancestors have !*ga* (iron)?"

"Are you joking? We didn't know !*ga*. If we needed arrows we used ≠*dwa* (giraffe) or *n!n* (eland) bones."

"Who gave Ju/'hoansi the iron?"

"We visited north and east and saw this wonderful stuff for arrows and knives; we asked Gobas for it and got some. It was very valuable; when others saw it their hearts were sad because they didn't have it; they wanted it so badly they would even fight other Ju for it. Parties went north to seek it; Gobas gave it to them in exchange for steenbok and duiker skins and other things."

"Where did Goba get iron from?"

Without hesitation /Kunta replied, "From the European."

"Are you saying that before Europeans came Gobas had no iron?"

"Yes, they had no iron."

❧❦❧

It is interesting that informants see iron coming ultimately from Europeans; they saw the appearance of iron and Europeans in their areas as so close in time that iron was associated with Europeans. While it is true that the amount of iron on Nyae Nyae-Dobe LSA sites is miniscule, it is striking that the long history of Iron Age occupation on their periphery, for example at the Tsodilo Hills with radiocarbon dates as early as 500 A.D., doesn't have much resonance with the Ju/'hoansi informants. When they did obtain iron from the Gobas, it was clearly an item of trade and not a marker of overlordship. In any event the very (post-European) regency of the trade in iron challenges the revisionist view of a deep antiquity of Ju/'hoan subservience.

Discussion

In all interviews there was repeated insistence that no Gobas or any other Blacks occupied their area or even visited prior to the late nineteenth century; several spoke of the Gobas' preference for staying on the river and avoiding the dry interior. All these accounts illuminate the pragmatic and matter-of-fact approach of Dobe and Nyae Nyae area people to questions of history. These, after all, are questions of the most general nature and the accounts agree closely, not only about the autonomy of the area from outside domination but also about the absence of cattle and agriculture in pre-colonial times (though not of pottery and iron). There are interesting divergences of opinion on whether pottery was imported or locally made, and on whether the Gobas had iron before the Europeans. Taken together these accounts along with others... constitute a fair representation of mid and late twentieth-century Ju/'hoan views of their forebearers' nineteenth-century history of autonomy.

One other indication of the Ju sense of their history is the largely positive self-image of their past. They see themselves as actors, not victims, and this contrasts with the negative self-imagery expressed by other San people, (such as Hai//om or Nharo views of their present and past.

Archaeological Tie-ins

The oral history interviews in both 1995 and 1997 accompanied archaeological excavation, designed to link archaeology with the knowledge that was part of the living tradition of the Ju/'hoansi. Professor Andrew Smith of the University of Cape Town started excavating a rich Later Stone Age archaeological site at Cho/ana, which provided a continual stimulus for oral history as new and interesting materials came to light in the excavations. The Ju informants' comments provided a valuable adjunct to the archaeological work (and vice versa). They identified plant remains, made tentative suggestions regarding fragmentary bone materials, and provided a social context in which the material could be interpreted. For example, the elders described a kind of white glass bead as one of the earliest of the European trade goods obtained through intermediaries to the north. A few days after the interview, precisely such a bead was found in a sealed level in association with an LSA industry.

But the most stunning confirmation of the direct late nineteenth-century encounter between people with advanced stone-working skills and colonialists was a piece of bottle glass (mouth and neck) showing signs of delicate micro-retouching that the South African Later Stone Age is famous for. This gave a further indication of the persistence of LSA stone-working techniques into the colonial contact period.

The oral history's insistence on the absence of cattle and Blacks in the interior was confirmed by the complete lack in the archaeological record of the presence of domesticated animals or of non-Ju/'hoan people in the area prior to the latter part of the nineteenth century....

Colonial Constructions of the Ju/'hoansi

Turning to the third body of evidence, what light do ethnohistoric documents shed on these Ju accounts of their own past? Do they support or contradict Ju accounts of relative autonomy? In general, the few historical accounts we do have support the Ju/'hoansi view of autonomy....

One of the earliest detailed accounts of the Nyae Nyae-Dobe Ju/'hoansi comes relatively late when Hauptman Müller, a German colonial officer, traveled through the Nyae Nyae area in 1911. Müller offers some unusually detailed observations on the situation of the Nyae Nyae-Dobe area Ju/'hoansi some 30 years after colonial trade had been established. In Müller's account (1912) the area remained remote and inaccessible. His visit was the first to the interior from the west in five years.

Most telling is Müller's ethnographic description of the bushman inhabitants of this stretch of land he calls "virginal" [jungfräulich]. He depicts their state as "noch uberuhrt von aller Zivilisation, in alter Ursprunglichkeit" [still untouched by all civilization in their old pristine state]. He reports with amusement how European objects such as matches and mirrors were unknown to them, as well as the camels of his troopers, which startled them and caused the women to grab their children and scatter into the bush. However, he did find them using such things as wooden bowls, glass and iron beads, cooper rings, and "Ovambo knives," all obtained through trade with Black neighbors.

Of particular interest is Müller's descriptions of the Bushman themselves. In his account they were well nourished and relatively tall, thanks to an ample diet of meat (hunted with bone-tipped arrows) and a variety of wild plants. There is no mention in Müller's account of any resident cattle or Bantu-speaking overlords, though BaTswana were visiting the area during his stay. For Müller the association of the Nyae Nyae Bushmen with the BaTswana was not ancient; it was of recent date and was based on trade and assistance rendered at the latters' hunting expeditions. The Bushmen were rewarded with gifts for their services and the relationship with the hunter/herders is described as equitable and friendly:

> The Bushmen seem, however, to be good friends with the BaTswanas. When I asked a Bushman if it didn't bother him that the BaTswanas were killing off so much game every year he said "Yes, but we are getting presents!" ...

Müller's is one of the earliest accounts to be based on actual reports of what he observed, as distinguished from second-hand accounts at a distance. And the preceding short quotation is among the very first to cite the actual words of a Ju/'hoan person.

⌇⊛⌇

To sum up this section, both German and Ju/'hoan testimony are consistent and mutually supportive. The detail presented by Müller and the others (such as Hans Schinz and James Chapman) attests to five propositions that accord closely with statements made by the Ju/'hoansi themselves:

1. The relative isolation of the Nyae Nyae-Dobe area from the West and the low volume of European traffic, 1880–1911
2. The absence of cattle in pre-colonial Ju subsistence
3. The absence of Bantu overlords or tributary relations
4. The relatively favorable terms of trade between Blacks and San
5. The relatively good foraging subsistence base and nutritional status of the San

These lines of evidence argue the case that the views of the Ju/'hoansi about their historical autonomy are not sharply at odds with the ethnohistoric sources.

Hunter-Gatherer Discourse and Agrarian Discourse

Both the Ju oral histories and the German and other historical texts are cultural constructions, and yet, how are we to account for the correspondences between these two bodies of evidence? Why do they corroborate one another? To argue that both are careful fabrications still leaves open the question of why they agree so closely. One would have to invoke conspiracy or coincidence, in either case a tough sell. Surely it would be more reasonable to assume that they agree because they are describing the same reality. If Kumsa's, the two /Ti!kai's, N!ae and /Kunta's and others' collective accounts of the Ju/'hoansi autonomous past gibe so closely with those of European eyewitnesses such as Müller, then on what grounds rests the view of the historic Ju/'hoansi as enserfed pastoralists? And why has this view gained such currency in anthropological circles?

A more fruitful approach to understanding the recent debates is to attempt to place them in the context of the intellectual currents of the late twentieth century. How does the current conjuncture shape our perceptions of the situation of indigenous "others"?

Obviously, by the 1990s, the processes affecting the Dobe Ju/'hoansi had brought them to becoming clients, laborers, and rural proletarians, subject to and dependent on regional and world economies. Their current predicament is well understood by recourse to theories arising from political economy, dependency theory, or colonial discourse. Current theorizing is much weaker, however, in understanding the antecedent conditions. Part of the inability of contemporary theory to encompass hunters and gatherers as historical subjects is the lack of attention to the *differences* between discourses about hunters and gatherers and the discourses concerning agrarian societies and the emerging world system.

In agrarian discourse the presence of structures of domination are taken as given; it is the *forms* of domination and the modes of exploitation and surplus extraction that are problematic. In the literature on the agrarian societies of the Third World, stratification, class and class struggle, patriarchy, accumulation, and immiseration constitute the basic descriptive and analytical vocabulary.

In hunter-gatherer discourse it is not the forms and modes of domination that are at issue; rather the prior question to be asked is whether domination is *present*. I have been struck by the eagerness of otherwise competent analysts to gloss over, sidestep, or ignore this question.

There is no great mystery about what separates hunter-gatherer from agrarian societies. The former usually live lightly on the land at low densities; they can move and still survive, an escape route not available to sedentary farmers. The latter, with high densities and fixed assets, can no longer reproduce themselves outside the system, and are rendered far more vulnerable to domination.

In the recent debate some analysts seem to have taken the world systems/ political economy position so literally that every culture is seen as nothing more than the sum total of its external relations. But surely there is more to a culture than its links of trade, tribute, domination, and subordination. There is the internal dynamic of the means by which a social group reproduces itself ecologically, socially, and in terms of its collective consciousness. . . .

An historically informed ethnography can offer an alternative to the totalizing discourses of world systems theory. The unself-conscious sense of their own nineteenth- and early twentieth-century autonomy expressed by Ju/'hoan hunter-gatherers and its corroboration by contemporaneous colonial observers is one example of how these powerful assumptions can be challenged. They bear testimony that in the not very distant past other ways of being were possible.

That said, autonomy should not be taken as an article of faith, nor is it an all-or-nothing proposition. It is, or should be, an empirical question, and each society may exhibit a complex array of more or less autonomy at stages in its history. Even in agrarian societies spaces are opened up, however small, for the expression of autonomous thought and behavior. Thus it need not be the exclusive preserve of non-hierarchical or noncolonized societies. . . .

With reference to the latter though, a final point: What is desperately needed is to theorize the communal mode of production and its accompanying world view. Without it there is a theoretical vacuum filled far too facilely by imputing capitalist relations of production, bourgeois subjectivity, or "culture of poverty" frameworks to hunter-gatherer peoples.

POSTSCRIPT

Are San Hunter-Gatherers Basically Pastoralists Who Have Lost Their Herds?

These selections express two radically different worldviews. Denbow and Wilmsen's view—which has been called the "revisionist" view—emphasizes the interconnectedness of societies and the tendency for powerful polities to exert control over their less powerful neighbors. On the other hand, Lee's view —called the "traditionalist" view—emphasizes the people's adaptation to their natural environment and sees their relations with outsiders as variable, depending on local circumstances. Most anthropologists recognize that all cultures are influenced by local conditions and by the larger social environment, including, to some extent, the entire "world system." The question is, How much weight should one give to these two types of influence?

The disagreement between these scholars and their supporters is not merely a matter of theoretical emphasis. They also disagree about the facts and their proper interpretation. In subsequent publications Wilmsen and Lee, in particular, have argued over such matters as the precise locations of groups and trade routes mentioned in travelers' journals and whether or not the presence of cattle bones, for example, in an archaeological site indicates trade or outside domination. For elaboration of Wilmsen and Denbow's views see "Paradigmatic History of San-Speaking Peoples and Current Attempts at Revision," *Current Anthropology* (vol. 31, no. 5, 1990) and Wilmsen's book *Land Filled With Flies: A Political Economy of the Kalahari* (University of Chicago Press, 1989). For Lee's critique of these sources see his and Mathias Guenther's "Problems in Kalahari Historical Ethnography and the Tolerance of Error," *History in Africa* (vol. 20, 1993) and "Oxen or Onions? The Search for Trade (and Truth) in the Kalahari," *Current Anthropology* (vol. 32, 1991).

The literature on the San is voluminous. Alan Barnard's book *Hunters and Herders of Southern Africa: A Comparative Ethnography of the Khoisan Peoples* (Cambridge University Press, 1992) is an excellent overview of the various San and Khoi (formerly called "Hottentot") peoples. Important expressions of the revisionist view include Carmel Schrire's article "An Inquiry Into the Evolutionary Status and Apparent Identity of San Hunter-Gatherers," *Human Ecology* (vol. 8, no. 1, 1980) and her chapter entitled "Wild Surmises on Savage Thoughts," in her edited volume *Past and Present in Hunter Gatherer Studies* (Academic Press, 1984). A crucial source on the history of the San is Robert Gordon's *The Bushman Myth: The Making of a Namibian Underclass* (Westview Press, 1992). Works supporting the traditionalist view include Susan Kent's "The Current Forager Controversy: Real vs. Ideal Views of Hunter-Gatherers," *Man* [n.s.] (vol. 27, 1992).

ISSUE 11

Do Sexually Egalitarian Societies Exist?

YES: Maria Lepowsky, from *Fruit of the Motherland: Gender in an Egalitarian Society* (Columbia University Press, 1993)

NO: Steven Goldberg, from "Is Patriarchy Inevitable?" *National Review* (November 11, 1996)

ISSUE SUMMARY

YES: Cultural anthropologist Maria Lepowsky argues that among the Vanatinai people of Papua New Guinea, the sexes are basically equal, although minor areas of male advantage exist. Men and women both have personal autonomy; they both have similar access to material possessions, influence, and prestige; and the activities and qualities of males and females are valued equally.

NO: Sociologist Steven Goldberg contends that in all societies men occupy most high positions in hierarchical organizations and most high-status roles, and they dominate women in interpersonal relations. He states that this is because men's hormones cause them to compete more strongly than women for high status and dominance.

In most of the world's societies, men hold the majority of leadership positions in public organizations, from government bodies, to corporations, to religious institutions. In families, husbands usually serve as heads of households and as primary breadwinners, while wives take responsibility for children and homes. Is the predominance of men universal and inevitable, a product of human nature, or is it a cultural fact that might vary or be absent under different circumstances? Are sexually egalitarian societies—in which men and women are equally valued and have equal access to possessions, power, and prestige— even possible?

Some nineteenth-century cultural evolutionists, including J. J. Bachofen and J. F. MacLellan, postulated that a matriarchal stage of evolution, in which women ruled, had preceded the patriarchal stage known to history. Today most anthropologists doubt that matriarchal societies ever existed, but it is well established that some societies trace descent matrilineally, through women, and that in these societies women generally play a more prominent public role than in patrilineal ones, where descent is traced from father to children.

Whether or not matriarchal societies ever existed, by the twentieth century European and American societies were firmly patriarchal. Most people considered this state of affairs not only natural but God-given. Both Christian and Jewish religions gave scriptural justification for the predominance of men and the subordination of women.

The anthropology of women (later termed "feminist anthropology"), which arose in the early 1970s, challenged the claim that the subordination of women was either natural or inevitable. The rallying cry of feminists was "Biology is not destiny." Women, it was said, could do anything society permits them to do, and patriarchal society, like any other social institution, could be changed.

Some feminist anthropologists considered male dominance to be universal but attributed it to universal cultural, not biological, causes. The groundbreaking volume *Woman, Culture, and Society,* Michelle Rosaldo and Louise Lamphere, eds. (Stanford University Press, 1974) presents some possible cultural reasons for universal male dominance. Rosaldo and Lamphere proposed that all societies distinguish between "domestic" and "public" domains and that women are always associated with the domestic domain, with the home and the raising of children, while men are active in the public domain, where they have opportunities to obtain wealth, power, and ties with other men.

Some anthropologists contend that sexually egalitarian societies once existed (e.g., Eleanor Leacock's "Women's Status in Egalitarian Society: Implications for Social Evolution," *Current Anthropology* [vol. 19, 1978]). They attribute the scarcity of such societies today to historical circumstances, particularly the spread of European patriarchal culture to the rest of the world through colonialism and Christian missionization.

In her selection, Maria Lepowsky argues that in the Vanatinai culture of Sudest Island in Papua New Guinea, the sexes are basically equal. She describes the numerous features of Vanatinai culture, including social practices and beliefs, that make this possible. She contends that matrilineal descent is one contributing factor, but that it alone does not guarantee sexually egalitarian social relations.

Steven Goldberg counters that males have more of the hormones that cause individuals to strive for dominance than women do. Therefore, regardless of cultural variations, men occupy most positions in hierarchical organizations and most high-status roles, and they are dominant in interpersonal relations with women. Goldberg would argue that even in a matrilineal society like the Vanatinai, more men than women would occupy positions of power and prestige.

While reading these selections, ask yourself whether or not the Vanatinai case actually contradicts Goldberg's assertion that all societies are male dominated. Do you know of any other societies in which men and women are apparently equal? Would a single sexually egalitarian society disprove Goldberg's thesis? If you accept Goldberg's contention that males have an innate tendency toward domination, do you think that any cultural arrangements could neutralize this or keep it in check?

Maria Lepowsky

Gender and Power

$\mathbf{V}$anatinai customs are generally egalitarian in both philosophy and practice. Women and men have equivalent rights to and control of the means of production, the products of their own labor, and the products of others. Both sexes have access to the symbolic capital of prestige, most visibly through participation in ceremonial exchange and mortuary ritual. Ideologies of male superiority or right of authority over women are notably absent, and ideologies of gender equivalence are clearly articulated. Multiple levels of gender ideologies are largely, but not entirely, congruent. Ideologies in turn are largely congruent with practice and individual actions in expressing gender equivalence, complementarity, and overlap.

There are nevertheless significant differences in social influence and prestige among persons. These are mutable, and they fluctuate over the lifetime of the individual. But Vanatinai social relations are egalitarian overall, and sexually egalitarian in particular, in that at each stage in the life cycle all persons, female and male, have equivalent autonomy and control over their own actions, opportunity to achieve both publicly and privately acknowledged influence and power over the actions of others, and access to valued goods, wealth, and prestige. The quality of generosity, highly valued in both sexes, is explicitly modeled after parental nurture. Women are not viewed as polluting or dangerous to themselves or others in their persons, bodily fluids, or sexuality.

Vanatinai sociality is organized around the principle of personal autonomy. There are no chiefs, and nobody has the right to tell another adult what to do. This philosophy also results in some extremely permissive childrearing and a strong degree of tolerance for the idiosyncrasies of other people's behavior. While working together, sharing, and generosity are admirable, they are strictly voluntary. The selfish and antisocial person might be ostracized, and others will not give to him or her. If kinfolk, in-laws, or neighbors disagree, even with a powerful and influential big man or big woman, they have the option, frequently taken, of moving to another hamlet where they have ties and can expect access to land for gardening and foraging. Land is communally held by matrilineages, but each person has multiple rights to request and be given space to make a garden on land held by others, such as the mother's father's matrilineage. Respect and tolerance for the will and idiosyncrasies of individuals is reinforced by fear of their potential knowledge of witchcraft or sorcery.

Anthropological discussions of women, men, and society over the last one hundred years have been framed largely in terms of "the status of women," presumably unvarying and shared by all women in all social situations. Male dominance and female subordination have thus until recently been perceived as easily identified and often as human universals. If women are indeed universally subordinate, this implies a universal primary cause: hence the search for a single underlying reason for male dominance and female subordination, either material or ideological.

More recent writings in feminist anthropology have stressed multiple and contested gender statuses and ideologies and the impacts of historical forces, variable and changing social contexts, and conflicting gender ideologies. Ambiguity and contradiction, both within and between levels of ideology and social practice, give both women and men room to assert their value and exercise power. Unlike in many cultures where men stress women's innate inferiority, gender relations on Vanatinai are not contested, or antagonistic: there are no male versus female ideologies which vary markedly or directly contradict each other. Vanatinai mythological motifs, beliefs about supernatural power, cultural ideals of the sexual division of labor and of the qualities inherent to men and women, and the customary freedoms and restrictions upon each sex at different points in the life course all provide ideological underpinnings of sexual equality.

Since the 1970s writings on the anthropology of women, in evaluating degrees of female power and influence, have frequently focused on the disparity between the "ideal" sex role pattern of a culture, often based on an ideology of male dominance, publicly proclaimed or enacted by men, and often by women as well, and the "real" one, manifested by the actual behavior of individuals. This approach seeks to uncover female social participation, overt or covert, official or unofficial, in key events and decisions and to learn how women negotiate their social positions. The focus on social and individual "action" or "practice" is prominent more generally in cultural anthropological theory of recent years. Feminist analyses of contradictions between gender ideologies of female inferiority and the realities of women's and men's daily lives—the actual balance of power in household and community—have helped to make this focus on the actual behavior of individuals a wider theoretical concern.

In the Vanatinai case gender ideologies in their multiple levels and contexts emphasize the value of women and provide a mythological charter for the degree of personal autonomy and freedom of choice manifested in real women's lives. Gender ideologies are remarkably similar (though not completely, as I discuss [later]) as they are manifested situationally, in philosophical statements by women and men, in the ideal pattern of the sexual division of labor, in taboos and proscriptions. myth, cosmology, magic, ritual, the supernatural balance of power, and in the codifications of custom. Women are not characterized as weak or inferior. Women and men are valorized for the same qualities of strength, wisdom, and generosity. If possessed of these qualities an individual woman or man will act in ways which bring prestige not only to the actor but to the kin and residence groups to which she or he belongs.

Nevertheless, there is no single relationship between the sexes on Vanatinai. Power relations and relative influence vary with the individuals, sets of roles, situations, and historical moments involved. Gender ideologies embodied in myths, beliefs, prescriptions for role-appropriate behavior, and personal statements sometimes contradict each other or are contradicted by the behavior of individuals.

As Ortner points out, a great deal of recent social science theory emphasizes "the centrality of domination" and the analysis of "asymmetrical social relations" in which one group has more power than the other, as the key to understanding a social system. A focus upon asymmetry and domination also tends to presuppose its universality as a totalizing system of belief and practice and thus to distort analyses of gender roles and ideologies in places with egalitarian relations.

Gender Ideologies

... More men than women are widely known for their wealth of ceremonial valuables and their involvement in exchange and mortuary ritual. Still, Vanatinai is an equal opportunity society where this avenue to prestige and renown is open to both sexes. A few women are well known throughout the archipelago for their exceptional wealth, generosity, and participation in ritualized exchanges. All adult women as well as men are expected to participate in exchange to a certain minimum, particularly when a father, spouse, or close affine dies. Besides the opportunity to be the owner or the eater of a feast, women have an essential ritual role as life-givers, the role of principal female mourner who represents her matrilineage in the ritual work of compensating death to ensure the continuity of life.

Women have a complementary power base as life-givers in other spheres that counterbalances the asymmetry of men's tendency to be more heavily involved in exchange, an advantage that results in part from male powers to bring death. The most exclusive is of course the fact that women give birth to children. These children enrich and enlarge the kin group of the mother and her mothers, sisters, and brothers, ensuring the continuity and the life of the matrilineage itself. Her role of nurturer is highly valued, and the idiom of nurturing or feeding is applied as well to fathers, maternal uncles, and those who give ceremonial valuables to others. In ideological pronouncements she is called, by men and women alike, the owner of the garden, even though garden land is communally held by the matrilineage, and individual plots are usually worked with husbands or unmarried brothers. She is, in verbalized ideology of custom, the giver of yams, the ghanika moli, or true food, with which all human beings are nurtured, whether she grew them or her husband or brother. She is likely to raise pigs, which she exchanges or sacrifices at feasts. She is prominent in the life-giving work of healing, a form of countersorcery. And life-giving, Vanatinai people say, is more highly valued than the life-taking associated with male warfare and sorcery....

An overview of the life courses of males and females on Vanatinai and the ideologies of gender associated with them reveals two more potential sources of contradiction to prevailing ideologies of gender equivalence. One seems clear to an outside observer: men may have more than one wife, if they are strong enough to fulfill multiple affinal obligations and if the co-wives consent to enter into or remain in the marriage. Women may not have two husbands. Even though polygyny is rare, and women need not, and do not necessarily, agree to it, it is a customary and continuing form of marriage and an indication of gender asymmetries. A big man may distribute his procreative power and the strength of his affinal labor and personal wealth to two or more spouses and matrilineages, enlarging his influence and his reputation as a gia. Women may not....

Vanatinai menstrual taboos, such as those prohibiting the menstruating woman from visiting or working in a garden and, especially, from participating in the communal planting of yams, are multivalent cultural markers of female power. The symbolic complexity and multiple meanings of such taboos have been emphasized in recent writings on the anthropology of menstruation. Earlier anthropological constructions have emphasized the relation of menstrual taboos to ideologies of female pollution and thus, directly, of female inferiority or gender asymmetry. In the Vanatinai case there is no ideology of contamination through physical contact with the menstruating woman, who continues to forage, prepare food, and have sexual intercourse. Both men and women who have had intercourse in the last few days are barred from the new yam planting, and the genital fluids of both sexes are inimical, at this earliest and most crucial stage, to the growth of yams. (Later on, marital intercourse in the garden will help the yams to flourish.) Vanatinai menstrual taboos, which bar women from what islanders see as the most tedious form of subsistence labor, weeding gardens, are not regarded by women as a burden or curse but as a welcome interlude of relative leisure. Their predominant cultural meaning may be the ritual separation of the sacred power of female, and human, fertility and regeneration of life from that of plants, especially yams, whose parallels to humans are indicated by anthropomorphizing them in ritual spells. Menstrual taboos further mark woman as the giver of life to human beings.

The Sexual Division of Labor

Vanatinai custom is characterized by a marked degree of overlap in the sexual division of labor between what men normally do and what women do. This kind of overlap has been suggested as a primary material basis of gender equality, with the mingling of the sexes in the tasks of daily life working against the rise of male dominance.

Still, sorcerers are almost all male. Witches have less social power on Vanatinai and are blamed for only a small fraction of deaths and misfortunes. Only men build houses or canoes or chop down large trees for construction or clearing garden lands. Women are forbidden by custom to hunt, fish, or make war with spears, although they may hunt for possum and monitor lizard by climbing trees or setting traps and catching them and use a variety of other fishing methods. Despite the suppression of warfare men retain greater control of the powers that come with violence or the coercive threat of violent death.

Some Vanatinai women perceive an inequity in the performance of domestic chores. Almost all adult women are "working wives," who come home tired in the evening, often carrying both a young child in their arms and a heavy basket of yams or other produce on their heads for distances of up to three miles. They sometimes complain to their husbands or to each other that, "We come home after working in the garden all day, and we still have to fetch water, look for firewood, do the cooking and cleaning up and look after the children while all men do is sit on the verandah and chew betel nut!" The men usually retort that these are the work of women. Here is an example of contested gender roles.

Men are tender and loving to their children and often carry them around or take them along on their activities, but they do this only when they feel like it, and childcare is the primary responsibility of a mother, who must delegate it to an older sibling or a kinswoman if she cannot take care of the child herself. Women are also supposed to sweep the house and the hamlet ground every morning and to pick up pig excrement with a sago-bark "shovel" and a coconut-rib broom. . . .

Vanatinai is not a perfectly egalitarian society, either in terms of a lack of difference in the status and power of individuals or in the relations between men and women. Women in young and middle adulthood are likely to spend more time on childcare and supervision of gardens and less on building reputations as prominent transactors of ceremonial valuables. The average woman spends more of her time sweeping up the pig excrement that dots the hamlet from the unfenced domestic pigs wandering through it. The average man spends more time hunting wild boar in the rain forest with his spear (although some men do not like to hunt). His hunting is more highly valued and accorded more prestige by both sexes than her daily maintenance of hamlet cleanliness and household order. The sexual division of labor on Vanatinai is slightly asymmetrical, despite the tremendous overlap in the roles of men and women and the freedom that an individual of either sex has to spend more time on particular activities—gardening, foraging, fishing, caring for children, traveling in quest of ceremonial valuables—and to minimize others.

Yet the average Vanatinai woman owns many of the pigs she cleans up after, and she presents them publicly during mortuary rituals and exchanges them with other men and women for shell-disc necklaces, long axe blades of polished greenstone, and other valuables. She then gains status, prestige, and influence over the affairs of others, just as men do and as any adult does who chooses to make the effort to raise pigs, grow large yam gardens, and acquire and distribute ceremonial valuables. Women who achieve prominence and distribute wealth, and thus gain an enhanced ability to mobilize the labor of others, are highly respected by both sexes. An overview of the life course and the sexual division of labor on Vanatinai reveals a striking lack of cultural restrictions upon the autonomy of women as well as men and the openness of island society to a wide variety of lifestyles....

Material and Ideological Bases of Equality

Does equality or inequality, including between men and women, result from material or ideological causes? We cannot say whether an idea preceded or followed specific economic and social circumstances. Does the idea give rise to the act, or does the act generate an ideology that justifies it or mystifies it? . . .

On Vanatinai, where there is no ideology of male dominance, the material conditions for gender equality are present. Women—and their brothers— control the means of production. Women own land, and they inherit land, pigs, and valuables from their mothers, their mothers' brothers, and sometimes from their fathers equally with men. They have the ultimate decison-making power over the distribution of staple foods that belong jointly to their kinsmen and that their kinsmen or husbands have helped labor to grow. They are integrated into the prestige economy, the ritualized exchanges of ceremonial valuables. Ideological expressions, such as the common saying that the woman is the owner of the garden, or the well-known myth of the first exchange between two female beings, validate material conditions.

I do not believe it would be possible to have a gender egalitarian society, where prevailing expressions of gender ideology were egalitarian or valorized both sexes to the same degree, without material control by women of land, means of subsistence, or wealth equivalent to that of men. This control would encompass anything from foraging rights, skills, tools, and practical and sacred knowledge to access to high-paying, prestigious jobs and the knowledge and connections it takes to get them. Equal control of the means of production, then, is one necessary precondition of gender equality. Vanatinai women's major disadvantage is their lack of access to a key tool instrumental in gaining power and prestige, the spear. Control of the means of production is potentially greater in a matrilineal society.

Matriliny and Gender

. . . Matrilineal descent provides the preconditions favorable to the development of female political and economic power, but it does not ensure it. In the cases of Vanatinai, the Nagovisi, the Minangkabau, and the Hopi, matriliny, woman-centered postmarital residence (or the absence of a virilocal residence rule), female autonomy, extradomestic positions of authority, and ideologies of gender that highly value women seem closely connected. Nevertheless matriliny by itself does not necessarily indicate, or generate, gender equality. As earlier comparative studies of matrilineal societies have emphasized, in many cases brothers or husbands control the land, valuables, and persons of sisters and wives....

Gender Ideologies and Practice in Daily Life

... The small scale, fluidity, and mobility of social life on Vanatinai, especially in combination with matriliny, are conducive of egalitarian social relations between men and women and old and young. They promote an ethic of respect for the individual, which must be integrated with the ethic of cooperation essential for survival in a subsistence economy. People must work out conflict through face to face negotiation, or existing social ties will be broken by migration, divorce, or death through sorcery or witchcraft.

Women on Vanatinai are physically mobile, traveling with their families to live with their own kin and then the kin of their spouse, making journeys in quest of valuables, and attending mortuary feasts. They are said to have traveled for these reasons even in precolonial times when the threat of attack was a constant danger. The generally greater physical mobility of men in human societies is a significant factor in sexual asymmetries of power, as it is men who generally negotiate and regulate relationships with outside groups.

Vanatinai women's mobility is not restricted by ideology or by taboo, and women build their own far-ranging personal networks of social relationships. Links in these networks may be activated as needed by the woman to the benefit of her kin or hamlet group. Women are confined little by taboos or community pressures. They travel, choose their own marriage partners or lovers, divorce at will, or develop reputations as wealthy and generous individuals active in exchange.

Big Men, Big Women, and Chiefs

Vanatinai giagia, male and female, match Sahlin's classic description of the Melanesian big man, except that the role of gia is gender-blind. There has been renewed interest among anthropologists in recent years in the big man form of political authority. The Vanatinai case of the female and male giagia offers an intriguing perspective.

In the Massim, except for the Trobriand Islands, the most influential individuals are those who are most successful in exchange and who gain a reputation for public generosity by hosting or contributing significantly to mortuary feasts. Any individual on Vanatinai, male or female, may try to become known as a gia by choosing to exert the extra effort to go beyond the minimum contributions to the mortuary feasts expected of every adult. He or she accumulates ceremonial valuables and other goods both in order to give them away in acts of public generosity and to honor obligations to exchange partners from the local area as well as distant islands. There may be more than one gia in a particular hamlet, or even household, or there may be none. A woman may have considerably more prestige and influence than her husband because of her reputation for acquiring and redistributing valuables. While there are more men than women who are extremely active in exchange, there are some women who are far more active than the majority of men.

Giagia of either sex are only leaders in temporary circumstances and if others wish to follow, as when they host a feast, lead an exchange expedition, or organize the planting of a communal yam garden. Decisions are made by consensus, and the giagia of both sexes influence others through their powers of persuasion, their reputations for ability, and their knowledge, both of beneficial magic and ritual and of sorcery or witchcraft....

Images of Gender and Power

... On Vanatinai power and influence over the actions of others are gained by achievement and demonstrated superior knowledge and skill, whether in the realm of gardening, exchange, healing, or sorcery. Those who accumulate a surplus of resources are expected to be generous and share with their neighbors or face the threat of the sorcery or witchcraft of the envious. Both women and men are free to build their careers through exchange. On the other hand both women and men are free not to strive toward renown as giagia but to work for their own families or simply to mind their own business. They can also achieve the respect of their peers, if they seek it at all, as loving parents, responsible and hard-working lineage mates and affines, good gardeners, hunters, or fishers, or skilled healers, carvers, or weavers....

⋅⁄⊚⋅

What can people in other parts of the world learn from the principles of sexual equality in Vanatinai custom and philosophy? Small scale facilitates Vanatinai people's emphasis on face-to-face negotiations of interpersonal conflicts without the delegation of political authority to a small group of middle-aged male elites. It also leaves room for an ethic of respect for the will of the individual regardless of age or sex. A culture that is egalitarian and nonhierarchical overall is more likely to have egalitarian relations between men and women.

Males and females on Vanatinai have equivalent autonomy at each life cycle stage. As adults they have similar opportunities to influence the actions of others. There is a large amount of overlap between the roles and activities of women and men, with women occupying public, prestige-generating roles. Women share control of the production and the distribution of valued goods, and they inherit property. Women as well as men participate in the exchange of valuables, they organize feasts, they officiate at important rituals such as those for yam planting or healing, they counsel their kinfolk, they speak out and are listened to in public meetings, they possess valuable magical knowledge, and they work side by side in most subsistence activities. Women's role as nurturing parent is highly valued and is the dominant metaphor for the generous men and women who gain renown and influence over others by accumulating and then giving away valuable goods.

But these same characteristics of respect for individual autonomy, role overlap, and public participation of women in key subsistence and prestige domains of social life are also possible in large-scale industrial and agricultural societies. The Vanatinai example suggests that sexual equality is facilitated by an overall ethic of respect for and equal treatment of all categories of individuals, the decentralization of political power, and inclusion of all categories of persons (for example, women and ethnic minorities) in public positions of authority and influence. It requires greater role overlap through increased integration of the workforce, increased control by women and minorities of valued goods —property, income, and educational credentials—and increased recognition of the social value of parental care. The example of Vanatinai shows that the subjugation of women by men is not a human universal, and it is not inevitable. Sex role patterns and gender ideologies are closely related to overall social systems of power and prestige. Where these systems stress personal autonomy and egalitarian social relations among all adults, minimizing the formal authority of one person over another, gender equality is possible.

NO

Steven Goldberg

Is Patriarchy Inevitable?

In five hundred years the world, in all likelihood, will have become homogenized. The thousands of varied societies and their dramatically differing methods of socialization, cohesion, family, religion, economy, and politics will have given way to a universal culture. Fortunately, cultural anthropologists have preserved much of our present diversity, which may keep our descendants from too hastily allowing their natural human ego- and ethno-centricity to conclude that theirs is the only way to manage a society.

However, the anthropological sword is two-edged. While diversity is certainly apparent from anthropological investigations, it is also clear that there are realities which manifest themselves no matter what the varied forms of the aforementioned institutions. Because these universal realities cut across cultural lines, they are crucial to our understanding of what society *by its nature* is and, perhaps, of what human beings are. It is important, then, that we ask why, when societies differ as much as do those of the Ituri Pygmy, the Jivaro, the American, the Japanese, and a thousand others, some institutions are universal.

It is always the case that the universal institution serves some need rooted in the deepest nature of human beings. In some cases the explanation of universality is obvious (e.g., why every society has methods of food gathering). But there are other universalities which are apparent, though without any obvious explanation. Of the thousands of societies on which we have any evidence stronger than myth (a form of evidence that would have us believe in cyclops), there is no evidence that there has ever been a society failing to exhibit three institutions:

1. *Primary hierarchies always filled primarily by men.* A Queen Victoria or a Golda Meir is always an exception and is always surrounded by a government of men. Indeed, the constraints of royal lineage may produce more female societal leaders than does democracy—there were more female heads of state in the first two-thirds of the sixteenth century than there were in the first two-thirds of the twentieth.

2. *The highest status roles are male.* There are societies in which the women do most of the important economic work and rear the children, while the men

seem mostly to hang loose. But, in such societies, hanging loose is given higher status than any non-maternal role primarily served by women. No doubt this is partly due to the fact that the males hold the positions of power. However, it is also likely that high-status roles are male not primarily because they are male (ditch-digging is male and low status), but because they are high status. The high status roles are male because they possess—for whatever socially determined reason in whichever specific society—high status. This high status exerts a more powerful influence on males than it does on females. As a result, males are more willing to sacrifice life's other rewards for status dominance than are females.

In their *Not in Our Genes,* Richard Lewontin, Leon Kamin, and Stephen Rose—who, along with Stephen Jay Gould are the best-known defenders of the view that emphasizes the role of environment and de-emphasizes that of heredity—attempt to find fault with my work by pointing out that most family doctors in the Soviet Union are women. However, they acknowledge that in the Soviet Union "family doctoring [had] lower status than in the United States."

Which is precisely the point. No one doubts that women can be doctors. The question is why doctors (or weavers, or load bearers, etc.) are primarily women only when being a doctor is given lower status than are certain roles played mostly by men—and furthermore, why, even when this is the case (as in Russia) the upper hierarchical positions relevant to that specific area are held by men.

3. Dominance in male-female relationships is always associated with males. "Male dominance" refers to the feeling, of both men and women, that the male is dominant and that the woman must "get around" the male to attain power. Social attitudes may be concordant or discordant with the reality of male dominance. In our own society there was a time when the man's "taking the lead" was positively valued by most women (as 30s' movies attest); today such a view is purportedly detested by many. But attitudes toward male-dominance behavior are causally unimportant to the reality they judge—and are not much more likely to eliminate the reality than would a social dislike of men's being taller be able to eliminate men's being taller.

Over the past twenty years, I have consulted every original ethnographic work invoked to demonstrate an exception to these societal universalities. Twenty years ago many textbooks spoke cavalierly of "matriarchies" and "Amazons" and pretended that Margaret Mead had claimed to find a society in which sex roles were reversed. Today no serious anthropologist is willing to claim that any specific society has ever been an exception.

It is often claimed that "modern technology renders the physiological differentiation irrelevant." However, there is not a scintilla of evidence that modernization alters the basic "motivational" factors sufficiently to cast doubt on the continued existence of the universals I discuss. The economic needs of modern society probably do set a lower limit on the status of women; no modern society could give women the low status they receive in some non-modern societies. But modernization probably also sets an upper limit; no modern society is likely to give women the status given to the maternal roles in some other matrilineal societies.

Scandinavian nations, which have long had government agencies devoted to equalizing women's position, are often cited by social scientists as demonstrating modernization's ability to override patriarchy. In fact, however, Norway has 454 municipal councils; 443 are chaired by men. On the Supreme Court, city courts, appellate courts, and in Parliament, there are between five and nine times as many men as there are women. In Sweden, according to government documents, men dominate "senior positions in employer and employee organizations as well as in political and other associations" and only 5 of 82 directors of government agencies, 9 of 83 chairpersons of agency boards, and 9 per cent of judges are women.

One may, of course, hope that all this changes, but one cannot invoke any evidence implying that it will.

Of course, there are those who simply try to assert away the evidence. Lewontin *et al.* write, "Cross cultural universals appear to lie more in the eye of the beholder than in the social reality that is being observed." In fact, with reference to the universalities mentioned above, they do not. If these universals were merely "in the eye of the beholder," the authors would merely have to specify a society in which there was a hierarchy in which males did not predominate and the case would be closed.

The answer to the question of why an institution is universal clearly must be parsimonious. It will not do to ascribe causation of a universal institution to capitalism or Christianity or modernization, because many hundreds of societies lacked these, but not the universal institutions. If the causal explanation is to be at all persuasive, it must invoke some factor present in every society from the most primitive to the most modern. (Invoking the male's physical strength advantage does meet the requirement of parsimony, but does not counter the evidence of the central importance of neuro-endocrinological psycho-physiological factors.)

When sociologists are forced to acknowledge the universals, they nearly always invoke "socialization" as explanation. But this explanation faces two serious problems. First, it does not explain anything, but merely forces us to ask another question: *Why* does socialization of men and women always work in the same direction? Second, the explanation implicitly assumes that the social environment of expectations and norms acts as an *independent* variable capable of acting as counterpoise to the physiological constituents that make us male and female.

In individual cases, of course, anything can happen.

Even when a causation is nearly entirely hereditary, there are many exceptions (as tall women demonstrate). Priests choose to be celibate, but this does not cast doubt on the physiological basis of the "sex drive." To be sure, there is also feedback from the environmental to the physiological, so that association of physical strength with males results in more males lifting weights.

However, in principle, a society could find itself with women who were physically stronger than men if women lifted weights throughout their lives and men remained sedentary.

But, in real life, this can't happen because the social environment is a *dependent* variable whose limits are set by our physiological construction. In real life we all observe a male's dominance tendency that is rooted in physiological differences between males and females and, because values and attitudes are not of primary causal importance here, we develop expectations concordant with the male–female behavioral differences.

Most of the discussion of sex differences has emphasized the neuro-endocrinological differentiation of males and females and the cognitive and behavioral differentiation this engenders. This is because there is an enormous amount of evidence demonstrating the role of hormones in fetally differentiating the male and female central nervous systems, CNS response to the potentiating properties of certain hormones, and the thoughts and actions of males and females.

There is not room here for detailed discussion of the neuro-endocrinological mechanism underlying dominance behavior. But a useful analogy is iron and magnet. Iron does not have a "drive" or a "need" to find a magnet, but when there is a magnet in the area, iron, as a result of the very way it is built, tends to react in a certain way. Likewise, the physiological natures of males and females predispose them to have different hierarchies of response to various environmental cues. There is no response that only one sex has; the difference between men and women is the relative strengths of different responses. Males react more readily to hierarchical competitiveness than do females; females react more readily to the needs of an infant-in-distress. Norms and socialization do not cause this difference, but reflect it and make concrete a specific society's specific methods for manifesting the response. (Cleaning a rifle and preparing Spaghetti-Os are not instinctive abilities).

The iron–magnet analogy makes clear the role of social environment. Were there to be a society without hierarchy, status, values, or interdependence of the sexes, there would be no environmental cue to elicit the differentiated, physiologically rooted responses we discuss. But it is difficult to imagine such a society and, indeed, there has never been such a society.

Even if we had no neuro-endocrinological evidence at all, the anthropological evidence alone would be sufficient to force us to posit a mechanism of sexual psycho-physiological differentiation and to predict its discovery. We do, however, possess the neuro-endocrinological evidence and the anthropological evidence permits us to specify the institutional effects—the limits of societal variation that the neuro-endocrinological engenders.

For thousands of years, everyone, save perhaps some social scientists and others ideologically opposed to the idea, have known perfectly well that men and women differ in the physiological factors that underlie masculine and feminine thought and behavior. They may not have known the words to describe the linkage of physiology with thought and behavior, but they knew the linkage was there. (I recently read a comment of a woman in Pennsylvania: "They keep telling us that men and women are the way they are because of what they've been taught, but you can go a hundred miles in any direction and not find a single person who really believes that.") And even the most feminist parent, once she has children, can't help but notice that it is nearly impossible to get small boys to play with dolls not named "Killer Joe, the Marauding Exterminator," or at least with trucks—*big* trucks.

None of this is to deny tremendous variation on the level of roles. Even in our own society, in just a century the role of secretary changed from virtually solely male to virtually solely female. With the exception of roles associated with child nurturance, political leadership, warfare, security, and crime, virtually every specific role is male in some societies and female in others. No one doubts that the women who exhibit the dominance behavior usually exhibited by men encounter discrimination. But the question remains: why is dominance behavior usually exhibited by *men*?

The implication of all this depends on context. Clearly the correctness or incorrectness of the theory I present is important to an understanding of human behavior and society. But to the individual man or woman, on the other hand, the universals are largely irrelevant. The woman who wishes to become President has a sufficient number of real-life equivalents to know that there is not a constraint rendering impossible a female head of state. But there is no more reason for such a woman to deny that the motivation to rule is more often associated with male physiology than there is for the six-foot woman to pretend that women are as tall as men.

POSTSCRIPT

Do Sexually Egalitarian Societies Exist?

In these two selections, Lepowsky and Goldberg disagree both on the interpretation of the facts and on the types of forces, cultural or biological, that determine relations between the sexes. Lepowsky argues that Vanatinai culture is basically sexually egalitarian and that this is due to a particular constellation of social and ideological features of their culture. Goldberg contends that men are dominant in every culture—the Vanatinai people would be no exception—and that men's innate drive to dominate would lead them to occupy most of the positions of authority and high status and to dominate women in interpersonal relations.

During the last 30 years, anthropologists have conducted many studies focusing specifically on gender ideas and roles in particular societies, especially in non-Western and tribal societies. Their general finding is that gender relations are much more complicated and variable than scholars thought in the early days of feminist anthropology. For example, studies have shown that not all societies make a simple distinction between domestic and public domains, associate women exclusively with a domestic domain, or evaluate activities outside the home as superior to those inside it. Scholars have also realized that analytical concepts like "male dominance" and the "status of women" are too crude. They have attempted to break them up into components that can be sought and measured in ethnographic field studies.

The question of whether or not males are dominant in a particular society is not as clear-cut as it once seemed. One important distinction now made, and reflected in Lepowsky's excerpt, is that between the actual practice of male-female roles and interactions and the ideologies that contain bases for evaluating the sexes and their activities. Studies show that in some societies women and men have similar amounts of influence over daily life, but the cultural ideology (or at least the men's ideology) portrays women as inferior to men. In some cases men's and women's spheres of activity and control are separate and independent. Some societies have competing ideologies, in which both men and women portray their own gender as superior. And some societies, such as the Hua of Papua New Guinea, have multiple ideologies, which simultaneously present women as inferior, superior, and equal to men (see Anna Meigs's book *Food, Sex, and Pollution: A New Guinea Religion* [Rutgers University Press, 1984]). Despite these complications, it may still be useful to term a culture in which both practice and ideology consistently point to equality or balance between the sexes as "sexually egalitarian," as Lepowsky does in the case of the Vanatinai. Of course Goldberg would say that such societies do not exist.

For more information on the Vanatinai people, see Lepowsky's book *Fruit of the Motherland: Gender in an Egalitarian Society* (Columbia University

Press, 1993). A very readable introduction to feminist anthropology is Henrietta Moore's book *Feminism and Anthropology* (University of Minnesota Press, 1988). An interesting collection of articles showing variations in male-female relations is Peggy Sanday and Ruth Goodenough's edited volume *Beyond the Second Sex: New Directions in the Anthropology of Gender* (University of Pennsylvania Press, 1990). For a discussion of gender equality and inequality among hunter-gatherers, see Karen L. Endicott's article "Gender Relations in Hunter-Gatherer Societies," in *The Cambridge Encyclopedia of Hunters and Gatherers,* Richard B. Lee and Richard Daly, eds. (Cambridge University Press, 1999).

For a full explication of Goldberg's theory of innate male dominance, see his book *Why Men Rule: A Theory of Male Dominance* (Open Court, 1993). Other works that argue for a biological basis for male dominance include Lionel Tiger's book *Men in Groups* (Holt, Rinehart & Winston, 1969); Lionel Tiger and Robin Fox's book *The Imperial Animal* (Holt, Rinehart & Winston, 1971); Robert Wright's article "Feminists Meet Mr. Darwin," *The New Republic* (November 28, 1994); and Barbara Smuts's article "The Origins of Patriarchy: An Evolutionary Perspective," in A. Zagarell's edited volume *Origins of Gender Inequality* (New Issues Press, in press).

ISSUE 12

Is It Natural for Adopted Children to Want to Find Out About Their Birth Parents?

YES: Betty Jean Lifton, from *Journey of the Adopted Self: A Quest for Wholeness* (Basic Books, 1994)

NO: John Terrell and Judith Modell, from "Anthropology and Adoption," *American Anthropologist* (March 1994)

ISSUE SUMMARY

YES: Adoptee and adoption rights advocate Betty Jean Lifton argues that there is a natural need for human beings to know where they came from. Adoption is not a natural human state, she asserts, and it is surrounded by a secrecy that leads to severe social and psychological consequences for adoptees, adoptive parents, and birth parents.

NO: Anthropologists John Terrell and Judith Modell, who are each the parent of an adopted child, contend that the "need" to know one's birth parents is an American (or Western European) cultural construct. They conclude that in other parts of the world, where there is less emphasis placed on biology, adoptees have none of the problems said to be associated with being adopted in America.

The 1976 television miniseries *Roots*, based on the book by Alex Haley, led many Americans to try to search out their own family stories, to find their own "roots." For most the effort merely meant asking grandparents about their ancestors. But for adopted children in America, information about their forebears was sealed by court order, and there was rarely any knowledge about their birth parents available to them from their adopted parents. Information about birth parents was usually kept secret to protect the birth parents from public scandal, since most adopted children were conceived out of wedlock and quietly put up for adoption with the understanding that the child and the public would never be able to link the birth parents with the adoptee. As social mores have changed in the United States, relatively little stigma now surrounds being an unwed mother or a single parent. But court records for most adoptions remain sealed, leading to a growing movement advocating open adoption records.

For several decades, adoptees' attempts to find their birth parents have become a growing social movement, with advocacy organizations, support groups, and self-help groups all attempting to help adoptees find their birth parents and which often help birth parents find the children they put up for adoption in their youth. Many of these groups insist that there is an inherent human right for adoptees to know their biological parents and for parents to know their natural children. These groups contend that there is a natural bond between parents and children that has been severed by adoption.

In the following selection, Betty Jean Lifton considers the psychological factors at play when children are put up for adoption, where knowledge of their birth parents is denied them. Drawing on her personal experiences as an adoptee as well as on interviews with dozens of other adoptees, Lifton considers how psychologically damaging this veil of secrecy is on adoptees, both as children and as adults. For her, people have a natural need to know where they came from. It is unnatural to grow up separated from and without knowledge of one's natural clan, she argues. The lack of such knowledge of one's roots has a negative impact on the child's psyche and leads them to seek out their roots, concludes Lifton.

Anthropologists John Terrell and Judith Modell counter that the "natural" need to know one's parents, as so often discussed by the adoption rights movement, is an American cultural construct. American and Western European culture emphasizes the difference between biological and adoptive families, viewing adoptive relationships as less real than biological ones. In most non-Western societies, people have very different views of adoption, typically viewing adoptive relationships as equal to biological ones. Citing examples from Hawaii and other parts of Oceania, they challenge the primacy of blood relationships over all other kinds of kinship ties. They argue that in America open adoptions would probably be healthier for all concerned parties but that it would be better still if Americans had a better understanding of the diverse ways other peoples have for understanding and dealing with adoption.

Are kin relations based on biology stronger than relationships based on other ties? Is there something in our genes that makes us have a more important relationship with our biological or birth parents than with others? Are adoptees likely to have stronger bonds with their adopted parents than with their birth parents? What do the experiences of Hawaiians and other Pacific Islanders say about how natural it is to want to know one's birth parents? Is the adoption rights movement in America a social phenomenon that could only emerge in America or does it touch on universal values and psychological needs?

Betwixt and Between

"Then I shan't be exactly human?" Peter asked.
"No."
"What shall I be?"
"You will be Betwixt-and-Between," Solomon said, and
certainly he was a wise old fellow, for that is exactly how
it turned out.

— James Barrie, *Peter Pan in Kensington Gardens*

Many people identify with the familiar condition of being Betwixt and Between, just as they identify with Peter Pan, the boy who did not want to grow up and face the responsibilities of the real world.

Peter, James Barrie tells us, is "ever so old," but really always the same age: one week. Though he was born "so long ago," he never had a birthday, nor is there the slightest chance of his having one. He escaped from his home when he was seven days old by flying out the window to Kensington Gardens.

Barrie doesn't tell us what was going on in Peter's family that after only seven days he knew he had to take off. But adoptees recognize Peter Pan as a brother. They, too, became lost children when they separated as babies from their natural families and disappeared into a place very much like never-never land. Like Peter, they are fantasy people. Denied the right to see their real birth certificates and the names of those who brought them into the world, they can't be sure they ever had a real *birth* day. They can never grow up because they are always referred to as an "adopted child."

I didn't realize that, like Peter, I wasn't "exactly human" until I was seven *years* old. It was the moment my mother told me I was adopted. Like most adoptive parents faced with breaking such bleak news, she tried to make adoption sound special, but I could feel the penetrating chill of its message. I was not really her child. I had come from somewhere else, a place shrouded in mystery, a place that, like myself, was Betwixt and Between.

As I listened, I could feel a part of myself being pulled into the darkness of that mystery—a place already carved out by Peter and the lost children. I would never be the same again.

From Betty Jean Lifton, *Journey of the Adopted Self: A Quest for Wholeness* (Basic Books, 1994). Copyright © 1994 by Betty Jean Lifton. Reprinted by permission of Basic Books, a member of Perseus Books, LLC. Notes omitted.

This was to be our secret, my mother said. Hers and mine. I was not to share it with anyone—not even my father. It would break his heart if he suspected I knew. In this way I learned that secrecy and adoption were inextricably mixed, as in a witch's brew. By becoming a keeper of the secret, I was to collaborate in the family conspiracy of silence.

I didn't know then that our little family secret was connected to the *big* secret in the closed adoption system, just as our little conspiracy was connected to the larger social conspiracy around adoption. My mother and father had been assured that my birth records would be sealed forever, that I would never be able to learn the identity of my original family. Secrecy was the magic ingredient that would give our adoptive family the aura of a blood-related one. Secrecy was the magic broom that would sweep away all feelings of grief and loss on the part of any of the parties involved.

As I played my role of the good daughter—repressing a natural need to know where I came from—I was unaware that the secrecy inherent in the adoption system was shaping and constricting the self through which I organized my perception of reality. By denying my natural curiosity about where I came from, and my grief for my lost birth parents and for the child I might have been, I was shrinking my emotional space to the size permitted by that system. So, too, were my adoptive parents forced by the secrecy to shrink their emotional space as they denied their need to grieve for the natural child they might have had.

We were trapped in a closed family system where secrecy cut off real communication. We were not unlike those families who keep secrets around alcoholism, divorce, incest, and all the other things that family members are prone to hide from their neighbors and from one another.

I had no idea of this as a child. Having repressed my real feelings, I was not consciously aware of my pain. And as a consequence, I was not consciously aware of myself, except as someone unreal pretending to be real. I did things that my human friends did, even looked real in my high school and college graduation pictures, and in the photographs taken at my wedding, before I flew off with my husband to the Far East.

Perhaps I might have never been in touch with my feelings if, shortly after my return from Japan, a relative, recently married into my adoptive family, had not remarked about something she heard—that my natural parents had been killed in a car accident. Her statement was like a Zen slap, knocking me into another state of consciousness. I had been told my parents were dead, but I had not been told this story. When I tried to clear up the mystery of how they died, I was shocked to learn that they had been very much alive at the time of my adoption—and might still be.

Much that had lain repressed in me now began stirring. I started to wonder how my mind had been able to cut off the primal subject of who my parents were. Even if it were true that they were dead, why had I not asked any questions about them? After all, dead people have names; they have relatives they have left behind; they have graves. Why had I behaved as if death had wiped out all traces of their existence? It was my first conscious brush with the psychological mystery that forms the core of this [selection]: How does a child's mind close down when it senses danger, and stay closed until some life event or crisis inadvertently jars it open? And what traumatic effects does this have on the child's growing sense of self?

⁂

As a writer, I set out to explore the psychological complexities of being adopted in my book *Twice Born: Memoirs of an Adopted Daughter.* I was amazed, even alarmed, at what surfaced. The compliant adopted child within, as elusive as ever, was in many ways a stranger to the adult I had become. The anger, barely contained under what passed as irony and wit, could no longer be disguised as I dredged up memories of that child's helplessness in the face of mysteries too dark to comprehend. Even as I wrote about my search and reunion, I felt burdened with guilt, as if it were a disloyalty to my deceased adoptive parents. Nor had I fully absorbed the depths of what I had been through. I found a birth mother who had tried to hold on to me but, as an unmarried seventeen-year-old with no emotional or financial support, finally had to let go. Once she was defeated, she put on the scarlet letter—S for secrecy and shame—and did not tell either of her two husbands or her son about me. We met secretly twice before I had to leave for a summer in Japan. The psychic chaos I felt during those two months in Tokyo—as if I had fallen into a black hole—was so great that when I returned to the States I did not call her for fear of falling back into that dark place: a place, as we will see, that is not unfamiliar to many adoptees who have internalized the taboos of the closed adoption system. At the time of my reunion, there were no books to sanction my search for my mother or to prepare me for what I might experience.

My next book, *Lost and Found, the Adoption Experience,* was an attempt to write such a book and, in so doing, to illuminate the existential condition of being adopted. I explored the psychological pitfalls that await adoptees all through the life cycle when they are forced to close off their real feelings and live *as if* their families of origin were not an inherent part of their identity. I laid out the difficult stages of awakening that adoptees experience before they dare to set out in search of the missing pieces in their lives.

As the search phenomenon was still relatively new at that time, the last part of the book gave an overview of the varieties of reunion experience and the psychological growth and accommodation that everyone—adoptee, adoptive parents, and birth parents—has to make. . . .

⁂

[Looking at my own life,] I found an adopted woman waiting there, one who was more sensitive than ever to the lack of respect for the rights of adopted children to know who they are, and who was still absorbed with the psychological mysteries inherent in adoption. Once again I was faced with the same questions I had been grappling with earlier: Why do adopted people feel so alienated? Why do they feel unreal, invisible to themselves and others? Why do they feel unborn? Now, however, I had a new question that I felt would shed light on the others: How do adopted people form a sense of self in the closed adoption system?

The psychoanalyst Karen Horney defined the real self as the alive, unique, personal center of ourselves that wants to grow. When the real self is prevented from free, healthy growth because of abandoning its needs to others, one can become alienated from it. She quotes Kierkegaard on the alienation and loss of self as "sickness unto death." Adoptees, who often say they feel they have no self, can be seen as expressing this despair. Having abandoned their need to know their origins for the sake of their adoptive parents, they are left with a hole in the center of their being. They feel they don't exist.

Of course, everyone has some kind of self. The adoptee born psychologically into the closed adoption system and shaped by its myths, secrets, and taboos from first conscious memory, and even before, has a unique self, an adopted self. But this fragile self has a basic inner division brought about by the need for denial that is built into the closed adoption system.

When I began research for this [selection], I was primarily interested in how secrecy affects the formation of the adopted self. I saw it as emotional abuse (of which adoptive parents are unaware) because it distorts the child's psychic reality. In the course of interviewing adoptees, however, I realized that it is not just secrecy that affects their sense of self but rather a series of traumas. This "cumulative adoption trauma" begins when they are separated from the mother at birth; builds when they learn that they were not born to the people they call mother and father; and is further compounded when they are denied knowledge of the mother and father to whom they were born.

I was not unfamiliar with the literature on trauma. My husband, Robert Jay Lifton, has been preoccupied with trauma on a massive scale. As a journalist, I have reported on the war-wounded, orphaned, and traumatized children of Hiroshima, Korea, Vietnam, and the Holocaust. Still, as an adopted person, loyal to my adoptive parents, I didn't allow myself to see that closed adoption is also a form of trauma—an invisible and subtle one—until years later when I began noticing parallels between adopted children and children of alcoholics, children of survivors (even survivors themselves), and children who have been abused.

There has already been some misunderstanding about the linking of adoption to trauma. Far from being regarded as traumatic, adoption is still widely viewed as fortunate for the child who is rescued from homelessness, and for the adoptive parents who are rescued from childlessness. And in most cases it is. Yet the word *trauma* has been slipping into the psychological literature on adoption with increasing frequency in the last decade as clinicians come to realize the high psychic cost that both parent and child pay when they repress their grief and loss.

I have come to believe in the course of my research that it is unnatural for members of the human species to grow up separated from and without knowledge of their natural clan, that such a lack has a negative influence on a child's psychic reality and relationship with the adoptive parents. By enveloping their origins with secrecy, the closed adoption system asks children to disavow reality, to live *as if* they were born to the parents who raise them. They grow up feeling like anonymous people cut off from the genetic and social heritage that gives everyone else roots.

⌣⊙⌢

As I write this, we are Betwixt and Between change and stasis in the adoption field. We are between two systems: the traditional closed one that for almost half a century has cut adopted children off from their heritage, and an open one in which birth mothers choose the adoptive parents of their baby and maintain some contact with the family. It is a time when the best interests of the child, for which the adoption system was originally created, have become subordinate to the best interests of the adults, as fierce custody battles are waged over the few available healthy white infants.

Meanwhile, adoption records remain sealed in all but two states due to the influence of a conservative lobby group, the National Council for Adoption, that has managed to polarize the field by labeling those who seek reform as "anti-adoption." Reformers who are working to open the system, as well as the records, however, are not anti-adoption but rather anti–closed adoption and pro–adopted children.

While no amount of openness can take away the child's trauma of being separated from his mother, or save the child from the trauma of learning she was not born into the adoptive family, we can remove the secrecy that compounds those two traumas. We can begin to demystify the adoptive family and to see it with much of the strengths and weaknesses of other families. The conservatives argue for the myth of the happy adoptive family that has no problems because love conquers all. But we will see that something more is expected of the adopted family: an excess of happiness that is meant to make up for the excess of loss that everyone in the triad experiences, and an excess of denial to cover that loss. Exposing the myths of the adoptive family while still holding on to the very real need and love that parents and child have for each other has been the challenge facing me....

The adoptees [I studied] are mostly successful people in that they are productive in their work and their private lives. But, ... much of their psychic energy has been taken up with adjusting to the mystery of their origins by disavowing their need to have some knowledge of and contact with their blood kin....

The adoptive family has managed to "pass" until now; it remains, for the most part, an unexplored constellation that has escaped psychological detection. Many professionals regard its psychodynamics as being the same as that of other families, overlooking the trauma that the parents as well as the child experience due to the conspiracy of silence built into the closed system.

Because it is a social rather than a natural construct, we can see the strengths and malfunctions of the adoptive family as a laboratory to illuminate some of the most fundamental issues around mothering and mother loss, attachment and bonding, separation and loss, denial and dissociation, and the human need for origins. We can see the deep need that parents and child fill for each other, but we can also see the problems that occur between parents and child when secrets prevent open communication between them.

In *Lost and Found* I spoke of what I called the Adoption Game, a family system that operates by unspoken rules that require everyone in it to live a double life. While seeming to exist in the real world with their adoptive family, the children are at the same time inhabiting an underground world of fantasies and fears which they can share with no one. The adoptive parents also live a double life. Believing themselves to be doing everything for their children, they withhold from them the very knowledge they need to develop into healthy adults. This double role of savior/withholder eventually works against the adoptive parents, estranging them from their children. So, too, the birth mother is forced to live a double life from the moment she surrenders her baby. Advised to go on as if nothing has happened, she keeps secret what is probably the most important and traumatic event of her life.

In [*Journey of the Adopted Self: A Quest for Wholeness*], I speak not of adoption games but of adoption ghosts. In many ways [the] book is a ghost story, for it tells of the ghosts that haunt the dark crevices of the unconscious and trail each member of the adoption triangle (parents and child alike) wherever they go. Unless one is aware of these ghosts, one will never be able to understand or to help the child who is adopted, the parents who adopt, or the parents who give up a child to adoption.

Who are these ghosts?

The adopted child is always accompanied by the ghost of the child he might have been had he stayed with his birth mother and by the ghost of the fantasy child his adoptive parents might have had. He is also accompanied by the ghost of the birth mother, from whom he has never completely disconnected, and the ghost of the birth father, hidden behind her.

The adoptive mother and father are accompanied by the ghost of the perfect biological child they might have had, who walks beside the adopted child who is taking its place.

The birth mother (and father, to a lesser extent) is accompanied by a retinue of ghosts. The ghost of the baby she gave up. The ghost of her lost lover, whom she connects with the baby. The ghost of the mother she might have been. And the ghosts of the baby's adoptive parents.

All of these ghosts are members of the extended adoptive family, which includes the birth family....

[The] book, then, is about the search for the adopted self. It is not about the literal search in the material world, where one sifts through records and archives for real people with real names and addresses; but rather about the internal search in which one sifts through the pieces of the psyche in an attempt to understand who one was so that one can have some sense of who one is and who one can become. It is the quest for all the missing pieces of the self so that one can become whole.

It is the search for the answer to that universal question—Who am I?—behind which, for the adoptee, lurks: Who is the mother who brought me into this mysterious world?

John Terrell and Judith Modell  **NO**

Anthropology and Adoption

Anthropologists, we believe, are likely to forget that "what every anthropologist knows" is not necessarily what everyone else knows. In the quest for tenure, professional visibility, and academic achievement, anthropologists may also overlook the possibility that what they know could be important to people who are not anthropologists, too, if only they know. Here is one example.

Adoption in America

In North America, most children grow up living with at least one of the parents they were born to; most children grow up assuming they will live with children born to them. Consequently, perhaps, many people in our society think of adoption as a second-best way of becoming a family (Schaffer and Lindstrom 1989:15). The psychological and social ties binding an adoptive family together are looked on as weaker than "natural" ties of blood. And adoption is seen as difficult and risky. The risk is held to be especially great when a child does not "match"—look like or share the background of—its adoptive parents (Bates 1993). This is preeminently true of transracial and international adoptions, in which a child, who has no say in the matter, is severed not only from its "real" family but also from ethnic roots and cultural heritage: in a word, from its true identity.

Recently, advocates of adoption have been emphasizing the difference between adoptive and biological families (e.g., Melina 1986; Register 1991; Schaffer and Lindstrom 1989), often as a way of helping parents through such "alternative parenthood" (Kirk 1984). Adoptive families are different, for one thing, because adoption is not typical in American society. They are more profoundly different because, it is said, all parties in the "adoption triad" (birth parents, adoptees, and adoptive parents) must cope with psychological pain and feelings of loss. Adoptive parents "lose" the chance to have a biological child and the perpetuation of their blood line. An adopted child loses its natural heritage. And birth parents lose their children.

Moreover, it is presumed that adoptive parents must deal with feelings of inadequacy, and birth parents with feelings of incompetence or frustration. Adoptees, in this argument, suffer throughout their lives because "adoption cuts off people from a part of themselves" (Brodzinsky et al. 1992:3). Even children who were adopted in the first days or weeks of life "grieve not only for the parents they never knew, but for the other aspects of themselves that have been lost through adoption: the loss of origins, of a completed sense of self, of genealogical continuity" (Brodzinsky et al. 1992:11–12). Because they have not been raised by those who gave them life, even the most well-adjusted adoptees, we are told, go through predictable ups and downs of psychological adaptation that distinguish them as a recognizable class of persons who may need special counseling and professional help (Brodzinsky et al. 1992; Samuels 1990:87–113).

Adoption in Oceania

Anthropologists know that what is problematic or self-evident in one society may not be so in another. Oceanic societies—Hawaii among them—are well known in anthropological literature for the frequency and apparent casualness of adoption. What most Americans know about our 50th state, however, does not usually include the information that the last reigning monarch was an adopted, or *hanai,* child. Moreover, this was a crucial fact in her story and remains significant in the interpretations Hawaiians make of their culture and history. In her autobiography, Queen Liliuokalani wrote:

> Immediately after my birth I was wrapped in the finest soft tapa cloth, and taken to the house of another chief, by whom I was adopted. Konia, my foster-mother, was a granddaughter of Kamehameha I., and was married to Paki, also a high chief; their only daughter, Bernice Pauahi, afterwards Mrs. Charles R. Bishop, was therefore my foster-sister. In speaking of our relationship, I have adopted the term customarily used in the English language, but there was no such modification recognized in my native land. I knew no other father or mother than my foster-parents, no other sister than Bernice. [Liliuokalani 1990:4]

She goes on to say that Paki treated her exactly as any other father would treat his child, and that when she would meet her biological parents, she would respond with perhaps more interest, but always with the same demeanor that was due all strangers who noticed her.

Liliuokalani adds that her biological mother and father had other children, ten in all. Most of them were adopted into other chiefs' families. She says it is difficult to explain to outsiders why these adoptions seem perfectly natural to Hawaiians. "As intelligible a reason as can be given is that this alliance by adoption cemented the ties of friendship between chiefs. It spread to the common people, and it has doubtless fostered a community of interest and harmony" (Liliuokalani 1990:4).

Given what anthropologists know about adoption throughout Oceania, (for example, Brady 1976; Carrol 1970; Howard 1990; Levy 1973; Mandeville 1981; Webster 1975), what this royal informant says about the place and popularity of adoption in her native land is not peculiar. For her—and not uniquely —adoption was a loving and generous transaction, not a response to need or crisis. Furthermore, such a loving and generous gesture benefited the whole society as well as the particular individuals involved.

The point of view represented by Queen Liliuokalani—and by other peo-ple in Pacific Island societies who share her experiences (Modell 1994a)—ought to be a lesson for Americans, with our quite different story of adoption. As Bartholet (1993) argues, birth parents, adoptive parents, and adoptees should know that people elsewhere in the world may look on adoption in a variety of ways that do not resemble our assumptions and biases about this form of kin-ship. They need to know that what adoption means, and what it signifies for participants, is malleable, contingent, pragmatic: a "social construction," not a natural fact or a universal cultural given.

Anthropology and Adoption

Anthropologists are likely to find this observation self-evident; adoption is made —*fictio*—by those who practice this mode of child having and child rearing. But, with some exceptions (e.g., Modell 1994b), anthropologists have not been drawn to study the politics and practice of adoption in Western societies: appar-ently what anthropologists find interesting elsewhere may be less interesting, or deeply private, at home. A glance over the abundant published literature on kinship, in fact, suggests that studying adoption generally plays a peripheral role in anthropology: as a way of illuminating a kinship system, as a mecha-nism of social mobility, or as a way of transmitting property. Little disciplinary attention has been paid to the diverse ways people think about, react to, and represent the meaning of adoption.

This is not to say that nothing exists on the subject. In the early 20th cen-tury, Lowie remarked on the frequency of adoption in Pacific Island societies, forgetting his cultural relativism to claim that child exchange in such societies went "well beyond the rational" (Lowie 1933). His surprise prompted others to inquire into the consequences of the unfamiliar behavior of moving large num-bers of children from household to household. Three decades later, in the early 1960s, Levy discovered in a small village in Tahiti that more than 25 percent of children were adopted; this was not untypical for Polynesian societies. Levy went on to analyze the impact of this generous "transaction in parenthood" in his path-breaking account of Tahitian culture and personality (Levy 1973).

Anthropologists such as Marshall picked up other threads in the (slowly) growing tapestry on adoption in the Pacific. In an article examining created kin in Trukese society, Marshall concludes that what is common to kinship is a notion of sharing, differently enacted and represented in different contexts (1977:656–657). To analyze kinship cross-culturally and without bias, he argues, one must explore the nature of nurture and of sharing. His article demonstrates the significance of creating kin through constructed sibling and parent-child bonds for revealing the meanings of kinship. To act like kin is to be kin; to care for reciprocally is to have a relationship. Conduct and performance make (and unmake) kin, with a fluidity that differs from "biogenetic" notions of kinship characteristic of American society (Marshall 1977).

Marshall's article confirms the extent to which kinship is not "natural" but "cultural," representing an intense experience of love and of obligation be-tween individuals. Moreover, these experiences may change over the course of a person's life, depending on circumstances and on perceptions of the "useful-ness" and rewards of being related.

Two volumes on adoption in Oceania underscored the importance of created kinship in Pacific Island societies: [Vern] Carroll's *Adoption in Ocea-nia* (1970) and [Ivan] Brady's *Transactions in Kinship* (1976). In both volumes the contributing anthropologists explore the structure and the functions of adoption, with varying degrees of attention to Carroll's initial warning about applying the single term *adoption* to diverse arrangements across cultures. The goal of challenging the universality of a definition of *adoption* is, as Ward Good-enough concludes in the epilogue to the 1970 volume, only imperfectly met. Treating adoption largely as a social institution, the articles in these volumes tended not to explore the meanings of the experience for the individuals in-volved or to establish a framework for interpretive analysis of the cultural and personal significance of "child exchange" wherever, and however, it occurs.

Silk offers an alternative to the conventional treatment of adoption in an-thropological literature. In a 1980 article, she notes the frequency of adoption in Pacific Island societies compared with almost all others in the world, and asks why. Her answer draws on sociobiological theory. Silk argues that as a way of modifying extreme family size, adoption is adaptive for the group, though it may be a risk for the individual child. Following her theoretical premise, the risk lies in the tendency of parents to treat their biological—more *closely related* —children differently from the way they treat an adopted child (Silk 1980:803). She further suggests that, consequently (and necessarily), biological parents re-tain an interest in the child they have given away; thus, bonds are maintained, not severed, by adoption. In offering a sociobiological explanation, Silk does not mean to exclude the social and cultural factors that affect the transaction; her primary aim is to distinguish societies in which adoption occurs frequently from those in which it occurs rarely (Silk 1980:816). She does not question the concept of adoption itself.

Frequency has continued to be a feature that brings adoption to the atten-tion of anthropologists, most of whom come from a society in which adoption affects "only" about 2 or 3 percent of children in any one year (Adamec and Peirce 1991). Anthropologists of Eskimo (Inuit) societies, sounding rather like anthropologists of the Pacific, remark on the astonishing ease with which chil-dren are moved from parent to parent, for shorter or longer stays (Guemple 1979). Several of these studies inquire into the impact of this movement on the affective as well as the structural and functional domains of social life.

The frequency of adoption in large-scale, complex societies has also piqued anthropological interest, though without major impact on the disci-pline. In 1980, for instance, [Arthur] Wolf and [Chieh-shan] Huang published an exhaustive study of adoption in China whose importance has mainly been acknowledged by other Sinologists. *Marriage and Adoption in China 1845–1945* traces trends in the transactions of women and of children as these reflect social and political changes. With a century's worth of historical records, Wolf and Huang had data other anthropologists might envy. Yet their analysis remains conventional, assuming that the meaning of adoption can be transferred from "us" to "them" and describing the social to the exclusion of the psychological ramifications of the phenomenon.

The silence accorded to full-scale studies of adoption continues. To take a final example: Esther Goody's pioneering analysis of "child exchange" in West African societies and among West Africans in London recognizes the range of meanings and functions moving a child may have (Goody 1982). Discussing numerous particular cases in which parenthood is delegated, Goody reminds her readers that words like *adoption* and *fosterage* are culturally and historically relative as well as individually negotiated. Her book speaks a quiet warning against assuming that the meaning of adoption holds from group to group, time to time, or even person to person.

One cannot, of course, leave the subject of adoption and kinship without referring to the work of Jack Goody—especially his under-appreciated article, "Adoption in Cross Cultural Perspective." The point he made in this 1969 piece remains all too appropriate: "For I know of no attempt to do a systematic survey of the distribution of this phenomenon, which is not for example included in the data recorded in the Ethnographic Atlas (1967) nor mentioned in Goody's study of changing family patterns (1963)" (Goody 1969:56). As far as we know, his agenda for the comparative study of adoption has not been followed. Nor have the issues raised in the ethnographic writings cited above been taken as far as they might.

If anthropologists embrace the goal of examining rather than imposing meanings of core concepts on others—or, for that matter, our own society—then adoption would seem to be a crucial area of study. For it is here that the multivocal meanings of personhood and identity, of kinship and social bonds, can be thoroughly explored—and from the point of view of those who "make" these kinds of relationships. Existing writings on adoption suggest there is more to be said about the self-conscious gesture involved in creating kin and its diverse manifestations. Virtually everywhere it occurs, adoption inscribes and perpetuates understandings of birth, blood, and belonging, of essence and accident or choice. In the late 19th century, the British jurist Sir Henry Maine articulated the premise of his own culture's understanding of adoption: fictive kinship, he wrote, replicates "real" kinship; the bond of law "imitates" the bond of birth and the child is "as if begotten" (Maine 1861). The ramifications of this premise in Western society, and the import of transferring it to other societies, have too rarely been seen as problematic.

The treatment of adoption in anthropological literature perpetuates a sense that the concept is nonproblematic. The transaction of a child, evidently, is not considered either a major social event or a key cultural text; rather, child exchange is analyzed as "only" an aspect of kinship, form of social solidarity, or response to demographic conditions. The neglect also speaks to a conservatism about our methods and categories of analysis, despite (or perhaps because of) the popularity of postmodernist writings in the discipline. Further confirming this is the modest reception given to several recently published radical reexaminations of kinship, of kinship and gender, and of theories of identity and ethnicity (e.g., Collier and Yanagisako 1987; Linnekin and Poyer 1990a; Schneider 1984; Weston 1991). These studies do show, however, that at least some anthropologists are drastically rethinking the context and meaning of fundamental aspects of social life.

Kinship and Adoption

Adoption as a category of meaning, like adoption as social practice, is problematic. Western common sense says the distinction between kin and non-kin is self-evident, a distinction that allows for the concept of "*as if* begotten." Adoption is thus a phenomenological category betwixt categories, a category that straddles the fence, a category in our society that dooms those who fall within it to be both kin and non-kin—real and "fictive." As Schneider has demonstrated through his brilliant analysis of the cultural unit on Yap called *tabinau*, there is much to be gained by recognizing how considerably varied and flexible the meanings of words can be (Schneider 1984:21).

Although Western ideas about kinship and adoption assume the primacy of blood ties and biological inheritance and see people as discrete and bounded individuals (Linnekin and Poyer 1990b:2, 7), anthropologists know that these presuppositions are not universal. Pomponio, for example, notes that while children on Mandok Island, Papua New Guinea, are thought to share the substance of their parents and other kin, "substance" means more than it does in Western thought: not just shared biogenetic endowment but the combination of blood, food, and work. "The transubstantial nature of Mandok personhood is evidenced by their belief that firstborns can be 'created' through adoption, and adoption is not limited to married couples." Many children (13 of 81, or 16 percent of her sample), in fact, are adopted specifically for this purpose. She concludes, "The important substance here is not contained in blood or semen, but food and work (i.e., caretaking). By feeding and caring for a child, the substance of the adult is transferred to that child" (Pomponio 1990:54).

Lieber argues that what Pomponio observes about the nature of kinship and adoption on Mandok may be true of Oceanic societies generally. What it means to be a person in many Pacific Island societies is structured, he says, by local theories of ontogeny (Lieber 1990:71) in which what a person becomes is not "in their blood," but is credited instead to the nurturing social and physical environment within which they mature. In other words, as Howard has summarized the argument, kinship in Oceania is considered to be contingent rather than absolute.

> Thus, on the one hand, kinship has to be validated by social action to be recognized; on the other, kinship status can be achieved through social action (i.e., by consistently acting as kinsmen even though genealogical linkages may be questionable or unknown). [Howard 1990:266]

A similar argument made by Sahlins chastens anthropologists for separating adoption—and kinship—from all aspects of culture and social structure. In Hawaii, where belonging comes from action and relationships are contingent, Sahlins claims: "From family to state, the arrangements of society were in constant flux, a set of relationships constructed on the shifting sands of love" (Sahlins 1985:20). The civil state, he might have added, rests upon chosen attachments much like the relationship between parents and child.

Anthropology and the Public

The process of rethinking theories of the person, of kinship, and of social and cultural life that is essential to our discipline also bears on current debates about multiculturalism occurring throughout the American university environment. Anthropologists have expressed amazement that scholars from across the disciplinary spectrum have discovered "the other," "multivocality," and "multiculturalism" without discovering anthropology (Perry 1992). But it is equally fair to argue that anthropologists have not actively guided the debate or introduced an anthropological vocabulary to a public that will feel the effects of such debate.

Anthropologists—or at least anthropologists who read the *Anthropology Newsletter*—do not need to be told that it is important to be "public or perish" (Givens 1992). Nevertheless—all too often, it seems—anthropologists focus on what their colleagues will say about their work and overlook opportunities to be heard and appreciated by others. Even when they cannot grab newspaper headlines with startling news about lost tribes, missing links, or the oldest potsherds in the world, they need to ask themselves: who might be interested to know what I know?

Thanks to anthropologists such as Schneider, it may no longer be intellectually strategic to study adoption simply to refute the conventional wisdom that the bonds of kinship are genealogical—given by "birth" (Schneider 1984:169–177). Studying adoption can also be a way of discovering the meanings and implications of aspects of culture and social order that remain problematic for both anthropologists and the public. Adoption not only belies what Schneider has called "biologistic" ways of marking and defining human character, human nature, and human behavior (Schneider 1984:175), it also reveals interpretations of concepts like identity, family, and ethnicity.

Thus, for instance, a study of adoption can shed light on definitions of and criteria for "citizenship": What does it mean to belong to a group or nation, and is this linked with ideas about what it means to belong to a family? Nor is adoption irrelevant to larger concerns about assimilation, "true" cultural identity, and ethnic purity, raising as it does the problem of being "*as if* begotten" when contract has been the mode of entry. At core, adoption is about who belongs and how—a subject of immense political as well as disciplinary significance. It is also, and increasingly, about power, privilege, and poverty. Concerns are properly raised about babies moving from the poor to the rich, or, a new version of the old "baby-selling" cry, about residents of impoverished nations and regions putting their babies on the international market. But anthropologists have not addressed those concerns. Moreover, these are issues that touch the lives of a general public, well beyond those who may experience, or know about, an adoptive relationship.

Conclusion

In societies such as ours where caring for children who are not one's own by birth is seen as risky, painful, and unnatural, learning through anthropology's eyes that what adoption does to people is not written in stone would undoubtedly be beneficial to birth parents, adoptive parents, and adoptees. It seems equally apparent that studying adoption in different societies can be a window through which anthropologists may learn about other facets of life.

Our own interest in adoption (beyond the powerful consideration that we are both adoptive parents) lies in both these directions. We are interested in adoption as an empirical question. What are the meanings, values, and contexts of caring for children "other than your own" in different societies? What determines the place and popularity (or lack thereof) of adoption in different societies? The agenda Jack Goody set over twenty years ago can benefit from recent literature on reflexivity and multivocalism, so that adoption is considered not only a social transaction but also a cultural text. The comparative task, then, will involve analyzing the forms of attachment and the representations of experience constituted by adoption—or, broadly, "child exchange"—as practiced by diverse cultural groups.

A study of adoption becomes an inquiry into fundamental beliefs about the person and personal connections as these intertwine with political, economic, and historical developments. Taking the perspective of constructed kinship and making the most of the "construction" it entails, so that adoption is not assumed to be univocal or universal in meaning, can advance theories of culture creativity, human agency, and identity formation. Ideally, studying adoption will preserve the centrality of individual experiences in the composition of social worlds and cultural texts.

We also want to strengthen public awareness of the diverse ways that people in different parts of the world—and in different ethnic communities here in North America—build and value human relationships and family ties and obligations. In the process we should demonstrate that anthropology importantly is, as it historically has been, a "way of seeing" for those other than its practitioners.

References

Adamec, Christine, and William Peirce, 1991, The Encyclopedia of Adoption. New York: Facts on File.
Bartholet, Elizabeth, 1993, Family Bonds. Adoption and the Politics of Parenting. Boston: Houghton Mifflin.
Bates, J. Douglas, 1993, Gift Children. A Story of Race, Family, and Adoption in a Divided America. New York: Ticknor and Fields.
Brady, Ivan, ed., 1976, Transactions in Kinship: Adoption and Fosterage in Oceania. Honolulu: University of Hawaii Press.
Brodzinsky, David M., Marshall D. Schechter, and Robin Marantz Henig, 1992, Being Adopted. The Lifelong Search for Self. New York: Doubleday.

Carrol, Vern, ed., 1970, Adoption in Eastern Oceania. Honolulu: University of Hawaii Press.

Collier, Jane Fishburne, and Sylvia Junko Yanagisako, eds., 1987, Gender and Kinship. Essays toward a Unified Analysis. Stanford: Stanford University Press.

Givens, David B., 1992, Public or Perish. Anthropology Newsletter 33(5):1, 58.

Goody, Esther, 1982, Parenthood and Social Reproduction. New York: Cambridge University Press.

Goody, Jack, 1969, Adoption in Cross-Cultural Perspective. Comparative Studies in Society and History 2:55–78.

Guemple, D. L., 1979, Inuit Adoption. Ottawa: National Museums of Canada.

Howard, Alan, 1990, Cultural Paradigms, History, and the Search for Identity in Oceania, *In* Cultural Identity and Ethnicity in the Pacific. Jocelyn Linnekin and Lin Poyer, eds. Pp. 259–279. Honolulu: University of Hawaii Press.

Kirk, H. David, 1984, Shared Fate. A Theory and Method of Adoptive Relationships. Port Angeles, WA: Ben-Simon Publications.

Levy, Robert, 1973, The Tahitians: Mind and Experience in the Society Islands. Chicago: University of Chicago Press.

Lieber, Michael D., 1990, Lamarckian Definitions of Identity on Kapingamarangi and Pohnpei. *In* Cultural Identity and Ethnicity in the Pacific. Jocelyn Linnekin and Lin Poyer, eds. Pp. 71–101. Honolulu: University of Hawaii Press.

Liliuokalani, 1990, Hawaii's Story by Hawaii's Queen. Honolulu: Mutual Publishing.

Linnekin, Jocelyn, and Lin Poyer, 1990a, [eds.] Cultural Identity and Ethnicity in the Pacific. Honolulu: University of Hawaii Press.

____, 1990b, Introduction. *In* Cultural Identity and Ethnicity in the Pacific. Jocelyn Linnekin and Lin Poyer, eds. Pp. 1–16. Honolulu: University of Hawaii Press.

Lowie, Robert, 1933, Adoption. *In* Encyclopedia of the Social Sciences. E. A. Seligman and A. Johnson, eds. Pp. 459–460. New York: Macmillan and Company.

Maine, Sir Henry, 1861, Ancient Law. London: Macmillan.

Mandeville, Elizabeth, 1981, Kamano Adoption. Ethnology 20:229–244.

Marshall, Mac, 1977, The Nature of Nurture. American Ethnologist 4(4):643–662.

Melina, Lois Ruskai, 1986, Raising Adopted Children. A Manual for Adoptive Parents. New York: Harper and Row.

Modell, Judith, 1994a, Nowadays Everyone Is *Hanai:* Child Exchange and the Construction of Hawaiian Urban Culture. *In* Urban Cultures in the Pacific. C. Jourdan and J. M. Philibert, eds. Forthcoming.

____, 1994b, Kenship with Strangers: Adoption and Interpretations of Kinship in American Culture. Berkeley: University of California Press.

Perry, Richard J., 1992, Why Do Multiculturalists Ignore Anthropologists? Chronicle of Higher Education 38(26):A52.

Pomponio, Alice, 1990, Seagulls Don't Fly into the Bush: Cultural Identity and the Negotiations of Development on Mandok Island, Papua New Guinea. *In* Cultural Identity and Ethnicity in the Pacific. Jocelyn Linnekin and Lin Poyer, eds. Pp. 43–70. Honolulu: University of Hawaii Press.

Register, Cheri, 1991, "Are Those Kids Yours?" American Families with Children Adopted from Other Countries. New York: Free Press.

Sahlins, Marshall, 1985, Islands of History. Chicago: University of Chicago Press.

Samuels, Shirley C., 1990, Ideal Adoption: A Comprehensive Guide to Forming an Adoptive Family. New York: Plenum.

Schaffer, Judith, and Christina Lindstrom, 1989, How to Raise an Adopted Child. A Guide to Help Your Child Flourish from Infancy through Adolescence. New York: Penguin Books.

Schneider, David M., 1984, A Critique of the Study of Kinship. Ann Arbor: University of Michigan Press.

Silk, Joan, 1980, Adoption and Kinship in Oceania. American Anthropologist 82(4):799–820.

Webster, Steven, 1975, Cognatic Descent Groups and the Contemporary Maori: A Preliminary Reassessment. Journal of the Polynesian Society 84:121–152.

Weston, Kath, 1991, Families We Choose: Lesbians, Gays, Kinship. New York: Columbia University Press.

Wolf, Arthur, and Chieh-shan Huang, 1980, Marriage and Adoption in China, 1845–1945. Stanford: Stanford University Press.

POSTSCRIPT

Is It Natural for Adopted Children to Want to Find Out About Their Birth Parents?

Lifton's argument is clearly situated within the adoption rights movement and draws upon her personal experiences as much as on the experiences of those she has interviewed. She and her American informants clearly have a burning need to know who their birth parents are, and she concludes that it is unnatural for anyone to be deprived of this information. She and her informants feel a certain amount of psychic pain and emptiness, as well as lack of wholeness.

Terrell and Modell, on the other hand, argue that however real such feelings may be, they are cultural constructs rather than natural, biological ones. They cite examples from Pacific Island societies to show that such feelings are not human universals but culturally specific responses to a particular normative kinship structure.

This issue raises questions about just how "natural" are kinship systems in different societies. American society has long placed emphasis on biological families, just as Americans have long accepted biologically or physiologically based illnesses as more real than psychological ones. As Terrell and Modell note, some anthropologists have not found it easy to ignore their own culture's views on adoption. Nevertheless, they argue that anthropologist David Schneider was essentially correct in his description of American kinship. In *American Kinship: A Cultural Account* (Prentice-Hall, 1968), he argues that while Americans contend that kinship is about biological relatedness, in practice it is those who "act" like close kin who are accepted as one's closest kinsmen. Thus, it is the social behavior rather than the genetic relationship that is most important in shaping our social worlds.

To what extent do significantly higher rates of adoption in Oceania or other parts of the world challenge American views that biologically based parent-child relationships are inherently more "real" than socially constructed relationship created by adoption? How are we to explain the strongly held views of Lifton and other adoption rights advocates, who clearly feel something lacking in their own lives if they do not and cannot know who their birth parents are?

Some of Lifton's other books include *Twice Born: Memoirs of an Adopted Daughter* (Penguin, 1977) and *Lost and Found: The Adoption Experience* (HarperCollins, 1988). Somewhat earlier versions of the same argument are provided by John Triseliotis's *In Search of Origins: The Experiences of Adopted People* (Routledge & Kegan Paul, 1973) and H. David Kirk's *Adoptive Kinship: A Modern Institution in Need of Reform* (Butterworths, 1981), as well as his *Shared*

Fate: A Theory and Method of Adoptive Relationships (Ben-Simon Publications, 1984). See also David M. Brodzinsky, Marshall D. Schechter, and Robin M. Henig's *Being Adopted: The Lifelong Search for Self* (Doubleday, 1992).

Modell has written a more extended view of the cultural construction of American adoption in *Kinship With Strangers: Adoption and Interpretations of Kinship in American Culture* (University of California Press, 1994). For similar perspectives, see Karen March's *The Stranger Who Bore Me: Adoptee-Birth Mother Relationships* (University of Toronto Press, 1995) and Katarina Wegar's *Adoption, Identity and Kinship: The Debate Over Sealed Birth Records* (Yale University Press, 1997). For a survey of current views of the problems of modern adoption, readers should consult a special issue of *Family Relations* (vol. 49, no. 4, October 2000), edited by Karen March and Charlene Miall.

For discussions of adoption in Pacific Island cultures, see *Adoption in Eastern Oceania* (University of Hawaii Press, 1970), edited by Vern Carroll. See also Jocelyn Linnekin and Lin Poyer's collection, *Cultural Identity and Ethnicity in the Pacific* (University of Hawaii Press, 1990), and Mac Marshall's essay "The Nature of Nurture," *American Ethnologist* (vol. 4, 1977).

ISSUE 13

Has the Islamic Revolution in Iran Subjugated Women?

YES: Parvin Paidar, from "Feminism and Islam in Iran," in Deniz Kandiyoti, ed., *Gendering the Middle East: Emerging Perspectives* (Syracuse University Press, 1996)

NO: Erika Friedl, from "Sources of Female Power in Iran," in Mahnaz Afkhami and Erika Friedl, eds., *In the Eye of the Storm: Women in Post-Revolutionary Iran* (Syracuse University Press, 1994)

ISSUE SUMMARY

YES: Iranian historian Parvin Paidar considers how the position of women suffered following the 1979 Iranian Revolution because of the imposition of Islamic law (shari'a), as interpreted by conservative male clerics. She contends that the Islamic Revolution marked a setback in the progressive modernist movements, which had improved women's rights during the secular regime of the Shah; new rights and opportunities have emerged since 1979 only in opposition to conservative interpretations of Islamic law.

NO: American anthropologist Erika Friedl asserts that men in Iran have consistently tried to suppress women's rights since the 1979 Iranian Revolution. Despite these efforts to repress them, women in all levels of society have access to many sources of power. In fact, argues Friedl, women have considerably more power available to them than either Western or Iranian stereotypes might suggest, even though they must work within Islamic law to obtain this power.

Perhaps nowhere has Islam's role in shaping the position of women been more obvious than in Afghanistan where the theocratic Taliban regime prevented women from working outside the home, from attending school, and from participating in the political process in any meaningful way. In Iran one of the effects of the 1979 revolution was that women suddenly lost most of the rights they had gradually obtained over the previous century. In both countries religious leaders have defended their actions and policies in terms of Islamic law, or *shari'a*, leading many Western observers to argue that this legal code inherently subjugates women. However, Muslim clerics have long argued that Islamic law does not subjugate women but merely defines men's and women's roles in society in complementary ways as prescribed by God.

At issue is whether or not Islamic customs, such as wearing head scarves, necessarily subordinate and subjugate women, as many feminist observers have argued. Or does Islamic law as interpreted by conservative male clerics merely delineate complementary social roles for men and women, as many Muslim scholars and religious leaders insist? Most importantly, if *shari'a* does not inherently subjugate women, why is it that the reimposition of *shari'a* law in the late twentieth century has so often included the loss of rights for Muslim women rather than enhancing their legal protections? In these countries, the more anti-Western and fundamentalist the religious and political leaders have become, the lower the apparent position of women.

Islam has traditionally depicted women as the weaker sex, in need of protection from the men in their lives. Such a view has shaped the social roles available to Islamic women in both conservative and progressive Muslim countries. Women in most Muslim countries have a much less obvious political voice in the affairs of the state than in Western countries, since politics is defined in Islamic law as the domain of men. But many observers have argued that within the household, women have considerably more power than Western observers have generally acknowledged.

The following selections consider the role and position of women in Iran. Parvin Paidar, herself an Iranian, documents the changing position of women since the nineteenth century. Here, she shows how women were able to draw on Western feminist ideas during the reign of the Shah to gain individual rights and improve the status of women. But when the Ayatollah Khomeini took control following the 1979 revolution, women's rights were sharply and suddenly curtailed. All of these changes were justified by the need to return to the "true" faith, as outlined in *shari'a* law. For Paidar, improvements in women's position in society have only been possible following Khomeini's death, when less conservative and more secular voices have emerged.

Erika Friedl acknowledges that Iranian women do not have the rights enjoyed by most Western women. But she argues that, working within conservative readings of Islamic law, Iranian women have many sources of power available to them. Such power can emerge in part through resistance to male authority. Or Iranian women can achieve control over their own lives and over the lives of their sons and husbands through work, religion, and the government itself. In a male-dominated society such as Iran, women have many "weapons of the weak" at their disposal, believes Friedl, with which they can achieve power within their households.

Parvin Paidar

 **YES**

Feminism and Islam in Iran

Feminism(s) in the Middle East and their articulations with Islam have attracted substantial interest in recent years. This [selection] will focus on the interaction between feminism and Islam in Iran. It will trace, in general terms, the development of feminism in that country and the ways in which it has interacted with Islam at various historical moments since the turn of the century. While in recent decades feminisms in the Arab Middle East by and large make reference to utopian Islam(s) to defend women's rights, in Iran the interaction between feminism and Islam has taken place in the context of a militant Shi'i state which claims to have implemented 'true Islam'. The contrast between these contexts may provide a useful contribution to an understanding of the interaction between feminism and Islam in various Middle Eastern contexts.

The approach adopted in this [selection] emanates from the view that far from being an optional extra, gender is situated at the heart of political discourses in Iran. Indeed, any political discourse aiming at the social reorganization of Iranian society has necessarily entailed a redefinition of gender relations and of women's position in society. Therefore, this [selection] will place the interaction between Islam and feminism in the broader context of political process in twentieth-century Iran.

Early Twentieth-Century Nationalist Feminism

In tracing the historical development of feminism in relation to Islam, a natural starting point would be the constitutional movement of the early twentieth century, since this was the context within which the 'woman question' was first explicitly raised in Iran.

The Constitutional Revolution of 1906–11 took place against the background of Western intrusion and the rise of nationalism. It revolved around the demand for constitutional monarchy to curb the power of the monarch in favour of the power of parliament and the rule of law on the one hand, and to protect Iran's national interests in the face of Western economic and political intervention on the other. It rested upon a diverse urban alliance which included merchants, traders, land owners, secular intellectuals and the Shi'i clergy. The importance of the constitutional movement for women was in the creation of a particular vision of modern Iran. The concept of modernity encapsulated justice, democracy, independence and women's emancipation. The movement created a conceptual link between national independence and progress and women's emancipation. It constructed women as social actors for the first time and facilitated the formation of a network of women's rights activists which gradually developed into a loosely formed women's movement.

Since the very idea of women's emancipation was grounded in the need for national progress, women activists prioritized the general developmental gains implicit in the improvement of women's position. The main demands of the women's movement included education and the abolition of practices such as seclusion and early marriage, which were regarded as serious impediments to women's contribution to national development. The way in which women's emancipation became associated with national progress during the constitutional period, created a generic link between feminism and nationalism which has shaped the course of Iranian feminism ever since. This has had at least two consequences. First, it has made it impossible to talk about the interaction between feminism and Islam without taking into account the links between Islam and nationalism. Second, this has been one of the main reasons why individualistic types of feminism based on women's personal experience and individual choice, a stance commonly associated with feminism in the West, have not developed in Iran.

The type of nationalism that developed in Iran in the first half of the century was on the whole secular. It was constructed as an alternative discourse, as Islam was associated with traditionalism and backwardness. During the constitutional period, secular intellectuals played an important role in constructing concepts such as constitutionalism, nationalism, modernity and women's emancipation.... Babism was ... one of the main indigenous sources of inspiration for women's emancipation at the turn of the century since one of its female protagonists Tahereh Qorrat ol-Eyn took off her veil in public and challenged the *ulama* (Muslim clergy) to debate women's position with her.

From the beginning of this century, then, the concept of women's emancipation became grounded in concepts associated with nationalism and modernity.... However, the debate on women was conducted in a way which avoided outright confrontation with religion. Feminists of this period complained against social conservatism rather than Islam as such. For example, Bibi Khanum Astarabadi argued that 'The obstacle to women's emancipation is not Islam but the male interest to preserve his privileges....'

Although the secular debate on women avoided outright opposition to Islam, nevertheless the expression of ideas inspired by non-Islamic sources was considered to be a serious threat by many Shi'i clerics. The Shi'i establishment focused on opposing the practical steps taken to emancipate women. For example, the opening of each new school for women was accompanied by a campaign by local mollahs to close it down. This is not to say that the clergy were united on the question of women's education—on the contrary....

[W]hile women's protests against subordination were conducted within an acceptable cultural framework which avoided overt criticism of Islam, the main point of reference for these women was secular nationalism. The secular nature of early twentieth-century feminism was strengthened further in the post-Constitutional period as a result of two particular developments; the rise of socialism and establishment of the Bolshevik state across the border in Russia and the emergence of the state as an agent of social reform. . . .

The emergence of the state as an agent of social reform was an even more important development affecting Iranian feminism in the early part of the century. The state established by Reza Shah Pahlavi in 1925 had a national-ist outlook and valorized pre-Islamic Iran. It set out to transform Iran from a dependent, backward society to a modern, independent nation-state and as a result the state became the initiator and implementor of social reform and as-sumed responsibility for the health, welfare and education of the population, at least in rhetoric.

Statist Feminism and the Rise of Cultural Nationalism in Mid Twentieth-Century Iran

However, in imposing reform on women's position, Reza Shah's state adopted a forceful and centralist approach and ended an era of women's independent activities by creating a state-sponsored women's organization to lead the way on women's emancipation. The measures proclaimed included compulsory un-veiling, free education and, potentially, the creation of new employment oppor-tunities. These measures had been demanded by many constitutionalists and feminists since the turn of the century, and by implementing them the state took the initiative on women's issues away from independent socialists, liberal nationalists and feminists. With a silent Shi'i establishment, co-opted national-ism, a suppressed socialist movement, and a partly co-opted, partly suppressed women's movement, the only voice allowed on behalf of women was that of the state.

The second Pahlavi state, established in 1941 after the abdication of Reza Shah in favour of his son, Mohammad Reza Shah, continued the same pattern of modernization, co-option and political suppression. The initial period of constitutional rule under the Shah resulted in the formation of a short-lived liberal nationalist government by Mohammad Mosaddeq who led a coalition of nationalist forces. The nationalist government, however, did not have a spe-cific gender agenda and its half-hearted attempt to introduce a new electoral bill which included enfranchisement for women failed. A CIA-sponsored coup in 1953 against Mosaddeq restored the Shah's autocratic rule. The post-coup pe-riod of 1960s and 1970s witnessed heightened suppression of most autonomous political groupings. But it also resulted in further state initiatives on women's rights. The campaign for political rights conducted by prominent feminists, such as Fatemeh Sayyah, had some success despite substantial opposition by the clergy.

The 1960s and 1970s also saw the growth of cultural nationalism and Islamic modernism. This occasioned a shift in the interaction between femi-nism, nationalism and Islam. The rise of cultural nationalism as a new political force closely associated with Islam resulted in the Shi'i establishment reclaiming lost moral ground on women and family issues as a result of several new developments.

First, on the religious front, after the death in 1961 of Ayatollah Borujerdi, the highest Shi'i authority of his time, a group of high-ranking clerics shared similar high status and gained their own followers. These Ayatollahs, including Khomeini, published and circulated widely their religious opinions on a broad range of issues, including women and the family. These religious views about women's position found political expression in a campaign by an Iranian version of the Muslim Brotherhood in the 1960s which presented a new fundamentalist defence of the Shi'i *shari'a* on women.

Second, on the political front, reformist clerics such as Ayatollah Motahhari and lay religious radicals such as Ali Shari'ati articulated new models of Muslim womanhood for Iranian women. The ideas of Shari'ati were adopted by the Mojahedin-e Khalq, who represented the Islamic tendency within the Marxist-Leninist guerrilla movement of the 1960s and 1970s which led a crusade against the Pahlavi state.

The success of these new Islamic trends in regaining the initiative on women and the family was due to both ideological and political factors. The Pahlavi state's unwillingness to introduce fundamental changes on women's position within the family enabled the Shi'i establishment to regain the initiative fairly easily. Both Reza Shah and Mohammad Reza Shah focused their reforms on the civic aspects of women's roles as opposed to the familial ones. Despite tremendous opposition by the Shi'i establishment, both Pahlavi regimes pushed forward with women's education, unveiling and de-segregation, while the reforms that they carried out on the family remained relatively limited. Pahlavi reforms did not go beyond a codification of traditional Shi'i law on women and family as part of the Civil Code of 1936, and an attempt to limit arbitrary male power in the family through the introduction of Family Protection Laws in 1967 and 1975. These limitations were due not so much to clerical opposition as to deeper concerns about the wider implications of granting women real power and independence within the family. The Pahlavi regimes opposed women's independence in the family and their independent presence in the public sphere, and this influenced the logic behind state-sponsored women's organizations which made sure that women's lives inside and outside the home remained under the control of male guardians. This strengthened the clergy's ideological hold over matters concerning women and the family, which was translated so effectively into a successful political campaign by the Shi'i movement during the 1970s.

However, the existence of new Shi'i ideas on women would not by itself have affected feminism in Iran if the political developments of the 1970s had not pushed them to the forefront. The rise of Shi'ism as a serious modern political movement in the context of anti-Shah politics became a major factor in the adoption of Shi'i ideas on women. The revolutionary context provided fertile ground for the first serious confrontation of secular feminisms (such as statist and socialist feminism) by political Islam. For the first time, Islamic activism became a serious political option for Iranian women, and many women from the younger generation who were totally alienated from state feminism took it up. The Pahlavi state's claim to be liberating women was politically untenable; the nationalist opposition was not able to present an alternative gender policy to that of the state and the socialist alternative only attracted a small minority of women. As a result, the campaign on women's issues became the preserve of the Islamic opposition.

The Islamic campaign on women included appeals to reject 'Westerniza-tion' and the exploitation of women as 'sex objects' which was seen as the consequence of Iran's economic and cultural dependence on the West. Instead, women were urged to embrace the new Shi'i model of womanhood which rep-resented 'authenticity' and 'independence' and emphasized women's dual role as mothers and revolutionaries. This found credence with large groups among both religious and secular women because it promised political freedom, eco-nomic equality, social justice, cultural integrity and personal fulfilment. It facilitated women's massive participation in the Revolution of 1979.

The contrast between women's participation in the 1979 Revolution and the earlier Constitutional Revolution could not be sharper, and was rooted in the different interactions between Islam and feminism in each revolutionary period. The 1979 Revolution was the second attempt in this century, apart from the brief Mosaddeq period, to redefine and change existing relations between the state and Western powers with the aim of establishing independence and democracy in Iran. But while the former revolutionary movement aimed to achieve this through emulation of the Western liberal model of society, the lat-ter aimed to achieve it by constructing an 'indigenous' and 'authentic' Islamic model of society in Iran. Moreover, while the flavour of the first revolution-ary discourse was that of a liberal nationalism associated with secularism, the second revolved around a cultural nationalism associated with Islam.

In summary, Iranian feminism was essentially secular until the rise of Shi'i modernism in the 1970s. It was only then that the new trend of Islamist fem-inism (gender activism within an Islamic framework) joined other feminisms in Iran.

Islamist Feminism and State Policy in the Islamic Republic

Let us now consider the development of Islamist feminism under the Islamic Republic. After the establishment of the Islamic Republic, the new constitution gave a prominent place to women, defining them as mothers and citizens. It stressed that the establishment of an Islamic nation was dependent on the Is-lamization of women and constructed the ideal Islamic woman in opposition to Western values on womanhood. The constitution attempted to create harmony between the Islamic family and nation by advocating a set of patriarchal rela-tions to strengthen male control over women in the family on the one hand, and granting women the right to be active citizens on the other.

The link between nationalism and Islam was crucial in determining the gender policies of the Islamic Republic. After the Islamic Republic settled into a theocracy, nationalism as a mobilizing force was transformed and re-defined.

The state attempted this by constructing nationalism as synonymous with anti-imperialism on the one hand, and replacing nationalism with Islam as the main mass mobilization force on the other. The new alliance between Islam and anti-imperialism, for which historical precedents existed in Iran, constituted the cornerstone of the Islamization policy of the state. The context of revolutionary populism, anti-imperialism, the effects of a war economy and struggle for state power between Islamic factions determined which concepts and ideas on women were defined as 'Islamic' and which ones as 'un-Islamic'. The result was a significant reversal of the history of clerical opposition to women's participation in politics. For example, the same clerics who had in the 1960s objected to women's enfranchisement on religious grounds were in the 1980s prepared to grant women the right to vote in the name of Islam.

With regard to women's social role, the Islamic Republic formulated policies on women's education, employment and political participation to ensure the continuation of women's mass support. Women's political participation was approved because it legitimized the state's Islamization policies and created an image of popular support and stability internally and internationally. These policies, however, were based on the premise that women's presence outside the home had to be accompanied with a process of de-sexualization of male-female interaction to protect the Islamic family and nation from its harmful moral consequences. A number of policies were developed to ensure this.

First, the protection of the family required the strengthening of male privilege through the Islamization of the Iranian household. The Family Protection Law was abolished and the Civil Code of 1936 was reinstated. This meant that the modest safeguards created for women in matters of divorce, marriage, child custody and abortion were all revoked overnight. Second, an extensive policy of gender segregation and compulsory *hejab* (head cover and loose clothes) for women was implemented. Third, measures were introduced in order to police the integrity of the family. These measures became known as the 'anti-corruption crusade', with a broad definition of corruption covering any social mixing between men and women as well as adultery, homosexuality, consumption of drugs and alcohol, gambling and a whole range of leisure activities.

Having thus structured the social role of women, the post-revolutionary Islamic state encouraged the development of an Islamic women's movement to counter the threat posed by secular feminism. The spontaneous movement of secular women to defend their rights against the Islamic state was crushed and secular feminism was driven into exile. Like preceding secular regimes, the Islamic state has ensured that the women's movement remained under tight state control. Different factions of the state and the state-sponsored revolutionary organizations attempted to harness women's tremendous mobilization potential by creating platforms for Islamic women activists.

The hard-line factions of the state took control of women's mass mobilization by organizing mass rallies in support of state Islamization and against the secular and Islamic opposition. Women's mass support was also manipulated in relation to two other areas of importance to the survival of the state—elections and the war against Iraq.

While women from the lower classes provided the mass support that the Islamic regime needed, Islamic women leaders became involved in philanthropic, religious, and feminist activities. Many of the state-funded welfare agencies, health and education centres, charities and foundations were run by women. Women who managed such organizations often came from clerical families and were well-connected within the circle of Islamic leadership.

A third category of Islamist women took up feminist activities under the patronage of the moderate factions of the state. The Women's Society of the Islamic Revolution (WSIR) was founded soon after the Revolution by a group of women to preserve and build upon the revolutionary demand for a culturally authentic gender identity. The popular, formerly pro-Pahlavi, women's magazine, *Zan-e Ruz* (Woman of Today), was taken over by an editorial board of Islamic feminists and transformed into a popular Islamic women's magazine. These women tended to be highly educated, often with doctorates from Western universities, and professionals in various fields. Their activities included not only publishing women's magazines, but also running women's organizations and formulating Islamic policies on women.

During the post-revolutionary transitional period of 1979–81, Islamist feminists drew their support from the religious faction of the Provisional Government and later, in some cases, the office of President Banisadr. The same period witnessed the forceful imposition of a hasty Islamization programme by Ayatollah Khomeini. This went against the views of Islamist feminists who wanted instead a long-term, gradualist Islamization programme based on educating women about the values of Islam.

Islamist feminists set out to create a vision of the 'ideal Islamic society' and the role of women in it. The idealization of the future Islamic society entailed a critique of the past and the present. The Islamist feminist theory of women's oppression and liberation was constructed in opposition to 'traditional Islam'. 'True Islam', according to Islamic feminists, transcended the 'traditional, deviatory and colonized Islam' in relation to women. The failures of traditional Islam were seen as rooted in male-dominated culture and distorted interpretations of Islamic laws.

Ayatollah Khomeini's Islamization measures received coded criticisms from the Islamist feminists. Azam Taleghani and Zahra Rahnavard, two well-known activists, warned the authorities about the negative effects of forcing women to wear *hejab*. They proposed that the Islamic dress code should not be made specific to women but that both men and women should be required to wear simple and decent clothing which covers the body in a non-arousing, modest fashion. On the Islamic Republic's policy of excluding women from the judiciary, Islamic feminists argued that 'women's emotionality is not an acceptable ground for their exclusion from passing judgement,' and said that 'Muslim women should be able to take their legal problems to female judges as much as possible, just as they take their medical problems to female doctors.'

Despite the enormous enthusiasm of these women and initial expectation that they would make a major contribution to the Islamic Republic's gender policies, Islamist feminists were marginalized by the hard-line factions of the post-revolutionary government. Ayotallah Khomeini's tendency to ignore voices of moderation, together with repressive state policies, resulted in the radicalization of the feminist strand of the Islamist women's movement. During the politically extremist years of 1981–87 the voice of Islamic feminism was thus silenced almost completely.

This took place in the context of a diversity of Islamist opinions, political power struggles, political repression, ideological control, economic stagnation, war and international isolation. These developments affected the ability of the state to establish coherent policies or ensure their effective implementation. Although the general framework of state policies on women was defined by opposition to the Pahlavi regime and 'alien Western values', actual policies of Islamization were formulated in a heterogeneous and *ad hoc* manner by a variety of agents with different and sometimes conflicting interests. The way this affected women can be seen in the pattern of their education and employment in this period. Although strongly encouraged in official rhetoric, in reality women's education and employment suffered from contradictory policies, the imposition of gender quotas and support for male dominance, combined with lack of co-ordination between the multiple centres of decision-making and lack of financial resources. Nevertheless, although the opportunities available to women were reduced, Islamization policies and mismanagement did not stop women's participation in education and employment.

The state also failed to deliver 'Islamic justice' in relation to women's position within the family. Women had been promised support for their 'natural' rights and roles. They were to receive economic and legal protection from the Islamic state and its male representatives in the home. In return, women were expected to prove their credentials as obedient wives, self-sacrificing mothers and active citizens. However, this equation failed to work in the actual political and economic circumstances of the Islamic Republic. On the contrary, measures such as the strengthening of male authority in the family not only failed to increase women's protection, but actually resulted in the reduction of women's familial rights and the deterioration of their material condition. The Islamic Republic may have given its female supporters the opportunity for popular political participation and a sense of righteousness and self-worth, but it seriously undermined women's position within the family and restricted their human rights.

All this gave greater credence to the cause of Islamist feminism. To survive during particularly repressive periods, Islamist feminists tried to be as non-controversial as possible, and in doing so they colluded extensively with state attacks on women's rights. The degree of loyalty to the state expected from Islamist feminists proved to be much higher than that expected from the pro-state feminists of the Pahlavi era. Despite this, the extremist years had a maturing effect on Islamic feminists. They realized that unless they established an autonomous existence and spoke out against state policy, women would continue to get a raw deal despite the state's claim to represent 'true Islam'. Thus, a small but vocal Islamist feminist opposition re-established itself in the late 1980s.

Since the late 1980s, Islamist feminists have been able to campaign for women's rights in a much more open and direct manner than before. They have also proved more successful in pressurizing the policy-makers to revise earlier restrictions on women's legal rights and to consider positive proposals for greater rights for women within an Islamic framework. The issues on which they have campaigned have included family, education, employment, political participation and *hejab*. On education and employment, which seem to be the most sophisticated and successful issues on which Islamic feminists have campaigned, discriminatory practices towards women have been scrutinized and proposals made for their eradication. One important achievement in this area has been the lifting of restrictions that had been placed on women's entry to technical, scientific and medical fields soon after the Revolution.

Campaigns on the family have focused on improving the balance of power between men and women in the family. The emphasis has been put on the concept of 'partnership between husband and wife' as opposed to the concept of 'male guardianship', which is the basis of the Civil Code. Islamist feminists have protested against the failure of state policy to 'facilitate the growth of women's talents and personality', 'preserve their rights in the sacred institution of family', 'protect the rights of unprotected women' and 'remove obstacles in the way of women's participation in economic, social and political activities.' The policies advocated include state remuneration for housewives and unmarried women, monogamy, automatic custody rights for mothers, protection against divorce without the wife's consent, the right of wives to half the family assets, and women's rights to undertake education, employment or travel without the consent of husbands or other male guardians.

However, despite achieving relative independence for their movement and having some success in persuading policy-makers to extend women's rights, Islamist women leaders have on the whole had limited opportunities to take on decision-making roles and have had a hard time gaining authority or influence in the Islamic polity. Only a handful have entered the Islamic parliament or the government. Eleven elections during the first decade of the Islamic Republic have produced in total only six women representatives in parliament, an even more tokenist minority than in the Pahlavi era. . . .

Conclusion

This incursion into contemporary Iranian history demonstrates that gender issues have been at the heart of Iranian politics and that they have undergone complex and sometimes paradoxical transformations. This has been nowhere more apparent than under the Islamic Republic. Indeed, the transformation of Islamist feminism from post-Revolutionary idealism to realism and pragmatism of the late 1980s has been remarkable. This being the case it is no longer inconceivable to envisage strategic alliances between Iranian strands of secular and Islamist feminisms on women's rights issues. The frames of reference of the two traditions of gender activism are, of course, very different. Iranian Islamist feminism is theoretically rooted in cultural relativism and politically rooted in anti-imperialism, while the direction taken by Iranian secular feminism in exile in the last decade has been largely universalist, anti-religious and increasingly individualistic.

However, the severity and material reality of the problems faced by Iranian women have reduced the importance of these ideological differences. To illustrate this point, it will be useful to compare the experiences of feminists campaigning to improve family laws in the Pahlavi era with those under the Islamic Republic. It took about forty years for secular feminists of the Pahlavi era to change the family law from the Civil Code of 1936 to the Family Protection Law of 1975. In 1979, it took Ayatollah Khomeini one speech to demolish the Family Protection Law in a single blast; and since then it has taken Islamist feminists over twelve years to build it again bit by bit; the task has yet to be completed.

The same family laws which had been historically presented by the Pahlavi state as part of a process of secularization and which were opposed by the clergy as contrary to Islam and therefore demolished, are now being reinstated under the Islamic Republic. The difference does not seem to be in the Islamist or secular nature of the law but in the political priorities of the era. This has created a potential for co-operation and alliance amongst ideologically diverse feminisms. Old ideological enemies may turn into new political allies when it comes to resisting the onslaughts of male supremacy. Although these alliances may be fraught and fragile, they speak of Iranian women's will to act upon their gender interests.

Erika Friedl  **NO**

Sources of Female Power in Iran

Reports of the position of women in Iran and in other Middle Eastern countries contain a seeming paradox: women are said to be subordinate to men, second-class citizens, oppressed, veiled, and confined, unequal to men legally and in access to resources. This gender inequity further is said to be validated, supported, and mystified by local gender ideologies and a superstructure formed by the teachings of the Quran and other religious scriptures, by Islamic law, and by folk notions about male–female differences. Yet, on the level of everyday life and popular culture, Iranian women, especially mature matrons, are widely perceived as 'powerful.' They are described as running the political affairs of their sons and husbands, as controlling the lives of everyone in the household—omniscient, beloved, respected, and feared matrons much like the stereotypical Jewish mother of western folk culture.

No matter how contradictory the concept of the oppressed-yet-powerful woman might seem, the contradiction is contrived. Indeed, I will even argue that subordinated people, women in this case, not only can be both oppressed and powerful simultaneously, but that they can derive power to effect changes in their own and in others' affairs from the very relations of inequality that define their position: from concrete, adversarial circumstances in their lives, from the existential conditions to which they are confined, unfavorable as they might be.

Women arrive at their position of power vis-à-vis the power elite through dynamic processes, each with its own dialectic logic. In this [selection] I will trace a few of these processes. I will focus on some examples of the power that women in Iran are said to have: on how they access it, how they use it, and where it takes them. In so doing, I will try to show the connection between women's oppression and women's power and will attempt to put the discussion of this seeming paradox into the context of an analytic-methodological frame....

Specifically, I have selected four topics that illustrate the power-potential of women. The first topic, resistance, is an abstract concept, manifested through a bundle of tactics used to counter hegemonic domination. These tactics can be used in all life situations, and create specific power dynamics. The other three topics are concrete and specific: women's work and employment, religion, and political conditions. These three pertain to everyday circumstances of life and are examined for their potential power-content through the use of several brief, illustrative examples.

Resistance as Power

Resistance can take women in three different directions.

1. Power differences between dominants and subordinates—any dominants and their subordinates—inevitably lead to resistance against demands, control, and restrictions of superiors. Dominants in turn perceive the resistance as attempts to challenge, even usurp, their power (in a Zero-Sum game) and thus label resisters as 'bad.' In our case, women do resist domination; their resistance is anticipated, and hence women are said to be by nature obstinate, shameful, foolish, sinful, or childish. As such, it is argued, they must be carefully watched and treated with commensurate firmness if need be ('need' being determined by those in authority), with yet another commensurate backlash of more resistance to be expected. Resistance therefore can, and often does, lead to more suppression: to punishment, discreditation, loss of honor, and confinement rather than freedom, choice, or autonomy.

   For example, in Iran (as elsewhere) women's compliance with the dress code is taken as a measure of both state control on the national level, and of men's control over their families on the individual level. One of the duties of male and female Revolutionary Guards is to publicly enforce the dress code (including the men's dress code, which is much less restrictive and much less focused on than the women's). If a woman's hair shows from under her headscarf the transgression not only is proclaimed a private sin but is also taken as a political statement of resistance to the nation's moral code and to women's place in the social hierarchy of the Islamic Republic, and thus may be punished. By resisting the dress code, individual women do make a statement of protest, but unless they can turn their individual resistance into a mass protest, they cannot use their gesture as a source of power to effect a desired change in the dress code or in their personal position. Their lonely protest is easily quelched.

2. Suicide is one of the most dramatic gestures of resistance. Suicide as a strategy of resistance to demands or to mistreatment by figures of authority (usually within the woman's family) is ineffective for the woman who dies, but the suicide death of one woman can give weight to the resistance efforts of another woman who can use the threat of suicide as a source of power to get her will....

3. The third extreme direction resistance can take is women's own acceptance of the dominants' view of female resistance to hegemonic authority. Women in Iran who accept this view—and there seem to be many —believe that women are inherently weak in body, intellect, and emotional resilience. In extreme but by no means isolated cases, they maintain that all women are inherently 'bad,' probably even hell-bound, and

that women's only hope for salvation lies in proper guidance which will save them from themselves, as it were. Accepting the male paradigm, women paradoxically can turn the male view into a source of power for themselves in relation to others in low positions: women can use the paradigm to control, 'guide,' and subordinate other women. For example, female Revolutionary Guards patrolling the streets to watch over the propriety of other women, mothers-in-law critically watching their daughters-in-law, or *hezbollah* (Party-of-God) women in offices and schools controlling the dress and behavior of officemates or students are enforcing conformity and quelching resistance to male authority. By taking up the cause of male/state authorities, including the expectation of resistance to domination and the perceived need to nip it in the bud, these women can achieve a substantial measure of power over other women. But this support undermines the position of women in general, including their own vis-à-vis their husbands or brothers. Not even the collaborators can easily convert this male-derived power over other subordinates into autonomy in their private lives....

In very rare cases, women manage to turn restrictive orders against the authorities themselves. For example, a woman principal of an all girl's school I know was ordered by her male supervisor not to let any man enter the school premises. When the supervisor appeared a few days later to check on administrative matters, the principal refused him entry on grounds of his own order. Tongue-in-cheek (as in this case) or seriously, women can claim the fool's freedom more easily than men. Although resistance based on the acceptance of male rule in government or in the family may lead to small personal victories for individual women, it cannot be expected to alter the skewed power balance between dominants and subordinates in general. Such resistance is a tactic for getting by and getting even, not for redress.

Resistance can take a great many forms, each with different consequences for the generation of power. I will briefly discuss four such forms which I have found to be used frequently: disobedience, subversion, refusal, and crying for help.

1. Open disobedience of male orders leads to conflict, hidden disobedience to distrust. Both conflict and distrust lead to greater oppression and tighter control, thus creating a vicious circle of tyranny and rebellion.

   For example, a young woman in a small town in southern Iran who disobeyed her husband frequently and for good reasons, as she and many others thought, was often beaten by him in the course of the resulting fights. On one such occasion she fled to her brother, who ordered her to stop arguing and to do her husband's bidding. When she now refused to obey her brother, he beat her, and her relatives and neighbors called her 'crazy' for being disobedient in such a foolishly demonstrative way. Another young woman I know had for years refused all orders by her relatives to marry one of her suitors, on pain of severe punishment at each refusal and near ostracism by her family. Although successful in her resistance, she paid a high price in comfort and reputation. Moreover, when her eventual later marriage to a man of her choosing turned out disastrous, villagers characteristically saw a direct connection between her earlier disobedience and her eventual calamity....

Disobedience as a tool of power for women works best if it is supported by dominants against other dominants: a father supporting his daughter against her husband; a son backing his mother against a half-brother. It can also be successful if one woman's disobedience is backed by other women in an act of solidarity that the men find hard to break. But because solidarity requires more organizational structure than women in Iran, especially rural women, usually have, it is relatively rare outside of the family. Within the family, solidarity is easiest to achieve between mothers and daughters and among sisters, whereas between mothers-in-law and daughters-in-law, and among sisters-in-law, relationships are potentially so fraught with tensions that solidarity seems to be hard to attain.

2. Subversion, in the form of minimal compliance with controversial rules or the outright subversion of such rules is at once a form of testing the limits of the rules and the tolerance of the rule-makers and thus is an expression of one's dissatisfaction with them. This form of resistance can very easily be interpreted as disobedience requiring respective reprisals.

   In Iran, for example, the rule for women to cover their hair in front of unrelated men is subverted when a woman drapes a big scarf loosely over her head, holding it in place not by a tight knot or a safety-pin under her chin but by slinging one end of the scarf over the opposite shoulder. The headdress which is meant to conceal has become an ornament; the intent is subverted and the woman who wears it makes a political statement by turning an object of control into one of protest....

3. A woman's refusal to obey her husband's (or father's) orders or to perform expected services challenges the man and inconveniences him. A woman who refuses a demand hopes that her husband will try to prevent the inconvenience and remedy the contested situation before precipitating a showdown. However, any kind of refusal by a woman in everyday situations, from refusing to cook or to fetch a glass of water for her son, to denying sex to her husband, is sanctioned negatively in the Islamic moral code. For a woman, refusing obedience or services to her husband (or, in varying degrees, to other men in positions of authority over her), no matter how extreme the demand, is a sin, and a very 'female' sin at that. It is a sin said to be typical of women, and this notion in turn is part of the script by which women are socialized. Women who resort to refusal as a tool of power are told they are courting punishment in the afterlife as well as in this life.

In the most extreme and most effective case of refusal, a woman leaves her husband to live with her father, brother, or grown son. Her husband then must cope with women's chores, including the care of young children, and is greatly inconvenienced. His difficulty can be compounded if his own mother and other female relatives, in tacit solidarity with his wife, refuse to help him. Sooner or later, out of necessity, he will decide to negotiate for his wife's return, presumably agreeing to measures that will redress his wife's complaints and will improve her situation. Wright reports a case from the Doshman Ziari in which two sisters even left their husbands in order to force them to make a political move the women favored. . . .

4. A cry for help, that is, informing others of wrongs one is suffering, aims to involve outsiders in one's affairs in order to embarrass one's own people into addressing the problem. This form of resistance undermines indirectly a woman's standing, the more so the more people get involved: honorable people take care of their problems themselves.

   For example, a woman who has been beaten may choose to go to the public bathhouse where her bruises will tell her story without a word from her. The news will spread to her father who may then decide to have a word with her husband, usually with a little noise as possible. . . .

These examples suggest that resistance as a source of power for women is considered destructive to self and to others in Iran. Resistance supports the stereotyping of women's power as an inherently dangerous force that must be controlled. Women's resistance is taken by men and women (in what Wright calls the 'dominant model' for behavior and attitudes) as proof of women's inherent weaknesses, their unreliability, recalcitrance, childishness, and antagonism. Although all of these have to be feared as dangerous to the social and moral order, the fear is not a wholesome one, but rather leads to distrust and further curtailment of movement and options for women. Yet, despite its limited, at best short-range, benefits and high costs, resistance is the single most frequently used tactic of power, the most popular 'weapon of the weak' that women use when they feel wronged. Social developments in the Islamic Republic have neither led to equal access to resources for women and men nor to equal opportunities for self-determination and personal autonomy. Given the government's social and gender philosophy, gender equality is not even a sociopolitical agenda. Women therefore can be expected to continue to try to use traditional means to create power, such as resistance, in conducting their lives, even to intensify these power tactics when other sources of power are curtailed.

Work as Power

Women's participation in the labor market is generally taken as an indicator of the status of women, especially in developing countries, and employment of women is considered a means, even a necessity, for women's emancipation. True as this view might be in the long-range processes of women's liberation, my observations in Iran suggest that a woman's labor contribution is not in itself a reliable indicator of a woman's autonomy and power (let alone her status), at least not among the lower classes. This is especially true for manual labor, which generally is regarded as demeaning drudgery. But even clerical work has this connotation, at least among people in the lower classes. Hegland reports from a village in southwest Iran that 'employment outside the home was considered an indication of low socio-economic position and a source of shame both for the women involved and for their relatives.' Such women often find it necessary to assert that they don't *have* to work, that they are well taken care of and chose employment.

The work women do, be it in- or outside of the home, can be tapped by women as a source of power under certain conditions: (1) The work creates dependencies that the woman can exploit; (2) the work creates resources that the woman can control; (3) the work creates skills that enable the woman to access other sources of power and creates in her the self-confidence to shrewdly exploit them. I will briefly discuss [the first of] these conditions [here].

Dependencies

Within the family, it is easy for a woman to make others, for example, her children, husband, and aged parents-in-law, dependent on her services. A woman in a traditional rural household, by refusing to cook or to milk animals, for example, might force her husband to negotiate with her for better treatment. (This, however, happens at the cost of reinforcement of the negative stereotype of women as nags, or, in extreme cases, the threat of divorce.) On the other hand, as a willing, cooperative, and competent housekeeper, a woman can gain considerable manipulative power. She can gain control over most of the household resources (including even control over a co-wife). By wisely using her resources, she will build up her husband and earn the respect of relatives and others in her social circle, which in turn will empower her to have input in others' and her own affairs. In this way she will also accumulate knowledge about others, which she can incorporate into a power base that includes political as well as economic and emotional resources, and provides many angles for arranging her circumstances to the benefit of herself and her protégés. Hegland reports that the village women she observed used 'their verbal and intellectual skills in gathering information, spying, persuading, taunting, berating, threatening, shaming, discussing, interpreting, encouraging' in order to manipulate their power base. One result of such successful manipulation is the 'powerful' wife-mother figure of popular culture and folklore: the woman who knows everything, who controls children and relatives, who makes and breaks people, who keeps her sons on short emotional reins, and whom everybody loves and fears at the same time. A competent woman in this sense is using her talents, connections, and services—all her assets—to build up her husband (or sons) and herself simultaneously. The most successful will continue to give the impression of overt deferral to male authority, because it is important for the maintenance of 'face' *(aberu)* that her husband's dominance should not be challenged overtly. This pretense of submission in turn has to be accepted by the husband at face value along with his wife's manipulations which, after all, he recognizes as advantageous for himself. This is a power game which so-called successful couples seem to be playing all over the patriarchal world, and which, because of its success, makes other ways of assertion by women, including attempts at emancipation in a western sense, seem superfluous, even foolish, to many men and women in these systems.

In economically depressed post-revolutionary Iran, the household, the kin group, large families are more important than before in structuring the lives of people; the social life as well as economic assistance flow in the kind of close-knit social networks in which women operate very well. Thus, chances for wielding the kind of power that comes from cleverly creating and using dependencies have increased in importance for women....

Religion as Power

Religion can empower women insofar as the religious idiom can provide the means, justifications, and rationalizations for independent actions. Religious concepts thus can be and are used as manipulative devices.

For example, during the revolution, many Iranian women participated in demonstrations against the Pahlavi regime. Hegland reports that the women (and the men who allowed them to do so) saw protest as a religious rather than a political activity: women were giving testimony to Islam by supporting Khomeini.

The paucity of occasions for women in the Islamic Republic to congregate legitimately outside their homes seems to be one of the reasons for the rapid increase in women's participation in graveyard visitation parties on Thursday afternoons. During these visits, women socialize while ostensibly fulfilling a pious obligation. Likewise, *rowzeh* gatherings and *sofrehs* (parties given in honor of a saintly personage) are used extensively for what is elsewhere called women's networking.

Likewise, pilgrimages to saints' shrines are popular among women as religiously motivated social activities. Women consider visits to a neighborhood shrine to be like informal visits to a relative, close to home and easily fit between chores. Pilgrimages to distant, important shrines, however, involve considerable expense and logistical problems, which make male approval, support, and escort necessary for women. Indeed, a woman very likely must use her manipulative powers to make her husband or son take her on a pilgrimage. Frequently a woman can keep her vow to pay a visit to a saint only after she is widowed or has found a separate source of funding for the travel.

For example, an old widow in Deh Koh, an herbalist who had been living precariously on her own for many years, wanted to make the pilgrimage to Mashhad, but was very concerned about the possible impropriety in going alone. On the bus to Mashhad she met a mullah with his eight-year-old son and contracted a temporary, non-sexual marriage with the boy. This allowed her to make the journey as a well-chaperoned married woman. Thus, she used the combination of control over her finances and two religiously sanctioned customs to gain the autonomy to venture into an otherwise inaccessible world. Temporary marriage, which can be taken to demean women, in this case became a source of power that enabled a woman to realize her wish.

Women can use expressions of piety as a manipulative strategy. Since about 1983, a code of piety has developed in Iran, a politically-piously correct way of talking, dressing, reading; a politically correct body of knowledge and phrases that one can use to one's personal advantage.

For example, a young woman (or man for that matter) seeking acceptance at a university or promotion at work will avoid the slightest hint of resistance to the dress code. In public, she will wear the plainest outer garments, correct low-heeled shoes, and a dark scarf pulled over her forehead, completely covering her hairline. She will accept a scholarship to a special Quran course in the summer, no matter how boring she might find it. She will not tell others that at home she is looking at American videos smuggled in from Kuwait. She will pray and observe the fast ostentatiously. She will not be seen with men (other than close family members) in public, and will discourage male attention. Her impeccable behavior will be noted by those who report on her morality, and this will increase her chances for advancement. The restrictive code is thus turned into a tool with which she can manipulate her career.

In the Islamic Republic many women, especially those in the middle class and the former elite, have perfected the art of dissimulation and the use of the code of piety to the extent that their private and public personae are almost totally different.

Since the war, the status of 'Mother of a Martyr' has become a potential source of power for women who have lost a son in the war. The government has given these women the moral right to demand respect and consideration from other people. These women are given preferential treatment in the allocation of subsidized appliances, and they are enlisted as watchers over the correctness of their neighbors' behavior. Some of these women, especially those with limited access to other sources of power and respect, use their position as informer to the point where conversation in a room falters when they enter. These women are seen by others as using a government-bestowed power to the detriment of other women.

In a more traditional religious domain, the prestige of a successful pilgrimage to certain shrines (expressed in the titles *haji, karbela'i, mashhadi*) and that of a descendant of the Prophet Mohammad (*sayyed*) carry respect and are thus a potential source of power for women. A *sayyed* woman often is sought out as a mediator in disputes or as a peacemaker.

For example, in Deh Koh, a man whose wife had fled to her father after a fight enlisted the help of a *sayyed* woman to persuade his father-in-law to send back his wife. Although the young woman's family had vowed they would let her go only if her husband agreed to a list of demands, they found it impossible to resist the *sayyed*, whose invocations of piety, morality, and peace were strengthened greatly by her illustrious descent. In effect, this *sayyed* used her own male-derived powers (from her ancestor, the Prophet) to undermine the protest action of another woman who, as a young wife, had very little power over her fate.

Government as Source of Power

Women in Iran have the right to vote. Yet although voting gives women a voice in political matters equal to men, not all women, especially not rural ones, consider it a source of power. A woman's vote is often regarded as her husband's or father's second vote: he will determine how she is to vote.

Similarly, women do not regard law and the courts as sources of power and rarely use them, even if in a particular instance the law would indeed be on their side. Involving the court in one's affairs is taken as a sign of failure of the informal, traditional, honorable ways of dealing with problems and thus is easily seen as shameful, especially for women. Furthermore, few women have the economic and strategic-assertive resources to go to court alone and plead their case, especially against a male relative.

For example, when in a small town a young woman's husband died, his relatives sent her back to her father without her two infant children. Although the law gave her the right to keep her children at least for a specific time, and although she missed her children badly and fell into serious depression, her father decided not to press the issue in court to avoid the embarrassment of a public fight. The woman felt completely unable to deal with the problem herself, especially over the objection of her father. For similar reasons, women who are denied their legal share of the inheritance of their brothers usually 'pardon' it rather than face a court battle with them.

As mentioned before, politically correct demeanor helps a woman with professional aspirations. In this regard, one could say the government provides a script for women who want to attain power positions, be it as a school principal, a medical professional, an elected member of a village or town council, a Revolutionary Guard, an informer in an office, or an employee of an intelligence agency. In the last three instances, 'successful' women use their government-bestowed powers against other women in the interest of the male dominants, thereby supporting women's domination. Thus, the government makes it possible for some women to advance individually without emancipation. . . .

A final example of a government-generated source of potential power for women comes from an unexpected and controversial circumstance: the mandatory sex-segregation in schools. Although motivated by a restrictive code of sexual morality that otherwise works against women, sex segregated schools have the advantages of all-women's groups in general: they provide young women with an environment where they are not harassed, restricted, challenged, or intimidated by male teachers and male classmates. In such environments women can express themselves freely, they have more opportunity to practice leadership and intellectual skills than they would have if men were present, and they can develop confidence even in such subjects as mathematics and the sciences which in some societies are said to be the domain of men.

Summary

When legitimate sources of power for women become increasingly scarce in an androcentric, male-dominated society such as the Islamic Republic of Iran, and women's realm of action and influence becomes more restricted, women can be expected to intensify their use of the 'weapons of the weak,' that is, manipulation of resources and resistance to restrictive rules to exert control over issues important to them. Both strategies potentially lead to a reinforcement of the popular Iranian stereotype of women's negative character traits, from childishness to outright evil, and reinforce the cycle of antagonism and distrust characteristic of such power constellations. Women who use this system 'well,' that is, in such a way that men feel secure in their claim to control and superiority (regardless of how manipulated or subverted they may be) or else feel that their women's strategies and tactics are advantageous for them, can derive power to the extent that the dominant-subordinate constellation may even seem reversed. Such women are viewed not only as 'powerful' but as de facto rulers of the house. Women who control other women in the interest of dominant authority, either within the family or in public, do so to the detriment of women in general and cannot easily derive autonomy over their own lives from this position. In both cases, that of the successful wife-mother and the wielder of male-derived power, however, the existing hierarchy of domination remains not only unchallenged but is stabilized, and the gendered system of super- and subordination is cemented.

POSTSCRIPT

Has the Islamic Revolution in Iran Subjugated Women?

Since the 1970s feminist anthropologists have increasingly focused attention on the role of women in different societies. Earlier anthropologists, they have argued, had largely written women out of ethnographies, relegating women's roles to the domestic sphere while women's economic and political roles remained largely unstudied. As feminist theory developed in the West, feminist anthropologists attempted to account for and explain the subordination of women in different societies. Radical feminists developed a universal model of patriarchy—a pattern of male domination of women, their labor, their sexuality, and their reproductive capacities. Such models were invoked to explain how women continued to be oppressed in many parts of the world. Explanations of how patriarchal regimes have invoked Islamic law as justification for women being given a subordinate position in society often have emerged from this patriarchal model. Paidar's selection draws on this patriarchal model but avoids the strident, polemical stance that has characterized many feminist interpretations of Muslim society.

The most important reaction to the patriarchal model has been the view that whether these Muslim communities are patriarchal or not, women nevertheless lead rich and rewarding lives in spite of their segregation from men and their limited public role. Some ethnographers have argued that Islamic women even wield considerable informal influence and power. Some anthropologists, such as Lila Abu-Lughod in her *Veiled Sentiments: Honor and Poetry in a Bedouin Society* (University of California Press, 1986) have challenged stereotypes of Islamic women that often depict them as trapped in exploitative gender roles that have emerged from an unchanging form of Islam. Abu-Lughad has argued that we need more descriptive studies of Muslim women before we can understand whether or not these women are subjugated. Friedl suggests that even when women have little direct access to power, as in postrevolutionary Iran, women can and have been able to set agendas and define some of the parameters in which public debate over gender policy will be conducted. See *In the Eye of the Story: Women in Post-Revolutionary Iran* (Syracuse University Press, 1994), edited by M. Afkhami and Friedl, for other perspectives on women's rights and roles in Iran.

For a discussion of women's roles in pre-Taliban Afghanistan, see Nancy Tapper's *Bartered Brides: Politics, Gender, and Marriage in an Afghan Tribal Society* (Cambridge University Press, 1991). Ziba Mir-Hosseini's *Islam and Gender: The Religious Debate in Contemporary Iran* (Princeton University Press, 1999) discusses the rise of an indigenous Iranian feminism within postrevolutionary Iranian society. For a discussion of Middle Eastern feminism, see *Remaking Women: Feminism and Modernity in the Middle East* (Princeton University Press, 1998), edited by Abu-Lughod, and *Gendering the Middle East: Emerging Perspectives* (Syracuse University Press, 1996), edited by Deniz Kandiyoti.

ISSUE 14

Is Ethnic Conflict Inevitable?

YES: Sudhir Kakar, from "Some Unconscious Aspects of Ethnic Violence in India," in Veena Das, ed., *Mirrors of Violence: Communities, Riots and Survivors in South Asia* (Oxford University Press, 1990)

NO: Anthony Oberschall, from "The Manipulation of Ethnicity: From Ethnic Cooperation to Violence and War in Yugoslavia," *Ethnic and Racial Studies* (November 2000)

ISSUE SUMMARY

YES: Indian social researcher Sudhir Kakar analyzes the origins of ethnic conflict from a psychological perspective to argue that ethnic differences are deeply held distinctions that from time to time will inevitably erupt as ethnic conflicts. He maintains that anxiety arises from preconscious fears about cultural differences. In his view, no amount of education or politically correct behavior will eradicate these fears and anxieties about people of differing ethnic backgrounds.

NO: American sociologist Anthony Oberschall considers the ethnic conflicts that have recently emerged in Bosnia and contends that primordial ethnic attachments are insufficient to explain the sudden emergence of violence among Bosnian ethnic groups. He adopts a complex explanation for this violence, identifying circumstances in which fears and anxieties were manipulated by politicians for self-serving ends. It was only in the context of these manipulations that ethnic violence could have erupted, concludes Oberschall.

Since the 1960s anthropologists and other social scientists have debated the causes, origins, and necessary conditions for ethnic differences to erupt into ethnic violence. Such discussions have built on an older debate about the origins of ethnicity. In the earlier debate, two key positions emerged. The first is the *primordialist* view, in which ethnic attachments and sentiments emerge from the fact of being members of the same cultural community. Although cultural in origin, the primordialists see kinship, language, and customary practices as the source of ethnic identity and social bonds between people of the same ethnicity. Ethnicity in this view is something one is born with, or at least born into, because it develops as one learns kinship, language, and culture. A second position, often called the *circumstantialist* perspective, was developed by the Norwegian anthropologist Fredrik Barth in his book *Ethnic Groups and Social Boundaries* (Little, Brown, 1969). For Barth, a person's ethnicity is neither fixed nor a natural condition of his or her birth. One's ethnicity could be (and often was) manipulated under different circumstances. By dressing differently, by learning a different language, and by intermarriage, people in many ethnic groups within a generation or two could become members of another ethnic group and have a different ethnic identity. Later, if it became advantageous to be members of the first ethnic group, these same people could acknowledge their past and become members of the first group.

The following selections shift the ethnicity debate to the problem of whether or not ethnic conflict is inevitable. Sudhir Kakar uses a psychological approach to develop a primordialist argument to explain the frequent and almost continual problems of ethnic violence in India. For Kakar, ethnic sentiments and attachments emerge from deep psychological concerns at the unconscious or even preconscious level. He contends that psychologically there are primordial differences between Indians of different ethnic backgrounds, and such differences lead to conflicts over access to resources, jobs, and the like.

Anthony Oberschall considers possible explanations for the sudden appearance of ethnic conflict in the former Yugoslavia. He acknowledges that the primordialist variables of kinship, religion, and language may play some role in explaining why Serbs, Croats, and Bosnian Muslims behaved as they did once ethnic conflict broke out. Traditional animosities existed for centuries in the Balkans, and they reemerged suddenly after 50 years of peace and cooperation. But such variables cannot explain why these groups started fighting with one another in the first place, says Oberschall, after nearly half a century of living together peacefully, regularly socializing, and even intermarrying with one another; such ties as kinship, language, and religion do not explain why tensions flared up or why neighbors suddenly tried to eliminate people of other ethnic backgrounds from their towns and villages. Drawing on a complex pattern of circumstantial variables, Oberschall develops a circumstantialist model, arguing that politicians were manipulating local sentiments for their own ends. In the context of great uncertainty and crisis, people of all ethnic backgrounds bought into the anxieties suggested by their different leaders.

What leads people to hate people of different ethnic backgrounds? Is it deeply held fears of cultural differences? Or does conflict emerge because individuals fear losing what they have worked hard to obtain? How could people in Yugoslavia live together harmoniously for 50 years and then suddenly participate in the "ethnic cleansing" of their neighborhoods? Could the willingness to commit such acts of violence against neighbors have been suppressed for half a century by a strong central government? What is the source of this kind of group hatred, since differences in skin color and physical features are largely not present in either the Indian or Yugoslavian cases?

Sudhir Kakar

Some Unconscious Aspects of Ethnic Violence in India

The need to integrate social and psychological theory in the analysis of cultural conflicts, i.e. conflicts between ethnic and religious groups, has long been felt while its absence has been equally long deplored. Though everyone agrees on the theoretical questions involved—how do these conflicts originate, develop, and get resolved; how do they result in violent aggression—a general agreement on the answers or even on how to get these answers moves further and further away.

A large part of the problem in the study of these questions lies with the nature of and the crisis within the social sciences. The declining fortunes of logical positivism, hastened in the last twenty years by the widespread circulation and absorption of the views of such thinkers as Gadamer, Habermas, Derrida, Ricouer and Foucault, has led to a plethora of new models in the sciences of man and society. The dominant model of yesteryears—social science as social physics—is now only one among several clamouring for allegiance and adherents. It incorporates only one view among many on the nature of social reality and of social science knowledge. Anthropology, sociology, political science, psychology and even economics are all becoming more pluralistic and scattering into frameworks. In such a situation, the calls for a general theory of ethnic violence or indeed (as Clifford Geertz has remarked) of anything *social*, sound increasingly hollow, and the claims to have one science seem megalomaniacal. Thus, without taking recourse to other disciplines and even ignoring the grand theories of human aggression in psychology itself—those of animal ethology, sociology, Freudian Thanatos and so on—I would like to present some limited 'local knowledge' observations on ethnic violence in India from a psychoanalytic perspective.

In the manner of a clinician, let me begin with the concrete data on which I base my observations on the first question, namely the origins of ethnic conflict. The data for these observations, and those which follow, come from diverse sources: spirit possession in north India, dreams of psychotherapy patients, eavesdropping on group discussions at the Golden Temple complex in July 1984, and finally, personal participation in large religious assemblies.

The Other in Ethnic Conflict

Some years ago, while studying the phenomenon of possession by spirits in rural north India, I was struck by a curious fact. In a very large number of cases, 15 out of 28, the *bhuta* or malignant spirit possessing Hindu men and women turned out to be a Muslim. When, during the healing ritual, the patient went into a trance and the spirit started expressing its wishes, these wishes invariably turned out to be those which would have been horrifying to the patient's conscious self. In one case, the Muslim spirit possessing an elderly Brahmin priest vigorously insisted on eating kababs. The five women surrounding the man who had engaged the *bhuta* in conversation were distinctly disheartened that he had turned out to be a *Sayyad* and one of them lamented: 'These Mussulmans! They have ruined our *dharma* but they are so strong they can withstand our gods.' In another case, the *bhuta* inhabiting a young married woman not only expressed derogatory sentiments towards her 'lord and master' but also openly stated its intentions of bringing the mother-in-law to a violent and preferably bloody end.

Possession by a Muslim *bhuta,* then, seemed to reflect the afflicted person's desperate efforts to convince himself and others that his hunger for forbidden foods and uncontrolled rage towards those who should be loved and respected, as well as all other imagined transgressions and sins of the heart, belonged to the Muslim destroyer of taboos and were furthest away from his 'good' Hindu self. In that Muslim *bhutas* were universally considered to be the strongest, vilest, the most malignant and the most stubborn of the evil spirits, the Muslim seemed to symbolize the alien and the demonic in the unconscious part of the Hindu mind.

The division of humans into mutually exclusive group identities of tribe, nation, caste, religion and class thus seems to serve two important psychological functions. The first is to increase the feeling of well being in the narcissistic realm by locating one's own group at the centre of the universe, superior to others. The shared grandiose self, maintained by legends, myths and rituals, seems to demand a concomitant conviction that other groups are inferior.

India has not been exempt from this universal rule. Whatever idealizing tendencies we might have in viewing our past history, it is difficult to deny that every social group in its tales, ritual and other literature, has sought to portray itself nearer to a purer, divine state while denigrating and banishing others to the periphery. It is also undeniable that sharing a common ego-ideal and giving one's own group a super-individual significance can inspire valued human attributes of loyalty and heroic self-sacrifice. All this is familiar to students of culture and need not detain us further here.

For the psychoanalyst it is the second function of division into ethnic groups, namely the need to have other groups as containers for one's disavowed aspects, which is of greater significance. These disavowed aspects, or the demonic spirits, take birth during that period of our childhood when the child, made conscious of good and bad, right and wrong, begins to divide himself into two parts, one that is the judge and the other that is being judged. The unacceptable, condemned parts of the self are projected outside, the projective processes being primitive attempts to relieve pain by externalizing it. The expelled parts of the self are then attached to various beings—animals and human —as well as to whole castes, ethnic and religious communities. This early split within our nature, which gives us a future license to view and treat others as if they were no better than the worst in ourselves, is normally completed by the time the child is six to seven years old. The earliest defenses for dealing with the unacceptable aspects of the self—namely their denial, the splitting from awareness and projection onto another group—require the active participation of the members of the child's group-parents and other adults who must support such a denial and projection. They are shared group defenses. The family and extended group of a Hindu upper-caste child, for instance, not only provides him with its myths and rituals which increase his sense of group cohesion and of narcissism in belonging to such an exalted entity, but also help him in elaborating and fleshing out his demonology of other ethnic and religious groups. The *purana* of the Muslim demon, for instance, as elaborated by many Hindu groups, has nothing to do with Sufi saints, the prophet's sayings or the more profound sentiments of Islam. Instead, its stories are of rape and pillage by the legions of Ghazni and Timur as well as other more local accounts of Muslim mayhem.

The Muslim demon is, so to say, the traditional container of Hindu conflicts over aggressive impulses. It is the transgressor of deeply-held taboos, especially over the expression of physical violence. Recent events in Punjab, I am afraid, are creating yet another demon in the Hindu psyche of north India. Over the last few years, tales of [Sikh militant leader] Bhindranwale's dark malevolence and the lore of murderous terrorists has led to a number of reported dreams from patients where Sikhs have appeared as symbols of the patient's own aggressive and sadistic superego. A group of Sikhs with raised swords chasing a patient who has broken into an old woman's shop, a Nihang stabbing a man repeatedly with a spear on the street while another patient as a frightened child looks down upon the scene from an upstairs window—these are two of many such dream images. Leaving aside the role played by these images in the patients' individual dramas, the projection of the feared aggressive parts of the self on the figure of the Sikh is an unhappy portent for the future relationship between the two communities. The fantasy of being overwhelmed by the frightening aggressive strength of the Sikhs can, in periods of upheaval and danger—when widespread regression in ego takes place and the touch with reality is weakened—lead to psychotic delusions about Sikh intentions.

Sikh Militancy

Until this point I have used some psychoanalytic, especially Kleinian, concepts of splitting and projective identification to understand data that bears on the question of ethnic conflict. More specifically, I have outlined the origins of certain pre-conscious attitudes of Hindus towards Muslims and Sikhs. These attitudes reflect the psychological needs of the child, and the adult, to split off his bad impulses, especially those relating to violence, and to attach them to other communities, a process supported and reinforced by other members of the group. Let me now use another set of analytical concepts of group identity and narcissism, narcissistic hurt and rage, to understand the phenomenon of Sikh militancy. To avoid any misunderstanding let me state at the outset that I am primarily talking about the militant Sikh youth of Punjab, not of all Sikh youths, and certainly not of the Sikh community as a whole. Also, the word narcissism in psychoanalysis is not used in a pejorative sense but, together with sexuality and aggression, as the third major and fundamental motivational factor in human beings which is concerned with the maintenance of self-esteem. The data for these observations comes from being an observer of heated and anguished discussions among randomly formed groups which were being spontaneously held all over the Golden Temple complex in Amritsar, five weeks after Operation Blue Star.* said elsewhere, the aftermath of Blue Star, which heightened the awareness of their cultural identity among many Sikhs, also brought out in relief one of its less conscious aspects. I have called it the Khalsa warrior element of Sikh identity which, at least since the tenth guru and at least among the Jats, has expressed itself in images of 'lifting up the sword' against the 'oppression of a tyrannical ruler', and whose associated legends only countenance two possible outcomes—complete victory (*fateh*) or martyrdom (*shaheedi*) of those engaged in the battle. The surrounding society has of course reinforced this identity element over the years by its constant talk of Sikh martial process and valour. The Sikh youth's acceptance of these projections of heroic militancy made by the Hindu can lead to his overestimation of this aspect of his identity as he comes to feel that it is his very essence. All other qualities which may compromise heroic militancy, such as yearnings for passivity, softness and patience, will tend to be denied, split off and projected onto other, despised groups. The damage done to the Akal Takht —as much a symbol of corporate militancy as of religious piety—reinforced the two M's—militance and martyrdom—the inner counterparts of the well-known five K's which constitute the outer markers of the Khalsa warrior identity. The exaggerated value placed on martyrdom is hard to understand for Hindus since oppressors in *their* mythology—the Hindu equivalent of Sikh legendary history —tended to be destroyed by divine intervention rather than by the sacrifice of martyrs.

The army action was then a hurt to Sihk religious sentiments in a very different way from the sense in which a Hindu understands the term. It was an affront to group narcissism, to a shared grandiose self. The consequent feelings were of narcissistic hurt and rage. This was brought home to me again and again as I listened to groups of anguished men and women in front of the ruins of the Akal Takht. Most men stood in attitudes of sullen defeat, scorned and derided by the women with such sentences as 'Where is the starch in your moustache now?'

Given the collective need for the preservation of this core of the group identity, the Golden Temple action automatically completed a circle of associa-

---

* [Operation 'Blue Star' was the code name for the army action to clear the Golden Temple of Sikh militants in June 1984, in which Bhindranwale died. The operation resulted in extensive damage to the sacred site.—Ed.]

tions. The army action to clear Akal Takht from desperadoes became an attack on the Sikh nation by a tyrannical 'Delhi durbar'. It was seen as an assault designed to wipe out all its traces, its *nishan*—since this is how it was in the past. The Sikhs killed in the attack were now defenders of the faith and martyrs—since this too is a pattern from the past. The encounter was viewed as a momentous battle, an oppressive empire's defeat of the forces of the Khalsa. The relatively heavy army losses are not a consequence of its restraint but a testimony to the fighting qualities of the Khalsa warrior. Paradoxically, the terrorist losses were exaggerated to simultaneously show the overwhelming strength of the army and the Khalsa readiness to die in martyrdom when victory is not possible.

Bhindranwale, in dramatically exemplifying the two M's of militancy and martyrdom, has touched deep chords. His status with much of the Sikh youth today is very near that of an eleventh guru. Initially, Bhindranwale may have been one of many *sants,* though more militant than most, who dot the countryside in Punjab. What began the process of his elevation was his successful defiance of the government—echoes, again of Sikh history, of defiant gurus contesting state authority. In setting the date and terms of his arrest ('*Santji* gave arrest', and not 'He was arrested', is how the people at the Temple complex put it), and predicting the day of his release, Bhindranwale began to be transformed from a mortal preacher to a 'realized' saint with miraculous powers. (And the reputation of being able to work miracles is, we know, essential for those aspiring to enter the portals of gurudom in all religious traditions.) His 'martyrdom' has now cemented the transformation and made his elevation into the Sikh militant pantheon irreversible. The tortures and murders in the Temple complex or outside are no longer his responsibility, being seen as the doings of deluded associates, acts of which Santji was, of course, unaware.

It is obvious that after the army action there was a threat to the cultural identity of at least a section of the Jat Sikh youth. This led to regressive transformations in the narcissistic realm, where reality is interpreted only as a balm to narcissistic hurt and as a coolant for narcissistic rage. It needs to be asked what precisely constituted this threat. I would tend to see the threat to the Jat Sikh group identity as part of a universal modernizing process to which many groups all over the world have been and continue to be exposed. This group though has preferred to change a social-psychological issue into a political one. The cultural decay and spiritual disintegration talked of in the Anandpur resolution are then viewed as an aspect of majority-minority relations rather than as an existential condition brought on by the workings of a historical fate. A feeling of inner threat is projected outside as oppression, a conflict around tradition and modernity as a conflict around power.

Narcissistic rage, then, is the core of the militancy of Sikh youth and Sikh terrorism. As Kohut says about this rage: 'The need for revenge, for righting a wrong, for undoing a hurt by whatever means, and a deeply anchored, unrelating compulsion in the pursuit of all these aims, gives no rest to those who have suffered a narcissistic injury.' For the analyst, this becomes paramount in the understanding of youthful militancy, the foreground, while political, social and other issues recede into the background.

Let me now make a few observations on the question of ethnic conflict resulting in violent aggression, i.e on mob violence. My data for these remarks is, paradoxically, personal participation in largely peaceful and loving groups engaged in religious and spiritual endeavours. Yet many of the psychological processes are common to the two kinds of groups. Both emotionally charged religious assemblies and mobs on the rampage bring out in relief the vulnerability of human individual ego functions confronted with the power of group processes. In the face of these, the 'integrity', 'autonomy', and 'independence' of the ego seem to be wishful illusions and hypothetical constructs. Mobs, more than religious congregations, provide striking examples of the massive inducement, by group processes, of individuals towards a new identity and behaviour of the sort that would ordinarily be repudiated by a great majority of the individuals so induced. They illustrate, more clearly than in any other comparable social situation, the evanescence of rational thought, the fragility of internalized behavioural controls, values, and moral and ethnical standards.

The most immediate experience in being part of a crowd is the sensual pounding received in the press of other bodies. At first there may be a sense of unease as the body, the container of our individuality and the demarcator of our boundaries in space, is sharply wrenched away from its habitual way of experiencing others. For, as we grow up, the touch of others, once so deliberately courted and responded to with delight, increasingly becomes a problem. Coming from a loved one, touch is deliciously welcomed; with strangers, on the other hand, there is an involuntary shrinking of the body, their touch taking on the menacing air of invasion by the other.

But once the fear of touch disappears in the fierce press of other bodies and the individual lets himself become a part of the crowd's density, the original apprehension is transformed into an expansiveness that stretches to include others. Distances and differences—of class, status, age, caste hierarchy—disappear in an exhilarating feeling that individual boundaries can indeed be transcended and were perhaps illusory in the first place. Of course, touch is only one of the sensual stimuli that hammers at the gate of individual identity. Other excitations, channelled through vision, hearing and smell, are also very much involved. In addition, there are exchanges of body heat, muscle tension and body rhythms which take place in a crowd. In short, the crowd's assault on the sense of individuality, its invitation to transcend one's individual boundaries and its offer of a freedom from personal doubts and anxieties is well nigh irresistible.

The need and search for 'self-transcending' experience, to lose one's self in the group, suspend judgement and reality-testing, is, I believe, the primary motivational factor in both religious assembly and violent mob, even though the stated purpose is spiritual uplift in one and mayhem and murder in the other. Self-transcendence, rooted in the blurring of our body image, not only opens us to the influx of the divine but also heightens our receptivity to the demonic. The surge of love also washes away the defences against the emergence of archaic hates. In psychoanalytic terms, regression in the body image is simultaneous with regression in the superego system. Whether the ego reacts to this regression in a disintegrated fashion with panic that manifests itself (in a mob) in senseless rage and destructive acts—or in a release of love encompassing the group and the world outside—depends on the structure provided to the group. Without the rituals which make tradition palpable and thus extend the group in time by giving assurances of continuity to the beleaguered ego, and without the permanent visibility of leaders whose presence is marked by conspicuous external insignia and who replace the benign and loving functions of the superego, religious crowds can easily turn into marauding mobs. Transcending individuality by merging into a group can generate heroic self-sacrifice but also unimaginable brutality. To get out of one's skin in a devotional assembly is also at the same time to have less regard for saving it in a mob.

Some Implications

The implications of my remark, I know, are not too comforting. The need for communities, our own to take care of our narcissistic needs and of others to serve as recipients for our hostility and destructiveness, are perhaps built into our very ground-plan as human beings. Well meaning educative efforts in classrooms or in national integration seminars are for the most part too late and too little in that they are misdirected. They are too late since most of the evidence indicates that the communal imagination is well entrenched by the time a child enters school. They are misdirected in that they never frankly address the collective—and mostly preconscious—fears and wishes of the various communities. Demons do not much care for 'correct' interpretations of religious texts by scholars, nor are they amenable to humanist pleas of reason to change into good and loving beings. All we can do is accept their existence but reduce their potential for causing actual physical violence and destruction. The routes to this goal, the strategies for struggle with our own inner devils, are many. One strategy strives for the dissolution of small group identities into even large entities. Sikhs and Hindus in Punjab can move towards a group identity around 'Punjabiyyat', in which case the despised demon shifts outside to the *Purubia* or the *Madrasi*. One can go on to progressively larger identities of the nationalist Indian whose *bete-noire* can then be the Pakistani or the Chinese. One can envisage even larger groupings, for instance of the 'Third World', where the sense of narcissistic well being provided by this particular community needs a demonic West as the threatening aggressor.

A second strategy is, in a certain sense, to go the opposite way. By this I mean less the encouragement of various ethnic identities than in ensuring that all manifestations of ethnic group action—assemblies, demonstrations, processions—are given as much religious structure as possible in order to prevent the breakout of archaic hate. Vedic chants and Koranic prayers, *mahants, pujaris* and *mullahs* in their full regalia and conspicuous by their presence, are fully encouraged to be in the forefront of religious processions and demonstrations. Traditional religious standards, flags and other symbols are liberally used to bind the religious assemblies.

Yet another strategy (and let me note that none of these are exclusive) is to concentrate all efforts at the containment of the communal demon on the

dominant community. We know that the belief of the dominant party in a relationship often becomes a self-fulfilling prophecy, involuntarily changing the
very consciousness of the weaker partner. In India the Hindu image of himself
and of other communities is apt to be incorporated in the self image of non-
Hindu minorities. Even when consciously accepted, the denigrating part of the
image is likely to be a source of intensive unconscious rage in other communities. Their rage is stored up over a period of time, till it explodes in all its violent
manifestations whenever historical circumstances sanction such eruptions.

Anthony Oberschall  **NO**

The Manipulation of Ethnicity: From Ethnic Cooperation to Violence and War in Yugoslavia

Four views on ethnicity and ethnic violence are common. In the 'primordial' view, ethnic attachments and identities are a cultural given and a natural affinity, like kinship sentiments. They have an overpowering emotional and non-rational quality. Applied to the former Yugoslavia, the primordialist believes that despite seemingly cooperative relations between nationalities in Yugoslavia, mistrust, enmity, even hatred were just below the surface, as had long been true in the Balkans. Triggered by fierce competition for political power during the breakup of Yugoslavia and driven by the uncertainties over state boundaries and minority status, these enmities and hatreds, fuelled by fear and retribution, turned neighbour against neighbour, and district against district, in an expanding spiral of aggression and reprisals. Although the primordial account sounds plausible, and it is true that politicians activated and manipulated latent nationalism and ethnic fears, some evidence contradicts it. Ethnic cleansing was more commonly militias and military against civilians than neighbour against neighbour. In seventeen assaults against villages during the ethnic cleansing of Prijedor district in Bosnia in May/June 1992, we found that the aggressors wore military and paramilitary uniforms and insignia. In fourteen assaults, the survivors did not recognize any of the aggressors, who did not bother to wear masks or disguises. These 'weekend warriors' from central Serbia openly bivouacked at the Prijedor police station. The primordial theory omits the fact that ethnic hatreds can subside as a consequence of statecraft and living together. [President Charles] de Gaulle and [Chancellor Konrad] Adenauer managed to reconcile the French and German people. Why no lasting conciliation in Yugoslavia after forty years of ethnic peace?

In the second, 'instrumentalist' view, ethnic sentiments and loyalties are manipulated by political leaders and intellectuals for political ends, such as state creation. For Yugoslavia, the instrumentalist explanation highlights Serb nationalists' goal of a Greater Serbia, and a similar Croat nationalism. Ethnic cleansing resulted from a historical longing by Serbs in Croatia at first backed moderate nationalists, for a Greater Serbia, with deep cultural roots. [Slobodan]

From Anthony Oberschall, "The Manipulation of Ethnicity: From Ethnic Cooperation to Violence and War in Yugoslavia," *Ethnic and Racial Studies*, vol. 23, no. 6 (November 2000). Copyright © 2000 by Routledge Journals, Taylor & Francis Ltd. Reprinted by permission of the author and Taylor & Francis Ltd. http://www.tandf.co.uk/journals. Notes and references omitted.

Milosevic and Serb nationalists tried to implement it when the opportunity arose in the late 1980s and early 1990s. Greater Serbia required ethnic cleansing of non-Serbs from areas inhabited by a majority of Serbs and the corridors linking Serb population clusters. Although there is evidence that ethnic cleansing was a state policy, orchestrated by the highest authorities in Serbia and the Bosnian Serb leadership, this explanation ignores that many Bosnian Serbs did not want secession, that many Serbs in Croatia at first backed moderate nationalists, and that many Serbs evaded the draft. The instrumentalist view assumes an ethnic consensus that initially does not exist. But if many were reluctant to wage war and to participate in ethnic cleansing, how did ethnic extremists prevail over these moderates?

The third 'constructionist' view of ethnicity and ethnic conflict was originally formulated by [Leo] Kuper. It supplements the insights of the primordial and of the instrumentalist views. Religion or ethnicity are very real social facts, but in ordinary times they are only one of several roles and identities that matter. There is a great deal of variance in a population on ethnic attachments and identities. In the words of [Juan J.] Linz and [Alfred] Stepan 'political identities are less primordial and fixed than contingent and changing. They are amenable to being constructed or eroded by political institutions and political choices'. The constructionist view offers insights but is incomplete. How are nationality and ethnicity constructed and eroded by political mobilization and mass media propaganda?

A fourth model of ethnic violence centres on state breakdown, anarchy, and the security dilemma that such conditions pose to ethnic groups who engage in defensive arming to protect their lives and property against ethnic rivals, which then stimulates arming by other ethnic groups like an arms race between states. The driving motivations are not ethnic hatreds but fear and insecurity. In the Yugoslav crisis Michael Ignatieff puts it thus:

> Once the Yugoslav communist state began to split into its constituent national particles the key question soon became: will the local Croat policeman protect me if I am a Serb? Will I keep my job in the soap factory if my new boss is a Serb or a Muslim? The answer to this question was no, because no state remained to enforce the old ethnic bargain.

There is a security dilemma in ethnic conflict, but why so much ethnic violence without state breakdown? Can insecurity and fear be spread by propaganda even when daily experience contradicts the allegations of ethnic hostility and threat? Can the powerful fear the weak?

Building on the four views and mindful of [Rogers] Brubaker and [David] Laitin's criteria for a satisfactory theory of ethnic violence, I use the idea of latent nationalism at the grass roots, and show how it was activated; I highlight ethnic manipulation by political leaders, and explain why manipulation was successful; I take into account the variance in ethnic identities and analyse why extremists prevailed over moderates; I focus on the security dilemma and ethnic fears and insecurity, and show how fears and insecurity grew from lies and propaganda. To this arsenal of concepts and models for generating the dynamics of ethnicization and collective violence, I add 'cognitive frames'. Combining all, I seek to explain how forty years of cooperative ethnic relations ended with collective violence and war.

Prijedor: A Case-Study

To get a sense of what is to be explained about ethnic conflict and violence at the grass roots, consider the Prijedor district in Northwest Bosnia where major ethnic violence took place in the spring of 1992. In the 1991 Census, Prijedor district was 42.5 per cent Serb and 44 per cent Muslim. It was surrounded by districts that had either a slight Serb majority or were close to even, as Prijedor was. Prijedor Serbs were not an isolated Serb minority island surrounded by a sea of Muslims and Croats.

There had been no Serb complaints of mistreatment, discrimination, or intimidation in Prijedor by non-Serbs, or vice versa. On the contrary, as a bewildered Muslim refugee from Prijedor stated,

> In Prijedor there were no conflicts between nationalities. We didn't make the distinctions. My colleague at work was an Orthodox Serb, we worked together. When we were children we went to the Orthodox church or the mosque together... I don't understand. Before there were never any problems between us. We lived together. My sister is married to a Serb, and a brother of my wife is married to a Croat.

According to the [United Nations] Bassiouni Report, Serbs held the leading positions in Prijedor in 1991, as they had done for decades.... In the 1991 elections, the predominantly Muslim SDA [Party of Democratic Union in Bosnia] won thirty seats; the Serb SDS [Serbian Democratic Party] twenty-eight, and thirty-two went to other parties. The Muslims refrained from taking over a number of leading posts to which their electoral victory entitled them because they believed in power-sharing. Even so, the SDS blocked the work of the Prijodor Assembly and organized a parallel governance for Serbs, in alliance with the SDS leaders in nearby Banja Luka. In Bosnia as a whole, the Serbs shared political power and controlled the most important military forces.

As in other towns and cities in Bosnia, the SDS in Prijedor organized a successful Serb plebiscite for Greater Serbia. A parallel Serb governance, called the 'Crisis Committee', secretly created an armed force of Serbs with weapons obtained from Serbia. Serb crisis committees were also formed among Serbs in some of Prijedor district's towns and villages. On the night of 29 April 1992, without any provocation or a shot being fired, 1,775 well-armed Serbs seized the city of Prijedor in a *coup d'état*. By this time the Prijedor local government had completely lost power to various Serb groups. Paramilitaries had seized the radio and television transmitters and cut off all but Serb transmissions. The Serb *coup d'état* in Prijedor is similar to what happened elsewhere in Northern Bosnia.

Non-Serb leaders were arrested and shortly afterwards disappeared, presumed executed. The Muslim police and other officials were fired from their posts. Schools closed; the newspaper ceased publication, and a Serb paper was started. Non-Serbs were harassed, intimidated, fired from their jobs. Amid incessant house searches, weapons, mostly hunting guns, belonging to non-Serbs, were rounded up. After the attempt on 30 May by the Patriotic League of Croats and Muslims—an armed formation of 150 fighters—to retake the old city, many non-Serb inhabitants were arrested and sent to the infamous Omarskca camp. At Omarska, prisoners were tortured, brutalized, starved and killed. The guards were rural Serbs from nearby villages; the interrogators were Prijedor police inspectors.... People were rounded up and some were executed: those shot were Muslim leaders whose names appeared on a list. Atrocities took place elsewhere in the district.

Several observations should be made about the events in Prijedor. Muslims and Serbs had lived in peace before the conflict erupted. The Serbs were neither a numerical minority, nor discriminated against. They not only had a share of power, but they had the biggest share, and they were well armed. Why, then, did Serbs fear their fellow citizens in Prijedor? A cartoon from this period expresses the puzzle well. It shows a bearded Serb paramilitary, armed to the teeth, with guns, hand-granades, ammunition belts, knives, waving a machine gun, looking worried, and yelling at the top of his voice, 'I am being threatened!' There was no anarchy, no state breakdown in Prijedor. The Serbs used the police and military of a functioning government to subdue the non-Serbs. Serbs may have been apprehensive about their future in an independent Bosnia, but even in Bosnia they had a big presence—numerical, military, political, economic. There was no spontaneous violence initiated by Serb civilians against non-Serbs, nor vice-versa. Instead, there was a highly organized, secretly prepared *coup d'état*, like the 1917 Bolshevik seizure of power in Russia.... As in the Russian revolution with the Soviets, the Serb parallel government was not only an instrument for seizing power from non-Serbs but of stripping the moderate Serbs of any influence and authority.

What was the reaction of ordinary Serbs to these events? Though there is no information on Prijedor itself, one can learn from what observers recorded in nearby Banja Luka. Peter Maas reports that a Serb lawyer there estimated that 30 per cent of Serbs oppose such things [ethnic cleansing], 60 per cent agree or are confused and go along with the 10 per cent who 'have the guns and control the television tower'.... An armed, organized 10 per cent who control mass communications can have its way when the majority supports it overtly or tacitly or is confused, and when the opposition is unorganized, divided, and scared. One has to explain how it was that 60 per cent were supportive of or confused on ethnic cleansing, since their support and quiescence were necessary for the success of the extremist 10 per cent.

Was Violent Conflict Inevitable?

In a multinational state such as Yugoslavia, nationality will be a salient dimension of political contention, and there will be leaders and intellectuals with a nationalist ideology and agenda. The Yugoslav constitution and its political institutions were delicately balanced and crafted to deal with nationality. A nationalist challenge would inevitably zero in on stateness, minority rights and power-sharing: if accepted boundaries of political units are renegotiated or remade, who decides which peoples and territories belong to new and old political entities? Will all peoples in the new units be equal citizens for governance, or will majority ethnonational affiliation become the admission ticket for full citizenship?

Once unleashed, nationalism in Yugoslavia set on a collision course the two largest nationalities, the Serbs and the Croats. With a quarter of Serbs living outside Serbia, a centralized Yugoslav state was a guarantor of Serb security. For Croats and their history of opposition to Hapsburg rule, a decentralized state and weak federation meant control of their own destinies, unencumbered by inefficient state agencies and enterprises staffed and controlled by Serbs. Nevertheless, nationality issues could have been sorted out with democratic institutions in a confederation, with collective rights for minorities, and with systems of political representation in elections and collective decision rules in assemblies that would protect minority voice and favour coalitions rather than majority domination. With these reforms, nationalist leaders would have found it difficult to rally the citizenry to their cause.

In a country with great differences in economic development and standards of living between the Republics, there will be disagreements over economic policies, taxation, transfer, subsidies across regions, and abandoning socialism for a market economy. All Republics had experienced dramatic economic gains since World War II. Yugoslavia was not beyond economic repair.

As in other communist states in the late 1980s, the Yugoslav communist leaders wanted to remain in power. Some reprogrammed as reform communists, and hoped to move into European-style social democracy. Others chose ethnonationalism as the issue that would carry them to power and create a new principle of legitimacy for the post-communist regime. Moderate nationalists stood for conciliation among nationalities; extremists were willing to pursue their goals with force and violence. The defeat of the moderates was not inevitable. Why did xenophobic nationalism resonate with the citizenry? How is it that when the media unleashed the war of words and symbols before the war of bullets, so many believed the exaggerations, distortions and fabrications that belied their personal experiences?

Ethnic Relations Before the Crisis

Survey research on ethnic relations in mid-1990 found that in a national sample of 4,232 Yugoslavs, only 17 per cent believed that the country would break up into separate states, and 62 per cent reported that the 'Yugoslav' affiliation was very or quite important for them. On ethnonational relations, in workplaces, 36 per cent characterized them as 'good', 28 per cent as 'satisfactory', and only 6 per cent said 'bad' and 'very bad'. For ethnonational relations in neighborhoods, 57 per cent answered 'good', 28 per cent 'satisfactory', and only 12 per cent chose 'bad' and 'very bad'. For the majority of Yuogoslavs, on the eve of the Yugoslav wars, nationalist contention in the public arena did not translate into hostile interpersonal ethnic relations....

Ignatieff is puzzled, 'What is difficult to understand about the Balkan tragedy is how . . . nationalist lies ever managed to take root in the soil of shared village existence. . . . In order for war to occur, nationalists had to convince neighbors and friends that in reality they had been massacring each other since time immemorial.'

The Manipulation of Ethnicity

For explaining ethnic manipulation one needs the concept of a cognitive frame. A cognitive frame is a mental structure which situates and connects events, people and groups into a meaningful narrative in which the social world that one inhabits makes sense and can be communicated and shared with others. Yugoslavs experienced ethnic relations through two frames: a normal frame and a crisis frame. People possessed both frames in their minds: in peaceful times the crisis frame was dormant, and in crisis and war the normal frame was suppressed. Both frames were anchored in private and family experiences, in culture and in public life. In the normal frame, which prevailed in [Josip Broz] Tito's Yugoslavia, ethnic relations were cooperative and neighbourly. Colleagues and workers, schoolmates and teammates transacted routinely across nationality. Some did not even know or bother to know another's nationality. Intermarriage was accepted. Holidays were spent in each others' Republics. Except in Kosovo, the normal frame prevailed for most Yugoslavs throughout the 1980s.

The crisis frame was grounded in the experiences and memories of the Balkan wars, the first and second world wars—and other wars before that. In these crises, civilians were not distinguished from combatants. Old people, children, women, priests were not spared. Atrocities, massacres, torture, ethnic cleansing, a scorched-earth policy were the rule. Everyone was held collectively responsible for their nationality and religion, and became a target of revenge and reprisals. . . .

Tito had wanted to eradicate the crisis frame, but it simmered in the memories of older people, the families of victims, intellectuals and religious leaders. Milosevic, Tudjman and other nationalists did not invent the crisis frame; they activated and amplified it. . . .

If the normal frame prevailed in the 1980s as shown by . . . survey findings, how did nationalists activate and amplify the crisis frame after decades of dormancy? The emotion that poisons ethnic relations is fear: fear of extinction as a group, fear of assimilation, fear of domination by another group, fear for one's life and property, fear of being a victim once more. After fear comes hate. The threatening others are demonized and dehumanized. The means of awakening and spreading such fears in Yugoslavia were through the newsmedia, politics, education, popular culture, literature, history and the arts.

The crisis frame in Yugoslavia was first resurrected by Serb intellectuals over the plight of the Kosovo Serbs. . . .

Fear of extinction was spread with highly inflated figures on the ethnic killings in World War II. . . .

In my interview with a Serb refugee one can trace how the atrocities discourse switched on the crisis frame: 'We were afraid because nationalists revived the memory of World War II atrocities . . . nationalist graffiti on walls awakened fears of past memories; it was a sign that minorities [Serbs in Croatia] would not be respected and safe'.

Fears of domination, oppression and demographic shrinkage were roused by the incessant rape and genocide discourse. . . .

Ordinary people echo the intellectuals' and the media crisis discourse. . . . Peter Maas asks a Serb refugee couple why they had fled their village. Their answer: Muslims planned to take over, a list of names had been drawn up, Serb women were to be assigned to Muslim harems after the men had been killed. They had heard about it on the radio; the Serb military had uncovered the plan. The journalist probes: 'Did any Muslims in the village ever harm you?' They reply, 'Oh no, our relations with the Muslims in the village were always good, they were decent people'. In the minds of the Serb couple, the crisis frame had eclipsed the normal frame. What under peaceful circumstances were totally implausible events—young women become sexual slaves in harems for breeding janissaries; a fifteenth- and sixteenth-century style Turkish/Islamic invasion of Europe—become credible narratives of ethnic annihilation and domination within the crisis frame.

Fear and the crisis frame provided opportunities for nationalists to mobilize a huge ethnic constituency, get themselves elected to office, and organize aggressive actions against moderates and other ethnics. . . .

Populist nationalism worked. The Vojvodina and Montenegro party leaderships resigned and were replaced by Milosevic loyalists. Abolishing the autonomous provinces of Kosovo and Vojvodina precipitated a constitutional crisis. . . . The nationality balance in Yugoslav politics was thus disturbed. Serbia gained control of over half the votes in all federal bodies and institutions. Slovenes and Croats reacted with their own nationalism.

There was grass-roots resistance to nationalism and to activation of the crisis frame. A content analysis of news stories in *Oslobodjenje* for 1990 indicates that municipalities, youth and veterans' organizations, and trade unions repeatedly protested against ethnic polarization and hatreds. . . . Important as this opposition was, it was countered by the spread of populist nationalism. *Oslobodjenje* in 1990 is full of affirmations of national symbols and identities: the renaming of localities; the reburial of bones of atrocity victims from World War II; nationalist graffiti on churches, mosques, monuments and in cemeteries; fights over flags, ethnic insults, nationalist songs, ethnic vandalism. To many, these were signs that normal times were sliding into crisis, and the authorities had lost control.

Mass communications and propaganda research help to explain why ethnic manipulation worked and why the crisis frame eclipsed the normal frame. First, . . . fear arousing appeals, originating in a threat, were powerful and effective in changing opinion and belief. Furthermore, the most important reaction to fear is removing the source of threat, precisely what nationalists were promising to do in Yugoslavia. Second, studies of propaganda routinely find that repetition is the single most effective technique of persuasion. It does not matter how big the lie is, so long as it keeps being repeated.

Third, much of what we know is vicarious knowledge and not based on personal experience. We accept the truths of authorities and experts whom we respect and who have socially recognized positions and titles. Who could really tell or check how many Serbs had been massacred by Ustasha? Fourth, outright falsehoods were common and intentional. According to a media analyst, 'In Serbia and Croatia, TV fabricated and shamelessly circulated war crime stories ... the same victims would be identified on Zagreb screens as Croat, on Belgrade screens as Serb'. ...

Fifth, mass communications studies of the two-step flow of communication show that in ordinary circumstances crude propaganda from 'patriotic journalism' is discounted because people are exposed to a variety of broadcast messages and because they check media messages against the beliefs and opinions in their social milieus in interpersonal relationships and conversations. Ethnic crisis politics breaks down the two-step flow. ...

Nationalists Win the 1990 Elections

Second only to the mass media wars for the revival of the crisis frame were the 1990 elections. Every town and city experienced the founding of political parties, often at a huge rally in a public building or a sports stadium, during which speaker after speaker gave vent to exaggerated nationalist rhetoric and hostile pronouncements and attacks against other nationalities. ...

Nationalists persuaded voters not to 'split the ethnic vote' but to vote as a bloc for the nationalists because the other nationalities would bloc-vote and gain power. Bloc-voting became a self-fulfilling prophecy. ... The politicians elected were more nationalist than their voters. ...

Repression of Minorities and Moderates

The demise of the moderates was due to a combination of electoral defeats, loss of credibility about being effective in a crisis, and intimidation and threats from extremists. ...

The nationalist winners purged their ethnic opponents and moderates of their own nationality from party and state positions. The targets were sent anonymous threat letters, were fired from their jobs, forced into military service, charged with treason, subversion and plotting armed rebellion, and subject to office and house searches for weapons, radio transmitters and 'subversive' literature. ... In a Bosnian example reported by [Tadeusz] Mazowiecki, 'According to a witness [from Bosanska Dubica], the elected authorities who were moderates and who tried to prevent acts of violence were dismissed or replaced by Serbian extremists'.

Other methods were cruder. ... Ordinary people could not escape ethnic polarization. In an interview a Serb taxi driver explained: 'No one wanted the coming war, but if I don't fight, someone from my side [Serb] will kill me, and if my Muslim friends don't fight, other Muslims will kill them'.

The overthrow of moderates by extremists or radicals is well known in the great revolutions: Girondins were overthrown by the Jacobins in the French revolution and all groups were overthrown by the Bolsheviks in the Russian revolution. The means of seizing power are similar. The radicals create parallel governance to the state and come to exercise *de facto* authority in many institutions, and militias and mutineers execute a *coup d'état.* Then the remaining moderates are purged. It happens in ethnic violence as well. It did so in the mixed ethnic districts of Croatia and Bosnia, and it happened in Prijedor.

Militias Take Over

Militias and paramilitaries roamed far and wide and perpetrated ethnic cleansing, massacres, atrocities and other war crimes, as in the Prijedor district....

Militiamen were not necessarily fanatics filled with hatred to start with. [Tim] Judah described how a Serb militiaman got recruited by his peers from the local SDS who pressured him for weeks: 'We've all got to take up arms, or we'll disappear from here'. He had Muslim and Croat friends. Would they protect him against extremists of all nationalities? Not likely, if it got violent. So he 'took out a gun'. Peer pressure, fear, not only of Muslims but of extremist Serbs who might finger him as a 'traitor', were the major reasons for joining a militia. Some of these men were unemployed and expected a job in the coming Serb government as militia or police.

Once the young man 'took out a gun' he became encapsulated in a quasi-military unit subject to peer solidarity and ethnic loyalty. He was trained in weapons and indoctrinated with the beliefs and norms of the crisis frame about other ethnics:

a. *Collective guilt:*   'They' act in unison; children grow into adults; women give birth to future warriors; even old people stab you from behind; 'they' will never change.

b. *Revenge and retaliation:*   'They' massacred 'us' in the past, and are about to do it again, in fact they have already started. A setting of scores is justified; an eye for an eye.

c. *Deterrence/first strike:*   Disable them before they strike, which is what they are about to do, despite appearances, because they are secretive and treacherous.

d. *Danger/survival:*   These are extraordinary times, one's entire nationality is threatened, and extreme measures are justified.

e. *Legitimacy:*   Ordinary people and militias are justified in taking extreme measures because the constituted authorities have not come to the defence of our people.

These are the rationalization and the justifying norms for unrestrained, collective, ethnic violence. Other motives for collective violence were economic gain, peer pressure and lack of accountability. From being an ordinary man in normal times the militiaman changed into being a killer at crisis times.

The Bassiouni report (UN Security Council 1994) counted eighty-three paramilitaries in Bosnia alone operating between June 1991 and late 1993, fifty-three for Serbs, with an estimated 20,000–40,000 members, thirteen for Croats, with 12,000–20,000, and fourteen for Bosniac, with 4,000–6,000 men. In view of 700,000 Bosnian Serb men aged fifteen to thirty-five, militiamen were 10–20 per cent of the Serb men of military age in Bosnia. Ten to 20 per cent of adult males in militias, added to the military and police, are more than enough for death and destruction against civilians on a massive scale.

Conclusion

My account is not a narrative of events but an analytic explanation for the breakup of Yugoslavia amid collective violence.... On the eve of the wars, Yugoslavs reported cooperative interpersonal ethnic relations and opposed a breakup of the state. Nationalist leaders succeeded in manipulating ethnicity by spreading fear, insecurity and hatred, which advanced their political agenda of separate national states.

To explain their success I draw on elements from the primordialist, instrumentalist and constructionist views on ethnicity and on the theory of ethnic violence originating in fear and insecurity. To these I add the concept of a cognitive frame which clarifies élite-grass-roots linkage and ethnic manipulation. Nationalism, ethnic identity and attachment alone, however intense, do not explain grass-roots ethnic actions. Yugoslavs possessed two frames on ethnic relations: a cooperative frame for normal, peaceful times, as in the decades of the fifties to the eighties. They also possessed a dormant crisis frame anchored in family history and collective memory of wars, ethnic atrocities and brutality. Threats and lies that were implausible and dismissed in the normal frame could resonate when the crisis frame was switched on: they became persuasive, were believed, and inspired fear.

In the waning days of Communism, nationalists activated the crisis frame on ethnicity by playing on fears of ethnic annihilation and oppression in the mass media, in popular culture, in social movements, and in election campaigns. Élite crisis discourse resonated at the grass roots, made for ethnic polarization, and got nationalists elected. Once in office, nationalists suppressed and purged both moderates in their own ethnic group and other ethnics. They organized militias who perpetrated acts of extreme violence against innocent civilians. They conducted war according to the crisis script. Without the tacit, overt or confused support of the majority, the nationalist leaders could not have escalated ethnic rivalry and conflict into massive collective violence.

POSTSCRIPT

Is Ethnic Conflict Inevitable?

Although Kakar's argument draws heavily on psychology, he clearly adopts a primordialist perspective that ethnic differences are inherently threatening; such differences lead to tension and will ultimately emerge as conflict. Individuals may keep their fears and anxieties in check for a time, but preconscious fears and anxiety will eventually emerge. For Kakar, no amount of education or politically correct training will eliminate these anxieties or permanently overcome them.

Oberschall's argument accepts the reality of primordialist variables such as kinship, language, and religion as more important than did Barth in his original formulation of the circumstantialist perspective. But for Oberschall, such variables must be triggered by circumstantialist factors before they can be aroused. The Balkans case is a particularly apt one, as ethnicity in Bosnia is largely based on religious differences. All three "ethnic" communities have emerged from essentially the same pool of genetic material. The language spoken by all three groups is essentially the same language, often called Serbo-Croatian by linguists, though the Serbs use a Cyrillic alphabet and the Croats use a Roman one. The main "ethnic" differences emerge from their three different religions: Eastern Orthodox, Roman Catholic, and Islam. Religious differences in Bosnia correspond to traditional political alliances, but, as in the conflict in Northern Ireland, they are not fundamentally based on significant biological or linguistic differences. In Bosnia, unlike Northern Ireland, people of all three ethnicities had lived and worked side by side; they socialized together and had even intermarried. The primordialist variables are, in Oberschall's view, insufficient to trigger the ethnic violence and brutality that erupted in Bosnia. Ethnic violence, massacres, and ethnic cleansing could only have emerged if people in the towns and villages were manipulated into fearing their neighbors, concludes Oberschall.

Anthropologists and sociologists have long recognized that racial and ethnic tensions in the United States and other countries are linked to issues about access to jobs, land, resources, and opportunities. But it is not clear whether or not such circumstantialist variables are sufficient to explain why social conflict so often allows ethnic affiliations to become so central.

For further reading on genocide and ethnic cleansing, see Alexander L. Hinton's edited volume *Annihilating Difference: The Anthropology of Genocide* (University of California Press, 2002). For another view on ethnic conflict in India, see Ashutosh Varshney's *Ethnic Conflict and Civic Life: Hindus and Muslims in India* (Yale University Press, 2002). For a recent perspective about ethnicity, see André Burguière and Raymond Grew's edited volume *The Construction of Minorities: Cases for Comparison Across Time and Around the World* (University of Michigan Press, 2001). For more circumstantialist discussions of ethnic conflict, see Jack Eller's *From Culture to Ethnicity to Conflict* (University of Michigan Press, 1999) and *The Myth of "Ethnic Conflict": Politics, Economics, and "Cultural" Violence,* edited by Beverly Crawford and Ronnie D. Lipschutz (International Area Studies, University of California at Berkeley, 1998).

On the Internet ...

American Anthropological Association Code of Ethics

Created by the American Anthropological Association, the largest organization of anthropologists in the world, this American Anthropological Association
Code of Ethics Web site provides a code of ethics for its members and a
handbook on ethical issues faced by anthropologists.

http://www.aaanet.org/committees/ethics/ethcode.htm

Kennewick Man

This site contains an article on the controversy following the discovery of the
bones of a 8,400-year-old man, now called Kennewick Man. The article discusses whether the bones, which do not appear to be Native American, should
be protected under the Native American Graves Protection and Repatriation
Act (NAGPRA) and therefore be reburied. Links are provided to previous articles, which give further information from both sides of the debate on Kennewick
Man.

http://www.archaeology.org/9701/etc/specialreport.html

The Female Genital Mutilation Education and Networking Project

This site on the Female Genital Mutilation Education and Networking Project
provides an explanation of female circumcision and gives recent news on the
topic. The site also presents a number of perspectives and provides links to
further information.

http://www.fgmnetwork.org/index.html

The Yanomamö

Created by Brian Schwimmer, this Yanomamö (also spelled *Yanomami*) Web
site explores intergroup relations, alliances, and the role of warfare among the
Yanomamö. This site also provides links to additional sites on the subject.

http://www.umanitoba.ca/anthropology/tutor/case_studies/
yanomamo/

Exhibitions at the Smithsonian: National Museum of the American Indian

This Web site of the National Museum of the American Indian was created
by the Smithsonian Institution and provides images of current and recent exhibits about Native American art and society. The links provided on this site
allow students to evaluate how this museum represents the Native American
community.

http://www.nmai.si.edu/exhibits/index.html

PART 5

Ethics in Anthropology

*T*he ethical treatment of other peoples has come to play an increasingly important role in contemporary anthropology. Ethical issues directly affect how cultural anthropologists should treat their living human subjects. But similar issues also affect archaeologists and biological anthropologists because the artifacts of past communities often represent the ancestors of living communities. Here the interests of anthropologists and native peoples diverge, and we ask whether such bones should be reburied to respect the dead or if they should be studied for science. Similarly, we may ask what the ethical responsibilites of Western anthropologists should be when they find certain cultural practices abhorrent or unjust. Should anthropologists work to change these practices? All of these issues raise questions about how involved anthropologists should become with the peoples with whom they work. Should anthropologists take a passive, objective, and even scientific position or should they use what they know to support or change these native communities?

- Should the Remains of Prehistoric Native Americans Be Reburied Rather Than Studied?

- Should Anthropologists Work to Eliminate the Practice of Female Circumcision?

- Did Napoleon Chagnon and Other Researchers Harm the Yanomami Indians of Venezuela?

- Do Museums Misrepresent Ethnic Communities Around the World?

ISSUE 15

Should the Remains of Prehistoric Native Americans Be Reburied Rather Than Studied?

YES: James Riding In, from "Repatriation: A Pawnee's Perspective," *American Indian Quarterly* (Spring 1996)

NO: Clement W. Meighan, from "Some Scholars' Views on Reburial," *American Antiquity* (October 1992)

ISSUE SUMMARY

YES: Assistant professor of justice studies and member of the Pawnee tribe James Riding In argues that holding Native American skeletons in museums and other repositories represents a sacrilege against Native American dead and, thus, all Indian remains should be reburied.

NO: Professor of anthropology and archaeologist Clement W. Meighan believes that archaeologists have a moral and professional obligation to the archaeological data with which they work. Such data is held in the public good and must be protected from destruction, he concludes.

From the beginning, the relationship between Native Americans and anthropologists in the United States has been an uncertain one, ranging from mutually cooperative to overtly hostile in which Native Americans deeply mistrust anthropologists and feel that Native American culture is exploited.

Native American activists have invoked concerns about religious freedom, arguing that the excavation of bones is a desecration, a violation of native rights, and a sacrilege against Native American religion. These individuals and organizations demanded the immediate return and reburial of all Native American skeletons currently held in public museums and other repositories. They objected both to the exhibition of the remains and to research on remains by physical anthropologists. Many Native Americans have pointed out that the same museums that exhibit Native American skeletons do not simultaneously display the bones of white Americans.

Responding to the concerns of Native Americans, in 1990 the U.S. Congress enacted the Native American Graves Protection and Registration Act (NAGPRA), which mandates that all public collections of Native American remains must be returned to relatives or descendants for reburial. The return of bones and material culture has come to be called "repatriation."

James Riding In, himself a Pawnee, argues that anthropologists and archaeologists have consistently desecrated graves by excavating and studying the bones of Native Americans. He begins his discussion by outlining the history of many public museum collections of Native American skulls. Many of these, he maintains, were war dead from the Indian Wars of the 1870s, and they should have been reburied on the spot. Riding In says that Native Americans believe that the bodies of the dead must be reunited with "Mother Earth."

Clement W. Meighan counters that the debate over what should be done with bones from archaeological excavations is a conflict between science and religion. In the case of very early prehistoric sites, there is usually no evidence that links living tribes inhabiting the surrounding areas with the early community; many of these groups would either be unrelated to living tribal members or might even be the remains of enemy groups.

For Meighan the requirements of science must be defended, and the unraveling of humankind's prehistory in the New World is of public interest to all Americans, whether Native or not. He contends that the public's right to know about the past is important, and any reburial of archaeological material represents the destruction of scientific data that can never be recovered. Arguing that political motives are at the heart of Native American claims to religious interest in archaeological remains, Meighan views reburial as an attempt to censor archaeological and anthropological findings that conflict with Native American legends and myths.

Although NAGPRA has been the official law of the land for a decade, there remain many contentious concerns about just which bones should be repatriated and how they should be treated both legally and professionally. Riding In and Meighan raise a number of questions about the interests of science and Native American religions. Are Native American religious beliefs more important than those of secular scientists? Do archaeologists desecrate Native American sacred sites whenever they excavate? Should the religious concerns of one ethnic or cultural community override either the professional concerns of another group or the intellectual rights of the general public? Who should control information about the past? Who should control depictions of any ethnic group's past?

James Riding In

Repatriation: A Pawnee's Perspective

My opposition to scientific grave looting developed partially through the birth of the American Indian repatriation movement during the late 1960s. Like other American Indians of the time (and now), I viewed archaeology as an oppressive and sacrilegious profession that claimed ownership over many of our deceased relatives, suppressed our religious freedom, and denied our ancestors a lasting burial. My first encounter with an archaeologist occurred at a party in New Mexico in the late 1970s. After hearing him rant incessantly about the knowledge he had obtained by studying Indian remains, burial offerings, and cemeteries, I suggested that if he wanted to serve Indians he should spend his time excavating latrines and leave the graves alone. Of course, he took umbrage at the tone of my suggestion, and broke off the conversation. While studying history at the University of California, Los Angles [UCLA] in the mid-1980s, I became committed to pursuing the goals of the repatriation movement, which was gaining momentum. Like other reburial proponents, I advocated the reburial of all Indian remains warehoused across the nation in museums, universities, and federal agencies. I also promoted the extension or enactment of laws to protect Indian cemeteries from grave looters, including archaeologists.

While working to elevate the consciousness of the UCLA campus about the troubled relationship between archaeologists and Indians, a few of us, including students, staff, faculty, and community members, took advantage of opportunities to engage in dialogue with the anti-repatriation forces. During these exchanges, tempers on both sides often flared. Basically, the archaeologists were functioning on metaphysical and intellectual planes that differed from ours. We saw their professional activities as sacrilege and destructive, while they professed a legal and scientific right to study Indian remains and burial goods. We wanted the university to voluntarily return the human remains in its collections to the next-of-kin for proper reburial. They desired to protect excavation, research, and curatorial practices. Asserting profound respect for Indian concerns, beliefs, and values, members of the archaeology group offered a host of patronizing excuses for refusing to endorse our calls for repatriation. In this sense, the UCLA struggle mirrored the conflict over human remains ensuing throughout much of the country. In 1989, as the UCLA battle ensued, I accepted an offer to assist the Pawnee government in its efforts as a sovereign nation to reclaim the remains of its ancestors held at the Smithsonian Institution. Being a citizen of this small and impoverished nation of Indians, I welcomed the opportunity to join other Pawnee activists in the repatriation quest. Earlier that year, Congress had enacted a repatriation bill that provided a legal mechanism for Indian governments to reclaim ancestral remains and burial offerings held at the Smithsonian.

Despite the law, obdurate Smithsonian personnel sought to frustrate Indian repatriation efforts with such tactics as stonewalling, deceit, and misinformation. Although Smithsonian personnel claimed that the true identities of six skulls classified as Pawnee could not be positively established, subsequent research on my part uncovered a preponderance of evidence confirming the authenticity of the accession records. This research also showed that, after U.S. soldiers and Kansas settlers had massacred a party of Pawnee men who had been recently discharged from the U.S. army, a Fort Harker surgeon had collected some of the victims' skulls in compliance with army policy and shipped them to the Army Medical Museum for craniometric study

Since that report, I have written articles, given presentations, and, in conjunction with others, conducted research on behalf of Pawnee repatriation initiatives at Chicago's Field Museum of Natural History. I also have written a report from information found in the Native American Graves Protection and Repatriation Act (NAGPRA) summary letters showing the location of additional Pawnee remains, sacred objects, objects of cultural patrimony, and cultural artifacts.

This essay offers some of my views concerning the reburial aspect of the repatriation struggle. It seeks to show the intellectual and spiritual foundations behind the movement as a means for understanding the complexity of the controversy. It also attempts to demonstrate how repatriation advocates managed to effect discriminatory laws and practices. Finally, it conveys a message that, although old attitudes continue to function within the archaeology and museum communities, a concerted effort brought to bear by people who espouse cooperative relations is in place to bring Indian spiritual beliefs in conformity with non-Indian secular values.

At another level, I write with the intent of creating awareness about a pressing need to disestablish racial, institutional, and societal barriers that impede this country's movement toward a place that celebrates cultural diversity as a cherished and indispensable component of its social, political, and economic fabric. Despite the tone of skepticism, caution, and pessimism found within this study, I envision a society where people can interact freely, respecting one another without regard to race, color, ethnicity, or religious creed. Before this dream becomes a reality, however, America has to find ways to dissolve its racial, gender, cultural, and class barriers.

Pawnee Beliefs, Critical Scholarship, and Oppression

The acts committed against deceased Indians have had profound, even harmful, effects on the living. Therefore, as an activist and historian, I have had to develop a conceptual framework for giving meaning and order to the conflict. The foundation of my perspective concerning repatriation is derived from a combination of cultural, personal, and academic experiences. An understanding of Pawnee religious and philosophical beliefs about death, gained through oral tradition, dreams, and research, informs my view that repatriation is a social justice movement, supported by native spirituality and sovereignty, committed to the amelioration of the twin evils of oppression and scientific racism. Yet, I am neither a religious fundamentalist nor a left- or right-wing reactionary. Concerning repatriation, I simply advocate that American Indians receive what virtually every other group of Americans enjoys; that is, the right to religious freedom and a lasting burial.

My training as critical scholar provides another cornerstone of my beliefs about the nature of "imperial archaeology." My writings cast the legacy of scientific body snatching within the realm of oppression. Oppression occurs when a set or sets of individuals within the dominant population behave in ways that infringe on the beliefs, cultures, and political structures of other groups of people. Acts of stealing bodies, infringing on spirituality, and resisting repatriation efforts represent classic examples of oppression.

Although exposed to years of secular interpretations about the nature of the world and the significance of archaeology for understanding the past through formal Euroamerican education, I have continued to accept Pawnee beliefs about the afterlife. To adopt any other perspective regarding this matter would deny my cultural heritage. I cannot reconcile archaeology with tradition because of the secular orientation of the former as well as its intrusive practices. Unlike archaeologists who see Native remains as specimens for study, my people view the bodies of deceased loved ones as representing human life with sacred qualities. Death merely marks the passage of the human spirit to another state of being. In a 1988 statement, then Pawnee President Lawrence Goodfox Jr. expressed a common perspective stressing the negative consequences of grave desecration on our dead: "When our people die and go on to the spirit world, sacred rituals and ceremonies are performed. We believe that if the body is disturbed, the spirit becomes restless and cannot be at peace."

Wandering spirits often beset the living with psychological and health problems. Since time immemorial, Pawnees have ceremoniously buried our dead within Mother Earth. Disinterment can occur only for a compelling religious reason. Equally critical to our perspective are cultural norms that stressed that those who tampered with the dead did so with profane, evil, or demented intentions. From this vantage point, the study of stolen remains constitutes abominable acts of sacrilege, desecration, and depravity. But racist attitudes, complete with such axioms as "The only good Indian is a dead Indian," have long conditioned white society to view Indians (as other non-whites) as intellectually inferior subhumans who lacked a right to equal treatment under legal and moral codes. Complicating matters, value judgments about the alleged superiority of the white race became interlocked with scientific thought, leading to the development of oppressive practices and policies.

Consequently, orgies of grave looting occurred without remorse. After the Pawnees removed from Nebraska to Oklahoma during the 1870s, local settlers, followed by amateur and professional archaeologists, looted virtually every Pawnee cemetery they could find, taking remains and burial offerings. Much of the "booty" was placed in an array of institutions including the Nebraska State Historical Society (NSHS) and the Smithsonian Institution.

We have a right to be angry at those who dug our dead from the ground, those who established and maintained curatorial policies, and those who denied our repatriation requests. Last year, my elderly grandmother chastised white society in her typically reserved, but direct fashion for its treatment of our dead. After pointing to an Oklahoma bluff where many Pawnee relatives are buried, she declared, "It is not right, that they dug up all of those bodies in Nebraska." What she referred to can be labeled a spiritual holocaust. When anyone denies us our fundamental human rights, we cannot sit idly by and wait for America to reform itself. It will never happen. We have a duty not only to ourselves, but also to our relatives, our unborn generations, and our ancestors to act. Concerning repatriation, we had no choice but to work for retrieval of our ancestral remains for proper reburial and for legislation that provided penalties for those who disrupted the graves of our relatives.

Yet our initiatives sought redress in a peaceful manner. In 1988, Lawrence Goodfox expressed our goals, declaring "All we want is [the] reburial of the remains of our ancestors and to let them finally rest in peace and for all people in Nebraska to refrain from, forever, any excavation of any Native American graves or burial sites." In our view, reburying the disturbed spirits within Mother Earth equalizes the imbalance between the spiritual and physical worlds caused by the desecration.

National Challenges to Imperial Archaeology and Oppression

The Pawnee reburial struggle occurred within the context of a worldwide indigenous movement. What beset my people had affected Natives everywhere. In this country, few Indian nations escaped the piercing blades of the archaeologists' shovels or the slashes of the headhunters' knives. These operations infringed on Indian beliefs, burial rights, and sovereignty. The notion that this type of research had validity was so ingrained in the psyche of many non-Indians that rarely did anyone question the morality, ethics, or legality of these practices; that is, until the repatriation movement surfaced in the late 1960s. This movement stands on a paramount footing with the valiant struggles of African-Americans for civil rights and women for equality. Taking a leading role during the early stages of the repatriation movement, organizations such as the American Indian Movement (AIM), International Indian Treaty Council, and American Indians Against Desecration (AIAD) expressed in dramatic fashion Indian concerns about the excesses of archaeology and oppression. Committed to the causes of reburying all disinterred Indians and stopping grave disruptions, these groups often employed confrontational strategies. Near Welch, Minnesota, in 1972, for example, AIM members risked arrest by disturbing a dig site. In addition to burning field notes and tools, they confiscated unearthed artifacts and exposed photographic film. Throughout the 1970s and

1980s, AIAD challenged the human remains collections and curatorial policies of government agencies, museums, and universities. As time progressed,
many college campuses saw a dramatic increase in tensions between Indians
and archaeologists. These actions catapulted the repatriation movement into
the consciousness of sympathetic politicians, newspaper editors, and members
of the general public. Increased knowledge of the issues subsequently spawned
unprecedented levels of non-Indian backing of repatriation.

As the 1980s progressed, more conciliatory Indians, often coming from
the professions of law and politics, surfaced as leading figures in the movement. Unlike the universal reburial advocates, these moderates tended to see
compromise as the most expedient means available to acquire the desired legislation. They often sought a balance between scientific study of Native remains
and the need for Indians to gain religious, burial, and repatriation rights under
the law. Organizations such as the National Congress of American Indians and
the Native American Rights Fund espoused the moderate cause. Realizing that
public sentiments increasingly favored the Indians' views, some archaeologists
and museum administrators endorsed compromise as a means of cutting their
losses and saving face. With common ground beneath their feet, individuals and
organizations waged a series of intense political battles at the state and federal
levels.

With moderates in control, reform transpired relatively swiftly. By 1992,
more than thirty states had placed laws on the books extending protection to Indian cemeteries, including several with repatriation provisions. Congress passed
two pieces of legislation, the National Museum of the American Indian Act in
1989 and NAGPRA the following year. Collectively, these national laws provided
Indian nations a means to obtain human remains linked to them by a "preponderance of evidence" and associated funerary offerings held by institutions
that received federal funding. NAGPRA also provides penalties for individuals
convicted of trafficking in human remains.

Ongoing Reburial Initiatives

With legal avenues now open for Indian governments to reclaim stolen ancestral remains and associated burial objects, some of the old repressive policies
fell by the wayside. The change enabled relatives to begin the task of reclaiming stolen bodies and grave offerings for reburial. Collectively, Indian nations
thus far have interred thousands of stolen remains. To date (summer 1995), the
Pawnees alone have placed nearly a thousand bodies back in Mother Earth. The
total number of recovered bodies will surely reach the tens of thousands within
a few years.

Reinterment ceremonies, along with funeral feasts, evoke a gamut of emotional expressions ranging from sorrow to joy. When conducting reburials,
people rejoice at the fact that the repatriated remains are finally being returned
to Mother Earth, but, like modern funerals, an air of sadness pervades the ceremonies. In particular, reinterring the remains of young children causes grieving
and weeping. Mourning is part of the healing process in that reburials seek to

restore harmony between the living and dead by putting restless spirits to rest. At another level, reburials bring closure to bitterly contested struggles.

Future Concerns

Legislation emanating from the repatriation movement has changed the customary ways that archaeologists and museums operate. Most notably, Indian governments now have established a sovereign right to reclaim the bodies of their ancestors from offending museums, universities, and federal agencies. In this capacity, they have the power to grant and deny access to their dead. Additionally, the new laws make face-to-face interaction routine between museums and Indian nations in certain repatriation matters. Several observers have proclaimed that the common ground signals the dawning of a new era of cooperative relations between Indians and museums. Despite changing attitudes and practices, it is too soon to assess the long-term ramifications of the reburial controversy. Six problematic areas cause me concern about the future of repatriation:

First, the laws do not provide for the reinterment of ancient, unclaimed, or unidentified remains. In other words, the fate of tens of thousands of bodies, along with associated funerary offerings, is uncertain. Will those with authority take steps to provide for a proper reburial for these bodies or will they allow the continuance of old practices and policies?

Second, the absence of legislation and aggressive enforcement of burial protection laws in some states may send a message that grave looting can resume without fear of arrest, prosecution, or punishment.

Third, NAGPRA's graves protection stipulations apply only to federal lands and entities that receive federal funding. In states without both progressive reburial legislation and a substantial Indian populace, large-scale acts of grave desecration may continue....

Fourth, and perhaps most significant a pervasive attitude among elements of the archaeology and museum communities keeps repressive and archaic ideas alive. In fact, members of these groups have consistently disavowed any wrongdoing by themselves and their predecessors. Rather, some present their work to the public as neutral, impartial, and objective interpretations of distant Native American cultures. To counter claims that the digging and study is disrespectful, others assert that taking remains for study shows respect for Indian people and culture. In a twisted logic, still others insist that they are the "true spiritual descendants of the original Indians and the contemporary Indians [are] foreigners who had no right to complain about their activities." Like most other repatriation advocates, I reject these pleas as condescending and duplicitous acts of misguided people and lost souls....

Anti-repatriation advocates echoed a common refrain. They viewed their pursuits as being under attack by narrow-minded and anti-intellectual radicals who sought to destroy archaeology. Equating repatriation with book burning, some alarmists often charged falsely that Indians would not rest until they had stripped museums and universities of their Indian collections. These strategies contain elements of self-delusion, arrogance, and racism. A tacit message found in these paternalistic defenses of imperial archaeology was that Indians must, for their own good, learn to respect the work of archaeology. Equally disturbing is the notion that Indians need archaeology. However, the exact opposite is true. Beneath the self-serving rhetoric lay a deceptive ambiance of cultural imperialism that masked the stark reality of how archaeology and museums infringed on Indian religion and burial rights.

Fifth, imperial archaeologists have had substantial levels of support from real and pretend Indians. The phenomena of co-optation and self-interest reverberates loudly here. Usually found working in museums, universities, and government agencies, some of these individuals claim a heritage complete with a Cherokee princess, but they embrace the secular views and values of Western science. Others belonging to this camp clearly have significant amounts of Indian blood, but they rely heavily on the goodwill of their non-Indian colleagues to promote and maintain their careers. Non-institutional advocacy surfaced from some grassroots Indians. At meetings, conferences, and confrontations, archaeologists rarely failed to produce a reservation Indian or two who spoke passionately against reburial in an effort to convince the public and policy makers that Native communities lacked unanimity on the subject. Whatever their motive, degree of Indian blood, or cultural orientation, their willingness to endorse oppressive archaeological practices marks a radical departure from traditional Indian philosophy.

Collectively, "wannabes" and misguided Indians may be able to damage reburial efforts. As the movement pushed for national repatriation legislation in the late 1980s, we found them sitting on committees convened by anthropology and museum associations that issued reports condemning repatriation. In a worst-case scenario, NAGPRA and other committees stacked with them and imperial archaeologists could conceivably frustrate or undermine repatriation requests.

Finally, it seems that archaeologists have launched a campaign to convince the public, tribal leaders, and others that skeletal investigations are necessary for a variety of reasons. According to a recent *Chronicle of Higher Education* article, "More and more of those kinds of opportunities will occur, many scholars agree, when researchers learn to persuade American Indians and others that skeletal remains and artifacts represent something other than a publication toward a faculty member's promotion and tenure." In other words, we are seeing archaeologists adopt less abrasive tactics to get their hands on our dead. Succumbing to subtle pressure, aimed at convincing us to accept a secular view of the dead as research objects, will erode a cherished part of our belief systems and cultures. In any event, some Indian nations have allowed the creation of archaeology programs on their reservations.

Clearly, the repatriation movement has won some major victories, but the war is unfinished. United States history teaches the lesson that individuals who face the threat of losing a privileged status often will devise rationalizations and strategies to resist change. Southern slave owners, for example, argued against abolitionism by making the outlandish claim that involuntary servitude was a benevolent institution that saved millions of blacks from the savagery of Africa. Historians repeated this claim well into the twentieth century.

It is conceivable that at some point someone will challenge the constitutionality of NAGPRA. If this occurs, will the courts respect Indian beliefs and burial rights? America's long history concerning issues of Indian religious freedom and political rights makes the possibility of a legal suit a scary thought. The Supreme Court has occasionally protected Indian sovereignty, as well as hunting, fishing, and water rights, but it also has incorporated such imperialistic notions as the doctrine of discovery and the plenary power doctrine into U.S. law. Its decisions also have eroded the power of Indian self-government by allowing the imposition of federal jurisdiction over certain crimes committed on Indian lands.

In recent years, conservative justices appointed by President Ronald Reagan have endangered Indian religious freedom. In *Lyng v. Northwest Indian Cemetery Protective Association* (108 S. Ct. 1319 (1988)) Justice Sandra Day O'Connor wrote the majority decision stating that the U.S. government had the right to build a road through an area on federal lands sacred to Yurok, Karok, and Tolowa Indians even if such a construction project would destroy the ability of those people to worship. In *Employment Division Department of Human Resources of Oregon v. Smith* (110 S. Ct. 1595 (1990)) the court held that a state could abridge expressions of religious freedom if the state had a compelling reason to do so. In this case, the court paved the way for states to deprive Native American Church (NAC) members of the right to use peyote in connection with their worship. Fortunately, in 1994, Congress addressed the religious crisis caused by the court by enacting a law that sanctioned peyote use for NAC services.

History demonstrates that promises made by white America to help Indians have not always materialized. The administrative branch of the federal government has entered into 371 treaties with Indian nations and systematically violated each of them. The legislative record is another cause of concern. The Indian Reorganization Act of 1934 authorized Indian nations to restructure themselves politically but only in accordance with models and terms acceptable to Department of Interior officials. During the 1970s, Congress declared that Indian government could exercise more powers of self-government. Federal bureaucratic controls over Indian governments, however, actually became more stringent, if not suffocating, in this era. During that decade, Congress also enacted the American Indian Religious Freedom Act of 1978 in a half-hearted effort to encourage federal agencies to accommodate customary Indian worship practices at off-reservation sites. The act provided virtually no protection because federal agencies and the Supreme Court, as we have seen, have followed a tradition that sees nothing wrong with suppressing Indian religious freedom. Although Indians are pursing a legislative remedy to resolve these problems, Congress has yet to enact a true religious freedom law for them.

Conclusion

Facing overwhelming odds, the repatriation movement has achieved many noteworthy successes. United States society, including a growing number of sympathetic archaeologists and museum curators, has finally recognized that Indians are not disappearing, and that Indians are entitled to burial rights and religious freedom. Nevertheless, under the new repatriation laws, many non-Indian entities still "legally" hold thousands of Indians remains and burial offerings. With many archaeologists and museum curators committed to upholding oppressive operational principles, values, and beliefs, the fate of these bodies remains in question. Moreover, others, perhaps best described as wolves in sheeps' clothing, are seeking to gain our cooperation, a euphemism meaning the delivery of another blow to our revered philosophies about the dead.

Given the durability of imperialist archaeology and the new approaches being used to gain access to the remains of our beloved ancestors, we must remain vigilant and monitor their operations. Protecting our dead must remain a moral and spiritual obligation we cannot callously abandon for we cannot allow further erosions of our beliefs and traditions. Thus a need still exists for maintaining the cultural traditions that inspired the repatriation movement.

NO

Clement W. Meighan

Some Scholars' Views on Reburial

[T]here is something inherently distasteful and unseemly in secreting either the fruits or seeds of scientific endeavors.

— Judge Bruce S. Jenkins

Destruction of archaelogical collections through the demands for reburial presents a serious conflict between religion and science. Archaeologists should not deal with these matters by "compromise" alone, but must sustain their rights and duties as scholars.

The above quotation is from a court case having nothing to do with archaeology, yet if we believe that archaeology is a scientific endeavor we must agree that this statement applies to archaeology as well as medicine, chemistry, or other fields of scholarship. The recent increased attention given to the ethics of scientists and scientific organizations, with news accounts almost weekly in such journals as *Science*, requires archaeologists to examine their basic assumptions about the nature of science and their obligations to scholarship. This is brought forward most forcefully in the debate over the past 20 years about the problems of reburial of archaeological and museum collections.

The discussion by Goldstein and Kintigh (1990) is a valiant effort to unravel some of the strands of conflict inherent in the controversy over the destruction of museum collections in the name of Indian religious beliefs. They seek some sort of middle ground in which scholarly and ethnic concerns can coexist in a constructive way. However, in view of the massive losses of scientific data now legislated by the federal government and some of the states, it needs to be made clear that many archaeologists do not agree with some aspects of the philosophical position taken by Goldstein and Kintigh. In particular, their statement that "We must change the way we do business" (Goldstein and Kintigh 1990:589) is not justified, particularly since their suggestions for change involve the abandonment of scholarly imperatives and the adoption of an "ethical" position that accepts the right of nonscholars to demand the destruction of archaeological evidence and the concealment of archaeological data. Of course, changes in the way archaeology is done will inevitably take place, for both internal (professional) and external (social/legal) reasons. This

From Clement W. Meighan, "Some Scholars' Views on Reburial," *American Antiquity*, vol. 57, no. 4 (October 1992). Copyright © 1992 by The Society for American Archaeology. Reprinted by permission. Some references omitted.

does not mean that the basic rules of scholarly obligations to one's data should change as well.

Goldstein and Kintigh fall into the anthropological trap of cultural relativism. In asserting that we must balance our concerns for knowledge with "our professional ethic of cultural relativism," they argue that our values are not the only values or ethics, but only one legitimate belief system. The implication is that all belief systems are of equal legitimacy, therefore one cannot make a clear commitment to any particular values as a guide to action. However, most individuals do make a commitment to the values that will guide their personal action. Recognizing that other people may have other values does not mean that one must accept those values or compromise his/her own ethical standards. Indeed, the dictionary has a word for believing one way and acting another—it is "hypocrisy."

Those who affiliate with organized groups, whether the Church of the Rising Light or the Society for American Archaeology (SAA), supposedly accept the beliefs and goals of the organization as stated in their by-laws or scriptures. The SAA, as an organization dedicated to scholarly research in archaeology, is bound by the general rules of scholarship that require *honest reporting and preservation of the evidence*. If the research data are subject to censorship, how can there be honest reporting? If the evidence (collections) is not preserved, who can challenge the statements of the researcher? Who can check for misinterpretations, inaccuracies, or bias? Once the collection is destroyed, we have only an affidavit from the researcher; we can believe it or not, but there is no way that additional investigation or new laboratory techniques can be applied to the collection to gain a better understanding of the evidence. The astounding new methods for medical and genetic research on ancient populations require a piece of the bone—pictures and notes won't do. Similarly, laboratory advances in dating and determining the source of artifact materials require that the relevant objects be available for study. Since we commonly proclaim that archaeological collections are unique and irreplaceable, how can we ever justify the conscious and acquiescent destruction of our data?

The suggestion of Goldstein and Kintigh that we balance our own values with the professional ethic of cultural relativism by "compromise and mutual respect" is not realistic. Many archaeologists are not going to compromise away their most fundamental scholarly beliefs. Similarly, many Indian activists are not going to compromise away their beliefs (however unsupported by evidence) that every Indian bone of the past 12,000 years belongs to one of their ancestors. There are some instances in which compromise and mutual respect have led to satisfactory results for both sides; there are many more instances in which these valued qualities have been insufficient to prevent or postpone destruction of important archaeological finds.

Those who want to do away with archaeology and archaeological collections are of course entitled to their beliefs, and they are also entitled to use whatever political and legal machinery they can to bring about their stated goals. Originally, the goals were modest, but they have escalated every year since this discussion began more than 20 years ago, as reviewed by me in an earlier article (Meighan 1984). The present-day goals have repeatedly been made clear. For example, Christopher Quayle, an attorney for the Three Affiliated Tribes, stated in *Harpers* (Preston 1989:68–69): "It's conceivable that some time in the not-so-distant future there won't be a single Indian skeleton in any museum in the country. We're going to put them out of business." The "them" refers in this statement to physical anthropologists, but it is also extended to archaeologists. For example, the recent agreement between state officials in West Virginia and a committee representing Indian viewpoints (a committee which, incidentally, includes non-Indians) states that everything in an ongoing study of a 2,000-year-old Adena mound must be given up for reburial within a year—"everything" includes not only the bones of the mythical "ancestors" of the claimants, but also all the artifacts, the chipping waste, the food refuse, the pollen samples, the soil samples, and whatever else may be removed for purposes of scientific study. While the tax-payers are expected to pay for a 1.8-million-dollar excavation on the grounds that it is in the public interest for archaeological data to be preserved, *nothing* of the tangible archaeological evidence is to be preserved. Meanwhile, Indian activists are paid to "monitor" the excavation, and they were given the right to censor the final report and prevent any objectionable photographs or data from appearing.

If there is any doubt about the goals of the anti-archaeology contingent, consider the case of Dr. David Van Horn, charged with a felony in California for conducting an environmental impact study required by law, and being honest enough to report what he found in the site, including some small bits of cremated bone, which required hours of study by physical anthropologists to identify as human. Is the reporting of a legally mandated salvage excavation a felony? It can be in California, and there are many who would like to make archaeology a crime throughout the United States. Archaeologists who accept these situations or treat them as merely local concerns (apparently the position of most scholarly organizations including the SAA), have not just compromised, they have abandoned scholarly ethics in favor of being "respectful and sensitive" to nonscholars and anti-intellectuals. When the current round of controversy is over, this loss of scientific integrity will be heavily condemned.

So there are some situations in which compromise is not necessarily the best approach, and this is one of them. Archaeologists may well be legislated out of business, and museums may well lose all their American Indian collections, and indeed the Indians have been far more successful than the archaeologists in the political arena. Many archaeologists believe, however, that this should not occur with the happy connivance of the scholarly profession of archaeology. Over 600 of them are members of the American Committee for Preservation of Archaeological Collections (ACPAC), which has argued for over 10 years that archaeology is a legitimate, moral, and even useful profession, and that collections that were legally made should remain in museums as an important part of the heritage of the nation. Bahn may have had this group in mind in his news report on the "first international congress on the reburial of human remains," in his reference to "the extremists, who unfortunately did not attend the congress to put the case for rejecting the whole notion of reburial." Who are these extremists? Neither ACPAC nor any individual known to me has stated that no reburial of any kind should take place; everyone agrees that bones of known relatives should be returned to demonstrable descendants. The disagreement is over remains to which no living person can demonstrate any relationship. Museum materials 5,000 years old are claimed by people who imagine themselves to be somehow related to the collections in question, but such a belief has no basis in evidence and is mysticism. Indeed, it is not unlikely that Indians who have acquired such collections for reburial are venerating the bones of alien groups and traditional enemies rather than distant relatives.

If the present attacks on archaeological data were happening in engineering, medicine, or chemistry, they would not be accepted by the general public since destruction or concealment of the facts in those areas of scientific knowledge can lead to disastrous results for many living people. The general lack of public concern about the attack on archaeology arises from the perception that archaeological conclusions really do not matter—if someone's reconstruction of the ancient past is ridiculous or unsupported by evidence, who cares? It will not affect the daily lives of anyone now alive, no matter what we believe about what happened thousands of years ago. However, the principles of scholarship and scientific evidence are the same in all scholarly research, including archaeology and anthropology, and credibility of conclusions is an essential consideration for any field of scholarship, whether or not there are immediate practical effects of the conclusions that are reached.

In one of the polemics put forward by Indian spokesmen in the student newspaper at the University of California (Los Angeles), those of us on the archaeological faculty were accused of participating in an activity that was comparable to the "killing fields of Cambodia." Even allowing for the juvenile rhetoric characteristic of student newspapers, I was dumbfounded at such a statement. How could I harm any person who had already been dead for thousands of years? How could anything that my studies did with the bones of these ancient people harm any living person? The condemnation seems extreme for a "crime" that is merely a failure to invite mythical descendants to control my research and destroy museum collections held in the public interest. When issues of respect and sensitivity are raised, it needs to be pointed out that these work both ways.

Some Legal Issues: Constitutional Requirements

The first amendment states that Congress shall make no laws respecting an establishment of religion. Most state constitutions have similar clauses; that of California says the state will *never* pass such laws. Yet California, other states, and the federal government have numerous laws on the books that are specifically written to favor aboriginal tribal religious beliefs and compel others to act in accordance with them. Religious infringement also occurs when archaeologists are excluded from evaluating claims regarding repatriation because they do not hold particular religious beliefs. Until these statutes are challenged and overturned, they remain an opening for other groups to seek similar legislation making their religious beliefs enforceable by law. Creationists, for example, have been trying for over 60 years to outlaw the teaching of evolution because it is in conflict with their religious tenets.

That there is a science vs. religion aspect is clear in the religious justification for the claiming of bones and "sacred" artifacts, as well as the proclamation
of many activists that archaeologists and museums are committing sacrilege in
obtaining, storing, and studying archaeological remains. I discuss bone worship
elsewhere (Meighan 1990). Tonetti (1990) provides a case study of the situation
in Ohio, documenting the religious roots of the anti-archaeology movement.
He also reports a survey of Ohio legislators that reveals a frightening ignorance
of science in general and archaeology in particular: "As Zimmerman so dramatically stated in his op ed piece in the Columbus Dispatch, he does not want
the General Assembly making law dealing with science issues when over 75%
do not know what his 5 year old son has known for years—that dinosaurs and
humans did not coexist" (Zimmerman (1989), as quoted in Tonetti [1990:22];
recent news reports state that some Indians are now claiming dinosaur bones
recovered by paleontologists).

Some Legal Issues: Cultural-Resource Laws

There is a serious conflict between the laws mandating return and destruction of archaeological material (not just bones but also artifacts and anything
deemed "ceremonial" by the claimants), and those laws mandating cultural-
resource management and the study and conservation of archaeological sites
and remains. The Van Horn case previously mentioned put Van Horn in the
position of doing an environmental-impact report required by law, only to
find himself spending thousands of dollars defending himself against a felony
charge for violating laws based on Indian religious beliefs about cremated
bones. The judge agreed with defense witnesses that there was no basis for a
trial, but the state made its point that archaeologists will be heavily punished if
"Indians" request it, regardless of the validity of their complaint.

The legal dichotomy between science and religion as it pertains to archaeology may be related, as Goldstein and Kintigh (1990:589) point out, to the fact
that public perception does not include Indian history as part of the history
of the United States, even though they recognize that public policy and law
include the non-European past as an integral part of the history of the nation.
That part of American history that is Indian history is largely the contribution
of archaeology; *all* of it prior to 1492 is the contribution of archaeology. This
has been recognized and supported by the government since the Antiquities Act
of 1906, and it is the basis for all the environmental-impact laws dealing with
archaeological remains.

Many opponents of archaeological-resource laws believe that since archaeology has no effect on public health or safety, it ought to be excluded from
environmental impact laws. They are given considerable ammunition by laws
that state that it is in the public interest to spend a lot of money to get archaeological materials, and then state that such materials are not worth preservation
but are to be reburied as soon as possible after they are dug up, in some cases
within a few days or weeks of the fieldwork. Further, the belief that archaeology belongs to Indians removes it from the heritage of all of the citizens and
makes it less likely that the public will be interested in supporting activities not

seen to be in the broad public interest. In these times of stringent budgets, it is hard enough to convince the taxpayers that they should finance archaeological excavations without having to convince them that they should also finance the reburial of the items recovered.

There are major negative results for archaeology in the present situation where not only the federal government, but states, counties, cities, and a plethora of political agencies believe that they should pass regulations controlling archaeological research. These laws and regulations conflict with one another and vary from jurisdiction to jurisdiction. In some states the conduct of archaeological research is a risky business. The smart archaeologist in California does not find certain things. If they are found, they are either thrown away or not mentioned in his/her reports. Field classes are also careful not to expose students or teachers to criminal charges, meaning that students in those classes will never expose a burial or deal with any "controversial" finds. Chipping waste is still a safe area for study.

This chilling effect on research is creating an underground archaeology of ill-trained students, dishonest researchers, and intimidated teachers who are afraid to show a picture of a burial to their classes, let alone an actual human bone. Students, who are often more perceptive than their professors, rapidly catch on and change their major or move their archaeological interests to parts of the world where they will be allowed to practice their scholarly profession. There is an increasing loss to American archaeology, and of course to the Indians whose history is dependent on it.

Some Museum Issues

A negative effect of the ongoing shift to tribalism and the right of anyone to claim anything in museums is already happening. In the past, most of the support for museums came from private donors, who contributed not only money but collections. Donors of collections had the tacit (and sometimes written) agreement that their materials would be preserved in the public interest. Who would contribute anything to a museum if they thought the museum was going to give their material away for reburial or destruction? When even Stanford University and other respected repositories of scientific collections decide that their first obligation is to whatever Indian claimant comes along, the donor who wants his/her material *preserved* will seek a repository in a state or country that is dedicated to that aim. It is a paradox that the National Park Service is busily developing new standards of curation for government collections at the same time the new National Museum of the American Indian is declaring that it will not keep anything that Indian claimants declare that they want.

Reviewers of this article believe that only a very small part of archaeological collections will be taken away from museums and archaeologists. This is a pious hope in view of the escalation of claims previously noted, reaching the apex in the West Virginia case in which *everything* recovered by archaeologists is to be given up for reburial. There are numerous cases in which archaeologists or museum employees have given up entire collections rather than negotiate with Indian claimants; for example, one prominent California case (the Encino excavation) included reburial of a number of dog skeletons, not required by any statute. It is true that the Smithsonian and some other museums now have committees to evaluate claims against their collections; perhaps these will protect scholarly and public interests, but it remains to be seen whether they can withstand the political pressures brought to bear. While I am sure that not all collections will entirely disappear, under current legislation all physical remains, all mortuary associations, and all items claimed to have religious or ceremonial significance are at risk—these are the major sources of information in many archaeological studies. When claimants can get museum specimens merely by using the word "sacred," it should be apparent that anything can be claimed by someone. It does happen, it has happened, and scholars can only hope that it will not happen in the future.

Conclusions

When scholarly classes in United States archaeology and ethnology are no longer taught in academic departments (they are diminishing rapidly), when the existing collections have been selectively destroyed or concealed, and when all new field archaeology in the United States is a political exercise rather than a scientific investigation, will the world be a better place? Certainly the leadership in archaeological research, which has been characteristic of the last 50 years of American archaeology, will be lost, and it will be left to other nations to make future advances in archaeological methods, techniques, and scholarly investigations into the ancient past.

One reviewer of this paper commented that I am engaged in a "futile attempt to resurrect a bankrupt status quo." In this view, not only can nothing be done to improve the present situation, but nothing *should* be done, and we should all meekly accept the regulations, limitations, and restrictions of academic freedom that are brought forward by politicians and pressure groups. For the last 20 years, those who have attempted to change these restrictions in favor of scholarly ethics and the preservation of collections have been dismissed as a small group of outmoded discontents who cannot adapt to a changing world. This is a mistake; I may represent a minority view, but it is not confined to a small number and is growing rapidly as archaeologists see more and more of their basic data destroyed through reburial. ACPAC's 600 members (in 44 states) include a sizeable fraction of the leading archaeologists in the United States as well as physical anthropologists, museum workers, and yes, Indians.

I am, however, triggered by the accusation that my comments lead to nothing but intransigence to offer a few suggestions for action other than "compromise," which so far has mostly meant giving in to political demands. My suggestions:

1. Archaeologists negotiating with Indians or other groups should make an effort to be sure that *all* factions of the affected group are heard, not merely the group of activists who are first in the door. Many archaeologists have been doing this for years, and nearly all of us can report that we had little difficulty in finding Indians who would work

with us in a mutually agreeable and often rewarding relationship that respected Indian interests but at the same time preserved the archaeological collections. Unfortunately, numerous instances can be cited of savage personal attacks on those Indians who agreed to share the archaeologists' task, with attempts to force the archaeologist to use other consultants and claims that the one chosen was not a real Indian (see an example in Tonetti [1990:21]). When money is involved, this is probably inevitable. However, there is no reason for archaeologists to be controlled by enemies of their discipline when they can work with friends. The existence of Indian physical anthropologists, archaeologists, and museum workers, as well as the increasing number of Indian-owned museums with scientific objectives and high standards of curation, should offer opportunities for real collaboration that do not require the destruction of evidence nor the censorship of scientific reporting.

2. Professional organizations should work to amend the legislation dealing with archaeology to get a time cut-off inserted: Remains older than a certain age should not be subject to reburial. The present laws, which ignore time and assume that everything, regardless of age, is directly related to living people, are not scientifically valid, and the scientific organizations are in a position to make this clear, if necessary in court. The recent reburial of an Idaho skeleton dated at 10,600 years ago should never have happened, but as reported by the State Historic Preservation Office of that state, Idaho law requires *no* demonstration of any relationship between Indians and archaeological remains.

3. Professional organizations should point out the disagreements between "preservation" laws and "religion" laws and should try to strengthen the former and eliminate the conflicts. If they are unable to resolve the issue by negotiation, they should support court cases that address the matter.

4. If scholarly organizations are unwilling or unable to make a clear statement of their position with respect to the giving up of archaeological collections and data, it is left to the individual archaeologist to decide his or her own professional ethics in this matter. A clear review of the moral issues is given by Del Bene (1990). This should be considered, particularly by young archaeologists entering the profession, so that they are consciously aware of the decisions they are making and the consequences for their professional future.

References

Del Bene T.A. 1990. Take the Moral Ground: An Essay on the "Reburial" Issue. *West Virginia Archeologist* 42(2):11–19.

Goldstein, L., and K. Kintigh. 1990. Ethics and the Reburial Controversy. *American Antiquity* 55:585–591.

Meighan, C.W. 1984. Archaeology: Science or Sacrilege? In *Ethics and Values in Archaeology,* edited by E.L. Green, pp. 203–233. Free Press, New York.

1990. Bone Worship. *West Virginia Archeologist* 42(2):40–43.

Preston, D.J. 1989. Skeletons in Our Museums' Closets. *Harpers.* February: 66–75.

Tonetti, A.C. 1990. Ghost Dancing in the Nineties: Research, Reburial and Resurrection Among the Dead in Ohio. *West Virginia Archeologist* 42(2):20–22.

POSTSCRIPT

Should the Remains of Prehistoric Native Americans Be Reburied Rather Than Studied?

Since these two selections were written, many Native American groups have requested the return of human remains from museums, and these bones have been reburied. Other groups have expressed little interest in recovering the remains of ancestors or skeletons excavated from their lands because they do not share the same cultural beliefs as those expressed by Riding In. A number of museum curators and archaeologists have taken a much more tempered and conciliatory approach to dealing with these issues than the position expressed by Meighan.

Such possibilities suggest that there are a variety of alternative approaches to the issue of reburial besides the diametrically opposed positions expressed here. Many groups, both from museums and universities, have urged compromise. A number of Native American groups have also tried to find ways to accommodate anthropological interests without sacrificing their own rights. Several contentious issues remain. What should be done with the remains of prehistoric Native Americans who have no known living descendants or cultural groups? Should the religious beliefs of one group of Native Americans stand for the rights of all groups? Should modern Native American communities have rights to rebury any human remains found on their lands? What should happen to the remains of the very earliest settlers in North America who are unlikely to be biologically related to modern tribes?

One recent incident arose in 1996 when a prehistoric skeleton was found along the banks of the Columbia River near Kennewick, Washington. Kennewick Man, as this individual has been called, appears to have lived 9,000 years ago and has been the center of an intense academic, political, and legal debate.

At first the bones were thought to be a white settler's, but carbon-14 dating suggests a much earlier date, which has ruled out ancestry from some early-nineteenth-century settler. When forensic anthropologist James Chatters examined the bones he concluded that the bones were Caucasoid rather than Native American. If true, such a finding would require a revision of North American prehistory. Although archaeologists wanted to examine these bones more carefully, local Native American groups claimed the right to rebury this individual, and the courts have generally supported their motions. These legal wranglings have led some archaeologists to complain that the Native Americans simply want to rebury the evidence that Europeans may have reached the New World at some early prehistoric period and may have predated the arrival of Native American groups coming from Asia. Evidence that Kennewick Man is Caucasoid is slim at best, but without examination by physical anthropologists we will never know.

For a discussion of the Kennewick Man debate, see David Hurst Thomas's recent *Skull Wars: Kennewick Man, Archeology, and the Battle for Native American Identity* (Basic Books, 2000). Other sources on this controversy include Douglas Preston's "The Lost Man: Umatilla Indians' Plan to Rebury 9,300 Year Old Kennewick Man With Caucasoid Features," *The New Yorker* (June 16, 1997) and two articles in *Archaeology*, "A Battle Over Bones: Ancestry of Kennewick Man" (January/February 1997) and "Kennewick Update: Nondestructive Lab Tests on Controversial Skeleton to Begin" (November/December 1998).

For an excellent summary of anthropological interest in Native American remains, see Robert Bieder's *A Brief Historical Survey of the Expropriation of American Indian Remains* (Native American Rights Fund, 1990). J. C. Rose, T. J. Green, and V. D. Green's "NAGPRA Is Forever: Osteology and the Repatriation of Skeletons," *Annual Review of Anthropology* (vol. 25, 1996) provides a useful summary of NAGPRA.

Riding In has also explored the issue of repatriation and the imperialist nature of archaeology in "Without Ethics and Morality: A Historical Overview of Imperial Archaeology and American Indians," *Arizona State Law Journal* (vol. 24, Spring 1992).

Several essays in Karen D. Vitelli, ed., *Archaeological Ethics* (Altamira Press, 1996) are relevant to this debate. For an example of a more moderate approach that urges compromise, see Lynne Goldstein and Keith Kintigh's "Ethics and the Reburial Controversy," *American Antiquity* (vol. 55, 1990).

ISSUE 16

Should Anthropologists Work to Eliminate the Practice of Female Circumcision?

YES: Merrilee H. Salmon, from "Ethical Considerations in Anthropology and Archaeology, or Relativism and Justice for All," *Journal of Anthropological Research* (Spring 1997)

NO: Elliott P. Skinner, from "Female Circumcision in Africa: The Dialectics of Equality," in Richard R. Randolph, David M. Schneider, and May N. Diaz, eds., *Dialectics and Gender: Anthropological Approaches* (Westview Press, 1988)

ISSUE SUMMARY

YES: Professor of the history and philosophy of science Merrilee H. Salmon argues that clitoridectomy (female genital mutilation) violates the rights of the women on whom it is performed. She asserts that this operation is a way for men to control women and keep them unequal.

NO: Professor of anthropology Elliott P. Skinner accuses feminists who want to abolish clitoridectomy of being ethnocentric. He states that African women themselves want to participate in the practice, which functions like male initiation, transforming girls into adult women.

For more than a century anthropologists have seen cultural relativism as an essential antidote to ethnocentrism, a perspective that evaluates and judges the practices of other peoples according to the standards and sensitivities of one's own culture. This issue raises questions about the boundaries and limits of the anthropologist's cultural relativism. By evaluating cultural practices in a culture's own terms, anthropologists have long defended cultural diversity and the general principle that dominant cultures should not force members of weaker cultures to abandon traditional customs and practices, simply because practices appear peculiar, bizarre, or wrong to those in power. But today the world is increasingly integrated, and a number of international organizations have emerged whose purpose is to defend a single universal vision of human rights. Few anthropologists would object in principle to the notion that human rights should be defended for all people, but universal moral codes also challenge the rights of cultural groups to be different.

In this issue two scholars debate whether or not anthropologists should interfere with the cultural practice, found in many parts of Africa and the Middle East, of clitoridectomy and infibulation, variously called female circumcision or female genital mutilation. The practice is typically part of female initiation ceremonies and takes different forms in different ethnic groups, varying from relatively minor surgery to the clitoris (clitoridectomy) to the complete surgical removal of the clitoris and much of the woman's external sexual organs, after which the vagina is sewn up, leaving only a small opening (infibulation).

Merrilee H. Salmon refers to this practice as female genital mutilation and argues that it is fundamentally wrong, a violation of a woman's human rights. She contends that the practice is part of a male-centered power structure, which allows men to control women. Although Salmon acknowledges that women often control the ritual and even the surgery, the practice of female circumcision nevertheless supports male dominance within the community. In her view this cultural practice is an immoral one, and anthropological calls for moral relativism in this case are fundamentally ill-founded.

Elliott P. Skinner counters that female circumcision is only found in African societies where male circumcision is also practiced. Both practices involve mutilation of the genitals and are the means of transforming male and female children into adult men and women, respectively. Skinner maintains that not only are the female rituals entirely in the hands of other women, but that the practices empower women within a society where men might otherwise dominate them. Feminists who argue that this practice is an example of male power over women, in his view, have got it wrong. Calls for the abolition of female circumcision began with Western missionaries who found the practice repugnant. He states that Africans supported female circumcision as a form of resistance to white domination, and in Skinner's view current calls from Western people for the abolition of this practice is another example of Western domination of African societies.

At issue here are several key questions: Is female circumcision morally repugnant? Should anthropologists defend it or work to stop it? How should anthropologists deal with such practices when they see them occurring in their village communities where they work?

Although this issue seems very narrowly focused on a particular traditional custom in only one part of the world, it has important general implications for cultural relativism and universal human rights. Should anthropologists defend cultural practices simply because they are traditional? Do anthropologists have a responsibility to help end practices that they find morally abhorrent? If so, whose moral notions should be followed? Is moral relativism fundamentally flawed, as Salmon asserts?

Merrilee H. Salmon

 **YES**

Ethical Considerations in Anthropology and Archaeology, or Relativism and Justice for All

Cultural Relativism and Ethical Relativism

Respect for the beliefs, practices, and values of other cultures, no matter how different from one's own, is a hallmark of anthropological wisdom. Franz Boas, the father of American academic anthropology, rejected invidious comparisons between European "high culture" and indigenous American languages, myths, art forms, and religions. Boas, dismissing absolute scales of cultural development such as those proposed by Condorcet and L. H. Morgan, insisted on studying the culture of each group in the context of its own historical development. Boas's work forms the historical basis for the anthropological doctrine known as *cultural relativism*.

Many anthropologists regard *ethical relativism* as an easy corollary of cultural relativism. I show that this view is incorrect. Cultural relativism does not entail ethical relativism; an anthropologist can consistently embrace cultural relativism while rejecting ethical relativism. As most anthropologists understand it, ethical relativism identifies the concepts of good and evil, or right and wrong, with what a particular culture approves or disapproves. Because ethical standards arise within particular cultures and vary from culture to culture, ethical relativists deny any extracultural standard of moral judgments. According to them, moral judgments of good or bad are possible only within a given culture, because such judgments refer only to compliance or noncompliance with that culture's norms.

The fact that a belief arises within a cultural context, however, does not imply that it can have no other basis. Although moral beliefs, like all other beliefs, arise within a given cultural setting, some of those beliefs may transcend the cultures in which they arise. Condemnation of murder and recognition of obligations to help others who are in extreme need, for example, are common to many cultures. Moreover, societies that differ in derivative moral judgments about marriage between close relatives frequently agree about more fundamental moral judgments, such as the immorality of incest. This modicum of moral

From Merrilee H. Salmon, "Ethical Considerations in Anthropology and Archaeology, or Relativism and Justice for All," *Journal of Anthropological Research*, vol. 53, no. 1 (Spring 1997). Copyright © 1997 by The University of New Mexico. Reprinted by permission of the publisher and the author. Notes and some references omitted.

consensus has encouraged some critics to try to refute ethical relativism by identifying a set of universally acceptable moral principles.

Whether universal agreement exists on any specific basic moral judgment is partly an empirical matter and partly dependent on how such terms as "murder," "cruelty," and "incest" are defined. Colin Turnbull's (1962) admittedly controversial studies suggest that the Ik do not embrace the most likely candidates for fundamental moral principles, on any reasonable definition of such principles. In Turnbull's account, the Ik provide a striking counterexample to general views that cruelty to children, for example, is universally condemned. Even if Turnbull's account is rejected, the search for moral principles that are both reasonably specific and universally acceptable is problematic.

The lack of agreement about principles, however, is not sufficient to demonstrate the truth of ethical relativism. What a culture regards as right or wrong conduct depends to some degree on both the members' factual beliefs about the state of the world and their beliefs about the likely consequences of their conduct. The absence of any universally accepted standards would support ethical relativism only if cultures that shared all the same factual beliefs and agreed about the consequences of particular behavior nevertheless disagreed in their ethical judgments. This situation has not been demonstrated. In fact, many apparent differences in ethical matters are resolved by bringing forth pertinent facts about the conditions under which moral choices are made. Even Turnbull (1962) goes to considerable trouble to show that severe hardship and deprivation of material resources in Ik society have altered their perceptions of reality. Whereas lack of universally accepted moral principles does not prove ethical relativism, however, neither would the universal acceptance of some specific moral principles disprove ethical relativism. The agreement could be accidental instead of arising from some feature of the human condition. Berlin and Kay's (1969) refutation of the relativism of color classification was convincing only because they were able to demonstrate the physiological—and thus cross-cultural—basis for color classification.

Ethical relativism apparently accords with anthropologists' determination to reject ethnocentrism and maintain a nonjudgmental stance towards alien cultural practices. Nevertheless, both anthropologists and philosophers have noted a serious problem with relativistic ethics: it seems to rule out condemning even such obviously immoral acts as genocide so long as they do not conflict with prevailing cultural norms. Ethical theories about what constitutes right and wrong behavior are severely tested when they go against our deepest moral intuition in this manner; in such cases one naturally questions the theory rather than giving up the intuition. H. Russell Bernard (1988:117), for example, says that

> cultural and ethical relativism is an excellent antidote for overdeveloped ethnocentrism. But cultural relativism is a poor philosophy to live by, or on which to make judgments about whether to participate in particular research projects. Can you imagine any anthropologist today defending the human rights violations of Nazi Germany as just another expression of the richness of culture?

Bernard's use of "is" in the first sentence shows that he does not distinguish cultural from ethical relativism. If he had done so, his point would be less confusing. *Cultural* relativism, in Boas's sense of trying to understand and evaluate the practices of other cultures in their own historical context, is a good antidote for ethnocentrism. Identifying the practices of any culture as the ultimate moral standard for that culture, however, is a different matter and rightly raises problems for a reflective anthropologist. Bernard in mentioning Nazi Germany has offered the standard counterexample to the claim that morality recognizes no extracultural authority.

Despite its fatal flaw, however, ethical relativism still enjoys wide acceptance among practicing anthropologists. Ethical relativism, for example, played a role in testimony by a French ethnologist in the trial of Bintou Fofana Diarra for complicity in the genital mutilation of her infant daughter. As reported in the *New York Times* (Weil-Curiel 1993), the unnamed ethnologist testified that "Africans should not be punished [for genital mutilation of infant girls] because they act under social pressure." The principle implicit in this statement—that one should not be punished for acts done under social pressure—is uncomfortably similar to the defense offered by Nazi war criminals.

A second problem with making cultural standards the final arbiter of morality is that this practice presumes a uniformity in cultures that current research denies, even for small, isolated, and tightly knit societies, or it gives a privileged moral position to powerful subgroups within the society. In the latter case, for example, the power to set cultural norms may belong to a minority whose control of valuable resources enables it to force others to follow its standards. Conversely, the power to set norms may accrue to those who are members of the majority, while significant minorities have no voice. In either case, one can only refer to the norms of "the culture" by ignoring ethical disagreement within the culture.

Some anthropologists believe that relativism is the only ethical stance that is compatible with a scientific investigation of other cultures. A scientific anthropologist presumably formulates "neutral" descriptions of the culture, reporting such quantifiable information as the frequency of occurrence of behaviors and perhaps the observed attitudes (approval, disapproval) of members of the society, while refraining from judging the culture or interfering with it in any way. Whether such detachment is required to maintain scientific integrity and whether such detachment is even possible are points raised by D'Andrade (1995) and Scheper-Hughes (1995). D'Andrade (1995:399) points to the alleged subjectivity of ethical judgments and contrasts these with the objectivity of scientific judgments. Scheper-Hughes (1995), however, objects to a scientific detachment that would prevent anthropologists from taking an active role in alleviating suffering among their research subjects. This debate is somewhat at cross-purposes because D'Andrade's main concern seems to be with an epistemic relativism that claims that such notions as knowledge and truth have no extracultural basis.... Scheper-Hughes, in contrast, is worried about the behavioral implications of a relativist ethics that takes the existing social arrangements in a culture as the ultimate moral authority.

The strict separation of science and values, a cherished principle of logical positivism, is increasingly difficult to defend in the face of ethical problems raised by scientific advances in many fields. In particular, current biomedical techniques for genetic engineering and research on human embryos raise important problems that tend to blur lines between scientific and value judgments. Bernard (1988) notes that when resources are limited, the very choice of anthropological research topics is value laden. The possibility of an ethically neutral or completely value-free science of human behavior now seems to many scientists both unattainable and undesirable, but recognition of the interrelationships between science and values need not prevent the limited type of objectivity that D'Andrade argues is possible for anthropological research.

Anthropologists may continue to avow ethical relativism despite its difficulties because they have not articulated an alternative ethical theory that is consistent with their distaste for ethnocentrism and their respect for cultural diversity. Nevertheless, maintaining a consistent form of ethical relativism is highly problematic in the present research climate. Facing the loss of valuable anthropological and archaeological resources, anthropologists have reexamined traditional relationships with their subjects, their colleagues, and the general public. To resolve problems and achieve clarity, they are currently debating and revising professional ethical standards. Despite the traditional commitment of anthropologists to relativism, the ethical principles that underlie their professional codes are not relativistic. The codes refer to their duties and responsibilities, and—by implication at least—to the corresponding rights of their research subjects, colleagues, and the general public. The conflict, often unacknowledged, between the avowed relativism of anthropologists and their sincere concern with justice and rights can lead to confusion and ineffectiveness in achieving the important goals of preserving anthropological resources and protecting cultural minorities. . . .

An Anthropological Example—Female Genital Mutilation

The arguments of feminist anthropologists for altering discriminatory practices of other cultures similarly compromise a commitment to ethical relativism. In some cultures, all females are subjected to genital mutilation. In its severe form, this involves cutting away most or all of the external sex organs (euphemistically called "circumcision") and sewing or sealing (infibulating) the vagina so as to leave only a pinhole opening for urination and menstruation. The practice affects an estimated ninety-five million or more women in at least twenty-five countries, mostly, but not all, in Africa (Lightfoot-Klein 1989). Within the cultures that practice genital mutilation, little disagreement exists about its value, though different groups offer various justifications for the practice. Most, but not all, of the countries that engage in the practice are predominantly Muslim, but it is absent in many other Muslim countries. The operation typically is performed on girls from six to nine years old but also on younger girls and infants. Sometimes when a bride is an "outsider," she is infibulated just before she marries into a group that follows the custom.

Anthropologists have attempted to document, understand, and explain this practice, which, aside from its harshness, strikes most Westerners as extremely bizarre. Why do they do it? What possible benefit do they see from it? How could it be so widespread? In contrast to most accounts in the contemporary press which dismiss the practice simply as a way of oppressing women, anthropologists' explanations are appropriately complex. They refer to the cult of virginity, the cultural association between female purity and the society's honor, and the antiquity of the tradition—Herodotus, writing in the fifth century B.C., obliquely refers to its practice in Egypt, and some mummies show evidence of infibulation. Anthropologists also cite the symbolic role female circumcision plays in distinguishing the Arab-Muslim African societies that practice it from their culturally distinct neighbors.

In places such as the Sudan, where the practice is nearly universal, anthropologists discuss genital mutilation in the context of social practices that involve other forms of mutilation practiced upon both males and females, such as tribal scarring of the face and piercing of body parts. Anthropologists also emphasize the cultural value of enduring pain without complaint. Economic explanations are also proposed. Midwives who perform the operations are sustained by the fees not only from the original circumcision and infibulation but also from treatment of the inevitable medical problems that result. Other explanations are psychological, such as those that refer to the attitudes of older women who say that they have gone through the experience and therefore do not see why the younger ones should be spared.

Besides offering their own historical and cultural explanations, anthropologists report the explanations of the people who engage in the practice. These include such claims as we have always done it, our religion requires it, no one will marry an uncircumcised woman, it makes us clean, it makes us more beautiful, it improves health, it limits the sex drive, it is good for fertility, and—referring to reinfibulation after childbirth—it deters a husband from seeking additional wives.

Some—relatively few—women and men in such societies do question the practice or its supposed benefits, particularly if they have been exposed to modern Western culture. But when asked why they nevertheless have their daughters circumcised, they refer to tradition, or say that their female relatives insisted, or insist that no one would marry the girl unless she were circumcised. Most explanations of female genital mutilation come from women, since few men can be persuaded to discuss the issue, claiming for the most part that it is women's business. Jomo Kenyatta, the revered former leader of Kenya and member of the Kikuyu tribe, who earned a Ph.D. in anthropology under [Bronislaw] Malinowski, however, said, "No proper Kikuyu would dream of marrying a girl who has not been circumcised" (Kenyatta 1938, quoted in Lightfoot-Klein 1989:71).

Women in cultures that practice genital mutilation claim that it is done for the benefit of the men, but women alone are responsible for arranging and performing the operations. Even the question of the acceptability of bridal candidates is largely under control of the women since arranged marriages are the rule, with the groom's mother having a prominent voice. (Recently a young woman from Togo sought and was granted asylum in the United States to avoid genital mutilation. The woman became endangered, however, only after her father had died. Her guardianship then passed to her aunt, who attempted to commit the woman to an arranged marriage.) Thus the practice is unusual inasmuch as it is intended to control women, it affects them almost universally, and they suffer the greatest harm from it; but they manage and control it almost exclusively.

The presence in European cities of sizable African communities that maintain the practice—despite local laws that prohibit it—has brought female genital mutilation to the attention both of the courts and of feminists who see it as "butchery intended to control women" (Weil-Curiel 1993). Anthropologists who claim to be relativists face the ethical dilemma of whether their responsibility ends with describing the practice and placing it in a cultural context, whether they are obligated to protect the practice from outside interference, or whether they should help to end the practice. Relativism might suggest that they have a further responsibility to protect, or at least not interfere with, this culturally sanctioned practice. At the same time, as relativists, they must also consider their responsibility to cooperate with members of their own culture who are trying to end the practice on the grounds that human rights are being violated.

Although relativistic anthropologists are reluctant to try to alter the values of other cultures, many think it appropriate to try to correct mistaken factual beliefs when this would benefit the welfare of members of the culture. Value judgments that are based on mistaken factual beliefs may be revised without undermining the values themselves. Clearly some beliefs of cultures that practice genital mutilation are factually mistaken. Contrary to those who say the practice is beneficial to sanitation or health, mutilation causes severe medical damage in many cases. The operation can cause immediate infection, excessive bleeding, and even death. Delayed common effects of the operation are infections of the urinary tract, menstrual problems, painful intercourse, reduction in fertility, and complications in childbirth. Nor does the Muslim religion command infibulation, as some believe. The practice does not guarantee virginity, since reinfibulation, which simulates the virginal state, is widely practiced. Because sex drive is more a matter of endocrinology than external organs, the claim that infibulation limits sex drive is likewise questionable.

Insofar as genital mutilation is motivated by sanitary or medical considerations, therefore, knowledge of the facts would tend to undermine the practice without reducing the cultural commitment to the values of purity, fertility, or health. Insofar as genital mutilation is motivated by other factors, such as maintenance of cultural distinctiveness and increasing the ability to endure pain, its medical harm could be alleviated by practicing less severe forms of circumcision without infibulation and by performing the operation only in a sterile clinical setting.

Such a medical solution, while it would save lives and preserve health, does not address the ethical question, raised by feminists, of the right to control one's body and whether or to what extent this right is inalienable. Since genital mutilation is usually performed on children, an important issue is whether parents have the right to harm the child in this way. Parents and guardians cannot violate *inalienable* rights of their children even for some supposed benefit.

Parents may, however, subject children to some kinds of discipline, as well as to dangerous and sometimes painful medical treatment, when it is for the good of the child. Erroneous views about the supposed benefits of genital mutilation, of course, cannot justify harming the child.

Unlike mistaken claims about the medical benefits of mutilation, other claims are apparently correct. Marriage within the culture *as things now stand* may not be an option for an uncircumcised woman. Moreover, for females in that culture, marriage is a prerequisite for obtaining any other rights. So being able to marry is a clear benefit and may outweigh the harm of circumcision from the point of view of the girl. (According to principles of justice, the benefit that justifies a harm must accrue to the individual who undergoes the harm, not merely to her extended family. Thus, loss of a bride price for the family would not, without further argument, justify the harm to the child.) Feminist anthropologists, as well as others who are concerned with human rights, want to take both educational and legal means to end the practice of genital mutilation. Their attitude, however, is not consistent with a commitment to ethical relativism....

Individual Rights and the Common Good

... In looking at the question of genital mutilation, the following pertinent questions arise. How fundamental is the right not to have one's body altered? At what age does the girl have the right to decide for herself whether to undergo a mutilation? Young girls in the Sudan who are not circumcised by their eighth year usually ask to have it done. Should we disregard these requests because the children are mere dupes of the culture? If they are, can they ever reach an age of consent? Many Western cultures practice ear piercing on infant girls, and many others accede to the wishes of six or eight year olds to have their ears pierced. Circumcision of male infants is common. Bodily mutilations are as much a part of cultural identity for some cultures as distinctive styles of clothing. Some mutilations we regard as attractive, some as beneficial to health, some as harmless, some as aesthetically offensive, others as brutal. Severe genital mutilation surely falls into the brutal category. Moreover, its rationale is empirically flawed, and because its harms disproportionately affect females, it raises serious questions about violating rights. In cases such as this, anthropological understanding of the practice can legitimately be used to aid attempts to eradicate or modify it for the benefit of the members of the culture where it is practiced. Those who disagree should at least argue for the practice on stronger grounds than the value of cultural diversity....

Anthropologists who work in cultures that withhold fundamental human rights from women, children, or any other subgroup face difficult choices about taking any *action* to restore rights. Some anthropologists would say that their decision to work in such cultures obligates them to alleviate the problem. Others hold that their role as anthropologists is to observe cultural phenomena and record and analyze them as accurately as possible, but not to try to alter conditions. In either case, the anthropologist has a minimal obligation to report the observed and analyzed state of affairs in normal anthropological outlets for publication. Anthropologists do not betray secrets or violate confidences when they describe a custom that is almost universally practiced in the culture. By calling attention to an unjust practice, however, anthropologists at least implicitly invite groups devoted to the protection of rights to take action. By presenting the offensive practice in its full cultural context, which may involve revealing its latent functions in addition to its manifest or stated functions, anthropologists also provide valuable information about how to control or prevent the practice.

After the anthropologist acts to present information in an appropriate way to a suitable audience, his or her responsibility to try to alleviate the injustice seems to me neither greater nor less than that of any person who is in a position to help the victims of an unjust practice. Even if no further action is taken, I think that the anthropologist who refuses to recognize that the value of cultural diversity is morally subordinate to that of protecting rights is on shaky moral ground. The anthropologist who retreats into ethical relativism in such situations, as did the ethnologist at the trial of Bintou Fofana Diana, does not demonstrate tolerance by appealing to social pressures in another culture but instead risks being committed to the same morally untenable position as the "Nazi defense."

Conclusion

I have reiterated some criticisms of ethical relativism, a position which once seemed to offer anthropologists a way to profess tolerance and avoid criticizing the morality of some practices of other cultures. My arguments try to show not so much that ethical relativism is "false" but that its consequences conflict with our deepest held moral intuitions and that it cannot be held consistently while embracing those intuitions. I have tried to show also that anthropologists need not forego tolerance if they abandon relativism in favor of a morality based on principles of justice and fairness. The concern with justice that guides anthropologists' codes of professional conduct can provide the starting point for a more sophisticated analysis of rights, which can be used to analyze cultural practices. (The philosophical literature on rights is vast, but a useful entry for anthropologists is available in Baker 1994.) Ethical judgments of another culture's practices, especially when based on deep understanding of their life, customs, and tradition, are indicative neither of ethnocentrism nor of intolerance. Instead, they show respect for the basic anthroplogical belief in "the psychic unity of humans" and a commitment to justice and fairness for all.

References

Baker, J., ed., 1994, Group Rights, Toronto: University of Toronto Press.
Berlin, B., and P. Kay, 1969, Basic Color Terms: Their Universality and Evolution. Berkeley and Los Angeles: University of California Press.
Bernard, H. R., 1998, Research Methods in Cultural Anthropology. Newbury Park, N.J.: Sage Publications.
D'Andrade, R., 1995, Moral Models in Anthropology. Current Anthropology 36(3):399–408.

Kenyatta, J., 1938, Facing Mount Kenya. London: Secker and Warburg.

Lightfoot-Klein, H., 1989, Prisoners of Ritual: An Odyssey into Female Genital Circumcision in Africa. Binghampton, N.Y.: Haworth Press.

Scheper-Hughes, N., 1995, The Primacy of the Ethical. Current Anthropology 36(3):409–20.

Turnbull, C., 1962, The Forest People. New York: Simon and Schuster.

Weil-Curiel, L., 1993, Mutilation of Girls' Genitals: Ethnic Gulf in French Court. New York Times, November 23.

NO

Elliott P. Skinner

Female Circumcision in Africa:
The Dialectics of Equality

Culture and society must, of course, always take account of human biology, but they do so in complex ways. The distinctive characteristics of culture is that it transcends nature; but this does not mean that it has left it behind—rather, it has turned it upside down.

— Robert F. Murphy (1977)

Female circumcision or clitoridectomy, called by the Mossi, the *Bongo*, is [a] not too subtle mechanism of Mossi women to challenge the superiority of men. This was the thought that flashed through my mind, as I watched with amazement, the quiet pride of the women and girls performing the rituals of the graduation ceremonies of their own Bongo. Here were women doing things that they usually never did, and more importantly, should not have been doing. They had procured the drums from men and, much to my surprise and their amusement, were beating them. Where had they learned? Oh yes! They must have practiced these rhythms while pounding millet and sorghum in their mortars. Inexplicable was the source of their knowledge of the songs and dances of the Bongo which were allegedly the sole province of males, but which they performed equally well. True, I had learned both the dances and songs of the Bongo during my numerous visits to the circumcision lodge, but these female graduates did them better than I ever did. Surely some Delilah had tricked a Samson who had then revealed the secrets of arrogant men. During the Bongo ceremony, Mossi women were showing to the men publicly, that they knew male secrets, and moreover, these were not important after all. . . .

The subject of male circumcision and female clitoridectomy and infibulation in African societies has been the source of great speculation and controversy, primarily because it involves the "fundamental ontological differences between the sexes—conditions of simple *being*—based in the first instance on anatomical distinctions" and what flows from these. Questions raised have been: 1. Are these operations cruel? 2. Do they have anything to do with sex? 3. Do they reveal anything about the relative merits of various cultures' sexual sensibilities? and 4. Do male and female versions of the operations differ with

From Elliott P. Skinner, "Female Circumcision in Africa: The Dialectics of Equality," in Richard R. Randolph, David M. Schneider, and May N. Diaz, eds., *Dialectics and Gender: Anthropological Approaches* (Westview Press, 1988). Copyright © 1988 by Westview Press, Inc. Reprinted by permission of the author. Notes and some references omitted.

regard to the answers to questions 1 and 2? Some anthropologists and some non-anthropologists have already strong views on these questions.

Fran P. Hosken discussing "Genital Mutilation in Africa," severely criticized those "Anthropologists (mostly men) who have studied African traditions have done no service to women by utterly disregarding women's health while they attribute 'cultural values' to such damaging traditions as excision and infibulation." Considering these practices "deleterious to health and indeed dangerous," Hosken lamented that many African groups "subject their female children to genital mutilation for a multitude of 'reasons,' many of which conflict and all of which are based on total ignorance concerning reproduction." She wondered aloud whether it was really in the interest of such populations "that such damaging myths are perpetuated under the cloak of silence and are praised as 'culture' in the literature? I think not. The time has come to face the facts." (Hoskin 1976:6) Hosken is tired of, and angry about those "explanations" of men and of what she calls "brain-washed women" who attribute clitoridectomy "to the fear of female sexuality," and the need to "prevent adultery." (*Ibid.*)

Simon D. Messing, an applied anthropologist, feels that he and his colleagues "cannot evade the issue of such a serious and widespread problem as genital mutilation of females, if they are concerned with public health... they should not leave the burden of this task entirely on the shoulders of radical feminists—and the latter in turn should welcome our cooperation." (Messing 1980:296)

Neither the radical feminists nor the anthropologists have considered the possibility that in the frequent dialectics that we find in social life, female circumcision might well be one of the numerous ways in which women challenge the vaunted superiority of men....

Given the contemporary controversy surrounding "female" circumcision (really an interesting misnomer), it is generally ignored that circumcision is predominantly a "male" ritual. Many well-known ancient peoples, such as the Hebrews (who probably adopted this ritual in ancient Egypt as they borrowed other interesting aspects of that culture) limited circumcision to males. The same thing is true for many African populations. As far as I can ascertain, there is not a single African society in which female circumcision exists without its male counterpart. The reasons for this are as intriguing as they are germane to this article....

Initiation ceremonies preparatory to marriage, sexual relations, and the creation of families, are widespread in African societies, but are not necessarily linked to either circumcision or clitoridectomy.... Characteristic of this *rite de passage* is the customary withdrawal of the initiates from the world of people; their education into the knowledge and lore of their societies; and their subjection to a great deal of physical pain and other hardships....

The Mossi initiated and subjected their pre-pubescent youth to both circumcision and clitoridectomy. In the Manga-Nobere districts of Burkina Faso (formerly Upper Volta) in southern Mossi country, every three or four years, during December, the coldest part of the year, and depending upon the food supply, the Mossi opened the "Bongo" or the initiation ceremony for boys, in a secluded area in the woods. Here were gathered about twenty to thirty boys, age seven or eight to twelve years old, from the surrounding villages and their helpers. Known as Bankousse, these youths built a camp called the *Keogo,* placing barriers on the paths leading to it so as to warn off uncircumcised children and women. The mothers of the boys brought food daily to the barrier, but did not cross it.

The Mossi considered circumcision to be a simple surgical act which was only incidental to the Bongo—a veritable initiation to life involving a great many hardships. Almost immediately after arriving at the Keogo the boys were circumcised by the head of the camp, known as the *Nane* who used a sharp razor for the operation. As in other parts of Africa, the initiates were not expected to cry, and their wounds were cared for by the Nane. Then came the important post operation period called *komtogo* or "bitter water" by the Bankousse because of the pain involved. Despite the cold nights, they had use of only a small fire and were not permitted to use any covers. Every morning they were forced to bathe in a cold pool, and when they returned, they had lessons to learn involving history, nature study, and life.

The Bongo had its own mystery language whose words turned out on analysis to be synonyms for ordinary More (the language of the Mossi) with the prefix "na." The camp had its own rules on which rank was based, not on those on the outside, but on the order in which the youths were circumcised. What the Nane attempted to do was to forge a link between the boys in opposition to himself, who acted like a veritable ogre. Walking about the camp with a long stick, he whipped the youngsters into line, threw sand in the food brought by the women, and made the Bankousse dance and sing until they were exhausted.

Graduation ceremonies of the Bongo involved going into the woods, cutting grass for the horses of the chiefs, and wood for their fires. Then on the appointed day, the mothers brought new clothes for their sons, hoping that none of them had died during the ordeal of the Bongo. Then on the appointed day the graduates dressed in their new clothing marched through the market place, and visited the chief. Then they engaged in dancing and singing at a public place just outside the market place.

As usual in almost all parts of Africa, the Mossi women were in complete charge of their Bongo from which they excluded all men. Their *Keogo* was not in the woods, but was in the compound of a woman who lived by herself. But as usual for males, I could find out nothing about the nature of the excision that took place. I did hear the drumming and singing that took place there all night until the wee hours of the morning, and did observe the young girls going backward and forward to their homes. Invariably they carried a tufted staff, said to have been given to them by their prospective husbands. The women would say nothing about the symbolism involved, considering the information specific to women alone. The most that they would say about what went on in the female Bongo was that the males have their secrets and so did the women.

Like the graduation exercises of the male Bankousse, the female ritual was a village-wide affair, but strictly within the province of the women. Market days before, the relatives and prospective husbands of the graduates, shopped for the clothes and headties, and makeup for them. Then on the day of the exercise, the young girls went to the home of the female Nane and accompanied by their mothers and sisters who were beating drums and singing, went to the village square where the Bankousse danced and sang the traditional airs of the Bongo. From time to time, male relatives and husbands would detach themselves from the line of spectators and approach the dancers, giving them presents of money. To all intents and purposes, the female Bongo was structurally and functionally quite similar to that of the males. This ceremony demonstrated to all that the Mossi women were just as capable as the men in performing an initiation ceremony whose function was to transform girls into women, as the male version transformed boys into men. Moreover, they had more effectively kept men from knowing their secrets than did the males, whose secrets they had obviously shared. . . .

What is important about the puberty rituals in African societies, whether they involved painful initiation, and whether they involved genital mutilation with recognizable pain, are the emic and etic features involved. The Africans do have their own views of their rituals even though others have ignored these views and insist upon their own interpretations. This is perhaps par for human beings involving as it does relative power. There is no doubt that had they the requisite power, Africans would insist that the world accept their interpretation of their own rituals, as well as their views of the rituals of others. Anthropologists would do well to keep this in mind.

The Mossi are not much given to speculating on the imponderables of social life, or the world in general, judging such ratiocinations quixotic. To them the Bongo for men and for women have the same meaning and serve the same function for both men and women: preparation for marriage and rearing families. Indicative of this equality is that the two genders control their own initiation rituals, even though women have to borrow drums from the males. When badgered about the sexual features involved in genital mutilation, an admittedly chauvinist Mossi male might suggest that since females are inferior to males they are not permitted to touch the male organ during sexual congress, and that clitoridectomy makes sexual congress easier. This may be as good a rationalization as any other, but flies in the face of the anxiety of Mossi men over the conduct of their wives, and their stated axiom: "Women are so important that if a man receives as a wife, either a blind woman or a leper, he should close his eyes, close his mouth, and close his ears, and keep her."

The equally male chauvinist Dogon explicitly associate both circumcision and clitoridectomy with elaborate myths concerning creation and cosmology. Both operations are said to have been instituted as punishments and are indicative of the incomplete state of human beings resulting from the primordial crime of a godling. There is the removal of the opposite sex complement with which all human beings were originally intended to be equipped. Thus for the Dogon there is complementarity in the operation. Mary Daly criticizes the Dogon for what she considered an emic patriarchal obfuscation of the true purposes of the operation, namely the intimidation and humiliation of women. What she conveniently ignores is the fact that the Dogon forbid men to have intercourse with their wives against their will and that the sexual responses of wives are in large part conditioned by the treatment they generally receive from their husbands (Daly 1978).

Somewhat like the Dogon, both the Egyptians and the Northern Sudanese stress the complementarity of circumcision and clitoridectomy. Referring specifically to the Sudanese, [Janice] Boddy asserted that

> Through their own operation, performed at roughly the same age as when girls are circumcised (sic) (between five and ten years), boys become less like women: while the female reproductive organs are covered, that of the male is uncovered, or, as one Sudanese author states, of a child's sex ... by removing physical characteristics deemed appropriate to his or her opposite: the clitoris and other external genitalia, in the case of females, the prepuce of the penis, in the case of males. This last is emphasized by a custom now lapsed in Hofriyat wherein one of the newly circumcised boys' grandmothers would wear his foreskin as a ring on the day of the operation (Boddy 1982:687–8).

Paying special attention to the widespread African emic notion of complementarity in the rituals of circumcision and clitoridectomy, Boddy insists that

> By removing their external genitalia, women are not so much preventing their own sexual pleasure (though obviously this is an effect) as enhancing their femininity. Circumcision as a symbolic act brings sharply into focus the fertility potential of women by dramatically de-emphasizing their inherent sexuality. By insisting on circumcision for their daughters, women assert their social indispensibility, an importance that is not as the sexual partners of their husbands, nor in this highly segregated, male-authoritative society, as their servants, sexual or otherwise, but as the mothers of men. *The ultimate social goal of a woman is to become, with her husband, the cofounder of a lineage section. As a respected haboba she is "listened to," she may be sent on the* hadj *(pilgrimage to Mecca) by her husbands or her sons, and her name is remembered in village genealogies for several generations* (italics supplied) (*Ibid.*:687).

Although Boddy had her own etic views of female genital mutilation among the Sudanese, her ethnographic data support the etic argument of this paper, namely that in this instance of the dialectics of social life, clitoridectomy rather than a ritual performed by women, to demean their already low status in many African societies, is a declaration of equality. What is interesting is that there are few, if any, cases in the ethnographic record where African women (as contrasted to the normally sexist African men) see this ritual as reducing their status. Feminists may consider the African women who defend this practice as "brain-washed," but should be aware that many African women, as well as men, take the same jaundiced view of many rituals of Western Christendom. True, some contemporary African women object to clitoridectomy, but few had dared to confront their mothers and grandmothers over the issue for fear of being taken for "black" white women. The implication here is that these women have failed to assert that cultural equality for which Africans have fought long and hard.

What is important about the controversy about clitoridectomy in Africa is that African women were never part of it. The issue grew out of a Judeo-Christian concern over human sexuality, involved Christian missionaries in Africa, and was used by African men in their struggle for cultural autonomy from Europeans, and ultimately for political independence....

Missionary opposition to clitoridectomy among the Kikuyu was very much linked to their opposition to all aspects of African culture that could frustrate their attempts to impose Western Christendom. We are told that

> The missionaries recognized the significance of the initiatory rites, of which circumcision was the outward physical symbol, and they were appalled at what they saw in them. The physical operation they considered brutal and unhygenic and in the case of girls a barbaric mutilation with permanent ill-effects. *But the atmosphere in which the ceremonies were carried out seemed to them even more evil, with what they took to be the sexual innuendo of the dances and songs, the licentiousness of the old men and women and the gloating cruelty of the operators and their attendants. They taught against the practices and prayed that the people might forego them altogether* (Italics added) (Murray–Brown 1972:50–51).

... What had started out as an issue over clitoridectomy, and a practice which many African Christians were prepared to change, became a cause célèbre over the issue of African cultural and political freedom. Much to the alarm of the colonial government, it became known locally in October 1919 that "John [Jomo] Kenyatta" who had gone to Britain to protest settler colonialism, had been to Moscow and was "in close touch with Communists and Communist Organizations." Songs praising Kenyatta and ridiculing the governor were outlawed as seditious, creating anger among anti-mission Kikuyu....

The problem now was that clitoridectomy had become inextricably linked to the Kikuyu desire for equality in their homeland. The missionaries were insisting that Kenyatta "should tell his people to obey government officers, Kikuyu chiefs, and missions in control of schools...."

Kenyatta's subsequent defense of clitoridectomy as an operation in which the operator had "the dexterity of a Harley Street surgeon... with a stroke she cuts off the tip of the clitoris... the girl hardly feels any pain" (Jomo Kenyatta 1962) is only understandable in light of the role that clitoridectomy had played in the drive of the Kikuyu to achieve equality for their institutions in the face of Europe's arrogance. Like Bob Murphy, Kenyatta was very aware of the dialectics of social life. For him colonial tutelage was oppressive and alien. He wrote:

> In our opinion, the African can only advance to a 'higher level' if he is free to express himself, to organize economically, politically, socially, and to take part in the government of his own country. In this way he will be able to develop his creative mind, initiative, and personality, which hitherto have been hindered by the multiplicity of incomprehensible laws and ordinances (*Ibid.*:192).

What the conflict over clitoridectomy did was to bring to "an abrupt close the paternalistic phase of missionary activity; henceforth the emphasis would be on the growth of native churches. The high noon of imperialism... [and the attempt] to extend white dominion over all of East Africa, was over." (*Ibid.*:151)

Kenyatta has been pilloried by many female scholars and feminists, for defending a practice (which he was prepared to see abolished), in the greater interest of political equality for Africans. Few noted, as did Harriet Lyons, that Kenyatta had suggested, perhaps as an after thought, that clitoridectomy may have been practiced to prevent masturbation, a practice condemned in both Kikuyu boys and girls, and that his major emphasis was "largely on social structure." (1981:510) Moreover, he was fully prepared to use education to abolish it. A more intemperate view of Kenyatta's action is that of Fran Hosken who declared that

> An international feminist observer cannot help but wonder why the male African leadership does not speak out about the mutilation of women, a custom that was reinforced by Kenyatta in Kenya and is also supported by the independence movement under his leadership.... It clearly affects the status of women in political affairs (Hosken 1976:6).

Understandably, there are some African feminists who agree with Hosken. Nevertheless, it should be noted that "the resistance of African feminists to anti-clitoridectomy agitation—evident at the United Nations World Conference on women held in Copenhagen in 1980" accords fully with the demand of Kenyatta for African cultural autonomy. Like him, these women realize that African practices must be brought into line with those characteristics of the emerging global civilization. What they insist upon is respect, and the end of European arrogance.

The problem with blaming Kenyatta and other African men for clitoridectomy misses the important point that African women have always been in control of this ritual (until now when male doctors may perform it in modern hospitals), and probably used it, to declare their equality with men. Faced with discrimination for not possessing those characteristics with which dominant social strata have linked their dominance, African women, like other women, and subordinate groups, have striven to acquire the traits viewed as valuable. These practices vary cross-culturally in time and space, and can be as different as Japanese females surgically operating on their eyes to approximate those of American males during the occupation of their country; to certain American females bobbing their noses; other Americans bleaching or darkening their skins; and still others dressing like males, and creating female counterparts of such organizations as Masonic lodges, veteran groups, and institutions of higher learning. In many of these cases, the males or dominant groups whose characteristics were being imitated, were not aware of the attempts to achieve equality with them, or to win their favor. That they were responsible for the behavior in the first place may well have been true, but a dialectician like Robert Murphy, whose eyes were probably opened by his wife, Yolanda, would smile at the irony of it all.

References

Boddy, Janice, 1982. "Womb as oasis: the symbolic context of Pharaonic circumcision in rural Northern Sudan," *American Ethnology,* 9: 682–698.

Daly, Mary, 1978. *Gyn/Ecology: The Metaethics of Radical Feminism,* Boston: Beacon Press.

Hosken, Fran P., 1976. "Genital Mutilation of Women in Africa." *Munger Africana Library Notes,* #36, October, p. 6.

Kenyatta, Jomo, 1962. *Facing Mount Kenya,* New York, Vintage Brooks.

Lyons, Harriet, 1981. "Anthropologists, moralities, and relativities: the problem of genital mutilations." *Canadian Review of Sociology and Anthropology,* 18: 499–518.

Messing, Simon D., 1980. "The Problem of 'Operations Based on Custom' in Applied Anthropology: The Challenge of the Hosken Report on Genital and Sexual Mutilations of Females." *Human Organizations,* Vol. 39, No. 3, p. 296.

Murphy, Robert F., 1977. "Man's Culture and Woman's Nature," *Annals of the New York Academy of Sciences.* Vol. 293, 15–24.

Murray-Brown, Jeremy, 1980. *Kenyatta.* London, George Allen & Unwin Ltd.

POSTSCRIPT

Should Anthropologists Work to Eliminate the Practice of Female Circumcision?

The issue of female circumcision raises important questions about whether or not there are limits to cultural relativism. Critics of cultural relativism have often pointed to the Nazi atrocities during the Second World War as examples of immoral practices that can be understood in culturally relative terms but should not be condoned. Cultural relativists in such cases counter that unlike male or female circumcision in Africa, genocide was never morally acceptable in German society.

At issue here is whether or not an unhealthy practice should be suppressed because it is unhealthy. If anthropologists work to abolish female circumcision, should they also work to prohibit use of alcohol, tobacco, and recreational drugs in our own society because such products are unhealthy? Are there limits beyond which cultural relativism has no power? If anthropologists and international organizations are right to stop female circumcision, would they also be justified in working to abolish male circumcision in Jewish and Muslim communities on the same grounds?

Without dealing directly with issues of cultural and moral relativism, Skinner argues that anthropologists should take seriously the concerns of both African men and women, the majority of whom want to continue to practice clitoridectomy and resent Western attempts to suppress the practice. For another view from a similar perspective, see Eric Winkel's essay "A Muslim Perspective on Female Circumcision," *Women & Health* (vol. 23, 1995).

There are many essays by authors who wish to abolish female circumcision, and nearly all of them refer to the practice as female genital mutilation. A lengthy bibliography can be found at http://www.fgmnetwork.org/reference/biblio.html. Typical examples would include Harriet Lyons's "Anthropologists, Moralities, and Relativities: The Problem of Genital Mutilations," *Canadian Review of Sociology and Anthropology* (vol. 18, 1981) and Anke van der Kwaak's "Female Circumcision and Gender Identity: A Questionable Alliance?" *Social Science and Medicine* (vol. 35, 1992).

For a balanced anthropological view of female circumcision and cultural relativism, see Carole Nagengast's "Women, Minorities, and Indigenous Peoples: Universalism and Cultural Relativity," *Journal of Anthropological Research* (vol. 53, 1997).

For a discussion of issues dealing with cultural relativism and anthropological ethics, see *Ethics and the Profession of Anthropology,* Carolyn Fluehr-Lobban, ed. (University of Pennsylvania Press, 1991).

ISSUE 17

Did Napoleon Chagnon and Other Researchers Harm the Yanomami Indians of Venezuela?

YES: Patrick Tierney, from "The Fierce Anthropologist," *The New Yorker* (October 9, 2000)

NO: John Tooby, from "Jungle Fever," *Slate,* http://slate.msn.com/?id=91946 (October 25, 2000)

ISSUE SUMMARY

YES: Investigative journalist Patrick Tierney contends that geneticist James Neel caused a measles epidemic among the Yanomami Indians of Venezuela by inoculating them with a virulent measles vaccine. He also states that Neel's collaborator, anthropologist Napoleon Chagnon, exaggerated Yanomami aggressiveness and actually caused violence by indiscriminately giving machetes to tribesmen who helped him, sometimes even inducing them to break their own taboos.

NO: Anthropologist John Tooby counters that medical experts agree that it is impossible to produce communicable measles with the vaccine that Neel used. He also argues that Tierney systematically distorts Chagnon's views on Yanomami violence and exaggerates the amount of disruption caused by Chagnon's activities compared to that of such others as missionaries and gold miners.

In September 2000 a startling message flew around the e-mail lists of the world's anthropologists. It was a letter from Cornell University anthropologist Terry Turner and University of Hawaii anthropologist Leslie Sponsel to the president and president-elect of the American Anthropological Association (A.A.A.), with copies to a few other officers, warning them of the imminent publication of a book that they said would "affect the American Anthropological profession as a whole in the eyes of the public, and arouse intense indignation and calls for action among members of the Association." The book in question, which they had read in galley proofs, was Patrick Tierney's *Darkness in El Dorado: How*

Scientists and Journalists Devastated the Amazon (W. W. Norton, 2000). The letter summarized some of Tierney's charges that medical researcher James Neel, anthropologist Napoleon Chagnon, and others seriously harmed the Yanomami Indians of Venezuela, even causing a measles epidemic that killed hundreds.

The leaking of the letter and the subsequent publication of Tierney's article in *The New Yorker* caused great excitement at the annual meeting of the A.A.A. in San Francisco, California, in mid-November 2000. Discussion climaxed at a panel discussion. The panel included Tierney, anthropologist William Irons (representing Chagnon, who declined to attend), and experts on the history of science, epidemiology, and South American Indians. (Neel could not defend himself, as he had died earlier that year.) Numerous members of the audience also spoke. Most speakers argued that Tierney was wrong in his accusation that the measles epidemic in 1968 was caused by Neel's and Chagnon's inoculations, but opinions about whether or not Chagnon had treated the Yanomami in an ethical manner during his research were mixed. Later, the executive board of the A.A.A. established a task force to examine the allegations in Tierney's book. The 300-page *Task Force Final Report* was completed on May 18, 2001, and is posted at http://www.aaanet.org.

Why would a book about researchers' treatment of a small Amazonian tribe have caused such an uproar? The reason is that due to the enormous sales of Chagnon's book *The Yanomamö* (now in its fifth edition) and the prize-winning films he made with Timothy Asch, the Yanomami (as most scholars spell their name) are probably the world's best-known tribal people and Chagnon one of the most famous ethnographers since Margaret Mead. Chagnon's use of his Yanomami data to support his sociobiological explanation of human behavior has also had influence outside anthropology, for example, in evolutionary psychology. The idea that the most aggressive men win the most wives and have the most children, thus passing their aggressive genes on to future generations more abundantly than the peaceful genes of their nonaggressive brethren, is a cornerstone of the popular view that humans are innately violent. Thus, Tierney's attack on Chagnon's credibility sent shock waves through the scholarly community.

Is it inherently unethical for scientists to treat other people as mere subjects for investigation or experimentation? Should scientists always place the welfare of their subjects ahead of the success of their research? Do researchers have a moral obligation to compensate people for their help and information? Are researchers responsible for the sometimes harmful effects of those payments? Are there ways of doing research that are mutually beneficial? Finally, is it fair to condemn a scholar for breaking a code of ethics that was not in place at the time of the research?

Tierney charges that Neel and Chagnon deliberately exposed Yanomami to a potentially fatal disease in order to test their theory of natural selection. He also contends that Chagnon's ethnographic research harmed the Yanomami by pitting person against person and group against group, leading to the violent conflict that he attributes to their heredity. Tooby counters that Tierney's book is a hoax, a systematic attempt to distort the facts and to blame the researchers for events that were beyond their control, like the measles epidemic.

The Fierce Anthropologist

In November, 1964, Napoleon A. Chagnon, a twenty-six-year-old American anthropology graduate student, arrived in a small jungle village in Venezuela, to study one of the most remote tribes on earth—the Yanomami Indians. At the time, the boundaries between Venezuela and Brazil were still uncertain. The upper Orinoco, with its tumultuous rapids and impassable waterfalls, had frustrated conquistadores since the sixteenth century, making its mountain redoubts a perfect blank slate for the dream of El Dorado and other fantasies about the New World. The German naturalist Alexander von Humboldt, who visited the area at the turn of the nineteenth century, wrote, "Above the Great Cataracts of the Orinoco a mythical land begins . . . the soil of fable and fairy vision." The Yanomami themselves were rumored, by other tribes and by the earlier explorers, to be "wild" and dangerous—so dangerous that, in 1920, one of the first Americans to encounter them, the geographer Hamilton Rice, opened fire with a machine gun, fearing that the Yanomami were cannibals. Four years later, Rice met the Yanomami again and wrote that they "are not the fierce and intractable people that legends ascribe them to be, but for the most part poor, undersized, inoffensive creatures who eke out a miserable existence."

The reality that Chagnon encountered was, in many ways, stranger than anything previously imagined. In "Yanomamö: The Fierce People," which was published in 1968, Chagnon gave both a harrowing account of a prehistoric tribe and a sobering assessment of what life was like for people whom he later referred to as "our contemporary ancestors." "The Fierce People" eventually became one of the most widely read ethnographical books of all time, selling almost a million copies in the United States alone. Buttressed by subsequent films about the Yanomami made by Chagnon and a documentary filmmaker, Timothy Asch, the book became a standard text in anthropology classes worldwide, and it has gone through five revised editions, the last one in 1997.

"The Fierce People" was written with the verve of an adventure story but was grounded in extensive empirical research. The book opens with this description of Chagnon and an American missionary named James Barker, stumbling into a Yanomami village:

> I . . . gasped when I saw a dozen burly, naked, sweaty, hideous men staring at us down the shafts of their drawn arrows! Immense wads of green tobacco

were stuck between their lower teeth and lips making them look even more hideous, and strands of dark-green slime dripped or hung from their nostrils. We arrived at the village while the men were blowing a hallucinogenic drug up their noses.... I just stood there holding my notebook, helpless and pathetic.... What sort of a welcome was this for the person who came here to live with you and learn your way of life, to become friends with you?

By 1968, Chagnon had spent nineteen months with the Yanomami. During this time, as he writes, he "acquired some proficiency in their language and, up to a point, submerged myself in their culture and their way of life." He studied the Yanomami in a broad variety of aspects, from their travel habits to their technology, use of hallucinogens, agriculture, intellectual life, social and political structures, patterns of settlement, division of labor, marriage practices, trading, and feasting. What was most striking about them was, he wrote, "the importance of aggression in their culture." The Yanomami, he concluded, lived in a "state of chronic warfare":

I had the opportunity to witness a good many incidents that expressed individual vindictiveness on the one hand and collective bellicosity on the other. These ranged in seriousness from the ordinary incidents of wife beating and chest pounding to dueling and organized raiding by parties that set out with the intention of ambushing and killing men from enemy villages.

Between 1968 and 1972, Chagnon made five more expeditions into Yanomami country, exploring increasingly remote villages. In a 1974 book, "Studying the Yanomamö," and in subsequent editions of his first book, he describes surviving a murder attempt by his hosts—whom he frightens off with a flashlight—and a close encounter with a jaguar, which sniffs him in his hammock. Despite repeated death threats, he pushes on into uncharted territory, where he discovers an isolated group, whose members he calls "the Fiercer People." Abandoned by a Yanomami guide, he hollows out a log canoe and returns downriver.

Since the turn of the twentieth century, anthropologists had been inspired to venture farther and farther afield in search of "pure" people, uncontaminated by the Industrial Revolution. In the nineteen-twenties, Margaret Mead went to the South Pacific and wrote her bestseller "Coming of Age in Samoa." Mead described native life in idyllic terms that spoke to the war-weary mood of the time, while overlooking some of the less pleasant aspects of Samoan life, such as the high incidence of violent rape.

"The Fierce People" was the product of a different period. Chagnon, who was born in 1938, had spent an austere childhood in small-town, rural Michigan; his father was an undertaker, and he was the second of twelve children. He earned his doctorate in anthropology at the University of Michigan, and obtained a grant from the National Institute of Mental Health to study the Yanomami. "The Fierce People" was published at the height of the Vietnam War, when violence was the subject of national debate, and it became, in effect, the ethnographic text for the sixties. In 1997, Chagnon told an interviewer for the Los Angeles *Times* that he had written about the Yanomami in reaction to the "garbage" he had learned in graduate school about "noble savages."

When Chagnon first encountered the Yanomami, they were thought to be the largest unacculturated aboriginal group on earth. They slept on bark hammocks slung around the periphery of communal roundhouses with open centers, called *shabonos*. They practiced ritual combats—a graded series of exchanges, starting with chest pounding and escalating into duels with long poles. For gardening, they relied on cutting tools that had been obtained through circuitous trade links with the outside world. Their staple food, which constituted seventy per cent of their diet, was plantains, an import to the New World. Even their genetic makeup was unusual. The Yanomami lack the so-called Diego Factor, an antigen found in other Mongoloid peoples, including Amerindians. Some scientists have hypothesized that they are descended from the first people to cross the Bering Strait, twenty thousand years ago.

The Yanomami had developed a complex belief system about their origins, their afterlife, and their vulnerability to an underworld of demons who were out to destroy souls by spreading disease. (Like many tribal societies, the Yanomami believed that their souls were also threatened by the taking of photographs.) Each village had shamans who maintained constant vigil against the forces of evil by casting spells on perceived enemies.

Today, there are an estimated twenty-seven thousand Yanomami living in hundreds of villages, spread out over about seventy thousand square miles in southern Venezuela and northern Brazil. They speak four distinct dialects, and there are enormous regional variations in trade, warfare, and degrees of contact with the outside world. At the time of Chagnon's first expedition, most of the Yanomami were mountain dwellers. They did not have much in the way of metal tools or personal possessions. They practiced slash-and-burn agriculture, and they spent much of their time on long treks of hunting and gathering. They did not use canoes—there are no navigable rivers in the mountains—and they had little use for clothes, other than a cotton waistband for women and a penis string for men. Increasingly, however, the Yanomami were leaving the mountains to settle along the main course of the Orinoco. There, during the nineteen-fifties, missionaries had established outposts, and Venezuelan government workers had set up centers for treatment of malaria, which had become endemic along the river. Some of the Yanomami in the lowlands were beginning to wear Western clothes, and they had settled into a relatively sedentary life style, which they supported by growing crops, begging, and performing services for outsiders. It was among these Yanomami that Chagnon established his headquarters, at the confluence of the Orinoco and Mavaca rivers, next door to the Mavaca mission in the village of Bisaasi-teri.

Chagnon arrived in Yanomami territory in an aluminum rowboat with an outboard motor. He was carrying axes and machetes to give to the villagers as payment for their coöperation. Although the people of Bisaasi-teri were accustomed to receiving a trickle of trade goods in return for their work in the mission, the sudden windfall created a sensation. In a letter from the field, Chagnon writes that the first recipients of his gifts, all of whom were male, immediately left the village for remote settlements, where the axes and machetes could be used for trade. One of the most startling conclusions of "The Fierce People" is that Yanomami warfare was caused largely by competition among marriageable men over females, who—thanks to the widespread practice of female infanticide—were in scarce supply. In another letter from the field, Chagnon noted, "This particular war got started the day I arrived in the field (cause: woman stealing), and it is getting hotter and hotter." The Yanomami's need to wage war, he observed, encouraged the breeding of males—and this, in turn, led to more war. Among anthropologists, this conclusion contradicted the conventional wisdom that primitive warfare was the result of competition for hunting territories, cropland, or trade routes. Chagnon later said that his findings had come as a surprise to him, too. In 1988, he told a reporter for *U.S. News & World Report*, "I went down there looking for shortages of resources. But it turns out they are fighting like hell over women."

Over a period of thirty years, Chagnon led some twenty expeditions into Yanomami territory and collected an unparalleled body of data, which he presented in two books and more than thirty articles. Perhaps Chagnon's most enduring achievement was explaining the Yanomami's seemingly savage behavior in a way that shed new light on natural selection. In 1988, he published an article in *Science* entitled "Life Histories, Blood Revenge, and Warfare in a Tribal Population," in which he reported that the Yanomami men who murdered had twice as many wives and three times as many offspring as non-murderers had. He concluded that, among the Yanomami, the act of killing bestowed status.

This paper had considerable impact beyond the field of anthropology. Edward O. Wilson and other sociobiologists accepted it as important evidence of the genetic origins of human violence. In a preface to Chagnon's 1992 book, "Yanomamö: The Last Days of Eden," which is "The Fierce People" adapted for a general audience, Wilson lauded Chagnon's synthesis of evolutionary biology and culture as a "master work."

◦◦◉◦◦

Like most undergraduate anthropology students in the nineteen-seventies, I admired "The Fierce People" for its vivid research and unsentimental approach. In part inspired by Chagnon's example, I set out, in 1983, to do a study of ritual murder in the Andes. Like Chagnon, I concluded that, among some tribes, committing ritual murder was a prestigious act. In 1989, I decided to study the Yanomami, first in Brazil, where the Amazon gold rush had brought epidemics, guns, alcohol, and prostitution, and then in Venezuela, along the Orinoco and in the mountains. Over the next ten years, I made six trips to the Amazon-Orinoco region, spending fifteen months in the field and visiting thirty of the villages that Chagnon had studied. What I found was sharply at odds with what Chagnon described.

In "The Fierce People," Chagnon wrote that the Yanomami were "one of the best nourished populations thus far described in the anthropological/biomedical literature." Unlike Chagnon's "burly" men, the villagers I encountered were—as Rice had observed in 1924—tiny and scrawny, smaller than most

African Pygmies. According to data compiled by Darna L. Dufour, a biological anthropologist at the University of Colorado, the adult males average four feet nine inches in height, and the women four feet seven inches. The children have some of the lowest weight-for-height ratios among Amazonian Indians. Moreover, Chagnon's account of Yanomami warfare seemed greatly exaggerated. I visited a village on the Mucajai River, in Brazil, where Chagnon had spent some time in 1967, and where he claimed to have found a group that demonstrated the most extreme form of Yanomami "treachery." However, according to the authoritative sociologist John Peters, who lived there from 1958 to 1967, the group had participated in only four raids in half a century. These raids, he said, had been provoked not by competition for women, as Chagnon had written, but by the spread of new diseases, which prompted angry accusations of witchcraft.

Others, too, were bewildered by some of Chagnon's writings. The linguist Jacques Lizot, who had been encouraged by Claude Lévi-Strauss at the Collège de France, has lived for twenty-five years with the Yanomami. In 1994, Lizot criticized Chagnon in the *American Ethnologist* for obscuring the identity of twelve villages in his homicide study, making it difficult for other anthropologists to verify his data. The German ethnologist Irenäus Eibl-Eibesfeldt, a former head of the human-ethnology department at the Max Planck Institute, outside Munich, has been conducting research among the Yanomami since 1969. In 1994, he and another Yanomami researcher at the institute wrote a letter to the American Human Behavior and Evolution Society, which claimed that Chagnon had got important mortality-rate statistics wrong.

In the past decade, some of Chagnon's colleagues, as well as Catholic missionaries in the field, have expressed concern about the impact of his research on Yanomami culture. Kenneth Good, who worked with Chagnon while researching his Ph.D., has lived among the Yanomami for twelve years—longer than any other American anthropologist. Good calls Chagnon "a hit-and-run anthropologist who comes into villages with armloads of machetes to purchase coöperation for his research. Unfortunately, he creates conflict and division wherever he goes." During his years among the Yanomami, Good witnessed a single war, and the only time he felt endangered was on his first, nervous night in the field, in 1975, when Chagnon and another anthropologist, both drunk, burst into his hut, tore his mosquito netting, and pushed him out of his hammock in a mock raid.

⁓⊙⁓

In 1995, Brian Ferguson, an anthropologist at Rutgers University, published a book entitled "Yanomami Warfare: A Political History," which challenged the sociobiological theories drawn from "The Fierce People" and other studies by Chagnon. Ferguson, whose book analyzes hundreds of sources, wrote that most of the Yanomami wars on record were caused by outside disturbances, particularly by the introduction of steel goods and new diseases. Ferguson noted that axes and machetes became highly coveted among the Yanomami as agricultural tools and as commodities for trade. In his account, evangelical missionaries, who arrived in Yanomami territory during the fifties, inadvertently plunged the region into war when they disbursed axes and machetes to win converts. In time, some of the missions became centers of stability and sources of much needed medicine. But Chagnon, whose study of Yanomami mortality rates took him from village to village, dispensed steel goods in order to persuade the people to give him the names of their dead relatives—a violation of tribal taboos.

In a chapter entitled "The Yanomamo and the Anthropologist," Ferguson described how these methods destabilized the region—in effect, promoted the sort of warfare that Chagnon attributed to the Yanomami's ferocity. By Chagnon's own account, he shuttled between enemy villages and cultivated "informants who might be considered 'aberrant' or 'abnormal' outcasts in their own society," and who would give him tribal secrets in exchange for beads, cloth, fishhooks, and above all, steel goods. To get the data he wanted, Chagnon, by his own account, began " 'bribing' children when their elders were not around, or capitalizing on animosities between individuals." Ferguson writes that Chagnon stirred up village rivalries by behaving like a regional big man and an "un-Yanomami . . . wild card on the political scene."

This depiction of Chagnon was supported by many of the Yanomami with whom I spoke. In 1996, in the village of Momaribowei-teri, a man named Pablo Mejía told me that when he was twelve he had witnessed Chagnon's arrival in his village: "He had his bird feathers adorning his arms. He had red-dye paint all over his body. He wore a loincloth like the Yanomami. He sang with the chant of his shamanism and took *yopo*"—a powerful hallucinogen used by Yanomami shamans to make contact with spirits. "He took a lot of *yopo*. I was terrified of him. He always fired off his pistol when he entered the village, to prove that he was fiercer than the Yanomami. Everybody was afraid of him because nobody had seen a *nabah*"—white man—"acting as a shaman. He said to my brother Samuel who was the headman, 'What is your mother's name?' My brother answered, 'We Yanomami do not speak our names.' Shaki"—the Yanomami's name for Chagnon—"said, 'It doesn't matter. If you tell me, I'll pay you.' So, although they didn't want to, the people sold their names. Everyone cried, but they spoke them. It was very sad."

Ferguson described an incident, in 1972, when Chagnon arrived in the village of Mishimishimabowei-teri, approximately seventy miles upriver from Bisaasi-teri. In exchange for blood samples, which he was collecting for his genealogical study, Chagnon distributed machetes to a nearby rival village, whereupon the headman of Mishimishimabowei-teri, an aggressive man named Moawa, threatened, Chagnon wrote, to "bury an ax" in his head if he didn't give his last machete to a man Moawa designated. Chagnon complied, but when he was safely back at his home base, in Bisaasi-teri, he vented his feelings in a way that shows how deeply he had become enmeshed in local politics. In "Studying the Yanomamö," Chagnon writes, "I told the Bisassi-teri that I planned never to return to Moawa's village. . . . I was tired of having people threaten to kill me. I was alarmed at how close some of them had come. I told them that I would do 'the same' to Moawa as he did to me, should he ever venture to come to Mavaca [mission] to visit."

In a review of Ferguson's book in *American Anthropologist*, Chagnon blamed the missionaries for any destabilization, pointing out that the conflicts had broken out long before 1964, when he arrived. In the 1997 edition of "The Fierce People," he wrote that he had been something of a savior to the people of Mishimishimabowei-teri, helping to broker "neolithic peace" between them and the antagonistic people of Bisaasi-teri. He said that, in return, the Mishimishimabowei-teri had bestowed on him the name of their village—an honor usually reserved for chiefs. "I was their village," Chagnon writes. "Their village was me."

Chagnon, who retired this year as a professor of anthoropology at the University of California in Santa Barbara, still retains his eminence in the field. Irven DeVore, a professor of biological anthropology at Harvard, says, "Chag was both first and thorough. First in the sense that very, very few anthropological studies have been carried out by an anthropologist who was first on the scene. Thorough in the sense that Chag has visited at least seventy-five Yanomami villages on both sides of the Venezuela and Brazil borders. I cannot think of a comparably thorough survey among any cultural group by an anthropologist. Chag gathered very detailed and documented data on the villages—so much so that another investigator could study the same population and come to a different conclusion. Chagnon's study was 'scientific' in the best sense of the word."

In 1995, Chagnon agreed to meet with me in his office in Santa Barbara. By this time, I had become a human-rights activist on behalf of the Yanomami and other Amazon tribes. I had written a piece in the New York *Times* that was critical of one of Chagnon's Venezuelan friends and colleagues, Charles Brewer-Carías, and Chagnon was angry about it. In recent years, he had become such a controversial figure for his research among the Yanomami that the Venezuelan government had prohibited him from reëntering Yanomami country. Chagnon refused to answer any of my substantive questions about his troubles, saying that, at some later date, he planned to write about them himself. During the preparation of this article, he was again asked to answer questions about his work with the Yanomami. After first agreeing to talk in depth to *The New Yorker*, he changed his mind a few days later and declined to comment.

One of Chagnon's most important academic mentors was the celebrated geneticist Dr. James Neel, who was a member of Chagnon's Ph.D. advisory committee at the University of Michigan. Neel, who died earlier this year, first achieved fame in the field of inherited disease and then headed the Atomic Bomb Casualty Commission, which was established after the war to study survivors of the bombings of Hiroshima and Nagasaki. Between 1965 and 1972, he received more than two million dollars from the Atomic Energy Commission to compare the cellular-mutation rates of the Japanese survivors with those of the Yanomami and other "primitive tribes" that had not been exposed to radiation. The immediate goal was to determine the effects of radiation on the genetic material of cells. The ultimate goal was to help set radiation safety standards in the United States.

Chagnon became, as Neel put it, the "indispensable cultural anthropologist" in Michigan's Human Genetics Department. Between 1966 and 1971, Chagnon made six trips to Brazil and Venezuela, as a member of a multidisciplinary team led by Neel to make what Neel described as the most comprehensive study of a tribal people ever attempted.

Neel had long been interested in unadulterated societies. A self-professed eugenicist, he believed that modern democracies, with their free breeding among large populations, violated the process of natural selection and promoted genetic entropy. Tribal people, in his view, were likely to have superior genetic material because they lived according to the survival-of-the-fittest principle—that is, they were ruled by polygamous chiefs who had triumphed over their rivals. He hoped that by studying the Yanomami he might be able to isolate specific genes for male leadership—or, as he put it, an "Index of Innate Ability." This view of the Yanomami as a superior breeding stock was not generally shared by Neel's medical colleagues. Most of them believed that the Yanomami, like other Amerindian tribes, were immune-depressed.

In January, 1968, Neel's team, which included Chagnon, Asch, and a Venezuelan doctor, Marcel Roche, arrived on the upper Orinoco. Chagnon was sent ahead of the others to secure, as he later wrote, "agreements from the Yanomamo to provide endless outstretched brown arms into which many needles would be stuck for the next weeks." Asch described the process in notes for one of his films: "The villagers are studied on a production line: numbers are assigned to them; specimens of their blood, saliva, and stools are collected; impressions of their teeth are made; and they are weighed and measured by the physical anthropologists." Each person was also photographed and paid with what Neel called "a 'cash' transaction based on trade goods."

Neel had learned of an outbreak of measles that had occurred the previous fall among Brazilian Yanomami in villages more than a hundred miles from the Venezuelan missions. For what he later called "an exercise in preventive medicine," Neel's team brought a thousand doses of live measles vaccine into the upper-Orinoco region. Neel was eager to collect data on vaccine responses. At the time, geneticists wanted to study tribal people who had no measles antibodies, in order to determine how their immune responses differed from those in modern societies. In 1966, Francis Black, a geneticist at Yale, had vaccinated a Brazilian tribe, the Tiriyo, with a measles vaccine, in the hope of using the vaccine virus as "a model of natural measles." He found that the Tiriyo's post-vaccination fevers were extraordinarily high; the temperature elevations were nearly three times those of other races that had been given the same vaccine.

Black had chosen the widely used Schwarz measles vaccine, rather than an older vaccine, the Edmonston B, citing "the risk of severe febrile response" with the Edmonston B vaccine. In 1962, when an immune-compromised child with leukemia died after receiving Edmonston B, one of the vaccine's inventors, John Enders, of Harvard, had cautioned that the strain was dangerous for immune-depressed people. Measles vaccines were also known to produce unusually severe reactions in people suffering from anemia, dysentery, or chronic exposure to malaria—and the Yanomami suffered from all three.

Two years after Black conducted his study, Neel took the Edmonston B vaccine, rather than the Schwarz, into Yanomami territory. None of the other members of Neel's team seem to have participated in this decision, and there is no evidence that any of them would have known the difference between the two vaccines. In January, 1968, Venezuela had begun a national vaccination project, administering the Schwarz vaccine in three diluted doses, on the recommendation of the Centers for Disease Control, in Atlanta. In the United States, where many children still received the Edmonston vaccine—it is no longer used anywhere in the world—it was given with an accompanying dose of gamma globulin, which reduces the fevers by half. Neel had his researchers administer Edmonston B without gamma globulin to forty tribespeople at a mission on the Ocamo River. According to the director of Venezuela's vaccination department, Dr. Adelfa Betancourt, they did so without the department's permission. (A science historian at the University of Pennsylvania, Susan Lindee, was recently quoted in *Time* to the effect that Venezuelan officials gave permission for the vaccinations. She has since told *The New Yorker* that her evidence for the claim was erroneous.)

Over the next three months, the worst epidemic in the Yanomami's history broke out. On the basis of three mission journals, data of the expedition itself, and interviews with Yanomami survivors and with other witnesses, I determined that the course of the epidemic closely tracked the movement of Neel's team. It broke out in the three settlements that received the vaccinations—the Ocamo mission, the Mavaca mission, and a village called Patanowa-teri. Because quarantines were not rigorously imposed, the disease spread to dozens of villages scattered across thousands of square miles. It is estimated that between fifteen and twenty per cent of the Yanomami who contracted measles died in the epidemic.

A child's unmarked grave lies next to a dirt airstrip at the Catholic Ocamo mission. Thirty years ago, a small cross was erected at this spot, but it could not withstand the tropical weather. The remains in the grave are those of a year-old boy named Roberto Baltasar, who died on February 15, 1968; he was the first clearly diagnosed case of measles among the Venezuelan Yanomami recorded in the mission journals. According to Vitalino Baltasar, the boy's father, Roberto had come down with the disease after being vaccinated by Chagnon, under the direction of Neel.

In a 1970 paper entitled "Notes on the Effect of Measles and Measles Vaccine in a Virgin-Soil Population of South American Indians," Neel and Chagnon tell a different story. In their account, a single case of measles coincidentally broke out among the Venezuelan Yanomami as soon as Chagnon and Asch arrived at the Ocamo mission. The measles, Neel and Chagnon wrote, had been brought by a fourteen-year-old Brazilian worker, who had come to Ocamo with other workers. They said that Roche had made "a tentative diagnosis of measles" in the Brazilian teen-ager, and added that Roche's diagnosis was "uncertain," because the boy's symptoms could not be distinguished from "any of a variety of 'jungle fevers.' " (And the boy showed no signs of a measles rash.) Twenty-eight years later, I talked to Roche in Venezuela, in the offices of a scientific journal of which he was the editor. He told me that he did not remember having diagnosed measles in the Brazilian boy. Indeed, according to the Mavaca-mission records, Roche and another doctor reported that the team's arrival had coincided with an ongoing epidemic of bronchopneumonia, whose symptoms match those that Neel and Chagnon described in the fourteen-year-old boy.

Chagnon and Roche began vacinnating the Ocamo Indians with Edmonston B for purely "preventive" reasons, Roche later told me. According to Neel and Chagnon, cases of "moderately severe measles" appeared among the vaccinated Yanomami six days after they were inoculated. The fevers Neel and Chagnon recorded were, on average, far higher than previous responses to the Edmonston B vaccine—so high that they could not be distinguished from the fevers of natural measles. Then Roberto Baltasar died. According to his father, vaccinated Yanomami began fleeing the Ocamo mission, and going into the hills. "They already carried the disease," he told me, twenty-eight years later. "Few of them returned, because the majority died."

It cannot be determined with any accuracy how many died after receiving the vaccination. Chagnon has said that no one who was vaccinated got measles, and, according to the medical consensus at the time, the Edmonston B vaccine virus was not, in itself, contagious. Today, scientists still do not know whether people who have been vaccinated with Edmonston B can transmit measles. What is certain is that the effects of an epidemic, in which hundreds died in a relatively short period, were especially devastating on a people who believed that some new black magic must have brought on the disease and who, at the first sign of the measles rash, panicked and fled from their homes into the forests, away from further medical attention.

A government nurse who was in the area at the time, Juan González, helped the Yanomami collect the bodies of the dead for cremation. "They hung the children in baskets from the trees," he recalls. "The cadavers were placed inside the baskets, all rolled up tightly, like a metallic foil. The women were more loosely wrapped, in leaves, and they were left hanging in hammocks out in the wild among the trees. They tied the men up on poles, higher up in the branches. What a stench there was. Nothing but dead Yanomami. The Yanomami say that they died from that vaccine. That's why even now some of them don't want to be vaccinated. I don't know how to explain it either, because we initially believed that that first vaccine had come to help us. Instead, it came to destroy us."

Asch, who died in 1994, left about twenty thousand feet of raw footage of the expedition, along with the sound tapes, to the Smithsonian Institution. The first mention of the measles outbreak on the soundtrack is heard on the eighteenth of February, three days after Roberto Baltasar's death. On that day, Asch recorded Neel giving him instructions on filming measles victims at the team's base camp, at Mavaca, where a second vaccination center had been established. "Let me tell you what we want to get—extreme severe morbilliform rash," Neel says. "Can you get this? . . . Both eyes. He has the typical morbilliform rash on both cheeks. . . . I'm afraid you're going to [see] some severe cases of measles. . . . We're going to be able to document the whole gamut of measles in this group."

Later, Chagnon asks Neel to summon more doctors, from Caracas, to treat the measles, and Neel agrees. Their radio operator, whom they call Rousseau, says that he will contact people in Caracas and request antibiotics *"por los efectos de la vacuna"*—because of the effects of the vaccine—and adds that the vaccine may bring *"brotes de sarampión,"* outbreaks of measles. After listening to Rousseau, Chagnon cautions Neel, "But he's trying to interpret all of them to mean that it's a reaction to the vaccination, which I don't think is a wise thing to do." Chagnon seems bewildered by the extent of the outbreak. He says, "Now we have measles at Mavaca and Ocamo, and I don't know where else it is—I don't know when it arrived."

Later, he tells Neel that the Ocamo Yanomami could easily spread the disease to others by journeying to nearby villages to trade. (Apparently, this happened. A group of Ocamo Yanomami who had sold blood to Neel's researchers for knives, machetes, and other trade goods travelled upriver to visit a village called Shubariwa-teri, which was then devastated by measles.) Chagnon suggests that Neel take quarantine precautions at Mavaca, and he urges that doctors be flown in from Caracas to care for the Ocamo Yanomami. Neel agrees. He then orders his younger colleagues to move farther up the Orinoco, into the tribe's heartland.

❧

During the epidemic, Neel, Chagnon, and Asch made two award-winning films. One was "Yanomamö: A Multidisciplinary Study," which presents a general overview of Neel's research objectives. The other was "The Feast," which documents the celebration of a military alliance between two formerly hostile villages. "The Feast" is widely considered one of the finest ethnographic films ever made, because of how it depicts the Machiavellian underpinnings of tribal festivities. In Asch's notes, he explained the background to the film: "To conduct raids and to protect itself from attack, a Yanomamö village must ally itself with neighboring villages. The feast is a means by which these intervillage alliances are formed. To prepare for a feast, the village is first cleaned. Gallons of banana soup for the guests are cooked and stored in large troughs. The guests, waiting outside the village, send in an emissary who chants a greeting and brings back food to his people. The guests burst in, dancing and brandishing their weapons, while the hosts recline in their hammocks. Feasting, trading, and games of ritual violence then take place. Sometimes these 'games' escalate into real massacres."

Both "A Multidisciplinary Study" and "The Feast" were filmed in the village of Patanowa-teri. Twenty-eight years later, when I visited there, a tribal elder named Kayopewe told me, through a translator, that before Chagnon and Asch arrived with their equipment the village had fallen into ruins and was largely abandoned. It was reconstructed and reoccupied, he said, only after Chagnon promised that if the villagers moved back in and held a peacemaking feast with their neighbors from a hostile village called Mahekoto-teri he would give every man among them a machete. Kayopewe said that the whole affair had, in effect, been brokered by the filmmakers.

Asch partly confirmed this account in an article published in the film journal *Sightlines,* in 1972. In a description of the making of "The Feast," he said that Chagnon had sent him, three Yanomami, and a young Protestant missionary, Daniel Shaylor, on an eleven-day trek to Patanowa-teri, a "mountain hideout" far from the vaccination centers along the Orinoco. "After finding [the] Pataowa-teri we set up an aircraft radio and reached Napoleon at Mavaca. He convinced the headman to move back into an old garden near the Orinoco River where the genetics expediction could work with them and we could take film." A large shipment of metal pots duly arrived as payment for the villagers' coöperation. In 1995, according to an article in the *Visual Anthropology Review,* Chagnon said, "I did not 'stage' this—it happened naturally. They could not have cared less about our interests in filming and are the kind of people who would not do something this costly and time consuming for two whole communities simply to accommodate the filming interests of outsiders."

Other payments were required—so many that Chagnon radioed for another plane to bring in more trade goods. When Chagnon distributed the goods, he created what seems, on the soundtrack, to be pandemonium. Later, when Chagnon and Asch asked a group of Yanomami to cut some bananas in front of the camera, they suddenly burst into a frenzied dance—"screaming at the top of their lungs, waving branches of leaves in the air," as Asch later wrote in *Sightlines.* Asch filmed the scene, assuming that it was a "garden ritual." When the Yanomami finally stopped, Chagnon asked them, "What was that all about?"

"Isn't that what you just asked us to do?" the headman replied.

The filming of "The Feast" also had unforeseen consequences. When Chagnon invited the Patanowa-teri's former enemies, the Mahekoto-teri, to participate as guests, he created a new alliance. According to Chagnon, it is Yanomami custom for two villages to celebrate such a union by choosing a new enemy, and after feasting together the new allies launched a raid on a third village, killing a woman in the process. One day, when Asch tried to film a doctor who was treating a sick man from the village of Mavaca, Neel interrupted him. "I don't want any of this," he said. "You're here to document the kind of study we're trying to make. Anyone can walk into a village and treat people. This is not what we're here to do."

After Neel's researchers departed many of the Mahekoto-teri and Patanowa-teri became sick and died. It is not clear what they died of, because they may have been exposed to many different pathogens, including colds, the Edmonston B virus, and malaria. (Shaylor, the expedition's translator, had arrived in Patanowa-teri with malaria, where he became so sick that he had to be evacuated.) In 1996, when I showed the elders of both villages a video of "The Feast," many of the old men wept. Kayopewe said, "We broke out in sores and rash on our faces, and it burned really badly. One of us died at the village [where the filming took place]. We left him there and fled into the jungles. An old man would die. We would tie him up in the trees. And then a young woman would die, and we would leave her in a basket. We kept dying off and dying off." When the men heard a translation of the soundtrack of "A Multidisciplinary

Study," in which Neel claimed that the Patanowa-teri had been saved from measles, thanks to the vaccinations, there was a chorus of protest. *"Horemu! Horemu!"* ("Lies, lies.") One man told me, "Shaki stole our spirits, and we have never been the same."

⋅◦⟨◉⟩◦⋅

By the mid-seventies, the Yanomami had become the most intensively studied and filmed tribal group in the world. In Paris in 1978, a festival was devoted to films about them. As scientists, news teams, filmmakers, and others competed for footage and new data bout the tribe, some of the Yanomami along the Orinoco became part-time film extras and anthropological informants.

At the same time, native-rights advocates began to criticize outsiders—gold miners, journalists, missionaries, scientists—claiming that cultural disruption and epidemics invariably followed their visits into the tribal territories. The first group to defend Yanomami rights was formed in Brazil, and a split developed in anthropology between the researchers who wanted simply to observe tribal culture and those who wanted Indians to have land rights and health care. From 1976 until 1985, Chagnon was prohibited from reëntering Yanomami territory. During those years, he and his wife, Carlene, raised two children, and he became a popular lecturer at Northwestern and then at the University of California at Santa Barbara.

In 1985, Chagnon, accompanied by a University of California graduate student, Jesús Cardozo, who was Venezuelan, succeeded in reëntering Yanomami territory. He returned to Mishimishimabowei-teri, where he hoped to finish his long-term study of the relationship between Yanomami homicide and reproductive success. Cardozo, who no longer has cordial relations with Chagnon, went on to help create the Venezuelan Foundation for Anthropological Research, which promotes Yanomami education and land rights. As Cardozo later recalled of the expedition, "We hadn't even got our boat moored to the shore at Mavakita"—a Mishimishimabowei-teri village that had broken off from the main group following various epidemics in the early seventies—"when Yanomami started coming out and shouting, 'Go away! Shaki brings *xawara* [illness].' Within our first twenty-four hours there, three children died—two in the night and another in the morning." Although there was no connection between Chagnon's arrival and the deaths, the events were seen as further evidence of the anthropologist's malefic power. "On our second night, half of the village fled into the forest to get away from us."

After another day of searching for a community where he could continue his genealogical research, Chagnon found a village, Iwahikoroba-teri, that was willing to receive the expedition. "When we arrived at Iwahikoroba-teri, everybody was sick, throwing up and moaning and lying down in their hammocks," Cardozo said. "I remember a little girl, Makiritama. She was vomiting blood. She was defecating blood, too. I remember her husband—she was very young, she was to be his future wife—showed me where she was spitting up everything. And I went up to Chagnon and said, 'You know these people are really sick. Some of them could die. I think we should go and get medical help.' Chagnon told me that I would never be a scientist. He said, 'No. No. That's not our problem. We didn't come to save the Indians. We came to study them.' "

For the next several weeks, Chagnon collected homicide data, numbering each Yanomami's chest or arm with a Magic Marker, posing the Yanomami for identification photographs, and paying them with trade goods. He summarized his findings in an article in *Science,* which was published in February, 1988. The article was noted in *Scientific American* for providing a new, though grim model for human evolution: "Through violence a Yanomamö male seems to enhance his reproductive success and that of his kin: he becomes 'fitter.' "

But Yanomami specialists generally rejected the study. In a number of anthropological journals, they challenged Chagnon's findings on ethical, statistical, linguistic, and interpretive grounds. And Chagnon's presence in the media—he was mentioned in the Los Angeles *Times,* in February, 1988, as having said that when the Yanomami were not hunting, or searching for honey, they were often killing one another—became provocative. Less than a year after the *Times* article appeared, the Brazilian military chief of staff cited the Yanomami's trulculence as a reason for breaking up their lands. A past president of the Brazilian Anthropological Association, Maria Manuela Carneiro de Cunha, wrote a letter to the *Anthropology Newsletter* in which she held Chagnon accountable, in part, for the government's actions against the Yanomami. In an article entitled "The Academic Extermination of the Yanomami," which was published in the Brazilian cultural journal *Humanidades,* two anthropologists, Alcida Ramos and Bruce Albert, wrote, "Few indigenous people . . . have had their image as denigrated as have the Yanomami, who had the misfortune of being studied by a North American anthropologist named Napoleon Chagnon."

Chagnon responded to da Cunha in the *Anthropology Newsletter* by saying that he could not control the press's tendency to sensationalize his findings, and that he should not be held responsible for the failure of Brazilians to defend the rights of indigenous people. In his 1992 revised edition of "Yanomamö," for which he dropped the subtitle "The Fierce People," he drew a distinction between researchers who sought objective facts, like him, and other anthropologists, who were motivated by a sense of political activism and who "hold a romantic, Rousseauian view of primitive culture."

In 1989, Chagnon proposed bringing a BBC film crew to Bisaasi-teri to commemorate the twenty-fifth anniversary of his arrival in the village. By this time, many more Yanomami had left the highlands to live near missions along the Orinoco and its tributaries, where they could attend schools, get medical care, and eat a more varied diet. The Yanomami at the missions were considerably more robust than those in the hills, and they had learned how to market their own handicrafts through a trade coöperative run by elected representatives. Along the Orinoco and Mavaca rivers, it was no longer easy for researchers to hire Yanomami porters, informants, or film extras. When the Yanomami at Bisaasi-teri learned that Chagnon was returning, they instructed their representative, a former guide of Chagnon's named César Dimanawa, to write a letter asking the anthropologist to keep away, because his films contained so much "fighting and bloodshed." Dimanawa wrote, "We do not want you to make any more films." Again, the Venezuelan government cancelled Chagnon's permit, citing the "turmoil" that his vist would provoke.

                                                     ◦◉◦

Chagnon turned for help to Brewer-Carías, his old friend. A distinguished botanist, Brewer-Carías had been criticized by environmentalists and human-rights activists for allegedly acquiring, under the pretense of doing research in rain forests, land for gold mining—charges that he emphatically denies. Through Brewer-Carías, Chagnon made another powerful ally, Cecilia Matos, the mistress of the Venezuelan President, Carlos Andrés Pérez, and the head of a foundation that had been set up to assist indigenous and peasant families. Chagnon, Brewer-Carías, and Matos devised a plan to create a Yanomami reserve in the Siapa Highlands—an area of thousands of square miles in which the Indians would live in protected isolation. Only scientists would be allowed into the area, to study the Yanomami at a research center run by Chagnon and Brewer-Carías.

Between August, 1990, and September, 1991 Chagnon and Brewer-Carías organized a dozen expeditions by helicopter into the Siapa region for journal-ists and scientists, in order to build up national and international support for their project. Three of the villages that were visited by Chagnon, Brewer-Carías, and their entourage were badly damaged by the helicopters. In 1991, Chagnon described one of these events in an article for the magazine *Santa Barbara,* en-titled "To Save the Fierce People": "A few feet from landing, we aborted when we saw the leaves of their roofs being blown away by the chopper's downblast. We saw people fleeing in terror and men throwing sticks and stones at us as we retreated up and away."

Dr. Carlos Botto, the director of the Amazon Center for the Investiga-tion and Control of Tropical Disease, in Puerto Ayacucho, was in the village of Ashidowa-teri when Chagnon landed in his helicopter and part of the *shabono* collapsed. "When the poles of the roof fell, a number of Yanomami were in-jured, and we had to treat them," Botto recalls. "We had to rescue people who were buried under the poles and roofing of the *shabono.* The expedition left a tragic scar."

In September, 1993, Chagnon and Brewer-Carías were named to a Pres-idential commission, which was given broad powers over the Yanomami's land and political future. The attorney general's office, leaders of the Catholic Church, and native-rights groups opposed the appointments, and three hun-dred representatives from nineteen Indian tribes rallied in the streets of Puerto Ayacucho, the capital of the state of Amazonas, in an effort to have Chagnon and Brewer-Carías expelled from Yanomami territory. On September 30th, Chagnon was escorted to Caracas by an Army colonel, who confiscated his field notes and advised him to leave the country—which he did.

In the United States, Chagnon remained highly regarded. Earlier that year, he had been elected president of the prestigious Human Behavior and Evolution Society.

◦◦◦

In September of 1996, after undergoing a weeklong quarantine, I trekked for seventeen days into the Siapa Highlands with a Brazilian malaria-control worker, Marinho De Souza. We were the first outsiders to revisit the area since Chagnon's tumultuous helicopter descents, and we found the villages very different from his description. In articles and interviews, Chagnon had said that the Siapa Yanomami were healthy, well fed, and peaceful. Here, in the tribe's unspoiled heartland, steel goods were scarce, and the homicide rate among men was much lower than it was in the lowlands along the Orinoco.

What De Souza and I discovered, however, was a fearful, broken society. At Narimobowei-teri, the first village that Chagnon's helicopter had damaged, men with drawn arrows greeted us, fearing that we were enemy raiders. At night, we listened to the chanting of shamans who were trying to exorcise the demonic flying machine that had descended upon their village, dispensing both wonderful trade goods and, they believed, terrible disease. At another village, Toobatotoi-teri, which Chagnon described as "the last uncontacted group in this region," we came to a clearing where shamans were trying to induce helicopters to land by chanting and dancing. The plan, apparently, was to trick any outsiders into unloading their steel gifts and then to scare them into leaving—quickly, before they could infect the people with colds and fevers. Life in the Siapa Highlands had always been a struggle. The villagers had combatted malnutrition, intestinal parasites, and, more recently, malaria. But what they could not comprehend—and what had shaken their world—was the sudden arrival of visitors who seemed to offer an easier life and, at the same time, sowed so much confusion. For them, Chagnon had come to personify everything that both attracted and repulsed them about our culture. They wanted him, and they didn't want him, and they could not forget him.

After twelve days of trekking, we reached Ashidowa-teri, the village where a number of Yanomami had been injured when Chagnon's helicopter blew away a roof. They were living in what looked like woefully inadequate lean-tos, and they were the most sickly, dispirited Yanomami I had seen in Venezuela. As soon as we entered their clearing, a man grabbed by hand, held it to his feverish forehead, and cried, *"Hariri!"* ("Sickness.") Many of the people had painted their faces black, in mourning, and most of the children looked malnourished.

At night, in the firelight of circled hearths, the Yanomami sang about the mysterious arrival of the helicopters and their strange riders. Then the people around the campfires began mourning for their departed kin. The headman, Mirapewe, said to me, "If you could count the dead, you would see how many of us there were."

Jungle Fever

Lately I've been engrossed in—and in some sense involved in—the most sensational scandal to emerge from academia in decades. The scandal erupted last month when two anthropologists, Terry Turner and Leslie Sponsel, sent a searing letter to the president of the American Anthropological Association. The letter distilled a series of chilling "revelations" made by the journalist Patrick Tierney in his forthcoming book *Darkness in El Dorado: How Scientists and Journalists Devastated the Amazon.* According to Turner and Sponsel, the scandal unearthed by Tierney, "in its scale, ramifications, and sheer criminality and corruption," is "unparalleled in the history of Anthropology." Turner and Sponsel listed a horrifying series of crimes—"beyond the imagining of even a Josef Conrad (though not, perhaps, a Josef Mengele)"—including genocide, allegedly committed by U.S. scientists against the Yanomamö, an indigenous people living in the Venezuelan and Brazilian rain forest.

Turner and Sponsel's letter spread like a virus over the Internet, quickly driving the controversy into the mainstream press. A story in Britain's *Guardian* —"Scientist 'killed Amazon indians to test race theory' "—was followed by accounts in *Time* and the *New York Times,* on NPR's [National Public Radio's] *All Things Considered,* and so on. The accusations drew strength from two institutions that endorsed Tierney's credibility: *The New Yorker,* known for its obsessive fact-checking, published an adapted excerpt from the book;... and the fact that the book is scheduled for publication... by W.W. Norton, which is highly respected by academics.

Prepublication galleys of the book show why it inspired such trust. Tierney's argument is massively documented, based on hundreds of interviews, academic articles, and items uncovered under the Freedom of Information Act, not to mention his own visits among the Yanomamö. Through 10 years of dogged sleuthing, it would seem, Tierney dragged a conspiracy of military, medical, and anthropological wrongdoing into the light. [In October 2000], when finalists for [the] year's National Book Awards were announced, *Darkness in El Dorado* was listed in the nonfiction category.

There is only one problem: The book should have been in the fiction category. When examined against its own cited sources, the book is demonstrably,

From John Tooby, "Jungle Fever," *Slate,* http://slate.msn.com/?id=91946 (October 25, 2000). Copyright © 2000 by *Slate*/Distributed by United Feature Syndicate, Inc. Reprinted by permission of United Media.

sometimes hilariously, false on scores of points that are central to its most sensational allegations. After looking into those sources, I found myself seriously wondering whether Tierney had perpetrated a hoax on the publishing world. Of course, only he knows whether he consciously set out "to trick into believing or accepting as genuine something that is false and often preposterous"—the dictionary definition of a hoax. But the book does seem systematically organized to do exactly that. And, to a frightening extent, it has succeeded.

The accusations are directed primarily against James Neel, a physician and a founder of modern medical genetics (now dead), and Napoleon Chagnon, perhaps the world's most famous living social anthropologist. Tierney describes Neel as an unapologetic "eugenicist" who believed as a "social gospel" that "democracy, with its free breeding for the masses and its sentimental supports for the weak" is a eugenic mistake.

Tierney argues that, starting in the 1960s, Neel and his researchers were funded by the Atomic Energy Commission to conduct horrifying medical "experiments" on the Yanomamö. Far and away the most serious allegation is that the researchers killed hundreds or even thousands by knowingly releasing a contagious measles virus into the previously unexposed Yanomamö population. As Turner and Sponsel put it, "Tierney's well-documented account... strongly supports the conclusion that the epidemic was in all probability deliberately caused as an experiment designed to produce scientific support for Neel's eugenic theory." Chagnon—described by Tierney as a "disciple" of Neel's—was implicated in this crime and charged with inadvertently bringing other devastating diseases as well. What's more, Chagnon was said to have been the main cause of the violence he saw among the Yanomamö and more generally to have twisted his scholarly portrayal of them to bolster his Hobbesian theories of human nature.

I was an early recipient of this ethics complaint, in that small number of Internet nanoseconds when it was still considered confidential. As president of the Human Behavior and Evolution Society, of which Chagnon was a prominent member, I was obliged to investigate the allegations, just as the American Anthropological Association would be doing. Chagnon had been my departmental colleague since I moved to the University of California, Santa Barbara, a decade ago, and I consider him a friend. But I'd never met Neel, and for all I knew, he really was a eugenics crackpot, exploiting the isolation of his field site in some warped way. And as for Chagnon—well, how much do we really know about the person in the next office?

Starting with the most serious charge—genocide—I looked up what Neel himself wrote about the measles epidemic. Tierney alleged that a measles vaccine Neel's team administered to the Yanomamö, Edmonston B, was a dangerous agent—and was known to be so at the time—and triggered the epidemic. In Neel's account (a cover-up?), what Tierney finds suspicious—that a measles outbreak started around the time Neel first administered the vaccine—has a different explanation: After Neel learned about the incipient outbreak, he started vaccinating people, trying furiously to head off an epidemic.

To my nonspecialist ears, Tierney's theory sounded possible: Many vaccines, including measles vaccines (then and now), use attenuated live virus, which, when injected, gives the recipient an infection that is supposed to stimulate the immune system. So why couldn't a live virus have spread contagiously from Yanomamö to Yanomamö, launching a deadly epidemic?

I started putting in calls to the Centers for Disease Control and Prevention [CDC] in Atlanta. Conversations with various researchers, including eventually Dr. Mark Papania, chief of the U.S. measles eradication program, rapidly discredited every essential element of the Tierney disease scenarios.

For example, it turns out that researchers who test vaccines for safety have never been able to document, in hundreds of millions of uses, a single case of a live-virus measles vaccine leading to contagious transmission from one human to another—this despite their strenuous efforts to detect such a thing. If attenuated live virus does not jump from person to person, it cannot cause an epidemic. Nor can it be *planned* to cause an epidemic, as alleged in this case, if it never has caused one before.

Experts elsewhere have confirmed this—and have confirmed the safety of the Edmonston B vaccine under the conditions in which it was used. All told, the evidence against Tierney's genocide thesis is now so overwhelming that even Turner, its once-enthusiastic supporter, has backed off. He concedes that the medical expert he finally got around to consulting took Tierney's medical claims and "refuted them point by point."

You'd think the Tierney book, 10 years in the making, might mention the relevant and easily discoverable fact that, as the Michigan medical report puts it, "live attenuated vaccine has never been shown to be transmissible from a recipient to a subsequent contact." Somehow it omits it (even though this information is featured prominently in a paper Tierney cites five times!). The *New Yorker* piece also fails to mention it and instead says, "Today, scientists still do not know whether people who have been vaccinated with Edmonston B can transmit measles." This is literally true, but only because scientists use the word *know* very carefully. Scientists also do not *know* that *The New Yorker* is not riddled with a cult of pedophilic Satan worshipers or that the Pentagon is not in the control of extraterrestrials masquerading as generals. If you ask a *good* scientist about each of these allegations, she would be forced to answer, yes, it's possible. But she will consider it relevant and worth mentioning, as *The New Yorker* does not, that the failure to substantiate a hypothesis given millions of opportunities floats the hypothesis out toward the scientific neighborhood inhabited by ESP and UFOs.

Once I had seen Tierney's most attention-getting claim crumble, I started through the galleys of his book systematically, evaluating it against available sources with the help of various colleagues. Almost anywhere we scratched the surface, a massive tangle of fun-house falsity would erupt through.

We had to accept from the outset that scores of conversations reported in the book are with people scattered through the rain forest, virtually impossible to contact (even for *The New Yorker*'s energetic fact-checkers). So Tierney's veracity would have to be judged on the basis of sources that could be reached. I had already run into one such source—Papania of the CDC, whom Tierney had interviewed for the book. Papania told me that he was troubled to find, in galleys he'd recently been sent, that Tierney had misquoted him. Tierney had him endorsing the idea that the vaccine was a plausible cause of the epidemic, which was not, in fact, his view.

It soon became evident that Tierney was no more faithful to written sources than to oral ones. To begin with, comparing Neel's autobiography with Tierney's use of it is an education in audacity. Whatever Tierney might have wished to convey by calling Neel a "conservative" and claiming that "Neel's politics were too extreme for Reagan's council on aging," Neel's book shows him to be a supporter of Al Gore ("superb," "the most hopeful recent sign"), a Reagan-Bush basher ("chilling," "myopic"), pro-nuclear-disarmament, and an enthusiastic environmentalist. Neel's conflict with the advisory council on aging, it turns out, came when he objected to the diversion of money from poor children into research on how to artificially extend the human life span—research that, Neel speculated, would wind up benefiting mainly the affluent.

And what of Tierney's claim that Neel was a "eugenicist" who believed as a "social gospel" that "democracy, with its free breeding for the masses and its sentimental supports for the weak" was a eugenic mistake? It turns out that Neel had been a fierce opponent of eugenics for 60 years, since his student days. To dramatize his opposition, he labeled his beliefs *euphenics,* emphasizing the medical and social importance of environmental interventions. As Neel put it, the "challenge of euphenics is to ensure that each individual maximizes his genetic potentialities" through the creation of environments in which each can flourish, and "to ameliorate the expression of all our varied genotypes"—ameliorate the *expression* of our genes, not the genes themselves. Neel lists, as examples of good social investments, prenatal care, medical care for children and adolescents, good and equal education for all children, and so on.

There is not a word on any of the pages Tierney cites about how "democracy... violates natural selection." Indeed, though worried about overpopulation, Neel argues that there is no scientific or moral basis for preventing anyone from being a parent, and he says that guaranteeing the equal rights to reproduce would "preserve insofar as it's possible all of [our species'] poorly understood diversity." Neel even does an extended calculation to debunk the eugenicist fear that reproduction by those with genetic defects threatens the gene pool!

Neel does analyze, in the standard way population geneticists do, how unfavorable genetic mutations were "selected out" more rapidly before the invention of agriculture and subsequent creature comforts, and before the transition from polygamy to monogamy (which slows the form of natural selection known as "sexual selection"). Here, as elsewhere in the book, Tierney works feverishly to erase the simple distinction—basic to all scientific discussion—between describing something and endorsing it. In this case, it was a difficult erasure, since Neel, far from wanting to return humanity to a lost world where natural selection is more intense, had called this "unthinkable." (Incidentally, if you're wondering why Neel might have found a measles epidemic useful as a test of his supposed eugenic theories, as Tierney claims, the answer is that Tierney never provides a coherent explanation.)

This pattern of falsification—of which I have mentioned only a small sampling—extends to Tierney's assault on Napoleon Chagnon. To begin with, Tierney—like some other Chagnon critics—carcicatures Chagnon's view of human nature, as if Chagnon considered people innately violent, period. In reality, Chagnon, pondering the relative rate that "people, throughout history, have based their political relationships with other groups on predatory versus religious or altruistic strategies," concludes that "we have the evolved capacity to adopt either strategy," depending on what our culture rewards.

Still, there's no doubt that Chagnon has a more Hobbesian view of human nature than is popular in most anthropological circles. Tierney claims that Chagnon, to support this view, exaggerates Yanomamö violence. He doesn't mention the fact that the rates of violence Chagnon documents are not high compared with the rates found by anthropologists in other pre-state societies. Nor does he mention Chagnon's view that, if anything, the Yanomamö's rate of lethal violence is "much *lower* than that reported for other tribal groups."

Not only does Tierney generally ignore inconvenient data, citing only anthropologists who disagree with Chagnon. He also, time and again, has a way of magically turning anthropologists whose data support Chagnon into anthropologists who contradict him. For example, Tierney cites a study of the Jivaro by Elsa Redmond that he claims undermines one of Chagnon's Yanomamö findings: that the effective use of violence contributes to social status, the acquisition of multiple wives, and the having of many offspring.

Here is Tierney's summary of Redmond:

> Among the Jivaro, head-hunting was a ritual obligation of all males and a required male initiation for teenagers.... Among the Jivaro leaders, however, those who captured the most heads had the fewest wives, and those who had the most wives captured the fewest heads.

Here is what Redmond actually says:

> Yanomamo men who have killed tend to have more wives, which they have acquired either by abducting them from raiding villages, or by the usual marriage alliances in which they are considered more attractive as mates. The same is true of Jivaro war leaders, who might have four to six wives; as a matter of fact, a great war leader on the Upano River in the 1930s by the name of Tuki of José Grande had eleven wives. Distinguished warriors also have more offspring, due mainly to their greater marital success.

Similarly, Tierney cites anthropologist John Peters at various points in his argument that Chagnon exaggerates Yanomamö violence. But what Peters actually writes in his book *Life Among the Yanomamo* is far stronger than anything Chagnon has written: "Anyone who is even minimally acquainted with the Yanomami is familiar with the central role of war in this culture. Violence seems always just a breath away in all Yanomami relations."

Throughout the book, Tierney is comically self-aggrandizing, often presenting as his own discoveries things plainly described in Chagnon's publications. After complaining that Chagnon concealed the identity of villages from which some of his more controversial data were drawn, Tierney writes, "It took me quite a while to penetrate Chagnon's data, but, by combining visits to the villages in the field with GPS [Global Positioning System] locations and mortality statistics, I can identify nine of the twelve villages where all the murderers come from in his *Science* article." Or, if he didn't want to do all that walking and calculating, he could have gotten this information by consulting sources listed in his own bibliography, such as a 1990 Chagnon article and Chagnon's *Yanomamo Interactive* CD.

Although Tierney's many misrepresentations are riveting, his omissions are equally important—and harder for fact-checkers to spot, since omissions don't have footnotes. They figure centrally in two of Tierney's core accusations: that Chagnon inadvertently introduced various diseases besides measles into the region just by going there; and that Chagnon, by giving pots, machetes, and other steel tools to the Yanomamö, somehow exacerbated the rate of warfare, thus influencing the very data he gathered.

Both of these claims are logically possible. But Tierney fails to mention some relevant facts (well known to him) that call them into question.

Tierney presents the Yanomamö as if they were isolated in a petri dish, except when Chagnon visited and sneezed. In reality, the Yanomamö are tens of thousands of people, surrounded by other people with real diseases who have regular transactions with them. Moreover, this 70,000-square-mile area is penetrated by thousands of non-Yanomamö: missionaries, gold miners (over 40,000), highway workers, government officials, tin miners, loggers, ranchers, rubber tappers, drug smugglers, soldiers, moralists like Tierney, and on and on. This whole area is beset by epidemics of various kinds, as the Yanomamö tragically encounter diseases from the industrialized world. So, the probability that Chagnon or Neel or Tierney in particular is the source of any specific epidemic is, crudely speaking, one divided by these tens of thousands. Yet Tierney strangely insists that disease, like war, somehow specifically dogs Chagnon's movements.

To reliably identify the major sources of disease, one would need to collect demographic data in many villages and map it against the various forms of contact. As it happens, this is just what Chagnon did, and he gradually concluded that the Catholic missions were serious sources of disease, largely because of their regular roles as points of contact and entry. Yanomamö living at the missions benefited from the medical care, but those living close enough to catch their diseases yet too far to get the medical care suffered. When Chagnon saw the pattern, he blew the whistle. This did not endear him to the missionaries, who have ever since been the source of enough anti-Chagnon anecdotes to keep an enterprising journalist busy for years.

Similarly, Tierney says that competition over the pots and machetes and other steel tools that Chagnon gave the Yanamamö sometimes led to war. This too is logically possible. The Yanomamö certainly valued Chagnon's gifts, since cutting the jungle back for their crops was much easier with machetes. But Tierney fails to mention that Chagnon's contributions (made so that he would be allowed to collect data) were dwarfed by all the other sources of such items, such as the military, who hired Yanomamö laborers, and especially the vast mission system, which imports boatloads of machetes and other goods, and even has its own airline.

While Tierney considers Chagnon's distribution of steel tools an outrageous threat to peace, he amazingly gives a free pass to the introduction by others—including some missionaries—of hundreds of shotguns. These weapons are known to have been used by the Yanomamö in raiding from mission areas to the less well-armed villages where Chagnon worked. Chagnon blew the whistle on this, too.

In short, what Tierney leaves out of his story is that what his key sources have accused Chagnon of—causing disease and warfare—just happens to be what Chagnon had previously accused some of them of doing. Indeed, a prerequisite of Tierney's ability to do research in this restricted area was almost certainly his endorsement of one side in this feud. Tierney's translators, his guides, his selection of interviewees—all carry the strong implication that he received a guided tour drenched with these local politics. Throughout the book, Tierney goes to extraordinary lengths to explain away real causes of disease and violence that trace back to his patrons. (He has a whole appendix devoted to attacking evidence that the missionaries spread disease.) When this context is supplied, the unremitting denunciations of Chagnon start to sound different, and Tierney, *The New Yorker's* intrepid "Reporter At Large," appears in a less flattering light.

Chagnon has made enemies in academia as well as in the rain forest. Anthropology is full of people who still subscribe to Rousseau's "noble savage" view of human nature, and their battles with Chagnon have been intense. That is why Tierney could pepper his *New Yorker* article, and his book, with anthropologists who question Chagnon's Yanomamö data—a technique of great rhetorical power unless you know about all the anthropologists Tierney doesn't mention whose data support Chagnon. Chagnon's longtime critics include Turner and Sponsel, a fact that explains their uncritical and hyperbolic embrace of the Tierney book, and a fact that isn't mentioned in their incendiary letter to the American Anthropological Association.

With experts increasingly coming forward to debunk various aspects of the Tierney book, the accusations against Neel and Chagnon "are crumbling by the hour," as it was put by Lou Marano of UPI, one of the few reporters to deeply examine the credibility of Tierney's charges. But much damage has already been done—and not just to the reputations of Neel and Chagnon. Tierney's claim that an immunization program can start an epidemic has been carried around the world in media reports. This myth could compromise the ability of health workers to administer such programs, especially in poor countries, and people could die as a result. Moreover, indigenous cultures will not benefit from the public's impression that they are endangered only by the occasional anthropologist, when in fact they are victims of far more powerful forces, ranging from well-meaning missionaries to untrammeled modernization.

The slow-motion tragedy of the world's indigenous peoples continues, and Tierney's thoroughly dishonest book is just one more exploitation of them.

POSTSCRIPT

Did Napoleon Chagnon and Other Researchers Harm the Yanomami Indians of Venezuela?

This controversy exposed a deep rift in the anthropological community. The rift has been variously defined as between those who see anthropology as a science and those who consider it a humanistic discipline, between sociobiologists and cultural determinists, and, at the basest level, between scholars who personally like or dislike Neel and Chagnon. The battle lines are sharply drawn, and few anthropologists have remained neutral. The antagonists are pulling no punches in their charges and countercharges.

The El Dorado Task Force of the A.A.A., which investigated Tierney's accusations, concluded, among other things, that Neel and his associates should be praised, not condemned, for vaccinating the Yanomami against measles, an action that "unquestionably... saved many lives" (see the *Final Report* on the A.A.A. Web site at http://www.aaanet.org). However, the task force criticized Chagnon on ethical and professional grounds for working with a group of wealthy and corrupt Venezuelans to gain access to the Yanomami in 1990, despite having been denied a research permit by the Venezuelan government. It also criticized him for misrepresenting the Yanomami as the "fierce people," a view used by others to justify violence against them, and for not correcting that image or supporting their human rights. Not surprisingly, the report has been criticized by Chagnon's supporters as too harsh and by his enemies as too lenient.

An extremely comprehensive and balanced guide to sources is the Web site of Douglas Hume, a graduate student at the University of Connecticut (http://www.anth.uconn.edu/gradstudents/dhume; click on "Darkness in El Dorado"). It includes a full list of articles published from September 2000 to the present, an extensive supplementary bibliography, and links to relevant Internet sites and documents. The paperback edition of Tierney's book contains an 11-page "afterward" responding to his critics. Other printed publications include Terry Turner's "The Yanomami and the Ethics of Anthropological Practice," Cornell University Latin American Studies Program Occasional Paper (vol. 6, November 2001) and the *Current Anthropology* forum entitled "Reflections on Darkness in El Dorado," which presents comments by six scholars (vol. 42, no. 2, 2001). A relevant earlier source is Leslie Sponsel's article "Yanomami: An Arena of Conflict and Aggression in the Amazon," *Aggressive Behavior* (vol. 24, no. 2, 1998).

ISSUE 18

Do Museums Misrepresent Ethnic Communities Around the World?

YES: James Clifford, from *The Predicament of Culture: Twentieth-Century Ethnography, Literature, and Art* (Harvard University Press, 1988)

NO: Denis Dutton, from "Mythologies of Tribal Art," *African Arts* (Summer 1995)

ISSUE SUMMARY

YES: Postmodernist anthropologist James Clifford argues that the very act of removing objects from their ethnographic contexts distorts the meaning of objects held in museums. He contends that whether these objects are displayed in art museums or anthropological museums, exhibitions misrepresent ethnic communities by omitting important aspects of contemporary life, especially involvement with the colonial or Western world.

NO: Anthropologist Denis Dutton asserts that no exhibition can provide a complete context for ethnographic objects, but that does not mean that museum exhibitions are fundamentally flawed. Dutton suggests that postmodernists misunderstand traditional approaches to interpreting museum collections, and what they offer as a replacement actually minimizes what we can understand of ethnic communities from museum collections.

In the late nineteenth and early twentieth centuries, museums were a major focus of anthropological research. In the United States, for example, until after the First World War more anthropologists were employed in museums than in universities. By 1940 cultural anthropologists had largely moved out of museums as they focused on intensive fieldwork. This change was directly related to a shift in paradigms from cultural evolution to functionalism, which happened in the 1920s and 1930s.

As anthropologists later began to focus on functional questions about how societies and their institutions worked, museum collections became increasingly unimportant. Many anthropologists believed that differences in the bindings of stone axes have little to say about how marriages were contracted or how clans were linked together; objects cannot explain how leadership worked or what role religious ideas might have had in maintaining social order.

The following selections deal with the question of how museums should exhibit and interpret ethnographic collections that were obtained during the "museum period" of anthropology. Both authors are critical of certain exhibitions, particularly art historian William Rubin's "Primitivism" show from 1984, and both feel that a good exhibition should contextualize museum objects historically. But the authors differ profoundly in their approach to the study of museum objects.

James Clifford surveys several different kinds of museum exhibits in New York and asks, Do any of them do justice to the peoples who made and used these objects? For Clifford, objects and the cultures from which they come have histories. He questions how much of these histories are present in the several exhibitions he visited. By definition, each and every non-Western object in a Western museum has been removed from its original ethnographic context, a process often referred to as "decontextualization."

Clifford explains in his selection how museums offer a "representation" of tribal peoples as if these societies were timeless and without history. By focusing on particular features of tribal culture, each exhibition makes statements about the relationship between modern Americans and "primitive" peoples. For him, these are fundamentally misleading representations.

Denis Dutton accepts that exhibitions such as those discussed by Clifford are inevitably incomplete, but the lack of a full context does not completely invalidate the exercise of exhibiting objects from tribal societies. He argues that Clifford and the other postmodernist critics of museum exhibitions go too far in their criticisms and that they, too, have an agenda that is itself misleading. Referring to this postmodernist agenda as a "new mythology" about tribal art, Dutton contends that the new mythologists have exaggerated their interpretations of museum exhibitions.

Dutton argues that museums can never offer complete representations of ethnic communities; but this does not mean that exhibitions cannot be both informative and enlightening even if they are incomplete. He asserts that Clifford's analysis leads us away from any understanding of museum objects; instead Clifford prefers to present his understandings of the culture through museum curators in our own modern culture. For Dutton, the goal should be to discover the meanings and significance of objects from the point of view of their original communities, and such meanings will never emerge from critiques of museum exhibitions like Clifford's.

How serious are the inevitable distortions of a museum exhibit? Does the omission of the current historical and global economic context misinform the public? How much context can a museum exhibition realistically provide? If such misrepresentations do occur, would it be better not to exhibit "primitive" art at all? What solutions to the problem of distortion do Clifford and Dutton propose?

James Clifford  **YES**

Histories of the Tribal and the Modern

During the winter of 1984–85 one could encounter tribal objects in an unusual number of locations around New York City. This [selection] surveys a half-dozen, focusing on the most controversial: the major exhibition held at the Museum of Modern Art (MOMA), " 'Primitivism' in 20th Century Art: Affinity of the Tribal and the Modern." The ... "ethnographic present" is late December 1984.

The "tribal" objects gathered on West Fifty-third Street have been around. They are travelers—some arriving from folklore and ethnographic museums in Europe, others from art galleries and private collections. They have traveled first class to the Museum of Modern Art, elaborately crated and insured for important sums. Previous accommodations have been less luxurious: some were stolen, others "purchased" for a song by colonial administrators, travelers, anthropologists, missionaries, sailors in African ports. These non-Western objects have been by turns curiosities, ethnographic specimens, major art creations. After 1900 they began to turn up in European flea markets, thereafter moving between avant-garde studios and collectors' apartments. Some came to rest in the unheated basements or "laboratories" of anthropology museums, surrounded by objects made in the same region of the world. Others encountered odd fellow travelers, lighted and labeled in strange display cases. Now on West Fifty-third Street they intermingle with works by European masters—Picasso, Giacometti, Brancusi, and others. A three-dimensional Eskimo mask with twelve arms and a number of holes hangs beside a canvas on which Joan Miró has painted colored shapes. The people in New York look at the two objects and see that they are alike.

Travelers tell different stories in different places, and on West Fifty-third Street an origin story of modernism is featured. Around 1910 Picasso and his cohort suddenly, intuitively recognize that "primitive" objects are in fact powerful "art." They collect, imitate, and are affected by these objects. Their own work, even when not directly influenced, seems oddly reminiscent of non-Western forms. The modern and the primitive converse across the centuries and continents. At the Museum of Modern Art an exact history is told featuring individual artists and objects, their encounters in specific studios at precise moments. Photographs document the crucial influences of non-Western artifacts on the pioneer modernists. This focused story is surrounded and infused with another—a loose allegory of relationship centering on the word *affinity*. The word is a kinship term, suggesting a deeper or more natural relationship than mere resemblance or juxtaposition. It connotes a common quality or essence joining the tribal to the modern. A Family of Art is brought together, global, diverse, richly inventive, and miraculously unified, for every object displayed on West Fifty-third Street looks modern.

The exhibition at MOMA is historical and didactic. It is complemented by a comprehensive, scholarly catalogue, which includes divergent views of its topic and in which the show's organizers, William Rubin and Kirk Varnedoe, argue at length its underlying premises. One of the virtues of an exhibition that blatantly makes a case or tells a story is that it encourages debate and makes possible the suggestion of other stories. Thus in what follows different histories of the tribal and the modern will be proposed in response to the sharply focused history on display at the Museum of Modern Art. But before that history can be seen for what it is, however—a specific story that excludes other stories—the universalizing allegory of affinity must be cleared away.

This allegory, the story of the Modernist Family of Art, is not rigorously argued at MOMA. (That would require some explicit form of either an archetypal or structural analysis.) The allegory is, rather, built into the exhibition's form, featured suggestively in its publicity, left uncontradicted, repetitiously asserted —"Affinity of the Tribal and the Modern." The allegory has a hero, whose virtuoso work, an exhibit caption tells us, contains more affinities with the tribal than that of any other pioneer modernist. These affinities "measure the depth of Picasso's grasp of the informing principles of tribal sculpture, and reflect his profound identity of spirit with the tribal peoples." Modernism is thus presented as a search for "informing principles" that transcend culture, politics, and history. Beneath this generous umbrella the tribal is modern and the modern more richly, more diversely human.

❧

The power of the affinity idea is such (it becomes almost self-evident in the MOMA juxtapositions) that it is worth reviewing the major objections to it. Anthropologists, long familiar with the issue of cultural diffusion versus independent invention, are not likely to find anything special in the similarities between selected tribal and modern objects. An established principle of anthropological comparative method asserts that the greater the range of cultures, the more likely one is to find similar traits. MOMA's sample is very large, embracing African, Oceanic, North American, and Arctic "tribal" groups. A second principle, that of the "limitation of possibilities," recognizes that invention, while highly diverse, is not infinite. The human body, for example, with its two eyes, four limbs, bilateral arrangement of features, front and back, and so on, will be represented and stylized in a limited number of ways. There is thus a priori no reason to claim evidence for affinity (rather than mere resemblance or coincidence) because an exhibition of tribal works that seem impressively "modern" in style can be gathered. An equally striking collection could be made demonstrating sharp dissimilarities between tribal and modern objects.

The qualities most often said to link these objects are their "conceptualism" and "abstraction" (but a very long and ultimately incoherent list of shared traits, including "magic," "ritualism," "environmentalism," use of "natural" materials, and so on, can be derived from the show and especially from its catalogue). Actually the tribal and modern artifacts are similar only in that they do *not* feature the pictorial illusionism or sculptural naturalism that came to dominate Western European art after the Renaissance. Abstraction and conceptualism are, of course, pervasive in the arts of the non-Western World. To say that they share with modernism a rejection of certain naturalist projects is not to show anything like an affinity. Indeed the "tribalism" selected in the exhibition to resemble modernism is itself a construction designed to accomplish the task of resemblance. Ife and Benin sculptures, highly naturalistic in style, are excluded from the "tribal" and placed in a somewhat arbitrary category of "court" society (which does not, however, include large chieftainships). Moreover, pre-Columbian works, though they have a place in the catalogue, are largely omitted from the exhibition. One can question other selections and exclusions that result in a collection of only "modern"-looking tribal objects. Why, for example, are there relatively few "impure" objects constructed from the debris of colonial culture contacts? And is there not an overall bias toward clean, abstract forms as against rough or crude work?

The "Affinities" room of the exhibition is an intriguing but entirely problematic exercise in formal mix-and-match. The short introductory text begins well: "AFFINITIES presents a group of tribal objects notable for their appeal to modern taste." Indeed this is all that can rigorously be said of the objects in this room. The text continues, however, "Selected pairings of modern and tribal objects demonstrate common denominators of these arts that are independent of direct influence." The phrase *common denominators* implies something more systematic than intriguing resemblance. What can it possibly mean? ... The affinity idea itself is wide-ranging and promiscuous, as are allusions to universal human capacities retrieved in the encounter between modern and tribal or invocations of the expansive human mind—the healthy capacity of modernist consciousness to question its limits and engage otherness.

... The affinities shown at MOMA are all on modernist terms. The great modernist "pioneers" (and their museum) are shown promoting formerly despised tribal "fetishes" or mere ethnographic "specimens" to the status of high art and in the process discovering new dimensions of their ("our") creative potential. The capacity of art to transcend its cultural and historical context is asserted repeatedly. ...

At West Fifth-third Street modernist primitivism is a going Western concern. ...

Indeed an unintended effect of the exhibition's comprehensive catalogue is to show once and for all the incoherence of the modern Rorschach of "the primitive." ... [T]he catalogue succeeds in demonstrating not any essential affinity between tribal and modern or even a coherent modernist attitude toward the primitive but rather the restless desire and power of the modern West to collect the world.

⋅⧫⋅

... If we ignore the "Affinities" room at MOMA, however, and focus on the "serious" historical part of the exhibition, new critical questions emerge. What is excluded by the specific focus of the history? Isn't this factual narration still infused with the affinity allegory, since it is cast as a story of creative genius recognizing the greatness of tribal works, discovering common artistic "informing principles"? Could the story of this intercultural encounter be told differently? It is worth making the effort to extract another story from the materials in the exhibition—a history not of redemption or of discovery but of reclassification. This other history assumes that "art" is not universal but is a changing Western cultural category. The fact that rather abruptly, in the space of a few decades, a large class of non-Western artifacts came to be redefined as art is a taxonomic shift that requires critical historical discussion, not celebration. That this construction of a generous category of art pitched at a global scale occurred just as the planet's tribal peoples came massively under European political, economic, and evangelical dominion cannot be irrelevant. But there is no room for such complexities at the MOMA show. Obviously the modernist appropriation of tribal productions as art is not simply imperialist. The project involves too many strong critiques of colonialist, evolutionist assumptions. As we shall see, though, the scope and underlying logic of the "discovery" of tribal art reproduces hegemonic Western assumptions rooted in the colonial and neocolonial epoch.

Picasso, Léger, Apollinaire, and many others came to recognize the elemental, "magical" power of African sculptures in a period of growing *négrophilie,* a context that would see the irruption onto the European scene of other evocative black figures: the jazzman, the boxer (Al Brown), the *sauvage* Josephine Baker. To tell the history of modernism's recognition of African "art" in this broader context would raise ambiguous and disturbing questions about aesthetic appropriation of non-Western others, issues of race, gender, and power. This other story is largely invisible at MOMA.... Overall one would be hard pressed to deduce from the exhibition that all the enthusiasm for things *nègre,* for the "magic" of African art, had anything to do with race. Art in this focused history has no essential link with coded perceptions of black bodies— their vitalism, rhythm, magic, erotic power, etc.—as seen by whites. The modernism represented here is concerned only with artistic invention, a positive category separable from a negative primitivism of the irrational, the savage, the base, the flight from civilization.

A different historical focus might bring a photograph of Josephine Baker into the vicinity of the African statues that were exciting the Parisian avant-garde in the 1910s and 1920s; but such a juxtaposition would be unthinkable in the MOMA history, for it evokes different affinities from those contributing to the category of great art. The black body in Paris of the twenties was an ideological artifact. Archaic Africa (which came to Paris by way of the future—that is,

America) was sexed, gendered, and invested with "magic" in specific ways. Standard poses adopted by "La Bakaire," like Léger's designs and costumes, evoked a recognizable "Africanity"—the naked form emphasizing pelvis and buttocks, a segmented stylization suggesting a strangely mechanical vitality. The inclusion of so ideologically loaded a form as the body of Josephine Baker among the figures classified as art on West Fifty-third Street would suggest a different account of modernist primitivism, a different analysis of the category *nègre* in *l'art nègre* and an exploration of the "taste" that was something more than just a backdrop for the discovery of tribal art in the opening decades of this century.

Such a focus would treat art as a category defined and redefined in specific historical contexts and relations of power. . . .

Since 1900 non-Western objects have generally been classified as either primitive art *or* ethnographic specimens. Before the modernist revolution associated with Picasso and the simultaneous rise of cultural anthropology associated with Boas and Malinowski, these objects were differently sorted—as antiquities, exotic curiosities, orientalia, the remains of early man, and so on. With the emergence of twentieth-century modernism and anthropology figures formerly called "fetishes" (to take just one class of object) became works either of "sculpture" or of "material culture." The distinction between the aesthetic and the anthropological was soon institutionally reinforced. In art galleries non-Western objects were displayed for their formal and aesthetic qualities; in ethnographic museums they were represented in a "cultural" context. In the latter an African statue was a ritual object belonging to a distinct group; it was displayed in ways that elucidated its use, symbolism, and function. The institutionalized distinction between aesthetic and anthropological discourses took form during the years documented at MOMA, years that saw the complementary discovery of primitive "art" and of an anthropological concept of culture." . . .

Cultural background is not essential to correct aesthetic appreciation and analysis: good art, the masterpiece, is universally recognizable. The pioneer modernists themselves knew little or nothing of these objects' ethnographic meaning. What was good enough for Picasso is good enough for MOMA. Indeed an ignorance of cultural context seems almost a precondition for artistic appreciation. In this object system a tribal piece is detached from one milieu in order to circulate freely in another, a world of art—of museums, markets, and connoisseurship.

Since the early years of modernism and cultural anthropology non-Western objects have found a "home" either within the discourses and institutions of art or within those of anthropology. . . . Both discourses assume a primitive world in need of preservation, redemption, and representation. The concrete, inventive existence of tribal cultures and artists is suppressed in the process of either constituting authentic, "traditional" worlds or appreciating their products in the timeless category of "art."

⊷⦿⊶

Nothing on West Fifty-third Street suggests that good tribal art is being pro-duced in the 1980s. The non-Western artifacts on display are located either in a vague past (reminiscent of the label "nineteenth-twentieth century" that ac-companies African and Oceanian pieces in the Metropolitan Museum's Rocke-feller Wing) or in a purely conceptual space defined by "primitive" qualities: magic, ritualism, closeness to nature, mythic or cosmological aims. In this rel-egation of the tribal or primitive to either a vanishing past or an ahistorical, conceptual present, modernist appreciation reproduces common ethnographic categories.

The same structure can be seen in the Hall of Pacific Peoples, dedicated to Margaret Mead, at the American Museum of Natural History. This new per-manent hall is a superbly refurbished anthropological stopping place for non-Western objects. In *Rotunda* (December 1984), the museum's publication, an article announcing the installation contains the following paragraph:

> Margaret Mead once referred to the cultures of Pacific peoples as "a world that once was and now is no more." Prior to her death in 1978 she approved the basic plans for the new *Hall of Pacific Peoples*. (p. 1)

We are offered treasures saved from a destructive history, relics of a van-ishing world. Visitors to the installation (and especially members of *present* Pacific cultures) may find a "world that is no more" more appropriately evoked in two charming display cases just outside the hall. It is the world of a dated anthropology. Here one finds a neatly typed page of notes from Mead's much-disputed Samoan research, a picture of the fieldworker interacting "closely" with Melanesians (she is carrying a child on her back), a box of brightly col-ored discs and triangles once used for psychological testing, a copy of Mead's column in *Redbook*. In the Hall of Pacific Peoples artifacts suggesting change and syncretism are set apart in a small display entitled "Culture Contact." It is noted that Western influence and indigenous response have been active in the Pacific since the eighteenth century. Yet few signs of this involvement appear anywhere else in the large hall, despite the fact that many of the objects were made in the past 150 years in situations of contact, and despite the fact that the museum's ethnographic explanations reflect quite recent research on the cultures of the Pacific. The historical contacts and impurities that are part of ethnographic work—and that may signal the life, not the death, of societies—are systematically excluded.

The tenses of the hall's explanatory captions are revealing. A recent color photograph of a Samoan *kava* ceremony is accompanied by the words: "STATUS and RANK were [sic] important features of Samoan society," a statement that will seem strange to anyone who knows how important they remain in Samoa today. Elsewhere in the hall a black-and-white photograph of an Australian Arunta woman and child, taken around 1900 by the pioneer ethnographers Spencer and Gillen, is captioned in the *present* tense. Aboriginals apparently must always inhabit a mythic time. Many other examples of temporal incoherence could be cited—old Sepik objects described in the present, recent Trobriand photos labeled in the past, and so forth.

The point is not simply that the image of Samoan *kava* drinking and status society presented here is a distortion or that in most of the Hall of Pacific Peoples history has been airbrushed out. (No Samoan men at the *kava* ceremony are wearing wristwatches; Trobriand face painting is shown without noting that it is worn at cricket matches.) Beyond such questions of accuracy is an issue of systematic ideological coding. To locate "tribal" peoples in a nonhistorical time and ourselves in a different, historical time is clearly tendentious and no longer credible (Fabian 1983). This recognition throws doubt on the perception of a vanishing tribal world, rescued, made valuable and meaningful, either as ethnographic "culture" or as primitive/modern "art." ...

At the Hall of Pacific Peoples or the Rockefeller Wing the actual ongoing life and "impure" inventions of tribal peoples are erased in the name of cultural or artistic "authenticity." Similarly at MOMA the production of tribal "art" is entirely in the past. Turning up in the flea markets and museums of late nineteenth-century Europe, these objects are destined to be aesthetically redeemed, given new value in the object system of a generous modernism.

⚜

The story retold at MOMA, the struggle to gain recognition for tribal art, for its capacity "like all great art... to show images of man that transcend the particular lives and times of their creators," is taken for granted at another stopping place for tribal travelers in Manhattan, the Center for African Art on East Sixty-eighth Street. Susan Vogel, the executive director, proclaims in her introduction to the catalogue of its inaugural exhibition, "African Masterpieces from the Musee de l'Homme, " that the "aesthetic-anthropological debate" has been resolved. It is now widely accepted that "ethnographic specimens" can be distinguished from "works of art" and that within the latter category a limited number of "masterpieces" are to be found. Vogel correctly notes that the aesthetic recognition of tribal objects depends on changes in Western taste. For example it took the work of Francis Bacon, Lucas Samaras, and others to make it possible to exhibit as art "rough and horrifying [African] works as well as refined and lyrical ones." Once recognized, though, art is apparently art. Thus the selection at the Center is made on aesthetic criteria alone. A prominent placard affirms that the ability of these objects "to transcend the limitations of time and place, to speak to us across time and culture... places them among the highest points of human achievement. It is as works of art that we regard them here and as a testament to the greatness of their creators."

There could be no clearer statement of one side of the aesthetic anthropological "debate" (or better, *system*). On the other (anthropological) side, across town, the Hall of Pacific Peoples presents collective rather than individual productions—the work of "cultures." At the American Museum of Natural History ethnographic exhibits have come increasingly to resemble art shows. Indeed the Hall of Pacific Peoples represents the latest in aestheticized scientism. Objects are displayed in ways that highlight their formal properties.... While these artistically displayed artifacts are scientifically explained, an older, functionalist attempt to present an integrated picture of specific societies or culture areas is no longer seriously pursued. There is an almost dadaist quality to the labels on eight cases devoted to Australian aboriginal society (I cite the complete series in order): "CEREMONY, SPIRIT FIGURE, MAGICIANS AND SORCERERS, SACRED ART, SPEAR THROWERS, STONE AXES AND KNIVES, WOMEN, BOOMERANGS." Elsewhere the hall's pieces of culture have been recontextualized within a new cybernetic, anthropological discourse. For instance flutes and stringed instruments are captioned: "MUSIC is a system of organized sound in man's [sic] aural environment" or nearby: "COMMUNICATION is an important function of organized sound."

In the anthropological Hall of Pacific Peoples non-Western objects still have primarily scientific value. They are in addition beautiful. Conversely, at the Center for African Art artifacts are essentially defined as "masterpieces," their makers as great artists. The discourse of connoisseurship reigns. Yet once the story of art told at MOMA becomes dogma, it is possible to reintroduce and co-opt the discourse of ethnography. At the Center tribal contexts and functions are described along with individual histories of the objects on display. Now firmly classified as masterpieces, African objects escape the vague, ahistorical location of the "tribal" or the "primitive." The catalogue, a sort of *catalogue raisonné*, discusses each work intensively. The category of the masterpiece individuates: the pieces on display are not typical; some are one of a kind. The famous Fon god of war or the Abomey shark-man lend themselves to precise histories of individual creation and appropriation in visible colonial situations. Captions specify *which* Griaule expedition to West Africa in the 1930s acquired each Dogon statue.... We learn in the catalogue that a superb Bamileke mother and child was carved by an artist named Kwayep, that the statue was bought by the colonial administrator and anthropologist Henri Labouret from King N'Jike. While tribal names predominate at MOMA, the Rockefeller Wing, and the American Museum of Natural History, here personal names make their appearance.

In the "African Masterpieces" catalogue we learn of an ethnographer's excitement on finding a Dogon hermaphrodite figure that would later become famous. The letter recording this excitement, written by Denise Paulme in 1935, serves as evidence of the aesthetic concerns of many early ethnographic collectors. These individuals, we are told, could intuitively distinguish masterpieces from mere art or ethnographic specimens. (Actually many of the individual ethnographers behind the Musée de l'Homme collection, such as Paulme, Michel Leiris, Marcel Griaule, and André Schaeffner, were friends and collaborators of the same "pioneer modernist" artists who, in the story told at MOMA, constructed the category of primitive art. Thus the intuitive aesthetic sense in question is the product of a historically specific milieu.) The "African Masterpieces" catalogue insists that the founders of the Musée de l'Homme were art connoisseurs, that this great anthropological museum never treated all its contents as "ethnographic specimens." The Musee de l'Homme was and is secretly an art museum. The taxonomic split between art and artifact is thus healed, at least for self-evident "masterpieces," entirely in terms of the aesthetic code. Art is art in any museum....

The non-Western objects that excited Picasso, Derain, and Léger broke into the realm of official Western art from outside. They were quickly integrated, recognized as masterpieces, given homes within an anthropological-aesthetic object system. By now this process has been sufficiently celebrated. We need exhibitions that question the boundaries of art and of the art world, an influx of truly indigestible "outside" artifacts. The relations of power whereby one portion of humanity can select, value, and collect the pure products of others need to be criticized and transformed. This is no small task. In the meantime one can at least imagine shows that feature the impure, "inauthentic" productions of past and present tribal life; exhibitions radically heterogeneous in their global mix of styles; exhibitions that locate themselves in specific multicultural junctures; exhibitions in which nature remains "unnatural"; exhibitions whose principles of incorporation are openly questionable. The following would be my contribution to a different show on "affinities of the tribal and the postmodern." I offer just the first paragraph from Barbara Tedlock's superb description of the Zuni Shalako ceremony, a festival that is only part of a complex, living tradition.

> Imagine a small western New Mexican village, its snow-lit streets lined with white Mercedes, quarter-ton pickups and Dodge vans. Villagers wrapped in black blankets and flowered shawls are standing next to visitors in blue velveteen blouses with rows of dime buttons and voluminous satin skirts. Their men are in black Stetson silver-banded hats, pressed jeans, Tony Lama boots and multicolored Pendleton blankets. Strangers dressed in dayglo orange, pink and green ski jackets, stocking caps, hiking boots and mittens. All crowded together they are looking into newly constructed houses illuminated by bare light bulbs dangling from raw rafters edged with Woolworth's red fabric and flowered blue print calico. Cinderblock and plasterboard white walls are layered with striped serapes, Chimayó blankets, Navajo rugs, flowered fringed embroidered shawls, black silk from Mexico and purple, red and blue rayon from Czechoslovakia. Rows of Hopi cotton dance kilts and rain sashes; Isleta woven red and green belts; Navajo and Zuni silver concha belts and black mantas covered with silver brooches set with carved lapidary, rainbow mosaic, channel inlay, turquoise needle-point, pink agate, alabaster, black cannel coal and bakelite from old '78s, coral, abalone shell, mother-of-pearl and horned oyster hang from poles suspended from the ceiling. Mule and white-tailed deer trophy-heads wearing squash-blossom, coral and chunk-turquoise necklaces are hammered up around the room over rearing buckskins above Arabian tapestries of Martin Luther King and the Kennedy brothers, The Last Supper, a herd of sheep with a haloed herder, horses, peacocks.

NO

Denis Dutton

Mythologies of Tribal Art

Forty years ago Roland Barthes defined a mythology as those "falsely obvious" ideas which an age so takes for granted that it is unaware of its own
belief. An example of what he means can be seen in his 1957 critique of Edward
Steichen's celebrated photographic assemblage "The Family of Man." Barthes
declares that the myth this exhibition promotes first seems to stress exoti-
cism, projecting a Babel of human diversity over the globe. From this picture
of diversity, however, a pluralistic humanism "is magically produced: man is
born, works, laughs and dies everywhere in the same way...." The implicit
mythological background of the show postulates "a human essence."

Barthes is exactly on target about the philosophic intentions of "The Family of Man." In his introduction to the published version of the exhibition,
Steichen had written that the show was "conceived as a mirror of the universal
elements and emotions in the everydayness of life—as a mirror of the essential
oneness of mankind throughout the world." Such juxtapositions as that which
places Nina Leen's *Life* magazine image of an American farm family next to a
family in Bechuanaland (now Botswana), photographed by another *Life* pho-
tographer, Nat Farbman, are therefore meant to convey the idea that despite
all differences of exterior form, of cultural surface, the underlying nature of
all families and peoples is essentially the same. This position is what Barthes
views as the sentimentalized mythology of "classic humanism," and he contrasts it with his own "progressive humanism," which must try "constantly to
scour nature, its 'laws' and its 'limits' in order to discover History there, and
at last to establish Nature itself as historical." While classic humanism regards
the American and African families as embodying, beneath culture and skin
color, abiding natural relationships of kin and affection, progressive humanism would insist that these bourgeois conceptions of the natural are themselves
historically determined. Barthes claims that such imperialistic juxtapositions
ignore the political and economic roots of diversity.

Although "The Family of Man" had a potently relevant message for the
generation that had witnessed the genocidal horrors of the Second World War,
it was also worth paying attention to Barthes's claim that Steichen's collection, for all its antiracism and humanist charms, conveyed an implicit illusion

of equality of power among the cultures it portrayed. It is now two generations later, however, and critics who accept the importance of exposing cultural mythologies and covert ideologies have new work to do. One area of criticism that especially stands in need of fresh examination is the shell-pocked field where battles have raged over the status and understanding of ethnographic arts. Barthes's reaction to MOMA's "The Family of Man" is particularly pertinent in this regard, because much of what he says adumbrates reactions to another exhibition, " 'Primitivism' in 20th Century Art," which took place over a quarter of a century later in that same museum. That show displayed side-by-side images of Africa and Europe, not photographs of people, but works of art. And it too was denounced as complacently positing, without regard to cultural difference, a specious universalism—aesthetic instead of moral.

But a sea change in academic thinking separates Barthes's critique of "The Family of Man" from the more strident critics of the "Primitivism" show. In the middle 1950s, Barthes was nearly alone in his dissent against a much loved and widely praised exhibition. The generation of critics who questioned (or denounced) "Primitivism" represented a manner of thinking that had become a virtual academic fashion. Some of these later critics were arguing from a set of ideas that had themselves come to embody a virtual mythology in precisely the Barthesian sense. Their views presuppose and constitute, in point of fact, a New Mythology of tribal arts—a prevailing set of presuppositions, prejudices, and articles of political and philosophical faith which govern many discussions of these arts and their relations to European criticism, art, and aesthetics. A contemporary Africanist art historian [Sidney Kasfir] for example, writes in a recent *African Arts* article on the authenticity of African masks and carvings: "That from an African perspective, these objects are *not* art in the current Western sense is too well known to discuss here." The phrase "too well known to discuss here" is symptomatic of a mythology. Barthes claimed his intention to unmask "the mystification which transforms petit-bourgeois culture into universal nature." Today we should be just as willing to deal with those mystifications that transform prevailing conventions of academic culture into validated truth.

This vigorous New Mythology of tribal arts takes on its life against the backdrop of what it posits as the Old Mythology. As with other ideologies, the New Mythology would no more describe its precepts as "mythology" than would the Old: both operate according to the familiar adage "Your views are so much mythology; mine speak the truth." Nevertheless, much contemporary theorizing and criticism about tribal arts are founded on a complacent acceptance of a substrate of givens and unsupported hypotheses which constitute the central tenets of the New Mythology. To be sure, not all of the theses are false. On the other hand, not all of the beliefs the New Mythologists stigmatize as Old Mythology are false either. Independent, critical thinkers should want to choose the component ideas of these mythologies that are worth rejecting, preserving, or reviving.

Providing a disinterested assessment of these ideas is not easy in the present ideologically charged and factious atmosphere. This indeed is part of the problem: so many contemporary theorists of tribal arts posit enemies who have it all wrong, in contrast to themselves, who have it right. This lack of any generosity whatsoever toward one's perceived (or invented) opposition increasingly stultifies writing in this area. The New Mythology finds itself expressed by a wide range of writers, including, for example, the more vociferous critics of the "Primitivism" show such as Thomas McEvilley and Hal Foster; James Clifford in his treatment of museums and ethnographic art; Arnold Krupat in *Ethnocriticism;* Sidney Kasfir in her article "African Art and Authenticity," published in this journal; Sally Price in *Primitive Art in Civilized Places;* Marianna Torgovnick in *Gone Primitive;* and Christopher B. Steiner in *African Art in Transit.*

Mythologies, Old and New

There are actually two phases of the Old Mythology to which these writers tend to react. What I will call *premodernist* or *colonialist* Old Mythology includes the elements of nineteenth-century imperialism—racism, contempt for "childish" artifacts, and regard for "primitive" art as representing a lower evolutionary stage of human development, with missionaries burning "fetishes" and the wholesale looting of indigenous art, as in Benin. The later, more enlightened, *modernist* Old Mythology, exemplified by such figures as Picasso, Roger Fry, and the "Primitivism" exhibition itself, is, from a New Mythological perspective, perhaps even more insidious, because while it pretends to valorize these arts, it perpetuates acts of imperialism, appropriation, and ethnocentric insensitivity toward Third World peoples—all in the name of enlightened, magnanimous liberalism. The grounds for my three-fold distinction—between premodernist/colonialist Old Mythology, modernist Old Mythology, and the New Mythology —can be usefully developed in terms of the following key ideas. Again, some of these notions included within these mythologies are entirely valid, some constitute half-truths, and some are plainly false; no one of these sets of ideas has a monopoly on truth.

> *(1) According to the premodernist Old Mythology, at least as the New Mythology likes to imagine it, tribal artifacts weren't works of art at all, but merely "fetishes," "idols," "fertility symbols," "ancestor figures," and the like, which colonialists collected as they might botanical specimens. The later, post-Picasso modernist version of the Old Mythology insists, on the contrary, that they are works of art, embodying universal aesthetic values.*

Curiously, the New Mythology frequently sides with the colonialist Old Mythology by aggressively questioning the status of tribal artifacts as works of art: in the New Mythological view, the Old Mythology at least acknowledged difference. This convergence of opinion, however, is complicated. Philistine colonialists often regarded artifacts as demonstrating little skill and no sense of form: the colonialists were applying nineteenth-century European aesthetic criteria to genres of work they did not begin to comprehend, and so were reluctant to call them "art." The New Mythologists' reluctance to identify tribal artifact genres as "art" is based on the notion that this would be hegemonic or imperialistic. Such reluctance is frequently supported by unthinking repetition of the folk legend that pretechnological peoples have no art because they have no word that refers to what Europeans call "art." Patrick R. McNaughton recognizes another aspect of this New Mythologists' doctrine and has stressed the importance of challenging it, "because so many scholars still recite what has become a kind of maxim asserted by outsiders about Africans, that they unlike us treat what we call art as a functional part of life" rather than something for aesthetic contemplation.

(2) The Old Mythology essentialized the primitive, subsuming the endless variety of tribal cultures under a few crude stereotypes.

The New Mythology, on the other hand, while eager to recognize the diverse and frequently unique characteristics that distinguish tribal societies, essentializes "the West," creating, in an inversion of Edward Said's familiar formulation, a kind of Occidentalism. Thus, in the example cited earlier, Kasfir qualifies her discussion of authenticity with the remark that the artifacts in question should not be considered art "in the current Western sense." The quaintness of this last phrase should not go unnoticed: among Praxiteles, Donatello, Rembrandt, Judy Chicago, Duchamp, and Koons—not to mention the myriad genres of European folk craft and popular art—there is no "current Western sense" of art, but various, radically different, and rival senses of the concept, each partially implicated in competing social practices and theories of art. In fact, in its crudity, the very phrase "the West" is the New Mythologists' answer to "the Primitive" as that term might have been used a century ago. The latter was a lazy and misleading way of lumping together such cultures as Hopi, Sepik, Benin, and !Kung—even Aztec, in some understandings of "primitive." In the New Mythology, "the West" refers to twelfth-century French villages, horror movies, the Industrial Revolution, the theology of St. Augustine, New Zealand public education, the international banking system, modern toy retailing, medieval concepts of disease, Thanksgiving dinner, electronic mail, Gregorian chants, Linnaean botany, napalm, the Chopin études, and bar codes —as though the values and ideologies found therein can be the subject of useful generalization. The New Mythology replaces one set of stereotypes with another set, equally banal.

(3) In the Old Mythology, precontact tribal societies were seen as largely isolated, unchanging, coherent, and unbroken in their cultural tradition. Colonialism was supposed to have destroyed their structure and belief base. Their Golden Age of aesthetic and cultural achievement, and hence authenticity, predates European contact: Postcolonial culture and artifacts are culturally "inauthentic."

The New Mythology asserts to the contrary that these societies never were isolated, were not necessarily "unified" or "coherent," and underwent profound breaks in their traditions before European contact. The Old Mythology's "people without a history" view was a convenient colonialist construction. The New Mythology responds to claims of "inauthenticity" by variously claiming

(a) indigenous belief systems were not destroyed but only occulted during the colonial period, and are now coming again into flower; (b) what is truly authentic is now found in the process of mutual appropriation by indigenous and colonial cultures; and in any event, (c) authentic cultural values must always be defined by the people who hold them: therefore, whatever indigenous people claim as authentic is, *ipso facto,* authentic, whether traditional, postcolonial, or merely imported.

Old and New Mythologists for the most part agree that small-scale indigenous societies have been permanently altered or obliterated by the encounter with the West's political systems, media, missionaries, technology, commerce, wage labor, and so forth. New Mythologists, however, are especially keen to emphasize that this has involved imperialist domination and exploitation. What is awkward for them is the fact that less desirable elements of culture change have been enthusiastically (and voluntarily) embraced by many indigenous peoples: cigarettes, soft drinks, movies, pop music, and Jack Daniels. By stressing that tribal cultures were always borrowing and in a state of flux, the New Mythology places in benign perspective the obliteration (or active abandonment) of traditional indigenous values: all cultures, it seems, are in the process of being altered by history.

(4) The Old Mythology, especially in its colonial form, held it unproblematic that traders or travelers might buy or barter for artifacts. Alternatively, artifacts might be accepted as gifts. None of this disturbs their meanings in the Old Mythology, and if anything the native should be thankful for receiving payment for the work before the termites got to it.

The New Mythology sees buying, selling, and trading as essentially Western concepts. Even to accept these objects as gifts is to become, as Kasfir puts it, implicated in "the web of conflicting interests that surround them." There is hence no "noninterventionist" way of obtaining these artifacts, since somewhere in the scheme power relations will obtrude, leading to the exploitation of the indigenous maker or owner of the object. In other words, the native always gets cheated. The New Mythology seems to impute to precontact tribal societies a premercantile edenic state, as though trade and barter (not to mention theft or conquest) of ritual or other valuable artifacts did not occur among these peoples until Europeans came along.

(5) The only reason to collect primitive artifacts, according to premodernist Old Mythology, was as curiosities, examples perhaps of an early stage of Social Darwinist development: they were to be placed in a cabinet alongside fossils and tropical insects. After Picasso & Co., the Old Mythology proclaimed that primitive art embodied the aesthetic sensibilities found in all art, and therefore was as much worth collecting as Constables or Utamaros, and for precisely the same reasons.

The New Mythology displays an oddly ambivalent attitude toward collecting. On the one hand, collecting is persistently disparaged, for instance as a "hegemonic activity, an act of appropriation... a largely colonial enterprise... the logical outcome of a social-evolutionary view of the Other." McEvilley speaks of "captured" tribal objects, a trope suggesting they exist in Western collections as prisoners or slaves. Given the reprehensible nature of collecting, one would expect New Mythologists to demand that the trade in ethnographic art cease, but I have not encountered any such suggestions (except, of course, for the criminal trade in looted antiquities). Even those writers who take moral satisfaction from criticizing collecting appear themselves to have "captured" the occasional artifact.

(6) On puritanical grounds the Old Mythology often forbade taking pleasure in works of tribal art: the sexual element in carvings offended missionary and nineteenth-century colonial sensibilities. In New Zealand, as elsewhere, genitals were hacked off Maori figures, and some overtly sexual carvings were simply burned, lest prurient pleasure be aroused.

The New Mythology replaces this attitude with a new and asexual form of puritanism. Enjoyment of any sort derived from the experience of ethnographic art is considered a cultural mistake at best, a form of visual imperialism at worst: "the colonialist gaze." Angst-ridden New Mythologists are reluctant to record appreciation or enthusiastic emotional reactions to artifacts. Thus Torgovnick heaps contempt on Roger Fry, among many others, for his "insensitive" and "racist" readings in praise of African art, but she never provides, in her own voice, nonracist, sensitive readings to instruct us on how to do it right. Nicholas Thomas is simply bemused: of the museums crammed with indigenous artifacts —"carved bowls, clubs, spears, baskets, pots," etc.—he honestly admits that "I have never understood why people want to look at such things (although I often look at them myself)." Christopher B. Steiner makes the bizarre claim that the objects are valued by Westerners as a way to "celebrate" the loss of the utility they had in their original cultural contexts. Other New Mythologists, such as James Clifford and James Boon (whose article title "Why Museums Make Me Sad" is clear enough), write about ethnographic arts with such a brooding sense of guilt about the historical treatment of conquered cultures that no sense of joy or love for the art is ever allowed to emerge.

(7) Colonialist Old Mythology held that though primitive cultures were to some degree capable of adopting Western technologies and manufactured articles, they could not possibly understand Western culture. In fact, having no adequate comparative perspective, the primitives could not even fully understand their own cultures. Their simple little societies were, however, transparent to the educated, sophisticated Westerner.

The New Mythology, on the contrary, contends that it is the "educated" West which fails to grasp the vast subtleties offered by these cultures, ranging from ethnobotany and folk medicines to spiritual wisdom. Instead, the West ethnocentrically imposes on them its own categories, such as "individual," "religion," or "work of art," when in actuality these concepts have no place in the cultural landscape of the Other. In the matter of borrowing, the New Mythology holds that indigenous artists are, in its preferred parlance, free to appropriate from European culture, infusing their new work with "transformed meanings," fresh associations given to foreign elements introduced into a new cultural context. The reverse—Europeans borrowing from indigenous arts—is to be discouraged. This inversion of the Old Mythology means that an innovative Sepik dancer who incorporates cigarette wrappers in an elaborate headdress is participating in an exciting fusion of cultures, while a Swedish office-worker who wears a New Guinea dog-tooth necklace is implicated in hegemonic, colonialist appropriation.

As a frontispiece for *Gone Primitive,* Torgovnick presents a heavily ironic, not to say sneering, painting (by Ed Rihacek) of a stylish European woman wearing sunglasses and sitting before a zebra skin, surrounded by a collection of "primitive art." In his derisory essay on the "Primitivism" exhibition, Clifford reproduces a 1929 photograph of Mrs. Pierre Loeb, seated in her Paris apartment filled with Melanesian and African carvings. Clifford labels this as an "appropriation" which was "not included in the 'Primitivism' Show" (a curious observation inasmuch as this very photograph appears in the show's catalogue). Both of these images suggest a kind of disapproval of European cultural appropriation that it would be unthinkable to direct toward their cultural inversion —for example, the 1970s posed village photograph Susan Vogel has published showing a Côte d'Ivoire man seated before a wrinkled, painted backdrop of an airplane, a cassette radio proudly displayed on his lap.

(8) The Old Mythology at its colonialist worst posited an ethnocentric aesthetic absolutism: advanced, naturalistic European art forms were seen, especially because of their naturalism, as demonstrating a higher stage in the evolution of art. Modernist Old Mythology retained the idea of universal aesthetic standards, but argued that tribal arts fully met these criteria for excellence, which were formalist rather than naturalistic.

In rejecting both these positions, some New Mythologists urge the abandonment of any idea of transcultural aesthetic criteria (which would be implicitly imperialistic) in favor of complete aesthetic relativism. McEvilley imputes to Kant an epistemology which "tacitly supported the violent progress of 19th- and 20th-century imperialisms" and which justified a view of the Western aesthetic sense as superior to that of non-Western cultures. The New Mythology owes its aesthetic relativism entirely to the climate of poststructural thought rather than to any empirical study of ethnographic and other world arts.

(9) More generally, both colonialist and modernist Old Mythologies imply or presuppose an epistemic realism: they both presume to describe the actual, existent characteristics of tribal societies and their arts.

Under the influence of poststructuralism, the New Mythology often presupposes various forms of constructivism, the idea that categories of human existence are constituted entirely by our own mental activity: we "invent" or "construct" the "primitive," tribal "art," "religion," and so on. The knots into which theorists become tied in trying to introduce such poststructural rhetoric into the study of indigenous arts is illustrated by Barbara Kirshenblatt-Gimblett who writes: "Ethnographic artifacts are objects of ethnography. They are artifacts created by ethnographers. Objects become ethnographic by virtue of being defined, segmented, detached, and carried away by ethnographers." From her first sentence, a dictionary definition, Kirshenblatt-Gimblett deduces a constructivist howler: the trivial fact that ethnographers define the ethnographic status of artifacts does not entail that *they create the artifacts.* Nor do they create the artifacts' meanings; it is the people being studied who determine that, and this awkward reality gets obviously in the way of attempts by New Mythologists to relativize cultural knowledge and meaning. Constructivism is a strong force among New Mythologists most influenced by literary theory, and is less persistent among those who come from a background of academic anthropology. Despite their tendency to toy with the jargon of literary theory, anthropologists generally acquire a robust respect for the independent existence and integrity of the peoples they study.

> *(10) Finally, premodernist Old Mythology, especially in its Victorian colonialist guises, preached the superiority of Western culture. It proposed to bring moral enlightenment to people it viewed as savages, mainly through Christianity, but also with science and modern medicine. In this, it stands starkly apart from modernist Old Mythology, and even from some eighteenth-century explorers of the South Pacific, who claimed that the moral sense and intellectual capacities of "primitive man" were at least equal to those of Europeans.*

The air of smug moral superiority has returned with a vengeance with the arrival of the New Mythology, whose champions patronize, censure, and jeer at any Old Mythology text they find wanting. The New Mythology of tribal arts displays a sense of righteous certitude that would fit the most zealous Victorian missionary.

At Play in the Fields of the Text

In some respects, the New Mythology's frequent borrowing from poststructuralism and the general intellectual climate of postmodernism is healthy and appropriate. For example, the approach to tribal arts must necessarily involve "blurred genres" and fused disciplines, bringing together ethnography, art history, philosophical aesthetics, and general cultural, including literary, criticism. This is fully in the poststructural/postmodern spirit, as is calling into question the peculiarly European distinction between the so-called fine arts and the popular and folk arts and crafts, which normally has no clear application in understanding tribal arts. But there are other aspects of poststructuralism which sit uneasily with the study of tribal arts.

One such notion is the pervasive poststructuralist attack on the authority of the artist or author in aesthetic interpretation. Barthes, whose thinking was again seminal in this regard, proclaimed the death of the god-author, along with the end of the ideologies of objectivity and truth, insisting that the meaning of a literary text is a critical construction instead of a discovered fact. In the theory of literature and the practice of criticism, such constructivist ideas have had their uses, liberating criticism from traditional demands to invoke authorial intention as a validating principle for critical interpretation.

However, the poststructural abandonment of the notion that texts contain meanings placed there by their authors (which it is criticism's job to determine) is only possible in a cultural landscape in which there is enough prior agreement on meanings to allow criticism to become thus freely creative. The poststructural death of the author could only take hold in literary theory because there was already in place an extensive tradition of interpretation of, say, *Madame Bovary* or *Moby Dick*. These novels enjoy a canonical status as works of literary art: they observe the conventions of established genres and were written in European languages by recognized literary artists. The cultural conditions that form the context of their creation and reception are solid enough to enable a generation of critics—notably Barthes, Foucault, and Derrida, but also the New Critics of the Anglo-American world—to declare the hypothetical death of the author and advocate a liberated, creative criticism of *jouissance*.

But do these doctrines and strategies of contemporary theory provide useful models for the critical ethnography of indigenous arts? Hardly. Poststructuralism's image of the free-spirited critic at play in textual fields goes counter to one of the most strongly held (indeed, in my opinion, indispensable) principles of the New Mythology: respect for the autonomous existence of tribal artists, including respect for their intentions and cultural values. Declaring the death of the (European) author may be jolly sport for jaded literary theorists, but an analogous ideological death of the tribal artist is not nearly so welcome in the New Mythology, nor should it be in any anthropology department. The study of tribal arts—indeed, all non-Western arts—cannot presuppose a sufficiently stable, shared background understanding against which one might declare artists' intentions irrelevant or passé. Moreover, the New Mythology gains its sense of identity by pitting itself against what it takes to be the Old Mythology's ethnocentric disregard not only for the intentions of tribal artists but for their very names as well. (Price calls this "the anonymization of Primitive Art," and it was a major complaint lodged against the " 'Primitivism' in 20th Century Art" exhibition. If such ethnocentrism is not to be actively encouraged, the tribal artist's interpretations *must* enjoy special status, defining in the first instance the object of study. In order to respect the cultures and people from which tribal works of art are drawn, the New Mythology must treat indigenous intentions—ascertained or, where unavailable, at least postulated—as constituting the beginning of all interpretation, if not its exhaustive or validating end.

This deep conflict between doctrines of the New Mythology and the poststructuralism it seems so eager to appropriate keeps breaking out despite efforts to paper it over. McEvilley and Clifford enthusiastically adopt the discourse of constructivism, so long as they are talking about how "we," or "the West," or the "omniscient" curatorial mind, construct the generalized primitive, but New Mythologists are not nearly so keen to revert to constructivist parlance when it comes to discussing the actual meanings of works of tribal art. Thus Kasfir asks, "Who creates meaning for African art?," where "for" indicates "on behalf of," implying that Western collectors and exhibitors make a meaning for African art to satisfy the Western eye and mind.

This, however, avoids the more obvious wording of the question "Who creates the meaning *of* African art?" If there is any answer at all to this question, it must begin with the artists and cultures that produce the art. The West can "construct" in the poststructuralist manner to its heart's content, but its understandings will always be about the indigenous constructions of the cultures from which African works derive. It is indigenous intentions, values, descriptions, and constructions which must be awarded theoretical primacy. If an African carving is intended by its maker to embody a spirit, and that is an ascertainable fact about it, then any ethnography that constructs its meaning in contradiction to that fact is false. Of course, ethnography need not culminate with indigenous meanings and intentions, any more than literary criticism comes to an end when an author's intended meaning for a work of fiction has been determined. But ethnography has no choice except to begin with indigenous meanings, which it does not construct, but discovers.

POSTSCRIPT

Do Museums Misrepresent Ethnic Communities Around the World?

Clifford, like many critical theorists, is deeply suspicious of all representations of others. Dutton, in contrast, seems to question both the motives and the logic of this suspicion. He is especially critical of Clifford's lack of historical accuracy when describing the goals and motivations of museums and their curators. Are Clifford's postmodernist conclusions guilty of misrepresenting the museum world in ways that parallel his critique of particular exhibits? Does Dutton's critique of the postmodernists solve the historical problems that are present in both museums and the writings of their critics? Is there a middle ground that would allow for exhibitions with more sensitive context?

Clifford has also dealt with museum exhibits in his book *Routes: Travel and Translation in the Late Twentieth Century* (Harvard University Press, 1997). Related approaches to the problem of representation in museums include Sally Price's *Primitive Art in Civilized Places* (University of Chicago Press, 1989) and Shelly Errington's *The Death of Authentic Primitive Art and Other Tales of Progress* (University of California Press, 1998).

Nicholas Thomas's *Entangled Objects: Exchange, Material Culture and Colonialism in the Pacific* (Harvard University Press, 1991) considers the problem of representation among ethnographic objects in the Pacific. Enid Schildkraut and Curtis A. Keim's *The Scramble for Art in Central Africa* (Cambridge University Press, 1998), Ruth B. Phillips and Christopher B. Steiner's *Unpacking Culture: Art and Commodity in Colonial and Post Colonial Worlds* (University of California Press, 1999), and Michael O'Hanlon and Robert L. Welsch's *Hunting the Gatherers: Ethnographic Collectors, Agents, and Agency in Melanesia* (Berghahn, 2000) provide examples of the rich historical context of museum collections of the sort Dutton seeks.

Both Clifford and Dutton build their arguments on the premise that objects have complex histories, an idea that was originally developed in slightly different ways by anthropological historian George W. Stocking, Jr.'s *Objects and Others: Essays on Museums and Material Culture* (University of Wisconsin Press, 1985) and by anthropologist Arjun Appadurai's *The Social Life of Things: Commodities in Cultural Perspective* (Cambridge University Press, 1986). Both books make two crucial points: objects have histories, and the meanings of objects change when the objects themselves move from one context to another. Also, both argue that objects can take on many different meanings depending on context and viewpoint. Together these books have redefined museological studies and transformed what had been an anthropological backwater into a thriving specialization within the discipline.

Contributors to This Volume

EDITORS

KIRK M. ENDICOTT is a professor and the chairman of the Department of Anthropology at Dartmouth College. He received a B.A. in anthropology from Reed College in 1965, a Ph.D. in anthropology from Harvard University in 1974, and a D.Phil. in social anthropology from the University of Oxford in 1976. He has repeatedly conducted field research among the Batek people of Malaysia. He is the author of *An Analysis of Malay Magic* (Clarendon Press, 1970) and *Batek Negrito Religion: The World-view and Rituals of a Hunting and Gathering People of Peninsular Malaysia* (Clarendon Press, 1979), and is coauthor, with Robert K. Dentan, Alberto G. Gomez, and M. Barry Hooker, of *Malaysia and the "Original People": A Case Study of the Impact of Development on Indigenous Peoples* (Allyn and Bacon, 1997).

ROBERT L. WELSCH is a visiting professor of anthropology at Dartmouth College and adjunct curator of anthropology at The Field Museum in Chicago. He received a B.A. in anthropology from Northwestern University in 1972, an M.A. in anthropology from the University of Washington in 1976, and a Ph.D. from the same department in 1982. He has conducted field research among the Ningerum people of Papua New Guinea, the Mandar people of South Sulawesi, Indonesia, and the diverse peoples of the Sepik Coast of Papua New Guinea. He is the author of *An American Anthropologist in Melanesia* (University of Hawaii Press, 1998) and coeditor, with Michael O'Hanlon, of *Hunting the Gatherers: Ethnographic Collectors, Agents, and Agency in Melanesia* (Berghahn Publishers, 2000).

STAFF

Theodore Knight   List Manager
David Brackley   Senior Developmental Editor
Juliana Gribbins   Developmental Editor
Rose Gleich   Administrative Assistant
Brenda S. Filley   Director of Production/Design
Juliana Arbo   Typesetting Supervisor
Diane Barker   Proofreader
Richard Tietjen   Publishing Systems Manager
Larry Killian   Copier Coordinator

AUTHORS

RICHARD E. W. ADAMS is a professor of anthropology at the University of Texas at San Antonio. He has excavated many sites in Mesoamerica and is the author of numerous books and articles.

JAMES CLIFFORD is a professor of the history of consciousness at the University of California at Santa Cruz. He has written many books and articles about postmodern anthropology, including *Routes: Travel and Translation in the Late Twentieth Century* (Harvard University Press, 1997).

GEORGE L. COWGILL is a professor of anthropology at Arizona State University. He is best known for his archaeological research in central Mexico. He is coeditor, with Norman Yoffee, of *The Collapse of Ancient States and Civilizations* (University of Arizona Press, 1988).

JAMES R. DENBOW is an associate professor of anthropology at the University of Texas at Austin. He has conducted field research in southern Africa and was curator of archaeology at The National Museum of Botswana.

THOMAS D. DILLEHAY is a professor of anthropology at the University of Kentucky. He is best known for his excavations at Monte Verde, Chile, and in the southwestern United States. He is the author of *Monte Verde: A Late Pleistocene Settlement in Chile* (Smithsonian Institution Press, 1997).

DENIS DUTTON is associate professor of art theory in the School of Fine Arts at the University of Canterbury at Christchurch, New Zealand. He is a specialist on aesthetics and tribal art and is the author of *The Forger's Art: Forgery and the Philosophy of Art* (University of California Press, 1983).

STUART J. FIEDEL is an archaeologist working with John Milner Associates in Alexandria, Virginia. He is the author of many books and papers, including *Prehistory of the Americas,* 2d ed. (Cambridge University Press, 1992).

ERIKA FRIEDL is a professor of anthropology at Western Michigan University. She is a specialist on the lives of women and children in Iran. She is the author of many books and articles, including *Children of Deh Koh: Young Life in an Iranian Village* (Syracuse University Press, 1997).

CLIFFORD GEERTZ is a professor at the Insitute for Advanced Study in Princeton, New Jersey. He has conducted field research in Indonesia and Morocco. He is the author of *Works and Lives: The Anthropologist as Author* (Stanford University Press, 1988).

MARIJA GIMBUTAS is a late professor of European archaeology at the University of California at Los Angeles. She was the author of seventeen books and some two hundred articles on European prehistory, including *The Civilization of the Goddess* (HarperCollins, 1992).

STEVEN GOLDBERG is chairman of the Sociology Department at City University of New York. He has written many articles and books, including *Seduced by Science: How American Religion Has Lost Its Way* (New York University Press, 1999).

JOHN J. GUMPERZ is an emeritus professor of anthropology at the University of California at Berkeley. His research interests have concentrated on sociolinguistics and issues of language and culture. He is the author of numerous books and articles, including *Discourse Strategies* (Cambridge University Press, 1982).

MARVIN HARRIS was a professor of anthropology at Columbia University until 1980, when he was appointed graduate research professor of anthropology at the University of Florida. He is the author of many books on anthropology and anthropological theory, including *Cultural Materialism: The Struggle for a Science of Culture* (Random House, 1979).

JEAN-JACQUES HUBLIN is a professor of anthropology at the University of Bordeaux as well as the director of the Dynamics of Human Evolution Laboratory at France's Centre National de la Recherche Scientifique. He is the author of many articles and books on paleoanthropology, including *Les Hommes Préhistoriques* (Hachette, 1995).

JAMES RIDING IN is an assistant professor in the School of Justice Studies and acting director of the American Indian Studies Program at Arizona State University. A historian by training, he is also a member of the Pawnee tribe.

SUDHIR KAKAR is widely known as the father of Indian psychoanalysis and has practiced for many years in New Delhi. He has been a visiting professor of psychology at the University of Chicago and is currently a senior fellow at the Center for the Study of World Religions at Harvard University. His books include *The Colors of Violence: Cultural Identities, Religion, and Conflict* (University of Chicago Press, 1996).

RICHARD B. LEE is a professor of anthropology and chair of the African Studies Programme at the University of Toronto. He is best known for his research among the San peoples of the Kalahari Desert. He is senior editor of *The Cambridge Encyclopedia of Hunters and Gatherers* (Cambridge University Press, 1999).

MARIA LEPOWSKI is a professor of anthropology at the University of Wisconsin. She has conducted field research in Papua New Guinea and is the author of *Fruit of the Motherland: Gender in an Egalitarian Society* (Columbia University Press, 1993).

STEPHEN C. LEVINSON is director of the Language and Cognition Group at the Max Plank Institute for Psycholinguistics at Nijmegen in the Netherlands. His research has focused on linguistic anthropology and cognitive anthropology. He is the author of numerous books and articles, including *Presumptive Meanings* (MIT Press, 2000).

BETTY JEAN LIFTON is a therapist, freelance writer, and adoption rights advocate who has published widely on adoption in the United States. Her books include *Twice Born: Memoirs of an Adopted Daughter* (St. Martin's Press, 1998).

ROBIN McKIE is a science writer who has authored and coauthored many popular books about scientific topics, including *The Genetic Jigsaw: The Story of the New Genetics* (Oxford University Press, 1988).

CLEMENT W. MEIGHAN was a professor of anthropology at the University of California at Los Angeles (UCLA) and for many years director of UCLA's Archaeological Survey. He excavated numerous archaeological sites in California and Mesoamerica.

LYNN MESKELL is an assistant professor of anthropology at Columbia University. Her archaeological research is focused on Egypt and the Mediterranean. She is the author of *Archaeologies of Social Life* (Blackwell, 1999).

JUDITH MODELL is a professor of anthropology, history, and art at Carnegie Mellon University in Pittsburgh, Pennsylvania. Best known for her research on adoption, she has written many articles and books, including *A Sealed and Secret Kinship: Policies and Practices in American Adoption* (Berghahn Books, 2001).

ANTHONY OBERSCHALL is a professor of sociology at the University of North Carolina at Chapel Hill. He has written many books and articles dealing with social conflict, including *Social Movements: Ideologies, Interests, and Identities* (Transaction Books, 1993).

PARVIN PAIDAR works in international development and is currently with UNIFEM in Afghanistan. Her research has focused on gender and social development in developing countries, especially on feminism and Islam in Iran. She is the author of *Women and the Political Process in Twentieth-Century Iran* (Cambridge University Press, 1997).

DALE PETERSON is a professor at Tufts University. He is the author, with Jane Goodall, of *Visions of Caliban: On Chimpanzees and People* (Houghton Mifflin, 1993) and, with Richard Wrangham, *Demonic Males: Apes and the Origins of Human Violence* (Houghton Mifflin, 1996).

STEVEN PINKER is a professor of brain and cognitive sciences at the Massachusetts Institute of Technology. His research has focused on the relationship between language and cognitive function. He has written numerous books, including *Words and Rules: The Ingredients of Language* (Basic Books, 1999).

MERRILEE H. SALMON is a professor of the history and philosophy of science at the University of Pittsburgh. Her recent research concerns the philosophy of anthropology.

E. S. SAVAGE-RUMBAUGH is a researcher at Georgia State University. She is the author of many articles and books, including *Apes, Language, and the Human Mind* (Oxford University Press, 1998).

ELLIOTT P. SKINNER is an emeritus professor of anthropology at Columbia University. He has conducted fieldwork in Burkina Faso (Upper Volta) where he formerly served as United States ambassador. He is the author of *The Mossi of Burkina Faso* (Waveland, 1990).

CHRISTOPHER STRINGER is a paleoanthropology researcher at The Natural History Museum in London. He is the author of several books, including, with Clive Gamble, *In Search of the Neanderthals* (Thames and Hudson, 1993).

ROBERT W. SUSSMAN is a professor of anthropology at Washington University in St. Louis and is currently editor of *American Anthropologist*. He is the author of *Lemur Biology* (Plenum Press, 1975), which he coedited with Ian Tattersall.

JOHN TERRELL is curator of oceanic archaeology and ethnology at The Field Museum in Chicago. He has conducted extensive field research in Papua New Guinea as well as in New Zealand, Tonga, Samoa, and Fiji. He has written numerous articles and books, including *Darwin and Archaeology: A Handbook of Key Concepts* (Bergin and Garvey, 2002).

ALAN G. THORNE is a visiting fellow in the Department of Archaeology and Natural History, Research School of Pacific and Asian Studies, at the Australian National University.

PATRICK TIERNEY is a freelance journalist and center associate/visiting scholar with the Center for Latin American Studies at the University of Pittsburgh and has spent much of the past decade conducting research for his critique of Napoleon Chagnon's fieldwork with the Yanomami Indians of Venezuela and Brazil. He is the author of *Darkness in El Dorado: How Scientists and Journalists Devastated the Amazon* (W. W. Norton, 2000).

JOHN TOOBY is a professor of anthropology at the University of California at Santa Barbara (UCSB) and codirector of UCSB's Center for Evolutionary Psychology. He is a specialist on the evolution of hominid behavior and cognition. He is coeditor of *The Adapted Mind: Evolutionary Psychology and the Generation of Culture* (Oxford University Press, 1992).

JOEL WALLMAN is a program officer at the Harry Frank Guggenheim Foundation in New York. In recent years he has studied aggression and linguistic ability. He is the author of *Aping Language* (Cambridge University Press, 1992).

EDWIN N. WILMSEN is a research fellow at the University of Texas at Austin. He has conducted research in Botswana and is the author of *Land Filled With Flies: A Political Economy of the Kalahari* (University of Chicago Press, 1989).

MILFORD H. WOLPOFF is a professor of anthropology at the University of Michigan at Ann Arbor where he directs the paleoanthropology laboratory. He has written many books and articles on paleoanthropology, including a leading textbook *Paleoanthropology*, 2d ed. (McGraw-Hill, 1994).

RICHARD WRANGHAM is a professor of anthropology at Harvard University. He studies primate behavior and ecology and evolutionary biology. He is the author, with Dale Peterson, of *Demonic Males: Apes and the Origins of Human Violence* (Houghton Mifflin, 1996).

JOÃO ZILHÃO is the founder and former director of the Archeological Institute of Portugal. His research focuses on Neandertals in Paleolithic Iberia. He is a contributor to many academic journals and is the author of *Atomically Archaic, Behaviorally Modern: The Last Neanderthals and Their Destiny* (Oxbow Books, 2001).

Index

acculturation model, of Neandertal tool use and the controversy over whether, occurred between Neandertals and modern humans, 37

Adams, Richard E. W., on whether environmental factors were responsible for the Mayan collapse, 110–116

Adoption in Oceania (Carroll), 244–245

adoptive children, the controversy over, wanting to find their birth parents, 236–251

Adovasio, James, 70, 71

"Affinities Room," at the Museum of Modern Art, and the controversy over museums as misrepresenting ethnic communities, 374, 375

Africa: the controversy over whether *Homo sapiens* originated in, 4–21; female circumcision in, 328–332, 335–341

"African Eve" theory: the controversy over whether *Homo sapiens* originated in Africa only and, 6, 7, 13, 14, 15, 21; the controversy over whether Neandertals interbred with modern humans and, 29–31

aggression, the controversy over whether humans are inherently violent and, 44–61

American Committee for the Preservation of Archaeological Collections (ACPAC), the controversy over whether the remains of prehistoric Native Americans should be reburied rather than studied and, 315, 319

American Indian Movement (AIM), the controversy over whether the remains of prehistoric Native Americans should be reburied rather than studied and, 307

American Indian Religious Freedom Act of 1978, 311

American Indian repatriation movement, 304

American Indians Against Desecration (AIAD), the controversy over whether the remains of prehistoric Native Americans should be reburied rather than studied and, 307, 308

American Indians. *See* Native Americans

apes: the controversy over the origins of human violence and, 44–51; the controversy over whether, can learn language, 130–141

Araújo, Cristina, 27

Ardrey, Robert, 54, 56, 57

art, the controversy over museums as misrepresenting ethnic communities and, 372–390

Aurignacian tool kits, the controversy over whether, were made by Neandertals and modern humans, 31, 32–33, 36–37

austalopithecines, 52, 53, 54, 56

Baker, Josephine, 375–376

Bankousse, 337

Barrie, James, 236

Barthes, Roland, 55–56, 62–63

Basin of Mexico, 118, 119

Bernard, H. Russell, 327–328, 329

Bhindranwale, 282, 284

Black, Francis, 351–352

"blood lust," 56, 57

Boas, Franz, 326, 328

Boddy, Janice, 339

bonobos, 52, 56

Bosnia, the controversy over the inevitability of ethnic conflict and, 288–297

Brady, Ivan, 244–245

Braun, Marc, 38

Brewer-Carías, Charles, 360

Brown, Roger, 151

burial. *See* reburial

Carroll, Vern, 244–245

Cavalli-Sforza, Luca, 9

Chagnon, Napoleon A., the controversy over, and other researchers as having harmed the Yanomami Indians, 346–368

Châtelperronian tool kits, the controversy over whether, were made by Neandertals and modern humans, 35–37

childcare, the controversy over sexually egalitarian societies and, 222

chimpanzees, the controversy over whether humans are inherently violent and, 52, 53, 57, 58

circumcision, the controversy over whether anthropologists should work to eliminate female, 326–342

Clifford, James, on whether museums misrepresent ethnic communities, 372–380

climatic changes, disappearance of the Neandertals and, 39

Clovis culture, 72–73, 75

Clovis points, 69, 70, 71, 75

cognitive anthropology, 185–186

cognitive frames, the controversy over the inevitability of ethnic conflict and, 293–295

collecting, the controversy over museums as misrepresenting ethnic communities and, 385–386

color, linguistic determinism and, 151–152

componential analysis, 185–186

"conditional oddity discrimination," 141
conditioned discrimination learning, language learning of apes and, 131
constitutional requirements, the reburial of Native American remains and, 316–317
Constitutional Revolution of 1906–1911, in Iran, and women, 256–258
co-references, language and, 165
Cowgill, George L., on whether environmental factors were responsible for the Mayan collapse, 117–123
Croats, the controversy over the inevitability of ethnic conflict and, 292
Cro-Magnons, the controversy over whether Neandertals interbred with modern humans and, 26–40
cross-species homogeneity, 140
cultic figurines, the controversy over whether there was a Goddess cult in prehistoric Europe and, 100–103
cultural identity, bodily mutilations as, 332
cultural materialism, the controversy over whether cultural anthropology should model itself on the natural sciences and, 172–181
cultural relativism, the controversy over whether anthropologists should work to eliminate female circumcision and, 326–334
cultural resource laws, the controversy over whether the remains of prehistoric Native Americans should be reburied rather than studied and, 317–318

D'Andrade, R., 328, 329
d'Errico, Francesco, 31–32, 37
Dart, Raymond, 53–54, 56
Darwin, Charles, theory of natural selection of, 45
deixis, 165
demonic males, the controversy over whether humans are inherently violent and, 54–61
Demonic Males: Apes and the Origins of Human Violence (Peterson and Wrangham), 52
Denbow, James R., on whether San hunter-gatherers were pastoralists who have lost their herds, 196–205
Dillehay, Thomas D., on whether people first arrived in the New World after the last Ice Age, 77–84
disobedience, and the effect of the Islamic Revolution in Iran on women, 268–269
displacement, design feature, of language, and apes learning language, 138
DNA. See mitochondrial DNA
Dobe San tribe, the controversy over the San as pastoralists who have lost their herds and, 209–212
Dogon, female circumcision and, 338–339

duality of patterning, design feature, of language, and apes learning language, 138
Duarte, Cidália, 27, 28–29
Dutton, Denis, on whether museums misrepresent ethnic communities, 381–390

Edmonston B measles vaccine, 351–352, 355, 356
emics, of thought and behavior, 176
Employment Division Department of Human Resources of Oregon v. Smith, 311
environmental factors: the controversy over, as responsible for the Mayan collapse, 110–123; disappearance of the Neandertals and, 39
epistemological principles, 173–176
equality, the controversy over the existence of sexually egalitarian societies and, 218–231
Eskimos, words for snow of, 153–154
ethical relativism, the controversy over whether anthropologists should work to eliminate female circumcision and, 326–334
ethnic communities, the controversy over museums as misrepresenting, 372–390
ethnic conflict, the controversy over the inevitability of, 280–297
ethnoscience, 185–186
etics, of thought and behavior, 176
eugenics, 351–352, 355, 357
euphenics, 357
"evolution of hunting" theory, 54

falsifiability, 173–174
Family of Man, The (Steichen), 381–382
"Feast, The," 356–357
female circumcision, the controversy over whether anthropologists should work to eliminate, 326–342
feminism, the controversy over the effect of the Islamic Revolution in Iran on women and, 256–265
Ferguson, R. Brian, 350
Fiedel, Stuart J., on whether people first arrived in the New World after the last Ice Age, 68–76
fish, as cosmogenic myth, 92–93
fishtail points, 75
fluted projectile points, 77
Folsom, New Mexico, bones discovered in, 68
foragers, the controversy over the San as pastoralists who have lost their herds and, 196–214
Friedl, Erika, on whether the Islamic Revolution in Iran has subjugated women, 266–275

Geertz, Clifford, on whether cultural anthropology should model itself on the natural sciences, 182–191
gender, the controversy over the existence of sexually egalitarian societies and, 218–231
General Semantics, 157
generalizations, 175
genetic manipulation, 4
genetics: the controversy over an African origin for *Homo sapiens* and, 4, 5, 6, 7, 12, 19, 20, 21; the controversy over whether Neandertals interbred with modern humans and, 29–31, 35
Gimbutas, Marija, on whether there was a Goddess cult in prehistoric Europe, 88–95
Giver of All, 92–93
goddesses: contextualized, 91–92; the controversy over whether there was a Goddess cult in prehistoric Europe and, 88–106
Goldberg, Steven, on the existence of sexually egalitarian societies, 227–231
Goldstein, L., 312, 314, 317
Good, Kenneth, 350
Goodall, Jane, 58, 59
Goodenough, Ward, 185
Goody, Esther, 245–246
Goody, Jack, 190
Gumperz, John J., on whether language determines how we think, 146–156
gynocentric theories, 97, 98

Harris, Marvin, on whether cultural anthropology should model itself on the natural sciences, 172–181
Hawaiians, adoption and, 244–245
Hayakawa, S. I., 157
Homo erectus, 49
Hopi Indians, concept of time of, 152–153
Hosken, Fran P., 336, 341
Howard, Michael, 49–50
Huang, Chieh-shan, 245
Hublin, Jean-Jacques, 31; on whether Neandertals interbred with modern humans, 34–40
humanism, classic, 381
humanistic paradigm, 180
hunter-gatherers, the controversy over the San as pastoralists who have lost their herds and, 196–214

Ignatieff, Michael, 289
In, James Riding, on whether the remains of prehistoric Native Americans should be reburied rather than studied, 304–312
India, the controversy over the inevitability of ethnic conflict in, 280–287
Indian Reorganization Act of 1934, 311

Indo-Europeans, 58, 59
infrastructure, theoretical principles and, 177–178
inner ear, study of Neandertal versus modern humans, and the controversy over whether Neandertals interbred with modern humans, 38
insecurity, the controversy over the inevitability of ethnic conflict and, 289, 293–295
interbreeding, the controversy over whether, occurred between Neandertals and modern humans, 26–40
internal militaristic competition, the Mayan collapse and, 117–123
Iran, the controversy over the effect of the Islamic Revolution in, on women, 256–275
iron-magnet analogy, 230
Islamic Revolution, the controversy over the effect of the, in Iran on women, 256–275

Johnson, Samuel, 50–51

Kahama killings, 44–45
Kakar, Sudhir, on whether ethnic conflict is inevitable, 280–287
Kalahari, the controversy over the San as pastoralists who have lost their herds and, 196–214
Kasfir, Sidney, 382, 385, 390
Kenyatta, Jomo, 330, 340–341
Keogo, 337
Khomeini, Ayatollah, 262–263
Kikuyu tribe, female circumcision and, 330, 340–341
Kintigh, K., 313, 314, 317
Kirshenblatt-Gimblett, Barbara, 388
Kluckhohn, Clyde, 182
komtogo, 337
Kuper, Leo, 289
!Kung tribe, the controversy over, as pastoralists who have lost their herds, 196–214
Kurgan Penetration, 94

Lancaster, Chet, 54, 56
language: the controversy over whether language determines how we think and, 146–166; learning of, and the controversy over, of apes, 130–141
Largo Velho, the controversy over whether Neandertals interbred with modern humans and the remains found at, 26–40
Leakey, Louis S. B., 83
Lee, Richard B., on whether San hunter-gatherers were pastoralists who have lost their herds, 206–214
Lenneberg, Eric, 151

Lepowsky, Maria, on the existence of sexually egalitarian societies, 218–226

Levinson, Stephen C., on whether language determines how we think, 146–156

Life Among the Yanomamo (Peters), 366

Lifton, Betty Jean, on whether it is natural for adopted children to want to find out about their birth parents, 236–241

Liliuokalania, queen of Hawaii, 243–244

linguistic determinism, the controversy over, 146–166

linguistics, the controversy over the San as pastoralists who have lost their herds and, 197, 198–199, 204

Lizot, Jacques, 350

logical positivism, 329

Lyng v. Northwest Indian Cemetery Protective Association, 311

male-female bonds, 55

manufactured goods, the controversy over Napoleon Chagnon and other researchers as having harmed the Yanomami Indians and, 348, 359–360

Marriage and Adoption in China 1845–1945 (Wolf and Huang), 245

Martin, Laura, 153–154

matrifocal society, the controversy over whether there was a Goddess cult in prehistoric Europe and, 89–90

matrilineal society: the controversy over the existence of sexually egalitarian societies and, 223; the controversy over whether humans are inherently violent and, 46, 55; the controversy over whether there was a Goddess cult in prehistoric Europe and, 89–90

Maurício, Joao, 26–27

Maya, the controversy over environmental factors as responsible for the collapse of, 110–123

McKie, Robin, on whether *Homo sapiens* originated in Africa only, 4–11

Mead, Margaret, 377

measles vaccine, the controversy over Napoleon Chagnon and other researchers as having harmed the Yanomami Indians and, 351–352, 355–357

Mediterranean matriculture, 99–100

Meighan, Clement W., on whether the remains of prehistoric Native Americans should be reburied rather than studied, 313–321

Mellars, Paul, 31

men: bonding of, 46; circumcision of, 332, 335; the controversy over whether humans are inherently violent and, 44–61

menstrual taboos, among the Vanatinai, 221

Meskell, Lynn, on whether there was a Goddess cult in prehistoric Europe, 96–106

Mesolithic peoples, 17, 18

Messing, Simon D., 336

Metropolitan Museum of Modern Art (MOMA), the controversy over museums as misrepresenting ethnic communities, 372–380, 381–382

Milosevic, Slobodan, 288–289

Mirror of Man (Kluckhohn), 182

mitochondrial DNA: the controversy over an African origin for *Homo sapiens* and, 4, 5, 6, 7, 12, 19, 20, 21; the controversy over whether Neandertals interbred with modern humans and, 29–31, 35

mobs, the controversy over the inevitability of ethnic conflict and, 285

Modell, Judith, on whether it is natural for adopted children to want to find out about their birth parents, 242–251

modernism, 373

Monte Verde, 74, 75; battle of, 77–84

Mossi, female circumcision and, 335–338

"Mother Goddess," the controversy over whether there was a Goddess cult in prehistoric Europe and, 88–106

moulding, as a training method, and apes learning language, 131

Mousterian tool kits, the controversy over whether, were made by Neandertals and modern humans, 35–36, 37

Müller, Hauptman, 212–213

multiregionalists, 7, 10

Mungai, 71

museums, the controversy over, as misrepresenting ethnic communities, 372–390

mythical imagery, the controversy over whether there was a Goddess cult in prehistoric Europe and, 92, 94

National Museum of the American Indian Act, 308

Native American Graves Protection and Repatriation Act (NAGPRA), the controversy over whether the remains of prehistoric Native Americans should be reburied rather than studied and, 305, 308, 309, 310, 311

Native Americans, the controversy over whether the remains of prehistoric, should be reburied rather than studied, 304–321

"natural laboratory," 117–118

natural selection, 45, 51

Neandertals, 17; the controversy over whether, interbred with modern humans, 26–40

Neel, James, 351–352, 355–357

neuroendocrinological differentiation, of males and females, 230

Norway, the controversy over sexually egalitarian societies and, 229

Oberschall, Anthony, on whether ethnic conflict is inevitable, 288–297
oral histories, the controversy over the San as pastoralists who have lost their herds and, 206–214
Out-of-Africa model: the controversy over whether *Homo sapiens* originated in Africa only and, 6, 7, 13, 14, 15, 21; the controversy over whether Neandertals interbred with modern humans and, 29–31

Päabo, Svante, 30
Pacific islanders, adoption and, 243–244
Paidar, Parvin, on whether the Islamic Revolution in Iran has subjugated women, 256–265
Paleo-Indians, as the first Americans, 68–76
Paleolithic peoples, 17, 18; images of vultures and owls of, 93
Papania, Mark, 356–357
Papua New Guinea, adoption in, 247
paradigms, 173
pastoralists, the controversy over the San as, who have lost their herds, 196–214
Pawnee Indians, the controversy over whether the remains of prehistoric Native Americans should be reburied rather than studied, 304–321
"Periodic Regeneration," 93
Peters, John, 350, 366
Peterson, Dale, on whether humans are inherently violent, 44–51
Pinker, Steven, on whether language determines how we think, 157–166
Pleistocene age, 15, 68, 69, 70, 73, 74
possession, by spirits, and the controversy over the inevitability of ethnic conflict, 281
preprojectile point horizon, 70
"'Primitivism' in 20th Century Art: Affinity of the Tribal and the Modern," the controversy over museums as misrepresenting ethnic communities and, 372–380, 382, 387
principles, epistemological and theoretical, 173–180
progressive humanism, 381
projectile points, 72, 73
projective identification, the controversy over the inevitability of ethnic conflict and, 281–282
psychoanalytic perspective, of the controversy over the inevitability of ethnic conflict in India, 280–287
Pullman, Geoffrey, 153–154
pygmy chimpanzees, 52, 56

radiocarbon dates, 78
Ramapithecus, 12
rapid fading, design feature, of language, and apes learning language, 138

reburial, the controversy over whether the remains of prehistoric Native Americans should be reburied rather than studied and, 304–321
Redmond, Elsa, 358
refusal, and the effect of the Islamic Revolution in Iran on women, 269–270
religion, the controversy over whether there was a Goddess cult in prehistoric Europe and, 88–106
religious infringement, the controversy over whether the remains of prehistoric Native Americans should be reburied rather than studied and, 316–317
restrictive human-controlled feeding, 58
Rogers, Richard A., 8, 82
Ryle, Gilbert, 15

Salmon, Merrilee H., on whether anthropologists should work to eliminate female circumcision, 326–334
San, the controversy over the, as pastoralists who have lost their herds, 196–214
Sapir-Whorf hypothesis, the controversy over linguistic determinism and, 146–166
Savage-Rumbaugh, E. S., on apes learning language, 130–135
Scandanavia, the controversy over sexually egalitarian societies and, 229
Scheper-Hughes, N., 328
Schwartz measles vaccine, 351–352
science, epistemological principles and, 173–175
Serbs, the controversy over the inevitability of ethnic conflict and, 288–297
sexual division of labor, 221–223
sexual selection, human aggression and, 47, 49, 50
sexually egalitarian societies, the controversy over the possibility for, 218–231
Skinner, Elliott P., on whether anthropologists should work to eliminate female circumcision, 335–342
Snake Goddess, as cosmogenic myth, 92–93
social organization, of Old Europe, 58–60
socialization, sexually egalitarian societies and, 229
sociobiology, 55–56
Solway, Jacqueline S., on whether the San were pastoralists who have lost their herds, 206–214
South America, Paleo-Indians in, 74–76
Souto, Pedro, 26–27
spirit possession, the controversy over the inevitability of ethnic conflict and, 281–282
Sponsel, Leslie, 354, 360
Spoor, Fred, 38
steel tools, the controversy over Napoleon Chagnon and other researchers as having harmed the Yanomami Indians and, 359–360

Steichen, Edward, 381
stimulus-response psychology, 139
stresses, in Maya civilization, 111–112
Stringer, Christopher, 15; on whether *Homo sapiens* originated in Africa only, 4–11
structure, theoretical principles and, 177–178
subversion, and the effect of the Islamic Revolution in Iran on women, 269
suicide, and the effect of the Islamic Revolution in Iran on women, 267
superstructure, theoretical principles and, 177–178
Sussman, Robert W., on whether humans are inherently violent, 52–61
Sweden, the controversy over sexually egalitarian societies and, 229
symbolic systems, 100
syntax, teaching of, and the controversy over apes learning language, 131

Taborin, Yvette, 31
Tedlock, Barbara, 380
temples, the controversy over whether there was a Goddess cult in prehistoric Europe and, 90–91
Teotihuacan civilization, the Mayan collapse and, 117–123
Terminal Classic period, of Maya culture, 110, 112
Terrell, John, on whether it is natural for adopted children to want to find out about their birth parents, 242–249
territoriality, human aggression and, 55
testosterone, human aggression and, 49
theocratic monarchies, 58–59
theoretical principles, 174, 177–179
thick description, the controversy over cultural anthropology modeling itself on the natural sciences and, 182–191
Thorne, Alan G., 5, 7; on whether *Homo sapiens* originated in Africa only, 12–21
Tierney, Patrick, on Napoleon Chagnon and other researchers as having harmed the Yanomami Indians, 346–361
time, concept of, of Hopi Indians, 152–153
Tooby, John, on Napoleon Chagnon and other researchers as having harmed the Yanomami Indians, 362–368
traits, genetically based, 55
Transactions in Kinship (Brady), 245
transitional assemblages, the controversy over whether, occurred between Neandertals and modern humans, 35–36, 37
tribal art, the controversy over museums as misrepresenting ethnic communities and, 372–390
Trinkaus, Erik, 26, 28–29, 32, 38
Turnbill, Colin, 327
Turner, Terry, 360, 363, 364, 368

Twain, Mark, 151
Tyler, Stephen, 174–175

vaccine responses, the controversy over Napoleon Chagnon and others as having harmed the Yanomami Indians and, 351–352, 355–357
Vanatinai, the controversy over the existence of sexually egalitarian societies and, 218–226
violence, the controversy over whether humans have an inherent tendency toward, 44–61

Wallman, Joel, on apes learning language, 136–141
warfare, the controversy over Napoleon Chagnon and other researchers as having harmed the Yanomami Indians and, 346–368
Washburn, Sherwood, 54, 56
Washoe, language learning in apes and, 136–137
Weber, Max, 182–183
White, Randall, 31
Whorf, Benjamin Lee, 146, 149, 156–164
Wilmsen, Edwin N., on whether San hunter-gatherers were pastoralists who have lost their herds, 196–205
Wilson, Allan, 5, 6, 13, 15
Wilson, E. O., 55–56
Wilson, Edward O., 349
Wolf, Arthur, 245
Wolpoff, Milford H., 5, 7; on whether *Homo sapiens* originated in Africa only, 12–21
women: the controversy over the effect of the Islamic Revolution in Iran on, 256–275; the controversy over the existence of sexually egalitarian societies and, 218–231
work, effect of the Islamic Revolution in Iran on women and, 270–272
Wrangham, Richard, on whether humans are inherently violent, 44–51

Yanomami Indians, the controversy over Napoleon Chagnon and other researchers as having harmed the, 346–368
Yanomamö: The Fierce People (Chagnon), 346–347
Yugoslavia, the controversy over the inevitability of ethnic conflict and, 288–297

Zilhão, João, 37; on whether Neandertals interbred with modern humans, 26–33
Zuni Shalako ceremony, 380